RESOURCES FOR TEACHING

Literature
and Its Writers

A Compact Introduction to Fiction,
Poetry, and Drama

FIFTH EDITION

RESOURCES FOR TEACHING

Literature and Its Writers

A Compact Introduction to Fiction, Poetry, and Drama

PREPARED BY

Ann Charters
University of Connecticut

Samuel Charters

William E. Sheidley
University of Southern Colorado

Susan C. W. Abbotson
University of Connecticut

Bedford /St. Martin's   BOSTON ■ NEW YORK

4   3   2   1   0   9
f   e   d   c   b   a

For information, write: Bedford/St. Martin's, 75 Arlington Street, Boston, MA 02116
(617-399-4000)

ISBN-10: 0–312–55642–X
ISBN-13: 978–0–312–55642–6

Instructors who have adopted *Literature and Its Writers: A Compact Introduction to Fiction, Poetry, and Drama,* Fifth Edition, as a textbook for a course are authorized to duplicate portions of this manual for their students.

PREFACE

We have organized this manual into three sections — Fiction, Poetry, and Drama — to correspond with *Literature and Its Writers*, Fifth Edition. For individual stories, poems, and plays, we offer brief critical analyses and suggest ways to discuss the work in class. Like the questions that follow, these commentaries aim to promote a lively exchange of responses and perceptions without insisting on any particular interpretation or critical methodology. Among the Topics for Writing are questions we call "Making Connections," assignments that ask students to link selections in the anthology, and questions we call "Responding Creatively," assignments that ask students to think critically about a work through their own creative writing. These questions were designed to promote critical thinking and to provide both stimulating topics for writing assignments and material for fruitful class discussions. Instructors will readily see ways to rephrase, restructure, and reapply these assignments to suit their purposes and their students' needs. Some writing topics may serve equally well as discussion questions, and vice versa.

The lists of Suggested Readings that conclude many of the entries are neither exhaustive nor highly selective. They simply cite interesting and, when possible, readily available criticism that proved useful in preparing this manual or they contain information and approaches to the stories that could not be incorporated in the commentaries. Thanks are due to the authors mentioned, to whose insights and scholarship these resources are generally indebted.

In the section on Fiction, the commentaries, questions, and topics for writing were prepared by Ann Charters and William E. Sheidley, with additional help from Samuel Charters, Susan C.W. Abbotson, Martha Ramsey, and Robert Gaspar. Samuel Charters wrote the commentaries, questions for discussion, and topics for writing in the Poetry section, and Susan Abbotson prepared the section on Drama along with Ann Charters, who wrote about Lynn Nottage's *POOF!*. Suzy Johnson and David Wasser also contributed comments on the introductory material. For ease of access, you will find the hundreds of works of fiction and poetry in the first two sections organized alphabetically by author, while in the third section the nine plays are organized chronologically by author, to suggest the historical development of this genre. There is no discussion of individual works in the commentaries and conversation sections of *Literature and Its Writers*, Fifth Edition, because we believe these works speak for themselves.

The last section of this manual is the Appendix of Audiovisual Resources, which lists a wide range of materials that discuss either individual authors and works or literary genres.

Ann Charters
University of Connecticut

Samuel Charters

CONTENTS

Part Two ■ Poetry

Part Three ■ Drama

RESOURCES FOR TEACHING

Literature and Its Writers

A Compact Introduction to Fiction, Poetry, and Drama

NOTES ON TEACHING LITERATURE AND COMPOSITION

If you have not had a lot of experience teaching literature and writing to first-year college students, I offer the following notes in the hope that they may assist you in planning your course. My most vivid memory of the first freshman English course I taught more than forty years ago is an incident that turned out to be the most embarrassing moment in my teaching career. During a particularly long-winded, soft-spoken student's reply to a question I asked the class, I fell asleep. I don't know what made me return to consciousness after a few seconds of restful slumber in the stuffy New Hampshire college classroom — perhaps an instinct that the silence around me was unnatural. I woke up to find fifty eyes of various shades of blue, brown, gray, and hazel staring at me expectantly, more amused than shocked. I was so rattled that I don't remember whether I apologized for my mindless absence from the classroom, but I do recall that I felt like an idiot when I had to ask my student to repeat her answer. She made short work of it this time. I vowed to myself that I would never be inattentive in a classroom again, and the experience hasn't repeated itself, at least up to now.

I nodded off while teaching my first freshman English class because I was so anxious about being prepared that I had stayed up too late the night before creating my lesson plan. I had crammed so much into my outline for that single fifty-minute class that it would probably have taken me the next two weeks to cover the material. That's my first advice: Besides getting enough sleep to stay attentive to the ideas of your students, try to plan each class realistically. Even though you may fear the dead silence of a classroom, you will discover that your students can and will voice their ideas. Just give them time.

Also it will help the entire class to stay awake and alert if, during your first class meeting, you begin with a well-ventilated classroom and check that all the students can hear you and one another. Then settle in and enjoy the business and the pleasures of teaching. As Stuart Sherman wrote in "Time in Teaching, Teaching in Time" (*Academe*, September/October 1996), "Teachers perform the strange magic of doing something important while doing nothing tangible (and I suspect that this is why they generally prefer the airy enchantments of the classroom to the physical labor of paper-marking)." Here are some further suggestions to consider if you are beginning to teach a literature and composition course to freshmen.

Planning and Writing a Syllabus

Before you plan the semester, find out if your English Department has set goals for students to meet in freshman classes. These usually stress departmental policy concerning class attendance and taking roll and stipulate a minimum number of pages of writing and revision from each student. Often there is also a sample syllabus or a file of syllabi used previously by other instructors teaching the course. These can help you plan your semester.

When I first meet my classes, I find it most useful to distribute a syllabus describing only the early weeks of the semester. You needn't plan the syllabus for the entire course right away (unless your institution requires that you do so). Tell your students that you will provide them with additional syllabi as you go along. This way you won't find yourself committed to unrealistic reading or writing assignments if you discover after meeting your class that they are proceeding at a different pace than you had imagined when you began planning the course. Remember to include your office hours, office location, and telephone number on the syllabus.

Tell your students at the start of the semester how you will arrive at their final grade. They should be clear about the relative importance of class attendance, participation in discussions and group work, homework, essays, research papers, oral reports, quizzes, midterms, and final exams. State in the syllabus the percentage of the grade represented by each of the activities in the course. Consider including collaborative group work whenever feasible: Peer assessment of essays and papers, literary research and oral presentations to the class, and similar activities encourage students to take on some of the responsibility for the learning process.

Planning Essay Assignments

Focus attention on the writing assignments early in the semester by passing out guidelines for essay preparation along with your first syllabus. Such a guide might look something like the following.

Your Name and Course Number
Subject: First Paper

Date Paper Is Due and Topic of Essay

General Guidelines for Preparing the Paper:

- State the number of words or pages, typed or word-processed and double-spaced. Stipulate margins and type size as well.

- Suggest the importance of a descriptive title for the paper, which, if possible, should relate to the student's critical thinking about the subject. The student should use the title as a tool to help the reader focus on the topic.

- Remind students of the need to proofread essays carefully for spelling errors, punctuation, and factual details (accurate titles, authors' names, names of characters, quotations, and so forth).

- Assign specific pages in Part Four of *Literature and Its Writers* to help students get started. Emphasize the importance of developing a thesis or central idea that is clearly stated in the opening paragraph of each essay.

Teaching Students to Read Literature

Take time in an early class meeting to discuss how students should be reading their assignments. Assign and review the chapters on reading, thinking, and writing about short fiction/poetry/drama (the order will depend on your approach). Emphasize the importance of reading slowly and reading twice, so that students begin to notice the way that writers use language, as well as what they are saying. Demonstrate how you would read a text if you were doing a homework assignment. Tell students what the American poet Robert Hass has said about reading literature: "Reading is a gymnasium for the imagination where people can work out, get ready for the shocks of existence."

Teaching Critical Thinking and Writing

Assign student writing every time the class meets. Probably the most frequent problem encountered by new instructors is neglecting to allow sufficient time during the semester to help students with their essays. Discussing the stories, poems, and plays you've assigned becomes so absorbing that too little class time is left to assist students in developing their writing skills.

One of the most immediate ways to integrate composition and writing practice into an introductory literature course is to conclude your first meeting by asking students to produce a writing sample in the last fifteen or so minutes of class. You might ask them to reflect on the fiction, poetry, and drama they've read either in or out of class and list the three works they've enjoyed (or disliked) the most, citing their reasons why. This exercise helps you to get to know your students and allows them to see the difference between expressing their personal taste and exercising their critical skills.

Student writing throughout the semester can continue on a relatively informal basis, in addition to the finished essays. Consider, for example, asking students to write a sentence or a paragraph demonstrating their critical thinking about each reading assignment. These written statements can become the basis for class discussion about the literature, or you could require that students keep journals of their responses. They'll probably start out writing summaries without much thought in them. After a few class meetings, however, you can insist that they write about their assignments *as literature*, using their newly acquired critical vocabulary.

Challenge students to pack into a single sentence as much information about the work as they can. You can also ask them to write two different sentences in their journals expressing ideas about each assignment — the first one before class discussion and the second one after. If you prefer to assign specific questions for homework to help students focus their thinking, you will find questions for discussion after each entry in this manual, as well as topics for longer writing assignments.

Organizing Your Course

Plan to devote four weeks to each literary genre if your course runs for fourteen weeks. This allows you to introduce the class to your aims and get to know them a little during the first week and to use the last week for oral reports, discussion of research papers, and a general course summary that will help students prepare for the final exam. Of course, if you don't give a final exam or include oral reports, or if you assign only short essays instead of a longer research paper, your final week can take a different direction. Allow time during each four-week period to work with student writing about these genres. Incorporate peer discussion and reviews into class time to involve students in the process of evaluating and improving their essays.

Here are five approaches to using *Literature and Its Writers* to help you plan the semester.

FORMAL

With this method you assign the introductory chapters on fiction, poetry, and drama at the beginning of each of the weeks devoted to the specific genre. You go over these pages in the classroom, clarifying the definitions of concepts important to each genre (plot, character, setting, point of view, style, and theme in short fiction; the poet's means; the elements of drama; and so on) and discussing the examples of stories, poems, and plays in these introductory chapters. Then you assign individual works to explore aspects of these formal elements (see the study guide to short story elements). This is a somewhat traditional approach, but it gives you and your students a clear idea of your method. You can teach the different genres in the order in which they are presented in *Literature and Its Writers*, or you can introduce them in a different order. Many instructors begin the course with short fiction, because students find it easiest to read. Other instructors prefer to start with poetry, because it is the oldest literary form, followed by drama and fiction. Still others teach poetry last, after fiction and drama, so that they won't run out of class time in the middle of a long dramatic work.

HISTORICAL

You might want to mix the genres to stress the origins and development of literature in the Western tradition. You could investigate literature's role as a record of historical and ideological change and the continuing significance of this record to our culture. You could begin with the selections of epic poetry, move on to classical Greek drama and Shakespeare, read the Augustan and Romantic poets, and continue into modernism with James Joyce, Ernest Hemingway, and T. S. Eliot. Or you could proceed in the opposite direction, beginning with contemporary poetry, drama, and fiction and tracing a line back to the classics. A major drawback to this approach is that the end of the semester will probably occur long before you've worked your way back to Sophocles. Be prepared to make radical revisions in your syllabus as the semester progresses. Or you might decide as you plan the course that you want to structure it exclusively as a survey of recent literature, or that you're most intrigued by the thought of developing the concept of canon revision by pairing traditional literary icons with alternate cultural statements.

THEMATIC

You could devise a course in which the assigned reading illustrates important themes — for example, "Nature and Consciousness," in which you could read such authors as Leslie Marmon Silko, Percy Bysshe Shelley, and Susan Glaspell, or "Social Problems of Our Time," where the writing could include work by James Baldwin, Lawrence Ferlinghetti, and Arthur Miller. The possibilities are endless, depending on your interests.

WRITERS' COMMENTARIES

This anthology contains numerous commentaries that can be used to good purpose in helping your students think critically about literature. Part Four, for example, includes a discussion of how Eudora Welty's commentary can illuminate their understanding of "A Worn Path" and be used in a writing assignment. You could organize your course around stories, poems, and plays that have commentaries that can also serve as model essays for students, illustrating different ways to structure their writing about literature.

WRITERS' CONVERSATIONS

   Literature and Its Writers contains in-depth conversations on four fiction writers, three poets, and one playwright. A week or more spent on the literary work and conversation of each author could be a satisfying and well-defined way to proceed through the semester. The essays could serve as models of different types of student writing, and related works of literature could be assigned from the anthology. For example (and this is not meant to imply that this is the only choice of writers or use of the commentaries), students could also read the stories of southern writers Zora Neale Hurston, William Faulkner, and Eudora Welty while they are studying the work of Flannery O'Connor; they could read poems by Elizabeth Barrett Browning and Christina Rossetti in addition to those of Emily Dickinson; they could read the poetry of Langston Hughes along with the Lorraine Hansberry play and commentaries.

Emphasizing Critical Thinking

   Regardless of how you organize the course, you might want to introduce students to the usefulness and limitations of the different critical methods discussed in Part Four of the anthology, including formalist, gender, and cultural criticism, to help them understand stories, poems, and plays. We have selected commentaries that follow specific critical methods to serve as examples. When teaching poetry, remind the students that they should read every assigned poem through to the end, even if they don't completely understand it. Although they may not get every word, they will often find that the poem has made a strong emotional impression on them.

   Always allow sufficient time, if possible, for students to reflect on their reading after the class has discussed an assignment. Refer back to the work read for the previous class and ask if there are further questions or insights to share about that work before taking on the next one. The story writer John Cheever reminds us that "the basic test" of literature is "Is it interesting?" And "interest" connotes "suspense, emotional involvement and a sustained claim on one's attention."

   During the first weeks of the semester, consider giving a brief paraphrase of the story, poem, or play before asking students to discuss the work. This minimizes the loss of precious time while unprepared students mumble vague and halting answers to the question, "What is this story/poem/play about?" It will also head off student embarrassment in the classroom if the content of the work has been grossly misunderstood. Critical thinking and sound interpretation depend on a clear understanding of the text. A brief paraphrase by the instructor before opening up the work for questions will start everyone off on equal ground and allow the class to go on to more interesting matters. If students have brought in a written homework assignment based on what they now see is a faulty understanding of a work's content, give them the opportunity to revise their papers before turning them in. This will help them to sharpen their critical thinking and to get more writing practice. You might also want to include occasional quizzes in class to check if students are keeping up with the reading.

   In this manual you will find interpretive essays clarifying most selections in *Literature and Its Writers* and scores of discussion questions and writing topics. They have been designed to challenge students' understanding and to lead them to a more thoughtful appreciation of each writer's literary strategies. And this, at least in my experience, is what literature and composition courses are all about.

Ann Charters
University of Connecticut

PART ONE

FICTION

SHERMAN ALEXIE

The Lone Ranger and Tonto Fistfight in Heaven (p. 35)

Although students will have little difficulty understanding the content of Alexie's story, they may be unfamiliar with the reference of the story's title, which seems to have no immediate connection to the story itself. In the story there is no specific mention of the Lone Ranger or Tonto, and nothing about a fistfight, in heaven or on earth. Some students will be familiar with the fictional characters in the title, but there may be students who are not, since it has been many years since they were a ubiquitous presence in American popular culture.

The Lone Ranger was a member of the Texas Rangers, a law enforcement group that was instituted in the nineteenth century to bring justice to the wild Texas frontier. In the fictional story, a group of rangers riding in a deserted area was ambushed by bandits, and all but one of them was killed. The survivor, severely wounded, was found by an "Indian," Tonto, who nursed him back to health. Together they set out to find the killers, and then rode on together through a long career, bringing justice to the West in Saturday matinee film serials, books, comic books, radio programs, and television. The Lone Ranger wore a mask to protect his identity and fought his enemies with silver bullets. When they had accomplished their mission, he and Tonto would move on, always leaving behind one of the silver bullets as a sign to the people they had helped.

The characters have obvious connections to other figures of myth and legend, such as Robin Hood, who also reinforced the belief in the power of the lone individual to effect change in society. The role of the "Indian," who was usually played by a white actor in dark makeup, was secondary, even though Tonto saved the Lone Ranger's life again in several episodes. There was also a suggestion of the fictional characters Don Quixote and Sancho Panza in the Lone Ranger's idealism and in Tonto's dependent role. Despite their years together, Tonto never learned English, expressing himself in a kind of pidgin English dialect. With the title of the story Alexie seems to be telling the reader that the myth is dead, and with the death of the myth the natural antagonism between the white man and the Indian can now be openly expressed. Native Americans had long complained about Tonto's role as a virtual servant to the white ranger, and in the years when the figures became fixtures of popular culture there were already cynical jokes questioning the relationship.

As students read the story more closely, they will realize that on another level Alexie is suggesting that the fistfight between the Lone Ranger, who represents white society, and Tonto, who represents Indian society, reflects a deep conflict within himself. There is almost no plot to the story. The only thing that happens — and we don't learn about it until close to the end — is that the narrator receives a phone call from the white woman whom he once lived with, abused emotionally, and finally left in the middle of the night. The story is a series of remembered incidents through which the narrator is made conscious of the conflict he feels between his Indian background and the white culture he has chosen to enter. By presenting the story as memory, he is able to introduce other elements that his memory dredges up — from failed treaties between the Indians and the whites, to memories of old basketball games, to his self-conscious description of his attempt to frighten the clerk of an all-night store. The reader is aware that Alexie himself was a good basketball player, and that he consciously participated in white culture on many levels, so the story has a strong element of autobiography.

Questions for Discussion

1. Is the title of the story meant seriously or ironically?
2. Why does the protagonist purposefully frighten the clerk of the 7-11?
3. When he describes the clerk swallowing hard "like a white man does," is he suggesting that someone else — an African American or an Asian American — would not be frightened in the same situation?
4. In the italicized sentence beginning "We'll take Washington and Oregon," to what is the author referring? Is it a specific or a general reference?
5. When he describes three white soldiers playing polo with a dead Indian woman's head and compares this to the U.S. policy in Central America, what is the author saying about America's treatment of other races and peoples?
6. When he says that his failure to do anything with his life is normal "for almost any other Indian in the country," is the author speaking cynically or out of genuine despair?

Topics for Writing

1. Some critics have suggested that Alexie is making a career by manipulating white Americans' guilt over the destruction of the Native American peoples. Discuss this idea in terms of the actions of the protagonist in the story.
2. In the story, there are two examples of police mistrust of minority peoples. Discuss whether these are, or are not, valid descriptions of police attitudes.

Commentary

Sherman Alexie, "*Superman and Me*," p. 575.

Suggested Reading

Alexie, Sherman. *The Lone Ranger and Tonto Fistfight in Heaven.* New York: HarperCollins, 1994.

ISABEL ALLENDE

An Act of Vengeance (p. 40)

Allende has said that "a good short story begins with the overpowering need to communicate a single idea or feeling. . . . It's like shooting an arrow. There is no second chance, it's a make-or-break proposition." She also believes that writing clearly is the first duty of the storyteller: "Not simply — that only works with soap advertising; we don't have to sacrifice aesthetics for the sake of ethics. On the contrary, only if we are able to say it beautifully can we be convincing."

"An Act of Vengeance" begins clearly and powerfully with an opening paragraph foreshadowing the plot of the story while suggesting the individuality of the protagonist Dulce Rosa Orellano, the Senator's daughter. Her father's high position may have gotten her elected Carnival Queen, but she is no stereotype. She is an independent young woman who will be forced to confront her terrible destiny — committing an act of vengeance that will avenge her father's death by the man with whom she allows herself to fall in love thirty years later.

The setting of Allende's magical realist story could occur in any fantasy land of the author's imagination, but its details reinforce the stereotypes about the conventional separation of women's and men's lives in her fictional country south of the border — the women in the local Ladies' Club are peaceful and plant trees in the town square; the men are violent and shoot out the windows in the public buildings, bullheadedly determined "to teach everyone a lesson." Dulce Rosa, the untypical heroine, thinks for herself even if she follows her culture's code of honor. To avenge her family's good name, she must kill the lover who was the young man who raped her after murdering and dishonoring her father. Forced to choose between the Senator's ghost and the man she loves, she stabs herself in her wedding dress before the ceremony.

Questions for Discussion

1. Discuss the style of the opening paragraph. How does it foreshadow the conclusion of the story?
2. Discuss the irony of the title. Is Rosa avenging her father's death, or her own independent "melancholy" character because she found herself unable to carry out her "perfect plan of vengeance"?
3. Is Rosa's change of heart toward her father's killer realistic? Did Allende mean it to be realistic, or does it suit the magical realist circumstances of the story?

Topics for Writing

1. **MAKING CONNECTIONS**   Compare and contrast the character of Dulce Rosa in Allende's story with the character of Madeline Usher in Poe's "The Fall of the House of Usher" (p. 472) as examples of passive/active women characters in two symbolic tales.
2. **RESPONDING CREATIVELY**   Write a book review of Allende's novel *Eva Luna.*
3. Allende has said that "it's hard for a book to stand against the message of the mass media; it's an unfair battle. Writers should therefore look for other forms of expressing their thoughts, avoiding the prejudice that only in books can they make literature. All means are legitimate, not only the cultivated language of academia but also the direct language of journalism, the mass language of radio, television and the movies, the poetic language of popular songs and the passionate language of talking face to face with an audience. These are all forms of literature." Agree or disagree with her statement.

Commentary

Isabel Allende, *"Short Stories by Latin American Women,"* p. 579.

Suggested Readings

Allende, Isabel. *The Stories of Eva Luna.* Trans. Margaret Sayers Peden. New York: Atheneum, 1991.

Correas de Zapata, Celia, ed. *Short Stories by Latin American Women: The Magic and the Real.* Houston: Arte Público, 1990.

Zinsser, William, ed. *Paths of Resistance: The Art and Craft of the Political Novel.* Boston: Houghton, 1989. Contains Isabel Allende's "Writing as an Act of Hope."

MARGARET ATWOOD

Happy Endings (p. 46)

The first time students read "Happy Endings," they may miss the way Atwood connects the stories from "A" to "F." "B" is the first unhappy ending (as Atwood warns us in the third sentence), with the "worst possible scenario" worked out in John and Mary's love affair. Atwood's vocabulary here is deliberately harsh and unromantic, unlike the sentimental clichés of the "A" scenario.

As Atwood continues her permutations of the couples' possible relationships, her stories get shorter and more perfunctory. Her language becomes more elemental, preparing the reader for her summary dismissal of all plots, since they all end in death. In the final three paragraphs, Atwood drops all pretense that she is telling stories and directly addresses her readers, revealing that her true subject is not the emotional life she is creating for her characters but her awareness of the elements of fiction. She defines plot as "what" or "just one thing after another." Then, like the instructor's manual of a short story anthology, she leaves the rest up to her reader: "Now try How [character] and Why [theme.]"

Questions for Discussion

1. Atwood's authorial presence is the strongest element in "Happy Endings" — does this make the text closer to an essay than a short story? Explain.
2. How does Atwood elicit your curiosity, so that you continue to read this short story? Would you say that she has proven that plot is the most essential element in a story? Is there also an underlying, coherent theme to "Happy Endings"?
3. Would the story still be effective if Atwood omitted her direct address to the reader ("If you want a happy ending, try A.")? Explain.

Topics for Writing

1. **RESPONDING CREATIVELY** Rewrite the story, inventing additional outcomes for John and Mary's relationship.
2. Ray Bradbury, in his book *Zen in the Art of Writing: Essays on Creativity* (Capra, 1990), writes, "The writer must let his fingers run out the story of his characters, who, being only human and full of strange dreams and obsessions, are only too glad to run. . . . Remember: Plot is no more than footprints left in the snow after your characters have run by on their way to incredible destinations. Plot is observed after the fact rather than before. It cannot precede action. It is the chart that remains when an action is through." Apply Bradbury's analysis to "Happy Endings."

Suggested Readings

Atwood, Margaret. *Dancing Girls and Other Stories.* Toronto: Seal Books, 1978.

————. *Good Bones and Simple Murders.* New York: Doubleday, 1994.

Cooke, Nathalie. *Margaret Atwood: A Biography.* Toronto: ECW, 1998.

Davidson, Arnold E., and Cathy N. Davidson, eds. *The Art of Margaret Atwood: Essays in Criticism.* Toronto: Anansi, 1981.

Grace, Sherrill E., and Lorraine Weir. *Margaret Atwood: Language, Text and System.* Vancouver: U of British Columbia P, 1983.

Howells, Coral Ann. *Margaret Atwood.* New York: St. Martin's, 1996.

McCombs, Judith. *Critical Essays on Margaret Atwood.* Boston: G. K. Hall, 1988.

Nicholson, Colin, ed. *Margaret Atwood: Writing and Subjectivity: New Critical Essays.* New York: St. Martin's, 1994.

Rigney, Barbara Hill. *Margaret Atwood.* Totowa, NJ: Barnes, 1987.

Rosenberg, Jerome H. *Margaret Atwood.* Boston: Twayne, 1984.

Stouck, David. *Major Canadian Authors.* Lincoln: U of Nebraska P, 1988.

Wilson, Sharon Rose. *Margaret Atwood's Fairy-Tale Sexual Politics.* Jackson: UP of Mississippi, 1993.

JAMES BALDWIN

Sonny's Blues (p. 49)

The marvel of this story is the way the narrator — Sonny's older brother — narrows the physical and emotional distance between himself and Sonny until Sonny's plight is revealed and illuminated in a remarkable moment of empathy and insight. This story of drug addiction in the inner city's black ghetto is as valid today as it was when it was written. By juxtaposing the two brothers — a straight high school math teacher and a heroin-addicted blues pianist — Baldwin makes it possible for readers to enter the world of the story regardless of their racial background or their opinions about drugs. The author doesn't judge Sonny's plight. Instead, through the brother, he helps us understand it, sympathize with it, and transcend it in a brief shared experience of Sonny's inspired musical improvisation.

This is a long story, and its plot consists mostly of flashbacks, more "told" than "shown" in the reminiscences of Sonny's older brother. Yet the power of Baldwin's sympathy for his characters and his eloquent style move the reader along. Baldwin captures the African American culture of strong family allegiances in the face of American racism. Both Sonny and his brother are trying to survive, and we respect them for their courage.

One of the ways to discuss the story is through an analysis of the narrator's growing sympathy for Sonny. Baldwin tells us that the narrator thinks, after the death of his little daughter, Grace, from polio, "My trouble made his real." This realization motivates the first scene with the two brothers in which Baldwin begins to build the bridge between them. Separately they watch three sisters and a brother hold a revival meeting on the sidewalk opposite the narrator's apartment, and after they hear the gospel music, the silence between Sonny and his brother begins to give way to shared sound. The scene leads directly to the two brothers going to the bar where Sonny plays and creates an opportunity for the narrator (and the reader) to enter Sonny's world and satisfy his anguished need to share his music with someone who will listen to it and understand.

Questions for Discussion

1. Analyze the following speech, in which Sonny explains to his brother how he has survived (however tenuously) the experience of racism in America:

    "It's terrible sometimes, inside," he said, "that's what's the trouble. You walk these streets, black and funky and cold, and there's not really a living ass to talk to, and there's nothing shaking, and there's no way of getting it out — that storm inside. You can't talk it and you can't make love with it, and when you finally try to get with it and play it, you realize nobody's listening. So you've got to listen. You got to find a way to listen."

    How does this explanation make Sonny a sympathetic character?

2. Discuss Baldwin's comment on the blues Sonny plays with Creole and the two other musicians at the end of the story:

    Creole began to tell us what the blues were all about. They were not about anything very new. He and his boys up there were keeping it new, at the risk of ruin, destruction, madness, and death, in order to find new ways to make us listen. For, while the tale of how we suffer, and how we are delighted, and how we may triumph is never new, it always must be heard. There isn't any other tale to tell, it's the only light we've got in all this darkness.

    Baldwin's subject is the music, of course, but he is also talking about other forms of creation. What might they be?

Topics for Writing

1. Chinua Achebe describes Baldwin as having brought "a new sharpness of vision, a new energy of passion, a new perfection of language to battle the incubus of race" in his eulogy titled "Postscript: James Baldwin (1924–1987)" (Hopes and Impediments, 1990). How does "Sonny's Blues" embody these qualities?
2. **MAKING CONNECTIONS** Baldwin's commentary "Autobiographical Notes" (p. 580) states that he found it difficult to be a writer because he was forced to become a spokesman for his race: "I have not written about being a Negro at such length because I expect that to be my only subject, but only because it was the gate I had to unlock before I could hope to write about anything else." Yet Baldwin's depiction of the life lived by African Americans is unique and very different from Ralph Ellison's, Toni Cade Bambara's, or Alice Walker's accounts. Compare and contrast "Sonny's Blues" with a story by one or more of these writers to describe how each finds his or her own way to dramatize what Baldwin calls "the ambiguity and irony of Negro life." Could "Sonny's Blues" be set in an Italian American or Jewish American family?

Commentary

James Baldwin, "Autobiographical Notes," p. 580.

Suggested Readings

Bloom, Harold, ed. *James Baldwin.* New York: Chelsea House, 1986.

Burt, Nancy, ed. *Critical Essays on James Baldwin.* Boston: G. K. Hall, 1986.

Campbell, James. *Talking at the Gates: A Life of James Baldwin.* New York: Viking, 1991.

Chametzky, Jules, ed. *A Tribute to James Baldwin: Black Writers Redefine the Struggle.* Amherst: U of Massachusetts P, 1989.

Kinnamon, Kenneth, ed. *James Baldwin.* Englewood Cliffs, NJ: Prentice, 1974.

Macebuh, Stanley. *James Baldwin: A Critical Study.* New York: Third, 1973.

Pratt, Louis H. *James Baldwin.* Twayne's United States Authors Series 290. Boston: Twayne, 1978.

Standley, F. L., ed. *Conversations with James Baldwin.* Jackson: UP of Mississippi, 1989.

TONI CADE BAMBARA

The Lesson (p. 73)

Relationships are an organizational key to this story. "The Lesson" is narrated by Sylvia, one of a group of eight African American children living in an uptown slum in New York City who are "treated" by their neighborhood guide, Miss Moore, to an educational visit to the F.A.O. Schwarz toy store at Fifth Avenue and Fifty-seventh Street. The group consists of four girls (Sylvia and her best friend, Sugar, and the relatively affluent Mercedes and her friend Rosie Giraffe) and four boys (Big Butt [Ronald], Junebug, Little Q.T., and Flyboy).

The "lesson" of the story is learned first by Sugar and then by Sylvia. All along Sylvia has assumed Sugar to be her ally, sharing her hostility to all adults as authority figures and to the idea of education. There's a suggestion of foreshadowing when the girls pay the taxicab driver outside F.A.O. Schwarz and Sugar steps in when Sylvia can't figure out the 10 percent tip on the eighty-five-cent fare — "Give him a dime." (This is a taxi fare from the early 1970s, when the story was written.) But Sugar plays dumb as usual in her next appearance in the story, when she asks Miss Moore outside the toy store, "Can we steal?"

After the children learn about the high prices of the luxury toys at F.A.O. Schwarz, they return to their homes uptown. Sugar's remark to Miss Moore before they disperse reveals that the afternoon's lesson in economics hasn't been wasted: "This is not much of a democracy if you ask me. Equal chance to pursue happiness means an equal crack at the dough, don't it?" Bambara doesn't tell us whether Sugar intends to begin studying hard in school or to begin dealing drugs, but the blinders formed by her life in the inner-city ghetto have fallen away, and she's clearly dissatisfied with her customary smart-aleck role. In her first response Sylvia is dumbfounded by her friend's betrayal, but within a few minutes she awakens to a sense of rivalry: "But ain't nobody gonna beat me at nuthin." Again Bambara leaves the lesson unspecified, and the reader must imagine how Sylvia intends to win the new game she's playing.

Questions for Discussion

1. What is the effect of the inner-city language in the story?
2. Is Sylvia a reliable or an unreliable narrator?
3. How does Bambara evoke a sense of sympathy for the people enduring the poverty and filth in Sylvia's neighborhood through her descriptions of the relationship of the winos and the newly arrived families from the South?
4. Describe the eight children and their relationships within the neighborhood group. How dependent is Sylvia on her friend Sugar?
5. Who is Miss Moore? Why does she personify the hostile force of "education" to the ghetto children?
6. Why does Sylvia keep the four dollars' change from the taxi fare? What does she do with the money? Is this a convincing ending to the story?

Topics for Writing

1.   **RESPONDING CREATIVELY**   Write a story using a special dialect that you have learned from your family or friends.
2.   **MAKING CONNECTIONS**   Compare and contrast the authors' uses of African American speech in this story and in Zora Neale Hurston's "Spunk" (p. 230). Analyze the different ways the two writers keep the dialect from distracting readers and causing them to lose interest in the stories.

Suggested Readings

Bambara, Toni Cade. *The Sea Birds Are Still Alive: Stories.* New York: Vintage, 1982.
Bell, Roseann P., Bettye J. Parker, and Beverly Guy-Sheftall, eds. *Sturdy Black Bridges: Visions of Black Women in Literature.* New York: Anchor, 1979.
Butler-Evans, Elliot. *Race, Gender, and Desire: Narrative Strategies in the Fiction of Toni Cade Bambara, Toni Morrison, and Alice Walker.* Philadelphia: Temple UP, 1989.
Cartwright, Jerome. "Bambara's 'The Lesson.'" *Explicator* 47.3 (Spring 1989): 61–63.
Evans, Mari, ed. *Black Women Writers (1950–1980): A Critical Evaluation.* New York: Anchor, 1984. 41–71.
Giddings, P. "Call to Wholeness from a Gifted Storyteller." *Encore* 9 (1980): 48–49.
Lyles, Lois F. "Time, Motion, Sound and Fury in *The Sea Birds Are Still Alive.*" *College Language Association Journal* 36.2 (Dec. 1992): 134–44.
Morrison, Toni. "City Limits, Village Values: Concepts of the Neighborhood in Black Fiction." In *Literature and the Urban Experience: Essays on the City and Literature.* Ed. Ann Chalmers Watts and Michael C. Jaye. New Brunswick: Rutgers UP, 1981.
Tate, Claudia, ed. *Black Women Writers at Work.* New York: Continuum, 1983. 12–38.
Vertreace, Martha M. "A Bibliography of Writings about Toni Cade Bambara." In *American Women Writing Fiction: Memory, Identity, Family, Space.* Ed. Mickey Pearlman. Lexington: U of Kentucky P, 1989.
———. "Toni Cade Bambara: The Dance of Character and Community." In *American Women Writing Fiction: Memory, Identity, Family, Space.* Ed. Mickey Pearlman. Lexington: U of Kentucky P, 1989.

Russell Banks

Black Man and White Woman in Dark Green Rowboat (p. 79)

In an afterword to a recent collection of his short stories (*The Angel on the Roof,* 2000), Banks justified his interest in the short story by explaining, "I've written a dozen or so novels, but the story form thrills me still. It invites me today, as it did back then, to behave on the page in a way that is more reckless, more steadily painful."

"Black Man and White Woman in Dark Green Rowboat" is a painful story, although on its quiet surface it could be said that the prevailing mood is a calm that matches the day Banks describes. He has left it to the reader to intuit the pain of each of the protagonists. We know the boundaries and the dimensions of the pain because the story at its deepest level is about something we live with daily; it is a story about race. The event that the author narrates, the young woman's decision to have an abortion, is just one incident in lives that have known many similar decisions. To allow us to judge the effect of the woman's decision on the life of the man she is with in the green rowboat, as well as on her own life, the author has stripped the story of any secondary action. We see everything with the bright clarity of the sunlight on the hot summer day. A man swims, people leave for work, a woman sits and reads a book, a second woman walks to get her mail, a teenager sits on his trailer steps and smokes a joint, an old man scrapes paint from the bottom of a boat. The scene is set for the couple and their afternoon of fishing in the dark green rowboat.

Everything about the scene is completely ordinary, except that the man is black. His blackness, because of the reader's consciousness of the implications of this blackness, places him just outside the scene. As both the man and woman are aware, the decision she has made, despite her denials, will shut him outside of the scene forever. If the author had chosen to allow her any other explanation for her decision —she is young, they aren't married, she has recently been ill — we might have been presented with a plausible justification for her decision. She says that her mother is concerned because of her problems with depression, but she never offers a reason of her own, and so we are left with an awareness that to her race is in itself sufficient reason for what she is going to do.

One of the brilliant technical aspects of the story is its use of color as a series of symbols for the events of the afternoon. At no point in the story is the phrase African American or the word Negro used to describe the man. We are only told the color of his skin. The word nigger appears once, but it is used by the man himself in angry derision. Instead, the ordinary scene of the lake and the trailers is given a spare, stripped dimension that is clarified with moments of color. The title itself gives us colors — black, white, and dark green — and the other tonalities in the story are set against them. The morning haze is blue-gray, the swimmer is wearing a white bathing cap, the water is a dark green plain. The woman who comes out to read is wearing white shorts and halter, the skin of the swimmer is a chestnut color, the woman going for her mail is wearing a T-shirt that had turned pink in the wash. The boy smoking the joint is blond, the blonde girl who walks toward the rowboat is wearing a lime-green bikini, and her skin is tanned a light brown. The trailers, from the lake, are like "pastel-colored shoe boxes." The reader is given continual, almost subliminal hints throughout the story to be conscious of color.

Although students probably have no familiarity with other stories by Banks, they would be interested to learn that he has written about this group of people many times. The trailer park is outside a small, imaginary New Hampshire mill town named Catamount, and the people who have jobs work in the town. The man taking the early swim is a retired captain in the American army, Dewey Knox; the woman reading the book, the girl's mother, is named Nancy Hubner; and the girl herself is Noni Hubner. She is home from college and recuperating from a nervous breakdown. Her father died two years earlier, and she and her mother are still struggling to go on with their lives. The boy smoking the joint is named Bruce Severance, and he will be shot to death in a few months as the result of a bad drug deal. The manager's name is Marcelle Chagnon, and the man scraping down the boat is named Merle Ring. He brought considerable confusion to the trailer park the winter before by winning $50,000 in the state lottery and showing a complete lack of interest in what might become of the money. This is the world of the little trailer park backed up against the boundary of the state forest at the edge of the lake. Did the author mean to emphasize the black man's inability to enter the white world at even this level by having his rejection come from someone who would be described as "trailer trash"?

Students will find it interesting to contrast this story with Ernest Hemingway's "Hills Like White Elephants" (p. 224). This is also a story about a young woman who is about to have an abortion, but the circumstances and emotions of the two stories reflect entirely different social and personal conditions.

Questions for Discussion

1.   The author has been careful to describe the setting of his story in considerable detail, but could the same story have been set in another part of the United States with the same effect?
2.   How much of the emotional effect of the story depends on the events that are described, and how much depends on the reader's understanding of the implication of the woman's decision?
3.   Does the young woman's lack of interest in fishing and the contents of the magazine she is reading suggest some of the emotional uncertainties that have gone into her decision?
4.   Although no direct reference is made to the man's race, there is emphasis on the historical implications of his color, first when he ties his shirt over his head so that he looks, in her words, like an Arab sheik and in his words, like a galley-slave, then when his face is described as "somber and ancient." What is the author suggesting with these allusions?
5.   Is there any moment in the story when the man is given an opportunity to express his wishes regarding the situation? What is the implication of her statement, "Well. We've been through all this before. A hundred times"?

Topics for Writing

1.   Discuss the way in which colors are used in the story.
2.   **MAKING CONNECTIONS**   Contrast this story with Hemingway's "Hills Like White Elephants" (p. 224) and discuss the similarities and the differences in the woman's role in the decision she has made.
3.   Discuss how the reader's consciousness of race is crucial to his or her understanding of the story.

Connection

Ernest Hemingway, *"Hills Like White Elephants,"* p. 224.

Suggested Reading

Niemi, Robert. *Russell Banks.* New York: Twayne; London: Prentice-Hall International, 1997.

AIMEE BENDER

The Rememberer (p. 85)

"The Rememberer" in this story is the narrator, reminding us that often stories are what people tell to hold on to their significant past. Yet she begins with an absurd proposition: "My lover is experiencing reverse evolution. . . . one day he was my lover and the next he was some kind of ape. It's been a month and now he's a sea turtle." She's serious. As her narrative goes on, her lover regresses from a sea turtle to a salamander which she brings to the beach so he can swim out to sea. Having watched him de-evolve, she concludes with the hope that one day he will re-evolve to "wash up on shore. A naked man with a startled look."

As the editors Robert Shapard and James Thomas observe in *New Sudden Fiction* (2007), Bender is writing "an allegory of disintegrating relationships, one partner growing away from another as the primitive opposes the intellectual." Bender's casual style is poignantly surrealistic, blending magic and reality, and her tone is as darkly humorous as it is poetic. She has created a contemporary feminist fairy tale in which the woman's intelligent voice is more than equal to that of her troubled masculine partner. This makes her the responsible one in the relationship, and she reminds herself that "it is my job to remember." Cold comfort when she puts her "one self to bed" in the last line of the story.

Questions for Discussion

1. Trace the stages of how Bender develops her metaphor of human evolution into an allegory in "The Rememberer."
2. Discuss how Bender deconstructs the idea of rationality as the highest human virtue. What quality does her lover offer in its place?
3. Bender often employs short sentences in her narration to suggest her emotional vulnerability as she watches her lover regress into earlier evolutionary stages. How effective is this rhetorical strategy in making her a sympathetic character in the story? How effective is her use of humor?

Topics for Writing

1. "The Rememberer" is an example of the type of short story now labeled "sudden fiction," very short stories only a few pages long. Unlike O. Henry stories of the past, very short stories written for popular magazines with a surprise ending or an ironic twist at the end, the new "sudden fictions" written by contemporary writers such as Bender don't end with a bang. The writer Charles Baxter has said that these new stories exhibit a new vision "of where you think reality takes place" — reflecting the cramped, hectic pace of our lives today as well as the shorter attention spans of readers who have grown up with television, instant text messaging, and cell phone communication. Write an essay in which you discuss the advantages and disadvantages of this kind of very short story.
2. **MAKING CONNECTIONS** Compare and contrast "The Rememberer" with the earlier allegorical very short story "Jackals and Arabs" (p. 275) by Franz Kafka.

Connection

Franz Kafka, "*The Metamorphosis,*" p. 278.

Commentary

John Gardner, "*On Myths and Literary Fairy Tales,*" pp. 652.

Suggested Readings

Bender, Aimee. *The Girl in the Flammable Skirt.* New York: Doubleday, 1998.
Shapard, Robert, and James Thomas, eds. *New Sudden Fiction.* New York: Norton, 2007.

RAYMOND CARVER

Cathedral (p. 89)

"Cathedral" is a story about alienation, isolation, and the cure for both. The narrator is an insecure, jealous man, more dead than alive — a man who has constructed a virtual prison in which he exists emotionally detached from his wife and cut off from any active participation in what makes life worth living. He anesthetizes his pain with drink and marijuana while making comments that reveal his feelings of inferiority, confusion, and resentment.

When the story opens, the narrator's tone is anecdotal and familiar ("this blind man, an old friend of my wife's, he was on his way to spend the night. . . . I wasn't enthusiastic about his visit"); at the conclusion, however, his tone has become one of awe ("'it's really something,' I said"). We are aware that he has undergone an important transformation, an almost mystical experience that comes to him at an unexpected moment from an unexpected source and frees him from the prison his life had become. Despite his jealousy of blind Robert and his professed resistance to the other's intrusion, the narrator unwittingly makes a friend of the blind man and in the process comes to understand something about himself. As he begins, ironically, to see through Robert's eyes, to experience the world through Robert's perceptions, his own horizons are expanded ("my eyes were still closed. I was in my house. I knew that. But I didn't feel like I was inside anything"). Robert contradicts every stereotypical idea the narrator holds about the blind, and with his commanding presence, his vitality, his sensitivity, and his engagement with life, he forces the narrator to see.

Contrasts abound between Robert and the narrator and between their respective relationships with the narrator's wife. The blind man is infinitely more alive than the narrator ("I don't have any blind friends," the narrator tells his wife; "you don't have any friends," she replies. "The blind man was also a ham radio operator. He talked in his loud voice about conversations he'd had with fellow operators in Guam, in the Philippines, in Alaska, and even in Tahiti. He said he'd have a lot of friends there if he ever wanted to go visit those places"). Robert and the narrator's wife (whom the narrator never calls by name but refers to, significantly, as "my wife") have a special and long-lasting friendship that involves a level of intimacy conspicuously absent from the narrator's marital relationship, the cause of much jealousy and resentment. An underlying tension is constantly present in the conversations between the couple, but with Robert the woman is a different person: "I saw my wife laughing as she parked the car. I saw her get out of the car and shut the door. She was still wearing a smile. Just amazing." We infer from this observation that she does not laugh much with her husband. His wife and Robert approach the house, "talking all the way." Earlier the narrator had commented, "right then my wife filled me in with more detail than I cared to know." Talking and the emotional sharing that results have played a vital role in the enduring relationship between the woman and the blind man; they are obviously not an integral part of the marital relationship.

"I want you to feel comfortable in this house," the wife says to her friend. "I am comfortable," Robert replies. Oddly, it is the narrator who is uncomfortable, and this discomfort prompts his pathetic attempts to feel superior to the blind man. Offering him marijuana, the narrator observes, "I could tell he didn't know the first thing." But soon he grudgingly acknowledges, "it was like he'd been doing it since he was nine years old," and the dynamics of the relationship slowly begin to change. After his wife falls asleep, the narrator offers to take Robert up to bed, but Robert declines. The narrator politely responds with "I'm glad for the company," then realizes, "and I guess I was." They watch television together, Robert telling his host, "whatever you want to watch is okay. I'm always learning something. Learning never ends. It won't hurt me to learn something tonight," but it is the narrator, not the blind man, who will learn something important tonight. The image of the two men's hands tracing the cathedral together is dramatic, striking, and poignant. Robert asks him if he is religious, and the narrator realizes that he truly does not know how to talk to Robert, but the difference now is that he begins to care that he doesn't.

As the two men's hands trace the cathedral, we are reminded of the time when Robert touched the woman's face. Perhaps the connection that has been forged between the men will influence the marriage as well. The narrator's awkward and inadequate attempts at conversation with Robert are a form of engagement, and his hand speeding across the page drawing windows and arches and buttresses is a liberating experience. Inspired by the man who cannot see, he has drawn himself out of the prison to which his own limited perceptions had restricted him.

Questions for Discussion

1. Is the narrator a sympathetic protagonist? Does your opinion of him change as the story progresses?
2. What does the narrator learn from his encounter with Robert? Do you believe that there will be a significant change in his outlook from this point on?
3. What is the significance of Carver's choice of a cathedral as catalyst for the narrator's learning experience? What added dimension does this symbol bring to our understanding of the story? Can you tie it to any previous detail?
4. Contrast the author's tone and the narrator's mood at the opening of the story with the tone and mood at the end. How does the change in style reflect the change that has occurred in the narrator?
5. What is the narrator's attitude toward his wife? What kind of marriage do they have, and what evidence do you find to support your conclusion? Is the narrator's jealousy of Robert irrational?
6. What are the primary emotions displayed by the narrator throughout, and how can we understand them in terms of the life he leads? What are some adjectives you would use to characterize him? What role does alcohol play in his life?
7. What is it about Robert that unsettles the narrator? How do his appearance and bearing resist every stereotypical image the narrator has about blind people, and why is this so upsetting?

Topics for Writing

1. For Carver, salvation lies in human contact and connection. Comment critically.
2. **RESPONDING CREATIVELY** Create a conversation between the narrator and his wife after Robert's departure.
3. Discuss "Cathedral" as a story about "the blind leading the blind."

Commentaries

Raymond Carver, *"On Writing,"* p. 584.
Raymond Carver, *"Creative Writing 101,"* p. 587.

Suggested Readings

Adelman, Bob. *Carver Country — The World of Raymond Carver.* New York: Scribner's, 1991. A photographic essay with quotations from Carver's writing.
———. *Fires: Essays, Poems, Stories.* Santa Barbara, CA: Capra, 1983.

———. *Where I'm Calling From: New and Selected Stories.* New York: Atlantic Monthly, 1988.

Gentry, Marshall B., and William A. Stuff, eds. *Conversations with Raymond Carver.* Jackson: UP of Mississippi, 1990.

Halpert, Sam, ed. *When We Talk About Raymond Carver.* Layton, UT: Gibbs Smith, 1991.

Simpson, M. "The Art of Fiction: Raymond Carver." Interview. *Paris Review* 25 (1983): 193–221.

Stull, W. L. "Beyond Hopelessville: Another Side of Raymond Carver." *Philological Quarterly* 64 (1985): 1–15.

Lan Samantha Chang

Water Names (p. 100)

This is another very short contemporary story, like Bender's "The Rememberer," often labeled "sudden fiction." Chang uses an old-fashioned realistic style to frame her traditional narrative of a grandmother's ghost tale about the family's ancient past in China.

To begin the story, Chang evokes a sharp sense of the present situation of the three sisters in the family after their parents' emigration to the American Midwest. In this frame, she sketches in the childish rivalries between the three young girls, Ingrid, Lily, and the unnamed narrator, squabbling with each other on their back porch at the end of a hot summer day. Their grandmother Waipuo joins them to tell them a story, as she says, "just to keep up your Chinese," but her intent as a storyteller is to give them a sense of their long, distinguished ancestry and to instill a sense of the importance of the past as it has the power to evoke wonder at life's possibilities in the prosaic world of the present.

The grandmother's story of Wen Zhiqing's lovely but spoiled daughter — who became enchanted by the deep, flowing river after a cormorant dived for a fish that had a valuable pearl ring in its stomach, which the girl imagined was a gift from a handsome prince in the underwater kingdom — is perhaps meant as a cautionary tale to the three small, listening children. Waipuo refuses to explain her story, escaping back into her bedroom inside the house, where her granddaughters imagine that she stands, combing her beautiful long hair before the mirror like a fairytale princess grown old. Left alone on the porch, the girls sense the ground of the American prairie beneath them "as dry and hard as bone." They are growing up far from the deep, flowing river of infinite possibilities in the story they have just heard. The sound of the prairie crickets reminds the grandmother of the sound of the "rippling waters" of the great Chang Jiang river she has left behind in China, but the narrator senses correctly that her own future in the New Country will be very different from that of the lovesick Chinese daughter in her grandmother's tale of their shared family past.

Questions for Discussion

1. Why does Chang interrupt the grandmother's ghost story with interjections by her three small listeners? Would "Water Names" have been more effective without these interruptions?
2. Why does Waipuo ignore her listeners, for the most part?
3. What do you think happened to Wen Zhiqing's daughter? Why isn't her fate important to the story that Chang is telling?

4. Why didn't Chang give a name to Wen Zhiqing's daughter? Why are we told the names of the narrator's sisters, Lily and Ingrid?

Topic for Writing

1. **RESPONDING CREATIVELY**   Write a ghost story based on an incident in your childhood or in your family history.

Commentary

John Gardner, "*On Myths and Literary Fairy Tales,*" pp. 652.

Suggested Readings

Chang, Lan Samantha. *Hunger.* New York: Norton, 1998.
Shapard, Robert, and James Thomas, eds. *New Sudden Fiction.* New York: Norton, 2007.

Anton Chekhov

The Lady with the Pet Dog (p. 102)

Anna Sergeyevna comes to Yalta because she wants "to live, to live!" Gurov begins his affair with her because he is bored and enjoys the freedom and ease of a casual liaison. At the outset both are undistinguished, almost clichés — a philandering bank employee escaping from a wife he cannot measure up to, a lady with a dog and a "flunkey" for a husband. By the end of the story, however, after having been captured and tormented by a love that refuses to be filed away in memory, the two gain dignity and stature by recognizing that life is neither exciting nor easy; and, by taking up the burden of the life they have discovered in their mutual compassion, they validate their love.

Chekhov develops the nature of this true love, so ennobling and so tragic, by testing it against a series of stereotypes that it transcends and by showing a series of stock expectations that it violates. Anna Sergeyevna reacts differently from any of the several types of women Gurov has previously made love to, and Gurov finds himself unable to handle his own feelings in the way he is accustomed to. Anna Sergeyevna proves neither a slice of watermelon nor a pleasant focus of nostalgia. Most important, as the conclusion implies, she will not remain the secret core of his life, bought at the price of falsehood and suspicion of others.

In observing the evolution of the lovers, the reader is led through a series of potential misconceptions. We may want to despise Gurov as a careless breaker of hearts, but it is clear that he has one of his own when he sees Anna Sergeyevna as a Magdalene. Later, when Gurov is tormented by his longings for Anna Sergeyevna, we are tempted to laugh the superior realist's laugh at a romantic fool: Surely when Gurov arrives at S——, disillusionment will await him. And in a sense it does. Just as there was dust in the streets at Yalta, the best room in the hotel at S—— is coated with dust; reality is an ugly fence; and even the theater (where *The Geisha* is playing) is full of reminders of how unromantic life really is. But Anna Sergeyevna has not, as Gurov supposes at one point, taken another lover, nor has she been able to forget Gurov.

The antiromantic tone is but another oversimplification, and the story comes to rest, somewhat like Milton's *Paradise Lost*, at a moment of beginning. The lovers' disillusionment about the nature of the struggle they face creates in them a deep compassion for each other, which finds its echo in readers' final attitude toward them as fellow human beings whose lives are like our own and who deserve a full measure of our sympathy. Or perhaps they draw our pity; surely their fate, which Chekhov so skillfully depicts as probable and true, inspires tragic fear. Gurov and Anna Sergeyevna have met the god of love, and Chekhov awes us by making him seem real.

WILLIAM E. SHEIDLEY

Questions for Discussion

1. Why does Gurov call women "an inferior race"?
2. At the end of section I, Gurov thinks that there is "something pathetic" about Anna Sergeyevna. Is there? What is it?
3. Why is Anna Sergeyevna so distracted as she watches the steamer putting in?
4. How does Anna Sergeyevna differ from other women Gurov has known, as they are described in the paragraph that ends "the lace on their lingerie seemed to him to resemble scales"? Compare this passage with the paragraph that begins "His head was already beginning to turn gray."
5. In view of what follows, is it appropriate that Gurov should see Anna Sergeyevna as a Magdalene?
6. What is the function of the paragraph that begins "At Oreanda they sat on a bench not far from the church"?
7. What "complete change" does Gurov undergo during his affair with Anna Sergeyevna at Yalta? Is it permanent?
8. Explain Gurov's remark at the end of section II: "High time!"
9. Why is Gurov enraged at his companion's remark about the sturgeon?
10. Discuss the possible meanings of the objects Gurov encounters in S———: the broken figurine, the long gray fence, the cheap blanket, and so on.
11. Seeing Anna Sergeyevna enter the theater, Gurov "understood clearly that in the whole world there was no human being so near, so precious, and so important to him." What is Chekhov's tone in this statement?
12. Explain Anna Sergeyevna's reaction to Gurov's arrival. Why does she volunteer to come to Moscow?
13. Discuss the implications of Gurov's "two lives" as Chekhov explains them in section IV. Do you agree with the generalizations about the desire for privacy with which the paragraph ends? Relate these ideas to the story's ending.
14. What will life be like for Gurov and Anna Sergeyevna? Anna has previously said, "I have never been happy; I am unhappy now, and I never, never shall be happy, never!" Is she right?

Topics for Writing

1. Write an essay describing Chekhov's characterization of the wronged spouse in "The Lady with the Pet Dog."
2. Discuss the meaning of the three geographical locales in "The Lady with the Pet Dog."
3. On your first reading of the story, stop at the end of each section and write down your judgment of Gurov and Anna Sergeyevna and your prediction of what will happen next. When you have finished reading, compare what you wrote with what turned out to be the case and with your final estimate of the protagonists. To the extent that your initial impressions were borne out, what points in the text helped to guide you? To the extent that you were surprised, explain what led you astray. What might Chekhov have wanted to accomplish by making such misconceptions possible?

Connection

Joyce Carol Oates, *"The Lady with the Pet Dog,"* p. 394.

Commentary

Anton Chekhov, *"Technique in Writing the Short Story,"* p. 591.

Suggested Readings

Bates, H. E. *The Modern Short Story.* Boston: The Writer, 1972.

Eekman, Thomas, ed. *Critical Essays on Anton Chekhov.* Boston: G. K. Hall, 1989.

Friedland, Louis S., ed. *Anton Tchekhov's Letters on the Short Story, the Drama, and Other Topics.* Salem, NH: Ayer, 1965.

Kramer, Karl D. *The Chameleon and the Dream: The Image of Reality in Chekhov's Stories.* The Hague: Mouton, 1970. 171.

Matlaw, Ralph E., ed. *Anton Chekhov's Short Stories.* New York: Norton, 1979.

Meister, Charles W. *Chekhov Criticism, 1880 through 1986.* New York: St. Martin's, 1990.

Pritchett, V. S. *Chekhov: A Spirit Set Free.* New York: Random, 1988.

Rayfield, Donald. *Chekhov: The Evolution of His Art.* New York: Barnes, 1975. 197–200.

Smith, Virginia Llewellyn. "The Lady with the Dog." *Anton Chekhov's Short Stories: Texts of the Stories, Backgrounds, Criticism.* Ed. Ralph E. Matlaw. New York: Norton, 1979. Excerpted from Smith, *Anton Chekhov and the Lady with the Dog* (New York: Oxford UP, 1973). 96–97, 212–18.

Troyat, Henri. *Chekhov.* Trans. Michael Henry Heim. New York: Dutton, 1986.

KATE CHOPIN

Désirée's Baby (p. 117)
The Story of an Hour (p. 121)

DÉSIRÉE'S BABY

It is difficult to imagine a reader who would not be horrified and disgusted by the tragic results of the racism and sexism that permeate this story. No one could believe that Armand Aubigny's inhuman cruelty to his wife, Désirée, and his child is warranted. The only real uncertainty the reader confronts regards Armand's foreknowledge of his own parentage: Did he know that his mother had "negro blood" before he married Désirée, or did he discover her revealing letter later on? If he did know beforehand (and it is difficult to believe that he did not) his courtship of and marriage to Désirée were highly calculated actions, with Désirée chosen because she was the perfect woman to be used in an "experimental" reproduction. If their child(ren) "passed" as white, everything would be fine. If not, Désirée, the foundling, would be the perfect victim to take the blame.

This may seem to be judging Armand too harshly, because the narrator does describe his great passion for Désirée, so suddenly and furiously ignited. Certainly Armand behaves like a man in love. But Chopin inserts a few subtle remarks that allow us to question this, at least in hindsight: "The wonder was that he had not loved her before; for he had known her since his father brought him home from Paris, a boy of eight, after his mother died there." It does seem unlikely that a man of Armand's temperament would conceive this sudden intense desire for "the girl next door," a sweet, naive young woman whom he has known for most of his life. Right from the beginning, Chopin also reveals details about his character that are unsettling, even to the innocent and loving Désirée. The basic cruelty of Armand's nature is hinted at throughout the story, particularly regarding his severe treatment of "his negroes," which is notably in sharp contrast to his father's example.

Armand's reputation as a harsh slavemaster supports the presumption that he has known about his own part–African American ancestry all along. He did not learn this behavior from his father, who was "easy-going and indulgent" in his dealings with the slaves. The knowledge that some of his own ancestors sprang from the same "race of slavery" would surely be unbearable to the proud, "imperious" Armand, and the rage and shame that his knowledge brings would easily be turned against the blacks around him. In much the same way, when Armand realizes that his baby is visibly racially mixed, he vents his fury viciously on his slaves, the "very spirit of Satan [taking] hold of him."

Modern readers will find many disturbing aspects to this story. The seemingly casual racism is horrifying. And feminists will be likely to take exception (as they sometimes do to Chopin's "The Awakening") to Désirée's passive acceptance of Armand's rejection of her and his child, and her apparently deliberate walk into the bayou. Suicide is not the strong woman's answer to the situation, but Désirée is definitely not a strong woman. She does have wealthy parents who love her and are willing to take care of her and the baby. So why would she feel that she has to end her life? Discussion of this issue will have to focus on the historical period and social setting of the story. Gender and class roles and structures were so rigid that it was impossible for a woman to cross those lines very far. If she tried, what would the cost be to her children? And of course, the most rigid barrier of all was racial. No mixing of black and white blood would ever be condoned in that society (thus, Armand's mother remained in France, keeping her family secrets), so Désirée's baby would never have acceptance anywhere. Désirée isn't able to see any viable way out of her terrifying situation, and her view is not entirely unrealistic, considering her time and place. Once again, Kate Chopin realistically depicts the cruelty and horror of a social structure that totally denies power to women, children, the poor, and, most of all, to blacks.

Questions for Discussion

1. Describe your feelings toward Armand at the end of the story. What aspect of this last scene do you find the most shocking? Are you completely surprised by his behavior here? See if you can trace Chopin's gradual building of Armand's character, noting the things she chooses to reveal to us throughout the story.
2. What kind of person is Désirée? Does she seem to be a good match for Armand? Does your opinion of her change as the story progresses? How consistent is she as a character?
3. How do you feel about Désirée's final choice? Is suicide an understandable choice, or is she simply a weak character? What other options do you think she may have?
4. Should Madame Valmondé have told Désirée of her realization about the baby? When she sees the baby at four weeks of age, she obviously is startled by something in its appearance, but doesn't mention it. Then, she returns home and seems to wait for disaster to strike, never returning to visit Désirée. How do you explain this behavior coming from an obviously protective, loving mother?
5. Armand is shown to be a very cruel master to his slaves, a direct contrast to the way in which his father ran the plantation. Does learning his family secret in the last scene suggest any explanation for this?
6. Do you think Armand knew about his own mother's African American ancestry before he courted and married Désirée? Look for evidence from the story to support your opinion.

Topics for Writing

1. Discuss the way the setting affects the action in this story.
2. Should Désirée have returned to her family home with her baby? Consider the pros and cons of her future there.
3. According to the critic Wai-chee Dimock, the racial injustice in "Désirée's Baby" is "only a necessary background against which Chopin stages her deadly dramatic irony. . . . The injustice here is not the injustice of racial oppression but the injustice of a wrongly attributed racial identity." Agree or disagree with this interpretation of the story.

Commentary

Kate Chopin, *"How I Stumbled upon Maupassant,"* p. 592.

Suggested Readings

See page 26 of this manual.

THE STORY OF AN HOUR

Does the O. Henryesque trick ending of this story merely surprise us, or does Chopin arrange to have Louise Mallard expire at the sight of her unexpectedly still living husband in order to make a thematic point? Students inclined to groan when Brently Mallard returns "composedly carrying his gripsack and umbrella" may come to think better of the ending if you ask them to evaluate the doctors' conclusions about the cause of Mrs. Mallard's death. Although Richards and Josephine take "great care . . . to break to her as gently as possible the news of her husband's death," what actually kills Mrs. Mallard is the news that he is still alive. The experience of regeneration and freedom that she undergoes in the armchair looking out upon a springtime vista involves an almost sexual surrender of conventional repressions and restraints. As she "abandons herself" to the realization of her freedom that "approaches to possess her," Mrs. Mallard enjoys a hitherto forbidden physical and spiritual excitement. The presumption that she would be devastated by the death of her husband, like the presumption that she needs to be protected by watchful, "tender" friends, reduces Mrs. Mallard to a dependency from which she is joyful at last to escape. Chopin best depicts this oppressive, debilitating concern in what Mrs. Mallard thinks she will weep again to see: "the kind, tender hands folded in death; the face that had never looked save with love upon her, fixed and gray and dead." Although had she lived Mrs. Mallard might have felt guilty for taking her selfhood like a lover and pridefully stepping forth "like a goddess of Victory," Chopin effectively suggests that the guilt belongs instead to the caretakers, the "travel-stained" Brently, the discomfited Josephine, and Richards, whose "quick motion" to conceal his error comes "too late."

WILLIAM E. SHEIDLEY

Questions for Discussion

1. In view of Mrs. Mallard's eventual reactions, evaluate the efforts of Josephine and Richards to break the news of her husband's death gently.
2. What purpose might Chopin have in stressing that Mrs. Mallard does not block out the realization that her husband has died?
3. What might be the cause or causes of the "physical exhaustion that haunted her body and seemed to reach into her soul" that Mrs. Mallard feels as she sinks into the armchair?
4. Describe your reaction to the view out the window the first time you read the story. Did it change on a second reading?

5. Mrs. Mallard's face bespeaks repression. What has she been repressing?
6. Discuss the imagery Chopin uses to describe Mrs. Mallard's recognition of her new freedom.
7. What kind of man is Brently Mallard, as Mrs. Mallard remembers him? In what ways does he resemble Josephine and Richards?
8. Describe your feelings about Mrs. Mallard as she emerges from her room. Is the saying "Pride goeth before a fall" relevant here?
9. In what way is the doctors' pronouncement on the cause of Mrs. Mallard's death ironic? In what sense is it nonetheless correct?

Topics for Writing

1. Discuss the imagery of life and the imagery of death in "The Story of an Hour."
2. Write a paper analyzing "The Story of an Hour" as a thwarted awakening.
3. Describe the tragic irony in "The Story of an Hour."
4. On a second reading of "The Story of an Hour," try to recall how you responded to each paragraph or significant passage when you read it the first time. Write short explanations of any significant changes in your reactions. To what extent are those changes the result of knowing the story's ending? What other factors are at work?
5. RESPONDING CREATIVELY   Can falsehood be the key to truth? Narrate a personal experience in which your own or someone else's reaction to misinformation revealed something meaningful and true.
6. RESPONDING CREATIVELY   How long is a turning point? Tell a story covering a brief span of time — a few minutes or an hour — in which the central character's life is permanently changed. Study Chopin's techniques for summarizing and condensing information.

Commentary

Kate Chopin, *"How I Stumbled upon Maupassant,"* p. 592.

Suggested Readings

Bender, B. "Kate Chopin's Lyrical Short Stories." *Studies in Short Fiction* 11 (1974): 257–66.

Chopin, Kate. *The Complete Works of Kate Chopin.* Baton Rouge: Louisiana State UP, 1970.

Dimock, Wai-chee. "Kate Chopin." In *Modern American Women Writers.* Ed. Elaine Showalter et al. New York: Collier, 1993.

Fluck, Winfred. "Tentative Transgressions: Kate Chopin's Fiction as a Mode of Symbolic Action." *Studies in American Fiction* 10 (1982): 151–71.

Miner, Madonne M. "Veiled Hints: An Affected Stylist's Reading of Kate Chopin's 'Story of an Hour.'" *Markham Review* 11 (1982): 29–32.

Seyersted, Per. *Kate Chopin: A Critical Biography.* Baton Rouge: Louisiana State UP, 1969. 57–59.

Skaggs, Peggy. *Kate Chopin.* Boston: Twayne, 1985.

Toth, Emily. *Kate Chopin.* New York: Morrow, 1990.

JUNOT DÍAZ

How to Date a Browngirl, Blackgirl, Whitegirl, or Halfie (p. 123)

Díaz has chosen the second-person point of view for his narrative, and he keeps it short and simple, as if expecting his reader to be on the same educational level as his narrator. Yet the language of the story is deceptively simple; Díaz also slips in words such as "nemesis" (instead of "enemy") that give his story the smooth finish of a creative writing class exercise that's been polished in draft after draft. The audacity of Díaz's subject is what grabs the reader's attention: "If she's a whitegirl you know you'll at least get a hand job."

As the speaker continues to outline the action he anticipates happening on the date, he grows progressively less confident, expecting less and less from the girls he is with. The tone of the story darkens as he fails to make any significant human contact with his dates, even the white girl whom he imagines permits sexual intercourse. The clash of the different cultures isn't the only communication barrier; the speaker includes "a local girl" among the hypothetical dates he's describing, so he doesn't need to pretend with her that he's a "Spanish" guy instead of a Dominican.

The mood of disenchantment extends past the narrator's personal encounters into the broader area of politics — there are references to the United States' invasion of the Dominican Republic. While moving to the United States apparently hasn't given the narrator immediate access to the American Dream of economic prosperity — he lives "in the Terrace," a housing project in New Jersey — he still can dream of sexual conquest with the ready supply of "strong-headed" young girls he meets at school.

Questions for Discussion

1. What are the cultural differences in the expectations of a "Browngirl, Blackgirl, Whitegirl, or Halfie"?
2. How do their different expectations cause the narrator to treat them differently on dates?
3. To whom is the narrator talking in the story? Who is his ideal reader?
4. Why is the narrator so conscious of his hairstyle?
5. How does the narrator establish the setting of the story and give a sense of the atmosphere of the housing project where he lives?
6. Why does the narrator include his reference to the tear gas used by the United States when the Dominican Republic was invaded?

Topics for Writing

1. MAKING CONNECTIONS Compare and contrast Díaz's story with the story told in the second person by Lorrie Moore, "How to Become a Writer" (p. 362).
2. The syntax of the story is weighted with many contemporary colloquialisms. Discuss whether these terms will present difficulties for future readers or whether they help lend the story a stronger sense of verisimilitude.
3. Discuss this story in the context of other immigrant literature and the themes of assimilation and loss of identity.

Suggested Reading

Díaz, Junot. *Drown*. New York: Riverhead, 1996.

RALPH ELLISON

Battle Royal (p. 127)

In the headnote to his comments on "Battle Royal" reprinted in Chapter 5 (p. 593), Ellison is quoted expounding on the importance of "converting experience into symbolic action" in fiction. One of the major triumphs of "Battle Royal" (and of *Invisible Man* as a whole) is Ellison's success in the realistic rendering of experiences that are in themselves so obviously significant of larger social, psychological, and moral truths that explication is unnecessary. From the small American flag tattooed on the nude dancer's belly to the "rope of bloody saliva forming a shape like an undiscovered continent" that the narrator drools on his new briefcase, Ellison's account of the festivities at the men's smoker effectively symbolizes the condition of blacks in America while remaining thoroughly persuasive in its verisimilitude. Both the broader structure of the evening and the finer details of narration and description carry the force of Ellison's theme. The young blacks are tortured first by having the most forbidden of America's riches dangled before them, then by being put through their paces in a melee in which their only victims are their fellows and the whites look on with glee, and finally by being debased into groveling for money (some of it counterfeit) on a rug whose electrification underlines their own powerlessness. In one brief passage, the nightmare of such an existence appears in a strange subaqueous vision of primitive life: "The boys groped about like blind, cautious crabs crouching to protect their mid-sections, their heads pulled in short against their shoulders, their arms stretched nervously before them, with their fists testing the smoke-filled air like the knobbed feelers of hypersensitive snails."

Because his actual experience forms itself into such revealing images, the narrator's dream of his grandfather seems all the more credible as a statement of his position. He dreams that the message on his briefcase says "Keep This Nigger-Boy Running" — not far from "You've got to know your place at all times." The narrator's grandfather knew his place and played his role, but he never believed a word of it. It is this assurance of an inner being quite different from the face he turned toward the world that makes him so troubling to his descendants. In his effort to please the white folks and in so doing to get ahead, the narrator seeks alliance rather than secret enmity with his antagonists. As a result he subjects himself to the trickery and delusions the white community chooses to impose on him. Dependent for his sense of himself on his ability to guess what they want him to do, the narrator finds himself groping in a fog deeper than the swirls of cigar smoke that hang over the scene of the battle royal. When the smoke clears and the blindfold comes off, he will recognize, as he puts it at the start, that he is invisible to the whites and may therefore discover his own identity within himself.

The first episode of a long novel does not accomplish the narrator's enlightenment, but it constitutes his initiation into the realities of the world he must eventually come to understand. Ellison says (in his commentary on p. 593) that the battle royal "is a ritual in preservation of caste lines, a keeping of taboo to appease the gods and ward off bad luck," and that "it is also the initiation ritual to which all greenhorns are subjected." This rite of initiation bears a revealing relation to the primitive initiation ceremonies known to anthropologists. The battle royal, for example, separates the boys from their families, challenges them to prove their valor, and subjects them to instruction by the tribal elders in a sort of men's house. The boys are stripped and introduced to sexual mysteries. But the hazing of women that is a frequent feature of such initiations is not carried on here by the boys but by the gross elders, whose savagery is barely under control; the ritual ends not with the entry of the initiates into the larger community but with their pointed exclusion; and the sacred lore embodied in the narrator's recital of his graduation speech makes explicit the contradictions inherent in the society it describes. To cast down his bucket where he is forces him to swallow his own blood. The narrator is delighted with the scholarship to "the state college for Negroes" that he wins by toeing the line and knowing his place, and he does not object that the "gold" coins he groveled for are fraudulent. His education in the meaning of his grandfather's troubling injunctions will continue, but the reader has already seen enough to recognize their validity.

WILLIAM E. SHEIDLEY

Questions for Discussions

1. In the opening paragraph the narrator says, "I was naive." In what ways is his naiveté revealed in the story that follows?
2. Why does the narrator feel guilty when praised?
3. What is the message to the narrator behind the suggestion "that since I was to be there anyway I might as well take part in the battle royal"? Explain his hesitation. What is the most important part of the evening for the whites?
4. Who is present at the smoker? Discuss the role of the school superintendent.
5. What techniques does Ellison use to convey to the reader the impact that seeing the stripper has on the boys?
6. What does the stripper have in common with the boys? Why are both a stripper and a battle royal part of the evening's entertainment?
7. During the chaos of the battle, the narrator worries about how his speech will be received. Is that absurd or understandable?
8. Does the deathbed advice of the narrator's grandfather offer a way to handle the battle royal?
9. Why does Tatlock refuse to take a dive?
10. Explain the narrator's first reaction to seeing the "small square rug." In what sense is his instinct correct?
11. What is the meaning of the electric rug to the whites? What do they wish it to demonstrate to the blacks?
12. Explain Mr. Colcord's reaction when the narrator tries to topple him onto the rug.
13. Analyze the narrator's speech. What is the implication of his having to deliver it while swallowing his own blood?
14. Why is the school superintendent confident that the narrator will "lead his people in the proper paths"?
15. Why does the narrator stand in front of his grandfather's picture holding his briefcase? Who gets the better of this confrontation?

Topics for Writing

1. Make a study of seeing and understanding in "Battle Royal."
2. Analyze the role of sex, violence, and power in "Battle Royal."
3. Write an essay exploring the battle royal and black experience in America.
4. Describe the "permanent interest" of "Battle Royal." (See Ellison's commentary in Chapter 5.)
5. Examine the blonde, the gold coins, and the calfskin briefcase in "Battle Royal."
6. Select a passage of twenty or fewer lines from this story for detailed explication. Relate as many of its images as possible to others in the story and to the general

ideas that the story develops. To what extent does the passage you chose reflect the meaning of the story as a whole?

7.   **RESPONDING CREATIVELY**   Recall an experience in which you were humiliated or embarrassed. What motives of your own and of those before whom you were embarrassed put you in such a position? Narrate the incident so that these underlying purposes become evident to the reader.

8.   Write a description of a game or ceremony with which you are familiar. What set of principles or relationships (not necessarily malign) does it express?

Commentary

Ralph Ellison, *"The Influence of Folklore on 'Battle Royal,'"* p. 593.

Suggested Readings

Blake, Susan L. "Ritual and Rationalization: Black Folklore in the Works of Ralph Ellison." *PMLA* 94 (1979): 121–26, esp. 122–23.

Horowitz, Ellin. "The Rebirth of the Artist." In *Twentieth-Century Interpretations of Invisible Man.* Ed. John M. Reilly. Englewood Cliffs, NJ: Prentice, 1970. 80–88, esp. 81. (Originally published in 1964.)

O'Meally, Robert G. *The Craft of Ralph Ellison.* Cambridge, MA: Harvard UP, 1980. 12–14.

Vogler, Thomas A. *"Invisible Man:* Somebody's Protest Novel." *Ralph Ellison: A Collection of Critical Essays.* Ed. John Hersey. Englewood Cliffs, NJ: Prentice, 1974. 127–50, esp. 143–44.

LOUISE ERDRICH

The Red Convertible (p. 138)

The story takes place in 1974, when Henry Junior comes back to the Chippewa Indian reservation after more than three years as a soldier in Vietnam. He is mentally disturbed by his experiences in the war, and, as his brother Lyman (who narrates the story) says laconically, "the change was no good."

Erdrich has structured her story in a traditional manner. It is narrated in the first person by Lyman, who uses the past tense to describe the finality of what happened to his brother and the red Oldsmobile convertible they once shared. The plot moves conventionally, after a lengthy introduction giving the background of the two brothers and their pleasure in the car. They are Native Americans who work hard for what they earn, but they also enjoy their money. As Lyman says, "We went places in that car, me and Henry." An atmosphere of innocence pervades this part of the story. They enjoy sightseeing along the western highways, going when and where they please, spending an entire summer in Alaska after they drive home a female hitchhiker with long, beautiful hair.

The story moves forward chronologically (although it is told as a flashback after the opening frame of four paragraphs), organized in sections usually several paragraphs long. Its structure is as loose and comfortable as the brothers' relationship. Then, midway, the story darkens when Henry goes off to Vietnam. For three sections, Lyman describes Henry's disorientation after the war. Then Henry fixes the convertible, the boys get back behind the wheel, and it seems briefly as if the good times are again starting to roll. But Henry feels internal turmoil similar to that of the flooded river they park alongside. The story reaches its climax when Henry suddenly goes wild after drinking several beers, deteriorating into what he calls a "crazy Indian." Lyman stares after him as he jumps into the river shouting, "Got to cool me off!" His last words are quieter, "My boots are filling," and then he is gone.

The last paragraph of the story is its final section, Lyman describing how he drove the car into the river after he couldn't rescue Henry. It has grown dark, and he is left alone with the sound of the rushing water "going and running and running." This brings the story full circle, back to the beginning, where Lyman told us that now he "walks everywhere he goes." His grief for his brother is as understated as the rest of his personality. Erdrich has invented a natural storyteller in Lyman. We feel his emotional loss as if it were our own.

Questions for Discussion

1. In the opening paragraph, Lyman says that he and Henry owned the red convertible "together until his boots filled with water on a windy night and he bought out my share." When does the meaning of this sentence become clear to you? What is the effect of putting this sentence in the first paragraph?

2. Also in the opening paragraph, Erdrich writes: "His youngest brother Lyman (that's myself), Lyman walks everywhere he goes." If Lyman is narrating this story, why does he name himself? Does speaking of himself in the third person create any particular effect?

3. What is the function of the third section of the story? Why does the narrator tell us about their wandering, about meeting Susy? What associations does the red convertible carry?

4. Watching Henry watching television, Lyman says, "He sat in his chair gripping the armrests with all his might, as if the chair itself was moving at a high speed and if he let go at all he would rocket forward and maybe crash right through the set." How would you describe the diction in this sentence? What effect does the sentence's length — and its syntax — create? What is the tone? What does this line, and the paragraphs around it, tell you about Lyman's reaction to Henry's change?

5. Where do Lyman and Henry speak directly to each other in this story? Where do they speak indirectly? How do they communicate without speech? Describe how Erdrich presents the moments of emotion in this story.

6. Why is Lyman upset by the picture of himself and his brother? When does the picture begin to bother him? Do we know if it's before or after Henry's death? Does it make a difference to our interpretation of the story? What burden of memory does this picture carry?

7. Consider the tone of the final paragraph, in which Lyman is describing how he felt when he gave his car to his dead brother. Look at the diction surrounding the red convertible here: It plows into the water; the headlights "reach in . . . go down, searching"; they are "still lighted." What attribute does the diction give the car? How is the car different now from the way it's been in the rest of the story? Does this transformation of the car invoke a sense of closure in the story?

8. The closing sentence says, "And then there is only the water, the sound of it going and running and going and running and running." How does this statement comment on the relationship between the two brothers?

Topics for Writing

1. Write an essay considering brotherhood in "The Red Convertible."
2. Discuss Erdrich's use of setting to determine tone.

3.   **RESPONDING CREATIVELY**   Rewrite the story from the third-person point of view.

Suggested Readings

Erdrich, Louise. "Excellence Has Always Made Me Fill with Fright When It Is Demanded by Other People, but Fills Me with Pleasure When I Am Left to Practice It Alone." *Ms.* 13 (1985): 84.

———. "Where I Ought to Be: A Writer's Sense of Place." *New York Times Book Review,* 28 July 1985: 1+.

Howard, J. "Louise Erdrich." *Life* 8 (1985): 27+.

WILLIAM FAULKNER

A Rose for Emily (p. 146)

Few stories, surely, differ more on a second reading than does "A Rose for Emily," which yields to the initiate some detail or circumstance anticipating the ending in nearly every paragraph. But Faulkner sets the pieces of his puzzle in place so coolly that the first-time reader hardly suspects them to fit together into a picture at all, until the curtain is finally swept aside and the shocking secret of Miss Emily's upstairs room is revealed. Faulkner makes it easy to write off the episodes of the smell, Miss Emily's denial of her father's death, the arsenic, and the aborted wedding (note the shuffled chronology) as the simple eccentricities of a pathetic old maid, to be pitied and indulged. The impact of the final scene drives home the realization that the passions of a former generation and its experience of life are no less real or profound for all their being in the past — whether we view them through the haze of sentimental nostalgia, as the Confederate veterans near the end of the story do, or place them at an aesthetic distance, as the townspeople do in the romantic tableau imagined in section II.

In his interviews with students at the University of Virginia (excerpted in Chapter 5, p. 595), Faulkner stressed Miss Emily's being "kept down" by her father as an important factor in driving her to violate the code of her society by taking a lover, and he expressed a deep human sympathy for her long expiation for that sin. In the narrative consciousness of the story, however — the impersonal "we" that speaks for the communal mind of Jefferson — Miss Emily Grierson is a town relic, a monument to the local past to be shown to strangers, like the graves of the men slain at the battle of Jefferson or the big houses on what long ago, before they put the sidewalks in, was the "most select street." Because all relics are to a degree symbolic, one should not hesitate to take up the challenge found in Faulkner's ambiguous claim that "the writer is too busy . . . to have time to be conscious of all the symbolism that he may put into what he does or what people may read into it" (quoted in the headnote). Miss Emily, for example, may be understood to express the part of southern culture that is paralyzed in the present by its inability to let go of the past, even though that past is as dead as Homer Barron, and even though its reality differed from the treasured memory as greatly as the Yankee paving contractor — "not a marrying man" —differs from the husband of Miss Emily's desperate longings. Other details in Faulkner's economical narration fit this reading: the prominence of Miss Emily's iconic portrait of her father; her refusal to acknowledge changing laws and customs; her insistence that the privilege of paying no taxes, bestowed on her by the chivalrous Colonel Sartoris, is an inalienable right; her dependence on the labors of her Negro servant, whose patient silence renders him an accomplice in her strange crime; and, not least, her relationship of mutual exploitation with Homer, the representative of the North —a relationship that ends in a morbid and grotesque parody of marriage. In this context, the smell of death that reeks from Miss Emily's house tells how the story judges what she stands for, and the dust that falls on everything brings the welcome promise of relief.

But Faulkner will not let it lie. Seen for what she is, neither romanticized nor trivialized, Miss Emily has a forthright dignity and a singleness of purpose that contrast sharply with those representatives of propriety and progress who sneak around her foundation in the dark spreading lime or knock on her door in the ineffectual effort to collect her taxes. And as the speechless townsfolk tiptoe aghast about her bridal chamber, it is Miss Emily's iron will, speaking through the strand of iron-gray hair that lies where she has lain, that has the final word.

WILLIAM E. SHEIDLEY

Questions for Discussion

1. The story begins and ends with Miss Emily's funeral. Trace the chronology of the intervening sections.
2. Explain why Emily is called "a fallen monument" and "a tradition."
3. Why does the narrator label Miss Emily's house "an eyesore among eyesores"?
4. Define the opposing forces in the confrontation that occupies most of section I. How does Miss Emily "vanquish them"?
5. Discuss the transition between sections I and II. In what ways are the two episodes parallel?
6. Apart from her black servant, Miss Emily has three men in her life. What similarities are there in her attitudes toward them?
7. Why is Homer Barron considered an inappropriate companion for Miss Emily?
8. Consider Faulkner's introduction of the rat poison into the story in section III. What is the narrator's avowed reason for bringing it up?
9. At the beginning of section IV, the townspeople think Emily will commit suicide, and they think "it would be the best thing." Why? What is the basis of their error regarding her intentions?
10. Why do you think Miss Emily gets fat and develops gray hair when she does?
11. Why does Miss Emily's servant disappear after her death?
12. Describe Miss Emily's funeral before the upstairs room is opened. In what way does that scene serve as a foil to set off what follows?
13. Discuss the role of dust in the last few paragraphs of the story.
14. Why does Faulkner end the story with "a long strand of iron-gray hair"?

Topics for Writing

1. Contrast the various attitudes toward the past in "A Rose for Emily."
2. Discuss the meaning of time and Faulkner's handling of chronology in "A Rose for Emily."
3. Construct a profile of Emily Grierson. Is she a criminal, a lunatic, or a heroine?
4. Explain the title of "A Rose for Emily."
5. Consider the relationship between "A Rose for Emily" and the history of the South.
6. What can you discern about the narrator of "A Rose for Emily"?
7. Were you surprised by the story's ending? On a second reading, mark all the passages that foreshadow it.

8.   **RESPONDING CREATIVELY**   Imitate Faulkner by telling the events of a story that lead up to a climax out of chronological order. What new effects do you find it possible to achieve? What problems in continuity do you encounter?

Commentary

William Faulkner, *"The Meaning of 'A Rose for Emily,'"* p. 595.

Suggested Readings

Basset, John E. Vision and Revisions: *Essays on Faulkner.* West Cornwall, CT: Locust Hill, 1989.

Bloom, Harold. *William Faulkner.* New York: Chelsea House, 1986.

Blotner, Joseph. *Faulkner: A Biography.* New York: Random, 1991.

Brooks, Cleanth. *A Shaping Joy.* New York: Harcourt, 1971.

Gwynn, Frederick, and Joseph Blotner, eds. *Faulkner in the University.* Charlottesville: U of Virginia P, 1959.

Hall, Donald. *To Read Literature: Fiction, Poetry, Drama.* New York: Holt, 1981. 10–16.

Heller, Terry. "The Telltale Hair: A Critical Study of William Faulkner's 'A Rose for Emily.'" *Arizona Quarterly* 28 (1972): 301–18.

Hoffman, Frederick J. *William Faulkner, Revised.* Boston: Twayne, 1990.

Howe, Irving. *William Faulkner: A Critical Study.* 2nd ed. New York: Vintage, 1962. 265.

Leary, Lewis. *William Faulkner of Yoknapatawpha County.* Twentieth-Century American Writers. New York: Crowell, 1973. 136.

Millgate, Michael. *The Achievement of William Faulkner.* New York: Random, 1966.

RICHARD FORD

Leaving for Kenosha (p. 153)

Ford's bleakly realistic story set in post-Katrina New Orleans deftly captures the mood of this catastrophic turning point in U.S. history, when a sense of loss haunts the beleaguered survivors with no relief in sight. Unlike stories about middle class family relations a half-century earlier dramatized by another Southern writer, Flannery O'Connor, satire is too blunt a weapon for Richard Ford in his depiction of contemporary social collapse. His well-meaning, intelligently self-aware protagonist has a crystal clear sense of his own futility. In "Leaving for Kenosha," Walter Hobbes is a father trying to do his best for his thirteen-year-old daughter Louise, but they are a wounded pair, tenuously connected post-divorce survivors of overwhelming domestic losses.

Walter shrugs off the idea that Katrina was responsible for his wife's infidelity and their subsequent divorce. "It had become fashionable to blame bad things on the hurricane — things that would've certainly happened any way. . . . As if life weren't its own personalized storm." Walter Hobbes (his last name suggests the name of the English philosopher who believed that reason could explain the universe) is a sympathetic loser, a man who has voted Democrat in George W. Bush's America. Ford suggests that his protagonist's inability to save his marriage or even to choose an appropriate greeting card for his daughter at Wal-Mart are the inevitable results of his moral paralysis in a totally corrupt society. At the conclusion of the story he retreats into a tactful silence when Louise announces that she wants to move to Italy or China, far from the parents whose divorce has destroyed her sense of home.

Louise's intense friendship with her schoolmate Ginny, who is moving to Wisconsin with her father, is the one hopeful note in this discordant story. At least race relations have improved among middle-class youth in the city. But as Louise and Walter drive through the ruined streets of New Orleans there is little to inspire her adolescent thoughts of a positive future there with her parents. Ginny was a scholarship student at an exclusive private school in the city, the African American daughter of a UPS driver, and Louise is the sheltered white daughter of an affluent attorney, but even this friendship is overcast by the reader's knowledge of the sobering fact that Walter has made his comfortable income representing corporate gas and oil interests, a factor in the city's long-standing web of civic corruption. Ford seems to be saying that everyone is hopelessly compromised in our society. Occasionally good deeds get done — Ginny received a scholarship, her grandmother is living in the devastated Ninth Ward in a brand new air conditioned home built for her by volunteer laborers, and UPS has offered her father a chance to relocate in Kenosha — but the extent of the damage in Ford's fictional America is too great for these small triumphs to offer more than a slender hope for far-reaching, substantial social progress to occur in the future.

Questions for Discussion

1. In a series of flashbacks, Ford gives us a great deal of information about Walter Hobbes's career, his marriage, and his relationship with his family and friends in New Orleans. Discuss how this information contributes to the reader's sense of his character. In what ways is he shown to be both a sympathetic and unsympathetic character?

2. We know less about Louise Hobbes. In what ways is she a typically self-centered young teenager? How is she presented as a sympathetic character?

3. Discuss the importance of setting in the story. Could it have been set in Kenosha, with Ginny's father's job transferred to New Orleans?

Topic for Writing

1. **RESPONDING CREATIVELY** Rewrite the opening paragraphs of "Leaving for Kenosha" as a first-person narrative. Why do you think Ford chose to use third-person narration for his story?

Suggested Readings

Ford, Richard. *A Multitude of Sins*. New York: Knopf, 2001.
———. *Rock Springs*. New York: Atlantic Monthly, 1987.

GABRIEL GARCÍA MÁRQUEZ

A Very Old Man with Enormous Wings (p. 166)

The word "allegories" in the headnote presents a challenge to readers of this story, and the inevitable failure of any simple scheme of interpretation to grasp fully the mystery at its heart reflects García Márquez's central theme exactly. Like the crabs, which come into the human world from an alien realm, the "flesh-and-blood angel" constitutes an intrusion of something strange and unfathomable into the comfortable world of reality as we choose to define it. Everybody, from the "wise" woman next door to the pope, takes a turn at trying to find a slot in which to file the winged visitor, but no definition seems satisfactory. Even Pelayo and Elisenda, whom the angel's presence has made wealthy, spend their money on a house "with iron bars on the windows so that angels wouldn't get in." When at last the old man flies away, Elisenda feels relief, "because then he was no longer an annoyance in her life but an imaginary dot on the horizon of the sea."

In discussing how he receives artistic inspiration, García Márquez says, "There's nothing deliberate or predictable in all this, nor do I know when it's going to happen to me. I'm at the mercy of my imagination." Without intending to limit the story's implications, one might associate the angel with this sort of unpredictable intrusion of the visionary and wonderful into everyday life. As an old man with wings, the angel recalls the mythical symbol of the artist, Daedalus, except that his wings are "so natural on that completely human organism that [the doctor] couldn't understand why other men didn't have them too." Bogged down in the mud, the angel seems less an allusion to Daedalus's son, the overreacher Icarus, than a representation of the difficulty of the artistic imagination in sustaining its flight through the unpleasant circumstances of this "sad" world. True artists are often misunderstood, ill treated, and rejected in favor of more practical concerns or of the creators of ersatz works that flatter established prejudices. Just so, nobody can understand the angel's "hermetic" language, and when he performs his aggressively unpractical miracles, no one is delighted. Exploited by his keepers, to whom he brings vast wealth, the angel receives as royalties only his quarters in the chicken coop and the flat side of the broom when underfoot. Popular for a time as a sideshow attraction, the angel is soon passed over in favor of the horrible "woman who had been changed into a spider for having disobeyed her parents," a grotesque and slapdash creation of the lowest order of imaginative synthesis, whose "human truth" gratifies both sentimentality and narrow-mindedness. But the artistic imagination lives happily on eggplant mush, possesses a supernatural patience, and though functionally blind to the bumping posts of ordinary reality, ever again takes wing. The angel has, perhaps rightly, appeared to his human observers "a cataclysm in repose," but near the end, as he sings his sea chanteys under the stars, he definitely comes to resemble "a hero taking his ease," preparing to navigate the high seas beyond the horizon.

WILLIAM E. SHEIDLEY

Questions for Discussion

1. Why are there crabs in the house? Is it for the same reason the old man with enormous wings has fallen in the courtyard? What other associations does the story make between the old man and the crabs?
2. Pelayo first thinks the old man is a nightmare. What other attempts are made to put this prodigy into a familiar category?
3. How does the old man differ from our usual conceptions of angels? What is the essential difference?
4. Explain Father Gonzaga's approach to the angel. What implications — about the angel and about the church — may be derived from his failure to communicate with him effectively?
5. Comment on the angel's career as a sideshow freak. Who receives the benefit of his success? Why does he fail? Compare what he has to offer with what the spider-woman has. What reasons might people have to prefer the latter?
6. Why do you think the angel tolerates the child patiently?
7. What are the implications of the angel's examination by the doctor?
8. How do we feel as the angel finally flaps away at the end? Does Elisenda's response adequately express the reader's?

Topics for Writing

1. Consider the ordinary and the enormous in "A Very Old Man with Enormous Wings." (Consider the etymological meaning of "enormous.")
2. Is García Márquez's story of the fallen angel a fairy tale, a myth, or an allegory?
3. Recharging the sense of wonder: How does García Márquez make the reader believe in his angel?
4. Read the story aloud to a selected spectrum of people (at least three) of various ages and educational levels. Tabulate their responses and opinions, perhaps in an interview. Combining this evidence with your own response to the story, try to define the basis of its appeal.
5. **RESPONDING CREATIVELY** Select a supernatural being from a fairy tale or other familiar source (the cartoons involving talking animals that wear clothes and drive cars might be worth considering), and imagine the being as a physical reality in your own ordinary surroundings. Write a sketch about what happens.
6. **MAKING CONNECTIONS** Compare "A Very Old Man with Enormous Wings" with other presentations of the supernatural (Nathaniel Hawthorne's "Young Goodman Brown," p. 213, for example).

Suggested Readings

Bell-Villada, Gene H. *García Márquez: The Man and His Work.* Chapel Hill: U of North Carolina P, 1990.
Byk, John. "From Fact to Fiction: Gabriel García Márquez and the Short Story." *Mid-American Review* 6.2 (1986): 111–16.
Fau, Margaret Eustella. *Bibliographic Guide to Gabriel García Márquez, 1979–1985.* Westport, CT: Greenwood, 1986.
García Márquez, Gabriel. *Collected Stories.* New York: Harper, 1984.
———. *Strange Pilgrims: Twelve Stories.* New York: Knopf, 1993.
McMurray, George R. *Gabriel García Márquez.* New York: Ungar, 1977. 116–19.
McNerney, Kathleen. *Understanding Gabriel García Márquez.* Columbia: U of South Carolina P, 1989.
Morello Frosch, Marta. "The Common Wonders of García Márquez's Recent Fiction." *Books Abroad* 47 (1973): 496–501.
Oberhelman, Harley D. *Gabriel García Márquez: A Study of the Short Fiction.* Boston: Twayne, 1991.
Ortega, Julio. *Gabriel García Márquez and the Powers of Fiction.* Austin: U of Texas P, 1988.
Williams, Raymond L. *Gabriel García Márquez.* Boston: Twayne, 1984.
Zhu, Jingdong. "García Márquez and His Writing of Short Stories." *Foreign Literatures* 1 (1987): 77–80.

CHARLOTTE PERKINS GILMAN

The Yellow Wallpaper (p. 172)

Gilman wrote "The Yellow Wallpaper" between 1890 and 1894, during what she later recalled were the hardest years of her life. She had left her first husband and child to live alone in California after a nervous breakdown, and she was beginning to give lectures on freedom for women and socialism while she kept a boardinghouse, taught school, and edited newspapers. During this time, her ex-husband married her best friend, to whom Gilman relinquished her child. The emotional pressures and economic uncertainties under which Gilman lived contributed to the desperate tone of this story.

Early readers of "The Yellow Wallpaper" compared it with the horror stories of Edgar Allan Poe (William Dean Howells said it was a story to "freeze our . . . blood" when he reprinted it in 1920 in *Great Modern American Stories*). Like Poe's homicidal narrators, Gilman's heroine tells her story in a state of neurotic compulsion. But she is no homicidal maniac. Unlike Poe, Gilman suggests that a specific social malady has driven her heroine to the brink of madness: the bondage of conventional marriage.

Her husband is her physician and keeper, the father of her beloved but absent child, the money earner who pays the rent on the mansion where she is held captive for her "own good." When she begs to get away, he replies practically, "Our lease will be up in three weeks, and I can't see how to leave before." Insisting that he knows what is best for her, he believes that the cure for her mysterious "weakness" is total rest. The husband is supported in his view by the opinion of the foremost medical authority on the treatment of mental illness, Dr. S. Weir Mitchell, a name explicitly mentioned in the story. Gilman had spent a month in Dr. Mitchell's sanitorium five years before. In her autobiography she later reported that she almost lost her mind there and would often "crawl into remote closets and under beds — to hide from the grinding pressure of that profound distress."

Gilman transferred the memory of her physical debilitation and "absolute incapacity" for normal (read "conventional") married life into her heroine's state in "The Yellow Wallpaper." The story dramatizes Gilman's fear while living with her first husband that marriage and motherhood might incapacitate her (as it apparently had Gilman's mother) for what she called "work in the world." She felt imprisoned within her marriage, a victim of her desire to please, trapped by her wedding ring. Gilman left her husband, but in "The Yellow Wallpaper" her heroine is sacrificed to the emotional turmoil she experiences.

As a symbolic projection of psychological stress, "The Yellow Wallpaper" has resemblances to Kafka's "The Metamorphosis," although it is more specific in its focus on social injustice to women. Like Gregor Samsa, Gilman's heroine is victimized by the people she loves. The yellow wallpaper surrounding her is "like a bad dream." It furnishes the central images in the story. The reader can use it like a Rorschach test to understand the heroine's experience of entrapment, confinement, and sacrifice for other family members. Like Gregor Samsa, she regresses to subhuman behavior as a self-inflicted punishment following her psychological rebellion — the wallpaper's bad smell, its bars and grid, its fungus and toadstools, and its images of the creeping (dependent, inferior) woman. But unlike Gregor Samsa, Gilman's heroine thinks she is freed from the "bad dream" by telling her story, not to a "living soul," but to what she calls (nonjudgmentally) "dead paper."

Telling her story enables her to achieve her greatest desire — the symbolic death of her husband. The story ends, "Now why should that man have fainted? But he did, and right across my path by the wall, so that I had to creep over him every time!" The central irony of the story, however, is that by the time she realizes the twisted ambition fostered by obediently following "like a good girl" her passive role as a conventional member of the "weaker sex," she has been driven insane.

Questions for Discussion

1. Why have the narrator and her husband, John, rented the "colonial mansion"? What is its history, and what is the reaction of the heroine to this estate? Does she feel comfortable living in the house?

2. Give a description of John. Why does the heroine say that his profession is "perhaps . . . one reason I do not get well faster"? How does the narrator view her husband? Does she agree with John's diagnosis and treatment? Who else supports John's diagnosis? What effect does this have on the heroine?
3. What clue does the narrator's repeated lament, "what can one do?" give us about her personality? Describe other aspects of the woman's personality that are revealed in the opening of the story. What conflicting emotions is she having toward her husband, her condition, and the mansion?
4. How would you characterize the narrator's initial reaction to, and description of, the wallpaper?
5. Describe the narrator's state after the first two weeks of residence. Has John's relationship with his wife changed at all?
6. Who is Jennie? What is her relationship to the narrator, and what is her function in the story?
7. How has the narrator changed in her description of the wallpaper? Is it fair to say that the wallpaper has become more dominant in her day-to-day routine? Explain.
8. By the Fourth of July, what does the narrator admit about the wallpaper? What clues does Gilman give us about the education of the narrator and her increasingly agitated state? Is she finding it more and more difficult to communicate? Explain.
9. As the summer continues, describe the narrator's thoughts. What is her physical condition? Is there a link between her symptoms and psychological illness?
10. How does the narrator try to reach out to her husband? What is his reaction? Is this her last contact with sanity? Do you think John really has no comprehension of the seriousness of her illness?
11. Why do you think Gilman briefly changes the point of view from first person singular to the second person as the narrator describes the pattern of the wallpaper? What effect does the narrator say light has on the wallpaper?
12. Who does the narrator see in the wallpaper? How have her perceptions of John and Jennie changed from the beginning of the story?
13. Abruptly the narrator switches mood from boredom and frustration to excitement. To what does she attribute this change? How does John react to this? What new aspects of the wallpaper does she discuss?
14. By the final section of the story, what is the narrator's relationship to her husband? to Jennie? to the wallpaper? How has the narrator's perspective changed from the start of the story? What change do we see in her actions?
15. Identify what has driven the narrator to the brink of madness. How does she try to free herself from this element? What is her greatest desire? What is the central irony of the story?

Topics for Writing

1. **MAKING CONNECTIONS** Compare and contrast the husband-wife relationship and its outcome in Gilman's "The Yellow Wallpaper" and Henrik Ibsen's play *A Doll House* (p. 1309).
2. **MAKING CONNECTIONS** Compare and contrast the monologue in Gilman's "The Yellow Wallpaper" with that in Edgar Allan Poe's "The Cask of Amontillado" (p. 467).

Commentaries

Sandra M. Gilbert and Susan Gubar, "*A Feminist Reading of Gilman's 'The Yellow Wallpaper,'*" p. 600.
Charlotte Perkins Gilman, "*Undergoing the Cure for Nervous Prostration,*" p. 602.

Suggested Readings

Bader, J. "The Dissolving Vision: Realism in Jewett, Freeman, and Gilman." In *American Realism; New Essays.* Ed. Eric J. Sundquist. Baltimore: Johns Hopkins UP, 1982. 176–98.

Delaney, Sheila. *Writing Women: Women Writers and Women in Literature, Medieval to Modern.* New York: Schocken, 1983.

Feminist Papers: From Adams to de Beauvoir. Ed. Alice S. Rossi. New York: Columbia UP, 1973.

Hanley-Peritz, J. "Monumental Feminism and Literature's Ancestral House: Another Look at 'The Yellow Wallpaper.'" *Women's Studies* 12.2 (1986): 113–28.

Hill, Mary A. "Charlotte Perkins Gilman: A Feminist's Struggle with Womanhood." *Massachusetts Review* 21 (1980): 503–26.

———. *Charlotte Perkins Gilman: The Making of a Radical Feminist, 1860–1896.* Philadelphia: Temple UP, 1980.

Lane, Ann J. "Charlotte Perkins Gilman: The Personal Is Political." In *Feminist Theorists.* Ed. Dale Spender. New York: Pantheon, 1983.

Nies, Judith. *Seven Women.* New York: Viking, 1977. 127–45.

Shumaker, C. "'Too Terribly Good to Be Printed': Charlotte Gilman's 'The Yellow Wallpaper.'" *American Literature* 57 (1985): 588–99.

SUSAN GLASPELL

A Jury of Her Peers (p. 185)

Students will most likely profit from reading both Glaspell's story and her play, *Trifles,* included in Part Three of this anthology (p. 1362), along with Leonard Mustazza's commentary "Generic Translation and Thematic Shift in Glaspell's *Trifles* and 'A Jury of Her Peers'" (p. 1598). Class discussion can be based on the similarities and differences between the play and the short story. Mustazza finds Glaspell's story "a much more interesting, resonant, and disturbing [work] than the slighter drama from which it derives." You might begin in the classroom by asking if students agree or disagree with his judgment, expressed at the conclusion of his essay.

Mustazza bases his argument on the fact that when Glaspell converted her play into a short story, it became twice as long. This enabled her to do more than present the theme of *Trifles* in short story form. She was able to include another dimension in "A Jury of Her Peers" when she dramatized the separateness of Mrs. Hale (from whose point of view the story is told) and Mrs. Peters (the sheriff's wife) at the beginning of the story. The story becomes more substantial than the play because Glaspell develops her characterization of these two women more fully; over the course of the narrative she shows how Mrs. Hale wins over Mrs. Peters to her opinion that Minnie Wright should not be punished for killing her husband. As Mustazza summarizes his thesis, "'A Jury of Her Peers' is much more concerned with the separateness of the women themselves and their self-injurious acquiescence in male-defined roles."

Questions for Discussion

1. Why does Glaspell begin her story in Mrs. Hale's kitchen?
2. Why is Glaspell's choice of point of view particularly important in this story?
3. When do you first become aware of the conflict between the female characters' feeling about Mrs. Wright and the male characters' approach to justice?

4.   Why is Sheriff Peters so concerned with finding a motive for the crime?
5.   Why were the women invited to accompany the men to the Wright farmhouse?
6.   What does the strangled canary symbolize?

Topics for Writing

1.   Summarize Leonard Mustazza's commentary in a hundred words.
2.   MAKING CONNECTIONS   Compare and contrast Glaspell's play and short story in order to defend your opinion about which you prefer. You may agree or disagree with Mustazza's commentary. (See p. 1677 in Part Four, "Comparison and Contrast," for a sample student essay analyzing Glaspell's story and play.)

Connections

Susan Glaspell, *Trifles,* p. 1362.
Lynn Nottage, *POOF!* p. 1561.

Commentaries

Elaine Showalter, *"On Glaspell's* A Jury of Her Peers," p. 623.
Leonard Mustazza, *"Generic Translation and Thematic Shift in Glaspell's* Trifles *and 'A Jury of Her Peers,'"* p. 1598.

Suggested Readings

See page 337 of this manual.

NADINE GORDIMER

Some Are Born to Sweet Delight (p. 202)

The opening paragraphs of Gordimer's chilling story foreshadow the plot to come. Vera, the seventeen-year-old girl who will unknowingly carry the bomb in her hand baggage onto the airliner that explodes in midair, is the daughter of a man who is highly conscious "of the danger of bombs affixed under the cars of members of parliament and financiers." But these car bombs, set by radical IRA members fighting their guerrilla battles against the British who control Northern Ireland, are only a forerunner to the much more widespread terrorist battle against Western nations fought by the radicalized Muslims in Pakistan and other countries. "Some Are Born to Sweet Delight" was published in Gordimer's 1991 collection *Jump,* a decade before the events of September 11 in the United States. The story is a terrible omen of the things that will continue to happen in the world in the years after its publication.

Rad, the foreign lodger who becomes Vera's lover and uses her as a carrier for the explosive device that will destroy the airplane, remains a mysterious stranger throughout the story. Gordimer describes him through Vera's innocent eyes as possessing "the strange expression of a caged animal, far from wherever it belonged." When she asks him if he wants to go home, he says "No," looking at her "with the distant expression of an adult before the innocence of a child." When she tries to draw him out about his family, "He was not to be drawn; he was never to be drawn." Gordimer's words are weighted with irony, referring to Rad's ultimate plan to annihilate as many Westerners as possible. In England he might have encountered "the disadvantages young men like him had in an unwelcoming country," but he is revealed as a completely heartless enemy agent by the end of the story.

The theme of "Some Are Born to Sweet Delight" is suggested in the epigraph Gordimer has placed at the beginning, the two-line quotation from William Blake's *Auguries of Innocence:* "Some are Born to sweet delight, / Some are Born to Endless Night." The story brings together the world's politically innocent "haves" (like Vera) and the radicalized, initiated "have-nots" (like Rad) in an explosive mixture. In effect, the darkness is striking back against the light, using terrorism as the only weapon available to them in the unequal struggle: "a faction of the world's wronged, claiming the destruction . . . in some complication of vengeance for holy wars, land annexation, invasions, imprisonments, cross-border raids, territorial disputes, bombings, sinkings, kidnappings no one outside the initiated could understand."

Questions for Discussion

1. Why has Gordimer made Vera only seventeen years old? Is she a sympathetic character, or do you consider her too stupid and vapid to be the protagonist?
2. How does Gordimer make you aware of Vera's sexual interest in Rad in the scene where she offers him a slice of her mother's homemade gingerbread?
3. What do Vera's parents think of Rad? In what ways do they possess the typical prejudices of their social class? Why do the owners of the house celebrate Vera's engagement with a bottle of champagne?
4. From Rad's point of view, does Vera behave like a well-brought-up young woman at any time of their involvement? Considering his strict Muslim background, how does he regard her behavior? What do his friends think about Vera?

Topic for Writing

1. Write a short paper in which you analyze the opening paragraphs of the story, discussing how Gordimer foreshadows the characters and events to come.

Suggested Readings

Clayton, Cherry, ed. *Women and Writing in South Africa: A Critical Anthology.* Marshalltown: Heinemann Southern Africa, 1989, 183ff.

Cooke, J. "African Landscapes: The World of Nadine Gordimer." *World Literature Today* 52 (1978): 533–38.

Eckstein, B. "Pleasure and Joy: Political Activism in Nadine Gordimer's Short Stories." *World Literature Today* 59 (1985): 343–46.

Gordimer, Nadine. *Jump and Other Stories.* New York: Farrar, 1991.

Gray, S. "Interview with Nadine Gordimer." *Contemporary Literature* 22 (1981): 263–71.

Heywood, Christopher. *Nadine Gordimer.* Windsor, Ont.: Profile, 1983.

Hurwitt, J. "Art of Fiction: Nadine Gordimer." *Paris Review* 25 (1983): 83–127.

Jacobs, J. U. "Living Space and Narrative Space in Nadine Gordimer's 'Something Out There.'" *English in Africa* 14.2 (Oct. 1987): 31–43.

Lazar, Karen. "Feminism as 'Piffling'? Ambiguities in Some of Nadine Gordimer's Short Stories." *Current Writing* 2.1 (Oct. 1990): 101–16.

Mazurek, Raymond A. "Nadine Gordimer's 'Something Out There' and Ndebele's 'Fools' and Other Stories: The Politics of Literary Form." *Studies in Short Fiction* 26.1 (Winter 1989): 71–79.

Newman, Judie. *Nadine Gordimer.* New York: Routledge, 1988.

Ross, Robert L., ed. *International Literature on Major Writers.* New York: Garland, 1991. 762ff.

Smith, Rowland. *Critical Essays on Nadine Gordimer.* Boston: G. K. Hall, 1990.

Smyer, R. I. "Africa in the Fiction of Nadine Gordimer." *Ariel* 16 (1985): 15–29.

Trump, Martin. "The Short Fiction of Nadine Gordimer." *Research in African Literature* 17.3 (Fall 1968): 341–69.

NATHANIEL HAWTHORNE

Young Goodman Brown (p. 213)

Students often need help recognizing stories that are not intended to be read as realistic narrative. Some readers tend to take every word in the story literally; Hawthorne, however, meant "Young Goodman Brown" to be a moral allegory, not a realistic story. While most students will be able to recognize the use of symbolism, you might have to introduce them to the idea of allegory, in which the entire story is an extended metaphor representing one thing in the guise of another.

An allegory is a story that has a dual meaning — one in the events, characters, and setting, and the other in the ideas they are intended to convey. At first, "Young Goodman Brown" holds our interest on the level of the surface narrative. But the story also has a second meaning, which must be read beneath, and concurrent with, the surface narrative. This second meaning is not to be confused with the theme of the story — all stories have themes, but not all stories are allegories. In an allegory, the characters are usually personifications of abstract qualities and the setting is representative of the relations among the abstractions (Goodman Brown takes leave of his "Faith" at the beginning of the story).

A story is an allegory only if the characters, events, and setting are presented in a logical pattern so that they represent meanings independent of the action described in the surface story. Most writers of allegorical fiction are moralists. In this moral allegory, Hawthorne is suggesting the ethical principle that should govern human life. The *unpardonable sin* for Hawthorne is a "want of love and reverence for the Human Soul" and is typified by the person who searches the depths of the heart with "a cold philosophical curiosity." The result is a separation of the intellect from the heart, which is fatal in relationships, as shown in what happens to Goodman Brown when he returns to Salem village at the end of the story.

Questions for Discussion

1. When is a careful reader first aware that Hawthorne intends this story to be read as a moral allegory?

2. One of the characters in a Hawthorne story says, "You know that I can never separate the idea from the symbol in which it manifests itself." Hawthorne's flat characters — such as Deacon Gookin, Goody Cloyse, and the minister —represent social institutions. Why does Hawthorne include them in the story?

3. On page 214 Hawthorne writes, "But the only thing about him that could be fixed upon as remarkable was his staff, which bore the likeness of a great black snake, so curiously wrought that it might almost be seen to twist and wriggle itself like a living serpent. This, of course, must have been an ocular deception, assisted by the uncertain light." What is the assertion contained in the first sentence? What effect do the words "might almost" have on that assertion? Why does Hawthorne immediately qualify the first sentence in the second? On pages 219–220, Hawthorne

writes: "Either the sudden gleams of light flashing over the obscure field bedaz-
zled Goodman Brown, or he recognized a score of the church members of Salem
village famous for their especial sanctity." Discuss the function of this sentence
and find others like it throughout the story. What is their cumulative effect?

4.   Why is it important that most of the action in this story takes place in the forest?
Looking through Hawthorne's story, isolate the particular words that are associated with the woods. Consider the paragraph on pages 218–219 that begins "And,
maddened with despair." List the characteristics of forests that are responsible for
this long literary tradition. Consider, too, whether the idea of wilderness remains
static throughout history. In the late nineteenth century, with industrialization
such a potent force, would people have conceived of the forest in the same way the
early settlers did? Why or why not?

5.   Where does this story take place (besides in the forest)? On page 214 a man
addresses the protagonist saying, "You are late, Goodman Brown. . . . The clock of
the Old South was striking as I came through Boston, and that is full fifteen minutes agone." What does this detail — that the traveler was in Boston fifteen minutes ago — mean to our interpretation of the story?

6.   On page 220, "the dark figure" welcomes his listeners to "the communion of your
race." What is usually meant by the word "communion"? How is it meant here?
What does the speaker mean by the phrase in which he uses it? What kinds of
powers does the "sable form" promise the crowd? Discuss the kinds of knowledge
that will henceforth be accessible to his listeners' senses. Who is speaking in this
passage on page 221: "Herein did the shape of evil dip his hand and prepare to lay
the mark of baptism upon their foreheads, that they might be partakers of the
mystery of sin, more conscious of the secret guilt of others, both in deed and
thought, than they could now be of their own"? How does this sentence guide your
judgment of young Goodman Brown in the closing paragraph of the story? How
does the sable figure's sermon comment on the closing paragraph?

7.   How much time does this story cover? Where do the first seven paragraphs take
place? How many paragraphs are set in the forest? What do the final three paragraphs address? What might be some reasons for the story to be built this way?

Topic for Writing

1.   Show how knowledge of seventeenth-century New England history and Puritan
theology can enhance a reading of the story.

Commentaries

Herman Melville, *"Blackness in Hawthorne's 'Young Goodman Brown,' "* p. 615.
Edgar Allan Poe, *"The Importance of the Single Effect in a Prose Tale,"* p. 680.

Suggested Readings

Arvin, Newton. *Hawthorne.* New York: Russell and Russell, 1961.
Bloom, Harold. *Nathaniel Hawthorne.* New York: Chelsea House, 1990.
Cowley, Malcolm, ed. *Portable Hawthorne.* New York: Penguin, 1977.
Crowley, J. Donald, ed. *Centenary Edition of the Works of Nathaniel Hawthorne.*
    Columbus: Ohio State UP, 1974. Vol. IX, *Twice-Told Tales;* Vol. X, *Mosses from
    an Old Manse;* Vol. XI, *The Snow Image and Uncollected Tales.*
Ferguson, J. M., Jr. "Hawthorne's 'Young Goodman Brown.' " *Explicator* 28 (1969):
    Item 32.
Fetterley, Judith. *The Resisting Reader.* Bloomington: Indiana UP, 1978.

Gallagher, Edward J. "The Concluding Paragraph of 'Young Goodman Brown.'" *Studies in Short Fiction* 12 (1975): 29–30.

McIntosh, James, ed. *Nathaniel Hawthorne's Tales.* New York: Norton, 1987.

Newman, Lea Bertani. *A Reader's Guide to the Short Stories of Nathaniel Hawthorne.* Boston: G. K. Hall, 1979.

Robinson, E. Arthur. "The Vision of Goodman Brown: A Source and Interpretation." *American Literature* 35 (1963): 218–25.

Von Frank, Albert J., ed. *Critical Essays on Hawthorne's Short Stories.* Boston: G. K. Hall, 1991.

Whelan, Robert E. "Hawthorne Interprets 'Young Goodman Brown.'" *Emerson Society Quarterly* 62 (1971): 3–6.

ERNEST HEMINGWAY

Hills Like White Elephants (p. 224)

Hemingway wrote this story in May 1927, while on his honeymoon in the Rhône delta with his second wife, Pauline. According to his biographer Kenneth Lynn, the story was a dramatization of a fantasy he had about his first wife, Hadley: "[I]f only the two of them had not allowed a child to enter their lives they would never have parted." Throughout his biography, Lynn interprets the fiction in terms of Hemingway's relationships. How much this approach sheds light on the fiction each reader must judge.

This story is an early example of a minimalist technique. Characterization and plot are mere suggestions, and it is possible for some young readers to finish the story for the first time with no idea that the couple are discussing an abortion. The setting Hemingway chooses for the couple's conversation is more richly developed. The symbolism of the "two lines of rails" at the station (the choice either to end the pregnancy or have the child); the fields of grain and trees along the Ebro River, which the girl sees on the other side of the station (fertility, a settled life) compared with the barren hills, long and white like white elephants (something considered unlucky, unwanted, and rejected); the bar and the station building (the temporary escape offered by alcohol, the sense of people in transit) — one can interpret these details in perfect harmony with the couple's emotional and physical dilemma.

The man's bullying of the girl drives the story. His ignorance about abortion and his insensitivity to what she is feeling or will have to endure physically ("It's not really anything. It's just to let the air in") are not presented as weakness. They are simply part of his insistence on persuading Jig to do what he wants her to do. The girl is also worthy of discussion. Her vulnerability is idealized, yet she is not stupid. Without the suggestion of her intelligence, there would be no story.

Hemingway regarded "Hills Like White Elephants" as one of his best stories, reserving a prominent place for it in his second collection, *Men Without Women*, published in the fall of 1927. Lynn states that in choosing this title for the book, Hemingway meant to suggest "that the alienation of women from men (as well as vice versa) was one of his themes."

Questions for Discussion

1. In what ways could you categorize this story as a minimalist work?
2. What do we know about the man? About the girl? Why isn't Jig called "a woman" in the story?

3. What is a "white elephant"? How does this expression suit the story?
4. What do you think will happen to this couple after the story ends?
5. Read the story aloud in class, assigning two students the roles of the man and the girl. Is the story as effective read as dialogue as it is on the page as a literary text?

Topic for Writing

1. RESPONDING CREATIVELY   Rewrite the story in a different setting to discover the importance of the railroad station and the Spanish landscape in "Hills Like White Elephants."

Connection

Russell Banks, *"Black Man and White Woman in Dark Green Rowboat,"* p. 79.

Suggested Readings

Baker, Carlos, ed. *Ernest Hemingway: A Life Story.* New York: Macmillan, 1976.
———. *Ernest Hemingway: Selected Letters 1917–1961.* Scribner, 1981.
Beegel, Susan F., ed. *Hemingway's Neglected Short Fiction: New Perspectives.* Ann Arbor, MI: UMI Research Press, 1989.
Benson, Jackson. *The Short Stories of Ernest Hemingway: Critical Essays.* Durham, NC: Duke UP, 1975.
———, ed. *New Critical Approaches to the Short Stories of Ernest Hemingway.* Durham, NC: Duke UP, 1990.
Brenner, Gerry, and Earl Rovit. *Ernest Hemingway.* Rev. ed. Boston: Twayne, 1990.
Flora, Joseph M. *Ernest Hemingway: A Study of the Short Fiction.* Boston: Twayne, 1989.
Hays, Peter L. *Ernest Hemingway.* New York: Continuum, 1990.
Lynn, Kenneth S. *Hemingway.* New York: Simon, 1987.
Reynolds, Michael S., ed. *Critical Essays on Ernest Hemingway's "In Our Time."* Boston: G. K. Hall, 1983.

AMY HEMPEL

Church Cancels Cow (p. 228)

For many years Amy Hempel has been writing so-called minimalist stories, very short stories that dramatize her sense of human mortality, as if the heavy thought that life is too short and death too often hovering over our doorstep never left her time enough to plan, let alone write, a novel. Her story "Church Cancels Cow" is so brief that it could also be called "sudden fiction," or even be categorized by its even shorter forms "flash fiction," "skinny fiction," "mini fiction," "quick fiction," and "micro fiction." Of course in this story the first-person narrator opens by telling us that she lives across from a cemetery, so it is no surprise that she thinks all the time about death. Do we believe that she is telling us the truth? She supplies us with an answer in her story: "For peace of mind I will lie about any thing at any time."

Read this story aloud in the classroom with your students, as if it were a poem. It is a prose poem, as carefully constructed as a sonnet. There is a setting — the cemetery and the narrator's house and yard opposite — but no plot, unless you call the artful way Hempel has built her narrative around the confrontation of two women a plot. Their argument develops over several short paragraphs and then peters out after the narrator lies and her accuser counts three other dogs visiting the cemetery. This development leads smoothly to the conclusion of the story, where the narrator switches from counting dogs to counting cows as she describes a childhood memory of car trips with her brother. Inadvertently she makes the same mistake as her accuser, who she thinks had used the word *faces* when she meant *feces*. Our narrator confuses *church* with *cemetery*. Another Freudian slip, or something really heavy on her mind?

Questions for Discussion

1. Trace the development of Hempel's "plot" from its casual opening paragraph to its tense final sentence. How does she dramatize the emotional content of her story?
2. Four characters are mentioned in "Church Cancels Cow" – the narrator, her dog, her accuser in the red Honda Civic, and her brother. Choose any one character and analyze their role in the story.

Topic for Writing

1. **RESPONDING CREATIVELY**   Write an essay in which you describe a family trip you took as a child and the games you played to have fun and occupy the time.

Suggested Reading

Hempel, Amy. *The Collected Stories.* New York: Scribner, 2007.

ZORA NEALE HURSTON

Spunk (p. 230)

The title of Hurston's story has a double meaning. "Spunk" refers to Spunk Banks, the giant of a man who courts the married woman Lena and who "ain't skeered of nothin' on God's green footstool — nothin'!" But it also refers to the quality of "spunk" (courage) shown by Lena's timid husband, Joe, the sarsaparilla-drinking "round-shouldered figure in overalls much too large," who comes back from the grave after Spunk has shot him in order to take his revenge. It took spunk for Joe to try to get Lena back from her pistol-packing lover, and Joe's courage lasts until he succeeds at what he wanted to do.

Hurston has written a ghost story based on the revenge motif in the Florida black tradition of vernacular speech and folk superstition. Joe first comes back from the dead in the figure of a "big black bob-cat" (an unearthly color for a bobcat). In this animal form he frightens Spunk so much that Spunk can't shoot his army .45 pistol, a small revenge in itself. For the ultimate revenge, something pushes Spunk in the back onto the buzz saw. Spunk believes it's Joe's ghost and vows to get him in hell. As a storyteller, Hurston pulls out of the two men's quarrel at this point. She ends the narrative with Lena, the "small pretty woman" who is the object of the two men's affections and who holds a wake for her departed lover. Hurston's interest is firmly in this world, describing the scene with a poetic economy of detail:

> The cooling board consisting of three sixteen-inch boards on saw horses, a dingy sheet was his shroud.

The women ate heartily of the funeral baked meats and wondered who would be Lena's next. The men whispered coarse conjectures between guzzles of whiskey.

Questions for Discussion

1. Why is the main part of the story told through the conversation between Elijah Mosley and Walter Thomas? They are, after all, outsiders to the intimate action, depending on hearsay for the bulk of their information.

2. Look at the final paragraph: "The women ate heartily of the funeral baked meats and wondered who would be Lena's next. The men whispered coarse conjectures between guzzles of whiskey." How does this paragraph, one of the few scenes related by the narrator, influence your interpretation of this story? Is "Spunk" about events that happen, or is it about the stories about events that happen? What's the difference?

3. This story is split into four parts, yet it's only five pages long. What is the effect of this structure? What is the narrative burden of each section?

4. In the opening paragraph of section II, Hurston writes, "Lena wept in a frightened manner." What are some other ways of saying this? What effect does this particular way have on your estimation of Lena's character? In the next paragraph Hurston writes, "'Well,' Spunk announced calmly, 'Joe came out there wid a meat axe an' made me kill him.'" Is this statement factually true? Where does the language Spunk uses locate the responsibility for the killing?

5. What effect does the African American Florida dialect have on the setting and characterization of the story? How much physical description is present in "Spunk"? How does the dialect convey the same ideas that physical detail might?

6. Analyze the final paragraph in section II:

    > A clear case of self-defense, the trial was a short one, and Spunk walked out of the court house to freedom again. He could work again, ride the dangerous log-carriage that fed the singing, snarling, biting circle-saw: he could stroll the soft dark lanes with his guitar. He was free to roam the woods again; he was free to return to Lena. He did all of these things."

    Notice the sentence lengths: three long sentences followed by a short one. What sentence gains the emphasis in this arrangement and why? What effect does the repetition of both words and syntax create? Look at the list of adjectives that precedes "circle-saw." How would you describe the style of this paragraph? How does it relate to the kind of story Hurston is telling?

7. What do you make of the supernatural elements that are introduced into sections III and IV? What kinds of stories contain supernatural elements like this? What is a "h'ant"?

8. With whom does the narrator place her sympathies in this story: Spunk, Joe, Lena, Elijah, or Walter? Discuss the passages that support your conclusion.

Topics for Writing

1. Examine country humor in "Spunk."
2. Discuss courage in "Spunk."
3. Analyze supernatural elements in "Spunk."

4.   **MAKING CONNECTIONS**   Compare and contrast folk elements in "Spunk" and Ralph Ellison's "Battle Royal" (p. 127).
5.   **RESPONDING CREATIVELY**   Rewrite the story from Lena's point of view.

Commentaries

Zora Neale Hurston, *"How It Feels to Be Colored Me,"* p. 604.
Alice Walker, *"Zora Neale Hurston: A Cautionary Tale and a Partisan View,"* p. 629.

Suggested Readings

Edwards, Lee R. *Psyche as Hero: Female Heroism and Fictional Form.* Middletown, CT: Wesleyan, 1984.

Gates, Henry Louis, ed. *Black Literature and Literary Theory.* New York: Methuen, 1984.

Hemenway, Robert. *Zora Neale Hurston: A Literary Biography.* Urbana: U of Illinois P, 1977.

Howard, Lillie P. *Zora Neale Hurston.* Boston: Twayne, 1980.

Hull, Gloria T. *Color, Sex, and Poetry: Three Women Writers of the Harlem Renaissance.* Bloomington: Indiana UP, 1987.

Hurston, Zora Neale. *The Gilded Six-Bits.* Minneapolis: Redpath, 1986.

———. *I Love Myself When I Am Laughing . . . and Then Again When I Am Looking Mean and Impressive.* Ed. Alice Walker. Old Westbury, NY: Feminist, 1979.

———. *Mules and Men.* Westport, CT: Greenwood, 1969.

Lupton, Mary Jane. "Zora Neale Hurston and the Survival of the Female." *Southern Literary Journal* 15.1 (Fall 1982): 45–54.

Washington, Mary Helen, ed. *Invented Lives: Narratives of Black Women, 1860–1960.* Garden City, NY: Anchor, 1987.

Yates, Janelle. *Zora Neale Hurston: A Storyteller's Life.* Staten Island, NY: Ward Hill, 1991.

SHIRLEY JACKSON

The Lottery (p. 235)

The interpretive suggestions in the headnote should guide students toward a recognition of the main themes of "The Lottery." The near universality of the ritual sacrifice of year gods and scapegoats in primitive cultures to ensure fertility, the continuation of life, and the purgation of society has been a common assumption since the publication of James G. Frazer's *The Golden Bough.* Jackson does not explore the transmutations of these old ceremonies in the accepted religious practices and psychological mechanisms of modern humanity; rather, she attempts to shock her readers into an awareness of the presence of raw, brutal, and superstitious impulses within us all. A fruitful approach for class discussion might involve exploring how the story achieves its impact. Jackson's comments (included in Chapter 5, p. 607) provide incontrovertible documentation of the power of "The Lottery" to stir the dark instincts dwelling below the surface of the civilized psyche, perhaps the same regions from which the story emerged fully formed — as Jackson claims — in the mind of the writer. No wonder readers have found "The Lottery" disturbing.

But they have also found it compelling, fascinating, and irresistible, and the reason may be partly to do with Jackson's technical skill. For the inattentive first reader, the natural suspense of any drawing, contest, or lottery provides strong motivation to hurry through to the ending, and when the realization of what is at stake comes, it strikes with redoubled force because of the reader's increased velocity. For the more careful reader, or for the reader already aware of the ending, the subtle foreshadowing — the boys are gathering stones, the box is black, Tessie Hutchinson "clean forgot what day it was" — triggers an uncomfortable double awareness that also urges haste; such haste spurs Mr. Summers's final, horrible remark, "All right, folks. . . . Let's finish quickly," and the cries of "Come on" and "Hurry up" by other villagers.

Jackson has succeeded in gaining the reader's vicarious participation in the lottery. Even the backwoods New England quaintness of the setting draws not the kind of condescending laughter that would distance the reader but the warm sentimental indulgence we reserve for the cutest Norman Rockwell illustrations. Little boys are being little boys as they pick up the stones, the villagers are walking clichés, and even Tessie Hutchinson, singled out from the rest by her tardiness, is tardy for the most housewifely of reasons. (How different the story would be if she appeared nervous and flustered, a few moments ahead of, say, a disheveled Steve Adams!) The reader is drawn to sink into this warm bath of comfortable stereotypes, illusions intact. Totally off guard against the possibility that the good hearts of these neighborly folks might beat in time with an ancient and brutal rhythm, that superstitious fears of hunger and death might easily outweigh feelings of friendliness and compassion, the reader may well recoil from any previous fascination and, in an effort to deny involvement, recoil from the story, too. Except that we do not reject it; "The Lottery" continues to exert such power over the imagination of its readers that it clearly must be providing a catharsis for instincts similar to those that move the villagers to pick up stones.

WILLIAM E. SHEIDLEY

Questions for Discussion

1. What associations does the word *lottery* have for you? Are they relevant to the story?
2. Comment on the ending of the first paragraph.
3. On what other occasions might the people of the village gather in the way they do for the lottery? Mr. Summers is in charge of "civic activities." Is the lottery one of these? Explain.
4. Discuss the degree to which the tradition of the lottery has been kept. Why does no one want to make a new box? Why is the whole institution not abandoned?
5. Examine the character of Tessie Hutchinson. She claims that her fate is not fair. Is there any reason why she should be singled out? Is she a tragic heroine? Consider her cry, "There's Don and Eva. . . . Make them take their chance!"
6. On your first reading, when did you begin to suspect what happens at the end of the story? How soon might it become evident? What are the most important hints?
7. One reason the ending can surprise a reader is that the villagers never speak directly of what they are about. Why not? Are they ashamed? afraid?
8. Comment on the conversation between the Adamses and Old Man Warner. What is the implication of Steve Adams's last appearance in the story?
9. Does the rhyme "Lottery in June, corn be heavy soon" adequately explain the institution of the lottery? What other reasons might people have for such behavior? What is the social function of a scapegoat?
10. After her family has received the black spot, Tessie complains, but Mrs. Delacroix tells her, "Be a good sport, Tessie." Comment on this choice of words.
11. Discuss the reaction of the Hutchinson family. Why does the lottery single out a family first, then a victim?

12.   Old Man Warner says, "People ain't the way they used to be." Are they? What does he mean?
13.   Why are the people in such a hurry to "finish"?
14.   What is the implication of "someone gave little Davy Hutchinson a few pebbles"?

Topics for Writing

1.   Discuss Jackson's techniques for building suspense in "The Lottery."
2.   Write an essay exploring the usefulness of stereotypes in "The Lottery."
3.   **RESPONDING CREATIVELY**   Examine the behavior of groups of people with which you are familiar. Can you find actual instances of formal or informal practices similar to the one described in "The Lottery" — even though they may not lead to such a brutal finale? Have you or has anyone you know been made a scapegoat? Write an essay showing how one such case reflects and confirms the implications of Jackson's story.

Commentary

Shirley Jackson, "*The Morning of June 28, 1948, and 'The Lottery,'*" p. 607.

Suggested Reading

Freidman, Lenemaja. *Shirley Jackson*. Boston: Twayne, 1975. 63–67.

HA JIN

A Bad Joke (p. 242)

When interviewed about his stories, Ha Jin has said that he often bases his works of fiction on anecdotes he's heard from sources in China. "A Bad Joke" reads as if the short tale about the two peasants who inadvertently slander the leader of the Communist Party had its origin in an anecdote. The first time that students read "A Bad Joke," it might not register that the innocence of the two peasants is unquestionable. In the department store, after protesting the ten percent inflation in the price of a pair of rubber loafers, the tall peasant says "Damn, all prices go up — only our chairman never grows." His short peasant friend then adds, "Yeah, that dwarf won't change." The three salesgirls circulate the peasants' humorous comment using the specific name of the Party Chairman Comrade Deng Xiaoping, and the joke immediately spreads throughout the provincial town. Several weeks later the two peasants return to town and find themselves under arrest for counterrevolutionary slander. Despite their insistence that they meant no disrespect to the Party Chairman, their appeal to their provincial Chairman Lou is rebuffed and the local Chief of Police sends them to prison as political criminals for an unspecified length of time. They are told to be grateful that they aren't being executed, but the short peasant isn't having any of it. He manages one last curse, lustily insulting the ancestors of Chairman "Dwarf" Lou, before being hauled away to prison with his tall friend.

Ha Jin insinuates himself into the story after the slanderous joke "began haunting offices, factories, restaurants, theaters, bathhouses, alleys, neighborhoods, train stations" when he writes, "Within a day, thousands of people in our city had heard the joke." Ha Jin has been settled in the United States for many years, but by planting the suggestion that he was a participant in the spread of a counterrevolutionary joke in

China, he tries to create the impression of his anecdote's verisimilitude, insinuating that he was there and it had really happened. However, the way he sketches the unremitting physical ugliness and spiritual meanness of the characters and the unrelenting political repression of the Communist system might lead some alert readers in the classroom to suspect that "A Bad Joke" itself is a work of propaganda.

Questions for Discussion

1. The two peasants are introduced as "the two jokers" in the opening sentence of the story. Is this a fair description of them and their actions?
2. How does Ha Jin engage your sympathy for the two peasants?
3. The two peasants are described as "the tall peasant" and "the short peasant." Why do you think Ha Jin depersonalizes them in this way?
4. Food plays an important role in the story. What does the specific prison food suggest about the lives of the peasants?
5. How does Ha Jin suggest throughout "A Bad Joke" that humor has no place in a totalitarian regime?

Topic for Writing

1. Write a book report of the stories in Ha Jin's *The Bridegroom* (2000), the collection in which "A Bad Joke" appears. In what different ways is Ha Jin critical of Communist China in his stories?

EDWARD P. JONES

Bad Neighbors (p. 247)

This is a long, complex story with a cast of characters numbering nearly twenty people, inhabitants of the 1400 block of Eighth Street NW, a black neighborhood in Washington, D.C. Jones depicts the characters so skillfully that they are individuated for an attentive reader, but many students would probably be helped by listing the characters' names on the board before attempting a classroom discussion. As with an analysis of Kafka's "The Metamorphosis," which often becomes easier if students can visualize the placement of the rooms in the Samsa apartment, labeling the houses on the 1400 block with the family names of their inhabitants might also help students understand what is going on as Jones suggests the complex rivalries and loyalties existing in the neighborhood.

Besides the large cast of characters, unusual in most short fiction, Jones develops his narrative in "Bad Neighbors" by using multiple flashbacks and flashforwards in time. The first words of the story "Even before the fracas with Terence Stagg," hint at a confrontation that will change the dynamics of the neighborhood occurring in mid-January, three months after the Bennington family moves into the house at 1406 Eighth, the event that starts the story. Jones plays with time the way Alice Munro does in her fiction, introducing characters and depicting multiple events over lengthy, not always chronological, periods that thicken the texture of the narrative and suggest that there is no simple way to sort out life's complexity of personalities and motivations. Also, as with Munro's short fiction, the memory of the third-person narrator isn't omniscient, though it is trustworthy. Jones tells us in the opening paragraph that the house at 1406 Eighth "would be home to at least twelve people, though that number was fluid."

Gradually the reader meets the members of the Bennington family: a bunch of little kids, an older woman in sunglasses who rarely leaves the house, the mother Grace, the unnamed father dressed in the uniform of a train's sleeping-car porter, a high school boy named Neil, his eighteen-year-old sister Amanda, and the oldest brother Derek, introduced in the third paragraph as "a well-built and often shirtless loudmouth in his early twenties" who seems to have a job. Judging from the family's clothes, behavior, language, ramshackle furniture, and Derek's shabby car, they are poor and uneducated, well below the middle-class standard of the prosperous home-owning black families who live on the block. Jones is suggesting the ruthless social judgments of this community of post office supervisors, civil servants, and lawyers who look down on their shiftless black neighbors renting a house owned by a white man who has fled to the suburbs after middle-class blacks bought into the neighborhood.

Jones does not share the values of these middle-class blacks. That Terence Stagg, of 1407 Eighth Street, attends Howard University, becomes a physician, and comes into a fortune after his grandparents are killed in an automobile accident doesn't mitigate his smug, self-centered, uncaring treatment of his young wife Sharon, who grew up next door at 1409 Eighth Street. At the end of the story, it is Derek who comes to her rescue when she encounters three men — two white and one black — who accost her on the street after her late-night shift as a nurse's assistant in the hospital. She emerges physically unscathed after Derek is wounded fighting off her attackers, but she is scarcely emotionally unscathed after their meeting. As in a Munro story, Jones includes enough material to develop a novel, yet the reader finishes "Bad Neighbors" curiously satisfied. Jones seems to be saying that he has given us the most important events of the story, and he trusts us to make the connections.

Questions for Discussion

1. How difficult did you find sorting out the large cast of characters in "Bad Neighbors"? Could Jones have used this as a strategy to slow down his readers so they would not race through the pages of his complex story?

2. What does Neil Bennington's love of reading — shared by his fellow high school student Sharon Palmer — add to the characterization of the Bennington family? Why does Derek make fun of his younger brother Neil?

3. Why doesn't Sharon understand the shallow personality of Terence? How does her parents' response to him influence her feelings about Terence? Why are they so impressed with him?

4. Who is in the right during the quarrel about who can park in front of Staggs's house? How does Derek's behavior foreshadow his actions at the end of the story?

5. Why do the other black families on the block decide to buy the house at 1406 Eighth Street? Do you sympathize with their action? How do the later events in the story cast a new light on Jones's early sentence about Hamilton Palmer's installing a little gate on his porch "when his children were too small to know all the ways the world beyond the gate could hurt them"?

6. Discuss the importance of the setting to "Bad Neighbors." In what way does the neighborhood "tip" again by the end of the story?

7. What is ironic about the title "Bad Neighbors"?

Topics for Writing

1. Analyze the role in the story of the small hand-carved statue of the black girl that Sharon receives as a Christmas present.

2. **MAKING CONNECTIONS** Compare and contrast the depiction of contemporary American race relations in "Bad Neighbors" and "Leaving for Kenosha" (p. 153) by Richard Ford.

Commentary

Wyatt Mason, *"The Stories of Edward P. Jones,"* p. 613.

Suggested Reading

Jones, Edward P. *All Aunt Hagar's Children*. Amistad, 2006.

JAMES JOYCE

Araby (p. 264)

The rich texture of imagery and allusion that Joyce weaves into "Araby" may delight the sophisticated reader, but for the classroom instructor it represents a temptation comparable to the one brought to mind by the apple tree in the "wild garden" mentioned in the second paragraph. Students should not be asked to contemplate the story's symbolism until they grasp its plot. To begin class discussion of "Araby" with the question "What happens?" may well be to discover that, for a novice reader, no meaningful action seems to have been completed. When the confusion arising from this sense of anticlimax is compounded by the difficulties presented by the unfamiliarity of florins, bazaars, hallstands, and other things old and Irish, "Araby" may strike students as pointless and unnecessarily obscure.

Once it is seen, however, that the narrator's disappointment at the bazaar resolves the tension built up by his attraction to Mangan's sister and his quest to fetch her a symbol of his love, the many specific contrasts between the sensuous and romantic world of the narrator's imagination and the banal and tawdry world of actual experience become meaningful keys to understanding what has happened. The opposition between fantasy and reality continues throughout: "Her image accompanied me even in places the most hostile to romance." The story's pivotal paragraph ends with the narrator cooling his forehead against the window in one of the empty upper rooms, staring out not really at Mangan's sister but at "the brown-clad figure cast by my imagination." Before this moment, his excited fancy has transformed the "decent" and somewhat dilapidated neighborhood of North Richmond Street into a fitting backdrop for such a tale as one might find in a yellow-leaved romance. Mangan's sister, kissed by lamplight, becomes in his view a work of art like a painting by Rossetti. The narrator's soul luxuriates in a dream of exotic beauty soon to be possessed by means of a journey to Araby: "I imagined that I bore my chalice safely through a throng of foes." But after the protracted visit from the tedious Mrs. Mercer and the even longer delayed return of the narrator's uncle with the necessary coin, the limitations of the romantic imagination begin to emerge. The "chalice" is replaced by a florin, held "tightly in my hand"; the quest is made by "third-class carriage"; and the bazaar itself, its potential visionary qualities defeated by failing illumination, turns out to be an ordinary market populated by ordinary shop girls from no farther east than England. At Araby, what matters is not purity of heart but hard cash.

The pitiful inadequacy of the narrator's two pennies and sixpence to master "the great jars that stood like eastern guards" at the door of the bazaar stall completes his painful disillusionment, but Joyce allows his hero one last Byronic vision of himself "as a creature driven and derided by vanity." When the lights go out in Araby, its delusive magic collapses, and the bazaar becomes as "blind" as North Richmond Street. Well might the narrator's eyes burn, for they have been working hard to create out of intractable materials a much more beautiful illusion than Araby. This imaginative power cannot be entirely vain, however, since in the mind that tells the story it is capable of evoking experiences like those described in the story's third paragraph, against which even the hoped-for transports of Araby would have paled.

WILLIAM E. SHEIDLEY

Questions for Discussion

1. Why does the narrator want to go to the bazaar?
2. Why does he arrive so late?
3. Why doesn't he buy anything for Mangan's sister?
4. Enumerate the activities taking place at Araby. To what extent do they sustain its "magical name"?
5. What had the narrator expected to find at Araby? What was the basis of his expectation?
6. Define the narrator's feelings for Mangan's sister. To what extent is she the cause of those feelings? What, as they say, does he see in her?
7. What purpose might Joyce have had in choosing not to mention the object of the narrator's affections until the middle of the third paragraph? Describe the context into which she is introduced. In what ways is she part of the world of North Richmond Street?
8. What is the role of the narrator's uncle in the story? What values and attitudes does he represent? Are they preferable to those of the narrator?

Topics for Writing

1. Make a study of light, vision, and beauty in "Araby."
2. Compare "Araby" and the quest for the Holy Grail.
3. Analyze the function of nonvisual sense imagery in "Araby."
4. Explore Joyce's control of tone in "Araby."
5. On a second reading of the story, keep two lists. In the first record ideas, images, and allusions that suggest contexts remote from the immediate situation, jotting down associations that they bring to mind. In the second list note anything mentioned in the story with which you are unfamiliar. Look some of these items up. Then write an informal paragraph or two showing to what extent tracking Joyce's mind in this fashion helped you to understand and enjoy the story.
6. **RESPONDING CREATIVELY** Using the first three paragraphs of "Araby" as a model, write a recollection of the way you spent your evenings at some memorable period of your childhood. Use specific sensory images to evoke the locale, the activities, and the way you felt at the time.
7. **RESPONDING CREATIVELY** Narrate an experience in which you were disappointed. First show how your erroneous expectations were generated; then describe what you actually encountered in such a way that its contrast with your expectations is clear.

Suggested Readings

Anderson, Chester G. *James Joyce.* New York: Thames and Hudson, 1986.

Attridge, Derek, ed. *The Cambridge Companion to James Joyce.* New York: Cambridge UP, 1990.

Beck, Warren. *Joyce's* Dubliners: *Substance, Vision, and Art.* Durham, NC: Duke UP, 1969. 303–60.

Beckett, Samuel, et al. *An Examination of James Joyce.* Brooklyn, NY: Haskell, 1974.

Benstock, Bernard, ed. *Critical Essays on James Joyce.* Boston: G. K. Hall, 1985.

Brugaletta, J. J., and M. H. Hayden. "Motivation for Anguish in Joyce's 'Araby.'" *Studies in Short Fiction* 15 (1978): 11–17.

Cronin, E. J. "James Joyce's Trilogy and Epilogue: 'The Sisters,' 'An Encounter,' 'Araby,' and 'The Dead.'" *Renascence* 31 (1979): 229–48.

Ellmann, Richard. *James Joyce: New and Revised Edition.* New York: Oxford UP, 1982.

Levin, Harry. *James Joyce: A Critical Introduction.* New York: New Directions, 1960.

Mason, Ellsworth, and Richard Ellmann, eds. *The Critical Writings of James Joyce.* Ithaca, NY: Cornell UP, 1989.

Morrissey, L. J. "Joyce's Narrative Struggles in 'Araby.'" *Modern Fiction Studies* 28 (1982): 45–52.

Riquelme, John P. *Teller and Tale in Joyce's Fiction: Oscillating Perspectives.* Baltimore: Johns Hopkins UP, 1983.

Roberts, R. P. "'Araby' and the Palimpsest of Criticism, or Through a Glass Eye Darkly." *Antioch Review* 26 (1966–67): 469–89.

San Juan, Epifanio Jr. *James Joyce and the Craft of Fiction: An Interpretation of Dubliners.* Rutherford, NJ: Fairleigh Dickinson UP, 1972. 209–23.

Scott, Bonnie. James Joyce. Atlantic Highlands, NJ: Humanities Press International, 1987.

Stone, H. "'Araby' and the Writings of James Joyce." *Antioch Review* 25 (1965): 375–410.

Franz Kafka

A Hunger Artist (p. 269)
Jackals and Arabs (p. 275)
The Metamorphosis (p. 278)

A Hunger Artist

This "brief but striking parable of alienation" (to quote Kafka biographer Ernst Pawel) was probably written in February 1922, shortly before Kafka began *The Castle.* He had just returned to Prague after a four-week winter vacation prescribed by his doctor as a sort of "shock treatment" to arrest his advancing tuberculosis and deepening depression. Back at his desk, in his room in his parents' apartment, Kafka described his activities in a letter to a friend: "In order to save myself from what is commonly referred to as 'nerves,' I have lately begun to write a little. From about seven at night I sit at my desk, but it doesn't amount to much. It is like trying to dig a foxhole with one's fingernails in the midst of battle."

"A Hunger Artist" was among the few works Kafka allowed to be published in his lifetime. Ironically, he read the galley proofs only a few days before his death. Pawel describes the scene:

> On May 11, [his friend Max] Brod came for what he knew would be his last visit, pretending merely to have stopped off on his way to a lecture in Vienna so as not to alarm his friend. Kafka, by then quite unable to eat, was wasting away, dying of starvation [because of throat lesions] and immersed in the galley proofs of "A Hunger Artist." Fate lacked the subtle touch of Kafka's art.

> The effort drained him. "Kafka's physical condition at this point," Klopstock [a medical student] later wrote, "and the whole situation of his literally starving to death, were truly ghastly. Reading the proofs must have

been not only a tremendous emotional strain but also a shattering kind of spiritual encounter with his former self, and when he had finished, the tears kept flowing for a long time. It was the first time I ever saw him overtly expressing his emotions this way. Kafka had always shown an almost super-human self-control."

As a parable, "A Hunger Artist" may be interpreted in as many ways as there are readers finding words to describe their response to the text. Kafka created in his fiction a metaphorical language akin to music, touching emotions at a level beyond the denotations of the words he used to dramatize his imaginary characters' situations. The title is significant: "*A* Hunger Artist," not "*The* Hunger Artist." There are many kinds of hungers, and many kinds of artists expressing different needs for substance. Students may define the "hunger" as a desire for religious certainty and the "fasting" as the stubborn abstention from a faith without God. Or the key to the parable may lie in the Hunger Artist's statement at the end of the story: "Because I have to fast, I can't help it. . . . Because I couldn't find the food I liked. If I had found it, believe me, I shouldn't have made any fuss and stuffed myself just like you and everyone else." Kafka was tormented by a failure of nourishment — from his faith, his family, his talent, his art.

Questions for Discussion

1. What is a parable? Is "A Hunger Artist" a parable?
2. Is it possible to read Kafka's story literally, as a realistic tale? What gives you the sense that there is more to "A Hunger Artist" than its plot and characters?
3. Is Kafka describing an unimaginable situation? Explain.
4. Gaping spectators, butchers, theatrical managers, circus people — the world of the Hunger Artist is mercenary and materialistic. He is described as a "martyr." A martyr to what?
5. As the Hunger Artist loses his popularity, he joins the circus, and his cage is put on display near the animal cages. What does this symbolize? What does this action foreshadow?
6. Explicate the last paragraph of the story. Analyze the function of the panther and his "noble body."

Topics for Writing

1. **RESPONDING CREATIVELY** Write a parable of your own.
2. Agree or disagree with this statement by Primo Levi, the Italian author who translated Kafka's *The Trial*:

    > Now I love and admire Kafka because he writes in a way that is totally unavailable to me. In my writing, for good or evil, knowingly or not, I've always strived to pass from the darkness into the light. . . . Kafka forges his path in the opposite direction: he endlessly unravels the hallucinations that he draws from incredibly profound layers, and he never filters them. The reader . . . never receives any help in tearing through the veil or circumventing it to go and see what it conceals. Kafka never touches ground, he never condescends to giving you the end of Ariadne's thread.
    >
    > But this love of mine is ambivalent, close to fear and rejection: it is similar to the emotion we feel for someone dear who suffers and asks us for help we cannot give. . . . His suffering is genuine and continuous, it assails you and does not let you go.

3. **MAKING CONNECTIONS** "It was not the hunger artist who was cheating, he was working honestly, but the world was cheating him of his reward." Compare

and contrast "A Hunger Artist" and "The Metamorphosis," taking this statement as the theme of both stories.

Conversations on Meaning and Intention in Franz Kafka's Stories, pp. 635–655

See page 61 of this manual.

Suggested Readings

See page 61 of this manual.

JACKALS AND ARABS

Kafka wrote "Jackals and Arabs" early in 1917, during a period when he had begun the study of Hebrew in the hope that one day he could relocate from Prague to Palestine. As his friend Gustav Janouch reported in *Conversations with Kafka*, Kafka felt that

> The Jews today are no longer satisfied with history, with an heroic home in time. They yearn for a modest ordinary home in space. More and more young Jews are returning to Palestine. That is a return to oneself, to one's roots, to growth. The national home in Palestine is for the Jews a necessary goal" (105).

"Jackals and Arabs" was first published in October 1917 in the magazine *Der Jude [The Jew]* edited by the Zionist leader Martin Buber. The following year it was included in *Neue deutsche Erzahler (New German Stories)* edited in Berlin.

Janouch also recorded Kafka's comment on fairy tales: "There are no bloodless fairy stories. Every fairy story comes from the depths of blood and fear. In this all fairy stories are alike. Only the surface differs. Northern fairy stories lack the exuberant fauna of the imagination in the fairy stories of the African Negro, but the core, the depth of longing, is the same" (95). "The depth of longing" for Kafka was spiritual in nature. In the foreword to *The Complete Stories*, John Updike noted that in Kafka's shorter tales such as "Jackals and Arabs,"

> an affinity may be felt with the parables of Hasidism, that pietist movement within Judaism which emphasized, over against the law of orthodoxy, mystic joy and divine immanence. Certain of the parables share Kafka's relish in the enigmatic:
>
> A man who was afflicted with a terrible disease complained to Rabbi Israel that his suffering interfered with his learning and praying. The rabbi put his hand on his shoulder and said, "How do you know, friend, what is more pleasing to God, your studying or your suffering?"
>
> [Martin Buber, *Tales of the Hasidim*, Vol.II]

Updike concluded his Foreword by stating that "a century after his birth he [Kafka] seems the last holy writer, and the supreme fabulist of modern man's cosmic predicament" (xxi).

Questions for Discussion

The commentary by John Gardner, "On Myths and Literary Fairy Tales" (p. 652), can serve as the ground for a discussion and analysis of Kafka's enigmatic literary fairy tale.

1. Gardner defines fairy tales as "the place where myth and reality meet." Using his working definition of myth as "a general type," which are the mythic elements and which is the ground of reality on which they meet in "Jackals and Arabs"?

2. If both jackals and Arabs can be read as mythic figures in the story, then which one is a literary creation and which one comes from life? Does this distinction change the meaning of the story?

3. The character of the Northerner precipitates the conflict in "Jackals and Arabs," just as Gardner maintains in his commentary that "in fairy tales we always get a conflict between mythic figures and one or more real-life characters, the person or persons who serve as surrogate for the child to whom the story is addressed." Nowhere in Kafka's story is the Northerner (the "real-life character") presented as a Jew. Should this influence your interpretation of the fairy tale?

4. Gardner maintains that "fairy tales are neither myths nor realistic stories but a little of each. That is perhaps the secret of their lasting power. . . . [M]ythic figures in fairy tales — both opponents and helpers of the child-hero — help the child see his problem as common, not a result of his personal freakishness." In "Jackals and Arabs," Kafka has simplified the archetypal presence of Evil in the world in his dramatization of "the world of dreams and the so-called unconscious, a shifting, obscurely symbolic landscape outside time, peopled by archetypes: but the dreamer, represented by the child-hero, is like a character out of realistic fiction. . . ." How does the final sentence of Gardner's commentary in its entirety help you to understand Kafka's story?

Topics for Writing

1. Write an essay in which you analyze the meaning of the scissors as an important symbol in "Jackals and Arabs." What does it contribute to the meaning of the story?

2. Kafka never endorsed the psychoanalytic theories of his contemporary Sigmund Freud (1856–1939), but a reader interested in psychology can write an essay interpreting "Jackals and Arabs" as a dream taking the critical perspective of psychological criticism with jackals representing the Id, Arabs the Superego, and the narrator the Ego.

Conversations on Meaning and Intention in Franz Kafka's Stories, pp. 635–655

See page 61 of this manual.

Suggested Readings

See page 61 of this manual.

THE METAMORPHOSIS

This story admits the broadest range of explications — biographical, psychoanalytical, religious, philosophical. Here is one way it might be read: As the sole supporter of his family after the collapse of his father's business, Gregor Samsa has selflessly devoted himself to serving others. Bringing home "good round coin which he could lay on the table for his amazed and happy family" has given him great satisfaction, and his only ambition has been to send his sister, "who loved music," to study at the Conservatorium. After his metamorphosis, Gregor can no longer justify his existence by serving others. Instead, he must come to terms with himself as himself, an alien being whose own nature and needs are perhaps only by a degree more strange to Gregor than those of the human Gregor Samsa would have been, if somehow he had confronted them rather than deferring to the version of himself projected by the supposed needs of his family.

Kafka simultaneously traces Gregor's painful growth to self-willed individuality and the family's liberation from dependence upon him, for the relationship of dependence and exploitation has been crippling to both parties. Gregor learns what food he likes, stakes his sticky claim to the sexually suggestive picture of the woman with the fur muff (which may represent an objectification of his libido), and, no longer "considerate," at last *comes* out, intruding his obscene existence upon the world out of a purely self-assertive desire to enjoy his sister's music and to be united with its beauty. With this act Gregor has become fully himself; his death soon after simply releases him from the misery of his existence.

It is also a final release of the family from dependence and from the shame and incompetence that it entails. As an insect, Gregor becomes quite obviously the embarrassment to the family that they allowed him to be when he was human. Step by step they discover their ability to support themselves — taking jobs, coping with what is now merely the troublesome burden of Gregor, and learning finally the necessity of escaping from the prison that his solicitousness has placed them in. Gregor's battle with his father strangely transmutes the Oedipal conflict. It is triggered by Gregor's becoming a being for whom there is no longer room in the family, just as if he were a youth growing to sexual maturity, but the result is that the father, who has previously been reduced to a state of supine inertia by Gregor's diligent exertions, returns to claim his full manhood as husband and paterfamilias.

Emerging from their apartment, "which Gregor had chosen," the family members grow into an independent purposiveness that Gregor himself is never able to attain. The story may be said to end with a second metamorphosis, focused in the image of Grete stretching her young body — almost like a butterfly newly emerged from her cocoon. Gregor, left behind like the caterpillar whose demise releases her, is denied all but a premonitory glimpse of the sexual and reproductive fulfillment for which his sister seems destined.

WILLIAM E. SHEIDLEY

Questions for Discussion

1. Describe the effect of Kafka's matter-of-fact assertion of the bizarre incident with which the story begins. Are you very interested in how it came to pass? How does Kafka keep that from becoming an issue in the story?
2. What are Gregor's concerns in section I? To what degree do they differ from what would matter to him if he had not been transformed into an insect?
3. When Gregor is trying to get out of bed, he considers calling for help but then dismisses the idea. Why?
4. What seems most important to the members of Gregor's family as he lies in bed? Is it his health?
5. Describe the reaction of Gregor's parents to their first view of the metamorphosed Gregor. What circumstances in ordinary life might elicit a similar response?
6. Discuss the view from Gregor's window.
7. Trace Gregor's adaptation to his new body. In what ways do the satisfactions of his life as an insect differ from the satisfactions of his life as a traveling salesman?
8. When Gregor's father pushes him back into his room at the end of section I, Kafka calls it "literally a deliverance." Comment on the possible implications of that description.

9. Describe Grete's treatment of Gregor in section II. Is Gregor ill?
10. What are Gregor's hopes for the future? Is there anything wrong with those hopes?
11. For a time, Gregor is ashamed of his condition and tries to hide from everyone. In what way might this be called a step forward for him?
12. Discuss the conflicting feelings Gregor has about the furniture's being taken out of his room. Why does he try to save the picture? What might Kafka's intention be in stressing that it is on this occasion that Grete calls Gregor by his name for the first time since his metamorphosis?
13. "Gregor's broken loose." What does Gregor's father do? Why? Explain the situation that has developed by the end of section II.
14. How does the charwoman relate to Gregor? Why is she the one who presides over his "funeral"?
15. Compare the role of the lodgers in the family with that of Gregor. Have they supplanted him? Why does Gregor's father send them away in the morning?
16. Why does Gregor, who previously did not like music, feel so attracted to his sister's playing? What change has taken place in his attitude toward himself? What might Kafka mean by "the unknown nourishment he craved"?
17. Comment on Grete's use of the neuter pronoun "it" to refer to Gregor.
18. What is the mood of the final passages of the story?

Topics for Writing

1. Write an essay describing how Kafka gains the reader's "willing suspension of disbelief."
2. Consider Gregor Samsa's metamorphosis as a triumph of the self.
3. Analyze Kafka's "The Metamorphosis" as a study of sublimated incest.
4. **RESPONDING CREATIVELY** Consider Kafka's use of apparently symbolic images whose complete meaning seems impossible to state in abstract terms — the apples, the fur muff, or the hospital beyond the window, for example. Write a vignette in which symbolic objects play a role without becoming counters in a paraphrasable allegory. Some examples of symbols: a candle, a cup, the sea, broken glass, ants.

Conversations on Meaning and Intention in Franz Kafka's Stories, pp. 635–655

John Updike, *"Kafka and 'The Metamorphosis,'"* p. 638.
Gustav Janouch, *"Kafka's View of 'The Metamorphosis,'"* p. 637.
R. Crumb and David Zane Mairowitz, *"A Hunger Artist,"* p. 642.
John Gardner, *On Myths and Literary Fairy Tales,* p. 652.

Suggested Readings

Anderson, Mark. *Reading Kafka.* New York: Schocken, 1990.
Canetti, Elias. *Kafka's Other Trial: Letters to Felice.* New York: Schocken, 1988.
Greenberg, Martin. "Kafka's 'Metamorphosis' and Modern Spirituality." *Tri-Quarterly* 6 (1966): 5–20.
Gross, Ruth V., ed. *Critical Essays on Franz Kafka.* Boston: G. K. Hall, 1990.
Janouch, Gustav. *Conversations with Kafka.* New York: New Directions, 1971.
Kafka, Franz. *The Complete Stories.* New York: Schocken, 1983.
———. *The Diaries of Franz Kafka.* New York: Schocken, 1988.
———. *The Metamorphosis.* Trans. and ed. Stanley Corngold. New York: Bantam, 1972. (Contains notes, documents, and ten critical essays.)

Levi, Primo. "Translating Kafka." In *The Mirror Maker*. New York: Schocken, 1989.

Moss, Leonard. "A Key to the Door Image in 'The Metamorphosis.'" *Modern Fiction Studies* 17 (1971): 37–42.

Nabokov, Vladimir. *Lectures on Literature*. New York: Harcourt, 1980. 250–83.

Pascal, Roy. *Kafka's Narrators: A Study of His Stories and Sketches*. New York: Cambridge UP, 1984.

Pawel, Ernst. *The Nightmare of Reason: A Life of Franz Kafka*. New York: Farrar, 1984.

Spann, Meno. *Franz Kafka*. Boston: Twayne, 1976.

Tauber, Herbert. *Franz Kafka: An Interpretation of His Works*. Brooklyn, NY: Haskell, 1969.

Taylor, Alexander. "The Waking: The Theme of Kafka's 'Metamorphosis.'" *Studies in Short Fiction* 2 (1965): 337–42.

Wolkenfeld, Suzanne. "Christian Symbolism in Kafka's 'The Metamorphosis.'" *Studies in Short Fiction* 10 (1973): 205–7.

JAMAICA KINCAID

Girl (p. 312)

Kincaid's one-paragraph story is a dialogue between a mother and a daughter, consisting mostly of the mother's litany of advice about how to act in a ladylike manner. Students might enjoy reading it aloud. The West Indian prose rhythms are subtly beautiful, and the humor of the mother's advice is revealed in the audible reading process for anyone who has missed it by scanning too quickly. The conflict between the girl and her mother is evident in the mother's fears that her daughter will grow up to be a "slut." Everything the mother says is twisted in light of that fear. The daughter wonders, *"But what if the baker won't let me feel the bread?"* And the mother replies, "You mean to say that after all you are really going to be the kind of woman who the baker won't let near the bread?" The speech rhythm is reminiscent of James Joyce's interior monologues. In fact, we are not amiss to ask whether the mother is actually speaking to her daughter in the story, or whether the daughter has internalized her mother's voice and written it down for us to read to the accompaniment of our own laughter.

Questions for Discussion

1.   What are the major subjects in this litany of advice? What kind of life do they describe?

2.   The title of the story is "Girl," yet the girl seems to have only two lines of her own — one a protest and the other a question. Why might the author have decided to call the story "Girl" rather than "Mother" or "Woman" or "Advice" or "Memory"?

3.   Identify and discuss Kincaid's use of humor in "Girl." What contribution does it make to the story?

4.   What is the effect of fairly precise household rules alternating with comments such as "on Sundays try to walk like a lady and not like the slut you are so bent on becoming"? String together the lines that admonish the potential slut. What do we think of the mother? What connection is there between the subjects the mother is speaking of and the idea of a slut? Why does it keep popping up from the most innocuous of items? What does this refrain make us think of the daughter? Is the "slut" refrain a joke or is the author making a suggestion about the construction of self?

5. Some of the advice seems like it could never have been spoken, only inferred: "this is how you smile to someone you don't like too much; this is how you smile to someone you don't like at all; this is how you smile to someone you like completely." Throughout the whole piece, do you think the mother is speaking to her daughter? What other possibilities could underlie the story's composition?

6. Toward the end of the paragraph the kind of advice changes: "this is how to make a good medicine to throw away a child before it even becomes a child," says the mother. Surely she's not speaking to a young girl here. In the final line, the mother calls her a "woman," the only direct address in the story; earlier the listener has been addressed as a potential slut and been told she's "not a boy." What's the difference between the advice that precedes and follows the reference to aborting a child? Which is more concrete? more abstract? Why does the advice change because of the listener's age? What kinds of knowledge is her mother able to offer?

Topics for Writing

1. Analyze Kincaid's use of humor to indicate conflict in "Girl."
2. RESPONDING CREATIVELY   Expand the story through the use of descriptive prose. Is the result more or less effective than Kincaid's original?
3. RESPONDING CREATIVELY   Write a short story in which you use only dialogue.

Commentary

Jamaica Kincaid, "On 'Girl,'" p. 609.

Suggested Readings

Kincaid, Jamaica. *At the Bottom of the River.* New York: Vintage, 1985.
———. Interview. New York Times Book Review, 7 Apr. 1985: 6+.

JHUMPA LAHIRI

A Real Durwan (p. 314)

Lahiri is writing a character sketch of Boori Ma, the underappreciated sixty-four-year-old female caretaker or *durwan* (gatekeeper) of the stairwell in a shabby old building in Calcutta who insists she enjoyed a much better life before she became a refugee in India after being forced out of East Bengal during Partition. None of the building's inhabitants believe her stories of her prosperous previous life, but since she keeps the stairs "spotlessly clean" and guards the entry to the entrance door, she is allowed to sleep on her ragged quilts beneath the letter boxes downstairs and cook her simple meals with coal shared by the building's many tenants. It would seem her status could not be more lowly, but Lahiri chronicles her decline into homelessness with sad economy: first her quilts are destroyed by rain, a promised replacement is not forthcoming, her neighbors begin small renovations in the building — a couple of wash basins, yellow paint for the shutters — until so many workmen are coming to the building that Boori Ma is forced to move up to the roof. Bored and restless up there, accustomed to the distractions in front of the building's entranceway, she slackens in her duties as a *durwan*. Unwisely she leaves the building and begins to roam the streets until she is robbed of her life savings tied to the end of her sari. When she returns, the residents unfairly accuse her of informing the robbers who have stolen the wash basin on the first floor. They throw Boori Ma out into the street, intending to find what they call "a real *durwan.*"

How did Lahiri take this simple plot and turn it into such a gracefully told, emotionally absorbing story? One way to have your students appreciate the importance of Lahiri's remarkably sustained, compassionate Chekhovian tone is to have them write a one paragraph summary of the events of the story, and then ask them to write the first paragraphs of their own story about how a squatter living in a slum tenement in any American city becomes a homeless person.

Questions for Discussion

1. What details does Lahiri invent to turn her protagonist Boori Ma into a sympathetic but never sentimental character?
2. How important is the setting in the story?
3. How much information about the partition of India must a reader know to appreciate Lahiri's story? How do Boori Ma's memories of her experiences fill in our knowledge of that troubled time in India's history?

Topic for Writing

1. The fiction writer and critic Frank O'Connor once said in *The Lonely Voice* (1962), his famous pioneering study of the short story, that short stories were especially strong when representing what he called "the Little Man," the people in the "underclass," society's exploited and unsung members whether they be Indian, Irish, Russian, American, or citizens of any country on the planet. On pages 15–17 of his book, O'Connor stated that writers of this type of story "take the mock-heroic character," any absurd figure, "and impose his image over that of the crucified Jesus, so that even while we laugh we are filled with horror at the resemblance" because the story is telling us that "I am your brother." (The way that O'Connor phrased his insightful statement is unfortunately sexist, but surely he meant "I am your sister" as well.) Agree or disagree with O'Connor's view of the short story, using Lahiri's story and any others in this anthology.

Commentary

Jhumpa Lahiri, *"On Writing Fiction,"* p. 610.

D. H. LAWRENCE

The Rocking-Horse Winner (p. 322)

Lawrence's masterful technical control wins the reader's assent to the fantastic premise on which the story is built; without that assent, the thematic statement the story propounds would lack cogency. Rather than confronting us boldly with his improbable donnée, as Franz Kafka does in "The Metamorphosis" (p. 278), Lawrence edges up to it. The whispering voices in the house that drive Paul to his furious rocking begin as a thought in the mother's mind and then become a figure of speech that crystallizes imperceptibly into a literal fact — or rather, into an auditory hallucination heard by the children that expresses their perception of their mother's unquenchable need for funds. Paul's ability to pick a winner by riding his rocking horse to where he is lucky requires even more circumspect handling. Like the family members, we learn about it after the fact, putting together bits of information to explain a set of peculiar but at first not at all implausible circumstances — Paul's claim ("Well, I got there!"), his familiarity with race horses, Bassett's reluctance "to give him away" to Oscar, Paul's giving Oscar a tip on a long shot that comes in a winner, and only then, with Oscar's skepticism always pre-empting that of the reader, the revelation of how much he has won. It is not until the very end that we, with his astonished mother, actually witness Paul in the act of receiving revelation — just as he slips beyond the world of everyday probability for good and into the uncharted supernatural realm from whence his "luck" seems to emanate.

Although no explanation, supernatural or otherwise, is necessary to account for good fortune at the racetrack, Lawrence persuades the reader that Paul's success is caused by his exertions and therefore has a moral meaning. In Paul's household the lack of love is perceived as a lack of money and the lack of money is attributed to a lack of luck. Because luck is by definition something that happens to one, to blame one's troubles on luck is to deny responsibility for them and to abandon any effort to overcome them. As the event makes clear, Paul's mother will never be satisfied, no matter how much money falls her way, because no amount of money can fill the emptiness left by the absence of love. The "hard little place" in her heart at the beginning of the story has expanded until, at the end, she feels that her whole heart has "turned actually into a stone." Paul sets out by the force of will to redefine luck as something one can acquire. He places belief before evidence and asserts, "I'm a lucky person. . . . God told me," and then makes good on his promise by riding his rocking horse to where luck comes from. " 'It's as if he had it from heaven,' " Bassett says, "in a secret, religious voice."

In his single-minded devotion to winning money for his mother at the racetrack by riding his rocking horse (which W. D. Snodgrass has likened to masturbation as Lawrence understood it), Paul diverts his spiritual and emotional forces to material aims, and Lawrence symbolically represents the effect of this materialization in the process of petrification by which the mother's heart and Paul's blue eyes, which have throughout the story served as an emblem of his obsession, turn to stone. At the end Oscar states the case with epigrammatic precision: Hester's son has been transformed into eighty-odd thousand pounds — a tidy sum, but of course it will not be enough.

WILLIAM E. SHEIDLEY

Questions for Discussion

1. How is Paul's mother portrayed at the outset? Does Lawrence suggest that she is blameworthy? Why or why not?

2. Explain the family's "grinding sense of the shortage of money." Why do the voices get even louder when some money becomes available? What would it take to still the voices?

3. Discuss the implications of Paul's confusing *luck* with *lucre*. How accurate is his mother's definition of luck? What would constitute true good luck for him?

4. Explain Paul's claim to be lucky. In what sense is he justified? In what sense is he very unlucky?

5. What function do Oscar and Bassett play in the story, beyond providing Paul with practical access to the racetrack and the lawyer?

6. "Bassett was serious as a church." Is this a humorous line? Does it suggest any-thing beyond the comic?

7. What is the effect on the reader of the episode in which Oscar takes Paul to the track and Paul's horse Daffodil wins the race?

8. Explain the mother's response to her birthday gift. What is its effect on Paul? Why?

9.   Before the Derby, Paul does not "know" for several races. Can this dry spell be explained? What brings it to an end?

10. Analyze Paul's last words in the story. What does he mean by *"get there"*? Where, in fact, does he go? Is *absolute* certainty possible? How? Why is Paul so proud to proclaim that he is lucky to his mother? Finally, comment on her reaction.

11. Evaluate Oscar's remarks, which end the story. Was Paul a "poor devil"? in what sense?

Topics for Writing

1.   Describe the handling of the supernatural in Lawrence's "The Rocking-Horse Winner."

2.   Explore the religious theme of "The Rocking-Horse Winner."

3.   Consider luck, will, and faith in "The Rocking-Horse Winner."

4.   Analyze the realistic elements and the social theme of Lawrence's supernatural tale.

5.   Consider luck, lucre, and love in "The Rocking-Horse Winner."

6.   **RESPONDING CREATIVELY**   Look up a newspaper story about some unexplained phenomenon — perhaps a ghost or a poltergeist — and work it into a narrative whose meaning is finally not dependent on an interest in the supernatural.

Commentary

D. H. Lawrence, *"On 'The Fall of the House of Usher' and 'The Cask of Amontillado,'"* p. 683.

Suggested Readings

Boulton, J. T., ed. *The Letters of D. H. Lawrence.* New York: Cambridge UP, 1989.

Clayton, J. J. "D. H. Lawrence: Psychic Wholeness through Rebirth." *Massachusetts Review* 25 (1984): 200–21.

Harris, Janice. *The Short Fiction of D. H. Lawrence.* New Brunswick, NJ: Rutgers UP, 1984.

Hyde, G. M. *D. H. Lawrence.* New York: St. Martin's, 1990.

Jackson, Dennis, and Felda Jackson, eds. *Critical Essays on D. H. Lawrence.* Boston: G. K. Hall, 1988.

Lawrence, D. H. *The Portable D. H. Lawrence.* New York: Penguin, 1977.

Meyers, Jeffry. *D. H. Lawrence: A Biography.* New York: Knopf, 1990.

Olson, Charles. *D. H. Lawrence and the High Temptation of the Mind.* Santa Barbara, CA: Black Sparrow, 1980.

Rice, Thomas Jackson. *D. H. Lawrence: A Guide to Research.* New York: Garland, 1983.

Rose, S. "Physical Trauma in D. H. Lawrence's Short Fiction." *Contemporary Literature* 16 (1975): 73–83.

Sager, Keith. *D. H. Lawrence: Life into Art.* Athens: U of Georgia P, 1985.

San Juan, E., Jr. "Theme versus Imitation: D. H. Lawrence's 'The Rocking-Horse Winner.'" *D. H. Lawrence Review* 3 (1970): 136–40.

Schneider, Daniel J. *The Consciousness of D. H. Lawrence: An Intellectual Biography.* Lawrence: U of Kansas P, 1986.

———. *D. H. Lawrence: The Artist as Psychologist.* Lawrence: UP of Kansas, 1984.

Shaw, M. "Lawrence and Feminism." *Critical Quarterly* 25 (1983): 23–27.

Snodgrass, W. D. "A Rocking Horse: The Symbol, the Pattern, the Way to Live." In *D. H. Lawrence: A Collection of Critical Essays.* Ed. Mark Spilka. *Twentieth-Century*

Views. Englewood Cliffs, NJ: Prentice, 1963. Originally published in *The Hudson Review* 11 (1958).

Squires, Michael, and Keith Cushman. *The Challenge of D. H. Lawrence.* Madison: U of Wisconsin P, 1990.

Widmer, Kingsley. *The Art of Perversity: D. H. Lawrence's Shorter Fictions.* Seattle: U of Washington P, 1962. 92–95, 213.

JACK LONDON

To Build a Fire (p. 334)

While the protagonist of "To Build a Fire" lacks sufficient imagination to concern himself with "significances" or to "meditate upon . . . man's place in the universe," London's story leads us directly to these issues. Its setting and structure strip man's confrontation with death in an alien and indifferent or even hostile universe down to a starkly simple example, while its slow and detailed pace brings home the reality of that confrontation with all the force of actual experience.

The nameless traveler across the blank Arctic landscape is as well equipped as any man for coping with his situation. He is resourceful, cautious, tenacious, and able to tolerate a great deal of discomfort. More experience in the Yukon would not have improved his ability to cope. It would simply have supplied him with such wisdom as is propounded by the old-timer: Don't try it, or don't try it alone. But avoidance can be only temporary. Man must face death, and face it alone. London places his character on "the unprotected tip of the planet," exposed to the frigid emptiness of the universe, and the story details how it overcomes him.

London defines the man's condition by contrasting it with that of the dog, which is at home in the hostile environment. Fitted by nature with adequate defenses against the cold and guided by unfailing instinct in deciding what to do, the dog provides an unsentimental perspective on the man's struggles. Although the man's judgment is a poor substitute for canine instinct and although his improvised technology, despite its provision of fire, proves disastrously less reliable than husky fur, the man's consciousness of his situation, his errors, and his eventual dignity in accepting his death earn him a heroic stature impossible for the dog, which London portrays as a dog, not as a person deserving credit for his decisions and hence his survival. At the end, the husky has more in common with "the stars that leaped and danced and shone brightly in the cold sky" than with the human spirit that has passed from the frozen corpse, leaving behind its mark in the dignity of the posture that the corpse retains.

Readers may disagree over whether the story — which, as Earle Labor has shown, corresponds remarkably with Greek tragedy as defined by Aristotle — conveys a tragic sense of order or the black pessimism characteristic of the mature London. Surely all readers will, however, acknowledge the powerful effect that the story creates, thanks to London's artful use of foreshadowing, repetition, and close observation of authentic detail. As numbness and frost invade and gradually seize the body of the man, the metaphysical chill accompanying the recognition of mortality creeps irresistibly into the reader's mind. Each detail of the story contributes to this single impression — the atmosphere; the cold ironic voice of the narrator; and most poignantly, perhaps, the contrasting moments of warmth by the fire at lunch, the remembered comfort of which is strangely echoed in the repose of the dying man's last thoughts.

Questions for Discussion

1. Describe the atmosphere established in the first two paragraphs.
2. What techniques does London use to impress the reader with the man's solitude? Why does he refrain for so long from mentioning the dog?
3. How cold is it? How does London make clear what such cold is like? Why is it important for him to do so?
4. London tells us that the man lacks imagination. What good would imagination have done him?
5. Why is the dog reluctant to follow the man? Why does it follow him anyway? Trace the dog's attitudes throughout the story.
6. The man keeps close track of time and distances. Why are they important to him? What significance might they have for the reader?
7. What is the reason for London's careful introduction of the hazards of the hidden spots of water in such detail before the man actually slips into one? What would be the difference if he withheld these explanations until afterwards?
8. What does the man do at half past twelve when he arrives at the forks? What does his behavior reveal about his character? In what way are those traits important to the subsequent action?
9. The words of an old-timer from Sulphur Creek enter the man's memory at intervals in the story. Trace the changes in his response to them. What does the old-timer have in common with the dog?
10. Several times London associates the cold with outer space. Consider the possible implications of this connection.
11. Why does London wait until after lunch to have the man fall into the water?
12. What mistake does the man make in building his second fire? Why does he commit that error?
13. While his second fire is getting started, the man indulges in some distinctly prideful thoughts. Is pride his downfall? Explain.
14. How do we feel about the man as he struggles to build his third fire?
15. What is wrong with the man's plan to kill the dog, warm his hands in the dog's body, and then start another fire?
16. At one point the man crawls after the dog on all fours, like an animal; at another he feels that he is flying like the god Mercury. What do you think London means to imply by these comparisons?
17. Although the man readily accepts the likelihood that he will lose parts of his body to the frost, he refuses to acknowledge that he is going to die until nearly the end. Contrast his behavior before and after he makes that recognition.
18. By the end, does the man still lack imagination?
19. Explain the effect of the last paragraph's being narrated from the dog's point of view.

Topics for Writing

1. Write an essay contrasting the use of instinct and judgment in "To Build a Fire."
2. Discuss London's use of foreshadowing and repetition.
3. Discuss London's treatment of the partial source of the story, Jeremiah Lynch's *Three Years in the Klondike* (London, 1904). (Quoted in Franklin Walker, *Jack London and the Klondike*, pp. 256–57; see Suggested Readings, below.)
4. After reading the story, make a list of the elements that compose it, such as *man, dog, cold, old-timer, fire, water*, and so on. Read it again, classifying each passage into the appropriate category or categories. Invent new categories as needed, but keep your list as short as possible. Draw a diagram showing how the elements are

related. Does your diagram reveal or confirm anything about the meaning of the story?

5.   **RESPONDING CREATIVELY**   Write a story or vignette involving a human being and an animal. Imitate London by telling part of it from the animal's point of view but without anthropomorphizing the animal in any way.

Suggested Readings

Labor, Earle. *Jack London.* Twayne's United States Authors Series 230. New York: Twayne, 1974. 63–70.

McClintock, James I. *White Logic: Jack London's Short Stories.* Grand Rapids, MI: Wolf House, 1975. 116–19.

Walker, Franklin. *Jack London and the Klondike: The Genesis of an American Writer.* San Marino, CA: Huntington Library, 1966. 254–60.

GUY DE MAUPASSANT

The Necklace (p. 345)

"The Necklace" has long been one of the most popular of Maupassant's stories, and one of the most interesting aspects of the story is this popularity, since artistically it is far from his best. The story is little more than an anecdote. Mme. Loisel, a woman from the lower middle class, is deeply dissatisfied with her station in life. As she sits down to dinner with her husband — a "little clerk at the Ministry of Public Instructions" — she thinks of "dainty dinners, of shining silverware, of tapestry which peopled the walls with ancient personages and with strange birds in the middle of a fairy forest."

Her husband, sensing her unhappiness, secures an invitation for a grand ball, and, when she is miserable at not having a fine dress, he gives her money he has been saving for a gun and a shooting holiday with his friends. When she is still unhappy at not having jewels, he suggests she borrow some from a wealthy friend, Mme. Forestier. Mme. Loisel borrows what she thinks is a diamond necklace, is a great success at the ball, but loses the necklace on the way home.

Too ashamed to tell the friend what has happened, the couple borrow money to buy a diamond necklace like the one that was lost. They return the necklace and slowly repay the loan. After ten years, during which the wife has become "the woman of impoverished households — strong and hard and rough," she accidentally meets Mme. Forestier and learns that she had lent her only a paste copy of a diamond necklace. Mme. Loisel and her husband have destroyed their lives for nothing.

Unlike in his finest stories, Maupassant here stays on the surface of the characters. Mme. Forestier and Mme. Loisel's husband are only faintly sketched; they seem to exist merely to act out roles. The anecdote itself is so implausible that simple questions — why didn't Mme. Forestier notice that a different necklace had been returned to her? Why did M. Loisel allow his life to be destroyed without a protest? — would bring it to earth. But most readers are willing to suspend their disbelief.

When we place the story in the time it was written, its themes stand out even more sharply. On its most obvious level this is one of the tales of moral instruction that were so widespread in nineteenth-century popular literature. Mme. Loisel's dreams of clothes and jewels represent the sin of vanity, and someone who has such dreams must be punished. The punishment inflicted on the woman and her husband is memorably out of proportion to their sin, the better to serve as a warning to those reading the story.

A second theme, which may be less obvious to the contemporary reader, is that Mme. Loisel has dreamed of moving to a higher social level. French society was rigidly structured, and Mme. Loisel's ambitions represented a threat, however vague, to the story's privileged audience. They would, of course, want to see her punished for this ambition.

These facts help to explain why the story was so widely read when it was written — but for today's readers other factors seem to be at work. For example, to one young student the necklace became the symbol for everything the world of adults represents. Perhaps it is the story's weaknesses — its implausible simplicities, the lack of definition of its minor characters, the trite obviousness of Mme. Loisel's yearning, and the pious cruelty of her punishment — that make it possible for other generations to give "The Necklace" their own interpretations.

Questions for Discussion

1. Do we use anecdotes like "The Necklace" to point out moral lessons today? What other examples of this kind of moral instruction can you think of in popular literature?
2. How did an evening at a ball offer Mme. Loisel a chance to present herself in a new guise?
3. What do we learn from the story about the structure of French society at the time "The Necklace" was written?
4. What symbols for wealth and station could be used in a story like Maupassant's that was written for today?

Topics for Writing

1. Analyze the symbolic implications of the necklace.
2. Consider the contrast between the lives of Mme. Loisel and her friend Mme. Forestier.

Commentary

Kate Chopin, *"How I Stumbled upon Maupassant,"* p. 592.

Suggested Readings

Fusco, Richard A. "Maupassant and the Turn of the Century American Short Story." *Dissertation Abstracts International* 51.5 (Nov. 1990): 1612A.

James, Henry. *Tales of Art and Life.* Schenectady, NY: Union College P, 1984.

Lohafer, Susan, ed. *Short Story Theory at a Crossroads.* Baton Rouge: Louisiana State UP, 1989. 276–98.

Los Angeles Public Library Staff. *Index to the Stories of Guy de Maupassant.* Boston: G. K. Hall, 1970.

McCrory, Donald. "Maupassant: Problems of Interpretation." *Modern Languages: Journal of the Modern Language Association* 70.1 (Mar. 1989): 39–43.

Poteau-Tralie, Mary L. "Voices of Authority: The Criminal Obsession in Guy de Maupassant's Short Works." *Dissertation Abstracts International* 52.4 (Oct. 1991): 1353A.

Traill, Nancy Helen. "The Fantastic for the Realist: The Paranormal Fictions of Dickens, Turgenev, and Maupassant." *Dissertation Abstracts International* 50.9 (Mar. 1990): 2891A.

Troyat, Henri. *Maupassant.* Paris: Flammarion, 1989.

HERMAN MELVILLE

Bartleby, the Scrivener (p. 352)

Many students have trouble reading this story because they cannot accept what they consider the weirdness of Bartleby's character. On first reading, the story seems to yield this interpretation. Shortly after it appeared in the November and December issues of *Putnam's Monthly Magazine* in 1853, for example, Richard Henry Dana Sr. wrote to Melville's friend Evert Duyckinck saying that he admired the skill involved in creating the character of Bartleby because "the secret power of such an inefficient and harmless creature over his employer, who all the while has a misgiving of it, shows no common insight." Dana's interpretation will probably also be the way 99 percent of college students will respond to the story, sharing his lack of sympathy for Bartleby.

The question is: Did Melville intend the readers of his story to feel this way? Why did he conclude his tale with the lines "Ah, Bartleby! Ah, humanity!"?

Most sympathetic literary critics see this story as Melville's attempt to dramatize the complex question of an individual's obligation to society. Like the dead letters that Bartleby burned in his previous job after they were no longer needed, his life ends when he is no longer useful to his employer. What standards should we use to judge someone's worth? How should we view those who no longer accept the world they are offered?

Questions for Discussion

1. How does the narrator's viewpoint affect your feelings toward Bartleby? What details particularly influence you one way or the other?
2. Do your feelings toward Bartleby change when the narrator reveals Bartleby's previous job in the Dead Letter Office?
3. How does Melville's humorous description of the two other clerks in the law office relieve his heavy presentation of the Wall Street setting? How do these minor characters set off each other, the lawyer, and Bartleby?
4. Do you ever feel like saying "I would prefer not to" in reply to figures of authority? What do you do when you feel a bit of Bartleby in you?

Topics for Writing

1. Explicate the paragraph beginning "For the first time in my life a feeling of overpowering stinging melancholy seized me." A close reading of this passage may bring you closer to realizing the complexity of Melville's portrayal of the lawyer's relationship to Bartleby.
2. Analyze the conclusion of the story. How can Bartleby's life be compared to a dead letter?
3. This story has an unusually prolonged and discursive exposition before the title character is introduced. Also, Melville doesn't motivate his behavior until the end of the story, after he is dead and the lawyer finds out about his previous job. Breaking the customary rules of starting a short story with a brief exposition and

motivating the characters as they are introduced, Melville might be accused of writing a poorly structured tale. Argue for or against this accusation, remembering that the short story genre was in its infancy when Melville wrote "Bartleby, the Scrivener."

4.   Read the excerpt in Chapter 5 from Melville's review of Nathaniel Hawthorne's *Mosses from an Old Manse* (p. 615), discussing what Melville calls "the power of blackness" in Hawthorne's tales. Can you find the same "power of blackness" in Melville's description of Bartleby's situation?

Commentaries

Herman Melville, *"Blackness in Hawthorne's 'Young Goodman Brown,'"* p. 616.
J. Hillis Miller, *"Who Is He? Melville's 'Bartleby, the Scrivener,'"* p. 617.

Suggested Readings

Boswell, Jeanetta. *Herman Melville and the Critics: A Checklist of Criticism.* Metuchen, NJ: Scarecrow, 1981.

Budd, Louis J., and Edwin H. Cady, eds. *On Melville.* Durham, NC: Duke UP, 1988.

Dillingham, W. B. *Melville's Short Fiction, 1853–1856.* Athens: U of Georgia P, 1977.

Fogle, R. H. *Melville's Shorter Tales.* Norman: U of Oklahoma P, 1960.

Freeman, John. *Herman Melville.* Brooklyn, NY: Haskell, 1974.

Higgins, Brian. *Herman Melville: A Reference Guide, 1931–1960.* Boston: G. K. Hall, 1987.

Inge, M. Thomas, ed. *Bartleby the Inscrutable: A Collection of Commentary on Herman Melville's Tale "Bartleby, the Scrivener."* Hamden, CT: Shoe String, 1979.

McCall, Dan. *The Silence of Bartleby.* Ithaca, NY: Cornell UP, 1989.

Melville, Herman. *Correspondence.* Evanston, IL: Northwestern UP, 1991.

———. *"Pierre," The Piazza Tales, and Uncollected Prose.* New York: Library of America, 1984.

Vincent, H. P., ed. *"Bartleby, the Scrivener": Melville Annual for 1965.* Kent, OH: Kent State UP, 1967. Includes Henry Murray's "Bartleby and I," 3–24.

Whitehead, Fred A. "Melville's 'Bartleby, the Scrivener': A Case Study." *New York State Journal of Medicine* 90 (Jan. 1990): 17–22.

LORRIE MOORE

How to Become a Writer (p. 379)

Students reading this humorous story may regard it as a mirror reflecting a "sitcom" version of themselves. It is as familiar as an empty Diet Coke can. The setting of the story is both nonexistent and omnipresent: parents on the verge of divorce, a son in the armed services, a kid sister who's good with little kids. Life swirls around, full of plot action, and what's a crazy girl who wants to become a writer to do? The answer for this affluent family: Advance one painless step — go on to college.

The girl attends college as a child psychology major. Nothing much happens there except a fateful accident: A computer erroneously assigns the girl to a creative writing class instead of "The Ornithological Field Trip" on Tuesdays and Thursdays at 2 P.M. So begins her apprenticeship to her craft, for which she shows more enthusiasm than talent. She apparently never reads short fiction, yet she tries very hard to write it. After graduation, she flirts briefly with the idea of law school before settling for slow starvation at home. Her kind, divorced mother is resigned: "Sure you like to write. Of course. Sure you like to write."

Moore's decision to tell the story in the second person gives her narrative its sense of immediacy. Her sense of humor does the rest, as she carves and serves up her tender victim, a sacrifice to the creative spirit that lives within us all.

Questions for Discussion

1. What is the irony involved in the girl's inability to find good plots for her stories, in the light of her parents' troubled marriage and her brother's military service in Vietnam?
2. Judging from the girl's behavior in her writing classes, does she show any talent? Are creative writing classes in college a good place to find out if one can write?
3. What does Moore gain by organizing her story chronologically?
4. Do you think that the fragments the girl keeps in a folder can be developed into good stories?
5. How does the detail the girl notices about her date at the end of the story suggest that she might have the talent to become a writer after all?

Topic for Writing

1. **RESPONDING CREATIVELY**   Moore's story is a goldmine of possibilities for writing other stories. For example, experiment with the point of view of her narrative — rewrite it in the first or the third person. Or, develop her fragments into short stories of your own, humorous if possible, tragic if not.

Suggested Reading

Moore, Lorrie. *Self-Help.* New York: Knopf, 1985.

ALICE MUNRO

Dance of the Happy Shades (p. 385)

Margaret Atwood's introduction to *Carried Away* (2006), a selection of Alice Munro's stories published by Everyman's Library, can help the reader understand the Canadian community that is the setting for this story. Alice Munro was born in 1931 and grew up in Huron County in southwestern Ontario, known as Sowesto. Though she left the county for part of her life, she moved back there and, as Atwood wrote, "lives at present not far from Wingham, the prototype of the various Jubilees and Walleys and Dalgleishes and Hanrattys in her stories." Her ancestry was partly Scotch Presbyterian and partly Anglican so that, as Atwood notes:

> Munro's acute consciousness of social class, and of the minutiae and sneers separating one level from the next, is honestly come by, as is — from the Presbyterians — her characters' habit of rigorously examining their own deeds, emotions, motives, and consciences, and finding them wanting. In traditional Protestant culture, such as that of small-town Sowesto, forgiveness is not easily come by, punishments are frequent and harsh, potential humiliation and shame lurk around every corner, and nobody gets away with much. (xiv)

Munro's social and cultural background is so distant from that of most American college students that her short fiction usually is of little interest to them. But as Atwood acknowledges, this Canadian short story writer from little-known Sowesto is among the major writers of English fiction of our time. In fact, Munro has even been given the dubious honor of being considered an American writer when John Updike included her work in his recent best-selling anthology of American short stories (she is of course routinely included in the yearly volumes of *The Best American Short Stories*).

So what does Munro do in her short fiction that's so admirable? Atwood nails it in her introduction:

> What should we call the combination of obsessive scrutiny, archeological unearthing, precise and detailed recollection, the wallowing in the seamier and meaner and more vengeful undersides of human nature, the telling of erotic secrets, the nostalgia for vanished miseries, and rejoicing in the fullness and variety of life, stirred all together? (xii)

Most important in its usefulness to our understanding of "Dance of the Happy Shades" is that in Munro's fictional world, as Atwood is aware, "grace descends upon us without any action on our part. In Munro's work, grace abounds, but it is strangely disguised; nothing can be predicted. Emotions erupt. Preconceptions crumble. Surprises proliferate." In short, "Salvation arrives when least expected, and in peculiar forms" (xiv).

Poor Miss Marsalles and her vanished world of summer piano recitals is brought to life for us in Munro's early short story chronicling the tedium of provincial middle-class domesticity, time's merciless erosion, and the unremitting social snobbery inherited by the young narrator — probably still not a teenager, she nevertheless understands that her piano teacher's antique hairdo, make up, and gown "startled no one but the youngest children." All of this is true in its meticulous observation and depiction, and we continue to read the story, unsure of where it is taking us but hardly expecting anything much good to happen. The situation drifts from bad to worse with the entrance of the strange children in their uniforms from the Greenhill School, who are said to be "quite musical but of course they're not all there."

Their uninspired performances of the standard novice's recital pieces goes on in the crowded, stuffy, stifling room in an atmosphere "of some freakish inescapable dream" where no relief is possible. Then the moment of grace occurs. A "thin and plaintive-looking girl" sits down for her turn at the piano and surprises her listeners by being truly musical. Munro describes what her listeners hear in three long, wonderfully complete paragraphs depicting the transcendent experience of sublime art, an experience whose emotional content is as impossible to summarize in a few words as the sound of music itself. Like an accomplished magician, without taking a backward glance at what she has pulled off, Munro ends the story in two final short paragraphs, leaving the reader — if she or he has been paying attention — in shock, alone with the wish to hold on to the glorious epiphany shared with the room of fictional characters.

Questions for Discussion

1.   It's possible that your students didn't much enjoy this story and didn't get the ending. Don't despair. As Munro stated in her penultimate paragraph, after Miss Marsalles tells the listeners the title of the recital piece, she "leaves nobody any the wiser." You might open up the discussion by asking a student to explain what Munro meant by these words.
2.   In what way is the title of the story, "Dance of the Happy Shades," ironic?

3. What do we learn about the character of Miss Marsalles in the opening sentence, when we are told that she gives parties, not recitals?

4. We learn in the second sentence that Munro has chosen to tell her story as first-person narration, through the point of view of a minor character, a young girl who participates in the piano recital. How does Munro convincingly tell us so many details about the background of Miss Marsalles and her sister, if her narrator is so naive?

Topic for Writing

1. RESPONDING CREATIVELY   Write an essay or a story describing your participation in a piano or dance recital, or playing in an orchestra, in which you experienced what Munro called "the freedom of a great unemotional happiness." Examine the paradox implicit in her phrase.

Suggested Reading

Munro, Alice. *Carried Away: A Selection of Stories.* New York: Knopf, 2006.

JOYCE CAROL OATES

The Lady with the Pet Dog (p. 394)
Where Are You Going, Where Have You Been? (p. 406)

THE LADY WITH THE PET DOG

Starting from a central turning point in Anton Chekhov's linear narrative to which her story refers, Oates spirals out, passing the center again, cycling past various incidents more than once, and reaching an account of the beginning of Anna's affair shortly before the end of the story, where, like Chekhov's lovers, Anna finds herself at a new beginning. This method enables Oates to reflect Anna's sense that "Everything is repeating itself. Everything is stuck." At the same time, the recurrent incidents give different impressions each time they are narrated, demonstrating to the reader that forward progress is taking place in Anna's idea of herself, a progress as definite as that of Chekhov's Gurov.

"It was obvious to her that she had, all along, been behaving correctly; out of instinct." With this insight Anna finally achieves the repose within herself that she has previously sought, with inevitably incomplete success, in her husband and her lover alternatively. Oates treats the dissolution of Anna's marriage with the imagery of melting and flowing away. When her lover shows up at the theater, she feels filled with congealed mucus, which she identifies both with panic and with love, and she wants it to drain away. As it does, however, she feels her own identity dissolving. Her husband cannot provide it for her; he leads a life of his own within himself. "There was no boundary to her in this house," she feels, and she experiments with suicide. Her lover, by contrast, offers definition. He draws a picture of her; he makes confining, definite gestures with his hands. But allowing him to take her over brings alienation from herself in the form of shame, the bitter consequence of engaging in behavior of which one disapproves.

"What did it mean to enter into a bond with another person?" Anna ponders. "No person could save another," she recognizes. In their last rendezvous of the story, Anna and her lover cling together in a kind of hermaphroditic union that seems absurd to her.

When he breaks it off and complains that she is using him to take the blame for her misery, Anna once again contemplates suicide. But with her recognition of his separateness,
"that he existed in a dimension quite apart from her, a mysterious being," Anna is saved.
When she sees that she loves him not as a part of herself or as a definition of herself but
as something other than herself — and loves him nonetheless — "she was flooded with
a strange certainty, a sense of gratitude, of pure selfless energy." Thus she has not only
found her way through the psychological mine field that separates the frontiers of her old
life and her new one; she has also redefined herself for herself and learned what it should
mean, and what it should not mean, to enter into a bond with another person.

Questions for Discussion

1. How does Oates convey the impact on Anna of her lover's reappearance? What
    effect does she attain by starting the story with this event?
2. Contrast the way Anna's intercourse with her husband is described at the end of
    section I, near the middle of section II, and again, briefly, somewhat past the
    middle of section III. Why does Oates return twice to this event?
3. Anna and her husband feel "shame between them"; riding to Albany with her
    lover, Anna feels "a declaration of shame between them." Explain the role of
    shame in this story. What is shame, and what becomes of it here?
4. When Anna and her lover try "to figure out their past" because "there was no
    future," the lover says, "this is impossible." Explain.
5. At home, why does Anna feel "there was no boundary to her, no edge"?
6. The telephone conversation in section II, in which Anna finally tells her lover not
    to come over, fades off into a fantasy of a potential future that in turn modulates
    into a narrative of present events. Why does Oates handle Anna's decision to
    resume relations with her lover in this oblique manner?
7. Comment on the image of love as fluttering moth's wings. Why is it appropriate
    at this point in the story? Would it be equally appropriate at the end?
8. Why does Anna want to be free of her lover at the end of section II?
9. What is the effect of reading about the events on Nantucket after some of their
    consequences have already been narrated? How would our response to this section
    differ if we came to it first?
10. Is Anna's lover a reader of Chekhov?
11. What is the impact on Anna of her lover drawing her picture? Of his saying to her,
    "You have defined my soul for me"?
12. When Anna comes back from Albany, her luggage is brought to her husband "on
    a conveyer belt, to be claimed by him." When she goes to her lover in the hotel,
    he says, "I understand. I'm making no claims upon you." Do these passages
    reflect what is actually the case in her relations with the two men?
13. Explain why Anna's feelings for her lover keep pushing her toward suicide.
14. Some passage tracing Anna's consciousness consist of nothing but fluttering self-
    contradictions. How can we be sure her final resolution is not one more of these?

Topics for Writing

1. MAKING CONNECTIONS   Oates has said, of this and the other "reimagin-
    ings of famous stories" in Marriages and Infidelities, that "these stories are meant
    to be autonomous stories, yet they are also testaments of my love and extreme
    devotion to these other writers; I imagine a kind of spiritual 'marriage' between
    myself and them." In what ways is Oates's story married to Chekhov's? In what
    ways is it autonomous? Does that relationship have any connection with Oates's
    theme?

2.   Examine the function of repetition in "The Lady with the Pet Dog."
3.   Discuss Oates's use of the telephone in "The Lady with the Pet Dog" (and per-
     haps also in "Where Are You Going, Where Have You Been?").
4.   **RESPONDING CREATIVELY**   Select a story from the anthology and follow
     Oates's example by reimagining it as an autonomous story of your own.

Connection

Anton Chekhov, *"The Lady with the Pet Dog,"* p. 104.

Conversations on Revisions of Joyce Carol Oates, pp. 655–666

See page 80 of this manual.

Suggested Readings

See page 80 of this manual.

WHERE ARE YOU GOING, WHERE HAVE YOU BEEN?

Pointing to Oates's remark that she usually writes "about real people in a real society" should help to keep discussion away from premature allegorization or mythologiz-
ing, which — for all its eventual value and interest — smothers the story's impact by
diverting attention from its realism. Her further observation that she understands
Connie to be "struggling heroically to define personal identity in the face of incredible
opposition, even in the face of death itself," may suggest how to go about answering the
main question the story poses when considered in naturalistic terms: Why does Connie
go out to Arnold Friend?

Connie's life as Oates depicts it takes place in two realms. Within her home and
family Connie feels condemned and rejected, and she returns the disapproval. Outside
these familiar precincts lies a world defined by movies, the drive-in restaurant, and the
ever-present popular music. It is not the music of Bob Dylan, as Tom Quirk assures us,
but the comparatively mindless, sentimental, and romantic music against which in the
early 1960s Dylan stood out in such bold contrast. Connie's idea of the world into which,
at the age of fifteen, she is beginning to make her first tentative forays is shaped by these
songs and occupied by *boys:* boys who can be snubbed with impunity, boys who merge
into one undifferentiated and safe blur in her mind, boys who offer hamburgers and "the
caresses of love." And that love is "not the way someone like June would suppose but
sweet, gentle, the way it was in movies and promised in songs." To these boys Connie
presents herself as undifferentiated *girl,* and she is concerned that she look attractive to
them.

The world, however, is occupied not only by frank and tentative boys but also by
determined and deceitful men, by evil as well as by innocence, by hypocrisy, perversion,
and violence — an exponent of all of which Connie attracts in Arnold Friend. Although
in the course of their interview Connie sees through his disguise, the impoverishment of
her world provides her no way to resist his advances. Her home offers no refuge, her
father does not come when she needs him (he has always been essentially absent anyway), and she is unable to manipulate the telephone because of her panic. Meanwhile,
Arnold, who presents himself in the guise of a movie hero, a teenage "boy," and her
lover, offers to take charge of her. He places his mark upon her and gives her a role to play
in a world of his devising. Because she is cut off from her past and has no idea of a future,
she is at his mercy in determining what to do in the present. Like her cultural cousin,
Vladimir Nabokov's Lolita, sobbing in Humbert's arms, she simply has nowhere else to

go. Not only does Arnold show Connie that she is desired, he also provides her a way to be "good": By going with him, she will save her undeserving family from getting hurt. Connie does not so much decide to go out to Arnold as she watches an alien being that Arnold has called into existence in her body respond to his desires. The final ironic horror, of course, is that she will be raped and murdered and buried in the desert not as brown-eyed Connie but as the imaginary "sweet little blue-eyed girl" of Arnold's sick imagination.

Oates acknowledges that her inspiration for the story came in part from reading about an actual case, and Tom Quirk has demonstrated at length the degree to which the circumstances of "Where Are You Going, Where Have You Been?" seem to be derived from an article in *Life* (4 Mar. 1966) by Don Moser entitled (in a reference to some lyrics from a popular song) "The Pied Piper of Tucson." Even some of the most apparently allegorical details, such as Arnold's trouble with his boots, which has been attributed to his having cloven hooves or wolf paws, reflect the facts about Charles Schmid, a wiry gymnast of twenty-three who stuffed things in his boots, wore makeup, and drove around Tucson in a gold car playing the hero to a group of high school kids until he was arrested for the rape and murder of three young girls. Quirk's argument that Oates followed the magazine article's theme in relating this horror in the "golden west" to the emptiness of "the American dream" points out an important dimension of the story, and his emphasis keeps the real horror of the incident in focus.

Gretchen Schulz and R. J. R. Rockwood are aware of the *Life* article, but they focus instead on another acknowledged source of Oates's inspiration, the folktale. Their discussion of the story's allusions to and affinities with "The Pied Piper of Hamelin," "Cinderella," "Little Red Riding Hood," and other tales suggests why "Where Are You Going, Where Have You Been?" is such a disturbing work. Their article offers detailed interpretations of the psychological crises Connie passes through, based on psychoanalytic interpretations of the meaning and developmental function of the analogous tales. (They use Bruno Bettelheim as their chief authority.) But whereas folktales most often smooth the passage of their readers through Oedipal conflicts and reintegration of the childhood identity into the adult by working through to a happy ending, "Where Are You Going, Where Have You Been?" taps these powerful psychic forces in the reader only to pour them out on the sand.

WILLIAM E. SHEIDLEY

Questions for Discussion

1. Define Connie's relationships with her mother, sister, and father. What is missing from this family? Why does Connie wish "her mother was dead and she herself was dead and it was all over"?

2. What are Connie's "two sides"? Is Connie's case unusual for a girl her age in our society? In what ways is she atypical? What about June?

3. The girls enter the drive-in with "faces pleased and expectant as if they were entering a sacred building," and the popular music in the background seems "like music at a church service." Explore the drive-in religion further. What are its creeds, its mysteries? Is it a true religion? a guide to the good life? Does Connie believe in anything else?

4. Discuss the similarities between Eddie, who rotates on a counter stool and offers "something to eat," and the emblem of the drive-in on its bottle-top roof. What else does Eddie offer? Compare Eddie with Arnold Friend as we first see him at the drive-in.

5. What does Oates accomplish by returning briefly to Connie's relationship with her family before narrating what happens "one Sunday"?

6. Discuss Connie's daydreams, in which "all the boys fell back and dissolved into a single face that was not even a face, but an idea, a feeling, mixed up with the urgent insistent pounding of the music," and in which she associates sunbathing with the "sweet, gentle" lovemaking "in movies and promised in song." What is the source of the sexual desire reflected in these dreams? What is its object?

7. Asbestos was formerly used as a nonflammable insulating material. Trace the images of heat and fire associated with it in the story.

8. Compare Connie's gentle breathing as she listens to the "XYZ Sunday Jamboree" with her breath "jerking back and forth in her lungs" when she tries to use the telephone at the climax of the story.

9. Why does Connie whisper "Christ. Christ" when she hears a car coming up the driveway? Does the effort to see Arnold Friend as a Christ figure find further substantiation in the text? Does it yield any meaningful insights?

10. Where does Connie stand during the first part of her conversation with Arnold? Is Oates's blocking of the scene realistic? symbolic?

11. Describe Arnold's car and clothing. What purpose is served by his transparent disguise? Why does it take Connie so long to penetrate the disguise?

12. Does Arnold have supernatural knowledge about Connie, her family, and her friends? Can his apparent clairvoyance about the barbecue be explained in naturalistic terms?

13. Account for Connie's idea that Arnold "had driven up the driveway all right but had come from nowhere before that and belonged nowhere and that everything about him and even the music that was so familiar to her was only half real." Explain why that idea is important to our understanding of what happens to Connie.

14. Why does Connie's kitchen seem "like a place she had never seen before"? How has Arnold succeeded in making Connie feel cut off from her past and unprotected in her home? What is the implication of "the echo of a song from last year" in this context?

15. What is the role of Ellie in Arnold's assault on Connie?

16. Arnold implies that Connie can protect her family from harm by coming with him. How important a factor is this in his winning her over to his will?

17. Examine the passage in which Connie tries to telephone her mother and then collapses in panic and hysteria. Notice its associations with sex and birth. What is taking place in Connie at this moment?

18. Arnold asks rhetorically, "What else is there for a girl like you but to be sweet and pretty and give in?" In what sense is this true?

19. Explain Connie's feeling that she is watching herself go out the door. What has caused this split in her consciousness?

Topics for Writing

1. Discuss Arnold Friend's obvious masquerade, and why it succeeds.

2. Comment on popular music and religion in "Where Are You Going, Where Have You Been?"

3. Read the story once while bearing in mind that it is "based on fact" — something very much like this is known to have actually happened. After finishing the story, write a personal essay giving your reaction. What does this account imply about human nature? about the society reflected in the story?

4. Reread the story with an eye to its allusions to folktales and fairy tales with which you are familiar. Arnold's "coach" has a pumpkin on it; Connie is nearly asleep

when he awakens her; he has big teeth; and so forth. What are the tales alluded to about? Is this story a fairy tale, too?

5.   **RESPONDING CREATIVELY**   Select an item from the news that grips your imagination and ask yourself why it does. Does it have affinities with folktales or myths? Does it suggest disturbing ideas about human nature and society? Write a narrative of the event, perhaps from the point of view of one of the participants, that incorporates these larger implications.

6.   **MAKING CONNECTIONS**   Compare technique and theme in Oates's "Where Are You Going, Where Have You Been?" and Shirley Jackson's "The Lottery" (p. 235).

7.   **MAKING CONNECTIONS**   Compare and contrast Arnold Friend and The Misfit in Flannery O'Connor's "A Good Man Is Hard to Find" (p. 447).

8.   **MAKING CONNECTIONS**   Study the allusions to religion in Oates's story. How would O'Connor have handled this material?

Conversations on Revisions of Joyce Carol Oates, pp. 655–664

Joyce Carol Oates, " 'Smooth Talk': Short Story into Film," p. 656.
Don Moser, "The Pied Piper of Tucson," p. 660.
Matthew C. Brennan, "Plotting against Chekhov: Joyce Carol Oates and 'The Lady with the Dog,' " p. 664.

Suggested Readings

Bloom, Harold. *Joyce Carol Oates.* New York: Chelsea House, 1981.
Friedman, Ellen G. "Joyce Carol Oates." In *Modern American Women Writers.* Ed. Elaine Showalter. New York: Macmillan, 1991.
Gardner, John. *On Writers and Writing.* Reading, MA: Addison-Wesley, 1994. 75.
Gillis, Christina Marsden. " 'Where Are You Going, Where Have You Been?': Seduction, Space, and a Fictional Mode." *Studies in Short Fiction* 18 (1981): 65–70.
Johnson, Greg. *Understanding Joyce Carol Oates.* Columbia: U of South Carolina P, 1987.
Milazzo, Lee. *Conversations with Joyce Carol Oates.* Jackson: UP of Mississippi, 1989.
Oates, Joyce Carol. *New Heaven, New Earth.* New York: Vanguard, 1974.
———. *(Woman) Writer: Occasions and Opportunities.* New York: NAL-Dutton, 1989.
Pearlman, Mickey, ed. *American Women Writing Fiction: Memory, Identity, Family, Space.* Lexington: U of Kentucky P, 1989. 9–44.
Plimpton, George. *Women Writers at Work: The Paris Review Interviews.* New York: Penguin, 1989.
Quirk, Tom. "A Source for 'Where Are You Going, Where Have You Been?' " *Studies in Short Fiction* 18 (1981): 413–19.
Rozga, Margaret. "Threatening Places, Hiding Places: The Midwest in Selected Stories by Joyce Carol Oates." *Midwestern Miscellany* 18 (1990): 34–44.
Schulz, Gretchen, and R. J. R. Rockwood. "In Fairyland, without a Map: Connie's Exploration Inward in Joyce Carol Oates's 'Where Are You Going, Where Have You Been?' " *Literature and Psychology* 30 (1980): 155–67.
Urbanski, Marie Mitchell Olesen. "Existential Allegory: Joyce Carol Oates's 'Where Are You Going, Where Have You Been?' " *Studies in Short Fiction* 15 (1978): 200–03.
Wegs, Joyce M. " 'Don't You Know Who I Am?': The Grotesque in Oates's 'Where Are You Going, Where Have You Been?' " *Journal of Narrative Technique* 5 (1975): 66–72.

Wesley, Marilyn Clarke. "Transgression and Refusal: The Dynamic of Power in the Domestic Fiction of Joyce Carol Oates." *Dissertation Abstracts International* 49.11 (May 1989): 3365A.

Winslow, Joan D. "The Stranger Within: Two Stories by Oates and Hawthorne." *Studies in Short Fiction* 17 (1980): 263–68.

TIM O'BRIEN

The Things They Carried (p. 419)

In "The Things They Carried," O'Brien has found a brilliant solution to one of the most common problems a writer faces: how to find a new way to approach a subject that has been written about many times before. His subject is men at war, a topic that has occupied writers since remotest antiquity. The earliest epic in the European tradition is Homer's account of the siege of Troy, and the earliest griot narratives from the empires of Africa recount battles fought along the banks of the Niger River.

The Vietnam War has been treated in a stream of stories, books, articles, studies, and debates. O'Brien's innovation is to tell us directly not about the soldiers, or about the meaningless war they find themselves in, but about the things they are carrying on their shoulders and in their pockets — the author also tells us about the things they carry under different circumstances. This simple device is startling and effective. The things his "grunts" are carrying are one way to identify them, to bring them to life.

This use of the small detail to illuminate the whole picture would not be as effective if it were limited to a simple description of what each of the men is carrying. But as he discusses the items — their use, their importance to the men's assignment, and the significance of each thing to each man — O'Brien tells us about the war itself and the soldiers' attitudes toward what they are doing. By presenting each of these objects as a microcosm of the war, the author makes the experience more comprehensible. He has found a dimension that shows us the soldiers as human beings, and that is the most important task for a writer who wants to make us face this cruel reality again.

Questions for Discussion

1. What is the effect of O'Brien's use of abbreviations and acronyms: R&R, SOP, M&Ms, USO, Psy Ops, KIA?
2. When the author writes, "Afterward they burned Than Khe," what is he telling us about the attitude of the men toward the people in the villages around them?
3. Why is it important to specify the weight of the equipment each man is carrying?
4. Does the language of the soldiers sound "real"? the descriptions of the weapons?
5. Why does the lieutenant burn the letters he has been carrying?

Topics for Writing

1. Soldiers from both sides are fighting the war, but the author tells us only about the men from one side. Why doesn't he describe the North Vietnamese soldiers?
2. Discuss the attitudes toward the war in the United States as they are reflected in the attitudes of the soldiers in "The Things They Carried."
3. Stories about men at war usually emphasize heroism and heroic acts; these are completely absent in this story. What has caused this change in attitude?

Commentary

Bobbie Ann Mason, *"On Tim O'Brien's 'The Things They Carried,'"* p. 612.

Suggested Readings

Bonn, Maria S. "A Different World: The Vietnam Veteran Novel Comes Home." In *Fourteen Landing Zones: Approaches to Vietnam War Literature.* Ed. Philip K. Jason. Iowa City: U of Iowa P, 1992.

Calloway, Catherine. "Pluralities of Vision: *Going After Cacciato* and Tim O'Brien's Short Fiction." In *America Rediscovered: Critical Essays on Literature and Film of the Vietnam War.* Ed. Owen W. Gilman Jr. New York: Garland, 1990.

———. "Tim O'Brien (1946–): A Primary and Secondary Bibliography." *Bulletin of Bibliography* 50.3 (Sept. 1993): 223–29.

FLANNERY O'CONNOR

Good Country People (p. 433)
A Good Man Is Hard to Find (p. 447)

GOOD COUNTRY PEOPLE

In the world of O'Connor's fiction, characters are seldom who we think they are or even who they think they are. "Good Country People" provides an intriguing twist on the archetypal theme: Events and people are seldom as simple as they seem.

O'Connor revels in the idiosyncrasies of personality, peopling this story with three strong characters in Joy (Hulga), Mrs. Hopewell, and Manley Pointer, as well as an interesting subsidiary character, Mrs. Freeman, with her "special fondness for the details of secret infections, hidden deformities," and "assaults upon children." O'Connor's choice of names figures prominently. Joy changes her name to Hulga to symbolize her sense of her own ugliness. Mrs. Hopewell continually hopes well of things, blathering a stream of banal platitudes that reveal her own lack of depth. The name Manley Pointer strikes the reader as humorously phallic and predatory-sounding given the surprising turn of events in the storage barn.

We don't see how "right" the details of this story are until we reach its sardonic conclusion, with Pointer going Hulga's intellectual atheism one better, disappearing with her leg in his "Bible" valise, and Mrs. Hopewell in her ignorance commenting on "that nice dull young man." Looking back, we see the clever meticulousness of Pointer's con — the feigned heaviness of his satchel, his feigned simplicity (as in mistaking the name of the house for its owner), the rube suit. It turns out that this specimen of "good country people" reads people better than the highly educated Hulga or the self-aggrandizing Mrs. Hopewell.

The experience of losing her artificial limb to the perverted Manley Pointer is the loss of a certain kind of virginity for Hulga, and however harrowing the experience, we sense that it will be a valuable one. Prior to her victimization, we feel mainly revulsion for Joy/Hulga. We sympathize with her hunting accident, but O'Connor highlights the unpleasant abrasiveness of her personality; clearly Hulga's psyche, as well as her body, has been damaged. Hulga's low self-esteem is exacerbated by her mother's implications of Hulga's abnormality, which focus on her intellectualism as much as on her disfigurement. For all Mrs. Hopewell's assertions that "it takes all kinds to make the world go 'round," she resents her daughter's interest in philosophy (female education is for a "good time") as well as Hulga's individuation: "It seemed to Mrs. Hopewell that every year she grew less like other people and more like herself."

In this multifaceted story of moral blindness, Hulga experiences a physical intimacy with Pointer that forces her into a new mode of reacting and out of her customary detached intellectualism: "Without the leg she felt entirely dependent on him. Her brain seemed to have stopped thinking altogether and to be about some other function that it was not very good at." However dastardly Pointer's actions, he forces Hulga to feel and acknowledge her emotions for the first time. We go away from the story feeling that Hulga will be a changed (and humbled) person — a person less presumptuous and closer to psychic wholeness.

Questions for Discussion

1. What does Mrs. Hopewell mean by "good country people"?
2. Why does Joy change her name to Hulga?
3. In what ways do you expect Joy/Hulga will change after her experience in the barn with Manley Pointer?
4. Discuss O'Connor's choice of names for the characters in this story.
5. Is Manley Pointer a believable character? Have you encountered people who are entirely other than they seem? What is Pointer really interested in? Why does he carry off Hulga's leg?
6. Discuss the dramatic function of Mrs. Freeman and her two daughters.
7. Discuss the effects on characterization of O'Connor's choosing to give Joy a Ph.D. in philosophy and an artificial leg. How do these details predispose our expectations?

Topic for Writing

1. Discuss the function of Christianity in "Good Country People."

Conversations on Flannery O'Connor's Fiction, pp. 666–678

See page 86 of this manual.

Suggested Readings

See page 86 of this manual.

A GOOD MAN IS HARD TO FIND

O'Connor's comments (included in Chapter 6, p. 674) direct attention to the climax of her story and suggest how she intended the central characters to be viewed and what she meant the story to imply. Students may benefit, however, from struggling at first to interpret the text unassisted by authorial explanation. The effort should reveal dimensions of O'Connor's art that might otherwise be overlooked.

The grandmother's reawakening to reality, which leads to her gesture of grace as she reaches out to The Misfit as one of her own children, may be triggered by the violence of the murders going on just offstage and the extremity of her own case, but her conversion has been carefully prepared for. Throughout the story this old woman longs in various ways to go back *home* — to Tennessee, to the days of her youth, to the mansion with the imaginary secret panel, which is as much in heaven as it is down a hilly back road in Georgia. Death is seldom far from her thoughts, though for a long time she does not apprehend its reality. Her initial worries about The Misfit are disingenuous, but encountering him or returning to east Tennessee come to the same thing in the end. On the road, the grandmother dresses up in nice clothes so that "anyone seeing her dead on the highway would know at once that she was a lady," observes a graveyard, and remembers her mansion at a town named Toombsboro. The Misfit and his men approach in a "hearse-like automobile"; the family awaits them in front of the woods that "gaped like a dark open mouth." The grandmother is at odds with present times. She squabbles with the children (whose behavior even the reader may find unusually improper); easily upstages the cabbage-headed, slacks-wearing woman who is their mother; joins Red Sammy in deploring the state of world affairs; and disastrously deludes Bailey by smuggling the cat into the car. But she loves the world as well, in a selfish, childish way. She *will* have the cat along; she admires the scenery (including a picturesque "pickaninny" for whose poverty she is not yet ready to feel compassion); she wishes she had married Mr. *E. A.* Teagarden, who courted her with watermelon and would have supplied all her worldly needs from the proceeds of his Coca-Cola stock; and she even makes a play for Red Sammy, the only tycoon in sight.

These desires may be misdirected, but just as it takes very little to upset the valise, release the cat, flip the car off the road, and carry the story into an entirely new set of circumstances, so, under the intensifying presence of death, it takes only a moment for the grandmother's selfish love for and alienation from the world to flip over into the selfless love that leads her to open her heart to The Misfit. After all, she at least rationalizes bringing the cat to protect it; she supportively asserts that Red Sammy is "a good man" in the face of his own cynicism and despair; and she offers the same praise to The Misfit from the moment she recognizes him. Without a doubt the grandmother's motive in insisting that The Misfit is "a good man" and in urging him to pray is to divert him from his evident intention and so to save her skin. But as the bullets ring out in the background and the grandmother's maternal instincts burst forth in her repeated cries of "Bailey Boy!" she begins to act charitably in spite of herself. She offers The Misfit one of Bailey's shirts, listens to his confession (although she is the one who is about to die), and when he is wearing Bailey's shirt, she reaches out to him in his anguish. A good man is hard to find; Jesus may have been the only one who was intrinsically good. But when she loves and pities the radically fallen Misfit, the grandmother becomes for the moment a "good woman" through her Christ-like action, as The Misfit himself acerbically recognizes.

As O'Connor mentions in her commentary, The Misfit has evoked widely differing responses from readers and critics, who have associated him with the devil, the modern agnostic existentialist, or "the prophet he was meant to become," in O'Connor's own phrase. Perhaps The Misfit's daddy provides the best way of distinguishing him from the rest of the characters with his remark, "It's some that can live their whole life out without asking about it and it's others has to know why it is, and this boy is one of the latters." Unlike O'Connor, whose vision of the world was grounded in *belief,* The Misfit wants to *know.* With Faustian presumption, he seeks to comprehend the divine mysteries in terms of his own intellect and demands a kind of justice in life that he can understand. When he cannot find the answers to his questions, but only the implication of inexplicable guilt (like Original Sin) in the punishment he receives, The Misfit sees the world not as the charming place it has appeared to the grandmother but as a prison whose empty sky resembles the blank walls of his cell in the penitentiary. In his own calculus of guilt, The Misfit feels he has been excessively punished, and he seems to be going about the world committing crimes in order to right the balance. His most perverse principle, "No pleasure but meanness," is sustained surprisingly well by the world O'Connor portrays. (Is *this* the reason for the story's lack of anything or anyone to admire and its unremittingly ironic tone?) But it gives way after he has been touched by the grandmother to his first true prophecy: "It's no real pleasure in life" — no *real* pleasure in *this* life, though true goodness sometimes appears in those made conscious of death.

WILLIAM E. SHEIDLEY

Questions for Discussion

1. What is the grandmother's reason for bringing up The Misfit at the beginning of the story?
2. Describe "the children's mother." Why does O'Connor make her such a nonentity?
3. What about John Wesley and June Star? What would have been the result had O'Connor characterized them as something other than totally obnoxious?
4. Discuss the grandmother's reasons for her fatal decision to bring Pitty Sing on the trip.
5. Why does the grandmother dress so nicely for the trip?
6. Compare the grandmother's response to the scenery and the trip with that of the children. What does O'Connor accomplish by means of this distinction?
7. Just before the stop at The Tower, the grandmother reminisces about her old suitor, Edgar Atkins Teagarden. Specify the connections between the two episodes.
8. What tower might O'Connor have had in mind in choosing the name for Red Sammy's establishment? Why is there a monkey in a chinaberry tree feasting on fleas posted outside The Tower? What do we learn about the world at Red Sammy's?
9. Contrast The Tower with the mansion the grandmother awakens to remember "outside of Toombsboro."
10. What factors cause the accident? Consider its meaning as a consequence of the grandmother's choices and desires.
11. Describe the manner in which The Misfit arrives on the scene. What effect does his appearance have on the reader?
12. The grandmother's response to The Misfit's remark that "it would have been better for all of you, lady, if you hadn't of reckernized me" is "You wouldn't shoot a lady, would you?" Evaluate her question.
13. To what extent is the grandmother correct in her praise of The Misfit? In what ways is he a gentleman?
14. Describe the grandmother's reaction to Bailey's departure. Is her response consistent with her previous behavior?
15. Define The Misfit's experience of the world. To what extent can his criminality be blamed on the conditions of his life? Does The Misfit feel any more free outside the penitentiary than in it?
16. How can the logic of The Misfit's position that "the crime don't matter . . . because sooner or later you're going to forget what it was you done and just be punished for it" be attacked? To what extent does The Misfit's description of himself apply to everyone? Bear in mind that the whole family is being punished with death for no ascertainable crime.
17. Explain how, to The Misfit, "Jesus thown everything off balance."
18. What is the effect of O'Connor's comparing the grandmother to "a parched old turkey hen crying for water"?
19. Does The Misfit do or say anything to deserve the grandmother's gesture of concern?
20. Explain The Misfit's final evaluation of the grandmother: "She would of been a good woman . . . if it had been somebody there to shoot her every minute of her life."

21. Contrast The Misfit's "No pleasure but meanness" with his last words in the story.

Topics for Writing

1. What is the function of tone in O'Connor's story?
2. Describe techniques of characterization in "A Good Man Is Hard to Find."
3. **RESPONDING CREATIVELY** Write a parable or short tale designed to illustrate a religious or philosophical truth. Following O'Connor's example, portray your characters ruthlessly as embodiments of what you want them to represent.
4. **MAKING CONNECTIONS** Comment on the relationship between the grandmother and The Misfit in "A Good Man Is Hard to Find" and the relationship between Connie and Arnold Friend in Joyce Carol Oates's "Where Are You Going, Where Have You Been?" (p. 406).

Conversations on Flannery O'Connor's Fiction, pp. 666–678

Flannery O'Connor, *"The Element of Suspense in 'A Good Man Is Hard to Find,'"* p. 674.
Flannery O'Connor, *"From 'Letters, 1954–55,'"* p. 667.
Flannery O'Connor, *"Writing Short Stories,"* p. 669.
Sally Fitzgerald, *"Southern Sources of 'A Good Man Is Hard to Find,'"* p. 677.

Suggested Readings

Asals, Frederick. *Flannery O'Connor: The Imagination of Extremity.* Athens: U of Georgia P, 1982. 142–54.
Brinkmeyer, Robert H., Jr. *The Art and Vision of Flannery O'Connor.* Baton Rouge: Louisiana State UP, 1989.
Browning, Preston M., Jr. *Flannery O'Connor.* Crosscurrents/Modern Critiques. Carbondale: Southern Illinois UP, 1974. 54–59.
Burke, John J. "Convergence of Flannery O'Connor and Chardin." *Renascence* 19 (1966): 41–47, 52.
Church, Joseph. "An Abuse of the Imagination in Flannery O'Connor's 'A Good Man Is Hard to Find.'" *Notes on Contemporary Literature* 20.3 (May 1990): 8–10.
Clark, Beverly Lyon, and Melville J. Friedman, eds. *Critical Essays on Flannery O'Connor.* Boston: G. K. Hall, 1985.
Feeley, Sister Kathleen. *Flannery O'Connor: Voice of the Peacock.* New Brunswick, NJ: Rutgers UP, 1972.
Gatta, John. "The Scarlet Letter as Pre-Text for Flannery O'Connor's 'Good Country People.'" *Nathaniel Hawthorne Review* 16.2 (Fall 1990): 6–9.
Giannone, Richard. *Flannery O'Connor.* Boston: Twayne, 1988.
Grimshaw, James A. *The Flannery O'Connor Companion.* Westport, CT: Greenwood, 1981.
Hendin, Josephine. *The World of Flannery O'Connor.* Ann Arbor, MI: Books Demand UMI, 1986.
Nisly, P. W. "Prison of the Self: Isolation in Flannery O'Connor's Fiction." *Studies in Short Fiction* 17 (1980): 49–54.
Ochshorn, Kathleen G. "A Cloak of Grace: Contradictions in 'A Good Man Is Hard to Find.'" *Studies in American Fiction* 18.1 (Spring 1990): 113–17.
O'Connor, Flannery. *The Habit of Being.* Letters edited and with an introduction by Sally Fitzgerald. New York: Farrar, 1979.
———. *Mystery and Manners.* New York: Farrar, 1969.

Orvell, Miles. *Invisible Parade: The Fiction of Flannery O'Connor.* Philadelphia: Temple UP, 1972.

Paulson, Suzanne. *Flannery O'Connor: A Study of the Short Fiction.* Boston: Twayne, 1988.

Pyron, V. " 'Strange Country': The Landscape of Flannery O'Connor's Short Stories." *Mississippi Quarterly* 36 (1983): 557–68.

TILLIE OLSEN

I Stand Here Ironing (p. 460)

One way to begin discussing this story is to look at the ending. "I will never total it all," the narrator affirms and then pronounces the summary whose inadequacy she has already proclaimed. The summarizing passage clarifies and organizes the impressions the reader may have gleaned from the preceding monologue. It is so clear that if it stood alone or came first in the story the validity of its interpretation of Emily could hardly be doubted. But since it follows her mother's "tormented" meditations, the summary seems incomplete in its clinical precision and must give way to a final paragraph of comparatively obscure and paradoxical requests focused in the startling but brilliantly adept image of the "dress on the ironing board, helpless before the iron," which links the story's end to its beginning and directs attention to the true central character.

What is mainly missing from the summary is the love and understanding that Emily's mother feels for her daughter as a result of living through the experiences bracketed by the orderly generalizations. Just as much as Emily, her mother has been the victim "of depression, of war, of fear." By virtue of having had to cope with those circumstances, she can respect Emily's response to them. Doing so enables her to counter the suggestion that "she's a youngster who needs help" with "Let her be." A good deal of the help Emily and her mother have received so far has put them in separate prisons — as when Emily was incarcerated at the convalescent home — and cut them off from love. To let Emily alone is at least to allow her some freedom to grow at her own slow pace.

Her mother is tempted to blame herself for the deficiencies in Emily's childhood, since she learned things about being a mother with her second family that she did not know with Emily. But her consideration of a characteristic incident early in the narrative suggests a crucial qualifying factor: When she placed Emily in nursery school at the age of two, she did not know what she was subjecting her daughter to, "except that it would have made no difference if I had known. . . . It was the only way we could be together, the only way I could hold a job." As much a victim of rigid and unfavorable economic and historic circumstances as her daughter, Emily's mother can speak her concluding line with feeling. In pleading that Emily somehow be made to know "that she is more than this dress on the ironing board, helpless before the iron," Emily's mother asks that her daughter be spared a condition to which she herself has been subjected. But Emily's mother, unlike Whistler's, does not sit for her portrait passively in a rocking chair; she stands there wielding the iron, controlling the very symbol of the circumstances that have not yet flattened her, painting her own self-portrait, and calling for help not in adjusting Emily to the world but in making the world a place in which Emily can thrive.

WILLIAM E. SHEIDLEY

Questions for Discussion

1. Who is "you" in the first sentence? What is the mother's first response to the request to unlock the mystery of Emily? Does her position change?
2. Does Emily's mother feel guilty about how she has cared for Emily? Why? What factors have affected her dealings with her daughter?
3. Why is the passage in which Emily throws the clock so effective?
4. Discuss the "help" Emily gets at the convalescent home. How does it compare with the help her mother calls for at the end?
5. Emily has suffered from the absence of her father, the exhaustion of her mother, poverty, asthma and other diseases, sibling rivalry, and unpopularity, among other complaints. What is the effect of these hardships on the young woman she has become? What is the effect of her discovery of a talent?
6. What has her mother learned from Emily?
7. Does Emily's mother love her daughter? How can we tell?

Topics for Writing

1. Compare and contrast Emily's talent and her mother's.
2. Discuss the function of the interruptions in "I Stand Here Ironing."
3. Consider "I will never total it all" — the importance of indeterminacy in Olsen's analysis of Emily.
4. Analyze the politics of "I Stand Here Ironing."
5. **RESPONDING CREATIVELY**   Write a summary statement in general terms about the personality of a sibling, relative, or friend you have known closely for a long time. Put it aside and cast your memory back to three or four specific incidents involving your subject. Narrate them briefly but in specific terms. Read over your sketches and compare the personality of your subject as it emerges with what you wrote in your generalized summary. Do you still think your summary is accurate? What are its limitations?

Suggested Readings

Frye, Joanne S. "'I Stand Here Ironing': Motherhood as Experience and Metaphor." *Studies in Short Fiction* 18 (1981): 287–92.
O'Connor, William Van. "The Short Stories of Tillie Olsen." *Studies in Short Fiction* 1 (1963): 21–25, esp. 21–22.

EDGAR ALLAN POE

The Cask of Amontillado (p. 467)
The Fall of the House of Usher (p. 472)

THE CASK OF AMONTILLADO

Poe is the great master of the contrived suspense story, and "The Cask of Amontillado" is a model of narrative compression toward a single effect. Students should understand that Poe had a theory on the short story; its essential points are suggested in his commentary in Chapter 6 (p. 680).

Despite Poe's rational explanation of how a writer should compose a story, his own fiction is directed toward eliciting irrational emotions. Poe's literary style aims at using as many extravagances of character, setting, and plot as he could invent, exploiting the reader's emotional vulnerability to disturbing images of darkness and chaos. The hectic unpredictability of the carnival season, the creepy subterranean wine cellar, and the ancient family crypt with its moldering skeletons all challenge us emotionally and make us want to read further.

In the reading, our own fears become the true subject matter. As in a nightmare, Fortunato finds himself being buried alive, one of the most basic human fears. On a more conscious level, we rely on a social contract to bind us together as a human family, and Montresor's lawlessness plays on our fear that any person can take the law into his or her own hands without being checked by conscience. Poe doesn't have to give us a great number of details about his characters; our imagination draws from the depths of the common human psyche to supply all that we need.

This story is a good example to use in stressing the importance of the students' close reading of a text. It's easy for readers to miss, in the last paragraph, the sentence "My heart grew sick — on account of the dampness of the catacombs." Yet upon this sentence rests the interpretation of Montresor's character: Can we excuse his action on grounds of insanity? Was he insane at the time he buried Fortunato alive, or did he go insane in the half century during which, he tells us, his crime has remained undetected? If the reader has not paid careful attention to that sentence, he or she will have missed an essential detail in understanding the story.

The book *Mysterious New England,* edited by A. N. Stevens (1971), suggests that Poe first heard the anecdote on which he might have based this story when he was a private in the army in 1827. Supposedly, only ten years before, a popular young lieutenant named Robert F. Massie had also been stationed at Fort Independence in Boston Harbor; when Poe was serving there, he saw a gravestone erected to the memory of Lieutenant Massie, who had been unfairly killed in a duel by a bully named Captain Green. As Stevens tells it,

> Feeling against Captain Green ran high for many weeks, and then suddenly he vanished. Years went by without a sign of him, and Green was written off the army records as a deserter.

> According to the story that Poe finally gathered together, Captain Green had been so detested by his fellow officers that they decided to take a terrible revenge on him for Massie's death.

> Visiting Captain Green one moonless night, they pretended to be friendly and plied him with wine until he was helplessly intoxicated. Then, carrying the captain down to one of the ancient dungeons, the officers forced his body through a tiny opening that led into the subterranean casemate. His captors began to shackle him to the floor, using the heavy iron handcuffs and footcuffs fastened into the stone. Then they sealed the captain up alive inside the windowless casemate, using bricks and mortar that they had hidden close at hand.

> Captain Green shrieked in terror and begged for mercy, but his cries fell on deaf ears. The last brick was finally inserted, mortar applied, and the room closed off, the officers believed, forever. Captain Green undoubtedly died a horrible death within a few days.

WILLIAM E. SHEIDLEY

Questions for Discussion

1. How does Poe motivate the behavior of Montresor? Does the story provide any hints as to the "thousand injuries" he has suffered? Are any hints necessary?
2. Why is the setting of the story appropriate?
3. What does Montresor's treatment of his house servants tell us about his knowledge of human psychology, and how does it prepare us for his treatment of Fortunato?
4. How does Poe increase the elements of suspense as Fortunato is gradually walled into the catacombs?

Topics for Writing

1. Montresor doesn't tell his story until a half century after the actual event. Analyze how Poe adapts the flashback technique to affect the reader of "The Cask of Amontillado."
2. Explicate the passage in the story in which Montresor entices Fortunato into the crypt.

Conversations on Critical Views of Edgar Allan Poe's Short Stories, pp. 678–695

See page 93 of this manual.

Suggested Readings

See page 93 of this manual.

THE FALL OF THE HOUSE OF USHER

Although Poe was not the first writer to work within the genre of the psychological narrative, he was so dominant in this area that his name continues to be associated with this narrative form. Through Poe, and his influence on French and then other European writers, this type of narrative assumed a steadily larger role in the development of the modern story.

In Poe's time, writing such as that represented in "The Fall of the House of Usher" was designated as gothic, which for many of its readers reflected simply the gloom and the cluster of symbols in gothic architecture. Poe's own readers would have recognized his settings and the devices he used to set his tales in motion. What differentiates him from the forgotten authors of the gothic tales and romances that filled the journals of the period is a quality of obsessiveness in the writing. With Poe there is never the sense that he is using a descriptive phrase for its literary effect. The struggle within him always seems to be the need to find the phrase or the situation that would project the psychological truth of his scene. Poe, unlike other authors, was relentless in his descriptions and his characterizations, and in all of his successful tales the final scenes fulfill the forebodings of the opening sentences. This story is one of his most celebrated psychological studies, and there could be no more powerful description of a dismal landscape than his opening sentence: "During the whole of a dull, dark, and soundless day in the autumn of the year, when the clouds hung oppressively low in the heavens, I had been passing alone, on horseback, through a singularly dreary tract of country, and at length found myself, as the shades of the evening drew on, within view of the melancholy House of Usher."

The sentence is weighted with words symbolic of despair: *dull, dark, soundless, oppressively low, alone, dreary, shades of evening, melancholy.* The term often used to describe these kinds of scenes in Poe's writing is *hallucinatory*. Also, he has emphasized the symbolic premonitions of the scene by what he has omitted. A characteristic opening for a gothic tale would have included a suggestion of a date and a place. A typical opening might be, "During the whole of a dark and soundless day in autumn of 182—, when the clouds hung oppressively low in the heavens over the dark lands of Saxony . . ." With the device of these specific places and dates, the scene could be imagined within a familiar context. Poe, however, brings us only to a darkening, wild scene that is at once so minutely described that we can visualize every tree and cloud, and at the same time the place and time are left so vague, and the description is so exaggerated, so wildly overblown, that it is like no scene we have imagined before. He ultimately achieves a total effect of oppression and despair by the relentless repetition of images and phrases that remind the reader again and again of the barren lifelessness of the scene that greeted him at the opening of the tale.

During Poe's short and difficult lifetime, his work was extravagantly praised and as vehemently criticized, and some of the negative attitudes toward his writing focused on his unexpected imagery and unusual verbal linkages. He wrote so much, under such intense economic pressure — often writing under the influence of alcohol and laudanum, the mixture of opium and alcohol used by most of the period's cultural figures such as Coleridge and DeQuincy — that he was open to charges of carelessness and indifference to the niceties of grammar and vocabulary. Almost invariably, though, what could be considered a grammatically garbled phrase or sentence emerges as crucial to the effect he sustains so brilliantly throughout his tale. In this story he describes the furniture in the rooms with the sentence, "The general furniture was profuse, comfortless, antique, and tattered." As an example of parallelism the sentence is a catastrophe. None of the four adjectives could be said to relate to each other in any obvious interpretation. "Profuse" doesn't even seem to be an adjective that would apply to furniture — and yet we have immediately an image of a scattering of furniture, whatever it is. "Comfortless" is at a considerable distance from "profuse," but somehow it forces us to modify what we have imagined of the roomful of furniture. "Antique" presents fewer problems, and "tattered" completes our associations with the vision we now have of a great deal of uncomfortable, worn, old furniture scattered around a room. On this level of association, with his nudge to the reader to do some of his work for him, Poe's sentence becomes much more reasonable. What finally gives the sentence its power in the context is its insistent allusion to the psychological context of the narrative. Of the four adjectives, two of them, "comfortless" and "tattered," again project the despair and oppression of the story's opening. Poe will not slacken the hand that is gripping his reader's neck.

In our own day readers have found that the psychological penetration of Poe's narratives has become part of the emotional landscape. Of particular interest in this story is his careful description of Usher's small painting. It is a painting that at the time of his writing existed only in Poe's fantasy, but as a modern surrealistic canvas it would not be out of place in any contemporary art museum. For students there will also be a particular interest in the music that he describes Usher performing. The recordings made in the 1960s and 1970s by visionary guitarist-singers — artists such as Berkeley's Robbie Basho — sound like a fulfillment of Poe's description, although Basho was not conscious of any direct connection. Of less immediate importance will be the books that Usher and his friend read together in their last wild days in the house. The books themselves suggest the similar context today of films and videos that come under the loose heading of psychological studies, or more simply, horror films.

What the reader finally perceives, as the tale comes to its frightening conclusion, is that it has no substance as a realistic portrayal. It is "real" only in that it is a realistic projection of the author's dark fantasy. We follow the details and the narrative as though they were real — in the way that we consider all fictive writing to be real — but at the same time we understand that the house that has been destroyed was a house that never existed. As a symbol of our fears, however, the house will continue to stand in its "black and lurid tarn." In our imagination we will also continue to be disturbed at some level of emotion we barely understand by "the remodelled and inverted images of the gray sedge, and the ghastly tree-stems, and the vacant and eye-like windows" of the doomed House of Usher.

Questions for Discussion

1. The reader is not given a specific place or time in the story's setting. Is this a help or a hindrance to students' response to the story?

2. Poe mentions opium twice in the story. Does this reflect the general acceptance of the use of the drug in his time? Does opium seem to influence the narrative in any way?

3. Poe describes the recovery from opium intoxication as "the bitter lapse into every-day life." How would readers of his time interpret this? How would a modern reader respond?

4. Does Poe intimate that the Usher family suffers from an inbred genetic condition? How does this affect the narrative?

5. Poe writes, "There can be no doubt that the consciousness of the rapid increase of my superstition . . . served mainly to accelerate the increase itself." In psychological terms, what is he telling the reader?

6. What is the atmosphere that hangs over the house? Is this a phenomenon found in nature?

7. What is Poe suggesting in saying of the doctor that "his countenance . . . wore a mingled expression of low cunning and perplexity"? What is the meaning of the doctor's interest in the dead sister's body?

8. The account of Usher's emotional state would suggest that he suffers from what is known today as bipolar disorder or manic depression. How would students interpret this analysis?

9. Does the description of Madeline's illness, "transient affections of a partially cataleptical character," have any modern clinical counterpart?

10. How would we characterize the paintings of Roderick Usher today?

11. How would we characterize the music that Usher creates? Have we a modern term for this genre?

12. Poe writes of Usher, "I perceived . . . on the part of Usher of the tottering of his lofty reason upon her throne." What is Poe suggesting to the reader?

13. What is the meaning of Usher's contention that the stones of the house have become sentient?

14. What suggests to us that the house is to be taken as a symbol? Will it be destroyed by the death of the brother and sister?

Topics for Writing

1. In his writing Poe uses many little-known words, such as *sentience, trepidancy,* and *collocation,* and many words in unusual forms, such as *objectless, luminousness,* and *encrimsoned.* Discuss this aspect of Poe's syntax in this story.

2. It is unusual in a story about death from this period that there is no mention of God or of any external spiritual being. Comment on this anomaly.

3. Analyze the first sentence of the story and consider its symbolic as well as its psychological allusions.

4. In the story there are continual allusions to Usher's mental illness. Analyze the specific descriptions of his illness in relation to the modern diagnosis of bipolar

disorder. Include in this analysis the description of Usher's steady rocking as he awaits the approach of his sister.

5. Discuss the opening paragraphs of the story as a prefiguring of the tragedy to come. Discuss Poe's intent in this presentation of the story's foundations in symbol and metaphor.

Conversations on Critical Views of Edgar Allan Poe's Short Stories, pp. 678–695

Edgar Allan Poe, *"The Importance of the Single Effect in a Prose Tale,"* p. 680.

D. H. Lawrence, *"On 'The Fall of the House of Usher' and 'The Cask of Amontillado,'"* p. 683.

Cleanth Brooks and Robert Penn Warren, *"A New Critical Reading of 'The Fall of the House of Usher,'"* p. 687.

J. Gerald Kennedy, *"On 'The Fall of the House of Usher,'"* p. 689.

David S. Reynolds, *"Poe's Art of Transformation in 'The Cask of Amontillado,'"* p. 692.

Suggested Readings

Adler, Jacob H. "Are There Flaws in 'The Cask of Amontillado'?" *Notes and Queries* 199 (1954): 32–34.

Baudelaire, Charles P. *Baudelaire on Poe: Critical Papers.* University Park: Pennsylvania State UP, 1952.

Buranelli, Vincent. *Edgar Allan Poe.* Rev. ed. Boston: Twayne, 1977.

Carlson, Eric W., ed. *Critical Essays on Edgar Allan Poe.* Boston: G. K. Hall, 1987.

———. *Introduction to Poe: A Thematic Reader.* Glenville, IL: Scott, 1967.

Dillon, John M. *Edgar Allan Poe.* Brooklyn, NY: Haskell, 1974.

Fletcher, Richard M. *The Stylistic Development of Edgar Allan Poe.* New York: Mouton, 1974.

Gargano, J. W. "'The Cask of Amontillado': A Masquerade of Motive and Identity." *Studies in Short Fiction* 4 (1967): 119–26.

———. *The Masquerade Vision in Poe's Short Stories.* Baltimore: Enoch Pratt, 1977.

Hammond, J. R. *An Edgar Allan Poe Companion: A Guide to Short Stories, Romances, and Essays.* Savage, MD: B and N Imports, 1981.

Knapp, Bettina L. *Edgar Allan Poe.* New York: Ungar, 1984.

Levin, Harry. *The Power of Blackness: Hawthorne, Poe, Melville.* Columbus: Ohio UP, 1980.

Mabbott, Thomas Olivle, ed. *Collected Works of Edgar Allan Poe.* Cambridge, MA: Harvard UP, 1978.

May, Charles E. *Edgar Allan Poe: A Study of Short Fiction.* Boston: Twayne, 1990.

Muller, John P., and William J. Richardson, eds. *The Purloined Poe: Lacan, Derrida, and Psychoanalytic Reading.* Baltimore: Johns Hopkins UP, 1988.

Symons, Julian, ed. *Selected Tales.* New York: Oxford UP, 1980.

ANNIE PROULX

Job History (p. 486)

What a dire, funny tale! Proulx's decision to highlight the employment history of the Wyoming citizen Leeland Lee results in the depiction of a "typical American" character whose dogged attempts at survival in an unforgiving economic climate might have been chosen for celebration in the uplifting campaign speeches of a President George W. Bush or a Senator John McCain. Proulx's choice of a title for this character's story suggests her less than uplifting view of the same material. But then she is a writer of short fiction, instead of a politician, and she has the benefit of expressing her own personal views on the subject of the limited future offered to an at-risk, ordinary, white American high school dropout born in 1947 trying to support his family in a totally exploitative, deregulated "free" economy.

Proulx gives us just enough details about her protagonist's physical appearance, family background (his mother inherits a small ranch, his "irascible" father hits him with a flyswatter), and his limited intelligence (he can sing "The Doggie in the Window" all the way through). After an early marriage, he takes his first job, joins the army for six years during the war in Vietnam, and then goes back to Wyoming to resume life as a civilian in the volatile economic environment of the 1970s. In the 1980s "the economy takes a dive," Leeland and his wife Lori give up their business, move several times, and he settles into a job as a long-distance truck driver. Thirty years later, after trying and failing at various enterprises, Lori dies of cancer. Two years later, Leeland takes a job as a cook and discovers a "long-hidden skill" at grilling and frying meat. Always optimistic, he and his oldest son plan to go into business running "a motorcycle repair shop and steak house." As Kurt Vonnegut would say, so it goes, until the end of the story.

Questions for Discussion

1. In "Job History," Proulx has written a humorous story about the haphazard career of a typical American. Do you think Leeland Lee is a typical American? What is the average annual income today of an adult white male in Wyoming?
2. What is Proulx trying to say about the much-praised opportunity and "freedom" of the American lifestyle?
3. Why does Proulx tell us the national news Leeland hears on the radio along with the incidents of his career?
4. Where is the humor in Proulx's story?

Topic for Writing

1. Write a review of Proulx's *Close Range* (1999), her collection of Wyoming stories that includes "Job History."

Suggested Readings

Proulx, Annie. *Close Range*. New York: Scribner, 1999.
————. *Fine Just the Way It Is*. New York: Scribner, 2008.

Leslie Marmon Silko

Yellow Woman (p. 491)

This story is told in the first person and presented episodically in several sections. It takes place over two days, beginning the morning Yellow Woman wakes up beside the river with Silva, the stranger she has spent the night with. The story ends at sundown the next day, when she returns to her family in the Pueblo village.

"Yellow Woman" is built on different traditions from those in the cultural background of most American students. Silko writes fiction that preserves her cultural heritage by re-creating its customs and values in stories that dramatize emotional conflicts of interest to modern readers.

As Yellow Woman narrates the story of her abduction and return to her family, the reader comes to share her mood and her interpretation of what has happened. As a girl she was fascinated by the stories her grandfather told her about Silva, the mysterious kachina spirit who kidnaps married women from the tribe, then returns them after he has kept them as his wives. These stories were probably similar to the imaginary tales passed down in an oral tradition whose origins are lost to contemporary American folklorists. Silko has created their modern equivalent, her version of how they might be reenacted in today's world. The overweight, white Arizona rancher is familiar to us, as is the Jell-O being prepared for supper, and we have no difficulty imagining the gunnysacks full of freshly slaughtered meat bouncing on the back of Yellow Woman's horse.

The dreamlike atmosphere Silko creates in "Yellow Woman" makes such realistic details protrude sharply from the soft-focus narrative. Yellow Woman doesn't think clearly. She seems bewitched by the myths her grandfather told her, and her adventure following the man she calls Silva holds her enthralled. At the end she says, "I thought about Silva, and I felt sad at leaving him; still, there was something strange about him, and I tried to figure it out all the way back home." We are not told what — if anything — she does figure out.

Instead, action takes the place of thought in the story. Yellow Woman looks at the place on the riverbank where she met Silva and tells herself that "he will come back sometime and be waiting again by the river." Action moves so swiftly that we follow Yellow Woman as obediently as she follows her abductor, mesmerized by the audacity of what is happening. There is no menace in Silva, no danger or malice in his rape of Yellow Woman. The bullets in his rifle are for the white rancher who realizes he has been killing other men's cattle, not for Yellow Woman — or for us.

Questions for Discussion

1. Why is Yellow Woman so eager to believe that she and Silva are acting out the stories her grandfather told her?
2. How does Silko structure the opening paragraphs of the story to help the reader suspend disbelief and enter the dreamlike atmosphere of Yellow Woman's perceptions?
3. Why does Silko tell the story through the woman's point of view? Describe the Pueblo Indian woman we know as Yellow Woman. Is she happy at home with her mother, grandmother, husband, and baby? Why is Yellow Woman's father absent from the story?
4. Are there any limitations to Silko's choice to tell the story through Yellow Woman's point of view? Explain.
5. Why doesn't the narrator escape from Silva when she discovers him asleep by the river as the story opens? What makes her decide to return home the next day?

Topics for Writing

1. RESPONDING CREATIVELY Tell the story through a third-person omniscient narration.
2. Compare "Yellow Woman" with an Indian folktale about the kachina spirit who kidnapped married women.
3. MAKING CONNECTIONS Compare "Yellow Woman" and Joyce Carol Oates's "Where Are You Going, Where Have You Been?" (p. 406) as rape narratives.

Commentary

Paula Gunn Allen, *"Whirlwind Man Steals Yellow Woman,"* p. 578.

Suggested Readings

Allen, Paula Gunn. *The Sacred Hoop: Recovering the Feminine in American Indian Traditions.* Boston: Beacon, 1986.

———, ed. *Spider Woman's Granddaughters: Traditional Tales and Contemporary Writing by Native American Women.* Boston: Beacon, 1989.

Graulich, Melody, ed. *"Yellow Woman."* Women, Text and Contexts Series. New Brunswick, NJ: Rutgers UP, 1993.

Hoilman, Dennis. "The Ethnic Imagination: A Case History." *Canadian Journal of Native Studies* 5.2 (1985): 167–75.

Nelson, Robert M. *Place and Vision: The Function of Landscape in Native American Fiction.* New York: P. Lang, 1993.

Sands, Kathleen Mullen. "Indian Women's Personal Narrative: Voices Past and Present." *American Women's Autobiography: Fea(s)ts of Memory.* Ed. Margo Culley. Madison: U of Wisconsin P, 1992.

Silko, Leslie Marmon. *Almanac of the Dead.* New York: Simon, 1991.

Helen Simpson

Homework (p. 499)

A sweet love story told mostly through a dialogue between a schoolboy George and his mother who's helping him with his English homework, an assignment to write three pages about "An Event That Changed Your Life." As the mother understands, the assignment is unfair because thirteen year olds "can't know what a life-changing event is at their age." So she agrees to help her son write the essay "only this once." This is the story of a mother-son bond that is strong and healthy, instead of the standard tale of adolescent rebellion and parental despair.

The story is told in first-person narration through the voice of George's mother, who has loved him from birth (as Grace Paley, one of Simpson's predecessors in the business of lovingly depicting family life, might have said). As a mother the narrator isn't possessive, enjoying the fact that her son is growing up into manhood and that he isn't emotionally fragile. "You can tell him off and he won't immediately go into orbit like some I could mention." She suggests the way he could write his essay — describe the event of his parents' divorce — and insists that although it's a lie, it's a necessary one because it will fulfill his English assignment: "Well, you're just being creative."

The mother takes a feminist spin on the results of the imagined divorce by making "the mum" leave "the dad" for a change and go off by herself, leaving "the dad" to take care of the kids while she travels around the world. George isn't happy "with where the story line was going," but the narrator feels "powerful, like a magician pulling rabbits out of a hat." She explains the necessary technical stuff such as how to pad the essay and how to create events that keep the story moving, insisting that writing an autobiographical essay is "like a game, isn't it?" The teacher "shouldn't be able to tell what's real and what's made up."

Just like this story. The reader doesn't know what is real and what Simpson has imagined, but by the end of "Homework" we believe in the love between George and his mother. They are united, even if "the dad" and "the mum" in the boy's essay are not. We may even find ourselves wondering if Simpson doesn't have a thirteen-year-old son in real life. After all, that's the power of that wonderful lie we call fiction.

Questions for Discussion

1. Do you think it was fair for the mother to help her son with his essay?
2. How typical is George as a thirteen-year-old? In what ways does he differ from an American schoolboy of his age?
3. Interpret Simpson's sentences at the end of the story: "Beware heat without warmth. . . . strength without sweetness is no use at all." Put her idea into your own words. Is it the theme of her story?

Topic for Writing

1. **RESPONDING CREATIVELY**   Rewrite "Homework" from George's point of view.

Suggested Readings

Simpson, Helen. *Getting a Life.* New York: Knopf, 2001.
———. *In the Driver's Seat.* New York: Knopf, 2007.

JOHN STEINBECK

The Chrysanthemums (p. 507)

The instinctive life that Elisa Allen loves as she tends her chrysanthemum plants lies dormant under her fingers. She is good with flowers, like her mother before her. But it is December, and Steinbeck tells us it is "a time of quiet and of waiting." The Salinas landscape lies peacefully, but Elisa is vaguely unfulfilled. She begins to transplant her little chrysanthemum shoots, working without haste, conscious of her "hard-swept" house and her well-ordered garden, protected with its fence of chicken wire. Everything in her little world is under control. The tension in the scene is in herself, something she vaguely senses but refuses to face: the difference between her little world and the larger one encompassing it. Elisa is strong and mature, at the height of her physical strength. Why should she lie dormant? She has no fit scope for her powers. Steinbeck suggests the contradiction between her strength and her passivity in his description of the landscape: "The yellow stubble fields seemed to be bathed in pale cold sunshine, but there was no sunshine in the valley now in December." Like Hemingway, Steinbeck uses physical and geographical details to suggest the *absence* of positive qualities in his fictional characters. There is no sunshine in the valley, and the chrysanthemum plants aren't flowering, but what is natural in the annual vegetation cycle is out of kilter in Elisa. She experiences the world as a state of frustration.

Steinbeck has written an understated Chekhovian story in which ostensibly nothing much happens. It is a slice of life as Elisa lives it, sheltered and comfortable, yet — in Henry David Thoreau's words — life lived in a state of "quiet desperation."

The two male characters feel none of Elisa's lack of fulfillment. They live in a male world and take their opportunities for granted. Her husband, Henry Allen, is having a fine day. He's sold his thirty head of steer for a good price, and he's celebrating this Saturday night by taking his wife out to dinner and the movies in town. The traveling tinker is a trifle down on his luck, but it's nothing serious. He's found no customers this day so he lacks the money for his supper, but he knows a mark when he sees one. He flatters Elisa by agreeing with her and handing her a line about bringing some of her chrysanthemums to a lady he knows "down the road a piece." Elisa springs into action, delighted to be needed. Her tender shoots need her, but she is not sufficiently absorbed by her gardening. The men do the real work of the world in this story. Gardening is a hobby she's proud of, and her husband encourages her to take pride in it, but she needs to feel of use in a larger dimension. Elisa mistakes this need for the freedom she imagines the transient knows on the road. Steinbeck gives her a clue as to the man's real condition in the state of his horse and mule, which she as a good gardener shouldn't have missed: "The horse and donkey drooped like unwatered flowers."

Instead, Elisa is caught up in her romantic fantasy of his nomadic life. Her sexual tension reduces her to a "fawning dog" as she envisions his life, but finally she realizes the man doesn't have the money for his dinner. "She stood up then, very straight, and her face was ashamed." Ashamed for what reason? Her lack of sensitivity to his poverty? her sexual excitement? her sense of captivity in a masculine world, where apparently only motherhood would bring opportunities for work? Elisa brings the man two battered pots to fix and resumes talking, unable to leave him or her fantasy about the freedom she thinks he enjoys. He tells her outright that "it ain't the right kind of a life for a woman." Again she misreads the situation, taking his comment as a challenge. She defends her ability to be his rival at sharpening scissors and banging out dents in pots and pans.

When the man leaves, Elisa is suddenly aware of her loneliness. She scrubs her body as rigorously as she's swept her house, punishing her skin with a pumice stone instead of pampering it with bubble bath. Then she puts on "the dress which was the symbol of her prettiness" — an odd choice of words. Without understanding her instinctive rebellion against male expectations, Elisa refuses to be a sex symbol. Again she loses, denying herself pleasure in soft fabrics and beautiful colors. When Henry returns, he is bewildered by her mood and unable to reach her. She sees the chrysanthemums dying on the road, but she still can't face the truth about her sense of the repression and futility of her life. Wine at dinner and the idea of going to see a prize fight briefly bring her closer to the flesh and the instinctive life she has shunned outside her contact with her flowers, but they don't lift her mood. She feels as fragile and undervalued as her chrysanthemums. She begins to cry weakly, "like an old woman," as Henry drives her down the road.

Elisa is frustrated, cut off from the fullness of life by her physical destiny as a woman in a man's world. Does Steinbeck understand the sexual bias that undermines Elisa's sense of herself? He makes Henry as considerate a husband as a woman could wish for — he takes Elisa to the movies instead of going off to the prize fight himself. Steinbeck was sensitive to women's frustration, depicting it often in his fiction, even if he didn't look too closely at its probable causes.

Questions for Discussion

1. Based on Steinbeck's description in the first three paragraphs, how would you characterize the initial tone of the story? What do you associate with Steinbeck's image of the valley as "a closed pot"? In what way does this initial description foreshadow the events of the story?

2. What kind of character is Elisa Allen? What are the physical boundaries of her world? What is Elisa's psychological state at the beginning of the story?

3. Characterize the two men who are part of Elisa's world. In what ways are they similar and different? How do their lives compare and contrast with the life Elisa leads?

4.   What is the role of the chrysanthemums in Elisa's life? What do they symbolize?
5.   How does Elisa delude herself about the life of the tinker? What other fantasies does this lead her to indulge in?
6.   In what way does the tinker manipulate Elisa to accomplish his goals?
7.   When the tinker leaves, a change comes over Elisa. What has she suddenly realized, and what course of action does she adopt?
8.   As Elisa, both realistically and symbolically, goes out into the world, has she achieved any resolution of her problem? Why does she end the story "crying weakly — like an old woman"?

Topics for Writing

1.   Discuss Steinbeck's use of setting to establish theme in "The Chrysanthemums."
2.   Consider the isolation of Elisa Allen.
3.   Analyze Elisa's illusions about the tinker and his interest in her as contrasted with reality.
4.   **RESPONDING CREATIVELY**   Recall a time when you felt threatened and frustrated by events that isolated you. Write a narrative recounting this experience from a third-person point of view.

Suggested Readings

Marcus, Mordecai. "The Lost Dream of Sex and Children in 'The Chrysanthemums.'" *Modern Fiction Studies* 11 (1965): 54–58.
McMahan, Elizabeth. "'The Chrysanthemums': Study of a Woman's Sexuality." *Modern Fiction Studies* 14 (1968–69): 453–58.
Miller, William V. "Sexual and Spiritual Ambiguity in 'The Chrysanthemums.'" *Steinbeck Quarterly* 5 (1972): 68–75.
Renner, S. "The Real Woman behind the Fence in 'The Chrysanthemums.'" *Modern Fiction Studies* 31 (1985): 305–17.
Sweet, Charles A. "Ms. Elisa Allen and Steinbeck's 'The Chrysanthemums.'" *Modern Fiction Studies* 20 (1974): 210–14.

AMY TAN

Two Kinds (p. 515)

"Two Kinds," which was first published in the February 1989 issue of *The Atlantic Monthly*, is an excerpt from Tan's best-selling book, *The Joy Luck Club*. It is a skillfully written story that will probably pose no difficulty for most students; plot, characters, setting, and theme are immediately clear. The narrator states what she's "learned" from her experience in her final paragraph: She has come to realize that "Pleading Child" and "Perfectly Contented" are "two halves of the same song."

Looking back to her childhood, the narrator appears to be "perfectly contented" with her memories. Her interpretation of her relationship with her mother is presented in a calm, even self-satisfied, way. After her mother's death, she tunes the piano left to her in her parents' apartment: "I played a few bars [of the piano piece by Robert Schumann], surprised at how easily the notes came back to me." The painful memory of her fiasco as a piano student has dissipated. Now she is her own audience, and she is pleased with what she hears. There is no real emotional stress in "Two Kinds"; the girl has had a comfortable life. She has survived her mother and can dispose of her possessions as she likes. She is at peace with her past, fulfilling her mother's prophecy that "you can be best anything."

The mother earned her right to look on the bright side of life by surviving tremendous losses when she left China. Her desire to turn her daughter into a "Chinese Shirley Temple" is understandable but unfortunate, since it places a tremendous psychological burden on the child. A discussion about this story might center on parents' supporting children versus "pushing" them to succeed in tasks beyond their abilities or ambitions.

Still, the narrator doesn't appear to have suffered unduly from her mother's ambitions for her. By her own account she was more than a match for her mother in the contest of wills on the piano bench. After her wretched performance at the recital, the daughter refuses to practice anymore. When her mother shouts, "Only two kinds of daughters. . . . Those who are obedient and those who follow their own mind! Only one kind of daughter can live in this house. Obedient daughter!" the girl answers by saying the unspeakable: "I wish I'd never been born! I wish I were dead! Like them [the mother's twin baby girls lost in China]." This ends the conflict, but the narrator goes on to tell us that she was unrelenting in victory: "In the years that followed, I failed her many times, each time asserting my will, my right to fall short of expectations. I didn't get straight As. I didn't become class president. I didn't get into Stanford. I dropped out of college." She tells us that only after her mother's death can she begin to see things in perspective, when she is free to create her own version of the past.

Because most students in class will be of the age when they are also asserting their wills against parents in a struggle to take control of their lives, they will probably sympathize with Tan's narrator and accept her judgments uncritically. Will any reader take the mother's side?

Questions for Discussion

1. Why is the setting of this story important? What do you learn from it about the experience of Asian immigrants in their first years in the United States?
2. What advantages are offered to the child? What disadvantages?
3. How typical is Tan's story of the mother-daughter conflict? Explain.
4. Explain the meaning of the last paragraph of the story.

Topics for Writing

1. MAKING CONNECTIONS   Compare and contrast the theme of initiation in Ralph Ellison's "Battle Royal" (p. 127) and Tan's "Two Kinds."
2. Analyze the use of dialect in Tan's "Two Kinds."

Commentary

Amy Tan, *"In the Canon, for All the Wrong Reasons,"* p. 625.

Suggested Readings

Tan, Amy. *The Joy Luck Club.* New York: Ballantine, 1989.
———. "The Language of Discretion." In *The State of the Language.* Ed. Christopher Ricks. Berkeley: U of California P, 1990.

JOHN UPDIKE

A & P (p. 524)

Although Updike was a precociously successful writer who spent his apprentice-ship living in New York City and writing for *The New Yorker,* much of the strength of his writing stems from his ability to take the reader back to the atmosphere of the small town where he grew up. "A & P" showcases this ability. This story about a nineteen year old at a checkout counter in an A & P supermarket skillfully sustains the point of view of a teenage boy from a small-town working-class family.

The incident the story describes is slight. What gives "A & P" its substance is the voice of the narrator. He is obviously what the author thinks of as an ordinary teenager: impatient with old people, not interested in his job, and deeply aroused by girls. The longest descriptive passage — almost a third of the story itself — dwells on the body of one of the girls; as the story's slight action unfolds, the bodies of that girl and one of her friends are mentioned several times. The narrator's adolescent desire and adoration are amusingly played off his clumsy bravado and the idiom of sexist stereotypes he is trying to master: "You never know for sure how girls' minds work (do you really think it's a mind in there or just a little buzz like a bee in a glass jar?)." His view of adult women is no less callow: "We're right in the middle of town, and the women generally put on a shirt or shorts or something before they get out of the car into the street. And anyway these are usually women with six children and varicose veins mapping their legs and nobody, including them, could care less."

It is probably true that when the story was written, in the late 1950s, its attitudes were not considered unusual. Today we have to ask ourselves whether the deplorable sex-ism is redeemed by the artfulness of the story, the technique Updike brings to construct-ing his narrator's voice.

Questions for Discussion

1. What does the language of the story tell us about the narrator's social background?
2. Are there any details in the story that place it in a specific part of the United States, or could it be happening anywhere within a few miles of a beach? Explain.
3. Is the boy's discomfort with older people limited to women, or is he also uncom-fortable with men? Is there anyone in the store he is comfortable with? Explain.
4. Do you think Updike shares the narrator's attitudes?

Topics for Writing

1. Analyze the strengths and limitations of the first-person narrative in "A & P."
2. **MAKING CONNECTIONS**   Compare and contrast adolescent narrators in Updike's "A & P" and James Joyce's "Araby" (p. 264).

Commentary

John Updike, "*Kafka and 'The Metamorphosis,'*" p. 638.

Suggested Readings

Cantor, Jay. "On Giving Birth to One's Own Mother." *TriQuarterly* 75 (Spring–Summer 1989): 78–91.
Detweiler, Robert. *John Updike.* Rev. ed. Boston: Twayne, 1987.

Fleischauer, John F. "John Updike's Prose Style: Definition at the Periphery of Meaning." *Critique: Studies in Contemporary Fiction* 30.4 (Summer 1989): 277–90.

Greiner, Donald J. *The Other Updike: Poems, Short Stories, Prose, Play.* Columbus: Ohio UP, 1981.

Luscher, Robert M. "John Updike's Olinger Stories: New Light among the Shadows." *Journal of the Short Story in English* 11 (Autumn 1988): 99–117.

Lyons, E. "John Updike: The Beginning and the End." *Critique* 14.2 (1972): 44–59.

Newman, Judie. *John Updike.* New York: St. Martin's, 1988.

Samuels, C. T. "The Art of Fiction: John Updike." *Paris Review* 12 (1968): 84–117.

Seib, P. "Lovely Way through Life: An Interview with John Updike." *Southwest Review* 66 (1981): 341–50.

Taylor, Charles C. *John Updike: A Bibliography.* Ann Arbor, MI: Books Demand UMI, 1989.

Thorburn, David, and Howard Eiland, eds. *John Updike: A Collection of Critical Essays.* New York: Prentice, 1979.

Updike, John. *Hugging the Shore.* New York: Random, 1983.

———. *Picked-Up Pieces.* New York: Knopf, 1976.

———. *Too Far to Go.* New York: Ballantine, 1979.

Wilhelm, Albert E. "Rebecca Cune: Updike's Wedge between the Maples." *Notes on Modern American Literature* 7.2 (Fall 1983): Item 9.

———. "The Trail-of-Bread-Crumbs Motif in Updike's Maples Stories." *Studies in Short Fiction* 25.1 (Winter 1988): 71–73.

HELENA MARÍA VIRAMONTES

The Moths (p. 530)

Although Viramontes has written in many styles, this story shows the influence of one of her teachers, Nobel Prize–winner Gabriel García Márquez. It has close affinities to the subject matter and the characters of a typical García Márquez story, and the literary style reflects García Márquez's commitment to magic realism. Viramontes's magic realism, however, is more rooted in the everyday than that of many other writers using this idiom, and her story about a girl's difficult relationship with her mother and her sisters reflects Viramontes's American upbringing. Students will likely have a strong response to the story's imagery and to the unyielding tale the girl tells of her grandmother's death. The image of small gray moths that come from her grandmother's soul and flutter out of her mouth at the moment of her death is unforgettable, and like so much of the metaphor and symbolism that is at the root of magic realist technique, it is never adequately explained. It is up to Viramontes's readers to make what they can of it.

Students will find it helpful in studying the story to follow one image through various points in the narrative. An image we can follow is the girl's hands. For Viramontes, the girl's hands become a symbol of her emotional difficulties with her family. Already in the second paragraph we are told that one reason the girl didn't fit in with her sisters was that her hands "were too big to handle the fineries of crocheting or embroidery." Her sisters have given her the cruel nickname "bull hands." The girl tells us casually that because she had doubted her grandmother's cure for her fever, her hands "grow like a liar's nose." Her grandmother cures her swollen hands with "a balm [made] out of dried moth wings and Vicks." When the girl tries to talk to her mother about the seriousness of her grandmother's illness, she feels her hands "hanging helplessly" by her side. She falls asleep and is awakened when her hands fall from her lap. As she crushes the chili peppers for her grandmother's tripe stew, she describes herself as doing it with her "bull hand."

Viramontes is not afraid to take chances, and her language is as startling as her imagery. The girl speaks of her grandmother's "pasty gray eye" beaming at her and "burning holes" in her suspicions about the old woman's folk medicines. She talks of a sunset as a moment when "the sun is finally defeated, finally sinks into the realization that it cannot with all its power to heal or burn, exist forever." Beneath the verbal fireworks, however, Viramontes has a simple story to tell. The girl is hardened by the verbal abuse and the whippings she has received at the hands of her family. Only her grandmother has let her escape from them into something like an ordinary life. When the grandmother dies the girl is alone, and she carefully cleans the old woman's body, taking her grandmother into the bathtub with her, holding her in her arms. Sitting in the water with the body, she is finally able to cry. Students will respond to the story's literary qualities — to its language and poetic imagery — but they will first be moved by the immediacy and the poignancy of the girl's experience.

Questions for Discussion

1. Discuss the image of the girl's hands and how the obsession with her hands follows her through the story.
2. One of the girl's difficulties with her family is her refusal to attend church. What does she experience the one time in the story she does visit a chapel?
3. Much of the girl's protest against her family sounds like a typical American teenager's complaints. What is different, or not different, about her complaints about her Latino family?
4. The story jumps from one time frame to another as the girl remembers her life with her *abuelita*. At what moment is the story occurring? How do we know it from the text?
5. How does the author relate the moment of the old woman's death to the eternal rhythms of life and our experience?
6. What is the contrast the author intends when she describes the water running into the bath as filled with "vitality and steam"?
7. Discuss what the author is telling us when she says that the girl, after her grandmother's death, "wanted to go to where the moths were"?
8. Discuss the symbolism of the moths.

Topics for Writing

1. In the same sentence in which Viramontes tells us that the protagonist's sisters have nicknamed her "bull hands," Viramontes describes her sisters' "waterlike voices," using a strong simile. Find other strong similes and metaphors in the text and discuss their importance to the story.
2. When the girl challenges her family's belief in the grandmother's folk medicine, she is challenging their adherence to old-fashioned traditions the way that many young people do. Analyze how this challenge is developed and resolved in the narrative.

Suggested Reading

Viramontes, Helena María, and Maria Herrera-Sobek, eds. *Chicana Creativity and Criticism: New Frontiers in American Literature.* Albuquerque: U of New Mexico P, 1996.

K‍urt V‍onnegut J‍r.

Harrison Bergeron (p. 534)

This humorous fantasy story deserves to become a classic in American literature, like James Thurber's "The Secret Life of Walter Mitty." Vonnegut has stretched the basic premise of American democracy — that all men (and women) are created equal — to its literal limit. In his opening paragraph he explains how this admirable social ideal was realized in the year 2081, and then he shows the consequences of the idea as experienced in the family life of George and Hazel Bergeron and their fourteen-year-old son Harrison.

As a storyteller, Vonnegut makes good use of the traditional elements of fiction in structuring a conventional plot, but you could point out to students that the most dramatic events of the plot (ironically enough) occur in a television program that George and Hazel are watching together in their living room, parodying the "normal" activities of the average twenty-first-century family. On the screen, they see their son shot and killed by the U.S. Handicapper General in a television studio after he has defied the law of the land by freeing himself, a beautiful ballerina, and several musicians of their handicaps.

The most memorable aspect of Vonnegut's story is his description of the effect of the handicap on George Bergeron — the various noises of buzzers, ball peen hammers, and riveting guns transmitted by his "ear radio" are guaranteed to keep him from thinking about anything for too long. Their effect is terribly painful, as it is meant to be. By destroying individual human thought, the government has created a nation of sheep, content in their passivity to accept whatever they see on television, including the murder of their only son.

Questions for Discussion

1. How does the "ear radio" worn by everyone possessing above-normal intelligence in Vonnegut's story anticipate the earphones worn now by people listening to tapes and CDs?
2. How do the noises transmitted by George Bergeron's earphones suggest the effect of the frequent television advertisements infiltrating programs broadcast by the media today?
3. In what way does "Harrison Bergeron" contradict the idea of human equality at the basis of democracy in the United States? How can you defend the idea, despite what happens in the story?
4. Why doesn't Hazel wear a handicap? How does George deal with his handicap?
5. Why isn't Harrison content with the status quo? Does his age alone (fourteen) adequately explain his rebellion against the laws of his society?

Topic for Writing

1. Analyze Vonnegut's use of simile and metaphor in "Harrison Bergeron" to suggest the emotional effect of the handicap radio on George Bergeron.

Suggested Reading

Vonnegut, Kurt, Jr. *Welcome to the Monkey House.* New York: Dell, 1968.

Alice Walker

Everyday Use (p. 540)

In this very accessible but powerful story, Walker deals with issues that college readers should find thought-provoking and relevant to their lives. It is a story about family, heritage, personal pride, and the way that one young woman's search for identity causes her to devalue the very aspects of her past that are most important. While searching for objects and symbols to enshrine as reflections of her zealous racial pride, Dee overlooks the human beings whose strength and courage she should really be interested in preserving and emulating.

Dee has always been seen, by herself and others, as different from her family and the people around her. She is smart, ambitious, wanting more out of life than her family seems to have. Of course, there is nothing wrong in any of this, and as many young people do, Dee moves away to find herself and a better life. The irony arises after she finds this new life. Then, her need to feel a connection to a past, a people, and a history asserts itself, and Dee searches for her identity in a socially trendy fashion, reaching back to African tradition in hairstyle, clothing, and name, "Wangero." The problem is that in "reaching back" to Africa, she reaches right past her own relatives, whose lives she considers common, ignorant, and unimportant.

This is illustrated most powerfully by her rejection of her birth name, which, she tells her mother contemptuously, is a name "after the people who oppress me." Her mother, puzzled, reminds her that she was named after her aunt, who was named after her mother, who was named after *her* mother . . . and reflects that the name could probably be traced back beyond the Civil War to slave days. You would think that a young woman who is so interested in preserving her "heritage" would show some interest in these women whose name she bears and whose lives of struggle and oppression she truly springs from, but Dee doesn't care at all. Dee is only interested in pieces of history that are aesthetically appealing and will enhance her life by making her (or her surroundings) look good. The stories of dead women, who lived (in Dee's view) in ignorance, poverty, and passive acceptance of oppression have no value for her.

Dee's shallowness and her superficial vision of family history are again displayed as we watch her select objects from her mother's house to take away as mementos. She takes the churn top and dasher, which her mother obviously still puts to practical use, without even asking permission, because she needs a centerpiece for a table. She places no value on the function of these objects or on another person's need for them, only on her own appreciation of their "artistic" qualities. Her mother allows her to have her way, but finally stands up to her and says no when she tries to take the handmade quilts. These quilts have been promised to Maggie, the rather pathetic younger sister who has always lived in Dee's shadow. Here, Mrs. Johnson's protective instincts are aroused, as she sees that Maggie will give in to Dee as she has always done unless her mother prevents it. She knows that Maggie is the one who will really value the quilts, putting them to "everyday use," as they were intended.

It is Maggie who is really in touch with her heritage, who has a "memory like an elephant" and who knows the family history because she knew and loved the people who created it. Maggie and her mother still live the same kind of life that their ancestors lived, in the same place, with the same kind of house, furniture, and food (which "Wangero" is so condescendingly "delighted" with). Dee, who is frenetically searching for objects that will make her feel connected to her roots, is smugly convinced that only she "understands her heritage." But, in reality, she doesn't understand anything about her family and in fact, has always looked down upon them all. Maggie is the one who deserves the family heirlooms, as she and her mother are the ones who really understand their meaning and who value their creators.

Questions for Discussion

1. Describe the mother in this story. What kind of person is she? How does she seem to feel about Dee? about Maggie?
2. How did Dee relate to her family before she left home? What role did she assume for herself? Does this change after she leaves home?
3. How do you feel about Dee? Do you sympathize with her desire to "improve" herself and her family? Where do you think she goes wrong?
4. Discuss the relationship between Maggie and Dee.
5. Why has Dee assumed African dress, hairstyle, and name? How would you characterize the attitudes of her and her new husband/boyfriend toward their race? positive or negative? honest or simply "politically correct"?
6. Discuss Dee's mother's and sister's reactions to her new persona, "Wangero." Do you sympathize with them?
7. How would you describe the way that Dee reacts to the food and objects in her mother's house?
8. Why does Mrs. Johnson decide to stand up to Dee and not allow her to take the quilts at the end of the story?
9. Why do you think Maggie is so content at the end?

Topics for Writing

1. Discuss Dee's final comment to her mother that she (the mother) "doesn't understand" her heritage.
2. **RESPONDING CREATIVELY** Argue with Mrs. Johnson, and try to convince her that Dee/Wangero deserves the quilts.
3. Discuss the positive and negative aspects of Wangero's and Hakim-a-barber's search for identity.

Commentary

Alice Walker, *"Zora Neale Hurston: A Cautionary Tale and a Partisan View,"* p. 629.

Suggested Readings

Banks, Erma Davis, and Keith Byerman. *Alice Walker: An Annotated Bibliography 1968–1986.* New York: Garland, 1989.
Bell, Roseann P., Bettye J. Parker, and Beverly Guy-Sheftall, eds. *Sturdy Black Bridges: Visions of Black Women in Literature.* New York: Anchor, 1979.
Bloom, Harold. *Alice Walker.* New York: Chelsea House, 1990.
Byerman, Keith, and Erma Banks. "Alice Walker: A Selected Bibliography, 1968–1988." *Callaloo: An Afro-American and African Journal of Arts and Letters* 12.2 (Spring 1989): 343–45.
Byrne, Mary Ellen. "Welty's 'A Worn Path' and Walker's 'Everyday Use': Companion Pieces." *Teaching English in a Two-Year College* 16(2) (May 1989): 129–33.
Cooke, Michael. *Afro-American Literature in the Twentieth Century: The Achievement of Intimacy.* New Haven: Yale UP, 1984.
Davis, T. M. "Alice Walker's Celebration of Self in Southern Generations." In *Women Writers of the Contemporary South.* Ed. Peggy Whitman Prenshaw. Jackson: UP of Mississippi, 1984. 83–94.

Erickson, P. "Cast Out Alone/To Heal/and Re-create/Ourselves: Family Based Identity in the Work of Alice Walker." *College Language Association Journal* 23 (1979): 71–94.

Evans, Mari, ed. *Black Women Writers (1950–1980): A Critical Evaluation.* New York: Anchor, 1984. 453–95.

Mariani, Philomena, ed. *Critical Fictions: The Politics of Imaginative Writing.* Seattle: Bay Press, 1991.

Petry, Alice Hall. "Alice Walker: The Achievement of the Short Fiction." *Modern Language Studies* 19.1 (Winter 1989): 12–27.

Stade, G. "Womanist Fiction and Male Characters." *Partisan Review* 52 (1985): 265–70.

Winchell, Donna Haisty. *Alice Walker.* Boston: Twayne, 1990.

DAVID FOSTER WALLACE

Good People (p. 547)

If Russell Banks wrote "Black Man and White Woman in Dark Green Rowboat" (p. 79) in order to re-imagine the exterior drama of Ernest Hemingway's "Hills Like White Elephants" (p. 224) using a contemporary American setting, then David Foster Wallace wrote "Good People" to dramatize his view of the interior emotional dilemma of Hemingway's story and give it a different ending. It is probably necessary to remind your students that it is likely that none of the three authors was motivated to write his story as an argument for or against abortion.

Told in the third person from the point of view of the protagonist Lane A. Dean Jr., Wallace tells the story of two young white middle class lovers "in trouble," nineteen-year-old Lane and twenty-year-old Sheri, two kids from respectable families dressed in squeaky clean blue jeans and button-up shirts who met in Peoria Junior College because they were both active in Christian ministries on campus. Both are hardworking and serious about their faith and what they still consider their promising futures. They couldn't be more different from the sexually involved pair of Hemingway's affluent European travelers in the early 1920s or Banks's lower-income trailer park inhabitants who find themselves in a similar predicament a half-century later.

As a devout Christian, Lane is obsessed with thoughts of Jesus Christ and the punishment of Hell after having impregnated his girlfriend by having sex outside of wedlock. Wallace makes it clear that Lane really likes Sheri and respects her, but does he love her enough to accept their child and get married? With Lane frozen in the shock of their predicament, serious and self-reliant Sheri makes a medical appointment at a clinic to get an abortion. Lane has tried to be supportive of her decision; he'd loyally "kept on about" how "he'd go with her and be there with her." But unlike Hemingway's protagonist, Lane is no selfish bully. He is sensitive and honest enough with himself to feel "like a ninny" when Sheri reminds him that he could never really "be there with her" since he'd be in the waiting room while she'd be the one having the procedure. He knows that "if he was the salesman of it and forced it upon her that was awful and wrong," yet he feels that his heart is frozen, since he has been unable to say that he loved her. If he had, then "it all would have been transformed," but he "could not say he did: it was not true." He knows that Sheri believes that he's an honorable man, but he's never been tested before. He senses that he doesn't know her true feelings for him, if indeed she even loves him.

Sitting together on the picnic bench as Sheri finally starts to turn toward him, Lane has what he later calls *"a moment of grace."* He believes he knows what she is going to say.

She is about to tell him that she cannot go through with the abortion, but that she releases him from all responsibility for the child. He imagines her saying that she "will carry this, and have it, and love it and make no claim on Lane except his good wishes and respecting what she has to do." His moment of grace is that while believing that he sees into her heart, he knows that she is lying. "She is gambling that he is good." Seconds later, at the conclusion of the story, Lane experiences a second epiphany: out of his sense of pity for Sheri's predicament, he is conscious of a question that he'd never thought to ask himself before: "why is he so sure he doesn't love her?" He realizes that he is just afraid, and that what he should be praying for is "not even love but simple courage, to meet both her eyes as she says it and trust his heart?" The story ends with a question mark. Even more than the other two stories, Wallace leaves the outcome of this couple's dilemma unresolved.

Questions for Discussion

1. What does Wallace tell you about Lane and Sheri that makes you suspect that they each love one another? Why haven't they been able to talk openly about their feelings in their relationship?
2. Is their predicament possible but improbable, or possible and probable, among college students?
3. How does Wallace ground his development of Lane's thoughts about his situation by having him notice his surroundings in the park? How does the shifting light on the young couple add drama to the narrative?
4. What is added to the scene by the presence of the adult male in the background?
5. Hemingway told his tale almost completely in dialogue. Wallace uses no dialogue in his retelling of the tale. What do these different narrative choices by each author contribute to the tone and mood of their stories?

Topic for Writing

1. Wallace structures his narrative as Lane's interior monologue, carried on in his thoughts as he scrutinizes the park by the lake where he and Sheri have gone to talk in the early morning before going to the abortion clinic in the afternoon. The author suggests the emotional weight of Lane's unhappiness in his opening sentence when he writes, "They were up on a picnic table at that park by the lake, by the edge of the lake, with part of a downed tree in the shallows half hidden by the bank." The symbolic overtones of the "downed tree in the shallows half hidden by the bank" echo the symbolic resonance in Hemingway's title of his story, "Hills Like White Elephants." The ragged repetition "at that park by the lake, by the edge of the lake," suggests Lane's ragged state of mind. Write an essay analyzing other instances of Wallace's rhetorical mastery at suggesting Lane's thought processes.

Connections

Russell Banks, *"Black Man and White Woman in Dark Green Rowboat,"* p. 79.
Ernest Hemingway, *"Hills Like White Elephants,"* p. 224.

Suggested Reading

Wallace, David Foster. *Brief Interviews with Hideous Men.* Boston: Little, Brown, 1999.

Brad Watson

Seeing Eye (p. 552)

"Seeing Eye" will probably be read by most students as an exercise in how an author can choose to tell a story using a point of view that isn't human. Buck is a seeing eye dog; he can see but he can't read the "Don't Walk" signal flashing out of the box across the intersection. Watson immediately grabs the reader's attention by stating that the dog's inability to interpret the eight letters blinking at him didn't matter in the least: "The dog saw the signal but paid little notice. He was trained to see what mattered: the absence of moving traffic."

What matters is Buck's ability to move his blind master safely through the world, which the dog is superbly able to do. He is a highly intelligent animal. Watson describes how the dog thinks — he listens to the buzz and tumbling of switches from the power box on the nearby pole and he alertly associates it "with the imminent stopping of the cars." When the light gets stuck, he patiently follows his master's command to wait at the corner. With the passage of time, his focus slips as the traffic and the blinking signal light "began to have a hypnotic effect upon him." As his attention begins to wander, sight becomes secondary to scent as he snuffles and sneezes at the various odors wafting past him on the breeze. When he lifts his head to watch the birds silhouetted against the sky darting between the tall buildings, we become aware that his canine responses are superior to that of humans: "He heard their high-pitched cries so clearly that he saw their beady eyes, their barbed tongues flicking between parted beaks. He salivated at the dusky taste of a dove he'd once held in his mouth." Finally, Buck's sensory equipment enables him to hear "the low hum beyond the visible world. His hackles rose and his muscles tingled with electricity."

Buck's blind master regrets the loss of sight and longs to recall what he terms "Panorama," the big picture. With all his senses intact in addition to a marvelously retentive memory, the dog lives in a bigger picture than his master can ever imagine. Watson's short story is more than a simple experiment in exploring a non-human point of view. His theme might be that all human beings are blind compared with the sensory perception and instinct of those creatures we consider lower animals, such as dogs. We also lack their qualities of patience and devotion. Would we human animals adjust so agreeably to being kept in a harness? Could we ever be trained to serve others before ourselves?

Questions for Discussion

1. The seeing eye dog has a name — Buck. In fact it has two names, since the reader is told he was called Pete before he was trained at school. Why doesn't the blind master have a name? How does Watson give you a sense of his character when he refuses to follow the woman and walk down a block to cross the street?
2. Why does Watson tell us about the dog's early life on the farm?
3. What does the man mean when he says he misses the ability to recall a "Panorama"?
4. Why does the blind man talk to his dog when he knows the dog can't talk back? What does this imply about the man's instinctive awareness of the dog's intelligence?

Topics for Writing

1. RESPONDING CREATIVELY   Rewrite "Seeing Eye" in its entirety from the perspective of the dog. Is it possible to do this without sentimentalizing your story?
2. Write a book review of Brad Watson's story collection, *Last Days of the Dog-Men* (1996).

Suggested Reading

Watson, Brad. *Last Days of the Dog-Men*. New York: Dell, 1996.

EUDORA WELTY

A Worn Path (p. 555)

Try not to force the Christian or mythological allegories the story supports until you encourage students to savor the beauty of the literal narration. Phoenix Jackson is an embodiment of love, faith, sacrifice, charity, self-renunciation, and triumph over death in herself, quite apart from the typological implications of her name or the allusions to the stations of the cross in her journey. Phoenix transcends her archetypal significance just as she transcends the stereotype of old black mammies on which she is built. Welty accomplishes this act of creation by entering fully into the consciousness of her character. There she discovers the little child that still lives within the old woman and causes her to dream of chocolate cake, dance with a scarecrow, and delight in a Christmas toy. Phoenix is right when she says, "I wasn't as old as I thought," but she does not merit the condescension of the hunter's exclamation, "I know you old colored people! Wouldn't miss going to town to see Santa Claus!" Even in her greatest discomfort, lying in the weeds, losing her memory, getting her shoes tied, "stealing" a nickel, or taking one as a handout, Phoenix retains her invincible dignity, an essential component of the single glimpse we receive of her triumphant homeward march, bearing aloft the bright symbol of life she has retrieved through her exertions.

In her comments on the story (included in Chapter 5, p. 632), Welty implies that the meaning of Phoenix's journey is that of any human exertion carried out in good faith despite the uncertainty of the outcome: "The path is the thing that matters." In keeping with this theme, Welty repeatedly shows Phoenix asserting life in the face of death. Her name itself, taken from the mythical bird that periodically immolates itself and rises reborn from its ashes, embodies the idea. (She even makes a noise like "a solitary little bird" in the first paragraph.) Phoenix makes her journey at the time of the death and rebirth of the year; her own skin color is like the sun bursting through darkness; she overcomes discouragement as she tops the hill; she extricates herself from a thorn bush (of which much may be made in a Christian allegorical interpretation); she passes "big dead trees" and a buzzard; she traverses a field of dead corn; she sees a "ghost" that turns out to be a dancing scarecrow; she is overcome by a "black dog" but rescued by a death-dealing hunter whose gun she faces down and whom she beats out of a shiny nickel; and she emerges from a deathlike trance in the doctor's office to return with the medicine her grandson needs to stay alive. Phoenix's strength lies in the purpose of her journey, and her spirit is contagious. The hunter, the woman who ties her shoes, and the doctor's attendant all perform acts of charity toward her, and lest the reader overlook the one word that lies at the heart of Welty's vision, the nurse says "Charity" while "making a check mark in a book."

Questions for Discussion

1. Notice Phoenix's identification with "a solitary little bird." What other birds does she encounter on her journey? Explain their implications.
2. What techniques does Welty use to suggest the laboriousness of Phoenix's trip?
3. Before she crosses the creek, Phoenix says, "Now comes the trial." Does she pass it? How? To what extent is this event a microcosm of the whole story? Are there other microcosmic episodes?
4. What effect do Phoenix's sequential reactions to the scarecrow, the abandoned cabins, and the spring have on the reader's view of her?
5. What is your opinion of the hunter? What conclusion might be drawn from the fact that even though he kills birds and patronizes Phoenix, he helps her in a way he does not know?
6. Interpret the passage that begins with Phoenix bending for the nickel and ends with her parting from the hunter.
7. Describe Natchez as Phoenix perceives it. Is it a worthy culmination for her journey?
8. In her comments reprinted in Chapter 5 (p. 632), Welty remarks that Phoenix's victory comes when she sees the doctor's diploma "nailed up on the wall." In what sense is this moment the climax of the story? What is different about the ensuing action from the action that leads up to this moment? Are there any similarities?
9. How does Phoenix describe her grandson? What is Welty's reason for using these terms?
10. Explain the irony in the way the nurse records Phoenix's visit.

Topics for Writing

1. Explain why many readers think that Phoenix Jackson's grandson is dead.
2. Discuss the symbolism of birds in "A Worn Path."
3. After your first reading of "A Worn Path," write a paragraph giving your opinion of Phoenix Jackson. Then study some symbolic interpretations of the story (such as those by Ardelino, Isaacs, and Keys, cited in the Suggested Readings). Reread the story and write another assessment of the central character. Does she bear up under the freight of symbolic meaning the critics ask her to carry? Does her relation to these archetypes help to account for your original response?
4. **RESPONDING CREATIVELY** Read Welty's account of how she came to write "A Worn Path." Following her example, write an account of what you imagine to be the day's experience of someone you glimpse who strikes your fancy. Use the intimate interior third-person limited-omniscient point of view that Welty employs for Phoenix Jackson.

Commentary

Eudora Welty, *"Is Phoenix Jackson's Grandson Really Dead?"* p. 632.

Suggested Readings

Ardelino, Frank. "Life Out of Death: Ancient Myth and Ritual in Welty's 'A Worn Path.'" *Notes on Mississippi Writers* 9 (1976): 1–9.

Bloom, Harold. *Eudora Welty.* New York: Chelsea House, 1986.

Desmond, John F. *A Still Moment: Essays on the Art of Eudora Welty.* Metuchen, NJ: Scarecrow, 1978.

Isaacs, Neil D. "Life for Phoenix." *Sewanee Review* 71 (1963): 75–81.

Keys, Marilynn. "'A Worn Path': The Way of Dispossession." *Studies in Short Fiction* 16 (1979): 354–56.

Kieft, Ruth M. *Eudora Welty.* Rev. ed. Boston: Twayne, 1987.

MacNeil, Robert. In *Eudora Welty: Seeing Black and White.* Westport, CT: Greenwood, 1990.

Phillips, Robert L., Jr. "A Structural Approach to Myth in the Fiction of Eudora Welty." *Eudora Welty: Critical Essays.* Ed. Peggy Whitman Prenshaw. Jackson: UP of Mississippi, 1979. 56–67, esp. 60.

Prenshaw, Peggy W., ed. *Eudora Welty: Thirteen Essays.* Jackson: UP of Mississippi, 1983.

Schmidt, Peter. *The Heart of the Story: Eudora Welty's Short Fiction.* Jackson: UP of Mississippi, 1991.

Turner, W. Craig, and Lee Harding, eds. *Critical Essays on Eudora Welty.* Boston: G. K. Hall, 1989.

Welty, Eudora. *The Eye of the Story.* New York: Vintage, 1990.

———. *One Writer's Beginnings.* New York: Warner, 1984.

WILLIAM CARLOS WILLIAMS

The Use of Force (p. 562)

Although Williams is best known as a poet, he also wrote a number of short stories, a successful play, and three novels chronicling the life of his wife's Norwegian immigrant family in the United States. Most of his short stories were written in the 1930s, during the Depression, and many of them were published in small magazines that were committed to the struggle for equality and social justice that dominated American intellectual life in those years. In the 1920s, when Williams was still thinking of himself as an experimental poet, he had written avant-garde prose, but the new stories, because of their political commitment, were written in a more direct style, and their subject matter was the ordinary life of the people who came to him as patients. The term for writing like this in the 1930s was "hard-hitting." Certainly Williams's new spare, unsentimental style was influenced by the stories of Ernest Hemingway, published several years earlier, but the setting in the poor neighborhoods of Rutherford, New Jersey, and the depressed, anxious people of the stories are his own.

The stubbornness of the girl in "The Use of Force" will remind some readers of the refusal of Melville's Bartleby to give in to authority in "Bartleby, the Scrivener" (p. 352), but Williams takes his story a step further. He reveals to the reader that the girl has a reason for her refusal to be examined. She is sick, and she is afraid of treatment. He also has the honesty to admit that he became so angry in the struggle with the girl that he felt pleasure in forcing her to give in.

The story certainly may suggest submerged sexual overtones to some readers in the fact that the patient is a girl and the doctor is trying to force a wooden instrument into her mouth, but there is nothing in the text to suggest that Williams intends to describe anything more than a professional visit to help a sick girl and her worried parents. Today we are more casual about infections like the one the girl is suffering from, but in Williams's time there were no antibiotics. He takes it for granted that his readers understand the necessity for him to get the girl's mouth open. To leave her as she is would probably be to leave her to die. As Williams writes, "I have seen at least two children lying dead in bed of neglect in such cases." He has to try to save her.

Questions for Discussion

1.   Today, would a doctor try to examine a child's throat during a house call, or would the patient come to a medical office to have the preliminary examination performed by a nurse?
2.   Williams tells us almost nothing about the kitchen where the girl is waiting or about the appearance of her parents. Why? (Students might suggest several possible answers.)
3.   When Williams writes that the girl's parents "weren't telling me more than they had to," what is he saying about the relationship between a doctor and his patients?
4.   The spare language of the story gives it some of the feeling of a medical report. Do students feel this is helpful or unhelpful in creating the mood of the story?
5.   Is it stubbornness or terror that is driving the girl to act the way she is?
6.   Why does the girl feel defeated when Williams finally is able to examine her throat? Does she comprehend that she is dangerously ill?

Topic for Writing

1.   There have been many changes in the relationship between doctors and patients in the United States since Williams wrote the story. Discuss whether you feel that Williams would have been happy with the changes, using examples from the story.

Suggested Reading

Coles, Robert, ed. *William Carlos Williams: The Doctor Stories.* New York: New Directions, 1984.

TOBIAS WOLFF

Say Yes (p. 565)

Wolff narrows the scope of "Say Yes" to zoom in on a seemingly ordinary evening in the life of a long-married couple. The unremarkable sequence of events nevertheless leads to the erotically charged atmosphere of the final paragraph. Through the routine domestic gestures of washing and drying dishes, attending to a cut finger, taking out the garbage, mopping the floor, and magazine reading, Wolff manages to reveal much about the inner lives of these people. Their namelessness emphasizes their ordinariness.

A conversation about interracial marriage sets the story in motion. Early in the dialogue, after suggesting that interracial marriage is a bad idea (without being able to fully articulate his reasons), the husband, observing his wife's expression, realizes he should back off from the subject but instead presses forward. These two know each other intimately — know how to needle, cajole, hurt, and apologize in subtle and not-so-subtle ways. In fact, this very intimacy — as with most marriages — carries negative as well as positive meanings. The husband's insistence that "a person from their culture and a person from our culture could never really know each other" reflects back on the couple's own relationship, leading the reader to question the extent to which any two people can know each other. Taking out the garbage and observing the night stars, the husband reflects on his marriage. Ashamed of fighting, he realizes the depth of the intimacy he shares with his wife as well as the transitoriness of their relationship with an intensity that affects him physically. This epiphany transforms at least his short-term behavior. Where normally he would "heave rocks" at the two dogs that topple his garbage, in this instance he lets them go unharmed.

Back in the house, he apologizes in the terms of the earlier discussion of interracial marriage, which now becomes a fantasy when he affirms that he'd marry her even if she were black. This openness to unexplored possibilities recharges the erotic life of the couple. When his wife enters the room in the darkness, "his heart pound[s] the way it had on their first night together," as if they were strangers.

Questions for Discussion

1. Why doesn't the husband "keep his mouth shut" when he knows he should?
2. What do you think the husband means when he says, "A person from their culture and a person from our culture could never really know each other"? Do you agree? What are some advantages and disadvantages of intracultural versus intercultural romantic relationships?
3. Why does the husband not "heave rocks" at the dogs that topple his garbage on this occasion, as he normally would?
4. In the final paragraph, why is the husband so excited? Does he experience a positive, erotic excitement, or does he realize that he doesn't know his wife as well as he thought he did?
5. Why is the question "Would you have loved me if I had been black?" so important to the wife?
6. To whom does the title apply? Who is expected to say yes?

Topic for Writing

1. Discuss the role of domestic details in advancing characterization in "Say Yes." What do these details reveal about this couple and their marriage?

Suggested Readings

Wolff, Tobias, *Back in the World: Stories*. Boston: Houghton, 1985.
———. *The Barracks Thief and Other Stories*. New York: Bantam, 1984.
———. *In the Garden of the North American Martyrs: A Collection of Short Stories*. New York: Ecco, 1981.
Woodruff, Jay, ed. *"In the Garden of the North American Martyrs." A Piece of Work: Five Writers Discuss Their Revisions*. Iowa City: U of Iowa P, 1993.

HISAYE YAMAMOTO

The Brown House (p. 569)

Yamamoto's story is like a Rorschach test, a diagnostic test of personality and intellect based on the reader's interpretation of what he or she has read. Do you interpret it as a realistic tale of the hardships suffered by the long-suffering Japanese wife Mrs. Hattori with her five young sons living in poverty in rural California in the late 1930s (after the Japanese military had invaded China and were involved in a war that predated their attack on American ships in Pearl Harbor), who is married to Mr. Hattori, another immigrant from Japan to the West Coast, a man who after their marriage becomes an impoverished compulsive gambler who beats her and impregnates her with their sixth child? Or is it a modern fairy tale that could just as well have begun with the formulaic words, "Once upon a time . . ." that would have emphasized the timeless quality of its account of the real cost of female endurance in the face of her mate's brutality and stupidity?

The story is a blend of the real and the surreal. The real includes the market price of the juicy and sweet strawberries in the California fields, so low in a bumper-crop year that even hard-working Japanese immigrants can't make a living wage for their families by picking them. Yamamoto describes the wonder of those strawberries in her opening paragraph with an unforgettable visual image when she writes that they were "as large as teacups." The real also includes the social reality that at the time this story takes place, during the Great Depression, families in the United States had no recourse to our current forms of social security such as unemployment insurance and food stamps. The surreal includes the Brown House surrounded by a few acres of asparagus, where "fortunes were made overnight," the dream of quick wealth irresistible to Mr. Hattori and its scores of other visitors — "white, yellow, brown, and black."

The Chinese running the gambling den send out a Chinese woman named Mrs. Wu with a plate of Chinese cookies to placate the car full of Japanese Hattoris. At first Joe, the oldest son, can't decide whether or not he likes the cookies since their flavor and texture are "unlike either its American or Japanese counterpart." As a Japanese American, he is being slowly acculturated in his new environment. By the end of the story, Joe and his brothers Bill, Ogden, Ed, and Sam acquire a taste for Mrs. Wu's Chinese cookies, since the boys and their mother find themselves waiting so often in the car for Mr. Hattori to come out of the Brown House. The strawberries and the cookies, both of them unique and yet familiar at the same time, keep the story grounded in the reality of family life, which motivates Mrs. Hattori's display of steadfast devotion. Yet she pays a high price for her selflessness, when the omniscient narrator tells us that Mrs. Wu notices her pregnant again sitting with her sons inside the car, once more waiting for her husband, and "had never before encountered a woman with such bleak eyes."

Questions for Discussion

1. In the middle of the story, when Mrs. Hattori can bear it no longer and leaves her husband, we are told that she takes the baby and the boy born before him with her, but she leaves her other two sons Bill and Ogden with Mr. Hattori. Yamamoto has told us that the Hattori family has five sons, but the name of the oldest son Joe isn't mentioned here. What do you suppose Yamamoto meant by this omission?
2. What do we learn about the Hattori family with the introduction of Mrs. Hattori's sister and nephew into the story?
3. Why doesn't Mrs. Hattori rejoice with her husband after he wins the lottery? How does he experience an illusion of a "wisp of steam" curling out of her nostrils at this time?
4. How does the repetitive depiction of the loyal Japanese American family waiting patiently in their old car outside the Brown house suggest that the narrative functions on one interpretive level as an archetypal fairy tale, with its bleak final words honestly replacing the traditional conclusion that "they all lived happily ever after"?

Topic for Writing

1. Write a review of Yamamoto's prize-winning book *Seventeen Syllables and Other Stories* (1988), in which this story appeared.

Suggested Reading

Yamamoto, Hisaye. *Seventeen Syllables and Other Stories*. Latham, NY: Kitchen Table, Women of Color P, 1988.

PART TWO

POETRY

ROLF AGGESTAM

Lightning Bolt (p. 741)
Fragments (p. 902)

Aggestam was born in the south of Sweden in 1941 and has lived since the early 1970s in Stockholm, where he was one of several important younger poets associated with the literary magazine *Lyrikvännen*. Following his debut with the book *Glimmer* in 1975, he published several collections of poetry and a prose memoir titled *Niagara*, which describes a disturbing journey back to his childhood village and to Denmark with his older brother, who was dying of a brain tumor. The book, published in 1994, won a major literary prize. In 1999, he was awarded the Gerd Bonnier Prize for his work as a poet.

LIGHTNING BOLT

Aggestam, who is married to the novelist and translator Annelie Fridell and has three children, also lives for extended periods in an isolated farmhouse in northern Sweden, and many of his poems, like "Lightning Bolt," reflect his life there. Unlike many poets who present a romantic view of life in the countryside, his writing describes a life that is hard and demanding. The poem is from *To Skin a Lightning Bolt*, published in 1998.

Questions for Discussion

1. The poem has lines and images that illustrate personification. What are they? Are there images in the poem that suggest other figures of speech?
2. The poem is written in direct, unpolished language. How does this help the reader understand what Aggestam is saying about the lightning bolt?
3. What is he suggesting about the lightning bolt when he says it could be stuffed and mounted like an animal? Does this suggest some of the living qualities of lightning?
4. What does he mean by saying the lightning wants to have "earth under the soles of its feet"?

Topic for Writing

1. MAKING CONNECTIONS Other poets in the text also describe nature. Compare this poem with a poem by Robert Frost or Emily Dickinson. Discuss the differences between Aggestam's view of nature and the other poet's views.

FRAGMENTS

Unlike many other contemporary poets, Swedish writer Rolf Aggestam has had as deep an interest in the poetry of the Near East and the Orient as he has in the European poetic traditions. For many years a special area of interest for him has been the early legends of King Arthur and his court as they first emerged in medieval French literature. "Fragments" appeared in his most recent, very successful collection of new work and it was generally considered a summation of many strands of his poetic philosophy.

Questions for Discussion

1. How does Aggestam's "Fragments" relate to other fragments of writing or art that have survived from earlier periods? Why does the first of the fragments end abruptly?
2. What is the inference of the phrase "even my silence / conceals nothing"?
3. What is Aggestam telling us about the poet Rumi that might be taken as a metaphor for the emotions of many poets as they struggle with the long traditions of poetry?
4. Are Rumi's attempts to escape his torment through sex and alcohol also common with other poets through the ages?
5. What is Aggestam inferring with his sly references to academicians and their "choice of words"? Is it clear that Aggestam is familiar with these more familiar areas of poetry studies?
6. How does this comparison with the poet Rumi lead Aggestam to make comparisons to a marathon runner?
7. In the third Fragment what does the poet say about words? Is this a contradiction of what many other writers have told us about the significance of words?
8. How could reading a poem be considered a "waste of time" for both the poet and the reader?
9. Does Aggestam seriously mean that the writing he has done could have been done by anyone? What does he mean to tell the reader with this?
10. What does the fourth Fragment tell us about silence? Often people use the expression *eloquent silence*. Is this an example of this, and how can we interpret it?

Topics for Writing

1. From outside reading compare these "Fragments" with what has survived of other older poets, particularly the classic Greek woman poet Sappho, whose work has survived only in fragments. Discuss how Aggestam has been influenced by these earlier fragments and discuss whether he conceived the poem as a larger metaphor for the meaning of these fragments for our cultural survival.
2. Discuss the consciousness Aggestam presents of that *poetic dimension* in our culture that is inexpressible. Quoting from his poem examine his attitude toward solitude.
3. Compare the experience of the poet Rumi to what we know of the experience of other rebel poets like Shelley and Coleridge and our modern Beat poets like Allen Ginsberg, drawing parallels between their lives and the older poet.
4. In the first Fragment, Aggestam writes of something that he doesn't reveal, even though nothing is concealed. Compare this to the myth of the Sphinx and relate the idea of "mysteries" to attitudes widespread in our own time.

ANONYMOUS

The Daemon Lover (p. 751)

Questions for Discussion

1. What is the ballad form? There are many irregularities in the rhyme as the ballad develops, what reasons could you suggest for this?
2. The ballad is credited to both the Scottish and the English folk traditions. What traces of its Scottish origins does the poem contain?
3. What might be some reasons for the creators of the ballad to set its action in Ireland?
4. At its earliest inception this ballad would have been performed as a song. What elements of the verses suggest this song background?
5. The traditional ballads were commonly the product of a long creative process by which other performers added or changed verses and lines. What signs of this process are there in the ballad's stanzas?
6. Why is the devil presented sympathetically in the opening verses? Does the reader become aware of his presence before the woman herself "espied his cloven foot"?
7. Would the people listening to the ballad at the time of its creation have been surprised by the appearance of the devil? Was this a familiar apparition to these audiences?
8. What is the ballad maker's view of women, as presented in the poem? Was this a prevalent attitude at the time?

Topics for Writing

1. Although the ballad is presented in simple terms it reflects a complicated view of morality and greed and their effect on the woman's decision to abandon her husband and family. Discuss this view of the woman's conduct and using other readings, draw parallels to similar narratives of appearances of the devil during this period.
2. Discuss the role of ballads like these in spreading knowledge as well as entertaining in a historical era when only a handful of people were able to read and write.
3. This ballad was popular in a period when belief in the devil was universal. Discuss how a ballad like this would have affected audiences in its time and whether these folk ballads were in conflict with the teachings of the church or were considered a complement to the scriptural texts.
4. Although the ballads were not written down at the moment they were created, they survived into modern times where they were discovered and documented by a generation of scholars. Describe how this folk tradition succeeded in preserving these songs, and discuss some of the performers who continue to present the old songs to modern audiences.

MATTHEW ARNOLD

Dover Beach (p. 907)

This well-known poem by one of the Victorian era's most important writers has continued to fascinate readers. Although its diction and complex rhyme scheme seem to place it in an older historical context, the poem is in many ways modern. There is no clearly sensed metric form. The first line, "The sea is calm tonight," is a matter-of-fact statement without any kind of hyperbole. Even with the enjambment of the second line — the phrase as the ear hears it is "the moon lies fair upon the straits" — there is still no sense that we are reading a poem from an era in which a poem's diction and vocabulary were expected to be different from everyday speech. It is only Arnold's use of ono-matopoeia in line 11, with its description of the waves streaming up the beach ("Begin and cease, and then begin again"), or the simile of line 23, when the poet writes that reli-gious faith was once like a sea that "Lay like the folds of a bright girdle furl'd," that the modern reader is reminded of the language and technique of the Victorian poets.

The poem is also modern in its disillusionment. The poet and the woman who has come with him to Dover are left alone without solace on a quiet night as they look out at the sea. It is not a difficult poem for modern readers to understand, although students may be confused by the leap in exposition that occurs after the third verse. To paraphrase the poem and its setting most simply, the poet is watching the sea as it sweeps up the beach on a moonlit night, and the sound seems to him to be filled with sadness. The rea-son for his sadness — his consciousness of "the turbid ebb and flow of human misery," as he describes it in line 17 — is not fully revealed until the last verse, but the mood weighs on him so heavily that he is reminded of Sophocles, who also heard the sea with this same mood of melancholy. If students have difficulty making this connection, the "it" of line 16 refers to this "eternal note of sadness," and the "it" of line 20 refers to the phrase again, but in this line Arnold has modified the reference by telling the reader that hearing the sound has given him "a thought." The thought is clarified in the third verse, when he says that religious belief, "The Sea of Faith," once covered the earth; now, how-ever, as the sea retreats from the beach, the poet hears the sound of faith retreating with it. The use of the phrase "naked shingles" to describe the beach in line 28 is a further extension of the mood of sadness that fills the poem's early lines.

Arnold leaps from the descriptive passages of the first three verses to the personal outcry of the last verse. What he has left out — to paraphrase the verse he might have written here — is the explanation that the mood of sadness he feels as he listens to the sea has made him conscious that there is no Sea of Faith surrounding him, and if there is no faith, then he and his loved one are left alone in a confused and frightening world, and for that moment they have only each other to cling to. This shift in mood can confuse readers, who become conscious that the last five lines of the poem seem sarcastic and angry. If there is no faith, then nothing, not even military heroism, has any meaning, and human history is simply the dark spectacle of an appalling world "Where ignorant armies clash by night." If students can supply the missing step in their minds, then the poem will become much clearer to them.

Perhaps the most helpful way to introduce students to the poem is to remind them that it was written in the mid–nineteenth century, when discoveries in geology, archeol-ogy, astronomy, and genetics had shattered the creation stories that Arnold, as a Christian, had been taught. Charles Darwin's *On the Origin of Species* was to become the most debated book of its time, and Arnold's poem is in many ways a direct, anguished response to the confusion and uncertainty that he felt at the new world he was facing — a world without religious faith at its center.

Questions for Discussion

1. In what ways do the questions of religious faith that trouble Arnold in this poem still trouble us today?
2. What is Arnold suggesting in the phrase "the folds of a bright girdle furl'd" in line 23?

3.   What is Arnold suggesting in the image of "the vast edges drear / And naked shingles of the world" in lines 27 and 28?
4.   What is meant in the contrast between the Aegean and "this distant northern sea" in the second verse?
5.   What is the significance of the reference to Sophocles in line 15?
6.   Is the despair Arnold expresses in the poem justified by the events of the years since it was written?

Topics for Writing

1.   "Dover Beach" has a symbolic importance to English readers, and the southern part of England has played an important part in English history. Analyze this role.
2.   At the time Arnold wrote the poem, England and France had been at peace with each other for only thirty-five years, after centuries of intermittent warfare. Explicate the line "ignorant armies clash by night" in terms of this history.
3.   Discuss the effect of the scientific discoveries of the nineteenth century on Christian beliefs.

MARGARET ATWOOD

Siren Song (p. 799)

Although modern translations of the two great epic poems, the *Iliad* and the *Odyssey*, written in pre-Christian Greece by the blind poet Homer, continue to be best-sellers in both the book and the audio-book versions, many students will not be familiar with the reference to the sirens in Atwood's poem. The *Iliad* recounts the story of the Trojan War, in which Greek warriors besieged the city of Troy for ten years to recover Helen, wife of King Menelaus of Sparta, who had been kidnaped by the Trojan prince, Paris. The Greeks entered the city by means of a wooden horse left on the field of battle, which concealed Greek warriors. When the Trojans drew the horse into the city, the warriors emerged during the night and opened the city gates to the Greek armies, who destroyed Troy.

The second part of the epic, the *Odyssey*, follows the wanderings of one of the Greek warriors, Odysseus, as he sails a meandering course home through the eastern Mediterranean Sea. Among the dangers he has to face is the song of the sirens, three maidens who live on a dangerous rocky island and tempt passing ships onto the shoals by the beauty of their singing. To escape the danger, Odysseus has his men tie him to the mast so he cannot yield to the temptation of their song. A modern reminder of the legend persists in the term *siren song*.

Atwood's poem is a humorous retelling of the legend from the point of view of one of the sirens, who demonstrates the effectiveness of the song by pretending to an unwary sailor that she wants to give up her life on the rocks. The sailor's fate is a wry comment on the power of the woman's seductiveness.

Questions for Discussion

1.   How would you describe the tone of the poem? Is it ironic? satirical? compassionate?
2.   Is Atwood commenting on the siren's lack of compassion for her victims or on the weakness of the men who are seduced by her song?

3. Why does the siren describe herself in unflattering terms, referring to herself as "squatting on this island" in her "bird suit"?
4. How does the siren play on the sailors' emotions?

Topics for Writing

1. Discuss whether the use of modern idiom in the poem brings it into our own times, or whether its effectiveness depends on our knowledge of the legend.
2. RESPONDING CREATIVELY   Paraphrase the legend of the sirens in a modern setting; you might consider presenting it in terms of a current musical style.

W. H. AUDEN

Musée des Beaux Arts (p. 908)
Stop All the Clocks (p. 909)
Lay your sleeping head, my love (p. 909)

MUSÉE DES BEAUX ARTS

The painting by the sixteenth-century Flemish artist Pieter Brueghel the Elder that Auden uses as the subject of his poem is in the Museum of Art in Brussels. The painting's full title is *Landscape with the Fall of Icarus*. In the poem Auden alludes to Icarus, a figure from Greek mythology who has fascinated writers and artists for centuries. Icarus attempted to fly, using wings of feathers that he fastened to his shoulders with beeswax. Despite his father's warnings not to go too high, he flew too close to the sun, so that the sun's warmth melted the wax and he fell into the ocean and drowned. The moral of the tale is that a son should listen to his father and not struggle against authority. A larger meaning is that humankind should not attempt to do things for which it was not made, and that challenging the order of the world will only lead to tragedy.

In the painting Auden describes, Icarus, who is ostensibly the composition's subject, is almost lost in a corner of the canvas. In the center foreground, peasant country life goes on in its ordinary way: A farmer is plowing, and behind him a shepherd is tending to a scattered flock of sheep. It is only after you look at the painting for several moments, reminding yourself that Icarus must be there somewhere because the painting is named for him, that you notice two naked legs protruding from the ocean in the lower right-hand corner, almost out of sight of the other people in the painting, who are paying no attention to what is happening. There is also a ship on the ocean, but there is no sign that anyone on board has seen anything. Even the ocean seems unconcerned. As Auden says in line 17, "the sun shone / as it had to on the white legs disappearing into the green / Water."

Auden is saying in his poem that despite suffering and tragedy, life goes on. The style of the poem, which is relaxed and conversational, matches Auden's theme, and the details he describes in the first stanzas are as ordinary as the lives depicted in Brueghel's painting. In his ironic comment, even the horse ridden by a torturer is not to be blamed for anything as it "Scratches its innocent behind on a tree."

Questions for Discussion

1. When Auden uses the word "suffering" in line 1, what is he describing?
2. To what do "miraculous birth" in line 6 and "dreadful martyrdom" in line 10 refer?
3. Auden spent most of his early years as a political activist. Does this poem express activist sentiments?
4. In lines 5 and 6 Auden suggests that it is the older generation who is waiting for something miraculous to happen, while young people are unconcerned. Is this a valid description of young people's attitudes today?

Topics for Writing

1. Discuss how painters and writers have used fables like the story of Icarus as the subject of their work.
2. **MAKING CONNECTIONS**   Many other poets — for instance, Anne Sexton in "The Starry Night" (p. 1008) — have described paintings. Compare Auden's poem with other poems about paintings.
3. Respond to the poem's suggestion that despite whatever miracles or disasters happen to us, life goes on.

STOP ALL THE CLOCKS

Although it is often said that poetry has lost its role as a living voice in contemporary culture, it is possible for a specific poem to make itself heard over the din of voices that dominate our society. Often, however, it is through some other medium that the poem first makes its modest entrance. With "Stop All the Clocks," it was its use in the popular film *Four Weddings and a Funeral.* The poem is recited at the funeral of one of the central figures, and it is perhaps the specific homosexual context of the performance that first attracted attention. The man who speaks the poem so movingly (in a broad Scots dialect) is reciting it for his male lover. The poem became so popular that there were separate printings of small collections of Auden's work taking the poem as the title, and the poem took on an iconic aspect. In the 1930s, when Auden wrote it, his own homosexuality was still a complex, unresolved issue, and the poem opens with what could be best described as a diffident shrug. The performance in the film beautifully captures this mood. The relationship between the two men, one older, the other younger, is presented with humor, almost as a comic undertone, and the first lines, "Stop all the clocks, cut off the telephone, / Prevent the dog from barking with a juicy bone," are rueful, not tragic. A line like "Let the traffic policemen wear black cotton gloves" is clearly intended to be read as satirical. With the next verse, however, beginning with the line "He was my North, my South, my East and West," the poem simply and directly presents us with the reality of a death. The closing line "For nothing now can ever come to any good," could have come at the conclusion of an anguished response to the death of a lover at any moment in the long traditions of English and American poetry. Although the poem would seem to have a specific subject in Auden's life, the Auden scholar Edward Mendelson, in his *The English Auden,* identifies it as a reworking of a song from the play *The Ascent of F6,* and the poem, in its first versions, referred to characters in the play

Questions for Discussion

1. What is the rhyme scheme of "Stop All the Clocks"? Many of the lines are in iambic pentameter, but there are also lines in tetrameter and hexameter, and there is a mingling of dactylic and trochaic meter. How does this metric variety affect your response to the poem? Do you perceive it as a conscious attempt to achieve a more natural speech rhythm in the lines or as a lack of discipline on Auden's part?

2. The final verse can be read as a metaphor for human grief. What personal equivalents could be substituted for the verse's grand proposals?
3. What is the term for the elevated suggestion of this verse?
4. Auden has substituted the word "moaning" for the sound of the airplane overhead. What is the term for this figure of speech?

Topics for Writing

1. In "Stop All the Clocks," there is a blending of public mourning and private grief. Discuss these elements of the poem and present alternatives to the gestures of public mourning that Auden suggests. Consider the reasons the poet presents many of these gestures of mourning as humorous.
2. Discuss the compositional elements of "Stop All the Clocks," analyzing the use of meter and rhyme. Notice particularly lines such as line 2. Auden could have kept the line to five metric stresses by dropping the adjective "juicy," but he chose to include the adjective and leave the line in hexameter. Discuss this choice.

LAY YOUR SLEEPING HEAD, MY LOVE

Questions for Discussion

1. Although the poem is not written in rhyme, Auden has used a consistent meter for the line length. What is the meter of the lines?
2. What is Auden implying in the second line, "Human on my faithless arm"? Is he telling the reader from the beginning that he does not intend to be faithful to this love? What might be his reasons?
3. How does the grave prove "the child ephemeral"?
4. Why does the poet insist that there shall be no punishment for this night? What is the "pedantic boring cry"?
5. Why does Auden contrast love's "enchanted slope" and the lovers' "ordinary swoon"? Is he being ironic?
6. What is the poet telling the reader of this night when he says "Certainty, fidelity / On the stroke of midnight pass / Like vibrations of a bell"? Is he intimating that this night is something that cannot be judged by ordinary moral constraints?
7. What consolations does Auden offer for the slights of the daytime hours and the "nights of insult"?

Topics for Writing

1. Auden has written a love poem that is not so much a declaration of love, but an explanation of why this night will do for a moment of love. Discuss the poem's stance toward the conventional social attitudes of fidelity and commitment. Compare it to Elizabeth Barrett Browning's "How Do I Love Thee?" (p. 775) and contrast the contradictory views of love the two poems present.
2. Auden's poem is a wry presentation of a night with a lover. There are a number of love poems in the anthology. Read several of them and try to find a common theme that unites them, or discuss what is different about each of them and their avowals of love, using citations from the poems themselves.
3. The language of Auden's poem is grounded in classic English verse. Discuss its use of metaphor and image, and relate it to the syntax of other poetry which would have been a model for Auden.
4. As an exercise in close reading, write a prose paraphrase of the first stanza of the poem, clarifying each of its ideas and emphasizing the moral stance which Auden has taken.

RONALD BAATZ

as though the whole earth (p. 790)
our beautiful old love (p. 790)
The Oldest Songs (p. 889)
Only for the Old and the Fragile (p. 890)

AS THOUGH THE WHOLE EARTH

OUR BEAUTIFUL OLD LOVE

Some students may have been introduced to the haiku in the lower grades, where there is an emphasis on a specific three-line haiku form in English, written with five syllables in the two outer lines and seven lines in the middle line. These haiku of Ronald Baatz conform to the three-line form, but the first haiku has fourteen syllables and the second sixteen, and there is no attempt at conformity in the syllable count of specific lines. Students should be reminded that the original poems in Japanese are written in ideograms which cannot be translated into precise English syllabic equivalents. A Japanese poet, who for some years was president of the American haiku society, simply wrote his haiku in English in a single line, following the Japanese form of one style of haiku. It is the concentration of language and the precision of the image evoked that is closer to the heart of the haiku.

In the first of his haiku, Baatz has achieved his effect by reversing the order in which the image would be presented in ordinary speech. He is saying "There were so many crickets singing that it sounded like the whole earth were ringing," but by beginning with the immensity of the sound itself — "as though the whole earth / were ringing" — he has given the reader a moment to savor the image, then he follows it with the explanation of the source of the sound. He has used a similar technique in the second haiku, emphasizing the opening line "our beautiful old love." Instead of writing "our beautiful old love / is on such thin ice," he has dropped the anticipated verb *is*, which leads to the next phrase — the reader's eye lingers a moment on the first image of a "beautiful old love." He then offers the reader a surprise with the image of himself and his estranged love standing on ice so thin that even to shiver would send them breaking through the fragile surface.

THE OLDEST SONGS

ONLY FOR THE OLD AND THE FRAGILE

Ronald Baatz lives in a farmhouse in the Catskill Mountains, not far from Woodstock in state of New York. He writes of the life around his house: the birds, the nearby pond, and the seasons with an acute consciousness of his own life in these surroundings.

Questions for Discussion

1.   Although Baatz's poems are written in open form they have a different appearance on the page. How does his spacing of the lines differ from other open-form poems you have read?

2. Why does Baatz title his poem "The Oldest Songs"? Is he presenting the reader with the idea that there is a life of the earth preceding the arrival of our species? How does this effect our reading of the poem?
3. Baatz has chosen to describe the birds calling to each other as "warnings." Does he know with any assurance what the songs of birds in March mean? Why might he have chosen to interpret them as warnings?
4. How does Baatz characterize the July sunlight? How does this differ from his description of the sunlight he enjoys sitting out on his porch in March?
5. In "Only for the Old and the Fragile" Baatz sets a series of goals for himself. Are these modest goals? How do they contrast with his idea that he would like to "charm the birds out of the trees"?
6. Why does Baatz say that people who have been said to "charm the birds" from trees are spoken of with "very / noticeable envy"?
7. Is there any reality in the fantasy Baatz presents of being lifted from the earth by birds?
8. What does he mean by "a painting by chagall"?
9. Is fame ever "completely out / of the question" for a writer or an artist? What is Baatz telling the reader about himself with this idea?
10. Is there an anachronism between Baatz's statement that he has no interest in ordinary goals like fame or money but he would like to achieve an entirely impossible dream of being lifted by birds as an old man?
11. Is there any reality in his idea of a "gracious death" as a "worthwhile act"? What is Baatz telling the reader by presenting it as an ideal goal?

Topics for Writing

1. Baatz writes in an everyday language. To emphasize the ordinariness of his expression, no two lines follow each other with the same spacing. At the same time, there is a precision and a clarity to the images he presents in his poems. Discuss the specific activities he mentions in "The Oldest Songs" and their relationship to each other and to what the student perceives as the theme of the poem.
2. Although Baatz is clearly an engaged observer of the natural life around his house he maintains an objective distance between himself and what he is describing. Using examples from the two poems, discuss the attitude he presents of himself as observer rather than participant in the activities he sees. Does this give the poetry a distinctive character or could his responses be considered typical of anyone who closely observes the natural world around them?
3. In "The Oldest Songs" the writer suggests the idea of the renewal of life after a difficult winter with his consciousness of the birds singing of "the earth's / oldest songs." Discuss this concept and include examples and images from his other poems in *Literature and Its Writers* to develop this idea.
4. In "Only for the Old and the Fragile" Baatz writes, "i have no desire to accumulate / wealth, and fame is completely out / of the question." This is a concept echoed by many poets and artists. Discuss its meaning in terms of their work and their attitude toward their society. Compare Baatz's statement to the decision of Thoreau to live alone in a cabin outside of his village of Concord.
5. The dream of communicating with nature has been a continual human fantasy, particularly in children's literature. Compare Baatz's image of himself and his wife being lifted by birds with other examples from the students' reading of human interaction with animals or birds. If possible, compare it to images from stories remembered from childhood.

AMIRI BARAKA

Legacy (p. 842)

Baraka was born as Leroi Jones in Newark, New Jersey, in 1934, and until he was thirty-one he lived in Greenwich Village with his wife Hettie Jones, who was white, and then with poet Diane di Prima, who also was white, fathering children with each of them. His writing reflected the moods and the stylistic mannerisms of the nascent Beat movement, and with Hettie Jones he was an important element of the new ferment with the magazine *Yugen* and Totem Press, which published many of the younger writers. In association with di Prima he continued his activities with *The Floating Bear,* a seminal publication that published much of the important experimental writing of the time. His response, however, to the assassination of black Muslim leader Malcolm X in 1965 led him to renounce his life with a wife who was not black and with his white friends, and to move to Harlem, where he founded the Black Arts Repertory Theater. A year later, after converting to the Kawaida branch of the Muslim faith, he changed his name to Amiri Baraka and moved to Newark, where he established a black community united in their struggle against what they conceived as the evil of American racism. His activism led to beatings and arrests by the Newark police, and his later years have been marked by controversy, which hasn't, however, led to his abandonment of his ideals. This early poem reflects his involvement with the aesthetics of the Beat movement and anticipates his later political commitment.

Questions for Discussion

1. "Legacy" is dedicated to the people who created the blues. What are some of the things that Baraka finds so moving in their way of life?
2. Is there a precise meaning to the image "cluttered eyes / of early mysterious night"? Is there some visual image that comes to mind?
3. Could a southern black man also reach for a lash, as in line 6? Could this refer to the man's work of plowing, or is Baraka here writing about a southern white?
4. When he describes riding to another town that is also black, what is he telling us? Does this relate to the fact that people are asleep "Down a road"?
5. Why does the poet describe the songs as having a "pretended sea" as a theme?

Topics for Writing

1. MAKING CONNECTIONS   In his other writing, Baraka has presented the idea of all African American culture as a "blues" culture. Discuss his definition of this concept, using examples from other work by African American poets in this anthology.
2. MAKING CONNECTIONS   "Legacy" has textual affinities to Etheridge Knight's poem "The Idea of Ancestry" (p. 841). Compare the two poems as examples of oral poetry, and examine the role of writing like this in the black consciousness.
3. MAKING CONNECTIONS   Baraka's writing continues many of the themes of the writers of the Harlem Renaissance. Compare his writing to the works of poets like Claude McKay and Langston Hughes, and discuss their attitudes toward the racial dilemma.

JUDITH BARRINGTON

Villanelles for a Drowned Parent, VI (p. 783)

Judith Barrington is one of a group of American poets who are drawn to the discipline of traditional poetic forms. In this poem, one of a series written, as she said, following the death of her mother by drowning, she turned to this discipline as a relief from her grief. The complicated effort to create the poems became an emotional catharsis, which is reflected in this villanelle.

Questions for Discussion

1. The form of the poem is the classic villanelle. What is its pattern of rhyme and repetition of lines?
2. What is she saying with the image "fathomed room"?
3. What other images does she use in the poem to refer to the sea?
4. In the fourth stanza she feels the sea drawing her closer. Is this an emotional response to her mother's death in the sea?
5. What pattern of waves is she describing in the image "like doors that slowly swing ajar"?

Topics for Writing

1. **MAKING CONNECTIONS** Compare this poem with Dylan Thomas's villanelle "Do Not Go Gentle into That Good Night" (p. 784). Each poem has death as a subject, but discuss the differences or similarities in their response to death's realities.
2. Discuss the poem's role in Barrington's struggle with her grief. The discussion could center around the fifth stanza, beginning "Your voice in the wind. . . ."

STEPHEN VINCENT BENÉT

1935 (p. 836)

It is sometimes hard to remember that poetry, like everything else in our culture, has its unpredictable fashions and abrupt, dazzling moments of temporary fame, because so much of the poetry we read in the classroom today seems to have been popular since the beginning of time. Stephen Vincent Benét was one of these writers whose fame, for a decade, seemed to assure his place among the dominant figures of modern American poetry. Today he is largely forgotten, and the book that established his reputation, the epic narrative poem *John Brown's Body,* is now read only as a piece from its own times. Benét, however, was a committed writer, with a clear eye and a balanced assessment of the social situation of the period between the two World Wars, and his best work, in both poetry and short stories, still has a distinct, incisive bite.

Benét was born in Pennsylvania in 1898, and in 1919 received his B.A. from Yale University. His first book, *Five Men and Pompey* (1915), was published when he was an undergraduate. In the stream of books that followed, critic Louis Untermeyer noted that "For a while [he] was too prolific to be critical." But in 1928, with the publication of *John Brown's Body,* a dramatic poetic retelling of the story of John Brown and the American Civil War, Benét reached hundreds of thousands of readers, was awarded the Pulitzer Prize, and found himself famous overnight.

During the Depression, which followed only brief years after his first success, Benét was insistent on continuing to point to what he perceived as the injustices and stigma of racism that were burning issues in the 1930s. He was also perceptive enough to see the threat of the approaching new World War, and this strongly imagined poem is his cry against the renewed carnage looming on the horizon.

Questions for Discussion

1. What is the metric structure of the poem? How does it resemble the meters of early traditional ballads, and how is it different from them?
2. Is the rhyme scheme also similar to older forms of the ballad?
3. What is the scene Benét is describing?
4. Why does he protest against what the dead soldiers are doing as they lay new barbed wire on old battlegrounds?
5. What is he referring to in the phrase "It is seventeen years"?
6. What do we understand about his attitude toward war in the harsh image "the last, blind war"?

Topics for Writing

1. Consider the historical context of the poem and discuss its relevance to its own times.
2. Some writers have insisted that the role of the poet is to stand above the political conflicts and the social movements of the day. Discuss how this attitude would affect the way some readers would look at this poem.
3. The poem continues to have relevance for our own times. Discuss how the date of the title and the poem's description of the men's weapons would be adapted to today's realities.

ELIZABETH BISHOP

The Bight (p. 736)
Sestina (p. 782)
The Fish (p. 911)
One Art (p. 913)

"The Bight" is analyzed in Chapter 9, and the form of "Sestina" is discussed in Chapter 11. The subject of "Sestina" is clearly Bishop's own childhood. Her father died when she was only eight months old, and after her mother suffered a mental breakdown Bishop was sent to live with her grandmother in Nova Scotia. Her grandmother's father had also died when she was a child, so although Bishop doesn't identify the reason for the grief that is so palpable in the poem, the fact that the child and her grandmother both feel it makes it clear that this is what Bishop is describing.

Bishop's poetry is popular with students because both her subject and the means with which she presents it are clear and immediately understandable. What makes her writing so useful for classroom discussion is that students also have no problem reading a Bishop poem for its technical skill and secondary meanings. On a first reading the class will have no difficulty with "The Fish." The narrator has caught a large ugly fish, and as she pulls it halfway out of the water, she sees from the old hooks and lines in its mouth that it has been caught before, but each time it has been strong enough to break free. When she realizes what an event it is for her to have caught a fish like this, she feels a sense of victory fill the air around her, and she lets the fish go.

If the class has already read the text's analysis of "The Bight," they are conscious of some of the imaginative ways in which Bishop works with diction and imagery. In the first line of "The Fish," the word "tremendous" is unexpected. It seems too momentous a word for the act of fishing. It does, however, prepare us for the ending of the poem, with its intonation of "rainbow, rainbow, rainbow!" — which is also more dramatic terminology than we'd expect. When you add the detail that the fish didn't fight at all, it seems that nothing about the fish is what you would expect. Line 7 is a remarkable example of Bishop's ability to compress words for effect. The line tells us that it's a very big fish that makes a grunt sound in only five words: "He hung a grunting weight." The three adjectives Bishop chooses to describe the fish are also chosen for effect. She gives us three points of description, almost like a triangulation, and where the three adjectives meet we have the fish, "Battered . . . venerable . . . homely."

Bishop has already managed to tell us so much about the fish that we almost don't need more, but she goes on to a brilliant simile: "his brown skin hung in strips / like an ancient wallpaper." Her description continues as she finds more and more to tell us about the fish, using simile and metaphor to compress and illustrate. She manages to show us a fish that is like most other fish, but at the same time she shows us how complex and miraculous a physical body is, and as we read about her fish we can't help being conscious of our own bodies. The fish deserves its medals of old bent hooks and frayed lines, and in the final lines is the consciousness that part of the victory belongs to the fish.

Although it is one of Bishop's later poems, "One Art" has so much of the arch tone and mocking self-irony of poetry written in the 1920s by women poets such as Elinor Wylie and Louise Bogan that it might have been an early poem that she didn't publish until this later date. It is also an exercise in rhyming virtuosity that is similar to many of Wylie's and Bogan's experiments. The poem is a villanelle; there are only two rhymes, aba, the same sounds occurring in each verse, and the a rhyme is repeated in the last line. It is probably no coincidence that one of the rhymes — *master, disaster, fluster, last or,* and so forth — is feminine, and the other — *intent, spent, meant,* and so forth — is masculine.

Questions for Discussion

1. What is similar between the ways the child and her grandmother each feels grief in "Sestina"?
2. In "The Fish," why does some of the narrator's feeling of victory also seem to have been won by the fish?
3. Although some of the details of "One Art" are very personal — "two cities . . . two rivers" — could this poem also have an emotional meaning for readers? Could they substitute personal details of their own?

Topics for Writing

1. Analyze each use of the word tears in "Sestina" and how these uses prepare for the phrase "Time to plant tears" in the poem's final stanza.
2. In his novella *The Old Man and the Sea*, Ernest Hemingway describes an old Cuban fisherman who also catches a "tremendous" fish, but he is so determined to bring it back to harbor that he keeps it tied to the side of his boat, even after sharks have stripped it and nothing is left of it but bones. Consider whether Hemingway's fisher performs a masculine act and Bishop's fisher performs a feminine act.

3. **MAKING CONNECTIONS** Marianne Moore, whom Bishop regarded as her mentor, also wrote a poem titled "The Fish" (p. 991). Compare and contrast the two poems.

Commentary

Brett C. Millier, *"On Elizabeth Bishop's 'One Art,'"* p. 1062.

WILLIAM BLAKE

From *Songs of Innocence*: Introduction (p. 914)
The Lamb (p. 914)
Holy Thursday (p. 915)
The Little Boy Lost (p. 915)
The Little Boy Found (p. 916)
From *Songs of Experience*: Introduction (p. 916)
The Sick Rose (p. 916)
The Tyger (p. 917)
London (p. 917)
A Poison Tree (p. 918)
The Garden of Love (p. 918)

It may be helpful to students if the instructor clarifies the connection between Blake's *Songs of Innocence* and *Songs of Experience*. Conceived as a children's book, *Songs of Innocence* (1789) consisted of thirty-one engraved and hand-colored plates, with illustrations of country scenes and floral decorations on every page. Only twenty-one copies are known to exist, so the work probably should be called a kind of art print multiple instead of a book, which suggests that copies went into bookstores and had some public circulation. There is no evidence of a separate publication of *Songs of Experience*. In 1794 Blake added the engraved plates of the new *Experience* poems to the original book and printed the two groups of poems together. Two different poems, "The Little Boy Lost" and "The Little Girl Lost," were added to the group of *Experience* poems. The title page of the complete collection read *Songs of Innocence and of Experience,* and there was a descriptive subtitle: "Shewing the Two Contrary States of the Human Soul." Over the next several years copies were printed and then hand-colored by Blake's wife to fill an order from a subscriber. Only twenty-four copies survive, so it had as small a circulation as the earlier version of the book.

The poems in these two small collections are so different from Blake's complex and difficult "prophetic" books that readers often assume that the *Innocence* and *Experience* poems are an earlier state of his development as a poet. The truth is, however, that before the *Innocence* poems he had already published an undistinguished collection of ordinary verse, followed by several works that many of today's readers consider "difficult," as did the few people who read them in Blake's time. Between the *Innocence* poems and the *Experience* poems Blake published or printed some of these ambitious longer works, again written in a visionary language that is often almost incomprehensible. The simplest explanation for the difference between these poems and the rest of his work is that he was writing the *Innocence* poems, at least in the first group, for children. As he writes in his Introduction to *Songs of Innocence,* "I wrote my happy songs / Every child may joy to hear." It is the quality of childish, innocent joy and experience that makes the poems unique.

Students usually have little difficulty reading Blake. During the Haight-Ashbury days of the 1960s, San Francisco rock bands would sometimes recite Blake from the stage, and Beat poet Allen Ginsberg recorded an entire album of his own musical settings of the poems. The "contrary states" Blake described in the subtitle are the metaphysical contradictions he found around him. In the book he matches pairs of poems to expose the harsh contrasts between the paradise of mankind's living in a natural state — the innocence of childhood — and the despair and constraints of eighteenth-century England.

FROM *SONGS OF INNOCENCE: INTRODUCTION*
FROM *SONGS OF EXPERIENCE: INTRODUCTION*
THE LAMB
THE TYGER

There are several paired poems in the volumes Blake printed later. In the Introduction to *Songs of Innocence,* he describes himself as a happy piper who responds to a child's laughing wish that he pipe a melody about a lamb. As the "child" vanishes, it asks the piper to write down his songs "In a book that all may read," and the poems that follow are his songs. The Introduction to *Songs of Experience,* on the other hand, is a somber, muffled, portentous call to "Hear the voice of the Bard." In the last verses he cries out to the earth to return, despite the night, as the night's "starry floor" and "watery shore" are still the earth's until sunrise.

One of the most obvious matched pairs of poems is "The Lamb" from *Innocence* and "The Tyger" from *Experience.* "The Lamb" is a gentle hymn praising Jesus Christ, and it wouldn't have been out of place in a children's prayer book of the time. The poem can be sung as a hymn in which the two lines that open and close each verse function as a chorus. These lines have three accents, and the six interior lines of each verse have four accents. The meter is trochaic throughout. The effect of the contrasting lines is like a softly breathed introductory chorus followed by a recitative; the verse closes with the repeated soft chorus. As a class exercise, students can perform the poem, reading the chorus line slowly and the interior lines more quickly. They will immediately hear the effect Blake intended. The poem's religious theme is echoed in its soft tones, its "l" sounds, and the internal alliterations of lines such as "Gave thee clothing of delight / Softest clothing, wooly, bright."

"The Tyger," with its hard accents and its strident, fearful imagery, is clearly something completely different, although there never has been any agreement as to how Blake meant the poem to be read. A collaborative note by two European scholars, John Chalker and Erik Frykman, presents one of the most widely held views: " 'The Tyger' expresses a sense of awe in the face of the mysterious and uncontrollable energy of life that the tiger symbolizes, and asks whether it is possible that animals so different as the lamb and the tiger should be the work of the same Creator. As well as symbolizing gentleness and energy, the lamb and the tiger express dual aspects of the personality of Christ." Many of the details of the poem — the "fire of thine eye" in line 6, "twist the sinews of thy heart" in line 10, "What the hammer? what the chain?" in line 13, and "When the stars threw down their spears" in line 17 — also suggest a visceral linking to the language and imagery of Milton's *Paradise Lost,* and if this was Blake's intention, then it is the figure of Satan that the tiger symbolizes. The stars, in this interpretation, would be the fallen angels who have thrown down their weapons after their defeat by God's angels.

Students may have difficulty following "The Tyger," but if they read it closely, they will find that it has many parallels with "The Lamb." In "The Lamb" the question is, Does the lamb know who created it? In "The Tyger" the question of lines 3–4 is, Who could have had the power to create something like this tiger? One of the immediate problems is the word *frame*. Blake means it in the way that a builder frames a house. A workable and helpful reading of lines 3 and 4 might be, What immortal force or skill could have shaped something of your fearful proportions? The fire in the eyes in line 6 is one of the materials that was brought to the tiger's creation, and the lines that follow ask who this powerful creator might be who could construct such a beast. The questions in the last line of the stanza, "What dread hand? and what dread feet?" are so compressed that they seem cryptic on first reading, but what Blake is asking is, What is the power that could have created that dread hand or foot? Blake doesn't answer the question of the first lines, because it is obvious to him that no other power than God could have created the tiger. It is the same power that created the lamb. Blake's final question, in lines 19–20, is, What did its creator think of the creature it had shaped and brought to life?

Questions for Discussion

1. Does Blake intend a contradiction in lines 7–8 of "The Lamb," when he says that the lamb has such a tender voice that it can make all the valleys rejoice? What does Blake mean here?

2. In "The Lamb" the question is answered about who created the lamb. In "The Tyger" the question is not answered, but Blake's questions about who might be the creator are only rhetorical. How do we know from the poem that Blake is certain of his answer?

3. How would students paraphrase Blake's wondering questions in lines 19–20 of "The Tyger"? What is Blake's meaning in lines 7–8?

4. Is there some similarity in what Blake is describing in "The Tyger" to the well-known story of the Frankenstein monster?

5. What is Blake suggesting when he tells us that the creator of the tiger would have to have had almighty power?

HOLY THURSDAY
THE LITTLE BOY LOST
THE LITTLE BOY FOUND

These poems from *Innocence* continue the collection's mood of childish joy, although one describes a gathering of London's workhouse children, and in the "Lost" and "Found" poems the child is frightened and tearful. "Holy Thursday" is a hymnlike celebration of the one day a year that children from the London workhouses are brought to St. Paul's Cathedral for a special service. The meter of the poem is unusual — iambic heptameter, seven accents to each line. Several of the lines, however, are punctuated to divide them into units of four and three stresses, which is the familiar meter of popular ballads. The lines that are not divided are heard with the same metrical division. Blake undoubtedly wrote the poem with the longer linear unit to give it a more imposing appearance on the page. It is one of his most sympathetic responses to children's life in the city. He describes them as "these flowers of London town" in line 5, and his sympathy even includes the church functionaries, the "Grey headed beadles," and the men who are responsible for the children's care, the "wise guardians of the poor." This is one of the few moments in Blake's writing where he accepts (or seems to accept) the church and its role in English society.

"The Little Boy Lost" and "The Little Boy Found" seem like simple lyrics of a child's experience of being lost at night on the fen. Because this poem is included in the *Innocence* section, it is followed immediately with the reassuring poem describing the boy, with God's help, being found by his mother. There is an ambiguous note in the poem. When the boy cries out for his father in line 5 of "The Little Boy Lost," "no father was there." In line 4 of "The Little Boy Found," God appears to the boy "like his father in white." Blake is probably suggesting that the boy's father is dead and that the father's spirit has led him to his mother, alone in the night, searching for him.

Questions for Discussion

1. Why does Blake use the image of the "Thames' waters" in line 4 of "Holy Thursday"?
2. What is Blake telling us about the children in line 7 of "Holy Thursday"?
3. How would you paraphrase the last line of "Holy Thursday"?
4. In "The Little Boy Lost" and "The Little Boy Found" there is an intimation that the boy's father is dead and that God has acted through his father's spirit to save the boy. Clarify this interpretation through the details in the two poems.
5. What is Blake telling us in the last line of "The Little Boy Lost," "And away the vapour flew"?

THE SICK ROSE
LONDON
A POISON TREE
THE GARDEN OF LOVE

Students will immediately notice how the mood in these poems differs from those of *Innocence*. "The Sick Rose" is clearly a metaphor for something that is eating at the heart of the rose, a symbol of love and joy. There are many interpretations of the poem, but one that perhaps comes closest to Blake's meaning is that the rose here symbolizes sexual love, described as "thy bed / Of crimson joy." Because the worm is described as "dark secret love," it is probably a metaphor for venereal disease, which Blake describes, again in oblique language, in the poem "London."

"London" is one of Blake's most explicitly political poems, and for many readers the London he describes could be any city in our modern world. The word "chartered" in lines 1 and 2 means for Blake the restrictions that hem in natural life in the city. It refers to the charter of the City of London, which is its basis for governing. In line 8 the "mind-forged manacles I hear" represent Blake's judgment that the chains that bind the people he sees on London's streets were created by the people themselves. The "youthful harlot's curse" in the last line can be taken in two ways — one meaning the curses of a street prostitute as she cries out to a customer, and the other the curse of venereal disease, which at the time was virtually incurable and raged through every level of society. Marriage, Blake suggests in the last two lines of the poem, will bring only sickness and death to the married couple and their child.

"A Poison Tree" is a paradox. The moral is that with a friend you can be open, and any anger between you will dissipate in your open exchange about it. With a foe you nurse your anger until it grows and grows. In Blake's parable, his anger blossoms into a flower, which tempts the foe and kills him when he comes too close. "The Garden of Love" demonstrates the other side of the feelings about churches and priests that Blake presented in "Holy Thursday." This is the same outrage at organized religion's denial of the human right to happiness that he intimates in the image of the "black'ning church" in "London."

Questions for Discussion

1. Although the "invisible worm" in "The Sick Rose" is usually interpreted as venereal disease, are there other possible interpretations?
2. In line 2 of "London," when Blake speaks of "the chartered Thames," what is he saying ironically about the river?
3. Explain Blake's meaning in line 8, "The mind-forged manacles I hear."
4. In the third verse is he blaming the church for the plight of the chimney sweeps and the government for the deaths of soldiers in battle?
5. What does he mean specifically in line 15 by "the new-born Infant's tear"?
6. In "A Poison Tree" what does Blake mean by "the pole" in line 14?
7. Is the first verse of "The Garden of Love" a metaphor for childhood or his early manhood?
8. In line 8, is Blake saying that organized religion is the death of love? Could there be other interpretations?
9. Blake creates an ironic singsong effect in the last two lines of the poem. What are the internal rhymes?

ROBERT BLY

Welcoming a Child in the Limantour Dunes (p. 786)

Questions for Discussion

1. This is an example of the poetic form called a *prose poem*. What is different about this poem from poems in open form? Is the difference in the form itself or is it also a difference in the poem's content?
2. Bly's description of the grains of sand is an example of the figure of speech called *personification*. How has he personified the sand? Does he have a reason for his statement that the sand grains "love a worried man"? Is this statement justified by the poem's theme?
3. What do you think is his meaning in the statement "Something loves even this planet"? Is it a statement of religious faith? Why has he used the word "something"?
4. What is the meaning in Bly's statement that this planet has been "abandoned"? Is this a contradiction of the phrase that precedes it, "Something loves even this planet"?
5. What is Bly telling us about the unborn child who "floats inside the Pacific of the womb"? What is his meaning in the image of the "Pacific of the womb"?
6. Why does Bly tell us that to be alone the girl must not have a horse with her? Is he referring to the cliché in films of a woman with a horse on the beach?
7. What is he telling us about the unborn child in his final image, that the child is "feeling the breakers roaring"?

Topics for Discussion

1. MAKING CONNECTIONS   Many poets have used the image of the ocean to suggest birth or life. Read other poems that also utilize this image, among them

Matthew Arnold's "Dover Beach" (p. 907 or Walt Whitman's "Out of the Cradle Endlessly Rocking" (which can be found in another source) and compare the use of the sea as an image, discussing reasons why the sea has been used so often by poets as an inspiration.

2. The poem has a number of references to religious faith, among them the image of the mole in his "Vatican" and Bly's statement that "Something loves even this planet." Discuss these references to religious faith in the poem and examine what can be inferred of Bly's own religious feelings from what he has written.

3. Discuss Bly's image of the unborn child floating in the "Pacific of the womb," examining its relation to the other sea images of the poem, using quotes from the text.

4. **RESPONDING CREATIVELY**   As a project in understanding the form of a prose poem, rewrite the poem in a series of lines as though it were an open form poem. Discuss the differences between the two ways of presenting the ideas of the poem and suggest the advantages or the disadvantages of writing the poem as a *prose poem*, as Bly has done.

ARNA BONTEMPS

A Black Man Talks of Reaping (p. 867)

Arna Bontemps was born in Louisiana in 1902, but when he was three, a racial threat to his father forced the family to flee to Los Angeles, where he grew up. His father was an active member of the Seventh Day Adventist church, and when Bontemps was fifteen, he was sent to study in a church-operated white boarding school, which had made some moves toward integration. Bontemps continued his education in California, then in 1924 he moved to Harlem to teach at the Seventh Day Adventist Academy. He began publishing poetry at this time, while also writing prose. His first novel, *God Sends Sunday,* published in 1931, had a secular tone that upset church officials, who transferred him to their Oakwood Junior College in Huntsville, Alabama. Bontemps left the school in 1934, moving first to California, then to Chicago. In 1943 he was awarded a master's degree in library science from the University of Chicago, and became a librarian at Nashville's Fisk University, where he continued to work, with occasional interruptions, until his death in 1973.

Questions for Discussion

1. What are the rhyme scheme and the meter of the poem? Is it written in a traditional English verse form?

2. What does Bontemps mean by the image "I have sown beside all waters in my day"?

3. What image does he employ to tell us what little he has to show for all his labor?

4. He has written only of the land from "Canada to Mexico." Could he just as well have included countries like Jamaica, Cuba, or Brazil?

5. Is there a sense of pride expressed in the line "I planted safe against this stark, lean year"?

6. How does he intend us to understand the phrase "My brother's sons"?

Topics for Writing

1. Beneath its studied tone, this is an angry poem of racial protest. Discuss the situation Bontemps has described.

2. Several of the poets of the Harlem Renaissance turned to poetry to express their anger at the racial situation of their day. Consider whether poetry is an effective medium for expressing these attitudes, using the poems in this section as examples.

ANNE BRADSTREET

To My Dear and Loving Husband (p. 919)
Before the Birth of One of Her Children (p. 920)
In Memory of My Dear Grand-Child Elizabeth Bradstreet, Who Deceased August, 1665, Being a Year and a Half Old (p. 920)

Students will find these poems easily comprehensible. The first is a love poem from a wife to her husband; the second and third respond to the harsh realities of death during childbirth and in early childhood. Although many of the physical circumstances of the poems have changed over the years, the emotions Bradstreet expresses continue to be with us today. For students, the points of difference and the points of similarity between their own experiences and the life of an American woman who lived four centuries ago can become a stimulating basis for classroom discussion.

What modern readers also sense in Bradstreet is an independence of spirit that seems at times almost contemporary, even though she is writing within the confines of her role as dutiful wife and practicing Christian in what was still virtually the wilderness of seventeenth-century Massachusetts. In his discussion of Bradstreet in the chapter "The Poetry of Colonial America" in *The Columbia Literary History of the United States* (1988), William J. Scheick writes,

> She apparently sensed within herself a somewhat rebellious disposition toward a number of features in her world, a rebelliousness she tended to think of as a manifestation of pride or vanity. Time and again her poetry reflects her personal search for humility, the virtue opposed to vanity. . . . In fact, Bradstreet seems to have been a very outspoken person, a quality that she liked in herself but that she worried about carrying to vain excess both in her life and her verse. It is a mistake to see her as someone subdued or see her poetry as work deflated by the pressure of an androcentric Puritan cul- ture. . . . It is this forthright, feeling person we especially meet in the late poetry, where she is more personally engaged in her quest for poetic form and technique.

Bradstreet's poetic achievement is all the more remarkable when we consider that she was isolated from any literary contacts and was raising eight children at a time when a woman in her social position was responsible for every aspect of household management. She seemed almost intuitively to grasp the principles of versification, even the complex idioms of the poetry of the period. "To My Dear and Loving Husband" is an example of what Elizabethan writers called "conceits" — clever and revealing ways of playing with words and ideas — and it ends with a paradox that is reminiscent of the poems of John Donne. The meaning of the first line, of course, is "it's as if we were the same person," but Bradstreet catches our attention with her wordplay, "then surely we." She follows it with a similar device in the second line, "then thee." The hyperbole of the wife's description of how much she prizes her husband's love and how much she loves him in return has the extravagances of Elizabethan rhetoric, and the paradox of the last line — "when we live no more, we may live ever" — echoes the theme of Donne's sonnet "Death, be not proud."

The two poems responding to childbirth and infant mortality are written more directly, as if her apprehension at the approach of yet another childbirth and the threat of death that hung over the uncertain lives of her small children required her to speak more directly, without conceit. The risk of death during childbirth was so great that in her "Before the Birth of One of Her Children" she says farewell to her husband, facing the possibility that she might not survive the ordeal. The poem in itself is a suggestion of the distances that our world has traveled since the lines were written.

Questions for Discussion

1. In line 6 of "To My Dear and Loving Husband," "Or all the riches that the east doth hold," to what is Bradstreet referring?
2. In line 9, "Thy love is such I can no way repay," the speaker suggests that she feels her husband's love is a gift to her. How does a modern reader respond to this concept of a husband's love as a gift?
3. What is the type of rhyme used in the last two lines?
4. Is the speaker suggesting in these lines that the reward she and her husband may expect for loving each other will be a shared eternal life?
5. In line 12 of the poem "Before the Birth of One of Her Children," Bradstreet writes, "I may seem thine, who in effect am none." What is she telling her husband? Was this a common belief at the time?
6. She speaks in the two poems about childbirth and her grandchild as though death were a constant presence in their lives. Is this an actual assessment of her daily reality?
7. Bradstreet uses a longer five-stress line in the poems that deal with mortality. What is the reason behind her choice of these meters?

Topics for Writing

1. Many of the emotions in Bradstreet's poetry will be familiar to modern readers. Other sentiments in her writing may seem to describe a woman's role as mother in ways that no longer reflect a woman's life and ambitions. Compare the differences and similarities between these two views of woman's role in society.
2. Discuss the consciousness of death in Bradstreet's poetry, and consider whether its presence is a reflection of her own emotions or whether it is a realistic response to the physical challenge of life at her time.
3. Compare the attitudes about childbirth as expressed in "Before the Birth of One of Her Children" and that of a modern mother, and discuss whether the medical advances of our period have affected the response of women to the experience.
4. MAKING CONNECTIONS The idea expressed in the last line of "To My Dear and Loving Husband" — Anne Bradstreet's assertion that "when we live no more, we may live ever" — has many affinities to ideas expressed in John Donne's sonnet "Death, be not proud" (p. 774). Compare the poems and analyze how this concept is presented by each poet.

Rᴉᴄʜᴀʀᴅ Bʀᴀᴜᴛɪɢᴀɴ

It's Raining in Love (p. 877)

Brautigan was one of the most popular of the writers who were part of the "flower-power" movement of the 1960s. His writing was an elusive combination of a sly, wide-eyed surrealistic consciousness and a down-to-earth sense of humor. This poem was included in his collection *The Pill Versus the Springhill Mine Disaster* (1968).

Questions for Discussion

1. How would you characterize the style of the poem? Is its seeming artlessness a conscious style adopted by Brautigan?
2. How would you describe the states of mind he is presenting in the verbs "to examine/evaluate/compute"?
3. What is the figure of speech he employs in his description of the rain's effect on the flowers and snails?
4. Why does it matter to him that "it's raining somewhere"? Is this an answer to the question, "Do you think it's going to rain?" which appears twice in the poem?
5. What is he telling us about the girl, when she asks about the chances of rain although the sky is clear?

Topics for Writing

1. Brautigan's poem is consciously humorous. Discuss the elements in his writing that make it humorous, and describe the serious considerations that lie beneath the surface.
2. In his wry, self-conscious manner, Brautigan has written a tender poem about love and its effect on people. Explain what he has told us, and compare this message with that in other poems about love in the anthology.

Eᴍɪʟʏ Bʀᴏɴᴛë

If grief for grief (p. 745)

Although modern readers know Emily Brontë primarily as the author of the classic novel *Wuthering Heights,* which she wrote in the late 1840s as she nursed her brother Bramwell through his last illness, she first published as a poet. In 1846 her sister Charlotte, author of the novel *Jane Eyre,* convinced a London publisher to issue a volume of poems by the three survivors of the family's five sisters. The poetry of Charlotte, Emily, and Anne was published in 1846 under the pseudonyms of Currer, Ellis, and Acton Bell. In a letter to the publisher Charlotte had claimed of Emily's poetry, "I know no woman that ever lived who wrote such poetry before." Despite Charlotte's assertion, the book was a complete fiasco. Only two copies sold in the first year after publication.

With the gradual interest in *Wuthering Heights* there was a response to the poetry as well, and Brontë's poetic voice — unsentimental but passionate, clear but tonally resonant — was to have a strong influence on some of the most important women poets of the Victorian era. Emily Dickinson, writing twenty years later, often seems uncannily to be echoing a phrase or an image of Brontë's poetry. Brontë wrote only a small body of verse, but it continues to be a presence in the world of English writing today.

Questions for Discussion

1. The poem is written almost as an Elizabethan song. What is the meter of the stanzas? How is the shorter final line like a song refrain?
2. The lines alternate masculine and feminine rhymes. What are the rhymes, and how would the lines scan?
3. There is a hint of an Elizabethan conceit in the first two lines. Could this reflect Brontë's reading? What is the meaning of "ruth" in the third line?
4. Would the Victorian world have been upset at her proclaiming the man she loved as "her angel" and her "idol"?
5. There is a use of near rhyme in the first stanza, but what appears to be near rhyme in the final stanza is the result in changes in pronunciation over the last century. How would the rhyme have sounded in Brontë's time, or in most of England today?

Topics for Writing

1. MAKING CONNECTIONS   Compare Brontë's poetry to the work of Emily Dickinson (pp. 937–942) and discuss the technical similarities and the distinctive "voice" of Brontë's poems, a voice that often seems to be echoed in Dickinson.
2. Relating the poem to the status of women in early Victorian England, discuss the open emotionalism of the sentiments and the undisguised passion of the poem's images.
3. MAKING CONNECTIONS   Read *Wuthering Heights* and compare the emotions depicted in the novel with the sentiments of Brontë's poetry.

GWENDOLYN BROOKS

Notes from the Childhood and the Girlhood (p. 712)
We Real Cool (p. 921)
The Mother (p. 922)
The Bean Eaters (p. 923)

NOTES FROM THE CHILDHOOD AND THE GIRLHOOD

Questions for Discussion

1. What is the rhyme scheme of the poem? Is it in regular meter? Why has she chosen to use both regular and irregular elements in the poem's form?
2. Brooks has chosen to tell her story in a series of figures of speech. What are some of them? How do they help her tell the story of the marriage?
3. What is the poet telling the reader with the line "Watch for porches as you pass"? What is the significance of "porches"?
4. It is a poem of acceptance, but is there bitterness in this acceptance?
5. What is the poet telling the reader in her personification of the "prim low fencing pinching in the grass"? What does she mean by "pinching in the grass"?
6. What is Brooks telling the reader with her phrase "pleasant custards"? Can the poem's final two lines be read as a summary of her own attitudes toward what she is describing?

Topics for Writing

1. Discuss the images that Brooks uses to convey the change in the lives of the couple she has described, and illustrate how she has presented this change in a series of descriptive images.

2. Many readers will see in this poem a reference to the rise of an African American middle class in an average American city. Discuss how the poem can be interpreted in this context and discuss how it could also be interpreted as having a larger context referring to any American working-class neighborhood.

3. Brooks has compressed a complex family situation into two sentences, "There are no swans and swallows any more. / The people settled for chicken and shut the door." Amplify these lines into the larger picture of the social situation she has implied in her images and discuss whether or not she might be making a negative comment.

4. The poem gives a precise description of the American middle-class dream, though the details are implied in a series of compact images. Discuss how the poet achieves this in a few brief phrases and expand the discussion into a consideration of how the writer herself seems to view this dream.

WE REAL COOL

"We Real Cool" is an excellent example of a poet's use of a persona. Brooks adopts the voice and the language of street adolescents to make her point that they are leading dead-end lives. The language is as sardonic and unsentimental as the life it describes, even though Brooks has slightly disguised the directness of her statement by ending each line with the first word of the next. The poem uses alliteration and compression, and a responsive class might even try reciting it as an athletic cheer. Repeated over and over, its bitter self-contempt becomes even more obvious.

Questions for Discussion

1. In the phrases "thin gin" and "jazz June" Brooks is using "thin" and "jazz" as verbs. What does she mean?

2. This poem is written in everyday slang, a language that changes continually. Do you recognize the poem's terms and phrases as language you would have used as adolescents? How would you change the poem to fit it into today's street language?

Topic for Writing

1. Because Brooks was an African American writer, most readers of the poem assume that she is describing black adolescents. Discuss the poem's implications for all adolescent dropouts, and consider whether other vernacular terms could give the poem a specific white identity.

THE MOTHER

In "The Mother" we enter a completely different emotional world from that of "We Real Cool." Brooks is presumably writing in the voice of a woman very much like herself. Although the first verse is in rhymed couplets, the meter is very free, and in the second verse there is so much emotion that the poet doesn't even retain the regular rhyme; she seems only to snatch at whatever rhyme occurs as she is writing. In "We Real Cool" she keeps an emotional distance from the poem by writing through a persona. In "The Mother" there is little emotional distance.

Questions for Discussion

1. What is Brooks referring to with the phrase "wind up the sucking-thumb" in line 7?
2. What does she mean by the images of line 10?
3. What does she mean by the adjective "dim" in lines 11 and 13?
4. What is suggested in the paradox of line 21, "in my deliberateness I was not deliberate"? Is the statement that she was not deliberate a possible reason for some of the complicated emotions expressed in the poem?
5. What is the truth she is trying to express in line 28?

Topic for Writing

1. Throughout the poem Brooks presents images of the life she has denied the children she didn't have. She also describes what is denied the mother —among other things, that she will never neglect or beat these children. Discuss the things that make up this life she describes, for both the mother and child.

THE BEAN EATERS

Brooks's poems often present unforgettable pictures of ghetto life, and this much anthologized poem is particularly vivid in its description of an old couple who have been reduced to bean suppers in rented rooms, but who still have memories of times of happiness and content.

Questions for Discussion

1. Although the moment that Brooks is describing could hardly be described as "poetic," she has used classic verse techniques of rhyme and meter. How is rhyme used in the poem? Does it add to the vividness of the scene, or does its presence come as an intrusion?
2. What is the meaning of the capitalization of the words "Mostly Good" in line 5?
3. Is she making a racial statement with her description of the couple as an "old yellow pair"?
4. What are the implications of the phrase "twinklings and twinges" in line 10?

Topics for Writing

1. Discuss the economic circumstances of a couple like this one. Brooks has related the poem specifically to an African American couple, but the scene could just as well involve an older white couple. Would there be differences in the scene she is describing?
2. In the last verse of the poem Brooks breaks out of the pattern of meter she used in the first two verses. Discuss how this changes the effect of the last lines.
3. MAKING CONNECTIONS   Brooks has been praised often for her authentic presentation of African American life. Using all of the poems in this sample of her work, discuss her view of the people and the scenes she describes and compare it with the poetry of other African American writers such as Rita Dove (p. 945) or Robert Hayden (p. 96).

Commentary

Robert Hayden, *"On Negro Poetry,"* p. 1050.

ELIZABETH BARRETT BROWNING

How Do I Love Thee? (p. 775)

Browning, born in 1806, was one of the most popular and respected poets of the Victorian period, and her name was seriously proposed for poet laureate at a time when women were expected to live in quiet subordination to their fathers and husbands. Much of her poetry was engaged in social issues, and she was at the front of the struggle against child labor in England and worked to end slavery in the United States. At the same time, she was a near invalid, sequestered in her father's house; it was only the determined courtship of a younger poet, Robert Browning, that succeeded in freeing her. The couple eloped and fled to France, and despite her poor health, she gave birth to a son at the age of forty-three. She died in her husband's arms in Italy in 1861. (Her father refused to forgive her throughout his lifetime.) In our century, the romantic story of her courtship and elopement are remembered more than her poetry, with the exception of a group of sonnets she wrote during Browning's courtship and presented to him as a gift after their marriage. The sonnets, titled *Sonnets from the Portuguese,* caused a sensation when they were first published in 1850, and despite changes in fashion and style they have been reprinted steadily ever since. Of all the sonnets, "How Do I Love Thee?" has been most enduring.

Questions for Discussion

1.   Is the sonnet English or Italian in form?
2.   The poem is framed within the conventions of Victorian religion. What elements and images in the poem reflect Browning's beliefs?
3.   Does the reference to "my lost saints" negate the poem's other references to religious faith? Does Browning intend to tell the reader that the speaker has lost her faith?
4.   In lines 7 and 8, "as men strive for Right," and "as they turn from praise," the poet has made assumptions about human conduct. What is she saying in these two figures of speech? What is the term for them?
5.   What is Browning saying in the phrase "with the passion put to use / In my old griefs"?
6.   The poem reaches an emotional conclusion that amplifies and develops the thought that opens it. What is the thought the poet develops in the fourteen lines?
7.   Is the development of an idea introduced in the opening lines a characteristic of the sonnet?

Topics for Writing

1.   MAKING CONNECTIONS   The sonnet describes love in ways that no longer entirely reflect today's attitudes. Write about the differences and similarities between Victorian and contemporary attitudes toward love expressed in poems by writers such as Sharon Olds (p. 995).
2.   MAKING CONNECTIONS   The sonnet form is complicated and tightly organized, but within its constraints poets have long been able to express themselves. Compare sonnets in the anthology by William Shakespeare, W. B. Yeats, e. e. cummings, and Rita Dove and discuss how each has used the sonnet form in his or her own way.
3.   The language of Browning's sonnet reflects the gender differences of the Victorian age. Discuss the changes a modern feminist poet might make in the poem's imagery.

Robert Browning

My Last Duchess (p. 795)

Robert Browning's family was able to support him in his decision to write, and he lived at home or traveled abroad until he married at the age of thirty-four. His early poetry was poorly received by critics, and during the years he was married to Elizabeth Barrett, she was much better known as a poet than he was. It was not until the publication of the long dramatic poem *The Ring and the Book* in 1869, eight years after her death, that he began to be considered as a poet in his own right.

"My Last Duchess" has always been popular with students, and some of them may have read it in high school. It is particularly effective read aloud, and as students listen to the poem, the skill of Browning's versification becomes more obvious. The poem uses end rhyme throughout, but with so much enjambment that the lines read like a casual conversation in which only one of the voices is heard. Some of the language may cause problems for students, but once they realize that the "plot" of the poem is familiar, they'll follow it to the conclusion.

The story reveals itself line by line, somewhat in the manner of a story by Edgar Allan Poe. As the poem begins, a duke is showing a portrait of his former wife to a visitor. Looking at the portrait upsets the nobleman because he sees again the expression of joy that the painter has depicted on his wife's face. As the duke talks about her, he becomes more and more angry. The smile, he fumes, should have been only for him, but she smiled that way at everyone and at everything pleasant in her life. Almost in disbelief, we listen to him tell the visitor that because she wouldn't stop smiling, he had her killed. Now — and he is all business in the last lines of the poem — we realize that the visitor is an agent working for another nobleman who is offering his daughter to the duke in marriage. As we are left with the realization that the daughter may be the duke's next victim, the duke takes the visitor down to dinner, talking again about his art collection.

Questions for Discussion

1. When do we realize that there is something about the portrait that upsets the duke?
2. Why does he keep the portrait behind a curtain?
3. What does he mean by "Who'd stoop to blame" in line 34?
4. What does he say about himself in the words "I choose / Never to stoop" in lines 42–43?
5. What does he tell the agent about a request for a dowry?

Topics for Writing

1. Develop the idea suggested in the poem that to the duke his wife was simply another possession, like the objects in his art collection.
2. The poem's setting seems to be a place that is not English. Discuss whether Browning would have written the same poem about an English duke.

CHARLES BUKOWSKI

beach boys (p. 833)
writer's block (p. 892)
huge ear rings (p. 893)

Charles Bukowski has long been an uncomfortable presence whom the community of poets writing with a consciousness of academic standards have ignored. He is probably the most influential poet of this era, with thousands of imitators everywhere in the world striving to write poetry with his incisiveness that captures his disruptive presence. Bukowski insisted on the right to be boorish, unpleasant, difficult, and insulting, and at the same time wrote poetry that reflects all of this but is often tender, self-deprecating, sympathetic, and funny. He had, as he wrote many times, a difficult childhood, which he assumed allowed him to be as difficult in his own way to anyone he met. He wrote thousands of poems and collections of unpublished work are still appearing years after his death in 1994 at the age of seventy-three. His writing — poetry and fiction — has been translated into dozens of other languages. His poems chronicle his habitual drunkenness, his obsession with sex, and his hapless inability to live within the conventions of ordinary life, all of which has made him an admired example for people who might lack the courage to act out these attitudes in their own lives. Whatever anyone thinks of Bukowski's writing, there is a vitality and a vein of humor in the best of his poetry that must be acknowledged.

BEACH BOYS

Questions for Discussion

1.   What are some of the implications of the title "beach boys"? What are the reader's expectations for a poem with a title like this? Does the poem fulfill these expectations?
2.   How is the theme of alienation presented in the poem? What are the examples Bukowski presents?
3.   How does the opening line, "only the young go to the beach now," prepare the reader for the theme of the poem?
4.   Much of the poem is constructed around contradictions. As an example, the speaker wouldn't go to the beach himself, but if his woman can go with him he "must have the courage to go there with her." How does he contradict the image he presents of the "young boys on their surfboards"?
5.   Is he asking that society provide some special place for people who feel alienated from the scene Bukowski describes? Could that happen? Why or why not? Is it desirable?
6.   In the poem Bukowski uses repetition for emphasis, as in the same flat phrase to introduce the "one-legged people," "the deformed," "the armless." How does he repeat this form in the poem's last five lines? What does he achieve with this effect?

Topics for Writing

1.   Discuss the alienation that is felt by many people who suffer from physical disability or deformity, and describe some of the efforts that have been made in recent years to draw them into the society.

2. Although Bukowski could have written a poem like this about many areas in modern life, discuss his reasons for setting it on the beach, where physical beauty is a major consideration.

WRITER'S BLOCK

Questions for Discussion

1. What is usually meant by the term "writer's block"? Is it something that afflicts many writers?
2. In the poem Bukowski makes use of a number of technical elements, like personification and simile. How are they used?
3. Although this is a consciously literary poem, we are reminded several times that Bukowski's life is as messy as always in images like "an unpaid gas bill" or the refrigerator sitting empty. Why does he do this?
4. Do writers usually try to present themselves in a consistent manner? Is this important to their reception by their readers?
5. What do you think draws him to the phrase "the Spanish bird sings"? What does the poem tell us about a writer's way of working and a writer's obsessions?
6. Why could it be considered an *oxymoron* for the poet to write a poem about suffering from writer's block?

Topics for Writing

1. Bukowski is sometimes considered more of a barroom drunk than a poet, but "writer's block" is written with considerable skill and uses a number of literary devices effectively. Discuss this "literary" side of Bukowski's writing and contrast it with criticism of his work found in other sources.
2. Discuss the French expression quoted in the poem, "without / literature / life is hell," and apply it to Bukowski's own life.
3. In this poem Bukowski has turned his typewriter into a protagonist through the use of *personification*. Discuss the figure he has created from his typewriter and develop the concept of *personification* using examples from this poem and the definition found in the Glossary of Literary Terms.

HUGE EAR RINGS

Questions for Discussion

1. Why has Bukowski chosen the woman's ear rings as the title for the poem? Is his use of the ear rings an example of *symbolism*? In this poem, what would elaborate ear rings symbolize?
2. What is it about the woman that causes Bukowski to compare her to a medieval witch? Is this how the woman would see herself?
3. How does the poet present himself in this encounter? Is it a sympathetic portrayal? Would Bukowski be concerned with the reader's opinion of him or does he think that many masculine readers can picture themselves in a similar situation?
4. What does Bukowski tell the readers about the woman that might describe a unique individual and not be used to apply to women as a gender? If she is as individual as he suggests, how could she be a figure reminding him of a witch?
5. Does the poem suggest that this is a situation that has happened to him before? Does the poet expect his readers to consider the incident as something that occurs daily on the streets of Los Angeles?

Topics for Writing

1. In the poem Bukowski alludes to the older attitudes that a woman's beauty was a snare for men, and that if they strayed from the path men set for them they were punished. Using other sources, develop this idea and discuss how the poem presents the idea in a modern guise, with his reference to the burning of witches.

2. Although the woman could be considered as a unique individual, Bukowski has described her in classic sexist terms — referring to her love of ornament like the "huge ear rings" and her insensitivity to the effect she might be having on other people. Discuss the poem in terms of its implied sexism, with a consideration of Bukowski's consciousness of this element in the poem.

GEORGE GORDON, LORD BYRON

She Walks in Beauty (p. 744)

Byron's life was so turbulent and so filled with extravagant gestures and disasters that the adjective *Byronic* was coined to describe a dangerously exaggerated lifestyle. At his birth in 1788 it was understood that he would inherit his title, but his father had squandered the family fortune, and Byron spent much of his childhood in poverty in Scotland. He was born with a clubfoot, and to compensate for his disability he stubbornly made himself into an excellent sportsman and swimmer. He was also handsome and daring, living much of his life in alternating periods of relative calm, when he did his writing, and chaotic excess, which included hundreds of affairs with women of every social class and experimental relationships with young men and boys. His books were enormously successful, despite the scandal over his incestuous relationship with his half-sister, which drove him from England. He died in 1824, at the age of thirty-five, trying to train and lead a small body of soldiers he had assembled at his own expense to fight for Greek independence.

Much of Byron's fame derives from his wildly colorful life, but his writing is even more interesting. His masterpiece is the long narrative poem *Don Juan*, but he also wrote drama, satiric verse, and short lyrics such as "She Walks in Beauty." Much of his writing is neoclassical, but the turbulence of his life and the simplicity of his lyric poetry place him in the company of the romantic poets. One of his few intellectual and spiritual friendships was with Percy Bysshe Shelley, during the years when they both lived in Italy.

Questions for Discussion

1. Although the poem is about the woman's physical beauty, Byron also writes of her spiritual beauty. What images or lines describe this spiritual beauty?
2. What is the term for the comparison in lines 1–2?
3. What is the poet saying about the woman's appearance in lines 5–6?
4. What does he mean with the phrase "nameless grace" in line 8? What words would you suggest to describe this grace?

Topic for Writing

1. MAKING CONNECTIONS The admiration Byron feels for the woman he describes in this poem contrasts sharply with the feeling expressed in Robert

Browning's dramatic monologue "My Last Duchess" (p. 795). Compare the two poems in their portrayal of women.

NICK CARBÓ

American Adobo (p. 797)

Nick Carbó has been an active proselytizer for poets and writers from the Philippine Islands, as well as an active poet whose own work reflects his background of family and traditions. He lives in Florida; he was named a Wallace Stegner Fellow at the University of Iowa and Stanford University, and he has been the recipient of a fellowship from the National Endowment for the Arts.

Questions for Discussion

1. What is adobo? What is Carbó implying by calling this "American adobo"?
2. What is Carbó's reaction to being introduced to other members of his family? Does this suggest that they don't have a close relationship?
3. His description of his cousin in the opening lines is dismissive and highly critical. What is his perception of her? How does this reflect on himself? Why is he being dismissive of her economic difficulties?
4. Is it common for some members of a family to have exaggerated ideas of the family's importance? What instances does Carbó name of his cousin's distortions of the truth?
5. What does he mean with the term "fallen leaves of our family tree" when he describes his cousin's memories?
6. When he names Central Avenue as the place where his aunt changed sheets in motels, what city is he mentioning? Was this one of the family's stops on the way to Albuquerque?
7. Does he intend the cruelty of the poem's final stanza, that his cousin was a poor cook? What is his motivation for dismissing her attempt to cook a family recipe for him?

Topics for Writing

1. In a short prose sketch, outline the events of the Carbó family's life in the Philippines and their journey to New Mexico, drawing on the places and the events mentioned in the poem.
2. Compare this poem to other writing by recent immigrants to the United States. Describe the things that seem common to their experience and discuss this poem in this context.
3. MAKING CONNECTIONS A number of poets in the anthology, among them Gary Soto (p. 1013) and Marilyn Chin (p. 847), write of their background as immigrants. Compare their writing and discuss the concept of this work as a distinctive new genre in American writing.

Lewis Carroll

Jabberwocky (p. 730)

Like everything else contained in Carroll's fantasy *Through the Looking Glass* (1871), the sequel to *Alice's Adventures in Wonderland* (1865), "Jabberwocky" has been discussed and analyzed for more than a century. Although there have been many ingenious interpretations, it seems to have been intended as a moment of teasing inspiration on the author's part. In the two books, C. L. Dodgson, who used the pen name Lewis Carroll to conceal his less-than-romantic identity as a university lecturer of mathematics, created a world of fantasy that still fascinates readers. As David Daiches commented in *A Critical History of English Literature* (1960), "Below a surface of attractive and quaint adventure lay rich patterns of parody, irony, sentimentalism, and symbolic suggestiveness which can keep the most cunning modern analytic critic fully occupied" (1086). Students will generally agree with Alice's comments when she heard the poem, "It seems very pretty . . . but it's rather hard to understand! . . . Somehow it seems to fill my head with ideas — only I don't know exactly what they are!"

Carroll is always credited with the invention of the word *chortled*, which first appeared in the poem; there are other words that the poem's popularity helped add to the language, including *whiffling, burbled*, and *galumphing*. As to what the poem means, no one has ever quite been able to agree.

Questions for Discussion

1. The words Carroll created *seem* reasonable. How has he given us the sense that the poem might be written in normal language?
2. The Jabberwock seems to be some kind of dragon. What words does Carroll create that seem to suggest a dragon? What does the dragon look like?
3. One technique Carroll uses to make his language seem reasonable is alliteration. What are some examples of alliteration in the poem?
4. Is it possible to create a mind picture of something that might be a "frumious Bandersnatch"? What syllables would you pick to create an image?
5. The repetition of the first and last stanzas suggests the form of a traditional ballad. Do you think this was Carroll's intention?

Topics for Writing

1. Carroll's poem seems to suggest how language is created — that we try out sounds, and by a communal consensus we agree on a meaning for the sound. Analyze any of the unusual words in the poem that are part of our common usage to determine what is in the sound that implies a meaning.
2. **RESPONDING CREATIVELY** Write a prose adaptation of the poem, using Carroll's language, telling the story of the Jabberwock and the adventures of the son as he carries out his father's wishes.

LORNA DEE CERVANTES

The Body as Braille (p. 761)

Lorna Dee Cervantes was born of Mexican and Native American parents in San Francisco in 1954. The family moved to nearby San Jose, where her mother cleaned houses, bringing her daughter with her. It was in the books she found while waiting for her mother to finish that Cervantes first began reading English poetry. She was discouraged from using Spanish when she was a child, but she identifies herself as a "Chicana" writer, and often employs Spanish phrases in her work.

Questions for Discussion

1. What does Cervantes mean by the title of the poem, "The Body as Braille"?
2. What is the meaning of the phrase in Spanish that Cervantes uses in line 6?
3. Does she anticipate difficulties in her relationship? How does she suggest this in the poem?
4. What is she telling us about the relationship in the final stanza? Why is she keeping her emotions hidden from her lover?
5. Why does she use the word "cauldron" in line 8? Is this also a metaphor for what she is feeling herself? What else in the poem might suggest this?

Topics for Writing

1. In the poem Cervantes contrasts two ways of describing the phenomenon of the ring around the moon. Discuss the two descriptions, her aunt's and her school book's, and contrast the knowledge that each represents.
2. **MAKING CONNECTIONS** Compare this poem with Hilda Morley's "I Remember" (p. 761), another description written by a woman of the effect of a man's touch on her body. Do these poems seem to express the physical or the emotional realities of the relationship?

SAMUEL CHARTERS

A Man Dancing Alone on an Island in Greece (p. 807)

This poem alludes to John Keats's "Ode on a Grecian Urn" (p. 762), and students should read it before turning to this contemporary response. The dance described in the poem was held in conjunction with a conference on the traditional acoustic Greek music known as *Rebetica* or *Rembetika* and the musicians and singers were considered among the finest performers of this style. The man dancing was one of the panelists from the conference and he was eating with his family at the restaurant, getting up from time to time to dance by himself. The conference was held on the island of Hydra off the coast of Peloponnesos in the fall of 2008. The concert was held outdoors at a popular *taverna* following a rainstorm. The writer was on the island visiting friends and was not participating in the conference.

Questions for Discussion

1. What is the specific setting of the poem that Charters is alluding to in the vase John Keats describes? Could the scene the poem depicts have occurred somewhere other than on a Greek island?

2.   What does the dancing man see, even though his eyes are closed as he moves?
3.   Although the man dances alone, are the people watching from the tables in their own way dancing with him?
4.   What does the description of the orchestra tell us about the nature of the music they are playing? Would a modern group use these instruments?
5.   Is there a contradiction between the everyday appearance of the musicians and the music they are performing? Is there music like it that students experience today?
6.   What is the writer alluding to in Keats's poem when he refers to the "stillness" of the man's dancing? What is the specific reference in Keats's poem?
7.   How does the poem's conclusion allude to the final lines of Keats's ode? Is it a valid comparison?
8.   What is the writer suggesting with the phrase "measured movement"?

Topics for Writing

1.   Discuss the process by which one poet can allude to the writing of another without copying or imitating the other poet's writing. Describe how this can broaden our understanding and response to the writing of each poem.
2.   Write a short paper about an impromptu performance that you have observed and relate it to a larger theme in literature or music.
3.   MAKING CONNECTIONS   Discuss the famous conclusion of Keats's poem that "Beauty is truth, truth beauty," and relate it to the events of Charters's poem, suggesting whether or not Charters's allusion seems valid.
4.   Write a short paper that compares your own feelings in a similar situation and discuss why someone would be embarrassed to stand up and dance alone. The discussion could be expanded to include standing up in front of others to speak or perform and conclude with any insights you might have gained from the experience.

Marilyn Chin

How I Got That Name (p. 847)

The subtitle of "How I Got That Name" is "An Essay on Assimilation," and students will find the poem's meaning even clearer if they understand that the subtitle's "essay" is only half serious. The poem is about Chin's own assimilation, as an Asian American with a difficult family background, into mainstream American life. As the poem also makes clear, her experience as a child of immigrant parents is a classic story of American life, and only the details would need to be changed for the story to fit Jewish immigrants or Haitian immigrants.

In lines 38–39 Chin emphasizes one of the details that is unique about the Asian American experience: "How we've managed to fool the experts / in education, statistics, and demography." Yes, the speaker is saying, we're considered a "model minority," but I'm just as unhappy as anybody else. She is so uncertain about herself and her role in America that in line 71 she declares, "I wait for imminent death." The death, she continues, is only "metaphorical," but the last long verse of the poem is her own wry epitaph.

Questions for Discussion

1.   What does Chin mean by "the resoluteness / of the first person singular" and the following three lines at the beginning of "How I Got That Name"?

2. In line 15, "lust drove men to greatness," is she being sarcastic?
3. What is the speaker saying about her father in line 26?
4. What does she mean when she says, in lines 38–39, that the Asian American minority has "managed to fool the experts"?
5. Line 57, "We have no inner resources," is a cliché. Does Chin mean it satirically here?
6. What does she mean in lines 72–73?
7. Discuss what has "swallowed her whole" in the last lines of the poem. Is it America, which has finally admitted her into its society? What other suggestions might you have?

Topic for Writing

1. To most outsiders, the fact that Asian Americans are a "model minority" and have higher average test scores, education, and income than Anglo-Americans is a mark of unusual success. Analyze Chin's assertion in her poems that these facts have no meaning for someone like herself.

Commentary

Marilyn Chin, *"On the Canon,"* p. 1044.

AMY CLAMPITT

Beach Glass (p. 899)

For many students part of the difficulty of reading Amy Clampitt's poetry is the richness of her vocabulary. She took from Marianne Moore a delight with words, for their sound and for their complicated meanings. Clampitt's poems themselves also pursue intellectual concepts that sometimes might not seem to be illustrated by the milieu of her poems, though on closer examination it is almost always clear that she has woven the two together and the poem becomes a physical expression of the idea that was pursuing her. It is also interesting that the beach where she is walking in this poem is in Maine, and it is not far from the beach where Rachel Carson walked when she wrote her masterpiece *Silent Spring*.

Questions for Discussion

1. Who was "Cassandra" in line 7? Why is she described as hearing nothing "but warning"?
2. There are many possible interpretations of the image in line 9 of the ocean "keeping open old accounts." What are some of them? Why do the old accounts never balance?
3. What does Clampitt mean by the "permutations of novelty"? How does she illustrate them herself?
4. What is Clampitt describing in her imaginative image of the sea playing "touch-last" with the shore?
5. Why does Clampitt turn her attention to beach glass? Where has it come from?
6. What are the kinds of glass that the poet finds in her search? Are they the kinds of glass that could be found on any beach? What is "chrysoprase"? Is it something that would normally be related to Almadén wine bottles?

7. What is the poet suggesting with the statement that "The process / goes on forever"? What is she telling the reader by linking the process to our own historical era, with the "treasuries / of Murano" as an example?
8. Why does she refer to the stained glass windows of the Chartres Cathedral as "the buttressed / astonishments"?

Topics for Writing

1. In her poem Amy Clampitt has given the reader a picture of a universe in continual renewal. Discuss the implications of her concepts with illustrations from the poem itself and extend the concepts into the scientific examination of the process of evolution.
2. In her consideration of a restless "intellect" that considers structures yet to be seen, Clampitt is implying that all she experiences is in flux, like the glass on the beach. Discuss this analogy and use quotations from the poem to demonstrate how she has prepared the reader for this summary.
3. The poem is a combination of intellectual concepts (its conclusion that there will be a prolonged examination of the process she describes) and visual images (the waves along the shore playing touch tag like a small dog). Discuss how these two elements of the poem interact and how they enlarge and extend the philosophical range of the poem's ideas.

LUCILLE CLIFTON

to ms. ann (p. 844)

Clifton is one of the many modern American poets whose backgrounds are more clearly working class than many of the writers of earlier generations. She was born in 1936, in Depew, New York, to a father who worked in a steel mill and a mother who worked in a laundry. Her most extended involvement with a literary apprenticeship was the period between 1953 to 1955 when she attended Howard University and was close to other young writers there at the same time, including Leroi Jones, later to be known as Amiri Baraka. In 1958 she married Fred J. Clifton and became the mother of six children.

She worked for many years as a claims clerk for the Unemployment Bureau in Buffalo, then became an assistant at the U.S. Office of Education in Washington, D.C. She began publishing books for children early, and her first poetry collection, *Good Times*, appeared in 1969. It was selected by the *New York Times* as one of the best books of the year, and since that time she has had an active literary career, both as a poet and a teacher. In *The Norton Anthology of African American Literature* (1996), Clifton commented on her writing:

> I use a simple language. I have never believed that for anything to be valid or true or intellectual or "deep" it had to be first complex. . . . I am not interested if anyone knows whether or not I am familiar with big words, I am interested in trying to render big ideas in a simple way. I am interested in being understood not admired.

Her insistence on writing in childlike idioms has tended to limit her subject matter, and occasionally eddies of sentimentality threaten to swamp the slight craft of her verse, but her clear perception of life's realities generally lends her work its own authenticity.

Questions for Discussion

1. Who is the woman addressed as ms. ann?
2. What is the intimation of the lines "I will have to forget / your face"? Why does she say "have to"?
3. What examples does Clifton give as reasons she has to forget the woman she worked for?
4. Among her various jobs Clifton does not seem to have ever been a housekeeper for a white employer. Why has she chosen to adopt this role for the poem? Why has she not written about her work in the employment office or as an assistant in the U. S. Office of Education? Is this poem intended as a metaphor for black experience?

Topic for Writing

1. Clifton has chosen to write in a simple, unnuanced style. Comment on the reasons why and discuss the strengths and the limitations of writing using such limited resources.

Samuel Taylor Coleridge

Kubla Khan: or, a Vision in a Dream (p. 924)
Frost at Midnight (p. 925)

Kubla Khan: or, a Vision in a Dream

This introduction to "Kubla Khan" — written in 1797, when Coleridge was living in Somerset — is included in the *Bloomsbury Guide to English Literature* (1995) and is a useful way to begin a closer study of this complex and enigmatic poem:

> Coleridge recorded that he fell asleep after reading a description in *Purchas his Pilgrimage* (1613) of the pleasure gardens constructed in Xanadu by the thirteenth-century Mongol king of China, Khan (king) Kublai. While he was asleep "from two to three hundred lines" came to him, which upon waking he hastened to write down. However he was interrupted by "a person on business from Porlock," and afterwards could recall nothing of the remainder, "with the exception of some eight or ten scattered lines and images." It is difficult to know how much of this account to believe. One element Coleridge suppresses is his addiction to opium, which is certainly relevant to the hallucinatory clarity of the poem's exotic images. Because of the oddness of Coleridge's account "a visitor from Porlock" has become a byword for any kind of intriguing, possibly evasive, excuse.
>
> Despite its designation "A Fragment" the work is artistically complete. The first three sections rework phrases from the Jacobean travel book to describe a strangely primal landscape. An awesome "mighty fountain" forms the source of the "sacred river" Alph, on the banks of which Kubla has built a "stately pleasure-dome" surrounded by orchards and gardens. After watering the garden the river continues its course, entering "caverns measureless to man" and sinking "in tumult to a lifeless ocean." The clarity and primitiveness of these images gives the poem an archetypal resonance. The river can be seen as the river of life or creativity; the fountain symbol-

izes birth (of an individual, civilization, poetic inspiration), and the "lifeless ocean" death or sterility. The dome stands for the precarious balance between. It is possible that the final fourth section of the poem, which seems to be a commentary upon the preceding lines, were "the eight or ten lines or images" written after the departure of Coleridge's visitor, if he or she ever existed. The poem ends by imputing magical qualities to the poem itself and its bardic author: "Weave a circle round him thrice, / And close your eyes with holy dread, / For he on honey-dew hath fed, / And drunk the milk of Paradise." (726)

If the reader continues with this explication of elements of the poem, it could be suggested that "honey-dew" and "milk of Paradise" describe opium, which would clarify much of the poem's imagery. This is the opening sentence of the book that Coleridge was reading: "In Xamdu did Cublai Can build a stately Palace, encompassing sixteene miles of plaine ground with a wall, wherein are fertile Meddowes, pleasant Springs, delightful streames, and all sorts of beasts of chase and game, and in the midst thereof a sumptuous house of pleasure." In Coleridge's time, *Can* was the usual spelling of the word, and it was pronounced as it was spelled, so there is a perfect rhyme between *Khan* and *man* in lines 1 and 4.

Questions for Discussion

1. "Kubla Khan" could be described as a rhapsody on a visual theme, which is the imagined pleasure garden. What are some of the visual images Coleridge associates with his theme?
2. What might he be describing in lines 15–16, "As e'er beneath a waning moon was haunted / By woman wailing for her demon lover"?
3. What is he describing as the source of the sacred river?
4. Is there anything in the poem that suggests what he might be comparing with the metaphoric image "caves of ice"?
5. What is Coleridge saying about this unknown figure in the last two lines?
6. Is there any way to identify the figure from the poem itself?

Topics for Writing

1. In its use of specific details — for instance, "five miles of fertile ground" —that contrast with its imaginative setting, "Kubla Khan" could be described as poetic science fiction. Develop a paper around this theme.
2. One of the most unusual aspects of the poem is its rhyme, which occurs throughout but not in a regular pattern. Analyze the rhymes and describe the way they enhance the poem's musicality.
3. The poem's first five lines are usually admired for their euphony (musicality). Analyze how alliteration, assonance, rhyme, and meter illustrate the musical effect of these lines.

Connection

Richard Leighton Green, *"Apropos Coleridge's 'Kubla Khan,'"* p. 780.

FROST AT MIDNIGHT

This poem is a fireside meditation exemplary of early romantic poetry. It describes a humble event in everyday language, and it leads the writer to profound thoughts about nature and human life. The baby sleeping beside Coleridge is his son Hartley. The poem is written in blank verse, but the play of thought is so richly imagined that it often seems as though the poem was written in rhyme. The only difficulty for the student will probably be the image of the "film," or coat of soot, on the grate in line 15. Coleridge himself supplied a gloss on the term: "In all parts of the kingdom these films are called Strangers and are supposed to portend the arrival of some absent friend."

Questions for Discussion

1. What does Coleridge mean in the image of line 1, "The Frost performs its secret ministry"? Why does he call this ministry "secret"?
2. What is described in lines 8–9, when the quiet around the speaker disturbs his meditation?
3. What is meant by the phrase "makes a toy of Thought" in line 23?
4. What is he saying about childhood and the city in line 51 to the end of the verse?
5. What is he saying with the word "pent" in line 52? What are its connotative meanings here?
6. What word is used to define the belief, expressed in line 62, that God is present: "Himself in all, and all things in himself"?

Topics for Writing

1. **MAKING CONNECTIONS** Coleridge's pantheistic beliefs were widespread among artists and intellectuals of his time. Compare his belief in nature with the beliefs of other romantic poets — for instance, Percy Bysshe Shelley and John Keats.
2. **MAKING CONNECTIONS** Analyze the poem for elements that characterize romantic poetry, referring to William Wordsworth's definition in his Introduction to his *Lyrical Ballads* (p. 1075).

BILLY COLLINS

American Sonnet (p. 776)
Tuesday, June 4th, 1991 (p. 927)
Memento Mori (p. 929)
By a Swimming Pool Outside Siracusa (p. 929)

Collins is that rare creature in the poetic establishment — a new writer whose poems are passed from reader to reader with pleased recognition of their individuality and impeccable style, and whose work is equally admired by many critics. Since his appointment as American poet laureate there has grown a steadily widening network of admirers who begin conversations with the excited question, "Have you read the Billy Collins poem about . . . ?" On a first reading, the seeming artlessness of the writing and the ordinariness of the subject matter can be disconcerting, but Collins is a writer whose work reveals itself more fully on second and third readings, and students are especially cautioned to look past the first impression to the literary themes that lie beneath the poem's surface.

The directness of the writing is also deceiving. Collins has spent years honing his style, and he has mastered every nuance of his language. At the same time he has persisted despite continual questioning of his work during the long years of his literary apprenticeship. It took him twenty years of submissions before he had a poem accepted by *Poetry* magazine. Probably what wins him most of his readers is the fact that many of his poems are, quite simply, funny. He is one of a handful of serious poets who allow you to laugh as you read their work. Among American poets, only e. e. cummings, Lawrence Ferlinghetti, and occasionally Allen Ginsberg offer their readers this rare pleasure. Which of his poems are the funniest? The only answer to the question is the general response of the committed Collins fan: "Have you read the Billy Collins poem about . . . ?"

Questions for Discussion

1. Do the poetic means of rhyme and meter play a role in Collins's poems? Does this affect the reader's response to the poetry, or is the modern poetic idiom sufficiently free of preconditions that any style of writing can be considered seriously?

2. What are some of the other poetic means that Collins employs? Can you find examples of poetic elements like metaphor, simile, poetic image, and allusion?

3. In his poem "American Sonnet," does Collins's sly suggestion that a picture post-card could be considered the American sonnet form seem naive, or is it a shrewd presentation of the means and the forms of the sonnet itself? Could this be considered a "literary" poem, even if the approach seems to deny a literary quality to his American sonnets?

4. In the fourth stanza of "Tuesday, June 4th, 1991," Collins presents an image of himself as a sort of "stenographer" of the morning — waiting to take notes of what is happening around him. Why does he use the word "contraption" to describe a courtroom dictation machine? How does the poem reflect this view of himself as a taker of notes?

5. In line 19 of the poem he uses the phrase "amnesiac waters of the Thames." What is the term for this figure of speech? What is his intention in this description of the Thames?

6. Why does Collins end his poem about an ordinary morning with an allusion to ancient mythology? Does he convince us of its applicability?

7. He takes as a title for his poem about his desk lamp joining the mourners at his funeral the Latin term "Memento Mori." What is he inferring with this term?

8. In his poem about the limits of language, "By a Swimming Pool Outside Siracusa," Collins often presents portentous phrases with mock seriousness. What is he telling us about the "burning questions" he asked the two men he is talking with? What is happening at the end of the poem, when he asks his listeners to "give him a minute"?

Topics for Writing

1. Part of the effect of Collins's poems is their subtle skill in the sound of his lines. He is a master of assonance. Discuss this aspect of his poetic craft.

2. **MAKING CONNECTIONS** Discuss Collins's use of classical allusion and relate it to other poems that draw on this rich vein of poetic subject matter.

3. **MAKING CONNECTIONS** In his poem "Tuesday, June 4th, 1991," Collins describes himself as a kind of "stenographer" to the morning. This could be considered a metaphor for the work of any poet. Discuss this concept with examples from other poems in the anthology.

GREGORY CORSO

I am 25 (p. 872)

Corso will always be known as the "jailkid" whom Allen Ginsberg met in a Greenwich Village bar when he was a twenty year old who had just been released from a New York State prison for his part in a finance company robbery. Although Corso dropped out of school in the sixth grade, he began to read and write poetry while still in prison. This poem was included in his collection *Gasoline,* published by Lawrence Ferlinghetti's City Lights Books in 1982.

Questions for Discussion

1. Who are the poets Corso includes in his first lines: Shelley, Chatterton, and Rimbaud? What do they have in common? Why would Corso respond to them?
2. Are these the writers Corso includes in his category of "OLD POETMEN"?
3. What does he mean by the line "who speak their youth in whispers"?
4. Is this a young writer's poem? Would Corso have written the same lines when he was older himself?
5. Is he being serious when he declares that he intends to "steal their poems"? Is this an attitude shared by other poets?

Topic for Writing

1. Comment on his statement, "what you once were, thru me / you'll be again," and relate it to other poetry as an explanation of what poets take from each other.

STEPHEN CRANE

War Is Kind (p. 834)

Crane was known in his brief life for the brilliantly imagined evocation of a young soldier's experience in the American Civil War, *The Red Badge of Courage,* published in 1895, but his bitter antiwar poem "War Is Kind" reflected his changed attitudes a few years later. Crane was born in New Jersey in 1871, and his career began with considerable promise, but he contracted tuberculosis and died in England in 1900 at the age of twenty-nine.

Question for Discussion

1. Discuss what is going on in stanzas 2 and 4 in comparison with stanzas 1, 3, and 5. Who are the persons in each stanza? How are they presented?

Topic for Writing

1. Read some of Crane's other poetry or fiction about war and write an essay discussing his characteristic attitudes and images.

ROBERT CREELEY

Ballad of the Despairing Husband (p. 756)

Robert Creeley was always known as a poet of short, terse statements, of verses that began and ended in a few brief lines, but suggested a storm of emotions. At the same time, like most poets of his generation, he had a broad background in the traditions of English verse. In this poem he draws on this background to create a ballad in traditional forms that has also the sardonic sting of a contemporary poem. Although most of the poem's stanzas are in a recognizable English or Scottish ballad form, he breaks off, and begins again, this time using the language and verse forms of the medieval troubadour.

Questions for Discussion

1. What is the verse form of the opening stanzas? What are the verse forms of the medieval troubadour's voice that takes over the poem?
2. What is he inferring with the line that precedes his stylistic switch to the florid language of the troubadour, "And I will tell her, and tell her right . . ."
3. Why were the conventions of the troubadour songs considered of a higher artistic rank than the ballad style which began the poem?
4. In the forced lines and the inept rhyming of the first troubadour-style verse is Creeley attempting a parody of the troubadour conventions or is he allowing the angry and tempestuous rhymer of the opening stanzas to make fun of himself?
5. In the opening stanzas there are occasional forced lines and rhymes, like "to her / answer," in which the rhyming syllable of "answer" falls on a weak cadence, rather than the strong cadence of the poem's other lines. Has Creeley included these fumbles purposefully? Is he allowing the reader to glimpse the annoyed husband behind his pretense of civility?
6. What is Creeley telling the reader with his final lines?

Topics for Writing

1. Outline the three different stanza forms that are represented in Creeley's ballad, explaining their differences in both rhyme and meter. Research the troubadour tradition, and place the stanzas in a historical perspective.
2. Discuss the humorous aspects of Creeley's ballad, both in the language and in the situation itself, suggesting reasons why the poet might have chosen to write a humorous poem as one side of a marital quarrel.
3. Creeley's ballad is considerably baudier than the majority of the early ballads that have made their way into the literary canon. After reading the early ballad in this anthology, "The Daemon Lover" (p. 751) discuss whether Creeley's ballad could be drawing on some earlier and earthier tradition as its inspiration, or whether its coarse language might reflect the reality that the author lived in our modern era, in which language again is used with fewer constraints.
4. Using the stanza form of the ballad's opening, write a description of some recent event, and discuss why this is or is not a helpful method of writing a narrative.

COUNTEE CULLEN

Yet Do I Marvel (p. 775)
From *Heritage* (p. 865)
Incident (p. 867)

During his life there was a continual discussion of Cullen's divided role as an advocate of traditional European verse techniques and a passionate defender of African American rights and values. As Robert Stepto has summed up the situation in his chapter "Afro-American Literature" in *Columbia Literary History of the United States,*

> . . . while he [Cullen] was obviously a serious and frequently anguished observer of *social* conventions, he was also an unquestioning and for the most part uninventive practitioner of established *poetic* conventions. In other words, though his quarrel with society yielded moving expressions of anger and irony, they did not instigate a comparable, idiosyncratic skepticism about the shape a poem might take. New themes came, but new forms did not. (790)

In essence, the contradiction is summed up in lines like these from "Heritage," which present the confusions that confronted him daily as a black individual, but that he describes in a language that is only coincidentally expressive of this reality:

> So I lie, whose fount of pride,
> Dear distress, and joy allied,
> Is my somber flesh and skin,
> With the dark blood dammed within . . .

The discussion now has broadened to include the other conflicts that are known about Cullen's life. It is clear that he was a much more complex figure than the courtly writer who won an enduring literary reputation while still a university student. In his years as a teacher, although his literary reputation declined, he was revered by his students. The complicated background of his birth in Louisville and his adoption as a teenager by a Harlem minister make it clear that his struggles were to an extent against his own hidden background. In his concealed homosexuality, there was also a perceived necessity to evade the problems that his sexual orientation could have caused him in the society of the period. His marriage to the daughter of W. E. B. Dubois was an effort to present a more expected image to his community, and its abrupt failure led to even more uncertainty in his literary career.

"Yet Do I Marvel" illustrates the contradictions that Cullen set out to resolve, and in this poem he achieves a masterful balance between his identification with European culture and his African American heritage. The form — a sonnet — and the literary allusions are European, but the subject is his racial identity. It is, again, the racial emphasis of his long poem "Heritage" that popularized the poem with its many readers, and it should be read with a consciousness of its importance to the debate of that period on the role of the African American in American mainstream culture. "Incident" is a wry, laconic masterpiece, which in its perplexed small dimension sums up long centuries of the American black experience.

Questions for Discussion

1. What is the model for Cullen's sonnet "Yet Do I Marvel"? English? Italian? What is its rhyme scheme?

2.   What is the meaning of line 4, "Why flesh that mirrors Him must some day die"?
3.   Explain Cullen's reference in lines 9 and 10, "immune to catechism." Why is the word "catechism" a useful allusion in the context of the poem?
4.   In line 11, is "to slightly understand" meant ironically?
5.   Is the vision of Africa in "Heritage" a description of a real land, or is it a dreamed reality?
6.   What is the meter and the rhyme scheme of the poem "Heritage"? The strict counting of accents leads Cullen to the enjambment of lines 4 and 5: "regal black / women from." Does this strengthen or weaken the effect of the opening stanza?
7.   What is the meaning of the phrase in line 15, "Juggernauts of flesh"? What term describes this figure of speech?
8.   In lines 31 and 32, "Africa? A book one thumbs / Listlessly, till slumber comes," the poet seems to suggest that he has tired of the question of Africa and his racial background. Does this contradict the emotional message of the rest of the poem?
9.   The mood of the poem seems to reflect an older and wiser disillusionment, but Cullen was a college student when he wrote it. How could he have achieved this effect while he was still so young?
10.   What is the poetic form of "Incident"? Is it similar to other poems of the same type in the anthology?
11.   Why might Cullen have chosen this verse form for a bitter poem about racial prejudice?
12.   How does the phrase "Heart-filled, head-filled with glee" describe an eight-year-old boy? Is it appropriate? Is it useful as a description of an African American boy of the 1920s?

Topics for Writing

1.   Discuss the verse forms that Cullen uses in each of these poems and relate them to the poetic elements discussed in Chapter 9.
2.   **RESPONDING CREATIVELY**   Imagine a debate between supporters and detractors of Cullen's poetic idiom and present what might be the arguments of the opposing groups.
3.   The issues that present themselves in "Heritage" still divide the African American community. For Afrocentrists, Cullen's vision of an idyllic African past is central to their reconstruction of black history. With the realities of modern-day Africa in mind, discuss the idealized view of Africa in the poem.
4.   **MAKING CONNECTIONS**   Compare the poems of Cullen, in terms of poetic technique, to the poems of Langston Hughes, and discuss also the differences or similarities in their response to their racial situation in America at the time.

E. E. CUMMINGS

O sweet spontaneous (p. 759)
somewhere i have never travelled (p. 931)
Buffalo Bill 's (p. 931)
in Just- (p. 932)

In his need to be continually upsetting to conventional readers, cummings experimented with typography in ways that often pushed his poems beyond comprehension. It is possible to puzzle out what he means in lines such as these from "XAIPE" (1950):

```
tw

o o
ld
o

nce upo
n
```

Too often, however, the poem the reader is left with is simplistic and banal. A more serious problem that cummings's desire to present himself as a "bad boy" projects into the poetry is his insistence on maintaining social attitudes that are offensive to many readers and certainly will cause problems for students. cummings was anti-Semitic and racist, and his view of women was limited. On the one hand, cummings could create poems of great sensitivity and beauty. Certainly "somewhere i have never travelled" is one of the most beautiful love poems in the English language. Students glancing through the table of contents of his collected writing, however, will encounter such titles as "IKEY (GOLDBERG)'S WORTH I'M" and "a kike is the most dangerous," which is certainly one of the most offensive anti-Semitic poems to be found outside of the hate literature of militia groups. African American students will find titles such as "one day a nigger" or "theys so alive / (who is / ?niggers)" especially reprehensible.

cummings's politics presents as many difficulties as his social attitudes. A reader encountering his work as an adolescent finds cummings's thumbing-of-the-nose toward authority a refreshing sign of youthful high spirits. His antiwar poems of the 1920s, such as "my sweet old etcetera" or "next to of course god america I," and the anti-Americanism of a poem like "POEM, OR BEAUTY HURTS MR. VINAL" seem less startling after the angry writing of the 1960s and 1970s. At the time, however, cummings's poems were a useful antidote to the unthinking jingoism that was pervasive in America. They are also very funny. Reading more of his writing, however, makes it clear that his view of America is not shaped by compassion or tolerance. He dislikes salesmen, politicians, businessmen, and academics as much as he does minority groups and unfriendly women. The cummings of much of the poetry is an elitist and a snob, a man who angrily denounces a society that gets up in the morning and goes to work and doesn't have time for his poems about his love affairs — many of them chance encounters with prostitutes — or the sunsets and sunrises he finds so breathtaking.

It will be helpful to the instructor presenting cummings to a class to realize that many critics, since the publication of cummings's first book in 1923, have made these same criticisms — that his work is often immature, sentimental, dismissive, and arrogant — just as they have praised the best of his poetry for its sensitivity and technical skill. One aspect of cummings's writing that has always fascinated readers is its blend of a modern, slangy, jazz-rhythmed style with traditional verse forms.

O SWEET SPONTANEOUS

Questions for Discussion

1. What is the dilemma the Earth faces in the poem?
2. What role do philosophy and religion play in this torment?
3. What is Earth's answer to its tormentors?
4. The poem is constructed around a series of images using figures of speech. What are these figures of speech and how do they bring the poem to life?
5. What does cummings wish to convey to his readers with his impudent and idiosyncratic use of the elements of grammar, spelling, and spacing?
6. Is he sending a contradictory message with his use of archaic terms like "thee" or "answerest"?

7.   Although he expresses some misgivings about philosophers, the poem expresses a philosophic point of view. What is it?

Topics for Writing

1.   In the poem cummings uses the adjective "prurient" to describe the response of philosophers to spring. Discuss how he illustrates this term in the conduct of both philosophy and religion toward the Earth.
2.   The poem could be said to typify an anti-intellectual point of view. Discuss this aspect of the poem and compare it to the other poetry by cummings in the anthology.

SOMEWHERE I HAVE NEVER TRAVELLED
BUFFALO BILL 'S
IN JUST-

For much of his life, cummings was married to a beautiful model named Marian Moorehouse, and many of his love poems reflect his deep and genuine emotion for her. "somewhere i have never travelled" is one of his most affecting love poems, and it is technically one of his most skillful. Students can follow the image of the rose through cummings's descriptions of how his loved one's fingers can open him, as spring opens "her first rose," to the last image, "the voice of your eyes is deeper than all roses." They should also be able to respond to the use of words like "frail" and "fragility," which suggest the softness of flower petals. Also, they will respond to the care with which cummings introduces rhyme into the last verse, subtly intensifying the beauty of the poem's language.

"Buffalo Bill 's," from cummings's first collection, *Tulips and Chimneys* (1923), is one of his most popular poems. There is marked contrast between the seriousness of the poem's subject, the death of famed frontier scout and showman William "Buffalo Bill" Cody, and the flippancy of the language. Buffalo Bill isn't dead; he's "defunct." And when cummings asks the Angel of Death how he responds to the death of someone as heroic as Cody, the question is presented in the unforgettable phrase "how do you like your blueeyed boy / Mister Death." Students will also find it appealing that cummings, despite his seeming flippancy, expresses a real admiration for Buffalo Bill. Cody rode a "watersmooth-silver / Stallion," and as cummings remembers the posters of Cody that advertised his Wild West Show, he bursts out, "Jesus / he was a handsome man."

"In Just-" is another poem from cummings's first book. In it he creates the sudden excitement of a spring day when a balloon seller comes to a place where children are playing and whistles to get their attention. As students will realize as they finish reading the poem, this balloon man is no ordinary street peddler. The "goat footed" figure ushering in spring is the god Pan, who whistles with his syrinx, bound-together hollow reeds known as pan pipes, to call up Persephone from the underworld. The names of the children in the poem — "eddieandbill," "bettyandisabel" — could easily be the names of children from anywhere in the world. Students will be able to picture the spring in such phrases as "mud-luscious" and "puddle-wonderful," and the opening image "in Just-/ spring," which means that spring has just arrived, will help students to understand some of the ways that cummings's best poems are a discovery of the possibilities of language. Students will also notice the use of run-together word phrases in both this poem and "Buffalo Bill 's," with the latter's "onetwothreefourfive pigeonsjustlikethat." This device helps cummings suggest that sometimes things happen so quickly that you can't really be sure of what you've seen.

Questions for Discussion

1. In the poem "in Just-" cummings uses wide spaces between the words *whistles, far,* and *wee.* Why did he leave that space?
2. What other unusual typographical devices does cummings use in the poem? Do you think they help us to understand what he is writing about?
3. In "Buffalo Bill 's," is cummings describing William Cody as a frontier scout or as a showman? What in the poem tells us this?
4. What kind of pigeons is cummings referring to in the line describing Buffalo Bill's shooting abilities?
5. What is the effect of the words that are run together in this same line?
6. In "somewhere i have never travelled," why do you think cummings chose the rose for his image of a flower?
7. Why do you think cummings sets so many of his poems in the spring?
8. Some critics have suggested that "somewhere i have never travelled" is like a sonnet. Why do they make that comparison?

Topics for Writing

1. Discuss several of cummings's typographical devices and judge their effectiveness in his poetry.
2. The pose of the "bad boy" that cummings adopts in his poetry has close links to such classic American archetypes as Mark Twain's Tom Sawyer and J. D. Salinger's Holden Caulfield. Analyze this persistent American image and try to explain its meaning.
3. Some of the brashness in cummings's poems is also reflected in the popular visual arts and the jazz music of the 1920s. Compare cummings's attitudes with the images and forms of the decade's other arts.
4. One of the criticisms of cummings is that essentially his work didn't change as he grew older — in other words, he never grew up. Compare an early and a late poem to see what, if any, changes occurred in the poet's attitudes.
5. Explicate the flower imagery in "somewhere i have never travelled."

H.D. [HILDA DOOLITTLE]

Mid-day (p. 758)
Oread (p. 791)

In the early poetry of H.D., the reader recognizes the schoolgirl who sat down in a rainstorm, stretched out her arms, and cried, "Beautiful rain, welcome." In "Oread," one of the first poems H.D. wrote as an imagist, she cries out to the sea to engulf the land, and herself with it. Although the poem is only a few lines long, it presents us with a complex series of images. In "The Poetry of Modernity," the English literary historian Linda Ruth Williams analyzed the poem in its imagist context:

> "Oread" is often tendered as the exemplary imagist poem, with the complex of sea, pines and nymph fusing as image. Pound had defined the image as "that which presents an intellectual and emotional complex in an instant

of time"; H.D.'s text pares down superfluity to a series of discrete, spare phrases. What the poem "is" is the relation between these phrases, how they build up into an image which does not come from individual key words or vague feelings but from the ways in which the component elements of the poem relate. (*Bloomsbury Guide to English Literature* [1995], 272)

In "Mid-day," written two years later, when she was no longer as closely involved with the original imagist group, H.D. describes how the smallest things in nature, like the sunlight or the crackling of a leaf, are overwhelming. The speaker feels the wind scattering her being, just as it scatters seeds, and she becomes aware of other things around her that have been split or bent, cracked or blackened. But then she sees a poplar tree on a distant hillside and remembers that the poplar is deep-rooted. The poplar is strong enough to withstand the wind that has scattered her, as seeds are scattered in the crevices of the stones. It is not explicit in the text, but seeds left in stone crevices can never grow.

Questions for Discussion

1. What is H.D. describing in "Oread" when she writes "pointed pines," "great pines," and "pools of fir"? What is the term for this kind of description?
2. What could students suggest as emotional equivalents for the waves she is asking to splash on "our rocks"?
3. In "Mid-day" H.D. writes, "I am anguished — defeated." What does she mean?

Topics for Writing

1. Write a paper discussing how "Oread" fits into the imagist program as outlined in Chapter 11, using images and lines from the poem as illustrations.
2. Both poems discussed include extensive images of nature, used in a very emotional context. Analyze these images and make some suggestions as to their symbolic meaning for H.D.
3. MAKING CONNECTIONS   In "Mid-day" some of the imagery is related to images in Percy Bysshe Shelley's "Ode to the West Wind" (p. 764). In his poem he asks the wind to drive his thoughts over the universe, "Like withered leaves," and "Scatter, as from an unextinguished hearth / . . . my words among mankind!" Compare and contrast the sections of the two poems that describe the wind as it whirls around each poet.

EMILY DICKINSON

You love me — you are sure — (p. 937)

I'm "wife" — I've finished that — (p. 937)

I taste a liquor never brewed — (p. 937)

Wild Nights — Wild Nights! (p. 938)

"Hope" is the thing with feathers — (p. 938)

There's a certain Slant of light, (p. 939)

I'm Nobody! Who are you? (p. 939)

After great pain, a formal feeling comes — (p. 939)

Much Madness is divinest Sense — (p. 940)

I died for Beauty — but was scarce (p. 940)

I heard a Fly buzz — when I died — (p. 940)

Because I could not stop for Death — (p. 941)

A narrow Fellow in the Grass (p. 941)

I never saw a Moor — (p. 942)

Students should read the Conversations commentaries while they are reading the poems. It can be difficult to picture the elusive Dickinson in her writing, but Thomas Wentworth Higginson's description is helpful in giving her a physical reality. Higginson was even more open in the letters he wrote to his wife shortly after his meeting with Dickinson, responding to an inner resiliency he sensed in the reclusive poet. He quoted Dickinson as saying, "How do most people live without any thoughts? There are many people in the world (you must have noticed them in the street). How do they live? How do they get the strength to put on their clothes in the morning?" She also said to him, "Women talk: men are silent: that is why I dread women."

Thomas H. Johnson was the editor who finally had the opportunity to work with the entire body of Dickinson manuscripts, and his description of his problems deciding on a final version of some of the poems will help students understand the way any poet works. Richard Wilbur discusses some of the underlying themes in the poems, and Linda Gregg responds to Dickinson's use of verbal resources.

Although the following is a concept that has not been previously suggested, it might help students if they think of Dickinson's poetry as being of two different types. During the years she was writing poetry at a feverish pace, from 1860 to 1863, she produced almost a poem a day, and she kept no other diary. This work could be described as "diary poems" — lyrics that Dickinson used to express or conceal her most personal emotions and descriptions of things that were happening in her personal life. These poems are usually loosely written, with irregular meter, uneven stanza length, and rhymes that often stretch even her very elastic consideration of slant or near rhyme. The other poems, which could be called her "public" writing, often have a general philosophic theme or a response to nature as their subject, and they tend to be more tightly written, usually in the four-line stanzas of alternating four- and three-stress lines that constituted the commonplace hymnal verse of the time. The poems Dickinson sent to Higginson were generally her "public" poems, and when Helen Hunt Jackson persuaded her to publish a single poem anonymously a few years before her death, the meter and rhyme had been elegantly "smoothed" to current fashion, although there is no way to know if the smoothing was done by Jackson or Dickinson herself.

In early letters to her brother Austin's wife, Susan Gilbert, Dickinson's language was extravagantly emotional, and in a series of passionate letters she wrote a few years later to a "master" (probably Charles Wadsworth), she expresses herself in fervent images. Her poetry, however, is often more guarded, often calculating in its evasions and silences. Dickinson also uses her poetry to debate with herself questions of religious faith and philosophy. So much in her poetry is concealed, but because so much is also told "slant," as she termed it, her work continues to fascinate and challenge her readers.

You LOVE ME — YOU ARE SURE —
I'M "WIFE" — I'VE FINISHED THAT —
I TASTE A LIQUOR NEVER BREWED —
WILD NIGHTS — WILD NIGHTS!

Of these four poems, three could be considered "diary poems," as they clearly are "an overflow of emotion" — as Wordsworth expressed it — and were left in such a rough state that there was no way they could have been considered for publication at the time they were written. It was only when modern readers began to read them as contemporary poems that the irregular rhyme, oblique phrasing, and startling use of metaphor were appreciated. "I taste a liquor never brewed —" is the one "public" poem of the group, and it is written in regular meter and rhyme. The end rhyme of the first and third lines to which an early critic objected, "Pearl" / "alcohol," can be read as one of Dickinson's characteristic slant rhymes.

The date of 1860 coincides with Charles Wadsworth's visit to Amherst, and if the interpretation of this period in Dickinson's life is correct, the poems relate to her emotional response to their relationship. However she intended the poems to be read, their power lies in their imagery and in a poetic form that matches the immediacy of Dickinson's thought. Few poets have written so spontaneously and so directly. A term that Dickinson applied to her poetry was "bolts of melody," and it is a useful description of her technique. If she had used the usual poetic diction and guarded emotional expression of the popular poets of her day, she would have never achieved the lyric extravagance of "I taste a liquor never brewed —" or the abrupt gust of emotion of "Wild Nights — Wild Nights!"

Questions for Discussion

1. In "You love me — you are sure —" Dickinson seems to cast herself in the role of a small girl. What images in the poem suggest this?
2. What is Dickinson describing with "grinning morn" in line 4?
3. What is the term for the metric pauses she indicates by dashes in the middle of some of the lines?
4. Discuss the poem's rhymes and half-rhymes. Is there a pattern to the rhyme?
5. Discuss what Dickinson might mean in "I'm 'wife' — I've finished that —" by using the word "wife" to describe herself. What might she mean by "Czar" and "It's safer so" in lines 3–4?
6. What is she describing with "soft Eclipse" in line 6? Why does she use the word *eclipse* for her metaphor?

7. What is she comparing in line 11?
8. Discuss the meter and rhyme scheme of "I taste a liquor never brewed —." Does it vary from its regular metric pattern? Why would Dickinson make any changes in the meter?
9. What is she referring to in line 3, "Vats upon the Rhine"?
10. What use does she make of alliteration in lines 4–6?
11. What is the metaphor she is introducing in lines 7–8, "Reeling . . . From inns of Molten Blue"? How does she develop this metaphor in the stanzas that follow?
12. Why do you think Dickinson didn't use the "correct" rhyme by Thomas Bailey Aldrich, quoted in the headnote?
13. We would use the term *hyperbole* for the poem's last stanzas. Discuss why we would describe them this way.
14. If we ignore the dashes in scanning the meter of "Wild Nights — Wild Nights!" the poem is written in regular dimeter except for the penultimate line. Why did Dickinson write the line differently?
15. What is the metaphor of the second and third stanzas?
16. What is Dickinson saying with "Futile — the Winds — / To a heart in port —" in lines 4–5?
17. How could line 9, "Rowing in Eden —," be interpreted?

Topic for Writing

1. Compare "You love me — you are sure —" and "I taste a liquor never brewed —" for their differences in meter and rhyme.

"HOPE" IS THE THING WITH FEATHERS —
THERE'S A CERTAIN SLANT OF LIGHT,
I'M NOBODY! WHO ARE YOU?
AFTER GREAT PAIN, A FORMAL FEELING COMES —
MUCH MADNESS IS DIVINEST SENSE —

" 'Hope' is the thing with feathers —" is one of Dickinson's most imaginative poems, and one that expresses reassurance. Whatever else has (or has not) happened in Dickinson's life, there is still hope — hope that is everywhere and never asks for anything. "There's a certain Slant of light," is more ambiguous, as it depicts a mood, a sense of depression the poet feels on winter afternoons. There is, however, no ambiguity about the darkness of her mood. One of Dickinson's biographers, Richard B. Sewall, notes that in their editing of the poem, Higginson and Mrs. Todd changed "Heft" to "weight" and

> included the poem in the section [of the 1890 Poems] entitled "Nature," even though it would have been more at home in their very next category, "Time and Eternity." Actually, the poem straddles both categories. The New England scene is sharp and clear, while the long, long thoughts it induces control our response to it. But what is the response? Are we left in a bleak, hurtful, hopeless world? When the light goes, are we in utter darkness? . . . I am reminded of the psychologist Carl Jung's phrase as he opposes the powerful, dangerous factors in our lives to the "grand, beautiful, and meaningful": he refers to this opposition as "the terrible ambiguities of immediate experience" (*Psychology and Religion* 55). Here, the poem seems to say, "If in the midst of life we die, it is also true that in the midst of death, we live." The oppressive tunes are "Cathedral," the hurt is "Heavenly," the despair is "imperial," of the "Air." And in this awareness we live more intensely, closer to the divine in our nature. It takes the shock

of such awareness — the "look of Death" — to wake us up. (qtd. in *Voices and Visions: The Poet in America*, ed. Helen Vendler [1987], 80)

In early poems written when she was a teenager, Dickinson was often wickedly funny, and in her mature poetry she could still be intentionally humorous. "I'm Nobody! Who are you?" is one of her poems dealing with the themes of fame and adulation, and she dismisses them with the arch comparison of public acclaim with a frog's croak.

"After great pain, a formal feeling comes —" is loosely composed, like the diary poems, and could be an emotional response to a moment of despair. Her comparison with a numb happiness as a "Quartz contentment" is one of her most startling images and sets up the contrast with the despair she is feeling, which is "Lead." The final line of the poem is one of her most deeply unhappy images. The hour of lead — if outlived — is like freezing to death in the snow.

"Much Madness is divinest Sense —" is one of Dickinson's most popular poems. It was included in the first collection of her work in 1890 and has been anthologized many times since then. It is one of her few poems that show a flash of anger — for a moment she lets us glimpse her impatience with the everyday world and its contradictions.

Questions for Discussion

1. What is Dickinson describing in line 3 of " 'Hope' is the thing with feathers —": "And sings the tune without the words"?
2. What is she saying in the last two lines?
3. In "There's a certain Slant of light," what does Dickinson mean by "Heft / Of Cathedral Tunes"? Discuss why she might find them oppressive.
4. What can she be referring to with her "Heavenly Hurt" that leaves no scar?
5. What is the term for the figure of speech Dickinson is using in "the Landscape listens" in line 13?
6. What is she suggesting in the juxtaposition of the words "Distance" and "Death" in the last lines?
7. Do we have any idea to whom Dickinson is speaking in "I'm Nobody! Who are you?" Is this an important consideration in our reading of the poem? Why or why not?
8. What does she mean by "they'd advertise" in line 4?
9. Discuss Dickinson's implied comparison in the poem of public life to a bog.
10. "After great pain, a formal feeling comes —" could be classed as a diary poem. What are the elements that would put it in this category?
11. Discuss Dickinson's meaning in the poem, clarifying her comparison between quartz and lead.
12. What does she mean in line 2, "Nerves sit ceremonious, like Tombs"?
13. Are the last two lines a metaphor of her own death?
14. What is the paradox she is describing in the first lines of "Much Madness is divinest Sense —"?
15. Could the poem be considered a statement of a political philosophy? What would that philosophy be?
16. Is this an angry poem, or is it only expressing an ironic observation?

Topics for Writing

1. Describe in a short paper the emotions Dickinson expresses in " 'Hope' is the thing with feathers —."
2. Discuss Dickinson's images of pain and death in "After great pain, a formal feeling comes —."

3. In "Much Madness is divinest Sense —" discuss the implications of "'Tis the Majority / In this, as All, prevail."

I DIED FOR BEAUTY — BUT WAS SCARCE

This poem can be grouped with Dickinson's other "public" poetry. Its theme is derived from the last lines of John Keats's "Ode on a Grecian Urn," indicating that Dickinson was not as isolated from the main poetic influences of her time as her other poetry suggests. Keats's lines "'Beauty is truth, truth beauty,' — that is all / Ye know on earth, and all ye need to know" are echoed in her whispered conversation between two people who have just died. Of all the romantic poets, it was Keats that Dickinson read and admired the most. In a later poem she said that she told the truth in her poetry, but that she told it "slant," so it is perhaps not an unconscious choice that she describes herself here as dying for beauty, while the man beside her has died for truth. The final lines also edge closely to another of her themes — her hidden disappointment that she would not have any recognition for her writing, even if this was a resolve she had made herself and to which she held firmly throughout her life.

Questions for Discussion

1. What is the form of the poem? Compare it to "I taste a liquor never brewed —."
2. What does Dickinson mean by "an adjoining Room" in line 4?
3. What does she mean when she calls death a failure in the second stanza?
4. What is the image she presents in lines 9–10?
5. Is the last line suggesting that the speaker's name would be lost after her death? Does she express disappointment in this knowledge?

Topic for Writing

1. **MAKING CONNECTIONS**   Relate the poem to the last lines of John Keats's "Ode on a Grecian Urn" (p. 762).

I HEARD A FLY BUZZ — WHEN I DIED —

Many meanings have been suggested for "I heard a Fly buzz — when I died —," among them that the fly represents the spirit of Christ entering her death chamber, or that the fly is the symbol of temporal reality breaking into the poem's spirituality. As with many of Dickinson's poems, there is probably no entirely satisfactory explanation for all of its imagery.

Questions for Discussion

1. In "I heard a Fly buzz — when I died —," what is happening in the room?
2. What is Dickinson describing in lines 7–8?
3. What is meant by her signing away her "assignables" in line 11?
4. What is meant with the color image of the fly's buzz, "With Blue — uncertain Buzz —," in line 13?

BECAUSE I COULD NOT STOP FOR DEATH —

Although there is no agreement among other poets about so many of Dickinson's poems, there is no disagreement about this one. In a 1932 essay Allen Tate wrote,

If the word "great" means anything in poetry, this poem is one of the greatest in the English language. The rhythm charges with movement the pattern of suspended action back of the poem. Every image is precise and,
moreover, not merely beautiful, but fused with the central idea. Every
image extends and intensifies every other. The third stanza especially
shows Miss Dickinson's power to fuse, into a single order of perception, a
heterogeneous series: the children, the grain, and the setting sun (time)
have the same degree of credibility; the first subtly preparing for the last.
The sharp *gazing* before *grain* instills into nature a cold vitality of which the
qualitative richness has infinite depth. The content of death in the poem
eludes explicit definition. He is a gentleman taking a lady out for a drive.
But note the restraint that keeps the poet from carrying this so far that it
becomes ludicrous and incredible; and note the subtly interfused erotic
motive, which the idea of death has presented to most romantic poets, love
being a symbol interchangeable with death. (qtd. in *Emily Dickinson*, ed.
Richard B. Sewall [1964], 22)

Questions for Discussion

1. What is the form of the poem? Is the rhyme scheme regular? What half-rhymes
    does Dickinson use?
2. What term would we use to describe the entire poem?
3. What does Dickinson mean by "My labor and my leisure too" in line 7?
4. What term would we use for the phrase "Gazing Grain" in line 11?
5. What is Dickinson saying about their ride in line 13, "Or rather — He passed us
    —"?
6. Discuss what she is saying in the fifth stanza, beginning "We paused before a
    House."
7. Is she suggesting in the last line that eternity is a goal? Does this mean that she
    wants us to think of eternity as a place rather than a measure of time?

Topics for Writing

1. Discuss the figure of death in the poem.
2. Dickinson mentions or describes death in many poems, including examples in this
    selection. Compare this poem with any of the others.
3. There are many images of time and its passage in the poem. Analyze and discuss
    them.

A NARROW FELLOW IN THE GRASS

This is one of the handful of Dickinson's poems published in her lifetime, but it
was printed by her friend Samuel Bowles in his newspaper, the *Springfield Republican*,
without her permission. Dickinson often worked in clusters of poems, and this is one of
several she wrote about snakes. Despite her unhappiness at seeing the poem in print, it
has many of the characteristics of her public poems, even though there is a subtle shift in
the poem's metric pattern after the second stanza. It does seem likely that when she wrote
it she saw it as something that could be published, as the style and subject matter are similar to popular magazine verse with which she was familiar. What suggests this even
more strongly is that she presents herself as a barefoot boy, one of the popular personae
for poems of this type.

Questions for Discussion

1. Scan the poem for its metric form and discuss Dickinson's use of rhyme and half-rhyme.
2. What is she saying in line 4?
3. What is she describing in the second stanza? How could this be paraphrased?
4. What reasons might be suggested for her use of the "Boy, and Barefoot" as a persona?
5. What is she saying about the poem's persona in the stanza beginning with line 17, "Several of Nature's People"? Does this seem consistent with Dickinson's own feelings about the natural world?
6. What does she mean by "Zero at the Bone" in line 24?

Topics for Writing

1. Discuss why a barefoot boy would be a popular persona for a poem about nature.
2. Discuss the feeling Dickinson describes as a "transport of cordiality" toward "Nature's people."

I NEVER SAW A MOOR —

In many of her poems written after the turmoil of the early 1860s, Dickinson's subject is eternity or heaven. This is one of her most direct expressions of her religious faith.

Questions for Discussion

1. Is the meter regular throughout "I never saw a Moor —"? How would the stanzas be scanned?
2. There are changes in the word order of lines 3 and 7. Why has Dickinson made these changes?
3. Why would she choose a moor as an image?
4. What does she mean by "Checks" in line 8?

Topic for Writing

1. Discuss Dickinson's concept of God and heaven in "I never saw a Moor —."

Conversations on Interpreting Emily Dickinson, pp. 1079–1096

Thomas Wentworth Higginson, *"Emily Dickinson's Letters,"* p. 1080.
Thomas H. Johnson, *"The Text of Emily Dickinson's Poetry,"* p. 1087.
Thomas Bailey Aldrich, *"In Re Emily Dickinson,"* p. 1089.
Richard Wilbur, *"On Emily Dickinson,"* p. 1091.
Linda Gregg, *"Not Understanding Emily Dickinson,"* p. 1093.

DIANE DI PRIMA

Revolutionary Letter #57 (p. 875)

Diane di Prima was born in New York in 1934. In rebellion from her Italian American family, she dropped out of college and became part of the generation that would create the Beat consciousness in scruffy apartments and in bars and on the streets of Greenwich Village and New York's Lower East Side. Her first book, *This Kind of Bird Flies Backwards,* was published in 1958 by Totem Press, a small press operated by Hettie and LeRoi Jones. Some months later di Prima had a child by Jones and lived with him until he adopted the name Amiri Baraka and moved to New Jersey to begin a new life as an activist for black freedom. Diane di Prima had children with other lovers, continued to write, and eventually moved to San Francisco, where she has had a long, productive career as teacher, counselor, and inspiration to two generations of women, as well as continuing to write and publish both poetry and prose. The *Revolutionary Letters,* which were written over a period of several years, reflect her response to the Vietnam War and her insistence on making her voice heard in the continuing debate over the direction the United States should take in this moment of crisis.

Questions for Discussion

1. How would you describe di Prima's conclusions about the deeper motives and events in the history found in "Revolutionary Letter #57"?
2. What is she telling us in the final line, "& watch the hills flicker like dreamskin"?

Topic for Writing

1. In her "Revolutionary Letter #57" di Prima presents a deeply personal contemplation on the realities and contradictions of American history. Discuss her conclusions, and place them in the context of the debate over the Vietnam War that dominated the political discourse in the United States at the time the poem was written.

JOHN DONNE

Death, be not proud (p. 774)
Excerpt from "Meditation XVII" (p. 943)
A Valediction: Forbidding Mourning (p. 943)
The Sun Rising (p. 944)
Batter my heart, three-personed God (p. 945)

Anyone who spends a little time with Donne's poetry soon becomes aware of the contradictions in both his life and his writing. In his early poetry he writes as "Jack" Donne, a young and passionate adventurer and London man-about-town. In his later poems and sermons he writes, just as passionately, as Dr. Donne of St. Paul's Cathedral. When the biographer Lytton Strachey described the contradictions of the Elizabethan age in which Donne lived, he found that Donne was a particularly complicated example of these contradictions. Strachey wrote,

> It is above all the contradictions of the age that baffle our imagination and perplex our intelligence. Human beings no doubt cease to be human beings unless they were inconsistent; but the inconsistency of the Elizabethans exceeds the limits permitted to man. Their elements fly off from one another wildly. . . . By what perverse magic were intellectual ingenuity and theological ingenuousness intertwined in John Donne? (qtd. in *Donne,* ed. Sir Herbert Grierson [1933], xiii)

In discussing the near hopelessness of Donne's situation — a Catholic in a Protestant country who converted to the Anglican Church and attempted to satisfy the emotional complications of his decision — the critic and editor of Donne's poetry, Sir Herbert Grierson, wrote, "His was a poetic temperament, imaginative, susceptible, impulsive, served by an acute and subtle intellect, and under the influence of diverse elements in his nature he complied with circumstances more than once in his life; but such compliance does not make for peace of mind" (*Donne* xv). If students have difficulty understanding these disparate elements in Donne's writing, they should understand that Donne, and all his later critics, had some of the same difficulties.

A Valediction: Forbidding Mourning

Donne wrote this poem for his wife, admonishing her not to mourn while he was away from her on a diplomatic mission. It is a characteristic Elizabethan conceit, finding a paradox in the true nature of their union, which is a love so refined that "Like gold to airy thinness beat" it joins them together even as they are separated. The poem also presents what is certainly an erotic symbol in the next to last stanza, even though Donne has presented the image as though it were his wife who waited and "grows erect" as he "comes home."

Questions for Discussion

1. Donne has used a word from the title, *mourning,* to introduce the image of dying men's last words in the first stanza. Does death frighten him, or do the people standing around the deathbed?
2. The word "melt" in the first line of the second stanza was commonly used in this period to mean having an orgasm. Is this Donne's meaning in this line? How is this interpretation strengthened or weakened in later lines of the poem?
3. In line 14 he writes of ordinary lovers, "Whose soul is sense." He seems to be saying that there is nothing to their love but pleasure of the senses. Does he regard this as negative?
4. What is he saying to his wife in stanza 6, "Our two souls . . ."?
5. Is his vision of their love weakened by his earlier lines, ". . . a love so much refined / That our selves know not what it is"?
6. Paraphrase the final stanza in terms of the paradox Donne presents.

Topics for Writing

1. Discuss the Elizabethan conceit and find other instances in Donne's poetry where he uses a conceit as a complicated paradox.
2. Compare Donne's view of love in this poem with that in his earlier love poems.

Death, be not proud
Batter my heart, three-personed God

John Chalker and Erik Frykman, in the notes to *An Anthology of English Verse* (1969), are helpful in their description of Donne's Holy Sonnets. They write,

> Like his other verse they show an impassioned mind expressing itself in forceful, colloquial terms, with the usual admixture of ingenious imagery. They are pervaded by a tortured sense of sin and unworthiness counterbalanced by the hope of divine mercy. Terror of death is a frequent theme in these sonnets: in the most often quoted of them it is overcome by a triumphant assurance of death's powerlessness. (245)

Students will notice that the form of the sonnets combines the English and Italian models. The first two quatrains rhyme in the Italian style, *abba / abba,* and the last six lines rhyme in the English style, either *cddc* or *cdcd,* with a new rhyme, *ee,* in the final two lines. Although the sonnets are concentrated and sometimes complex in their imagery, students usually find that with a few moments of discussion they can follow their attitudes and ideas. Perhaps because of their religious themes, or perhaps because Donne was older, the sonnets are less crabbed and difficult than most of his secular verse. They still, however, are filled with paradox.

"Death, be not proud" develops a paradox that was common at the time — that because at death human beings wake to live eternally, it is death that dies: "One short sleep past, we wake eternally / And death shall be no more."

In "Batter my heart, three-personed God" the speaker asks God to hammer at his heart until He gains admittance. He has labored to give himself to God, but he still is filled with doubt. This is usually interpreted to mean the doubts that torment many Christians, but it could also be a veiled reference to Donne's difficulties with his divided faith. The sonnet expresses its theme in paradoxes that are as effective as the language of "Death, be not proud." If the man is to rise and stand, then God must overthrow him. In the powerful final lines he says that he never will be free until God fetters him, and he never will be chaste until God ravishes him.

Questions for Discussion

1. In lines 5–6 of "Death, be not proud," Donne says that rest and sleep are a pleasurable picture of death. What will death itself be like?
2. What is he saying in line 7, with "soonest our best men with thee do go"? Is this similar to the familiar saying "Only the good die young"?
3. What does he mean by calling death a slave in line 9?
4. In "Batter my heart, three-personed God," what does Donne mean by "three-personed God"?
5. What is meant in line 2, with the list of words like *knock* and *breathe* that failed to open the speaker's heart?
6. What does he mean in line 5, that he is "to another due"?
7. In line 7 Donne describes reason as God's viceroy. What does he mean by this?
8. What is the meaning in line 11 of the speaker's request that God divorce him?

Topics for Writing

1. **MAKING CONNECTIONS**   This sequence of Donne's sonnets was written not long after the collection of Shakespeare's sonnets was published. Compare the two writers' sonnets.
2. Write a paper comparing and contrasting Donne's various uses of paradox in the Holy Sonnets.

THE SUN RISING

Also read Wendy Cope's humorous limerick (p. 779) alluding to Donne's poem "The Sun Rising."

Questions for Discussion

1. Donne's poem is written in a complex scheme of rhyme and rhythm. Are each of the stanzas written in a similar form? What is the rhyme scheme? Does the poet

allow himself some liberties with the rhymes? Where are they irregular or what is called *near rhymes*?

2. The poem is a dense construct of metaphor. What are some of the metaphors and figures of speech Donne uses to create the scene of the poem? Could we characterize the language of the poem as an example of *hyperbole*?

3. What are some of the things Donne tells the sun to do in the first stanza, instead of wasting its efforts on Donne and his mistress? Are any of these reasonable?

4. What is he saying to the sun about eclipsing its rays with a wink? Why does he choose not to lose "her sight"?

5. What is he calling a "Saucy pedantic wretch"? What is he intimating with the phrase?

6. What does the poet mean with his lines "Love, all alike, no season knows nor clime, / Nor hours, days, months, which are the rags of time"? What could be some meanings for his phrase "rags of time"?

7. What is he saying about himself and his mistress in the line "She is all states and all princes I"?

8 What does he mean by his statement that "Princes do but play us"? Does he intend it to sound egotistical, or is it a repetition of his theme that there is nothing more universal than what they are experiencing together as the day passes?

9. A modern term for poetry of this style is *metaphysical*. What is the meaning of the term and is it applicable to a poem like Donne's?

Topics for Writing

1. There is an extravagance in this poem's claims on the powers of physical love. Summarize what Donne claims to find around them and within their bed chamber as he and his mistress spend the day together. Discuss his justification for these boasts and consider their real meaning.

2. Donne in this and other poems sets himself up to challenge the major elements of time and nature that are commonly felt to dictate the world's seasons and events. Discuss whether this is an attitude widespread in England during the Elizabethan period or whether it was Donne himself who proclaimed it? Compare this poem to Donne's sonnet "Death, be not proud" (p. 774) which challenges the power of death in the same way he challenges the power of sun in this poem. Is there any justification for his attitudes?

3. This is the type of poem often called *metaphysical*, and at the time the poems were written the extravagant metaphors and similes were called *conceits*. Describe the poem's use of language and decide whether or not the terms are appropriate.

FROM "MEDITATION XVII"

For modern readers this excerpt is certainly the best-known selection from Donne's writings, and the phrase "No man is an island" has become part of the general vocabulary, even though in a Feminist reading the use of the term "man," meaning all of the human race, is no longer considered acceptable. It is ironic that the paragraph first became widely known as the epigraph for the novel by Ernest Hemingway, *For Whom the Bell Tolls,* which told the story of a man fighting a hopeless rearguard action as part of a Communist guerrilla force battling the Fascist army of General Franco in the 1930s Spanish Civil War. Hemingway was telling the reader that everyone must be engaged in the struggle against Fascism. The statement is now a larger challenge — we all must engage ourselves in society because we are all affected. The paragraph is taken from a sermon written by Donne after he had entered the church, and it refers to the funeral bells that were heard throughout London during a season of disease and death.

Questions for Discussion

1. What is the larger metaphor of the paragraph? Why does he say "no man is an island"?
2. What is he telling the reader in the phrase "any man's death diminishes me"?
3. His example of a "clod" washed away leaving Europe the "lesse" is an example of hyperbole. Are there other figures of speech in the paragraph?

Topics for Writing

1. Discuss the feminist reaction to the use of the term "man" in writing that intends it to mean the entire human race. Does this reading diminish our response to the writing?
2. Rewrite the paragraph using a gender neutral term instead of Donne's general term "man." Discuss the relative effectiveness of the statement using either the general term or a gender neutral term.
3. Compare the humility of this writing with Donne's assertions of power over the universe in his poems "The Sun Rising" (p. 944) and "Death, be not proud" (p. 774). Discuss the contradictions that these different writings seem to suggest and offer an explanation as to why Donne seems to have altered his views.

Connection

Wendy Cope, *"The fine English poet, John Donne,"* p. 779.

RITA DOVE

Sonnet in Primary Colors (p. 776)
Singsong (p. 946)
Maple Valley Branch Library, 1967 (p. 946)
The Pond, Porch-View: Six P.M., Early Spring (p. 947)

SONNET IN PRIMARY COLORS

Dove was born in Akron, Ohio, in 1952, and has had an enviable career. She has been the recipient of nearly every major grant and fellowship; she has studied in Europe as a Fulbright-Hays scholar; her book *Thomas and Beulah,* a collection of short poems about her grandparents, won the Pulitzer Prize in 1987; and in 1993 she received a two-year appointment as poet laureate of the United States. Her poetry is so clear and so immediately accessible that students should have no trouble understanding her writing, though they may not be familiar with Frida Kahlo, the Mexican painter who is the subject of "Sonnet in Primary Colors." Kahlo was married to the painter Diego Rivera, and during her lifetime her own painting was not considered to be on a level with his artistic achievement, a judgment that has been largely reversed in recent years. Her work fused elements of Mexican folklore with her strongly held political beliefs, and she used herself, usually dressed in peasant costume, as the subject of all her canvases. She was injured in an accident as a young woman and spent her life in continual pain from spinal injuries. It is the injury and her self-portrait *The Broken Column* that is referred to in line 5 of the poem, "the plaster corset / her spine resides in." The poem also refers to another of Kahlo's works, *Me and My Parrots,* and to the fact that she and Rivera paid tribute to communism — assembling the photos of Stalin, Lenin, Marx, Engels, and Mao at the foot of their bed.

Dove has written many poems in what she considers a modern sonnet form. Students will note that this poem has fourteen lines, but it is otherwise written without the classical sonnet's rhyme or meter. It is the intellectual mode of the sonnet that Dove considers to be its most important aspect for modern writers.

Questions for Discussion

1. Although in her poem Dove is describing details from paintings of Frida Kahlo, is it possible for us to visualize Kahlo through the descriptions in the poem?
2. What is the figure of speech Dove is using in "stern petticoats" in line 3?
3. Can we tell from the poem what Kahlo has given herself as a present?
4. What do the political figures named in the poem tell us about Kahlo's political ideals?
5. Why does Dove use the term "primary colors" in the title of the poem?

Topics for Writing

1. **MAKING CONNECTIONS**   Discuss the elements in Dove's poem that are close to the classic sonnet and those elements that are different from it, using other sonnets in the anthology for comparison.
2. In a research paper developed from library materials, write a short biography of Frida Kahlo and discuss the relation between her life and Dove's depiction of it in the sonnet.

SINGSONG
MAPLE VALLEY BRANCH LIBRARY, 1967
THE POND, PORCH-VIEW: SIX P.M., EARLY SPRING

In her early collections, Dove sometimes seems poised between her two worlds — the African American experience of her youth and the European cultural world she entered with her univerity studies in Austria and her marriage to a European writer. A poem with a sensitivity to black speech and culture was often followed by a poem derived from modern European attitudes and concerns. Critic Helen Vendler, however, in her discussion of Dove's work in *The Given and the Made* (1995), emphasizes the crucial role of race in her work, while making it clear that this imposed choice of subject matter does not in itself necessarily lift the work to the level of art.

> No black artist can avoid, as subject matter, the question of skin color, and what it entails; and probably the same is still true, if to a lesser extent, of the woman artist and the subject matter of gender. Yet if these important subject matters are not presented by a dispassionate eye and a trained hand, the result will not be art, and will not exert a gaze prompting the beholder to examine his own conscience.

In the recent collection from which these three poems are taken, *On the Bus with Rosa Parks* (1999), Dove seems to have created a synthesis for the sources of her writing, which enables her to approach her unique background with a new assurance.

Questions for Discussion

1. What is Dove suggesting with the title of the poem "Singsong"?
2. Is there something songlike about the poem, or is she inferring a state of consciousness?
3. Is there a contradiction in her descriptions of her young self as a "new toy / waiting for my owner to pick me up" and "I was narrowly sweet, infinitely cruel"?
4. Would many people describe themselves as "infinitely cruel" in their childhood? Why does Dove present this judgment to the reader?
5. What is she telling us in the line "tongued in honey and coddled in milk"?
6. The last lines of the poem echo a well-known song by Bob Dylan. Does Dove mean to remind the reader of Dylan's lyric?
7. In her remarkable description of her reading in "Maple Valley Branch Library, 1967," there is an almost indigestible variety of subjects and enthusiasms. How does a young reader like Dove relate to such a range of interests?
8. Her description of the librarian makes it clear that what Dove wanted to know was what the woman had read that made it possible for her to constantly smile. Does this suggest that Dove was turning to the books she read in a search for something inside herself?
9. What does she mean by the metaphor of eating the elephant by taking small bites? Is this a symbol for Dove's own ambitions?
10. "The Pond" is an unexpected poem. Instead of describing an evening of calm contemplation that the reader might expect from the title, the poem is a disappointed lament about the place to which her life has brought her. Is there anything in Dove's other poems that prepares us for this unhappiness?
11. The tone of "The Pond" veers between the familiar and the literary. What are the connotations of a word like wending in line 2? Does it have literary associations?
12. What is Dove describing in the image "The sunset ticks another notch / into the pressure treated rails"? Why does she specify "pressure treated rails"?
13. What is a child's "backseat universe"?

Topics for Writing

1. MAKING CONNECTIONS   Like the poet Countee Cullen, Dove also writes from a consciousness of her blackness and at the same time from a deep response to European culture. Compare the writing of the two poets and discuss the differing strategies they bring to their synthesis of these two creative sources.
2. Discuss the range of reading that Dove describes in her library poem, and try to find a common thread that holds the material together. Comment on the material's uses to a young poet.
3. In "Singsong," the poet writes that "I ran the day to its knees." Discuss her meaning, and relate it to the experience of childhood she describes here.
4. The woman of "The Pond" has lost the optimism and excitement of the girl who read so widely in the Maple Valley Branch Library. Compare the two poems and imagine what disappointments could have caused the change. Include in the discussion a response to the image of the "dear goose / come honking down / from Canada."

Commentary

Rita Dove, "An Intact World," p. 1045.

Paul Laurence Dunbar

Sympathy (p. 840)

Dunbar was a complex, brilliant man who lived his short life under the shadow of institutionalized racism. He was born in Dayton, Ohio, raised by an attentive mother, and achieved early recognition when he was elected president of his high school graduation class and delivered the graduation poem — despite being the only African American in the student body. He became successful as a poet, writing, however, in a sentimental "coon" dialect that is uncomfortable for many readers. Although he revered many classic English and American poets, among them Keats, Tennyson, and Longfellow, his most obvious influence was the immensely popular white American poet James Whitcomb Riley, whose writing typified the style of vernacular poetry in a stylized rural dialect. With the collection of dialect verse *Lyrics of Lowly Life* (1896), Dunbar reached some of this same mainstream audience, both white and black, and he spent much of his time and energy in subsequent years traveling and reading from his dialect collections. He began writing prose in 1898 and published both short fiction and novels. Despite a happy marriage and considerable recognition, he was unable to resolve the tensions of his situation and his already weakened health was further damaged by his alcoholism. Since his death, at the age of thirty-four in 1906, the difficulties of placing him in a literary category have persisted. As the introduction to Dunbar's writing in *The Norton Anthology of African American Literature* (1996) suggests:

> Although African American schools, cultural societies, and literary prizes were named in Dunbar's honor in the wake of his untimely death, during the last half-century Dunbar has frequently been treated as a cautionary example: a black artist co-opted by white media hype, a poet who by singing "serenely sweet" to whites only postponed the bitter realization resonant in his most poignant line: "I know why the caged bird sings." (884)

Questions for Discussion

1. What is the meter of the opening line? The final line of each stanza is one metric foot shorter than the first six lines of the stanzas. Why does Dunbar use this shorter length?
2. The poem is written entirely in the English romantic idiom. Is there an incongruity between the poem's subject and the language Dunbar has used to express it?
3. Many of the word choices — such as "opes," "chalice," and "fain" — are deliberately archaic. Why would Dunbar use these older locutions?
4. There are specific comments in the poem on racial injustice, such as the line "And a pain still throbs in the old, old scars." How would Dunbar have expected his audience to respond to these references? Is the audience for his poetry a southern working-class audience?
5. The poem is an extended metaphor, which is reinforced by the distancing of the poet from the subject in the poem's title. What is the metaphor that Dunbar presents?

Topics for Writing

1. Discuss the importance of the English romantic tradition to many African American poets, and examine the concepts of freedom and revolt in the romantic tradition that made it more acceptable to black writers.

2.   **MAKING CONNECTIONS**   Both Dunbar and Countee Cullen (p. 865) chose to write in the language and style of the English poets they loved. Discuss this anomaly and examine the response of modern readers that is suggested by the comment quoted from *The Norton Anthology of African American Literature.*

Robert Duncan

The Ballad of Mrs Noah (p. 753)

The story of Noah and the ark is one of the central myths of Judeo-Christian culture, and it has been the source of paintings, poems, comic illustrations, songs, and commentary for more than a thousand years. Duncan is better known as one of the representative poets of the 1950s modernist movement, and this ballad has a loose, affectionate tone that sets it apart from his other work.

Questions for Discussion

1.   Could this poem be read to children? Even though Duncan has written his ballad in this deceptively naive style, he still develops new themes about the ark's voyage. What does he introduce that is not usually part of the myth?
2.   The central feature of the myth is that on the ark there are two of each of the world's creatures, so they can reproduce and multiply when the ark finds dry land. Do we expect to find that Mrs. Noah also has two of everything in her kitchen?
3.   Although it is the animals that are always represented in illustrations of the ark's voyage, it is obvious that plants would be needed as well. Should we feel grateful to Mrs. Noah for including "apple, apricot, cherry and peach" in the cargo? Is it also necessary to have two of each of the plants?
4.   The poem is loosely rhymed and there is considerable variety in the meter, but it still presents its fresh story with control and economy. How does Duncan present his Mrs. Noah and her story? Does the story have a beginning, a middle, and an ending?
5.   What does Mrs. Noah find when she returns to the city she left? Is it a different ending to the myth to have the ark return to its starting place?

Topics for Writing

1.   Discuss other versions or adaptations of the Noah myth, perhaps a version you remember from your childhood. Compare these different versions to Duncan's approach.
2.   Mrs. Noah speaks in a country dialect. List some of the words and expressions she uses that reflect this personal way of speaking, and discuss what this verbal play adds to the picture Duncan presents of his unlikely heroine.

T. S. Eliot

The Love Song of J. Alfred Prufrock (p. 949)

Students should read the commentary on the poem by Cleanth Brooks and Robert Penn Warren (Chapter 17, p. 1039). They offer an interesting insight into the character of the poem's protagonist. Students will be surprised to learn that although the poem was not published until Eliot had moved overseas, it was written while he was still an under-graduate at Harvard College. The poem's mingling of many of Eliot's literary interests — from Renaissance writing to traditional English poetry to the fashionable new poetry of the French symbolists — is so free and spontaneous that some of the poem's images seem as startling to Eliot as they do to modern readers. When he used this method of organization again for the long poem *The Wasteland* a few years later, the new poem achieved worldwide success and made him famous, but it now seems mannered and self-conscious, whereas "Prufrock" still has the brash excitement of fresh discovery.

What Brooks and Warren do not make clear in their analysis is that the poem is not only a maze of allusion but also a maze of quotation, direct and indirect. Students may feel that in some sections it reads like a pastiche or a collage, and their instincts here are right. Except for the passage from Dante that he used as an epigraph to the poem, Eliot chose not to identify the quotations, unlike Marianne Moore, who was writing at the same time and who also used quotations liberally in her work. Eliot's decision *not* to identify the sources of many of the lines of the poem was useful to his reputation. Because only literary specialists could identify them, Eliot was often praised for images and lan-guage that he took from other sources. One of the most arresting images of this poem is the despairing cry "I should have been a pair of ragged claws / Scuttling across the floors of silent seas," but it isn't made clear that this image is actually from a poem by Jules Laforgue, a symbolist poet whom Eliot had translated. For most students, however, sim-ply mastering the most obvious details of this long and complex poem will be enough of a challenge in the classroom.

The opening line of the poem poses a question that has never been satisfactorily answered: Who is the "you" Eliot asks to go with him for the evening? In *Modern American Poetry, 1865–1950* (1989), Fred Moramarco has summarized the various inter-pretations:

> To whom he is speaking in the poem is purposefully ambiguous. It is pos-sibly someone else in the room, most likely a woman he's trying to seduce; it could be to the reader, so that the "you" in the first line — "Let us go then, you and I" — becomes everyone who reads the poem; and it could be to another part of Prufrock himself, so that the poem becomes an internal monolog between two parts of a self — a nervous chat between the Ego and the Id. Each of these interpretations has advocates. It is a measure of the poem's strength that it can be read consistently with any of these three premises in mind. (99)

Questions for Discussion

1. The poem is a dramatic monologue. What elements place it in this category?
2. At the time the poem was published, the image of line 3 was considered very shocking. Is it still shocking to readers today?
3. What is Eliot describing in line 7, "sawdust restaurants with oyster-shells"? Do places like this exist today?
4. What does he mean in lines 26–27, "there will be time / To prepare a face to meet the faces that you meet"?
5. What is Eliot telling us with the repetition of the lines "In the room the women come and go / Talking of Michelangelo"?
6. What is he describing in line 39, "Time to turn back and descend the stair"?
7. In line 86, "And in short, I was afraid," what is the narrator afraid of?
8. What is the narrator saying about himself in line 125, "I do not think that they will sing to me"?

Topics for Writing

1. Although the language of the poem is ironic, self-deprecating, and often humorous, the person described in the poem is deeply tragic. Analyze the tragedy of the poem.
2. Many commentators have written about the last three lines of the poem. Write your own responses to these lines.

Connection

J. Walker, *"On T. S. Eliot's* Prufrock," p. 780.

Commentaries

Cleanth Brooks and Robert Penn Warren, *"On Eliot's 'The Love Song of J. Alfred Prufrock,' "* p. 1039.
T. S. Eliot, *"From 'Tradition and the Individual Talent,' "* p. 1046.

Martín Espada

Soliloquy at Gunpoint (p. 953)
Public School 190, Brooklyn 1963 (p. 953)
Sleeping on the Bus (p. 954)

Questions for Discussion

1. Why does Espada use the word "soliloquy" in the title of his poem describing a robbery attempt?
2. What makes him feel that he and the young man threatening him are only acting out roles that they are familiar with? How have scenes like this become familiar to them?
3. Is it realistic to accept his conclusion that the young man simply handed his weapon to him?
4. In a poem like "Public School" Espada seems to give himself as a child the knowledge he has now as an adult. Does this seem like an accurate description of his perspective as a Hispanic in an American school? Could he have known what he was experiencing even when he was so young?
5. What is he telling us about the immigrant experience in "Sleeping on the Bus"? Would someone who had a more established place in the society expect to sleep on a bus?
6. In Espada's poetry is there a directness and clarity of speech that would seem to contradict the economic circumstances of his youth? Does he write as you would expect someone in his circumstances to speak? What does this tell us about the uses of conscious artistic skills in a poet's work?

Topics for Writing

1. In these three poems Espada gives us an insight into the feelings and experiences of someone like himself who struggles against patterns of discrimination in American society. Discuss the images he has given us, and present the poetic means he has used to help us "see" them.

2. Many of the things Espada describes in the poems are a result of economic factors. In a short paper using library and Internet sources, present a more detailed picture of the economic circumstances of Hispanic families in the United States, referring to points he raises in the poems.

LAWRENCE FERLINGHETTI

Constantly Risking Absurdity (p. 703)
The World Is a Beautiful Place . . . (p. 828)

CONSTANTLY RISKING ABSURDITY

Ferlinghetti has chosen a trapeze artist's performance as a metaphor for a poet's performance with words. Each must present himself to his audience, and if the poet fails to be convincing and entertaining as he performs on his "eyebeams" over the heads of his audience, he and his little act will appear ridiculous. There above the people's heads he is constantly risking the embarrassment of appearing absurd. Ferlinghetti makes it clear that even though the poet is the performer, his poet's role is modest. There waiting for him is Beauty, and he — a little figure looking like Charlie Chaplin — might be lucky enough to catch her as she leaps. If students have read the e. e. cummings poem "Buffalo Bill 's," (p. 931), they will notice that, like cummings, Ferlinghetti has run together words — for instance, *charley-chaplin* — and certainly his poem has some of cummings's playfulness and humor.

Questions for Discussion

1. What does Ferlinghetti mean when he writes in line 8 that the poet "climbs to a high wire of his own making"?
2. What is the association between the trapeze artist and Charlie Chaplin?
3. What is Ferlinghetti telling us in line 12 when he writes that the poet's act goes on "to the other side of day"?
4. In lines 16–18, what is he saying about a poet's depiction of reality?
5. To what is he comparing the truth in the metaphor "taut truth" of line 21?

Topics for Writing

1. As a modern poet, Ferlinghetti uses lines of different lengths and patterns in his writing. Some of the lines are written and spaced on the page so that they seem to suggest the high wire of a trapeze act. Comment on this.
2. Much of the poem is presented in a lighthearted manner, and it seems that there is no larger issue than the risks poets take in presenting their work to an audience. In the final lines, however, Ferlinghetti says that Beauty has leaped into "the empty air / of existence." Write a paper centered on the idea that our existence is only "empty air."

THE WORLD IS A BEAUTIFUL PLACE . . .

Questions for Discussion

1. What is the tone of the poem? Is it a political poem?
2. What is the contradiction of the lines that begin "if you don't mind happiness" and end with "so very much fun"?

3. Why does Ferlinghetti write, later in the poem, that "the world is the best place after all"? What does he name to illustrate this idea?
4. Why is his tone again ironic when he says the world is the best place, "even for thinking"?
5. Why does he put "living it up" in quotation marks?
6. What is the ending of everything he has described in the poem? Why is the mortician "smiling"?

Topics for Discussion

1. The poem could be seen as presenting a deeply cynical attitude, but then again the tone of the poem could also be considered an expression of a veiled idealism. Present in a paper evidence drawn from the poem to support either of these responses.
2. MAKING CONNECTIONS   On one level the poem is a fierce condemnation of our current society and its consistent failure to live up to its promise. Illustrate this idea with examples from the poem and relate them to other poems in the anthology that also probe our society's problems.

CAROLYN FORCHÉ

The Colonel (p. 830)

Carolyn Forché was born in 1950 and teaches at George Mason University. In the 1970s she worked in El Salvador as a human rights advocate and journalist for Amnesty International. Her anthology *Against Forgetting* (1993) is a major gathering of twentieth-century protest poetry against injustice and inhumanity.

Questions for Discussion

1. What poetic elements strike you in this prose poem?
2. Describe the character of the colonel and how it emerges through the poem.

Topic for Writing

1. MAKING CONNECTIONS   Compare the emergence of the characters of Forché's colonel and the duke in Robert Browning's "My Last Duchess" (p. 795).

ROBERT FROST

A Time to Talk (p. 713)

The Pasture (p. 958)

Mending Wall (p. 958)

Home Burial (p. 958)

Birches (p. 962)

Fire and Ice (p. 963)

To Earthward (p. 964)

Stopping by Woods on a Snowy Evening (p. 964)

The Road Not Taken (p. 965)

After Apple-Picking (p. 965)

Most students will already have read some of Frost's poetry in high school, and they will be able to discuss some of the themes and backgrounds in the poems. Many aspects of Frost's writing, and Frost himself, are contradictory and elusive, and it will be challenging to the instructor to present a more balanced and perhaps less immediately appealing view of Frost to the class.

The Nobel Prize–winning Irish poet Seamus Heaney has summed up the complicated response of many other poets to Frost in his essay "Above the Brim" in *Homage to Robert Frost* (1996):

> Among major poets of the English language in this century, Robert Frost is the one who takes the most punishment. "Like a chimpanzee" is how one friend of mine remembers him in the flesh, but in the afterlife of the text he has been consigned to a far less amiable sector of the bestiary, among the stoats, perhaps, or the weasels. Calculating self-publicist, reprehensible egotist, oppressive parent — theories of the death of the author have failed to lay the ghost of this vigorous old contender who beats along undauntedly at the reader's elbow. His immense popular acclaim during his own lifetime; his apotheosis into an idol mutually acceptable to his own and his country's self-esteem, and greatly inflationary of both; his constantly resourceful acclimatization of himself to this condition, as writer and performer — it all generated a critical resistance. (61)

As is well known, Frost set out from the beginning to make himself a success as a writer. As he wrote in a letter in 1913, "There is a kind of success called 'esteem' and it butters no parsnips. I mean a success with the critical few who are supposed to know. But really to arrive where I can stand on my legs as a poet and nothing else I must get outside that circle to the general reader who buys books in their thousands. I may not be able to do that. I believe in doing it — don't you doubt me there. I want to be a poet to all sorts and kinds. I could never make a merit of being caviar to the crowd the way my quasi-friend Pound does."

He felt he deserved success because, as he said in another letter, "to be perfectly frank with you I am one of the most notable craftsmen of my time. . . . I am possibly the only person going who works on any but a worn out theory (principle I had better say) of versification. . . . I alone of English writers have consciously set myself to make music out of what I may call the sound of sense."

Frost, however, faced a problem in his hunger for fame and recognition. The kind of familiar, pastoral poetry he might have wanted to write was already being written by poets who will not be familiar to students but who were much more successful than Frost at the time, among them Vachel Lindsay, Carl Sandburg, and Edgar Lee Masters. In the 1930s Frost had to contend with the enormous success of the populist poet Stephen Vincent Benét. He was also painfully conscious of the work of such modernist poets as T. S. Eliot and Ezra Pound, who were beginning their careers at the same time as he, and his difficulties with Eliot's poetry lingered for most of his life.

Faced with the competition of poets working on either side of him, Frost was left with little room to reach the audience he desired. His strategy was to write with a modernist clarity of diction and syntax, retaining, however, the traditional forms of meter and rhyme, and to strip his work of the sentimental clichés that had stifled late Victorian verse and, indeed, had been the deadening characteristic of his own verse. In his sense of verse structure and verbal nuance, Frost was as good as he said he was, and he carefully constructed a body of work that was narrow in scope but tightly concentrated around a recognizable persona as a crafty New England cracker-barrel sage. Frost's major poems usually were skillfully constructed to present readers with a homily — a "detachable statement," in poet Lawrence Raab's words — that they could take away from the reading. The most famous of Frost's homilies is "Good fences make good neighbors" from "Mending Wall." It was, as poet Robert Lowell described it, a "great act."

Students should read the Conversations section on Frost and his writing, which includes an early interview with Frost and a close reading of one of his major poems, "After Apple-Picking."

A TIME TO TALK

Questions for Discussion

1. Frost has written the poem in a seemingly casual rhyme scheme. What is the pattern of the rhymes? What is the meter of the lines?
2. Does the casualness of the poem give some latitude with the meter? What are some of the lines that don't follow a regular pattern?
3. The poem is an anecdote, a description of a daily meeting. What is Frost saying about himself in the poem? Has he forgotten the work still to be done, "the hills I haven't hoed"?
4. What does the poet mean with the adjective "mellow" describing the ground he is hoeing?
5. Even in Frost's day the use of automobiles was widespread in country areas. Why does he speak of his friend coming by on horseback? Is it a conscious nostalgia for earlier times?

Topics for Writing

1. The incident in the poem has some similarities to the incident in his more famous poem "Mending Wall." Compare the two poems and describe the difference between the two meetings.
2. As a writing project, try to re-create the conversation the two friends might be having beside the road, using references from the poem as a source for their talk.
3. All of the activities that the poem describes, the journeying and the hoeing, are now done by machines — the automobile for most journeys, and a variety of

mechanical diggers for work like hoeing. In a paper discuss some of these changes and decide whether or not Frost could have written this poem in our own day.

The Pasture

Mending Wall

Frost liked "The Pasture" very much, and he used it to open several collections. "Mending Wall" is one of his best-known poems, and it has been quoted on occasions as solemn as President John F. Kennedy's inspection of the Berlin Wall, when he recited its first line, "Something there is that doesn't love a wall." As critics immediately noted, the Russians could quote the last line of the poem, "Good fences make good neighbors," to justify the building of the wall. Frost himself was amused by the differing interpretations and said that he should have written the opening lines "for the generality," as he sometimes referred to his readers: "Something there is that doesn't love a wall / Something there is that does."

In an extended discussion of "Mending Wall" in the book *Touchstones* (1996), Lawrence Raab examines the "riddle" of the opening line:

> "Mending Wall" opens with a riddle: "Something there is . . ." And a riddle, after all, is a series of hints calculated to make us imagine and then name its hidden subject. The poem doesn't begin "I hate walls," or even "Something dislikes a wall." Its first gesture is one of elaborate and playful concealment, a calculated withholding of meaning. Notice also that it is the speaker himself who repairs the wall after the hunters have broken it. And it is the speaker each year who notifies his neighbor when the time has come to meet and mend the wall. Then can we safely claim that the speaker views the wall simply as a barrier between human contact and understanding? (204)

Most students will immediately identify with the attitude of the poet rather than that of the neighbor, who is presented as "an old-stone savage." When asked by the English novelist Graham Greene what he meant by "Good fences make good neighbors," Frost replied, "I wish you knew more about it, without my helping you." If they think more closely about what Frost seems to be saying — that it isn't really important to be so concerned about property rights — a few students may come to identify with the more conservative views of the neighbor.

Questions for Discussion

1. Discuss what might be called the "suspended rhyme" of the last lines of each stanza of "The Pasture" that ties together the overall rhyme scheme. Is it effective?
2. In line 3, Frost has changed the word order for the sake of the rhyme. Would the line have been as effective if it had been left in the normal word order?
3. What is the metric form of "Mending Wall"?
4. What elements of assonance and alliteration can be found in the first line?
5. What is meant by "To each the boulders that have fallen to each" in line 16?
6. What is suggested by "outdoor game" in line 21?
7. What is meant in line 24, "He is all pine and I am apple orchard"? What is the term for this figure of speech?
8. Discuss Frost's phrase "Spring is the mischief in me" in line 27.
9. In his use of the word "Elves" in line 36, is Frost being serious, or is this more of his spring mischief?
10. Discuss his description of his neighbor, beginning with line 40. Is this a fair description?

Topic for Writing

1.   In a short paper discuss the contradiction between the two "detachable statements" in "Mending Wall": "Something there is that doesn't love a wall" and
"Good fences make good neighbors."

HOME BURIAL

As Robert Frost grew older he became an exasperated defender of rhymed verse,
but in the early collection of his poetry which brought him his first fame, *North of
Boston*, written in England and published in 1914, only a handful of the poems were written in rhyme. Perhaps because of his isolation from the United States he had missed the
debate that was raging among American poets over the newly popular *free verse* and the
first stirrings of the *Imagist* movement, which favored short lyrics written in unrhymed
stanzas with some of the feeling of Japanese haiku. The heart of Frost's collection were
eleven long poems written in the accepted narrative style known as *blank verse*, which
had been introduced into English poetry before the Elizabethan era and was the language
of the Elizabethan dramatists, Shakespeare among them. Blank verse is generally written
in iambic pentameter, although virtually every poet who wrote in this form allowed
themselves some freedom in the meter of their lines. Frost also took liberties with the
meter, as students will find, especially as the husband and wife of this despairing tale
become increasingly angry and disturbed with each other. "Home Burial" is the most
emotional of the long poems in the collection, and its tensions could be a reflection of the
unhappiness of Frost's own marriage.

Two of the poems from *North of Boston* have become among Frost's best known
works. One, "After Apple-Picking," is rhymed; the other, "Mending Wall," is in blank
verse.

Questions for Discussion

1.   What is the form of the poem? How does blank verse differ from the familiar
unrhymed verse used by most contemporary poets?
2.   Does Frost allow himself some freedom in the use of the pentameter? What are
some instances where he varies the meter?
3.   What is the fear the husband sees in his wife as she stands at the top of the stairs?
4.   What is she is looking at, that after some time he notices as well? Were home-
burial grounds common in this period? What was the reason?
5.   In line 29 what does Frost mean when he writes "We haven't to mind *those*"?
6.   Is the husband already attacking the wife when he cries out in line 37 "Can't a man
speak of his own child he's lost"?
7.   What is Frost telling us about the husband when he says in lines 52–53 "A man
must partly give up being a man / With women-folk"? Was this a widely accepted
attitude at this time? Is it still acceptable today?
8.   What the wife remembers of the day their child was buried was her husband saying, in lines 96–97, "Three foggy mornings and one rainy day / Will rot the best
birch fence a man can build"? Why has this upset her? Does her husband understand her accusations?
9.   In the three lines that begin with line 79, "Making the gravel leap and leap in air,
/ Leap up, like that, like that . . . ," is the wife being obsessive? Is there any way
either of them can win their desperate argument?
10.   Is there any justification for the husband's final declaration in line 120, "I'll follow
and bring you back by force. I *will*"? Can there be any future for their relationship?

Topics for Writing

1. Often blank verse was used for extended narratives that didn't fit into the limits of shorter lyrics. Outline the story that Frost has told us, rewriting some of his verse as prose to make the story line easier to follow.
2. Analyze the meter of Frost's lines and note instances where he has varied the pattern of iambic pentameter. In a paper, explain why he has allowed himself these variations and discuss what he might have gained by it, using examples from the poem.
3. Analyze the reasons for the difficulties between the husband and wife, and discuss whether or not a modern couple might have come to the same deadlock in their relationship. Which of the two is more to blame?
4. Discuss the reasons why the husband might have made the statement "A man must partly give up being a man / With women folk?" In today's more gender-neutral climate, are there still elements of these judgments lingering in our attitudes? Use examples from your own experience and illustrate your discussion with examples from the poem.

BIRCHES

If students find this poem difficult to follow, they will be encouraged to learn that Frost composed it using two fragments, and he later confessed being unable to remember where the two were joined. Of all his major poems, it is the least well-constructed, and a closer reading may convince students that it may have been patched together from several fragments.

It was a joke among Frost's students at his Bread Loaf Writing Program that you always could tell when you were coming close to Frost's farm because all the birch trees along the road were bent down. The poem, however, is better read as a metaphor or allegory than as a simple description of climbing birch trees. It is one of his most complex poems and one of his most sentimental. It is also a poem that displays all his masks.

As they begin to study the poem, students will find that one section detaches itself from the rest — the sixteen-line description of birches in a coating of winter ice, beginning with "Often you must have seen them" in line 5. It is one of his most brilliantly imagined passages, and it fits so uncomfortably with the other segments of the poem that Frost himself breaks it off with a comment by the crusty old farmer persona he was so carefully nurturing: "But I was going to say when Truth broke in / With all her matter-of-fact about the ice-storm." He capitalizes *Truth* to suggest a note of derision for the "factual" description.

In terms of the poem's overall structure, Frost is correct in dismissing his extended descriptive passage, as the poem is about something else, but there is a brilliant clarity to the description. The poem's wordy iambic pentameter almost disguises the imaginative verbal skill of the imagery, but if the lines are rewritten in terms of the imagist credo that Ezra Pound published at about the same time that Frost was writing the poem — "No unnecessary words" — the effect of the imagery is more obvious:

> You must have seen them
> Loaded with ice on a sunny winter morning,
> Clicking upon themselves as the breeze rises,
> Turning many colored as the stir cracks
> And crazes their enamel . . .

The passage ends with the unforgettable simile of the birches bent down and trailing their leaves on the ground, "Like girls on hands and knees that throw their hair / Before them over their heads to dry in the sun."

The subject of the poem is Frost's desire to return to the simplicities of childhood. Although there are darker hints of masturbation and a fierce Oedipal conflict in lines 26–32, Frost ends the poem on a self-satisfied note: "One could do worse than be a swinger of birches."

Questions for Discussion

1. In his description of fallen birches in lines 1–2, Frost intimates that the concept of a boy swinging on birches is an imagined construct. Is this concept developed in the rest of the poem?
2. In his extended description of the leaves covered with ice, what does he mean by "many colored" in line 8? What are the "heaps of broken glass" in line 12?
3. What is the antecedent of the word "They" in line 14?
4. What is Frost referring to with "matter-of-fact" in line 22?
5. Discuss the Oedipal overtones of lines 28–33.
6. What is Frost saying in line 50, "May no fate willfully misunderstand me"? Could the previous lines be interpreted as a wish for death? What does he mean by "get away from earth awhile"?
7. Why has Frost emphasized "Toward" in line 56?

Topics for Writing

1. "Birches" seems to present a factual description of something Frost remembers from his childhood, but the poem also suggests that this is all a metaphor for a dream of childhood. Explore these contradictions in a paper.
2. **MAKING CONNECTIONS**   Frost's relationship to nature, as expressed in the line "I'd like to go by climbing a birch tree," is the opposite of the relationship the poet Percy Bysshe Shelley expresses in "Ode to the West Wind" (p. 764) in the line "I fall upon the thorns of life! I bleed!" Compare these two responses.

FIRE AND ICE
TO EARTHWARD

"Fire and Ice" is almost an epigram, but its corrosive cynicism is more strongly weighted than most epigrams. Part of the effect of this poem and "To Earthward" is the concentrated language and the obvious skill with rhyme and meter. In concise lyrics like these, Frost was able to strip away the wordiness and occasional padding of his poems in blank verse. The lines in "Fire and Ice," as is usual in Frost's shorter lyrics, are end-stopped, but "To Earthward" is one of his most ingenious displays of enjambment, often across the gap between the stanzas. Students should scan the poems to understand their metric subtlety. In its passion and yearning, "To Earthward" is as close to the traditional lyric mode as Frost allowed himself to come.

Questions for Discussion

1. "Fire and Ice" is often considered an example of Frost's cynicism. Why would the poem be considered cynical?
2. What is the speaker saying about himself in line 3, "From what I've tasted of desire"?

3. Frost was almost fifty when he wrote "Fire and Ice." Could it be considered the words of an old man? Why would we feel this?

4. The poem has an unusual structure. What is the meter of the lines?

5. In the poem, the speaker matches hate with ice. What is he telling the reader about the nature of anger?

6. Each of these poems mixes lines of unequal length. In "Fire and Ice" it is a mixture of two- and four-stress lines, dimeter and tetrameter; in "To Earthward" the mixture is two- and three-stress lines, dimeter and trimeter. Why does Frost mix the lines? Is there a pattern he follows throughout each poem? What is the effect of the shorter lines?

7. In "To Earthward" the break between the last line of the first stanza and the first line of the next is an enjambment. Where else in the poem does Frost use enjambment?

8. What is the speaker saying with the poem's opening image, "Love at the lips"? What is the term for this figure of speech?

9. What does "swirl and ache" mean in line 9?

10. What is the antecedent of the word "those" in line 13?

11. Is there a paradox in lines 15–16, "The petal of the rose / It was that stung"? What is Frost saying about love in this phrase?

12. What does "the aftermark / Of almost too much love" mean?

13. What does "The sweet of bitter bark" mean in line 23?

14. In emotional terms, what is the speaker longing for in the poem's final lines?

Topics for Writing

1. "Fire and Ice" has as its subject the destruction of the world. An African American gospel song also describes the destruction of the world in the lines "God gave Noah the rainbow sign / No more water, fire next time." Explore the concept of the end of the world as described in Frost's poem and in the gospel song.

2. **MAKING CONNECTIONS** This poem expresses many of the attitudes of the typical carpe diem poem — for instance Andrew Marvell's "To His Coy Mistress" (p. 742) or A. E. Housman's "Loveliest of trees, the cherry now" (p. 711). Analyze these elements in Frost's poem.

STOPPING BY WOODS ON A SNOWY EVENING

Students familiar with old popular songs may be interested to know that student waiters at Frost's Breadloaf Conference discovered that this poem can be sung to the melody of "Hernando's Hideaway."

There have been many suggestions as to the significance of the repeated final line of the poem. Frost said that he had planned for the poem to have another stanza, but he couldn't think of one, so he brought the poem to a close by repeating the last line he'd written. The poem's rhyme scheme is carefully planned, and this could be the reason for the repeat. If they study the poem, students will find that it has an intricate, interlocked rhyme scheme that calls for the third line of each stanza to set the rhyme for the first two and final lines of the next. The only way Frost could finish the rhyme of his final stanza was to repeat the third line, which would otherwise be left without a rhyme for closure. The poem's regular meter is unusual for Frost, who normally employed subtle shifts of syntax, but there is no interruption in the metric flow.

The setting of the poem seems simple — a man stops his horse in the woods on the year's shortest day, the winter solstice of December 21, and looks into the darkness. There are many vague elements to the poem, however, and readers have noted the implied death wish of the first line of the final stanza. Frost tacitly accepted this interpretation but always insisted that because the man continued on his journey, the poem also expressed a life wish. The poem's homily is the line "But I have promises to keep" and the repeated two final lines, "And miles to go before I sleep."

Questions for Discussion

1. Outline the poem's rhyme scheme and scan its meter.
2. Why is there a change in word order in the first line?
3. Discuss the alliteration of the first stanza.
4. Why does Frost use the adjective "his" to describe the woods? Does he intend some larger meaning?
5. Is there any significance to the fact that the poem describes something happening on the night of the winter solstice?
6. In line 12 there seems to be contradiction between the poet's earlier description of the dark, cold night and his description of "easy wind and downy flake." What does he mean by this?
7. What is the implication of the adjective "lovely" in line 13? Discuss whether this line expresses a wish for death.
8. To whom has the speaker made his "promises"? Is the poem specific about this?

Topic for Writing

1. This poem could be read as an allegory of human life, with the interpretation that we are only travelers through a world that is often dark and lonely. Explore this interpretation in a paper.

THE ROAD NOT TAKEN

Students who have read the introductory note to Frost's poetry in the text know that the poem was originally written as a joke for his friend Edward Thomas, who never could decide which road he wanted to take and always regretted whichever choice he made. It is more obvious as a joke if students read the two outer stanzas and the two inner stanzas separately. It is in these two inner stanzas that Frost depicts his friend trying to decide which road to take, even though, as Frost makes clear, they are just about the same. The reader is left with a homily in the last lines, "I took the one less traveled by, / And that has made all the difference," and the muddle of the middle stanzas is quickly forgotten.

The last two lines exemplify the persona Frost spent his life shaping — that of the outsider who has gone his own way and who has become a different person because of it. This is what Frost's audiences expected of him, and these two lines of the poem fulfill those expectations.

Questions for Discussion

1. What does Frost mean in lines 2–3, "I could not travel both / And be one traveler"?
2. Outline the descriptions of the two roads Frost describes in the poem's two middle stanzas, especially emphasizing the first two lines of the third stanza. Does he contradict these lines with his famous assertion later in the poem that he "took the one less traveled"?
3. What is Frost saying in the passage "how way leads on to way" in line 14?
4. What is the effect of the dash that ends line 14?

Topics for Writing

1. RESPONDING CREATIVELY   Part of the reason Edward Thomas didn't understand that the poem was intended as a joke is that the middle two stanzas aren't clearly funny in their attempt to portray his indecision. Rewrite these stanzas to make the joke more obvious.
2. The first two lines of the final stanza can be read as a prophecy of Frost's later life. Discuss what this foretells about his future.

AFTER APPLE-PICKING

Philip Gerber's commentary on "After Apple-Picking" discusses the question of whether Frost intended the poem to be read as an allegory of his death.

This is one of Frost's most memorable poems, with a sonority that has some of the quality of Keats's "To Autumn" and an "ice mirror" image and a "nightmare" section that stretch to depths of imagination Frost seldom allowed himself. Although he vigorously rejected free verse, some of the poem's strength comes from its technical freedom. It is as close to free verse as Frost could get without stepping over the line. He has resorted to irregular line lengths to emphasize rhyming words, but there is no regular rhyme pattern, and the poem could almost have been written in free verse, as this recasting of the first lines shows:

> My long two-pointed ladder's sticking
> through a tree toward heaven still,
> And there's a barrel that I
> didn't fill with apples beside it,
> and there may be two or three apples
> I didn't pick upon some bough.

Students should discuss the nightmare of lines 18–27 and also look closely at the ice/glass/pane imagery of lines 10–15. This imagery constitutes some of Frost's most vague, and it is highly effective for this very reason. This is one of those moments when Frost trusted his intuition. As he wrote in a letter, "You get more credit for thinking if you restate formulae or cite cases that fall easily under formulae, but all the fun is outside: saying things that suggest formulae that won't formulate —that almost but don't quite formulate." If he was pressed to explain images such as these, he always maintained that explaining them would just say the same thing but in words that were not as good.

Questions for Discussion

1. Discuss whether the poem is meant as an allegory of Frost's life or death.
2. What does he mean by "Essence of winter sleep" in line 7?
3. Discuss the possible meanings of the ice/glass/pane imagery in lines 10–17. Why does Frost say he was already on his way to sleep before the melted piece of glass fell from his fingers?
4. Discuss the nightmare of lines 18–27 and Frost's use of imagery: tactile, visual, and aural. The only type of image missing in the section is olfactory, but he has already used it earlier in the poem. Where is the olfactory image?
5. What is Frost suggesting with line 30, "There were ten thousand thousand fruit to touch"? If the poem is an allegory, what could be the meaning of this line and of the beginning of the next line, "Cherish in hand"?
6. Discuss what Frost could mean by "trouble" in line 37.
7. Is the sleep he describes in line 38, "This sleep of mine, whatever sleep it is," a metaphor for death? Does the "long sleep" in the penultimate line describe only the woodchuck's hibernation?

Topics for Writing

1.   This is a poem of regret and resignation. Analyze the way these emotions are presented in the poem.
2.   Write about Frost's dream of the apple harvest and describe the ways in which its details take on a nightmarish quality.

Conversations on Robert Frost's Poetics, pp. 1096–1107

Rose C. Feld, "*An Interview with Robert Frost,*" p. 1097.
Robert Frost, "*The Figure a Poem Makes,*" p. 1100.
Robert Lowell, "*On Robert Frost*" (poem), p. 1102.
Joseph Brodsky, "*On Grief and Reason,*" p. 1102.
Philip L. Gerber, "*On Frost's 'After Apple-Picking,'*" p. 1104.
James Wright, "*The Music of Robert Frost's 'Stopping by Woods on a Snowy Evening'*" p. 1107.

Margaret Gibson

October Elegy (p. 770)

Margaret Gibson has taught poetry for many years at the University of Connecticut, which is set in rural surroundings in central Connecticut. The October that she describes in such lyric terms is one of the moments of beauty that marks the passage of each year. The poem was included in her collection *Earth Elegy,* published by Louisiana State University Press in 1997.

Questions for Discussion

1.   Why does Gibson title her poem an "elegy"? What distinguishes an elegy from other poetic forms?
2.   In the opening lines, what is she saying when she writes that the leaves "spindle and settle"? that "The woods open"?
3.   Although the language of the poem is clear and direct, Gibson makes skilled use of many figures of speech, among them simile and metaphor. What figures of speech does she employ in the first stanzas?
4.   What is she suggesting with the term "*no one*" in the third stanza?
5.   Does she prepare us for the reference to her father and mother and the glance between them in the fourth stanza? Is there something she has said in the poem that might have led us to expect this moment of personal tenderness?
6.   What is she implying by using the word "nakedly" when she describes the look between them?
7.   What is her meaning when she writes of the "word/ I am opening with careful incision"?
8.   Is there an element of earth magic in her suggestion that fire might crack "from common stones"?
9.   Does she intend to present us with a paradox in the final image of a "sunrise in evening," or is she employing a vivid description of the last light on the stones?

Topics for Writing

1. In a paper, discuss the elements that define an elegy, illustrating your presentation with examples from the poem.
2. In the poem's final stanzas Gibson asks us to understand that for people like the old woman of ninety there is still the expectation of a moment when they'll "wake." Discuss what Gibson means by this, and project what someone experiencing this moment might come to understand.
3. She writes in the fifth stanza, "Interpret in a moment's/ surrender your heart." Discuss what she is asking the reader to do, and follow its implications in the poem's closing stanzas.
4. MAKING COMPARISONS   Compare Gibson's elegy with Thomas Gray's famed "Elegy Written in a Country Churchyard" (p. 766), citing their similarities and explaining their differences of poetic and philosophical intention.

ALLEN GINSBERG

A Supermarket in California (p. 811)
From *Kaddish* (p. 871)

It should be emphasized in any discussion of Ginsberg's poetry that these are performance pieces, and to experience their whole effect students should hear them read aloud, preferably in one of the many recordings that Ginsberg made of his poetry.

A SUPERMARKET IN CALIFORNIA

This, like all of Ginsberg's best-known poems, is a skillfully constructed performance piece. It uses a "line breath," as Ginsberg called it, that reminds the listener of the cadence and breadth of Walt Whitman's lines. The poem describes a night in Berkeley when Ginsberg had been reading Whitman's poetry. He was tired and hungry, so he walked the few blocks from his back garden cottage on Milvia Street to the all-night supermarket on University Avenue. In the poem he brings Whitman to his audience, not as a distant literary figure but as an old man the speaker overhears in the next aisle propositioning the grocery clerks. Ginsberg's readings are a careful balance of poems that are humorous, scandalous, and wryly moving, and in this tribute to Whitman he expresses his feeling of companionship with the "lonely old grubber" and his consciousness that part of what they share is loneliness. He also expresses his ultimate feelings of detachment from the America he finally agrees to join in his poem "America."

Questions for Discussion

1. What does Ginsberg mean by "shopping for images" in line 2? What are some of the images he finds in the supermarket?
2. In the second line he speaks of Whitman's "enumerations." What does he mean by this? Does it describe his own writing?
3. Who was García Lorca, and why does Ginsberg mention him here?
4. Why do the speaker and Whitman, in line 7, never pass the cashier?
5. What is he describing in line 10, "trees add shade to shade"?
6. What is the contrast suggested in line 11, "past blue automobiles in driv~

Topic for Writing

1.   Suggest an answer to the question Ginsberg asks in the last line of the poem. Explain your answer.

FROM *KADDISH*

Questions for Discussion

1.   What is a Kaddish?
2.   Why does Ginsberg speak of his mother's "corsets & eyes" in the opening lines? What do these two physical things symbolize to him?
3.   What is the tone of Ginsberg's writing? What technical means has he used in this poem to express his grief?
4.   What is he referring to in "Adonais' last triumphant stanzas"?
5.   What is he describing when he writes of "cries of Spaniards now in the doorstoops doors and and dark boys on the street"? What is the change that has occurred since his mother was part of this world?

Topics for Writing

1.   Early in this selection from the poem, Ginsberg says he is "Dreaming back thru life." Discuss what he means by this and illustrate your discussion with examples from the poem.
2.   Discuss the elegaic tone of the poem and suggest some traditional sources for it.
3.   Compare this poem to "A Supermarket in California" and comment on differences of style and artistic intention. Place the poem in the context of Ginsberg's concept of the world about him and his place in it.

NIKKI GIOVANNI

Adulthood (p. 826)

In her long and distinguished career as a writer and spokesperson for the black community in America, Giovanni has moved from the militancy of her early poems to writing that reflects her adult experience as a woman and the changes she sees in American society. This poem clarifies the emotional realities that pushed her out of the life that had been anticipated for her and radicalized her when she was still a student. It was an experience that she shared with many students her age and it has left a lasting legacy with our society.

Questions for Discussion

1.   Giovanni has written this poem in a style approximating street dialect. Why has she chosen to do this? Does it give the poem an authenticity? Could she have achieved the same effect with the poem if she'd written it in standard English grammar?
2.   What do the poem's details tell us about her family's economic situation? Would she be considered middle class?
3.   She uses the term "colored bourgeois." What does she mean by this? Is it meant in a positive or a negative sense? Why didn't she use the term "Black bourgeois"?
4.   What forced her to abandon her idealism and adopt a more activist stance?

5. In lines 36–49 Giovanni lists those who were killed, beginning with the head of the UN, the Swedish diplomat Dag Hammarskjöld. The majority are blacks but there are also white and an Asian. What is the reason for including these other names on her list of Africans and African Americans who were murdered? Who are the people on the list?

6. What life is she leaving behind as she becomes a political activist? Is it a life that still feels familiar today?

7. Does Giovanni show any sign of regretting the choice she has made?

8. Why does she conclude that a "real Black person . . . must now feel / and inflict / pain"? Does this still seem like a reasonable statement now that the United States has elected a black president?

Topics for Writing

1. Giovanni writes of finding a new life for herself by withdrawing from anything that wasn't in her own "image." Discuss what this withdrawal means in emotional terms and examine the things she turned to instead. Compare her experience with someone you know.

2. Giovanni's experience in college enabled her to change her viewpoint about many things. In an essay discuss specifically what happened to her, using examples from the poem.

3. Identify each of the persons named in her list of the killed, telling why they are on the list and what their role was in the world struggle for equality and justice that she felt they represented.

LOUISE GLÜCK

First Memory (p. 846)

The strength of Glück's poetry is its directness and clarity. The images are compressed and burnished, with any distracting elements stripped away. It is this unflinching objectivity that makes it possible for her to express feelings and attitudes that would be difficult for her readers to accept if she explained why she wrote the poems the way she did — or if she asked us to sympathize with the people in her poems. The hard light she shines on them is often cruel, but it is the cruelty of honest emotion.

In the short poem "First Memory" — which ended the book *Ararat* (1990) — she allows herself to confront her own pain. She understands that if she hadn't loved her father, she wouldn't have been wounded by what she felt as his inability to love her — she wouldn't have felt anything. It is a moving statement, and it has allowed Glück to go on to new themes in her poetry that reach beyond her early obsessions with self and family.

Question for Discussion

1. What is the irony of the poem "First Memory"? Does the poem tell us that the speaker has found a way to accept what she remembers?

Topics for Writing

1. The language in Glück's poetry is stripped bare. There are no figures of speech, no shifts in syntax, no startling imagery, hardly any use of adjectives or adverbs, but still we feel that what she writes is intensely poetic. Discuss the elements in Glück's style that create this effect.

2.   **MAKING CONNECTIONS**   "First Memory" describes a painful memory of a difficult relationship with a father. Compare this poem with Sylvia Plath's "Daddy" (p. 998), another poem about a failure of a father to reach a daughter emotionally.

Commentary

Louise Glück, *"Poems* Are *Autobiography,"* p. 1049.

JORIE GRAHAM

I Watched a Snake (p. 904)

Some of the difficulty found in Jorie Graham's poetry is in the care with which she develops her images. Several lines will be devoted to a single visual description and then the reader will meet an intellectual concept that extends the implications of what she has described, often with what at first appears to be only a tenuous connection. With Graham, more than with many other poets, it is necessary for students to take time with the poem, to be certain of the ground they are standing on before they follow her along the next step in the poem's path.

Questions for Discussion

1.   The first twenty lines of Graham's poem are devoted to a description of a snake moving slowly through the grass behind her house. What are possible reasons she might have for setting the scene of the poem with such fidelity? Is the suggestion that the snake's movements might have "something to do / with lust" something she considers seriously or is this only a passing thought?

2.   What is Graham suggesting with her image that we "stitch the earth" with our own mortality? How does this relate to the snake she has been watching?

3.   How does Graham compare the snake's small search with a poet's work? Does she make the comparison seem useful?

4.   What is the implication of the image "It is the simplest / stitch this going where we must"?

5.   What is meant by the "necessary" (line 41) as it describes the capture of the dragonfly at the end of the snake's search?

6.   Why does the poet find that she isn't afraid of snakes at just that moment? What has given her a sense of kinship with the snake's small journey? Is she also alluding to the old superstition that women are fearful of snakes because of the snake that tempted Eve in the Garden of Eden?

7.   What does the poet mean with the simile "meanings like sailboats / setting out / over the mind"?

8.   What does Graham mean with her conclusion "Passion is work / that retrieves us"? How does Graham mean the word "passion" in this context? Does it have the same meaning here as the more usual inference of sexual passion? Why not?

Topics for Writing

1.   Although the poem describes the movements of a small snake hunting for food Graham relates this to the ordinary hungers which we all experience. Discuss the concept she is presenting in this image and relate it to the poem's conclusion "Desire / is the honest work of the body."

2.   Discuss the concepts of hunger, desire, and passion as Graham uses them in her poem, contrasting the more common uses of the words to describe more specific human concerns.

3.   Discuss Graham's concept of desire as "the honest work of the body / its engine, its wind" as she uses it in the poem, quoting from the poem itself.

4.   MAKING CONNECTIONS   Compare Graham's poem about a snake to Emily Dickinson's "A narrow Fellow in the Grass" (p. 941), noting the differences as well as the similarities. Consider whether or not some of the differences between the two poems reflect the change in women's status in the world. Could Dickinson have considered an image of desire as a subject for her poem?

Connection

Emily Dickinson, *"A narrow Fellow in the Grass,"* p. 941.

THOMAS GRAY

Elegy Written in a Country Churchyard (p. 766)

The poem's social and political attitudes are discussed in Chapter 10 (p. 769). Because of the sympathy for the lives of the common villagers that the poem expresses, students might question whether it is an Augustan or neoclassical poem, as some of its language and sentiments seem closer to the romantic poetry of a few years later. In a collaborative comment, however, Professors John Chalker and Erik Frykman make it clear in *An Anthology of English Verse* that Gray's work is "within the central Augustan tradition in its preoccupation with the large general truths of human nature, its avoidance of overt subjective feeling, its use of elevated diction and personification, and its cultivation of extensive literary reference to enrich the texture of the writing" (93).

Although the poem's effect is largely derived from the fact that the villager for whom the elegy is written is nameless and unknown, students will be interested to learn that Gray was moved to write the poem by the death of a friend, Richard West. The poem took Gray eight years to complete. The poem was an immediate success, and the most important literary figure of the time, Samuel Johnson, succinctly summed up the reasons for its popularity. The elegy, he wrote, "abounds with images which find a mirror in every mind and with sentiments to which every bosom returns an echo."

Questions for Discussion

1.   Although the poem is written in four-line ballad stanzas, which usually are written in tetrameter, the meter Gray has chosen is iambic pentameter. With regard to the discussion in the text as to the effect of different line lengths and meter, why did Gray write in this longer line?

2.   Why would the poem have been less effective if Gray had given a name and a history to the person buried in the cemetery?

3.   What ideas in the poem suggest the coming social changes that would culminate in the American and French Revolutions?

4.   Who is being addressed in lines 31 and 32?

5.   In lines 47 and 48 Gray uses the image of hands playing a harp to describe literary accomplishment. What is such an image called?

6.   What does Gray mean in lines 49 and 50 when he writes of knowledge as an "ample page / Rich with the spoils of time"?

Topics for Writing

1. Gray's poem expressed sentiments that for their time seemed revolutionary to many people. Analyze these sentiments and explain their significance for the mid–eighteenth century, when the poem was published.
2. MAKING CONNECTIONS   In lines 61–72 Gray suggests that the lowly role of the village peasants prevents them from having an effect on history, but he also writes that they won't be tempted to commit the crimes of the rich and powerful. They won't, for example, "wade through slaughter to a throne," as he writes in line 67. Discuss Gray's sentiments here and contrast them with the sentiments of writers of the same period — for instance, William Blake, who believed in the essential goodness and innocence of mankind.
3. The poem is filled with images of nature. Use these images in an analysis of the relationship between the physical setting of the poem and the sentiments it expresses.
4. The famous lines of the stanza beginning with "The boast of heraldry" (line 33) suggest sentiments that lie outside Gray's Christian beliefs. Explicate the philosophical implications of these lines.

ANGELINA WELD GRIMKÉ

The Black Finger (p. 863)
Tenebris (p. 864)

Angelina Weld Grimké was the child of an interracial couple. The marriage of her parents in Boston was encouraged by two white aunts who had been active in the abolitionist movement in South Carolina. The marriage began happily, but her white mother found the strains of an interracial relationship overwhelming and soon left her daughter with her husband and never saw her again. Grimké's father was a lawyer, and she was raised in a genteel Boston environment. She graduated from the Boston Normal School of Gymnastics in 1902 and became a high school teacher in Washington, D.C., continuing her career until her father's death in 1930, when she left Washington. She moved to New York intending to devote time to her writing, but although she lived for nearly thirty more years, her writing career was over. There had been an early play dealing with racial themes, and a long fictional treatment of the same situation, then during the Harlem Renaissance her poetry began appearing in the important journals *Crisis* and *Opportunity.* Her work also was included in *Caroling Dusk,* a widely hailed anthology edited by Countee Cullen during this period. Grimké wrote little poetry, but her work clearly responds to modernist ideas, and there is a quiet technical assurance. Despite the small scope of her poems she dealt with issues that continue to have relevance today.

Questions for Discussion

1. In "The Black Finger," what are the adjectives Grimké uses to describe the cypress tree? Are these the usual adjectives poets have used to describe trees?
2. What is the symbolism of the cypress's dark bark and its straight trunk?
3. How has she used this symbol to make a statement about race?
4. Why does she repeat the word "beautiful" in the opening line and in the penultimate line?
5. Describe what she is describing in "Tenebris." Is this a similar image to the cypress she described in "The Black Finger"?

6. In what way is the poem's title symbolic?
7. Grimké plays with the concept of the "hand huge and black." Is she telling us that the shape is only a shadow of the tree? Does she also want us to see it on other levels of meaning?
8. Does this poem contain an implied threat? What does Grimké want us to feel with the final two lines?

Topics for Writing

1. MAKING CONNECTIONS The open forms of Grimké's poems have some affinities with the poetry that Langston Hughes was writing at the same time. Compare their work and discuss both the technical means that each poet uses and the racial themes that are explicit in their work.
2. A rallying cry for black activists in the 1960s was the slogan "Black is Beautiful!" Discuss "The Black Finger" as an early example of this same statement.
3. Discuss the implications of the black hand attacking the white house in "Tenebris." Why did Grimké say that the shadow of the hand is "huge," while the bricks on the white man's house are "very small"?
4. In a short essay, place Grimké's ideas in the currents of thought that influenced the writers of the Harlem Renaissance.

THOMAS HARDY

The Man He Killed (p. 835)

Born in southern England in 1840, Hardy devoted himself to fiction for nearly fifty years, becoming one of England's most successful novelists. In his fifties, financially secure, he was able to devote himself to lyric poetry. He died in 1928.

Question for Discussion

1. Discuss the development of the speaker's attitude toward the man he killed.

Topic for Writing

1. MAKING CONNECTIONS Compare Hardy's use of irony with that of Stephen Crane in "War Is Kind" (p. 834).

ROBERT HASS

A Story about the Body (p. 788)

Former poet laureate Robert Hass is a Californian who often uses the California landscape as his theme. He has also written many psychologically insightful prose poems.

Questions for Discussion

1. What do the dead bees represent?
2. Could the bees be interpreted as the woman's comment on the man's love?

3. The poem is titled "A Story about the Body." Could it be interpreted as a comment on each of their bodies, not just his? Could it refer to a collective body? Would any of our bodies respond the same way?
4. What is the significance of the layer of rose petals the woman places over the dead bees?
5. Is the woman's gesture made in anger or in sad resignation?

Topic for Writing

1. So many love poems take as their theme the body of the loved one. Comment on how the injury to the woman's body ends the man's love and discuss whether it was an honest love.

ROBERT HAYDEN

Those Winter Sundays (p. 967)
A Letter from Phillis Wheatley (p. 968)
Night, Death, Mississippi (p. 968)

THOSE WINTER SUNDAYS
A LETTER FROM PHILLIS WHEATLEY

Hayden was not a prolific writer, and in some of his work he seems uncertain of his poetic voice, but "Those Winter Sundays" has become an American classic, and students find much in the poem that touches them.

Students should read the poem by Phillis Wheatley (p. 839) before turning to Hayden's "A Letter from Phillis Wheatley."

Questions for Discussion

1. In "Those Winter Sundays," what does Hayden mean by the first two words, "Sundays too"?
2. In line 3, what does he mean by "cracked hands"?
3. The emotional center of the poem is the short sentence at the end of line 5, "No one ever thanked him." Discuss what Hayden suggests in this sentence.
4. In line 6, "the cold splintering, breaking," what is Hayden describing?
5. What is the speaker saying about himself in the last verse of the poem? Why does he repeat the question in line 13?
6. How closely does Hayden's "A Letter from Phillis Wheatley" match Wheatley's own way of writing?
7. In line 20 Hayden's Wheatley describes herself eating alone, "like captive royalty." Is she being ironic? What are possible meanings for this line?
8. What is the importance of the signatures she mentions in lines 21–22?
9. Why does she think she should decline the honor of appearing at court?
10. In line 33, what does she mean by "no Eden without its serpent"?

Topic for Writing

1. The question of identity was a complex one for Hayden, who thought of himself simply as a writer, not an African American writer. As David Huddle points out

in his commentary on "Those Winter Sundays," there is nothing in the poem that ties it directly to the African American experience: Hayden describes a normal Sunday experience for many families in America. Write about the question of racial identity in this poem.

NIGHT, DEATH, MISSISSIPPI

A continuing subject for African American writers of Hayden's generation was lynching, which was one of the most appalling realities of the American racial situation. It has been estimated that over a forty-year period, a black man or woman was lynched somewhere in the South every two and a half days, and the lynchings often turned into public spectacles with thousands of witnesses. Hayden's poem presents the night thoughts of an older member of the Ku Klux Klan who is waiting for his son to return from a lynching, and the man is filled with regret that now he is too old to join the mob himself. In the second section, the son has returned and is describing the murder, and his father asks his grandchildren to bring water so their father can wash away the blood.

Questions for Discussion

1. Is it possible to discuss a poem like this in terms of its artistic qualities, or is the subject matter so strong that it dominates whatever could be said about the writing?
2. What is the figure of speech in the description "in his reek / and gauntness"?
3. The poem is presented in multiple voices: the poet, the old man, the old man's son, and the son's wife. Which of the voices do you hear in the different stanzas of the poem?
4. What is the comparison intended in the line "fevered as by groinfire"?
5. What is the poet saying in the final line, "*O night betrayed by darkness not its own*"?

Topics for Writing

1. This poem makes most readers uncomfortable. Does the writer have a responsibility to mute the tone of the writing to soften its effect? Discuss this question of the writer's responsibility to the truth of the poem's subject.
2. Discuss the question of separating the poem from the horrors it describes, and consider whether any poem written about lynching could not upset its readers.
3. The poem is a striking technical achievement. Discuss Hayden's use of imagery and the varying voices to create this vivid picture of a moment in the Mississippi darkness.
4. MAKING CONNECTIONS Read and compare this poem with the two other poems in the anthology with lynching as their subject: Claude McKay's "The Lynching" (p. 864) and Langston Hughes's "Song for a Dark Girl" (p. 979).

Commentary

Robert Hayden, "*On Negro Poetry*," p. 1050.

SEAMUS HEANEY

Digging (p. 970)
Mid-Term Break (p. 971)

"Digging" is Heaney's most frequently anthologized poem, although "Mid-Term Break" is very popular too. Each illustrates the sure poetic instincts that have shaped Heaney's career and earned him the Nobel Prize for literature at a relatively early age. As critic Sven Birkerts wrote in *This Electric Life: Essays on Modern Poetry* (1989),

> Linguistic authenticity is the very quality that we revere in the work of a poet like Seamus Heaney. Though his lines are seldom political in any overt sense, they retain an implicit — I would say even organic — sense of communal connectedness. The language has specific gravity; it is adequate to the felt reality of life in a world of severe natural and social conditions; it is aware of ancestral bonds and local, tribal, responsibilities. Heaney convinces me that these implicit linguistic recognitions can often transmit a more vital political meaning than can more obviously topical kinds of address. (84)

In each of these poems, there is the quality of connectedness that Birkerts describes. Each of the poems is also a skillful technical achievement in which Heaney balances the immediate and the banal with larger generalizations through his subtle control of language and dialect.

Like "Digging," "Mid-Term Break" plants the narrator into a family setting — but not the ancestral turf. Instead, Heaney is returning home from boarding school ("college") to attend the funeral of a little brother killed when he was struck by a car. The father here is not the sturdy, impassive shovel-wielder of "Digging" but a man whose grief cannot be contained. Heaney's bereaved mother's emotions are vented in "angry, tearless sighs." Perhaps the main pleasure and challenge of reading the poem is to track the poet's own emotions, implied in the details of the unfolding narrative. The last line packs the most emotional punch, with every syllable emphasizing how young, small, and helpless the victim was.

Questions for Discussion

1. "Digging" is usually read as an example of extended metaphor. What is the metaphor of the poem?
2. What is the implied comparison in the phrase in line 2, "snug as a gun"?
3. What is Heaney telling us in line 7, "comes up twenty years away"?
4. What is the speaker telling us about himself in the three lines beginning "The cold smell of potato mould . . ."?
5. In "Mid-Term Break," track the poet's emotions in the choice of images such as tolling bells, whispering strangers, and tearless sighs. What sort of tone is being set?
6. Why do you think the poet included the image of the cooing baby? How does it fit (or not fit) with the developing tone and story?
7. What lines in the poem most puzzled or surprised you — when you first read it and when you reread it after knowing what the poem was about? Explain.

Topics for Writing

1. Discuss the role of nature in Heaney's poetry, based on these two poems and any others you research.
2. Although "Digging" can be read as a nonpolitical poem, some critics have traced a political stance in the poem's imagery. Discuss these political elements in the poem.
3. Discuss the role of family and tradition in "Digging" and "Mid-Term Break."

GEORGE HERBERT

Easter Wings (p. 726)

This *shaped verse*, as poems written to form a representation of the title are called, is one of the best-known works of George Herbert, a modest clergyman whose mother had been a friend of John Donne. Herbert was born in 1593 and lived until 1633, when he died of tuberculosis while serving as curate of a small rural parish in southern England. His only book, *The Temple*, was published a few months after his death. Herbert's poetry is most often compared with Donne's, as they share the Elizabethan penchant for conceit and paradox. Herbert's faith, however, is less troubled than Donne's, and his conception of his relationship with God is direct and trusting. The poem is deceptively simple, but if read aloud with the line lengths carefully observed, it has the rise and fall of a bird's flight. The text is so skillfully presented that the diminution of line lengths — from pentameter to monometer, a foot lost with each line, and then the expansion again back to pentameter — seems entirely natural, even if on first glance the poem seems contrived.

Questions for Discussion

1. Scan the poem and analyze the steps by which Herbert reduces and expands the line lengths.
2. Analyze the first five lines and discuss how they suggest a diminution in the lines by their description of humankind's fall from grace.
3. Compare the two stanzas. What is the denotative meaning of lines 5 and 15 that justifies their short length?
4. What images in the poem continue the concept of wings?
5. Lines 10 and 20 say something very similar in images that are only slightly altered. Discuss what Herbert means in the two lines.
6. What is the symbolic meaning of the first line?
7. The second stanza may be read metaphorically as a reference to Herbert's illness. What images in the stanza suggest the physical effects of tuberculosis?
8. If the second stanza does describe his illness, how could the last line be interpreted?

Topic for Writing

1. MAKING CONNECTIONS   Compare Herbert's religious faith as expressed in this poem with the religious faith expressed in John Donne's "Batter my heart, three-personed God" (p. 945).

ROBERT HERRICK

To the Virgins, to Make Much of Time (p. 717)

Herrick was a Londoner, born in the city in 1591, who reluctantly spent his long life in the west of England as a modestly paid clergyman. His consolation seems to have been the hours he spent writing brief verse in the style of Ben Jonson. When the troubled years of the Puritan Commonwealth drove him back to London, he published in 1648 a volume containing 1,200 poems divided into two sections — *Hesperides,* the secular poems, and *Noble Numbers,* the religious poems. Following the restoration of the monarchy in 1660, he returned to his country parish, where he died in 1674 at the age of eighty-three.

The great majority of Herrick's secular poems would have to be classed among the silliest poetry in the English language, but a handful of short lyrics have given him a small but enduring reputation. The poems were ignored during his lifetime but became popular in the sexually repressive Victorian era as a kind of delicate erotica, thanks to poems with titles like "Upon the Nipples of Julia's Breasts."

"To the Virgins, to Make Much of Time" is the classic representative of the "carpe diem" poem in English (the term means "seize the day"). The Victorians understood that underneath the metaphors of rosebuds and flowers Herrick was telling young women to stop wasting their time and to get married as soon as possible. The Victorians also understood that the loss of virginity was the most important of the poem's suggestions.

Questions for Discussion

1. Herrick's poem contains veiled suggestions of regret and disappointment in his own life. What in the poem implies this?
2. The poem is a quatrain with a rhyme scheme of alternating masculine and feminine rhymes. Is there any implied meaning in this rhyme scheme?

Topics for Writing

1. MAKING CONNECTIONS   Compare this poem with Andrew Marvell's "To His Coy Mistress" (p. 742) and discuss the presentation of the carpe diem theme in each poem.
2. Herrick's statement in the poem that youth is the best age of life has echoes in today's culture. Discuss the idea in terms of current attitudes toward clothing, music, and the arts.

JOHN CLELLON HOLMES

Fayetteville Dawn (I) (p. 856)

John Clellon Holmes was born in 1926 and following his discharge from the U.S. Navy in 1945 he settled in New York City where he attended classes at Columbia University and began writing poetry. He was quickly recognized as one of the emerging young voices of the new American poetry scene, but after meeting young novelist Jack Kerouac at a party in 1948, Holmes became convinced his talents lay in prose. His friendship with Kerouac developed until they met almost daily, comparing their work on Holmes's *Go,* the first novel to describe the lifestyle of the new Beat Generation, and

Kerouac's own new novel, which was published several years later as *On the Road*. Holmes eventually moved from New York to Old Saybrook, CT, where he lived for much of his life. He published novels and literary journalism, taught writing at a number of universities, and in the late 1960s he returned to writing poetry. He became a tenured professor at the University of Arkansas, directing the university's writing program. He died of cancer in 1988.

"Fayetteville Dawn (I)" was written shortly after Holmes had moved to Fayetteville, Arkansas, to take up his position at the University of Arkansas. In these early months he responded to the sounds and the world of nature in his new surroundings.

Questions for Discussion

1. What is the poetic means that Holmes has used in the first line of the poem? Is this echoed in the second line?
2. In addition to alliteration, what other poetic means does he employ in this carefully compressed description of dawn?
3. The poet writes specifically of an apartment complex at the edge of town, and he is clearly experiencing dawn in a suburban environment. What images in the poem tell us he is waking in the suburbs?
4. What is the figure of speech employed in the image "radios asleep"? Are there other places in the poem where Holmes also uses this same figure of speech?
5. Does the poet intend us to hear other associations by including snoring in the "sounds of our machinery"?
6. Holmes uses the word "hubbub" to describe the sounds of the birds outside his window. Is this a word usually employed to describe the sounds of nature? Why has Holmes employed it here?
7. Suggest reasons why Holmes might have chosen to describe the insects and birds as "things with wings."
8. Have the insects and birds made a conscious decision to be silent against the human noise of the day? What is Holmes telling the reader about the interrelationship between the two worlds by suggesting that there is this larger consciousness?

Topics for Writing

1. Although the reader might say that Holmes employs a number of poetic techniques in this short lyric, compression determines the effect of the first verse. Paraphrase the physical scene of the poem's first seven lines and explain how Holmes has found ways to compress the essence of the experience into these short lines. What has he gained in poetic effect by reducing the scene to these images?
2. Holmes's poem is carefully poised between two rhythmic structures: the long lines of four stresses, among them the opening line itself; and answering lines of three or sometimes two stresses. There is a rhetorical structure introduced in this contrast, a kind of statement answered with its elucidation. Analyze the poem from this point of view.
3. In his images of the human "machinery" and the night creatures "recharging" Holmes suggests larger dimensions in our complex relationship to the natural world. Discuss the shifting boundaries between nature and our human lives that he intimates in his poem, quoting directly from the poem itself.

GERARD MANLEY HOPKINS

The Windhover (p. 972)
Pied Beauty (p. 973)
God's Grandeur (p. 973)
Thou Art Indeed Just, Lord (p. 973)

When Hopkins's writing was first published after World War I, most poetry was still being written in regular meter and rhyme, and there was a stormy controversy over his attempt to create new meters with what he called *sprung rhythm.* He intended for each line to have an equal number of stresses, regardless of whether the line could be scanned in a traditional form of meter, like iambic or trochaic. If he thought there would be some uncertainty about where the stress should fall, he wrote it in above the word or syllable.

Today Hopkins's poetry seems remarkable not for its metrical innovation but for its ecstatic mysticism. As English literary historian Linda Ruth Williams described his writing, "For Hopkins, poetry exceeds meaning; it is . . . his impulse to communicate with the 'isness' of things, to allow material language to touch the thing itself through a poetic experience of epiphany" (*Bloomsburg Guide to English Literature*, p. 228). Hopkins was a religious mystic, and to modern readers the openness of his poetic forms seems a natural expression of his religious fervor. There is a trance state in Christian worship known as *speaking in tongues,* and in "The Windhover," which Hopkins considered one of his most successful poems, the reader does get the sense of a man in an ecstatic trance at the sight of the hawk in the morning air.

"The Windhover" is a difficult poem, and many have attempted to interpret it. Students should read the commentary by Bernard Bergonzi (p. 1037), which might not answer the questions they have about the poem but will certainly illustrate the problems that critics have had interpreting it.

All of the poems included here are sonnets. It is almost as though Hopkins chose the strictest form to rein in his ecstatic outbursts. "Pied Beauty" is shorter, but he called its form a *curtal,* or shortened sonnet. It has been compressed into roughly two-thirds of the traditional sonnet. The first eight lines become six, and the last six become three and a half. The form gives the poet the opportunity to achieve the drama of the shortened last line.

Questions for Discussion

1. Although "The Windhover" is a difficult poem, students may be able to understand some of Hopkins's way of writing if they paraphrase the less complex lines. How would the class paraphrase the first four lines, continuing to the word "ecstasy" in the beginning of the fifth line?
2. Although much of the poem's imagery will become clear after a careful reading, critics have been unable to agree on the meaning of some of the images. Some critics feel that the word "chevalier" in line 11 is a metaphor for Christ. Can students find anything in the poem that supports or refutes this interpretation?
3. In "Pied Beauty," Hopkins cries out for glory to God for "dappled things." What are the dappled things he names in the next four lines?
4. What does he mean by "All things counter" in line 7?
5. In "Pied Beauty," what does Hopkins mean by the line "He fathers-forth whose beauty is past change"?

6.   In "Thou Art Indeed Just, Lord" Hopkins uses the phrase "Time's eunuch." Is he referring to himself?

Topics for Writing

1.   Like Emily Dickinson, Hopkins resisted pleas by friends to publish his poetry. Students might want to comment on whether his awareness that he would have to make changes in his poems for publication might have influenced his decision. Students could also suggest the kind of changes Hopkins might have had to make to his poems for them to be acceptable to a late-Victorian audience.
2.   In "Pied Beauty," Hopkins catalogues the things for which he wishes to praise God. Students could describe the things in more everyday terms and suggest what a list like this tells us about Hopkins.

A. E. HOUSMAN

Loveliest of trees, the cherry now (p. 711)

Housman was born in England in 1859 and died in 1936. His fame as a poet rests on two slender volumes, the first of which, *A Shropshire Lad,* he published himself in 1896. Shropshire is a rural county in the west of England, and the themes of the poems were inspired by everyday life in Shropshire villages. The book became very popular in England during World War I. In 1922, *Last Poems* appeared, including the last of the poetry Housman had written in the 1890s and a handful of newer poems. A few additional poems were included in a collected edition a few years after his death. Although it would appear from this small output that Housman lacked a serious commitment to literature, he was, in fact, a leading scholar of Latin poetry, publishing hundreds of articles and editing the works of several Roman poets. His own poems are wryly affectionate, but he was savagely critical of other scholars in his field, and some of his writing consists of vituperative attacks on what he considered "shabby" scholarship.

Because he lived a solitary bachelor's life, Housman is sometimes considered to have been homosexual. The truth is more complicated. While a student at Oxford, he suddenly realized that an intense friendship he felt for another male student could become physical, and he immediately withdrew from the relationship. He was so disturbed by what he had felt, however, that his Oxford studies suffered, and he failed to pass with distinction. Because of this he was unable to secure a teaching job immediately and was forced to work as a clerk in the London Patents Office for ten years while he produced his scholarly articles and editions in the evenings and on vacations. He finally was given a professorship at London University in 1892, when he was thirty-three, and in 1911 he became a professor at Cambridge University.

Housman's work has a deceptive simplicity that reflects the directness and immediacy of the Roman poets, particularly Horace and Catullus, whose work he studied. It was the unsentimental directness of Housman's poetry and the familiarity of his themes that attracted such a large readership during the war. Many of his readers today find that the way of life he described has disappeared from the English countryside, and a strong sense of nostalgia is part of the response to his writing. The poems read effortlessly, but Housman later commented that writing poetry with this deceptive ease was intensely difficult and that he couldn't sustain the immense effort.

Questions for Discussion

1.   "Loveliest of trees" is sometimes described as a "perfect lyric." Discuss the poem in terms of its meter and rhyme scheme, examining it to see if there is any use of enjambment or half-rhyme and discussing its occasional rhythmical irregularities.
2.   Although a gentle example of the genre, "Loveliest of trees" is a carpe diem poem. What in the poem places it in this genre?
3.   The middle stanza has some of the elements of Elizabethan paradox. How could this stanza be paraphrased?
4.   To what is Housman alluding in line 5, "of my three score years and ten"?

Topics for Writing

1.   MAKING CONNECTIONS   Housman's poetry could in many ways be considered a fulfillment of the poetic ideals William Wordsworth expressed in the Introduction to his *Lyrical Ballads* almost a hundred years earlier. Discuss Housman's themes and language in terms of Wordsworth's description of what he was trying to achieve with the "new" romantic poetry.
2.   MAKING CONNECTIONS   Compare "Loveliest of trees" with other carpe diem poems in the anthology and discuss why Housman's poem would be included in this category.

LANGSTON HUGHES

From *The Negro Artist and the Racial Mountain* (p. 860)

The Negro Speaks of Rivers (p. 865)

Mother to Son (p. 977)

I, Too (p. 977)

Bound No'th Blues (p. 978)

Song for a Dark Girl (p. 979)

House in the World (p. 979)

Florida Road Workers (p. 979)

Merry-Go-Round (p. 980)

Down Where I Am (p. 980)

Theme for English B (p. 981)

Dream Deferred (p. 982)

For a broader perspective on the poet and his writing, students should read "Conversations on Langston Hughes and His Legacy" (p. 1108), which emphasize Hughes's role as a social poet. Throughout his career he spoke for the African American community, confronting white society for its racism and an economic structure that led to inequality and injustice. Of all the major American writers of his era, Hughes was perhaps the most courageous, and his decision to write in a direct, simple language that spoke *for* as well as *to* the black community cost him the serious critical attention his work deserved. Hughes decided early what he wanted to do with his writing, and he never wavered from his course.

We sometimes forget that the circumstances of a writer's life play a crucial role in the work he or she is able to produce. Hughes was the only important American poet of this period who supported himself by writing, which meant that he wrote many poems and his work often responded to topical questions that interested his Harlem audience. Sometimes he deprecatingly called himself a "folk" poet, but this term overlooks his subtle but sure sense of words and their nuance, his sensitivity to vernacular speech, and his sure sense of form. Hughes used a great variety of structures, but always for the purpose of presenting the poem's voice most effectively. His poetry, as his biographer Arnold Rampersad wrote, was always at the service of the black community, and it continued to mirror the African American travail in America — the joys and angers, the disappointments and consolations — but always with a sure and conscious poetic skill and intelligence.

Students will not find many examples of traditional verse forms in Hughes's work, and there are no allusions or references that would not be obvious to most of his readers. His genius lies in his ability to present the voice of the speaker, the poem's persona, in a few deceptively simple lines. His gift to his readers is a world teeming with real people — young, old, rich, poor, angry, happy — whose voices mingle in the rich texture of his poetry.

THE NEGRO SPEAKS OF RIVERS

Hughes wrote this poem after he'd seen the Mississippi River for the first time, when he was on a train taking him to stay with his father in Mexico. He was nineteen years old, and when the poem was published a year later it attracted immediate attention in the Harlem intellectual community. It is still a poem that is read and loved. At his funeral the audience recited the poem aloud. The poem has an important meaning to many of its readers because it presents in a single haunting image — that of the world's ancient rivers — the concept of the antiquity of the African race, the unique differences between African American and European American cultures, and the spiritual depths that these factors have given to the African American community.

Questions for Discussion

1. How has the speaker's soul "grown deep like the rivers"?
2. In line 5, what does Hughes mean by "dawns were young"?
3. What connection is he making in the phrase "Nile of the Mississippi" in line 7?
4. Why does he include the image of Lincoln in the same line? Is this simply a historical reference, or does the phrase also contain a social message?
5. What are the connotations of the word "dusky" in line 12?

Topic for Writing

1. Discuss the poem's many references to black history.

MOTHER TO SON

In this poem Hughes speaks through the voice of an old woman worn down with her life but "still climbin'."

Questions for Discussion

1. What is the poem's extended metaphor?

2.   What kind of real staircase does Hughes describe in the poem? Where would he have seen a staircase like it?

3.   Why would we say that the line "Life for me ain't been no crystal stair" is an understatement?

4.   What is the woman telling her son in lines 18–19?

Topic for Writing

1.   Relate some of the images of the real staircase metaphor to life experiences the woman may have had.

I, Too

"I, Too" is one of Hughes's early poems. Its language and style reveal the influence of Walt Whitman. The instructor might ask students to draw comparisons between Whitman's work and this poem.

Questions for Discussion

1.   Is this poem, like "Mother to Son," an extended metaphor?

2.   Who is Hughes referring to as the other person who sings America when he writes "I, too"?

3.   Discuss the shift in emphasis from "I, too, sing America" to "I, too, am America."

4.   Is there a specific connotation of the word "company" in this context, or is it meant only metaphorically?

Topics for Writing

1.   An important political movement of the 1960s emphasized that "Black is Beautiful." Discuss the similarities between this poem and these attitudes and examine whether this poem might have been one of the movement's sources.

2.   Discuss whether the "tomorrow" in the poem has finally arrived.

BOUND NO'TH BLUES

Hughes was one of the first writers to apply the structure of a blues song to poetry. He has, however, written this poem in six-line stanzas that make it difficult to see immediately its relationship to the blues. Students might find it helpful if the instructor wrote the poem out in the way a blues song is usually sung. This is the first stanza of Hughes's poem written as a blues song:

> Goin' down the road, Lawd, goin' down the road.
> Down the road, Lawd, way way down the road.
> Got to find somebody to help me carry this load.

This is a typical blues verse:

> Woke up this morning with a heavy achin' head,
> Lawd, woke up this morning with a heavy achin' head,
> Nothin' but the blues, hangin' 'round my bed.

The essence of a blues verse is that the first two lines present a physical situation and the third line presents an emotional reaction to that situation. Blues songs are very seldom narrative. A blues song is usually — as in Hughes's poem — a series of associative verses that develop a single emotional theme.

In this poem Hughes uses the image of a Mississippi town as unfit for a "hoppin' toad." A well-known folk / blues song describes the water in Michigan as tasting "like sherry wine," while down south in Mississippi the water "tastes like turpentine." Hughes is using a rural black voice speaking in dialect, and he has captured the speech patterns with unerring accuracy.

Questions for Discussion

1. How does Hughes avoid the repetition that is inevitable in a blues song?
2. What is the situation and the emotional reaction to the situation of each of the stanzas? What single emotional theme do the stanzas develop?
3. What is the political import of the last stanza?
4. Discuss how these lines would be scanned for meter if the poem was sung as a blues song.
5. What are some of the changes in diction and syntax Hughes has made to capture the flavor of vernacular speech?

Topic for Writing

1. **RESPONDING CREATIVELY**   Collaborate with a fellow student on writing a blues song of your own.

SONG FOR A DARK GIRL
HOUSE IN THE WORLD

The strong social protest in "Song for a Dark Girl" is implicit in Hughes's use of the last line of the popular southern song "Dixie" as the opening line of each stanza. The instructor could emphasize the intent of the poet here by singing this line from the song as the poem is read aloud. "Song for a Dark Girl" expresses Hughes's rage at southern racial violence, and "House in the World" is as close as he would get to despair about the racial prejudices he faced.

Questions for Discussion

1. What statement is Hughes making with the phrase "white Lord Jesus" in line 7 of "Song for a Dark Girl"?
2. Why does he repeat the word "naked" in the last two lines of the poem?
3. What is the term for the figure of speech in the last lines? What is Hughes describing specifically?
4. Is there a contradiction in "white shadows" in "House in the World"? Does Hughes mean shadows in the denotative sense here, or is there a connotative meaning?
5. What does he mean by the word "house"?
6. In "Song for a Dark Girl" Hughes contrasts black and white; in "House in the World" the contrast is between dark and white. Discuss whether Hughes implies any difference in his use of *black* or *dark*.

Topic for Writing

1. **MAKING CONNECTIONS**   Contrast and discuss other poems in which quotation is used to express a specific political meaning, as it is in "Song for a Dark Girl."

FLORIDA ROAD WORKERS

In this poem Hughes presents us with another of his large cast of speakers, this time a worker building a road in Florida. Although this is a masculine voice, it is not in the same vernacular dialect as "Bound No'th Blues." The poem is as freely structured as "Mother to Son," but here the voice is distinctly masculine. Students should also note that in this poem Hughes describes class differences rather than racial differences, a theme that was to become stronger in the poems he wrote a short time later as the Depression deepened.

Questions for Discussion

1. In lines 6 and 7, what might be some of the reasons that Hughes breaks out of dialect?
2. The phrases "fly by on," "sweep over," and "light and civilization to travel on" are all metaphorical. What is the larger social metaphor of the poem?
3. Who is Buddy? Is it anyone specific named in the poem?
4. Although we hear the poem as written in black dialect, could this be the voice of any worker? Could it be a woman's voice? Why or why not?
5. What is the compensation the worker feels he is getting for his work on the road?

Topics for Writing

1. Discuss the social-class differences the poem describes in terms of the year in which it was written.
2. Compare the speech of the old woman in "Mother to Son" with the speech in "Florida Road Workers" and discuss what terms or phrases suggest the sex of the speaker.

MERRY-GO-ROUND
DOWN WHERE I AM

In these later poems there is a note of ironic humor, and even the anger has a wry resignation. Hughes still feels the humiliation of racism and discrimination but now seems to be lacking the weapons to fight this injustice — a situation he had not anticipated when he wrote his confident political poems of the early 1930s.

Questions for Discussion

1. Who is "Jim Crow" in "Merry-Go-Round"?
2. "Merry-Go-Round" and "Down Where I Am" are written in different voices. Which words or phrases in the first poem suggest the speaker's youth, and which in the second poem suggest the speaker's age?
3. What does Hughes mean by "Climbin' that hill" in line 10 of "Down Where I Am"?
4. Discuss the metaphor of line 13, "I'm gonna plant my feet."

Topics for Writing

1. "Merry-Go-Round" is a humorous poem, despite the seriousness of the subject. Analyze its humor.
2. Discuss the social implications of "door," "up there," and "that hill" in "Down Where I Am."

THEME FOR ENGLISH B

In this poem Hughes presents us with still another of his personas, this time a young African American university student. Although Hughes also studied briefly in New York, the poem is clearly not a description of his own experience. Students should note that in this poem race is not the only decisive issue — so are age and social role, as the older white man is the student's instructor.

Questions for Discussion

1. Do you think the instructor gave the class assignment as a poem? Why do you think Hughes turned it into a poem?
2. Why does the student describe the way back to his room in such detail in lines 11–15? Is this part of the assignment, "let that page come out of you"?
3. Who is the "you" that ends line 18?
4. Is the instructor as liable as the student to like "Bessie, bop, or Bach"? Who is Bessie? What is bop?
5. In lines 34–35, Hughes uses the word "sometimes" to describe the instructor's feelings and "Nor . . . often" to describe the student's feelings. What difference in attitude is Hughes implying here?
6. In lines 37–38, "As I learn from you, / I guess you learn from me —," is the student uncertain about how much the instructor is learning from him because of racial differences, or is it because the instructor is older?
7. What is the student saying in line 40, "Somewhat more free"?
8. Discuss what grade you would give the student for his paper.

Topics for Writing

1. The poem raises important issues of acculturation and cross-cultural identity, which the student sums up in line 33, "That's American." Discuss some of these issues.
2. Analyze the elements of speech and the details that create a young persona in the poem.

DREAM DEFERRED

In this poem Hughes speaks in an autobiographical voice, and the message is as determined in its opposition to racism as it was in his earliest poems. Fittingly, Lorraine Hansberry's play *A Raisin in the Sun*, which depicts a black family's struggle to assimilate in a white area, begins with a version of Hughes's poem.

Question for Discussion

1. Discuss the implications of strong images in the poem, such as "fester like a sore" or "stink like rotten meat."

Topic for Writing

1. Discuss whether this poem is a prophecy or a description of the racial situation as Hughes experienced it.

Conversations on Langston Hughes and His Legacy, pp. 1108–1116

Langston Hughes, *"A Toast to Harlem,"* p. 1109.
Jessie Fauset, *"Meeting Langston Hughes,"* p. 1110.

Arnold Rampersad, *"Langston Hughes as Folk Poet,"* p. 1112.
Carl Phillips, *"Langston Hughes and Poetic Identity,"* p. 1113.
Kevin Young, *"Langston Hughes (poem),"* p. 1115.

Commentary

Robert Hayden, *"On Negro Poetry,"* p. 1050.

T. E. HULME

Images (p. 791)

English poet Hulme is of interest to us today for his brief participation in the early imagist movement. His discussions with the young American poet Ezra Pound helped form the aesthetic basis for imagist poetry, although Hulme himself wrote very little and many of his poems stray from the strict imagist canon. In this poem, he presents an image that is striking for its use of a figure from everyday life, much like Pound's better-known "In a Station of the Metro." In his precise eight words, however, Hulme manages to present a progression from the past to the present, which perhaps has its inspiration in the Japanese haiku poetry that was an important influence on the imagists. Students should also read the discussion of imagism in Chapter 11 (p. 790), and Pound's formulation of imagist theory in the commentary section (Chapter 17, p. 1065).

Questions for Discussion

1. What is the poet describing in his phrase, "scaffolding once / and workmen whistling"?
2. How closely does Hulme follow the guidelines for imagist writing in the description of imagist theory by Ezra Pound?
3. Is there a suggestion of melancholy in the poem? Is this the poet's intent?

Topics for Writing

1. Discuss the ways this poem represents imagism as an aesthetic theory.
2. RESPONDING CREATIVELY   Paraphrase the poem in a prose paragraph that develops its emotional content and the details of physical activity it suggests.

Commentary

Ezra Pound, *"On the Principles of Imagism,"* p. 1065.

LEIGH HUNT

Jenny kiss'd Me (p. 809)

See entry for T. S. Kerrigan on page 226 of this manual.

RANDALL JARRELL

The Death of the Ball Turret Gunner (p. 837)

This short poem is Jarrell's best-known work. Much of the effect is its laconic, antiheroic stance. Nothing in the poem is what the reader would expect from a poem about war. The central figure has been dropped into the state, the way an animal is dropped, and the state becomes not a home but the belly of the turret where he crouches. He is not like a person but like an animal, with fur instead of skin. The final line, with its flat description, is the final deflation of any myth of the heroism of war. Although the poem is not autobiographical, Jarrell served England with the U.S. Air Force during World War II, and in the poem that opens *Little Friend, Little Friend*, a book about his life in wartime, he refers to his fellow pilots as "other murderers."

Questions for Discussion

1. What is Jarrell describing in the phrase, "my wet fur froze"?
2. What does he mean by "loosed from its dream of life"?
3. What is he telling us when he writes "dream of life," "I work," and "nightmare fighters"?

Topics for Writing

1. Many sociologists have written that without the social conditioning that young men receive through film, television, and books, they would not be so willing to sacrifice their lives in war. Consider how this poem would or would not influence someone's decision to go into military service.
2. MAKING CONNECTIONS   Compare the attitude expressed in this poem with that of two well-known antiwar novels of World War II, Joseph Heller's *Catch-22* and Kurt Vonnegut's *Slaughterhouse Five*, both of which center on pilots or bombing raids.

ELIZABETH JENNINGS

One Flesh (p. 719)

This poem by the English poet Elizabeth Jennings was written in 1967, at a time when the barriers to what could be written and published were breaking down. It is difficult to imagine that such an unembarrassed statement about the sexuality of the writer's parents could have appeared at an earlier time. This generation of women poets found themselves entering a new world in which they could express themselves with a new freedom, and they responded to their opportunity with a surge of creativity that still fuels women's poetry today.

Questions for Discussion

1. What is the rhyme scheme of the poem? There are also irregularities in the rhyme, where do they occur? Why do you think Jennings was not bound by her own rhyme pattern?
2. She has freely mixed rhyme with both strong and weak accents, what has she achieved with this flexibility?

3.   Although the meter is often irregular, what is the basic pulse of the poem?

4.   The poem is in the tradition of the closed form poem, with a rich use of poetic images and methods. What are some of the figures of speech she uses and how do they affect our reading of the poem?

5.   What is she suggesting in the phrase "All men elsewhere" and what could be the "new event" her parents wait for?

6.   Is she viewing the end of her parent's sexuality from a child's viewpoint or from an adult's? What does she suggest about their sexuality in the line "Tossed up like flotsam from a former passion"?

7.   What is the meaning in her suggestion that their entire lives were a preparation for chastity? Is there a negative sense in her attitude toward her parents and sex?

8.   What is she asking the reader in the question "Do they know they're old"?

Topics for Writing

1.   MAKING CONNECTIONS   The American writer Sharon Olds has written many poems in which she approaches the subject of her parents' courtship and sexuality. With poems in the anthology and the use of outside sources, compare this poem of English writer Jennings with Olds's perception of her own parents' relationship.

2.   Discuss reasons why this poem would not have appeared before the 1960s and what this tells us about the changed role of poetry for writers today, using examples from poems in the anthology.

3.   Although it is clear that Jennings is uncomfortable thinking of her parents' sexual relationship, her attitudes could also reflect her comparative youth. Discuss whether or not an older Jennings would make the same judgment of her parents lying companionably in separate beds.

4.   A student who has an interest in today's psychological theories could discuss how this poem represents the long history of repression by children of thoughts of their parents' sexuality.

JAMES WELDON JOHNSON

Sunset in the Tropics (p. 840)
The Creation (p. 861)

Although James Weldon Johnson grew up in a middle-class home in Jacksonville, Florida, he felt that his education at Atlanta University — unusual for the times — implied a responsibility to the strivings of the African American community that had made his education possible. Following his graduation he took a position as a teacher in a small backwoods Georgia schoolhouse, instructing the children of ex-slaves. Throughout his life he continued to credit the experience of these early years for his introduction to the vernacular speech and song of the black society. He had a long, varied, and successful career as poet, song lyricist, foreign service officer, and teacher, and in the early 1930s he was appointed to Fisk University's Adam K. Spence Chair of Creative Literature. As a song lyricist he joined his brother John Rosamond Johnson in New York in 1901, where his brother was having considerable success writing for the black musical stage with a partner, Bob Cole. The year before, James had written a poem for a commemoration of Abraham Lincoln at the Stanton School in Jacksonville, where he had become principal. The poem was titled "Lift Ev'ry Voice and Sing," which, set to music by his brother, came to be called the "Negro national anthem."

After five years of writing lyrics for the stage shows his brother and Cole were producing, Johnson was encouraged to join the U.S. diplomatic service. In 1906 he became an American consul in a coastal city in Venezuela, and three years later he became head of the consulate in Corinto, Nicaragua. He was publishing poetry in American periodicals, and his novel *The Autobiography of an Ex-Colored Man* was published anonymously in 1912. In 1913 he resigned from the foreign service and returned to New York to take over the editorial page of the *New York Age,* and he expressed his nostalgia for the tropical lands where he had been living in a group of poems titled *Down by the Carib Sea,* which included "Sunset in the Tropics." In 1916 he was asked to become the national organizer for the fledgling NAACP, and he committed himself to the struggle for racial justice. In 1927 when his ground-breaking collection of "sermons" — which included "The Creation" — written in the vernacular language of the African American church was published, he reprinted the *Autobiography,* this time acknowledging himself as the author.

Questions for Discussion

1. What is the form of "Sunset in the Tropics"? Although there is a use of rhyme, could this be described as a poem composed in a modernist style?
2. Although the poem is describing a remembered moment, could it be described as a "dramatic" poem?
3. There are many phrases in the poem that suggest a long familiarity with the scene that is being described. What are some of these phrases and descriptive passages?
4. Earlier in his career Johnson had written poems in the accepted "Negro" dialect of popular poets like Paul Laurence Dunbar. Is there a suggestion of this dialect style in this poem? Could you suggest reasons why it is or is not an element of this poem?
5. In "The Creation" Johnson uses an entirely different poetic idiom. Why does he write this poem in this new way?
6. How do the rhythms of the poem and its line breaks suggest the chanted sermons of the African American church? What is the effect of a poem written in this style?
7. In this poem Johnson is retelling one of the most widely known stories in the Christian world. Does his version bring new dimensions to the familiar tale?
8. Although "The Creation" is usually considered a "vernacular" poem, much of the language is drawn from older writing, including the Bible. How does this affect the poetic tone of the sermon?

Topics for Writing

1. These two poems are written in strongly contrasting literary styles. Describe the differences and discuss the reasons Johnson might have had for writing them in the styles he chose.
2. Although "The Creation" is usually described as a poem in dialect, it is also a skilled, richly conceived poem that employs many of the figures of speech and the stylistic techniques of classic Anglo-American poetry. Discuss these two aspects of the language of the poem.
3. Although "The Creation" is described as a "Negro" sermon, there is little in the poem to give a specifically African American setting until the image in the final lines of the poem, comparing God to a "mammy" bending down to shape the clay image of the first human being. Discuss this image and its effect in the context of the poem.

4. MAKING CONNECTIONS   This poem was published at the peak of inter-
    est in the poets of the Harlem Renaissance. Compare this poem to the work of
    other important writers from this movement, such as Langston Hughes and
    Countee Cullen, discussing their differences and their similarities.

Ben Jonson

On My First Son (p. 716)

In the December 1997 issue of *AWP Chronicle,* the poet Lawrence Raab offered a
helpful elucidation of Jonson's poem for his dead son:

> The most striking feature of "On My First Son" is the way it invokes
> poetry, the way it uses its own presence. The dead child, as if being put to
> bed, is told to "Rest in soft peace." But that peace is immediately broken:
> "and asked, say. . . ." The boy, about to sleep, is granted speech, then given
> a specific sentence: " 'Here doth lie / Ben Jonson his best piece of poetry.' "
> We recognize this as a tombstone epitaph, yet hear it spoken as well. But
> who is talking? The father, the poet, speaks for the son, about both father
> and son, joined in their shared name. The son lies under the stone, where he
> is not only a boy, but his father's "best piece of poetry." And as that he can
> continue to speak — of separation and diminishment, but of completion as
> well. . . . The devastating pain of the poem, most desperately present in "O
> could I lose all father now! For why / Will man lament the state he should
> envy," turns into a final, tender creative act: "Rest . . . and . . . say." If this
> is a small comfort, it is the truest Jonson can offer himself. (19)

Questions for Discussion

1. Although the poem is not written in strict sonnet form, it has some of the syntac-
    tical and conceptual elements of a sonnet. What are the similarities to the sonnet?
    Considering more than the formal difference of the number of lines, why would
    we not classify it as a sonnet?
2. In line 2, Jonson intimates that his son's death is a punishment for his own sin.
    What is his sin? What is the religious justification for his punishment?
3. Discuss the meaning of lines 3 and 4. Is Jonson clear in what he intends to say, or
    is there an ambiguity built into the lines?
4. What is the meaning of his cry, "O could I lose all father now!" The phrase has
    been compressed from a more complicated thought; how could it be paraphrased?
5. In line 9, Jonson suggests that his son might be asked a question. Who might be
    asking the question?
6. What word has been withheld from the last line to fit the meter? How does the line
    relate to the thought Jonson presents in line 2?

Topics for Writing

1. The concept of joy in life as a sin is unique to Christianity. Discuss the meaning of
    line 2 in terms of its justification in Christian doctrine.
2. RESPONDING CREATIVELY   A modern poet, using the same diction and
    vocabulary of Jonson's poem, would be less constrained by the requirements of
    rhyme and meter. Rewrite the poem using open form where it seems appropriate
    and discuss the changes you make.

Bob Kaufman

From *Jail Poems* (p. 873)

Bob Kaufman was so identified with San Francisco and the Beat movement that it is surprising to realize that he was born in New Orleans, one of thirteen children born to a German Orthodox Jew and a Catholic mother who herself came from Martinique. He shipped out in the U.S. Merchant Marine when he was thirteen, and remained a sailor for twenty years. He was thirty-three when he decided to settle in San Francisco and become a poet. His *Jail Poems* reflect his rough life as a seaman and give his response to Kerouac's definition of Beat as "Beatitude."

Questions for Discussion

1. What is the form of *Jail Poems*? Is it similar to other writing by the Beat poets?
2. What does the speaker feel toward the other prisoners? How do we know this?
3. How would you interpret his line "I become part of someone forever"?
4. What is he saying in the line "In a universe of cells — who is not in jail"?
5. Why is Saturday a good day to go to jail?
6. How can we interpret the modernist image of the final entry, "Come, help flatten a raindrop"?

Topics for Writing

1. Interpret Kaufman's lines "Cargo / Destined for ports of accusation, harbors of guilt," and relate them to the other poems in the sequence.
2. MAKING CONNECTIONS   Describe the prisoners he presents in the first entry and discuss Kaufman's attitude toward them. Relate this attitude to the concept of "Beatitude" as other writers define it.

John Keats

To Autumn (p. 734)
Ode on a Grecian Urn (p. 762)
On First Looking into Chapman's Homer (p. 803)
Ode to a Nightingale (p. 983)
When I have fears (p. 985)

As they read Keats's poetry, students should remember that the work of many creative artists — writers, composers, painters — can be divided into different periods; within each period, the artists work through a series of closely related ideas and concepts. Keats had only one creative period — the brief moment between his first mature poetry and his illness and death from tuberculosis less than three years later. As though he sensed from the beginning that his time was finite, he explored his central themes, ideas, images, concepts, and even ways to construct the poem in everything he wrote. This selection includes the first of Keats's major poems, the sonnet "On First Looking into Chapman's Homer," written in 1816 when he was twenty-one; the tragically prophetic sonnet "When I have fears," from 1818; two poems from 1819, his most richly productive year ("To Autumn" and "Ode to a Nightingale"); and "Ode on a Grecian Urn," which was finally completed in 1820, a year before his death.

Students should also read "Oatmeal" (Chapter 12, p. 813), Galway Kinnell's tribute to Keats. It will remind readers that Keats wasn't only the sensitive young man of his poems; he was also a London cockney who got into a lot of fights in school. The poetry was written under the shadow of Keats's poverty, hopeless love, and growing illness.

To Autumn

The imagery of "To Autumn" is discussed in the text. It was the last of Keats's great odes from 1819, and there is a calmness about the poem, as though, for a moment, Keats no longer felt the need to wrestle meanings or interpretations from what he was feeling and experiencing.

Questions for Discussion

1. What is Keats saying about the season and the sun in line 2?
2. What do we call the figure of speech he uses in line 12, "Who has not seen thee oft amid thy store"?
3. What would we call the figure of speech of the rest of the stanza, lines 12–20?
4. How would you paraphrase the description of autumn in this stanza?
5. In line 23, is Keats speaking of the songs of spring in a real or metaphoric sense? What would he refer to as "real" spring songs?
6. What is he describing in line 25, "barred clouds bloom the soft-dying day"?
7. Lines 27–29 evoke a striking picture of a cloud of gnats. What poetic devices does Keats use to bring this picture to life?

Topics for Writing

1. **RESPONDING CREATIVELY**   Develop a personified image of a different season of the year and a different kind of human occupation or interest.
2. Keats's poetry is rich in assonance and alliteration. Analyze these elements in the opening lines of "To Autumn."
3. Autumn is personified as a farmworker. Describe what we can tell of the worker's daily tasks from the details in the poem.

Ode on a Grecian Urn

The fullest expression of Keats's themes is the famous "Ode on a Grecian Urn." For more than a hundred years it was one of the best-known poems in the English language. Today's students are probably not so familiar with it, but its ideas and poetic idiom had an immeasurable influence on English and American poetry until the social turmoil that followed World War I threw so many of the poem's values into question. In the poem Keats contrasts his theme of the eternity of beauty with the turmoil of everyday life. What the vase depicts is life's "mad pursuit," "struggles to escape," and "wild ecstasy," but the vase itself is a "still unravished bride of quietness." The poem's sexual undertones — for instance, the description of the unfulfilled embrace in lines 16–20 and the physical passion in lines such as 26–27, "For ever warm and still to be enjoyed, / For ever panting and for ever young" — lend it an even more intense poignancy.

The beauty Keats describes in the poem is almost beyond our comprehension. He writes in lines 11–12, "Heard melodies are sweet, but those unheard / Are sweeter." Because the beauty is depicted on the vase, it will be eternal. Students have usually accepted the poem's last lines without question, but commentators on the poem have argued over whether there is a contradiction between the opening of the poem, in which the poet addresses the vase, and these final lines, in which the vase addresses humankind. Keats doesn't seem to have felt any contradiction himself. There is a more difficult problem of interpretation in line 45. Does the description "Cold Pastoral!" contradict the message of warmth and beauty Keats presents in the rest of the poem? The colon in the line suggests that he means the term as a description of eternity, the word immediately preceding the colon, but it is a vague passage. For most students the final lines will present no difficulties, even if they don't agree with Keats's message.

Questions for Discussion

1. What does Keats mean by "Sylvan historian" in line 3?
2. Discuss the meaning of lines 11–12, "Heard melodies are sweet, but those unheard / Are sweeter; therefore, ye soft pipes, play on."
3. In line 14, what is Keats referring to as "spirit ditties of no tone"?
4. What is he describing in line 30, "a burning forehead, and a parching tongue"?
5. Discuss possible interpretations of "Cold Pastoral!" in line 45. Is Keats describing eternity?
6. What is he suggesting about the power of art in line 44, "Thou, silent form, dost tease us out of thought"?
7. What does he mean in line 47 when he refers to the urn as "a friend to man"?
8. Discuss the ideas expressed in the poem's final two lines.
9. Discuss the moral implications of Keats's statement that "Beauty is truth, truth beauty."

Topics for Writing

1. Compare the various ways Keats uses the concept of beauty in his poems.
2. MAKING CONNECTIONS Compare the idea of line 19 in "Ode on a Grecian Urn," that the beauty of the woman depicted on the vase cannot fade, with the sentiments in Andrew Marvell's "To His Coy Mistress" (p. 742).
3. MAKING CONNECTIONS Interpret Emily Dickinson's "I died for Beauty — but was scarce" (p. 940) in terms of the last lines of Keats's poem.

ON FIRST LOOKING INTO CHAPMAN'S HOMER

Keats's creative years were so few that it's almost meaningless to think of early or late work, but "On First Looking into Chapman's Homer" is the first of his poems that is distinctly in his own voice. Here is the sensitivity to every nuance of rhythm and to the verbal tone of each word, the delicate balance between homage to classical literature and Keats's excited discovery of the new lyric style of poetry, the subtle technical mastery of meter and accent, and the rapture — almost a childish excitement — at beauty that has just been revealed to him. Students will find these elements present in some way in each of the poems. The comments in the text explain the circumstances of this sonnet. We know that Keats wrote it at dawn in less than two or three hours, hurrying from a night of reading with a friend, and somehow the poem feels like a dawning day, even if the only passage that might apply is "I felt like some watcher of the sky."

Questions for Discussion

1. When he writes "Much have I travell'd in the realms of gold" in the first line, is Keats writing metaphorically? What is he telling us in this image?
2. What is he describing in the first four lines of the poem?

3. What is the "wide expanse" of line 5?
4. What do we call the figure of speech in his phrase "its pure serene" in line 7?
5. Could the correct name of the Spanish explorer who first saw the Pacific Ocean, Balboa, be inserted to replace "stout Cortez"? Why was the poem never corrected?

Topic for Writing

1. One of the dominant themes of the poem is the importance of classical literature to young readers. Discuss this influence on Keats's writing.

ODE TO A NIGHTINGALE

With "Ode to a Nightingale" Keats expresses all of his major themes: beauty, its eternal freshness, and the contrast with the pain and death of mortal life. It is a complex poem. In musical terms it would be described as polyphonic. Its themes are presented; new themes take their place; then ideas return and are presented in new forms. As always with Keats, the opening phrase is immediately effective: "My heart aches." Lines 3 and 4 mean that the speaker feels as though a minute ago he drank some sort of depressant and he is drifting off to dreamland. Paradoxically, he insists that his heart aches not out of envy for the nightingale's "happy lot" but out of an excess of happiness that the bird "In some melodious plot . . . singest of summer with full-throated ease." The second stanza hints at death. He will take the draught, a wine, that he felt he might have drunk (the hemlock mentioned in the poem's opening lines), and leave the world.

In the first two stanzas Keats presents the reader with images of natural beauty, but in the third stanza they are contrasted with what he knows of life's realities, its "weariness, the fever." Line 26, "Where youth grows pale, and specter-thin, and dies," must refer to his brother, consciously intended or not. The fifth stanza is one of Keats's most startling poetic passages. The speaker can't see where he is walking, as it is night, but even in the darkness he can guess what flowers and wild growth are "at his feet."

In the sixth stanza Keats returns to the subject of death. In the next stanza he insists that the nightingale's song is immortal. He ignores the reality of any single nightingale's death: The song will be continued by another nightingale. It is the song — beauty — that is immortal. Then to end the poem suddenly he brings the reader back to the poem's opening, "My heart aches." This stanza begins, "Forlorn," and in a few words he is back in the drowsy, half-forgetful state of the poem's first lines. Was it all a dream? He leaves us with the confused suggestion "Do I wake or sleep?"

Questions for Discussion

1. Could Keats's suggestion of the use of an opiate in "Ode to a Nightingale" be compared with Coleridge's use of opium in "Kubla Khan"?
2. Is the speaker awake or dreaming?
3. In the first stanza he suggests that his heart is aching, but aching with "being too happy." Is this a contradiction? How is the contradiction clarified in the final stanza?
4. There is a seeming paradox in line 6, "But being too happy in thine happiness." Is this like the paradox of an Elizabethan conceit?
5. What is Keats asking for in the beginning of the second stanza? Is this like the opiate he describes in the first stanza, or are their effects different?
6. Who is he saying will fade away in the first line of the third stanza?
7. In the rest of the stanza is he saying that only human beings experience mortality?
8. What is the implication of line 27, "but to think is to be full of sorrow"?

9. In line 33, what is Keats telling us about "Poesy"?
10. Why is the speaker contemplating suicide in the sixth stanza?
11. Ruth, in line 66, is the first reference in the poem to something other than nature or the speaker's own feelings. Why is she an appropriate symbol here?
12. What is Keats saying in line 72, "the fancy cannot cheat so well"?

WHEN I HAVE FEARS

In our modern age we still face the dangers of disease, and the AIDS epidemic has traced a long trail across much modern American poetry. In Keats's time it was tuberculosis that was the relentless danger that was little understood and widely feared. He contracted the disease himself while nursing his brother through his own doomed struggle against the disease. When Keats accepted the reality of his own infection, he also was accepting the inevitable presence of death. This sonnet, in which he tries to rationalize his fears, was one of the most widely quoted of his poems in the nineteenth century, and it is still difficult not to feel the emotions of this supremely gifted young poet as he tries to accept that he will have so little time to fulfill his promise.

Questions for Discussion

1. What is the rhyme scheme of the sonnet? Is it English or Italian in form?
2. In its opening lines the imagery of the poem is based on the pastoral tradition. Does this explain the word "glean'd" in the second line? What other allusions are there to harvest and rural bounty?
3. What is the inference of the word "teeming" in line 2? Sometimes teeming is used in a negative sense. Is that the case here?
4. Is the shift of the poem to his vision of the love that he will never experience a contradiction of the mood of the opening images?
5. Is there an obvious relationship of love and fame, as Keats suggests in the last line?
6. Why does he describe love's power as "unreflecting"?

Topics for Writing

1. Keats had an indelible effect on English poetry for nearly a century after his death, and at some point in their development almost every young poet attempted to achieve the sonorities of a line like "Hold like rich garners the full-ripen'd grain." Analyze the line in terms of assonance and alliteration and its structural meaning in the poem.
2. MAKING CONNECTIONS Compare the brief years of Keats's literary production with those of his two most gifted contemporaries, Percy Bysshe Shelley and Lord Byron, who also died while they still were young. Each of the poets had a period of youthful experimentation before achieving a distinctive personal style. Examine a representative poem of each of them to compare their technical means and their poetic techniques.

T. S. KERRIGAN

Elvis Kissed me (p. 810)
WITH Jenny kiss'd Me (p. 809) by LEIGH HUNT

T. S. Kerrigan's poem was included in his collection *Another Bloomsday at Molly Malone's Pub*, published by The Inevitable Press in Laguna, California, in 1991.

Questions for Discussion

1.   What portion of Leigh Hunt's poem has Kerrigan chosen to parody most closely?
2.   Why did Kerrigan choose Elvis Presley as the subject of his own poem? Is it the inclusion of Presley that makes the poem humorous?
3.   What does Kerrigan imply in the line "easy pickings here"?
4.   What does Kerrigan parody of Hunt's line "Jumping from the chair she sat in"? Could Kerrigan have written an effective parody if he did not have a genuine familiarity with Hunt's poem?
5.   Could a modern poet have written a poem with the tone and the emotions of "Jenny kiss'd Me"? Why, or why not?

Topics for Writing

1.   Analyze Kerrigan's parody and show its similarities to Hunt's poem, then continue the discussion to examine the concept of parody itself.
2.   The two poems have a surface similarity, but Kerrigan has consciously given his own poem a different emotional tone. Discuss this difference and relate it to the nature of parody itself.

GALWAY KINNELL

The Road Between Here and There (p. 739)
Oatmeal (p. 813)

Kinnell was born in Providence, Rhode Island, in 1927, served in the Navy during the Second World War, and received his B.A. at Princeton University and his M.A. at the University of Rochester following his discharge. He had already begun writing poetry, but he quickly became dissatisfied with traditional verse forms and began to reach out to a more fluid and immediate mode of expression, much as poets like W. D. Snodgrass and Robert Lowell were doing at about the same time. Kinnell also had a strong sense of political commitment and worked for some time as a member of the Congress of Racial Equality (CORE), traveling in the South to register African American voters. He was actively engaged in the protest movement against the Vietnam War. For many years he has lived in rural Vermont. Like many poets in the United States, Kinnell has supported his writing by teaching, and he has taught at a number of universities and colleges. His poetry has won many prizes, including a Pulitzer Prize for his *Selected Poems* in 1983.

THE ROAD BETWEEN HERE AND THERE

Questions for Discussion

1. Why is this poem described as a metaphor? A term that is sometimes used for a longer example of this form is "extended metaphor." Would this term be applicable to Kinnell's poem?
2. What is the effect of the poem's use of the word "Here" to open each example? Would this repetition also make the poem more effective if it were read aloud?
3. We often use the term "the road of life" as an image for our own experience. How does this relate to Kinnell's poem? Could he have been conscious of this familiar metaphor when he began writing?
4. Many of the images in the poem describe events that occurred when he was driving. Would other writers, perhaps living in a large city instead of rural Vermont, use the automobile as a symbol of their lives in the same way?
5. How would we classify the image of "two piglets who rummaged inside the burlap bag like pregnancy itself"?
6. What is he suggesting in the image of the chimney "standing up by itself and falling down" in the last lines of the poem?

Topics for Writing

1. In the poem Kinnell is using examples from his mundane daily activities to symbolize the small dramas and tragedies of everyday life. Discuss some of the specific examples he names and examine how they take their place in the larger metaphor of the road as the story of his own experience.
2. **RESPONDING CREATIVELY** Using the images and symbols Kinnell has included in the poem, it would be possible to write a description of the life he has led in the countryside. In the description extend your ideas to include his thoughts and attitudes as they are reflected in the poem.
3. There is a vivid use of imagery throughout the poem. Discuss the elements of traditional poetic techniques he has employed to create a poem that is decisively contemporary in its allusions and summations.

OATMEAL

Although Kinnell writes in the modern open form, he uses structured techniques to achieve the intensity and the allusive power of traditional verse. He also feels himself part of the formal poetic tradition, and in the description of his imaginary breakfast with John Keats, he not only manages to give us a fresh and lively glimpse of what Keats must have been like but he also offers a shrewd commentary on one of Keats's most beautiful but complex poems, "Ode to a Nightingale."

Questions for Discussion

1. Although the ostensible subject of this poem is Kinnell's meeting with John Keats, it also has an underlying theme. Discuss this theme.
2. Is the imagery of line 19 in "Oatmeal" — "and the way here and there a line . . ." — a modern metaphor, or is Kinnell paraphrasing Keats's poetic style?
3. The denotative meaning of "amnion" is the innermost membrane enclosing the fetus before birth. What is Kinnell saying with line 28, "maybe there is no sublime, only the shining of the amnion's tatters"?

Topic for Writing

1.   Analyze the means Kinnell has used in "Oatmeal" to present us with a living portrait of John Keats.

CAROLYN KIZER

For Jan, in Bar Maria (p. 760)

Carolyn Kizer was born in Spokane, Washington, in 1925 and studied first at Sarah Lawrence College, then continued her graduate studies at Columbia University and the University of Washington. Though her early marriage failed, as a newly divorced mother with three children she had the financial resources to attend a poetry workshop led by Theodore Roethke. In 1961, Kizer published her first collection of poems, *The Ungrateful Garden*. She considers herself a feminist writer, and she has led poetry programs both in the United States and in foreign countries as well as acted as poet-in-residence at a number of American universities. Her collection *Yin* won the Pulitzer Prize for 1984.

Questions for Discussion

1.   What is Kizer suggesting with her note that this poem is in the style of a classic Chinese poet?
2.   Why is it important for the poet that the two women still can run up the hill from the beach "without getting too winded"? Where is Ischia and what does this tell us about their summer there?
3.   What does Kizer want us to know about her past when she speaks of Spokane as "That colorless town"?
4.   Why does Kizer use the term "trivial-hearted" as an explanation for the fact that they no longer fear death?
5.   What does Kizer tell the reader about them as younger women in her phrase "Mad as yearling mares in the full moon"? Does she intend this to be read as a description of their young sexuality?
6.   How does the image of the sexuality of young mares relate to the image from a preceding line of them dancing in "twin pinafores"? What is Kizer telling the reader by using the term "pinafores"?
7.   Is the image Kizer presents of herself and her friend a negative one? How does she present the reaction of the villagers?
8.   Is it probable that the villagers would have had the same reaction if the two women had been from the village themselves? What is Kizder telling the reader with her comment that they "shocked the people of Forio"?

Topics for Writing

1.   By opening her poem with the note that she is writing in the style of a classic Chinese poet, Kizer reminds the reader that poets consider themselves part of a long poetic tradition. Discuss this element of Kizer's poem, and using examples of poems in the sections "Address and Tribute" and "Allusion" describe this feeling which poets share, using examples from the writing.
2.   The poem is a lively description of one aspect of the new emancipation of women. Discuss the relationship between the two women and the men around them, both from the point of view of the two American young women themselves and the

point of view of the men of the village, considering the background of their own social mores.

3. In the poem Kizer also makes it clear that the two women are free of economic concerns. In Ischia they are "drinking together, sisters of summer." Discuss this aspect of women's emancipation and compare it to the lives of the people they left behind in "that colorless town."

ETHERIDGE KNIGHT

The Idea of Ancestry (p. 841)

Knight, who was born in Corinth, Mississippi, in 1931, lived a troubled, turbulent life that in many ways cut across the black experience of America during these years. He grew up in the rough environment of a southern black town, with its inescapable denigration of African American selfhood, and much that happened to him afterward continued to reflect this troubled background. He became addicted to drugs when he was still young, but he managed to come through four years in the U.S. Army, from 1947 to 1951, without becoming entangled with the authorities. In 1960 his habit finally led to his arrest for robbery. He was sentenced to eight years in prison, and it was during his prison years that he began to develop his verbal skills in black street language and finally turned to writing poetry. Two important figures in African literature at this time, Dudley Randall and Gwendolyn Brooks, became interested in his writing, and Randall published Knight's first book, the well-received *Poems from Prison*, in 1968.

Following his release from prison, Knight was encouraged to become one of the writers active in Detroit's black arts movement, and for a time was married to poet Sonia Sanchez. Sanchez had been an addict herself for some time when she was younger, and she had considerable experience with the difficulties he faced, but his addiction made it impossible for the marriage to survive. Knight continued his tumultuous career, performing his poems and creating new work, and his major 1973 volume *Belly Song and Other Poems* strengthened his reputation. His irregular life had damaged his health, however, and he died in 1985 at the age of fifty-four. Perhaps the finest summation of Knight's life and his determination to bring his writing to a black audience is the challenging cry that ends his 1969 poem "For Black Poets Who Think of Suicide":

> Let All Black poets die as trumpets
> And be buried in the dust of marching feet.

Questions for Discussion

1. Knight thought of his poems as oral recitations rather than written performances. How does the style of this poem reflect this attitude?
2. What does he achieve by presenting in detail the identity of the faces in the forty-seven pictures?
3. How do we interpret his declarations of love in the second stanza? Does his love for both his grandmother and his young niece find room under the wide umbrella of this love?
4. What is he telling us in line 27, "I almost kicked it with the kinfolks"? What are some of the things he describes that aided him in his struggle to get free of the drug?
5. He is making a statement about drugs in his line "I had almost caught up with me." What is his meaning? Does this seem like a realizable dream?

6.   In his simile of himself as a salmon returning to his "birthstream," he prepares us for the metaphor of line 35, "This yr there is a gray stone wall damming my stream." What is the meaning of the gray stone wall? Why is the first figure of speech a simile and the second a metaphor? What are the implications of the image of the stone wall "damming my stream"? How does this anticipate his statement a few lines later, "I have no sons"?

Topics for Writing

1.   The image that opens the poem, the forty-seven pictures of his family taped to the wall of his prison cell, is one of the strongest first lines in modern American poetry. Comment on its significance in a poem written by a convict, and discuss how it introduces the theme of family that is developed in the poem.
2.   In earlier black poetry, like Countee Cullen's *Heritage* (p. 865), the idea of ancestry is tied to a consciousness of an African past. Discuss this new concept in Knight's poem, that his past is the rural South.
3.   In his characterization of his grandmother, who has "no / place in her Bible for 'whereabouts unknown,'" he is making a statement about the role of black women in sustaining the black family. Discuss the role these women played in these difficult years.

Yusef Komunyakaa

Facing It (p. 838)

Komunyakaa was born in 1947 in Bogalusa, in eastern Louisiana, but his service in the Vietnam War in 1969 and 1970 took him out of Louisiana into a larger world. He began to publish poetry about his war experiences shortly after his discharge, and he is one of the most articulate of the poets who have described their combat experiences. This poem, written almost twenty years after the war, is a recounting of a visit to the controversial Vietnam Veterans Memorial in Washington, D.C. The memorial is an unadorned, highly polished black wall containing the names of the 58,022 service personnel known to have died in the Vietnam War. In the poem, Komunyakaa develops his imagery around the memorial's gleaming surface, which serves as a mirror for the people visiting the memorial at the same time as he.

Questions for Discussion

1.   Why does he tell us that his face hides "inside the black granite"?
2.   What is the emotional connotation of line 6, "My clouded reflection eyes me / like a bird of prey"?
3.   Is the color of the memorial symbolic? Why would Komunyakaa feel this?
4.   Why does he "half-expect" to find his own name chiseled on the wall along with the others?
5.   What is the symbolism of the final image, the woman brushing the boy's hair?

Topic for Writing

1.   MAKING CONNECTIONS   Compare the attitudes toward war implied in this poem with that in Wilfred Owen's poem "Dulce et Decorum Est" (p. 836).

TED KOOSER

Selecting a Reader (p. 706)

Although Ted Kooser is a prolific poet who has published several collections and chapbooks, as well as an accomplished memoirist, he spent his life working as an executive in the life insurance industry. Now retired, he lives in the Midwest.

Questions for Discussion

1. Is Kooser's poem in open or closed form? Would it have changed our appreciation of the poem if it had been written in a traditional form?
2. Why has he given us so many details of the appearance of his young reader? Could you describe her from what he has told us? Is this someone you would consider "pretty"?
3. Why has he stressed the precise moment when he wants her to read his poetry?
4. What is he telling us with his suggestion that he, as the writer, can select his readers? How realistic is this idea?
5. Has Kooser deliberately led us to expect a different conclusion to his poem, which tells us that the reader has more practical things to do with her money than buy a book of poems? What is the contradiction he has created?

Topics for Writing

1. Discuss whether it would be possible to object to Kooser's suggestion that his reader should be pretty. Refer to other poems in the anthology that also describe women in terms of their appearance.
2. Discuss the concept of the writer "selecting" his readers, and examine the content of other poems to describe how their choices of subject matter might have reflected the poet's concern with attracting readers to select what he has written.

TOM KRYSS

Of Dry Strings and Riverbeds (p. 885)
What Harmonica? (p. 886)
Night Storm (p. 887)

Although Tom Kryss was associated with the tumultuous poetry scene in Cleveland in the 1970s and 1980s his own poetry and art work expressed a more traditional emphasis. Often he wrote about current music and political events, but his poems found a fruitful balance between material and writing style. He also was active as a publisher and illustrator, creating cover illustrations for many chapbooks. He plays a continuing, vital role in the alternative poetry movement today.

OF DRY STRINGS AND RIVERBEDS

Questions for Discussion

1. Although the poem is written in open form, the line length is an informal succession of loosely stressed iambs in either four- or five-stress meter, though the pattern of the meter, as in ordinary speech, varies from line to line. Does this give the

poem a structure we sense as we read it? What is the effect of his division of the poem into verses of five and six lines?

2. The poem uses a rich variety of figures of speech. How are simile and metaphor used in the poem? Personification?

3. The guitar itself is used in many different ways in the poem. How does it appear as a symbol and a metaphor?

4. What is the inference of his image in the term "riverbeds" in the poem's title? How is it linked to the image of "a dry riverbed"? Does the reader's mind hear at the same time a more familiar phrase "Of Dry *Streams* and Riverbeds"? Was this ambiguity something the poet considered as he titled the poem?

5. What is the writer inferring with the line "but silence offers no assurances"?

6. The key to the poem its use of the guitar as a metaphor for the lives of people also living in the house. How is this expressed in the poem's imagery?

Topics for Writing

1. Although the subject of Kryss's poem is the musical instruments left behind in rooms and attics, within the poem's seeming quiet there is a sense of disappointment and loss. Discuss the syntax of the poem centering on phrases like "a few tense chords," "a silent boarder or eccentric family member," and summarize what you feel. What is the theme of the poem?

2. The student could write a paper about a musical instrument left in their own home, and if they choose, also use the instrument as a metaphor for someone left behind in the home, unused, "locked away."

3. We usually associate the guitar with today's popular music. Discuss the multiple meanings in the poem when the "guitar" is presented within a traditional syntax and used symbolically to make a statement about existence that has larger dimensions than the popular music world.

WHAT HARMONICA?

As in his poem "Of Dry Strings and Riverbeds," Kryss has again used a symbol of today's popular music world, though here the harmonica, unlike the guitar, is being played and is a living part of everyday life.

Questions for Discussion

1. What does Kryss mean with his first line, "Very forgiving, as instruments go"?

2. What similes does the writer use to compare the harmonica to other sounds? What is he telling us about life's larger themes in his image "nothing I'd want to pull out / at the wake, or walk the streets with"?

3. What does he mean with the line "first row, next to the pit"? How has he used the line as a metaphor?

4. Kryss consistently describes the harmonica as easy to play, but what is he telling the reader with his last lines, "not so low as to blow / disappointment all out of proportion"?

5. What is the writer inferring with the phrase "raw music"? Is this an apt description of the sound of someone blowing the open tones of a harmonica?

Topics for Writing

1. Discuss Kryss's characterization of the harmonica as what could be termed a "proletarian" instrument, easily mastered and carried around in a pocket. Compare this with the idea of instruments that are not "Very forgiving."

2. Kryss has employed a number of similes to describe the sound of the harmonica, including his note that it produces "raw music." Using the harmonica or some other instrument, write a variety of similes to describe the sound, comparing the results to other similes or metaphors relating to the sound of the instrument encountered in other reading.

Night Storm

Questions for Discussion

1. What does the poem tell the reader about the family relationships? Does the child seem conscious of her handicap?
2. What is the allusion in the term "Cyclopean eye"?
3. There is a vivid imagery of the storm's power. What are some of the phrases the poet employs? What is the meaning of the description that their daughter "rode each bolt into its memory"?
4. What does the poet infer with the phrase "the plague of the tongue"? Is there a historical allusion in the use of the word "plague"?
5. What could be a possible explanation of the child's ability to speak clearly during the excitement of the storm?

Topics for Writing

1. Discuss the image of the poem, a small child drawn to the enormity of a storm and being momentarily transformed by it, in terms of a larger symbolic meaning where our experience of life is conditioned by larger events of the world beyond us.
2. The student could write about similar experiences, moments when some natural event affected either themselves or a member of their family.

Maxine Kumin

Mother of Everyone (p. 812)

Maxine Kumin, who was born in Philadelphia in 1925, has lived for many years in rural New Hampshire. She has had a long and richly productive career as a poet, novelist, essayist, and author of children's books, and her writing has won many awards, including the Pulitzer Prize for her 1972 collection *Up Country: Poems of New England*. Although her poetry is largely written in modern, open verse forms, she has always been responsive to the older poetic traditions.

The student should also refer to the poetry of Muriel Rukeyser, p. 1005.

Questions for Discussion

1. What is the personal disability Kumin is comparing with Rukeyser's recovery from a stroke? What is similar about the two experiences?
2. What is the poet saying in the image "the bent sapling of my torso"? What is the figure of speech she is using?
3. Why does Kumin quote the line "it is time for the true grace of women" as an example of Rukeyser's speaking voice? What is Kumin telling us about her by using the word "declaiming" to describe her voice?

4.   What does Kumin mean by her description of Rukeyser's speaking difficulty as "a splinter whe worked past"? How does this relate to the title of the poem Kumin quotes, "Resurrection of the Right Side"?

5.   What is the figure of speech Kumin uses in her description of Rukeyser's stroke as "the earthquake that flattened her"? Does this figure describe the event clearly? How can the word "stammered" describe walking?

6.   What is the "rubble" that Rukeyser uses as she continues to write poetry?

7.   Would other women also consider Rukeyser as a "mother of everyone" or is it necessary to agree with the political aspects of Rukeyser's writing?

Topics for Writing

1.   Often poets encourage each other to approach difficult or sensitive subjects. In this poem it is the example of the older poet's courage and determination that has encouraged Kumin as she faces her own problem. Discuss how this exchange can take place and consider it as a kind of empowerment, defining the word and using examples from the poem in the discussion.

2.   **MAKING CONNECTIONS**   In her poem, Kumin describes many of the things that she admired about the older woman — "tough as a tree trunk," and "young and fervent" are some examples. Quoting from Kumin's comments, create a portrait in prose of Rukeyser and with this portrait clarify Kumin's final line of praise "Muriel, mother of everyone."

3.   Kumin has written a poem of tribute. Discuss the elements of Rukeyser's personality that she feels are valuable and compare them to values that you personally do or do not share. Consider the final line — is Rukeyser a mother to you as well?

4.   Discuss Rukeyser's political position, as described in Kumin's poem, and consider the relevance of this opinion to the position of women in the society.

JOANNE KYGER

October 29, 1963, Wednesday (p. 879)

Some time before this poem was written Kyger had joined Gary Snyder in Japan where he was engaged in a serious study of Buddhism. They were married there and then traveled together to India to meet a friend from California, Allen Ginsberg, who had been living in the holy city that was then known as Benares and is now called Varanasi. Already both men were well known, even though they had only begun to publish their work a few years earlier. Kyger's attitude toward the adulation they are receiving is clearly ambivalent.

Questions for Discussion

1.   What does Kyger mean by the term "elevated"? Is this usually thought to be possible? What might be some of her reasons for saying here that she is elevating? Is anybody noticing?

2.   What is the simile she employs to describe her husband and Ginsberg leading the crowd into the trees? Is she inferring that there are some characteristics of the historic adoration of sages in the behavior of the crowd? Does she find the two poets worthy of being considered sages?

3.   Is there a laconic tone in Kyger's suggestion that the reader may call the white wall Grecian, "if the fancy takes you"?

4. What is it Snyder and Ginsberg are drinking "up all day / in teacups"? Is it common for poets to be treated this way, even on the streets of India?
5. Why is no one noticing Kyger there against the wall? Does this upset her?
6. Does Kyger have the impression that the two poets would rather she didn't levitate at just that moment?
7. Why does she tell us she's wearing a Tibetan bathrobe?
8. Is her final comment, "Silence," meant as a sardonic complaint? Could there be other meanings to the use of the word?

Topics for Writing

1. Levitation is only one of many acts performed by Indian street performers. Discuss some of them and present arguments for why the crowds seeing them perform might choose to believe some of the things they see.
2. Kyger asks herself whether or not the practice of Buddhism by the three Westerners will have a good effect on the people crowding around them. Discuss whether the example of outsiders adopting a belief or political ideas can have an effect upon the people for whom these concepts have been part of their lives.
3. From further reading in the works of Ginsberg, Snyder, and Kyger discuss their Buddhist beliefs and extend the discussion to the effect their studies had on the intellectual zeitgeist of the 1960s.
4. The Buddhism introduced by the Beat writers often manifested itself in political action. Discuss how Buddhism and activism could complement each other with examples from the Beats' writing and activities during this period.

LI-YOUNG LEE

Eating Alone (p. 760)

Although Lee was raised in a Chinese family, his father, who had been one of the physicians attending Communist dictator Mao Tse-tung, was forced to leave China. The family lived in Indonesia, where Lee was born in 1957; Hong Kong; Macao; and Japan before finally settling in Pennsylvania. Lee received his B.A. at the University of Pittsburgh in 1979, and after further studies he settled with his family in Chicago, where his career combines teaching and writing.

Questions for Discussion

1. What is the vision Lee saw through the window the morning he is writing the poem?
2. Does the poet associate his father with his memories of gardening? Why does he make this association?
3. The details of the garden — the turning leaves, the bird he sees, the cellar door — all tell us that the poem is describing a pastoral scene. Why does the poem exclude the poet's city life?
4. What is he telling us with the image of the hornet trapped in the rotten pear?
5. Do the poem's final words, "What more could I, a young man, want," suggest that he is admonishing himself for perhaps wanting more than just this simple meal? Or is he truly suggesting that he is satisfied with this moment?

Topics for Writing

1.   Some writers have felt that the clarity and precision of Lee's observations of the physical scene around him are related to his Chinese background, and the directness and immediacy of the response to nature in Chinese poetry and art. Using library materials, compare Lee's descriptions to Chinese drawing or painting, or to Chinese classical poetry.

2.   **MAKING CONNECTIONS**   Compare Lee's close affinity with the natural world to the poetry of two poets in the anthology, Galway Kinnell and Maxine Kumin, who, like him, turn to the natural world for their inspirations, though they were also from the city.

3.   **MAKING CONNECTIONS**   Compare this poem, and Lee's thoughts about his father, to Seamus Heaney's poem "Digging" (p. 970), which also describes a poet seeing his father at work in the garden outside his window.

Denise Levertov

Mid-American Tragedy (p. 830)
From Matins (p. 898)

Levertov's imagination was so rich and her range of expression so wide that no one poem or single group of poems could capture the range and style of her writing. Her writing reflected the changes in her life as she moved from England to the United States and left the cosmopolitan, politically engaged life of her family in London. Although British and American English have many similarities, they also have many differences, and Levertov decided immediately to refashion her poetic language to encompass the American idiom. Her first book, *The Double Image*, published in England in 1946, was written in what she called the "neoromantic" style.

When her second book, *Here and Now*, was published eleven years later, Levertov had found the inspiration she needed in the work of William Carlos Williams, H.D., and the Black Mountain poets. She had become so much a part of this new American school of writing that *Here and Now* appeared as pamphlet number 6 in the City Lights series published by poet Lawrence Ferlinghetti in San Francisco. Allen Ginsberg's *Howl* was number 4 in the series, and the book that followed Levertov's as number 7 was a reprint of Williams's experimental text *Kora in Hell*. In the 1960s, as the Vietnam War became the crucial issue in America, Levertov became increasingly engaged in the antiwar movement. At least one of her old friends, poet Robert Duncan, broke with her over her commitment. She traveled to Southeast Asia to lead protests, and of her own work she wrote, "we need poems . . . to help us live the revolution." At the same time, she continued to write other poetry that was unaffected by her political engagement.

Mid-American Tragedy

Questions for Discussion

1.   Is the situation described in the poem a typical one, despite the tragedy of the son's illness? Is it usual for parents of a gay son to refuse to listen to his explanations or justifications?

2. Do his parents actually intend to take him for a trip to Disney World, or is this only a projection on Levertov's part?
3. What is she suggesting with her statement in the final line, "his life at last"?
4. Why did Levertov capitalize "Mom" and "Dad" in the second line?
5. Is there irony in her mention that the dying man must listen to "Jingle Bells" as he struggles against his illness?

Topics for Writing

1. Although Levertov has presented her portrait of the older couple in an almost humorous tone, this is an angry poem. Discuss the emotional stance the poet has taken to express this anger.
2. In a short essay, discuss ways that the poet could have expressed some sympathy for the parents, instead of an immediate dismissal of their standards and values.
3. Discuss what might have been exchanged between the son and his parents, if, as Levertov asked of them, they had sat quietly and listened to what he might say.

From Matins

Questions for Discussion

1. What is the denotative meaning of "matins"? What in the poem suggests why the poet chose it as a title? Does the poet mean it in the specific sense, or is the title a metaphor for the morning's activities?
2. What is Levertov implying in the phrase "Stir the holy grains" in verse V? Is she being ironic?
3. She introduces the poem with the term "The authentic!" What does she mean by the term? What are examples of it that she includes in the poem?
4. What does Levertov imply in her image of the egg that must be broken to supply nourishment? Does she also imply that experience must be lived before it becomes part of our lives?
5. Many of the details of the poem describe a mother's activities as she tends her family. Is the poem intended as a feminist statement? Why or why not? What is the larger woman's role in the household's life that Levertov is describing?
6. Is there a suggestion of liturgical language in her repetition of the line "call the child to eat"? Would this relate to the title of the poem?

Topics for Writing

1. This is a poem about daily life and the meanings one may draw from this life. Discuss Levertov's characterization of "The authentic" in the lines " . . . it's always / a recognition, the known / appearing fully itself and / more itself than one knew." Discuss the larger philosophic concept of inferring the whole from its parts that the poem expresses.
2. Discuss the image that as she eats she is thinking and thinking takes her into a realm of dream that "runs through us / faster than thought / toward recognition." Relate it to the larger theme of her poem, the quest for authenticity.
3. Discuss why Levertov has chosen ordinary activities to illustrate a poem that is about a poetic concept of reality and consider whether she has achieved her purpose in the poem.
4. "Matins" is the term for morning prayer in the Anglican Church. Discuss the religious implications of the title and trace any suggestion of this meaning in the events of the poem.

5.   **MAKING CONNECTIONS**   This theme of the intensity of experience has been approached by many poets, among them Robert Frost and Emily Dickinson. Find other poems with this theme and compare them to Levertov's exultant conclusion.

Primo Levi

Almanac (p. 851)

Questions for Discussion

1.   At its heart this is an angry poem. What is the cause of Levi's anger?
2.   In the opening lines he describes the forces of nature at work. What are these forces? How do they operate on the earth itself?
3.   What does Levi mean with his description of the sea, "Always miserly with its riches"?
4.   He does not describe an earth that is at peace with itself. What is the figure of speech he uses when he writes "Earth too will fear the immutable"?
5.   What is the poet saying when he declares that mankind will not fear the laws of the universe?
6.   What is Levi's final view of the fate of the human race?

Topics for Writing

1.   **MAKING CONNECTIONS**   Compare this poem to any of the other poems in this group relating to "The Living Earth" and contrast Levi's views with the views of that writer.
2.   Levi's view of Earth itself is that it is essentially an "indifferent" force. Comment on the effect of this belief on the poem he has created.

D. A. Levy

Perhaps (#5) (p. 874)

The writing of Cleveland's rebel poet d. a. levy reminds us that the Beat movement was much more chaotic and nihilistic than the recent emphasis on the optimistic aspects of Jack Kerouac's writing suggests. Of special importance for levy was the influence of Allen Ginsberg, who made an appearance in the city to support a local publisher who was facing an obscenity charge. An aspect of levy's writing that separates his poetry from much of the literary underground is that although he has clearly used illegal drugs himself he writes eloquently of their deadly consequences.

Questions for Discussion

1.   Much of levy's poem is a maze of references and allusions. What are some of them?
2.   levy also employs language in ways that allude to slang and even diction of different eras. What are some examples of this?
3.   What allusion is he employing in the phrase "A Grand Ole Memory"?

4. This style of writing is often called "underground" or "alternative." What is meant by the terms and how could they be applied to levy's writing?

5. Is there a contradiction in his description of the new arrivals as "unknown friends"? Was this a common experience in these years?

6. What is he telling us about the people in his simile "we finally put them to / bed like stuffed toys"?

7. What makes levy feel nauseated by the sight of the people injecting drugs in the morning?

8. What is levy telling the reader with his final lines, "someone in my head / KEEPS YELLING / *Laugh or You'll Die*"?

Topics for Writing

1. In the 1960s one definition of levy's writing style was *free association*. Discuss the term and use quotes from the poem to illustrate its different aspects.

2. The 1960s saw a corresponding musical movement in underground or alternative rock. Discuss this phenomenon in terms of both its political and aesthetic attitudes and relate it to contemporary music and literature.

3. **RESPONDING CREATIVELY**   Write a poem using the technique of free association. Explain what you have learned about this kind of writing in the process of writing your own poem.

4. Describe an experience similar to the arrival of the "unknown friends" in levy's apartment and compare your experience to what levy witnessed nearly a half century ago.

5. Discuss the two contradictory aspects of the Beat phenomenon that have emerged: today's appropriation of figures like Jack Kerouac for everything from advertisements for sports clothes to adulatory documentary films versus the awareness that the Beat movement was once considered a threat to most American values. Many of its leading figures were briefly jailed, and their writings were seized either for obscenity or political reasons. levy himself was driven to suicide by the efforts of the Cleveland authorities to silence him. Compare the attitudes of today's generation to what the Beats faced in their own time.

GERALD LOCKLIN

A Loser (p. 891)
So It Goes (p. 891)
Second-Hand Television (p. 892)

In his steadfast commitment to poetry as a university teacher, writer, reviewer, and editor/publisher, Gerald Locklin has played an important role as an influence to many new writers and as a spokesperson for the group of poets associated with the chapbooks and the magazines of the alternative press. His poems have a deceptive casualness, achieved by a consistent sensitivity to the syntax of the poem, however brief, and to his ability to create a scene in a few words. The most imitated feature of his poems is the sardonic last line — usually referred to by other poets as a "tag."

Questions for Discussion

1. The tone of Locklin's poetry could be described as "a resigned irony of annoyance." What does this term suggest to his readers?

2. In "A Loser" what kind of individual is he describing? Although the poem is brief, has he told us enough about the person with his final line for us to have a clear image of who he's describing?
3. Does Locklin make any moral judgment about his friend's addiction to sport? Although there is no annoyance in the poem, is there a clear resignation toward the situation?
4. In "So It Goes," what can we say of Locklin's relationship with his son? Would we say that he is being fair to his son?
5. Though Locklin's poems are often short and written in casual language, they are skillfully constructed. What elements in the poem help create an immediate impression of the conversation between father and son for the reader?
6. Is Locklin making a larger statement about the relevance of serious art in the life he and his son know?
7. The tone of "Second-Hand Television" is clearly expressing his annoyance at a social phenomenon that is beyond his ability to change. Why does he not raise the tone of the poem to anger?
8. Is "Second-Hand Television" a familiar term? Is it an accurate description of the presence of television sets in many public places? What is it about this that Locklin finds particularly annoying?
9. In these poems, does Locklin leave us with the impression that there might be other things that also annoy him?

Topics for Writing

1. Implicit in Gerald Locklin's poetry is a protest against those things in our society that contribute to a decline of the spirit he feels was present in this country's beginnings. Discuss how this effects his poetry and show how this "annoyance" plays a role in the poems.
2. Discuss Locklin's use of humor in his poetry and, particularly, in his last line "tags." Compare this use of a *tag* to the humorous last lines — the punch lines — we associate with stand-up comedy.
3. Locklin's resignation and annoyance serve as a cover for his deep sympathy for today's human situation. Discuss his role as an idealist in a society that despite its official rhetoric seems to have little place for personal idealism.

Audre Lorde

Hanging Fire (p. 843)

Just before her early death from cancer, Lorde felt that her acceptance as a writer was still in question because of her militant stance as a "black-woman-lesbian activist," as she called herself. Enough years have passed to put her work into a more sympathetic perspective, but it is useful to be reminded of the importance of this aspect of her work to other writers, especially because her militancy was one of the shaping forces of her poetry. In a review of the anthology titled *This Bridge Called My Back: Writing by Radical Women of Color* (1983) in which Lorde's work appeared, Julia Watson writes,

> Speaking as a white, midlife, sometimes academic single mother, I want to make clear that I can't speak of what *Bridge* has meant to, say, a Latina lesbian over the last decade — how it offered recognition, community, empowerment, sisterly voices. I can, however, speak to the audience of

white middle-class women who may feel we're on the outside looking in, with *Bridge*. *Bridge* forces us to deny the comfort of that distance by naming hard issues about white feminism's contribution to the oppression of women of color and its denial of difference that renders women of color invisible. Audre Lorde, for example, points out that white feminists can attend the conference at which she's the Black token because women of color are minding their houses and children. In a now-famous and all-too-prophetic essay, "The Master's Tools Will Never Dismantle the Master's House," Lorde rejects the *tolerance of differences* that she finds characteristic of white middle-class feminism and argues for understanding difference as *that raw and personal connection from which our personal power (as Black women, as lesbians) is forged*. (qtd. in *The Forbidden Stitch: An Asian Women's Anthology* [1989])

Today, in our evolving multicultural society, the moments when Lorde's poetry responds to a common feminine experience seem central to our understanding of her writing. This poem takes one such moment as its subject.

Questions for Discussion

1. What is the meaning of the term "hanging fire"? How does it apply to this poem?
2. List the agonies of adolescence Lorde describes. Are they typical of fourteen-year-old agonies? She is describing a black adolescent, but would a white fourteen-year-old girl's list be much different? What is the meaning of the second line, that her skin has "betrayed" her?
3. Is Lorde's doomed thought of dying before high school graduation typical?
4. What is Lorde intimating with the lines "and momma's in the bedroom / with the door closed"? Does this in part explain the intensity of her outburst?
5. Why does Lorde repeat these lines throughout the poem? Is this an effective technical device?

Topics for Writing

1. The anxieties of adolescence are not usually a subject for adult poetry. Discuss this anomaly and suggest some reasons for it.
2. Discuss the suggestion in the poem that many adolescents suffer from a fear of death. Quote from the poem and explain the meaning of the lines presenting this idea.

ROBERT LOWELL

Skunk Hour (p. 986)
For the Union Dead (p. 988)
Departure (p. 989)

One of the strengths of Lowell's poetry is its clarity and precision. Students will find that although the concepts Lowell presents have several dimensions, he doesn't end a poem until each of these elements has been integrated into the overall structure. Students should read his commentary on "Skunk Hour" (Chapter 17, p. 1058) for insight into the care and creative thought that are continual in his writing. Lowell's poem is structured like a letter; the language has been tightened in some lines, and there's a literary quality to others.

"For the Union Dead" depicts a moment in one man's consciousness. He is first at the site of the old South Boston Aquarium, where he remembers pressing his hand against the glass as a child. Now he presses his hand against the fence of a building site on Boston Common, a park in Boston's business district. A parking garage is under construction, and the work is disturbing the memorial to an African American regiment that was led by Robert Shaw, a young white Bostonian, during the Civil War. The 54th Massachusetts Regiment was defeated by Confederate forces, who refused to accept their surrender and killed everyone they could seize, including the commanding officer. Students may be familiar with the film *Glory* (1989), which dramatizes the regiment's development and eventual massacre at Fort Wagner, South Carolina, or they might have seen the regiment and its fate documented in the television series *The Civil War*. At the time the poem was written, the regiment's story had been almost forgotten. As Lowell wrote, the memory of it "sticks like a fishbone / in the city's throat."

Lowell sorts through images to show connections and relationships. On television African American schoolchildren defy school segregation; in a store window is a photograph of the atomic explosion that destroyed Hiroshima; and as the poem ends the speaker remembers the old aquarium where he began, but what he now sees are cars with fish fins, and the memory of the "cowed, compliant fish" is replaced with the "savage servility" of the new city.

SKUNK HOUR
FOR THE UNION DEAD

Questions for Discussion

1. What is Lowell telling us about the speaker's emotional state in lines 31–36 of "Skunk Hour"?
2. What is the significance of the title "Skunk Hour"?
3. Is the phrase "Sahara of snow" in line 2 of "For the Union Dead" an oxymoron?
4. In line 8 of the poem, what does Lowell mean by "cowed, compliant fish"?
5. What is the subject of the poem?
6. Does Lowell's description in lines 59–60 of the faces on television serve as a comparison with the faces in the memorial that he describes in line 22?

Topic for Writing

1. Relate Lowell's references to the African American regiment to the actual events.

DEPARTURE

Questions for Discussion

1. What is the quotation in Latin that Lowell uses as an epigraph for the poem? Does it prepare the reader for the lines later in the poem citing the Roman poet Horace?
2. What is the poet describing in the first lines? What would be a word to describe the things that come into his mind as he is waiting out the rain?
3. What is Lowell saying when he describes the rain as waiting to "hit / the fugitive in flight"? Is the line intended to be ironic?
4. What figure of speech is Lowell introducing with the line "Your books are rows of hollow suits"? What is he suggesting with the image?

5. What is Lowell describing with his image of Horace and the Ligurian girl? Was it a dream or was it something that might have happened? Why does or why does not the reader think so?

6. In the lines following his reference to Horace he breaks in "Can you hear my first voice." Is he referring to his early poetry? What is he saying about himself and poetry that is "amused in sorrow, / dramatic in amusement . . . "?

7. Does an image like this prepare the reader for Lowell's conclusion that "only by exaggeration / could I tell the truth"? Is his judgment of himself from his early years positive? Why or why not?

8. What is Lowell suggesting in his conclusion, "choice itself is wrong"?

Topics for Writing

1. Compare this poem to the other poems by Lowell in the anthology and contrast the tone and the conclusions of this poem with his other writing. Identify themes in each poem that develops similar ideas.

2. RESPONDING CREATIVELY   Paraphrase the opening lines of the poem, describing the scene that Lowell presents before he digresses into the image taken from Horace and *its* scene.

3. Discuss Lowell's use of figurative language in the poem, explaining and defining phrases like "the body's curative diversions," "flapping their paper wrappers," "catastrophies of description," and "augmenting storm."

4. In a paper examine whether this poem could be read as the statement of a resigned poet looking back at his early poetry. Discuss how the last moments of the rainstorm function as an illustration of the poem's mood and suggest reasons for the tears the poet finds "scattered on my cheeks" in the final line.

Commentaries

Robert Lowell, *"An Explication of 'Skunk Hour,' "* p. 1058.
Robert Lowell, *"Foreword to Plath's 'Ariel,' "* p. 1060.
Robert Lowell, *"On Robert Frost"* (poem), p. 1102.

MINA LOY

One O'Clock at Night (p. 845)

This fresh, unexpected poem was one of three published together as "Three Moments in Paris." Although it reads today as a feminist statement, it was written before there was a conscious feminist movement. It was left up to individual women, like Loy, to make their own statements about the situation in which women were placed in the early years of the twentieth century. Loy, who was born in London in 1882, lived for some time in Florence, Italy, writing as an art historian and publishing a manifesto demanding that women artists interpret the art of their time — which was Italian futurism — from a feminine point of view. She moved to New York in 1916, was briefly married, and became an active participant in the modernist art movements both in the United States and Europe. Her first book, *Lunar Baedecker*, a collection of experimental poetry and prose published in 1923, became a modernist classic and was reprinted in expanded versions in 1958 and, posthumously, in 1982. She died in New York City in 1966.

"One O'Clock at Night" is an amusing, tart glimpse of a familiar situation. A bored woman sits in a bar and listens — or pretends to listen — to the men with her talking animatedly to each other. Finally she is too tired to listen any more and, mercifully, she is taken home. This might be the first poem presenting this moment from the woman's point of view.

Questions for Discussion

1. Although it was written early in the twentieth century, the poem is modernist in style and tone. What are the elements that make it modernist?
2. Loy has used longer spacing at some points in the poem — for example, before "roars," "as it seems to me," and "so sleepy." What is she indicating with these longer spaces?
3. What is she telling us about the man she is with when she writes, "your indisputable male voice" and "you who make more noise than any man in the world when you clear your throat"?
4. What is the poet telling the reader about herself in the line "And cease to be a woman"?
5. Is she critical of the men and their argument?
6. What word describes her attitude toward the men's conversation? Does the word "indulgent" fit here? Is this an attitude that is familiar to women readers?
7. The discussion between the men begins with "Dynamic Decomposition" and ends with "Plastic Velocity." Is Loy making fun of the men or could this be the actual subject of the conversation?

Topics for Writing

1. Discuss her assertion "I have belonged to you since the beginning of time." Is there something in the tone of the line that suggests she is speaking metaphorically of women's situation in their relationship to men? Comment on this possiblity and consider whether, finally, Loy is simply being sarcastic.
2. This poem comes early in the effort of women to achieve recognition from men for their intellectual capabilities. Discuss the meaning of this poem from a feminist perspective.

ARCHIBALD MACLEISH

Ars Poetica (p. 700)

The New Critical methods of the 1950s that swept the record of American poetry clean of the great women poets of the 1920s also dismissed the politically committed poets of the 1930s, among them such writers as MacLeish. MacLeish was not only one of the decade's most widely read and influential poets, but he also won the Pulitzer Prize three times — twice for poetry (in 1932 for *The Conquistador* and in 1952 for his *Collected Poems*) and in 1958 for his play J.B., based on the Book of Job. He served as Librarian of Congress from 1939 to 1944 and held several important administrative positions in the government during World War II. Among his other works are the radio plays that spoke out against the rise of European fascism — *The Fall of the City*, first broadcast in 1937, and *Air Raid*, broadcast in 1938.

MacLeish was born in Illinois in 1892. He served as an artillery captain in France in World War I and after the war briefly practiced law before deciding to become a poet.

A younger brother was killed in aerial combat in 1918, which had a strong effect on MacLeish's writing. He was the Boylston Professor of Poetry at Harvard University from 1949 to 1962. He died in 1982, shortly before his ninetieth birthday.

"Ars Poetica" is still one of MacLeish's most popular poems, as much for its skilled use of language as for its insistence that the art of poetry is ultimately beyond analysis. Students may have difficulty with the poem, but a discussion developed around the following questions should assist them.

Questions for Discussion

1. Why does MacLeish use a Latin phrase for the poem's title?
2. What would we call the image of the first line: tactile? auditory? visual?
3. Does MacLeish use the same kind of image in lines 2–3?
4. Discuss the choice of diction in lines 5–6. What is MacLeish suggesting about the art of poetry in his word choice here? Does this relate to his choice of a Latin phrase for the poem's title?
5. Discuss the syntactical changes in lines 13–14, "Leaving, as the moon behind the winter leaves, / Memory by Memory the mind."
6. What is MacLeish saying in lines 17–18, "A poem should be equal to: / Not true"?
7. In lines 20 and 22, what is the name for the figure of speech MacLeish is using?
8. Discuss what MacLeish means with the poem's last two lines, "A poem should not mean / But be."

ANDREW MARVELL

To His Coy Mistress (p. 742)

Students should have no trouble understanding this poem. The only phrase that presents any difficulty is "slow-chapt" in line 40. Chap is an archaic word derived from the German; it means jaw, and Marvell is using it as a contrast to the verb "devour" in the line before. He is saying that he and his mistress would do better to eat up time quickly than to wait. Most of the poem is skillfully handled, but these two lines are clumsy, and if students have difficulties visualizing the image here, it is as much Marvell's fault as their own.

"To His Coy Mistress" is usually described as a carpe diem poem, and students might be asked to look at Robert Herrick's "To the Virgins, to Make Much of Time" (Chapter 8, p. 717) as a classic example of the genre. Certainly this is a theme in "To His Coy Mistress," but Marvell introduces it only as an attempt to seduce his hesitant mistress. He is so impatient with her that the reader gets the impression that if this idea doesn't work he'll try something else. Not only is Marvell impatient ("Had we world enough and time"), but he is also annoyed ("this coyness Lady were no crime"), jeering ("For Lady you deserve this state"), and insulting ("your quaint honor"). As he begins to run out of ideas, all he can think of to promise the woman is that they will share physical enjoyment like "am'rous birds of prey," which is almost an oxymoron. He doesn't even offer her any real sexual pleasure. His metaphor for her first sexual encounter is "tear our pleasures with rough strife," and although "iron gates of life" could be interpreted to mean the adversities of life, it can also be interpreted to mean the difficulties of piercing the hymen. The poem's last two lines seem to suggest that something will be shared out of the experience, but it seems mostly to be an image of days filled with sex, which Marvell assumes the woman will also enjoy. Certainly he doesn't offer her anything else.

Regardless of how one interprets Marvell's poem, it is still one of the most subtle and sophisticated seduction poems in English. Even in today's world, Marvell's poem is a vivid example of masculine impatience and persuasiveness.

Questions for Discussion

1. What does Marvell mean by "our long love's day" in line 4?
2. There is a double meaning in Marvell's use of the term "vegetable love" in line 11. What is he telling the reader by using it? How does it contrast with animal love?
3. In line 24, Marvell speaks of eternity as a vast desert, whereas in Christian theology eternity is usually regarded as the ultimate in pleasure — as unity with God. What is Marvell's intention in this image?
4. What is he suggesting to his mistress in the passage beginning in line 26, "Nor, in thy marble vault, shall sound / My echoing song"?
5. What is Marvell saying in the last two lines of the poem?

Topic for Writing

1. Discuss the concept of "carpe diem" and try to identify a modern equivalent of Marvell's message.

CLAUDE McKAY

If We Must Die (p. 864)
The Lynching (p. 864)

Although Claude McKay was born in Jamaica (in 1889) and lived and worked on the island until he was twenty-two, he is indelibly associated with the Harlem Renaissance, and his ability to fuse the forms and traditions of English and American poetry with an outspoken protest against American racism is generally considered an essential element in the shaping of the movement's early years. When he left Jamaica he had already published two collections of his poems, one in standard English and one in patois, which drew on his year as a police constable in the capital city of Kingston. McKay used the prize money awarded to his books in Jamaica to travel to the United States, where he planned to enter the Tuskegee Institute in Alabama. After two months of attempting to deal with southern racism, he fled to Kansas, where he studied agricultural science for two years at Kansas State College before deciding to try to support himself as a writer in Harlem.

Soon after his arrival, McKay became associated with many of the influential members of New York's avant-garde literary world, and unlike many of the Harlem Renaissance figures, he primarily published his poetry in white periodicals. In 1922, after living for two years in England, where he met George Bernard Shaw and published in many politically oriented journals, he returned to the United States, and with his defiantly militant collection *Harlem Shadows* he established many of the themes that were soon taken up by the Renaissance writers. Younger poets like Countee Cullen and Langston Hughes found the poetry an inspiration, and the collection is often considered the first important statement of what was to grow into the Harlem literary movement.

The sonnet "If We Must Die," which McKay had written after the widespread attacks in 1919 by white mobs on black Americans, became a rallying cry for many activists, and since it was written without a specific racial identity, it was recited by Winston Churchill in an address seeking to rally the British people against Hitler.

McKay made no attempt to hide his support for Soviet communism, and in 1923 he moved to Moscow, where he was received as a major literary figure and addressed the Fourth Congress of the Communist International. After a period, however, he tired of being presented as a spokesman for a cause, and he moved to Paris, where he lived for several years. He finally returned to the United States in 1934, but found that the economic collapse so overshadowed every other aspect of life in the United States that his work no longer had resonance with new readers. At the time of his death in 1948, he was living in Chicago, teaching at a Catholic Youth Organization.

Questions for Discussion

1. Each of these poems is a sonnet written in traditional form, although they differ in their rhyme scheme. What is the rhyme scheme for each of them?
2. What style of sonnet is each poem?
3. Neither of the sonnets makes a specific reference to race, but it is clear that "The Lynching" refers to the racial situation in the United States. How do we know that "The Lynching" expresses McKay's view of American reality, and how do we explain his unwillingness to specify the situation in "If We Must Die"?
4. How could we explain his use of the word "kinsman" in "If We Must Die"? Is it a word generally used in this context?
5. What is he saying in the lines "even the monsters we defy / Shall be constrained to honor us though dead"?
6. In "The Lynching" why does he tell us that the victim's spirit ascended "in smoke" to heaven?
7. What is he telling us in the lines that begin "The women thronged to look . . ."?
8. Is he being ironic by using the term "little lads" to describe the young boys dancing at the scene of the lynching?

Topics for Writing

1. Discuss the seeming contradiction of McKay's use of traditional verse forms to express inflammatory political views. Does this kind of poetry make an effective propaganda weapon?
2. Using library sources and the Internet, discuss the problem of lynching in the United States, referring to its long history and specific literary protests like McKay's poems.
3. MAKING CONNECTIONS Compare these poems to the writing of Langston Hughes, which deals with the same subject of racial injustice, and suggest how the attitudes of the two poets are similar or different.

ANN MENEBROKER

A Mere Glimpse (p. 704)
Repossessed (p. 883)
The Second Flood and Then the Fire (p. 884)
Love (p. 885)

For Ann Menebroker, whose home is in Sacramento, it was California poets like Charles Bukowski and Gerald Locklin whom she regarded as her literary mentors. Although she lives not far from San Francisco and its colorful Beat movement, she was aware that if things became too chaotic in Sacramento at least she could always find a way to get home, and so has remained in the smaller city. Her poetry has a directness and clarity that hides the attention she has given each word and each line. The straightforward poem "Love" is the most often reprinted of all her work.

A MERE GLIMPSE

Questions for Discussion

1. In this poem Menebroker is describing to a reader the way the inspiration for a poem comes to her. What does she tell us about these first steps? Can the first words be inspired by any physical action?
2. What does the poem tell us about the nature of poetry itself? How does she express it in the opening lines?
3. What is the significance of "those billions of stars"? What does she mean by "the vision we have / alters our perception"?
4. Is she thinking of the emerging poem in closed or open form? For her, what would be the difficulty of writing in closed form?
5. What is she telling us about the two realities — that of the poem and the glimpse of the man and the dog who inspired it?
6. Although the diction of the poem is direct and informal she uses figures of speech to develop her concept, among them simile. What are some examples of this in the poem?

Topics for Writing

1. RESPONDING CREATIVELY Compose a poem around the image Menebroker has presented — a man crossing the street with his dog.
2. Discuss Menebroker's concept that there is much more to be known than we are able to see, which she expresses in her image of the limitless numbers of stars in space.

REPOSSESSED
THE SECOND FLOOD AND THEN THE FIRE
LOVE

Questions for Discussion

1. "Repossessed" is a condensed narrative. What does she tell us about herself, her husband, and their economic circumstances? Is it necessary for her to say some-

thing specific about their income and their housing needs? What is the meaning of the word "Repossessed"?

2. What does she mean by the phrase "whatever small things can hide"? What kind of a scene is she describing?

3. Although the tone of the poem is terse and laconic it also expresses a strain of gentle nostalgia. How has she achieved this?

4. Can we interpret what she tells us about spiders and their webs and the couples' need to be caught in their own web as a symbol of the act of purchasing the house itself?

5. The catch of the poem is its final line, "Pray for us." What is she telling about herself and her husband in these words?

6. What story is Menebroker is telling us in "The Second Flood and Then the Fire"? Although she has told the story in modern terms, have the details she lends the story retained the meaning of the original narrative?

7. How should we interpret her lines "no one was being / overly good / or bad." Does the ordinariness of the glimpses of everyday life heighten the poignancy of her account?

8. How do we interpret her lines "It was a good enough / ending"? Is there a tone of resignation in the final image of the rain never stopping?

9. The poem "Love" opens with a metaphor and concludes with an unexpected simile. What are these two figures of speech, and why is the reader not expecting a reference to the Great Depression of the 1930s in a poem titled "Love"?

10. Is it true that we continue to act on things that we don't fully understand, as Menebroker suggests? Is love one of these things?

Topics for Writing

1. Discuss the inferences in Menebroker's phrase in "Repossessed," "Is this the capitalist in me?" in terms of the economic situation the poem describes, quoting specifically from the poem.

2. Discuss why a poem that quickly sketches the economic ruin of the house's previous owners and the precarious financial situation of Menebroker and her husband is told without sentimentality or reference to larger social issues like economic inequality or the cruelty of economic circumstances. Place the poem in a context of working-class vernacular writing, using Fred Voss's poem (p. 832) as a beginning.

3. **MAKING CONNECTIONS** Compare Menebroker's "The Second Flood and Then the Fire" with Robert Duncan's retelling of the same story in his poem "The Ballad of Mrs Noah" (p. 753). Contrast the view of the world as the rain begins and continues in each of the retellings with specific details from the poems.

4. Discuss the images in the poem of lovers who have forgotten to embrace and death touching their lips and calling out everyone's name.

5. **RESPONDING CREATIVELY** Write a poem on the same theme as Menebroker's "Love," choosing your own metaphor and simile to structure your poem.

6. Discuss why a poem with this theme would reach many readers and be often reprinted. Consider the effect of its poetic means, its joined metaphor and simile, as part of the response to the poem.

MARIANNE MOORE

Poetry (p.701)
The Fish (p. 991)
In the Public Garden (p. 992)

POETRY
THE FISH

    The comments in the text should help students read and interpret "Poetry." "The Fish," as students will quickly find, isn't about a particular fish and has no connection to Elizabeth Bishop's poem of the same title. Moore's poem is a description of the turmoil at the edge of the sea, where a cliff meets the water and the sea creatures tangle against one another. If the poem has an obvious subject, it is the cliff itself, which Moore introduces in the fourth stanza. The poem is a series of brilliant images, beginning with "wade / through black jade," the poet's metaphor describing the fish swimming in shallow dark water. The rhymes are obvious, despite Moore's comment that she often conceals them, and part of the poem's startling effect is the abrupt rhyme of single words and even partial words used as perfect rhymes. Her lines are, as she said, end-stopped, but a line can be a single syllable long.

Questions for Writing

1.   In the first two lines of "Poetry" — "I, too, dislike it; there are things that are important beyond all this fiddle" — what is Moore telling us about poetry?
2.   When she includes critics in her list of creatures we don't understand, what is she telling us about her opinion of critics?
3.   What is she telling us about "business documents and / school books" in line 17?
4.   In "The Fish," what is Moore describing in lines 8–9, "The barnacles which encrust the side / of the wave"?
5.   What is she telling us, in the fourth stanza of "The Fish," with her image of the sea driving an iron wedge into the cliff's iron edge?

Topics for Writing

1.   Discuss Moore's phrase "Imaginary gardens with real toads in them" in line 24 of "Poetry."
2.   Suggest some reasons that Moore shortened "Poetry."

IN THE PUBLIC GARDEN

    This admiring assessment of Moore's poetry by fellow poet Randall Jarrell, from his collection *No Other Book: Selected Essays* (1999), could have been written about "In the Public Garden," which is representative of so much that he describes here:

> The tone of Miss Moore's poems, often, is enough to give the reader great pleasure, since it is a tone of much wit and precision and intelligence, of irony and forbearance, of unusual moral penetration — it is plainly the voice of a person of good taste and good sense and good will, of a genuinely human being. Because of the curious juxtaposition of curious particulars,

most of the things that inhabit her poetry seem extraordinarily bright, exact, and there — just as unfamiliar colors, in unfamilar combinations, seem impossibly vivid. (127)

Questions for Discussion

1. The rhyme scheme for this poem is particularly ingenious. What is the rhyme pattern? Are the rhymes perfect rhymes or near rhymes? Is there a use of combinations of masculine and feminine rhyme?
2. Moore breaks the rhyme pattern in the three-line short stanza close to the end of the poem, "herbs which they can sell." Does she resume the pattern of rhyme for the final stanzas?
3. As she is driven to the festival at Harvard, she has a taxi driver who is "almost scriptural." What is she telling us about the driver?
4. Moore meets a variety of people at the festival, but reflects that her own tale is "without that radiance which poets / are supposed to have." What is the quality of radiance she refers to?
5. Is her mention of the swans as part of the setting of the Muses an afterthought, or has she prepared us for something as unlikely as swans as companions to poetry?

Topics for Writing

1. The poem concludes with the suggestion that "Art, admired in general, / is always actually personal." Discuss this statement and apply it to Moore's poetry.
2. This poem is itself a long tribute to poetry. Examine the statements she makes about poetry in this setting, and discuss how they relate to the scene she has described.
3. Although the poem is written with a carefully constructed rhyme scheme and a repeated form to the stanzas, it seems almost spontaneous in its freedom of expression. Discuss this seeming contradiction with examples from the poem itself, and apply the poet's own statement that freedom is "For 'self-discipline.' "

HILDA MORLEY

I Remember (p. 761)

In a biography of Hilda Morley, written at her death in 1998 at the age of seventy-nine, the *New York Times* wrote, "her poetry was shaped by the visions of Abstract Expressionism, which can create metamorphoses. Artists like Klee and Picasso, she said, gave her the means to create word canvases depicting the world around her."

Morley was born in New York City, but traveled widely and spent considerable time in London, both as a student and a teacher. Following her marriage to composer Stefan Wolpe in 1952, she became an instructor at the legendary Black Mountain College in North Carolina. She began publishing her poetry about this time, and her first collection, *A Blessing Outside Us*, was published in 1976. The poetry, from the beginning, had a luminosity, a clarity, and a power of evocative description. Poet Robert Creeley, who knew her from the period when they were both at Black Mountain, wrote,

> Poets are makers, they say. One's responsibility would then be, as Robert Duncan put it, "the ability to respond." Reading now, all the years passed seem an endless time that we have known one another, dear friend. Yet each

poem is still that moment which can have no other time ever. You've given everything you have. Here it comes back a thousandfold. (from *Preface for Hilda,* Robert Creeley's home page, 1998)

Questions for Discussion

1. This is a poem that could be said to have a clearly expressed moment of epiphany. What is the moment, and how has Morley prepared the reader for it?
2. Why has she left spaces in some of the lines, and indented others at irregular lengths?
3. Is this a technique to shape the reader's perception of the pauses in the poet's conception of the scene she remembers?
4. How has Morley made use of alliteration in the line beginning "enormous sky . . ."?
5. What is she suggesting in the series of verbs that open the poem, "buried," "hiding," and "clasping"? How does this prepare us for the word "gentle" that ends line 6?
6. Although this is a literary poem, the description of the scene is almost the way a painter might perceive it. Is there a contradiction between these two ways of "seeing"?

Topics for Writing

1. In the poem, Morley skillfully balances the immediacy of the small gesture of an embrace with the broad sweep of her description of the sea and the light. Discuss the means she employs to sketch both elements on this small poetic canvas.
2. This is a poem that evokes images of color. Discuss the colors Morley has described in the light and the sea, and contrast these with her lover's wonder at the whiteness of her breasts.
3. MAKING CONNECTIONS   This is a poem in open form, and Morley has said that an early meeting with the poet H.D. helped shape her idea of a poem's form. Compare this poem to H.D.'s "Mid-day" (p. 758), and discuss the similarities and differences in the styles of writing.

LES MURRAY

An Absolutely Ordinary Rainbow, (p. 901)

Les Murray is Australian and lives on a farm in the countryside not far from Sydney. Although he is not himself a farmer, the seasons and the incidents of farm life often are themes of his poetry. The setting of this poem is a city in Australia, but the poem itself is also proof again of the universality of human experience. The event he describes could have occurred in any city in the world and the effect of one person's open display of personal emotion could have the same effect on the passersby as it has here. The poem could be read as a parable, presenting to the reader one of our universal experiences, but in terms we can immediately identify. There is also a clear allusion to the mass emotions of religious experience. Although Murray has had a long and productive writing career, he is not yet well known to American readers, but he is widely translated and regularly appears in Europe on extensive reading tours. His name is often mentioned as a possible recipient of the Nobel Prize for Literature.

Questions for Discussion

1. The title of the poem is meant ironically, since no rainbow appears in the poem. What does Murray intend us to understand from his title? Is a rainbow ever an "absolutely ordinary" experience?
2. What is so startling that it causes people to stop what they are doing to go see what it is? The street names are Australian, from Sydney, but could they also be the names of streets from any city?
3. Is Murray's description of someone sitting and weeping to be taken literally, or is it intended as a metaphor for some more universal experience?
4. What is so unusual in this display of emotion? Why does Murray use the word "dignity" to describe it?
5. What is the poet telling the reader about the people surrounding the man when he speaks of them "longing for tears as children for a rainbow"?
6. What is the inference in the lines "Some will say, in the years to come, a halo / or force stood around him"? How does this relate to other narratives of immediate belief in crowds observing a singular event?
7. What is Murray telling the reader in his comparison of small children with "such as look out of Paradise"? Why is it that they can come sit near the weeping man, "with dogs and dusty pigeons"?
8. Is Murray consciously evoking religious conversion with his image of a woman "receiv[ing] the gift of weeping"? What is he telling us of the others who "weep for sheer acceptance" and still others who "refuse to weep out of fear of all acceptance"?
9. What terms does the poet use to describe sorrow? Does this justify, to Murray, the man's weeping in public?
10. How has it become necessary for the man to evade "believers" as he ends his weeping and hurries away? Is Murray suggesting that human emotions are so quickly and so easily stirred?

Topics for Writing

1. Discuss Murray's poem as a parable and connect it to other stories of mass religious conversions that are part of our culture. Quote particular images from the poem that have religious overtones and place them in the context of Murray's larger theme of the effect of a person's openly expressed emotions on a crowd.
2. **RESPONDING CREATIVELY**   Imagine this poem set in any other city — perhaps your own town or city — and describe in a paper the effect of a similar event on a passing crowd, taking Murray's point of view as a theme for development.
3. Although the title contains the most obvious use of ironic humor in the poem, there are many places in the poem where the same wry irony is expressed. Use some of these instances to discuss the use of irony in the poem and consider whether it would or would not be stronger if Murray had not allowed this hint of humor in the situation he is describing.
4. Write about the affect of an emotional outburst you have witnessed and compare this to what Murray describes in his poem.

Naomi Shihab Nye

Making a Fist (p. 799)

Nye's poem was collected in *Words under the Words*, published in Portland, Oregon, in 1995 by Far Corner Books.

Questions for Discussion

1.   Where is Tampico? Is this a poem by a woman immigrating to America?
2.   What is the meaning of the phrase "drum in the desert"?
3.   Nye writes that her "stomach was a melon split inside my skin." Is she describing car sickness or something more serious?
4.   Why does she characterize her mother's confidence as "strange"? Is she suggesting that her mother has some knowledge of the moment of death?
5.   Nye writes of "borders we must cross separately." Is she speaking of physical borders, or is she speaking metaphorically?
6.   Why does she lie in the back seat of the car, opening and closing her hand?

Topics for Writing

1.   This moment of fearing death is common to most children. Discuss why this feeling becomes an emotional barrier and how it is crossed.
2.   In her poem Nye uses the clenching of a fist as the symbol for continuing to live. Discuss other gestures we make to assure ourselves of our mortality.

Frank O'Hara

The Day Lady Died (p. 876)

O'Hara was born in Baltimore in 1926, but he is always associated with New York City, where he played an important role in the city's artistic life as an associate curator at the Museum of Modern Art and an active commentator on the contemporary art scene. He was also one of a group of New York poets, including John Ashbery, Kenneth Koch, and Ron Padgett, who collectively became known as the New York School. Although he was close friends with many of the Beat writers of the 1950s, and, as a homosexual, was linked in the public's mind with homosexual Beat poets like Allen Ginsberg and John Weiners, his poetry was closer in intellectual attitude to the work of then-current French and European writers. He died in a tragic accident on Fire Island in 1966, when a dune buggy drove over him in the darkness as he lay asleep on the beach.

The strength — and for some critics, the weakness — of O'Hara's poetry is its spontaneous flow of small details. He wrote quickly and compulsively, and he filled pages with poems that contain the germ of a poetic idea but often with what academic critics would consider little poetic shape or direction. For a younger New York poet like Todd Colby, "Frank O'Hara's writing embodies not just the rush and thrill of New York City, but the velocity of meaning and language colliding at the end of the century."

Certainly many students respond immediately to O'Hara's well-known poem about the death of singer Billie Holiday because they realize that O'Hara himself feels her death so intensely. Holiday's life had been troubled for many years, and she had become a legend to many in the artistic community through her recordings and her autobiography, *Lady Sings the Blues*. At the time of her death, Holiday had been hospitalized in New York for a general collapse aggravated by heavy drug use, and there had been banner headlines a few days before when traces of cocaine, smuggled into the hospital by a friend, were found on her pillow. In the poem, the contrast between the ordinariness of O'Hara's day, which he conveys with the laconic list of what he is doing, and the abruptness of his discovery of her death, forces his readers to be aware that death can come suddenly, as it did to O'Hara himself only two years later.

Questions for Discussion

1. What does the speaker tell the reader about himself in his description of the books he is considering for his train ride to Long Island?
2. What is the effect of all the detail he presents of the day before he becomes aware of Holiday's death?
3. What is the social scene he suggests with his lists of things he will buy for his evening?
4. Although the poem seems to be a random list, it is carefully limited to items and moments that demonstrate his emotional mood before he sees the newspaper. What is he excluding and what is he emphasizing in the things he presents?
5. O'Hara's poem is without overt poetic effects until the syntactic shift in the final line. Why did he keep the language of the poem so direct?

Topic for Writing

1. Discuss the relationship between the artistic expression of a musician like Holiday and the contemporary visual artists in New York in the 1950s.

SHARON OLDS

The Summer-Camp Bus Pulls Away from the Curb (p. 785)
Parents' Day (p. 995)
Summer Solstice, New York City (p. 996)
Sex without Love (p. 997)

THE SUMMER-CAMP BUS PULLS AWAY FROM THE CURB

Questions for Discussion

1. Although the poem is about a child's departure for summer camp, the subject of the poem is not the theme of the poem. What is the theme?
2. Could the poem be described as a poetic metaphor for this theme? Why or why not?
3. Why does Olds make a separation between the things "stored in his heart," and the things "laid up in his mind"? Is she inferring that the head and the heart are separate and they perceive impressions in different ways?
4. What is Olds suggesting with the image of the camp bus becoming "smaller and smaller" as it draws away?

5. What is she saying in her image of the folding of a flag at the end of a ceremony? This is a moment that is central to a military funeral, does she seem to be comparing the child's departure to a kind of death? Why do you think so or not? What is she implying with the phrase "only a heavy wedge remains"?

6. What is Olds telling us about her son with the terms "exuberance" and "arrogance"? Is she being pejorative with her use of the term "arrogance?"

7. What is she telling us about herself with her flat assertion that "What he does not have / he can lack"? Is she telling us that there is a point at which a parent's responsibilities end? Is this something that can happen as early as summer camp?

8. What are "Hardy Boys"? Are there different objects that you would imagine a boy taking with him to summer camp today? Would these newer items — a cell phone as an example — change the situation?

Topics for Writing

1. In the last three lines of her poem Olds has compared the nurturing of a child as similar to packing things into a trunk. Discuss this metaphor in terms of the details she has presented in the poem and in more general terms about your own life experience.

2. Although Olds has chosen to describe a separation of a child from parents with this description of a bus leaving for summer camp, there are other moments in a family's life which are more often considered as decisive steps toward emotional separation, like high school graduation or marriage. Discuss these other decisive moments and examine the details Olds has outlined to mark this separation in terms of these other moments of separation between parent and child.

3. MAKING CONNECTIONS In another poem of Olds's in this anthology, "Parents' Day" (p. 995), she has presented a similar situation from the point of view of the child. Compare the two poems and contrast the meanings she has read into the two similar, but different, situations.

4. The use of modern technology, like cell phones and online communication, have in some ways altered the situation of a child leaving for summer camp. In an essay, discuss whether or not these new technical possibilities have altered the emotional situation between the parent and child at this moment, or if the feeling of separation remains as strong.

PARENTS' DAY

Questions for Discussion

1. Although the poem is written in open form, Olds has used a number of poetic devices and language forms to heighten the emotional effect of the poem. What are some of them? What does the simile in the opening lines, "I strained / forward, like a gazehound . . . / then I raced toward her" tell us about Olds as a young girl waiting for her mother?

2. What do we call the use of language in the phrase "tucks and puckers"?

3. What is the figure of speech Olds has employed in the description of her chest as a "washboard front"?

4. Is it typical, in this situation, for children to compare their mothers to other mothers, to think of them as prettier than those who "looked like mothers"? Is a child as young as the girl in camp ready to make objective judgments about a parent? Does Olds question this herself?

5. What is the irony Olds has suggested with her comparison of her mother's beauty as "like a / goddess or an advertisement for California raisins"?

6. Olds has used the image of her mother's genes as a kind of DNA within herself, which she feels her mother must notice. How would her mother be able to notice something as individual as this?

7. What does Olds mean with her inference that these elements of DNA would be like "bits of undissolved sugar"?

Topics for Writing

1. In the final line of her poem, Olds says of her mother that "she was mine." Discuss the implications of this statement as seen from a child's perspective. Suggest what factors would lead a child to think they "own" a parent.

2. Olds's poem is an example of the skills and sensitivity to meaning that poets bring to their use of language. Discuss the figures of speech in the poem and how Olds has used them to imply meanings and inferences that would have required longer explanations if she had stayed within the bounds of figurative language.

3. MAKING CONNECTIONS   In another poem of Olds's in this anthology, "The Summer-Camp Bus Pulls Away from the Curb" (p. 785), she describes a similar moment from the point of view of the parent. Compare the emotional situation of the two poems and contrast the point of view of the child in one poem with the parent in the other. Discuss how they complement or contradict each other, using examples from the poems in your discussion.

SUMMER SOLSTICE, NEW YORK CITY

Olds's language is so immediately accessible, so close to everyday speech, that students may not be conscious of the artistic choices that shape the diction and syntax of this poem. In "Summer Solstice, New York City," the language is as direct as everyday speech, but much of the poem's imagery is built outside the body. The poem contains some of Olds's most imaginative figures of speech. In line 6, the social agencies that are summoned into action at emergencies are called "the huge machinery of the earth." In line 18, the edge of the roof where the man is threatening to jump is described as "the lip of the next world." Mingled with these images are images of birth and the body, which Olds brings to a resolution by comparing the way the police handle the man after he has abandoned his suicide attempt with the way a woman would handle a child who has been lost. In the poem's last lines she catches the emotions we feel at that brief moment when something frightening or threatening ends and we can begin to live again: Cigarettes the policemen had lit "burned like the / tiny campfires we lit at night / back at the beginning of the world."

Despite the cliché that "no one reads poetry," Olds's poems have found a steadily growing audience.

Questions for Discussion

1. In "Summer Solstice," what is Olds telling us about summers in New York City?

2. What is she saying about the policeman's feelings as he puts on his bullet-proof vest in line 10?

Topic for Writing

1. In "Summer Solstice," Olds mingles images of birth and death. Discuss the attitudes these images are expressing.

Sex without Love

This is one of Olds's most anthologized poems. It is a startling, upsetting poem, careening down an unsteady path between wonder and cynicism. In the opening lines the tone is of surprised wonder — Olds herself had never thought before of people who make love with no concern for emotion as performing artists. Their performance, she says, is as beautiful as dancers "gliding over each other like ice-skaters / over the ice," and for a moment we accept Olds's admiration. Then, after her lovers have reached orgasm, she asks, how can they not love the one who has made this journey with them? At that moment she understands their calculating selfishness. It is cynical to call what they are doing love when what they are feeling is only their response to themselves. In the final lines, her dancers and figure skaters have turned into runners who work out alone, and Olds makes us see that they are partaking in their own private sport. Olds's cynicism is obvious in the lines "They do not / mistake the lover for their own pleasure."

The poem works so well because she has taken something familiar and made us see it in a completely new way. Her frankness, her lack of squeamishness about physical details, which can sometimes unbalance her poetry, are beautifully suited to the subject.

Questions for Discussion

1.   Why does Olds choose dancers and figure skaters as examples of the beauty of sex without love?
2.   Why does she use as similes for the faces of the lovers: "red as steak, wine, wet as / the children at birth"?
3.   Why does she end the simile about children at birth with the phrase "whose mothers are going to / give them away"? Is Olds making a social judgment? What does she want to tell the reader?
4.   How do we know that she is being sarcastic when she speaks of "the purists, the pros"?
5.   Is "sex without love," as she describes it in the poem, only an empty exercise in narcissism? What implies this?

Topic for Writing

1.   "Sex without Love" has been considered a representative statement of the morality of the 1980s. Explore this idea with examples from other writing of the 1980s that either confirms or denies it.

Commentary

Sharon Olds, "*From the* Salon *Interview*," p. 1063.

Mary Oliver

Mussels (p. 853)

Questions for Discussion

1.   Oliver's poem is written in an unusual grammatical style. The first of the poem's four sentences comprises the first eighteen lines, and it is made up of a series of fourteen dependent clauses which embellish the sentence's basic meaning. Which

of the elements of the poem are the dependent clauses, and what has she gained in her poem by presenting the scene in this way?

2. She has chosen to present her poem in short phrases set into a pattern of four stepped lines. What are some reasons why she might have chosen this form?

3. What is "riprap" and is it an effective setting for the tone of the poem?

4. Oliver repeats three lines, "make a sound /not loud / not unmusical" but with a different context. Why might she have chosen this repetition and what are the contrasting ways that she continues each appearance of the lines?

5. What is Oliver telling the reader with the contradictory statement "they, who have no eyes to see with, / see me"?

6. How does Oliver personalize the mussels? Does she express any sympathy for them? Is this an attitude a reader might expect in a contemporary poem taking the natural world as its theme?

7. What does the poet mean with the phrase "not unmusical"? Why has she referred to music in this context?

Topics for Writing

1. The poet uses a strong word to tell the reader what she intends to do with her catch of mussels, she is going to "devour" them. Discuss what she might intend to tell the reader about herself by using this word, and consider the poem in terms of a more environmentally sensitive response to the presence of mussels on the rocks.

2. **MAKING CONNECTIONS**   Compare the response to the world of nature in this poem with the response of the nature poet Gary Snyder, using examples in this anthology.

3. The first sentence of the poem is simply telling the reader "In the riprap they cling in dark clusters and the orange bodies make a sound as they take nourishment." Discuss the poet's use of dependent clauses to embellish this statement, and how they contribute to the effectiveness of the poem.

CHARLES OLSON

Le Bonheur (p. 897)

Although this poem can be taken out of the context of Olson's major work *The Maximus Poems*, virtually all of his work revolves around the themes of the larger poem. This ecstatic celebration of spring is written with an immediacy of style and communication, and yet at the same time it suggests some of the extended dimensions of syntax and reference that inform his work. In conjunction with this poem the student should read the selection from Olson's influential essay "Projective Verse" (p. 896).

Questions for Discussion

1. This is a picture of spring created by fleeting impressions. What are some of them? What is the view of the spring they create?

2. Olson uses a number of linguistic references, including French quotations, in the poem. What is his purpose in telling us the bees "dig" the flowers? Is his use of contemporary slang a conscious placing of his poem in a vernacular context?

3. What is the poet telling us in his lines "Every time the cock crows / I salute him"? How does this relate to his next statement "I have no longer any excuse / for envy"?

4.   What is the implication of his image "the morning / stands up straight"?

5.   Olson suggests that his life has "been given its orders." Is this a fatalistic accept-
      ance of the regular cycle of the seasons, or is the poet making a larger statement
      about his life? Is fatalism a concept you would relate to the poem?

6.   What is the poet's suggestion in his image for the passage of the seasons "dis-
      persed effort"?

7.   Why does the poet tell us "Nobody studies / happiness"?

8.   What is the meaning of his final lines "The hour of death / is the only trespass"?

Topics for Writing

1.   After reading the selection from Olson's essay "Projective Verse" (p. 896) discuss
      its relevance to the compositional form of this poem.

2.   The series of impressions that Olson has chosen to illustrate the moment of spring
      are disjunctive, presented without a specific context. Discuss the interrelation-
      ships between the images and show they effectively give the poem its coherence.

3.   MAKING CONNECTIONS   Many poets have written about spring, and also
      many, like Olson, have found that there is also an intimation of death in the
      ecstatic response to the new season. Discuss why this has been a perennial theme,
      drawing on outside reading or materials in the anthology.

4.   Olson has included a complex image in the poem in his contrast of the work of the
      Diesel and the whippoorwill. Discuss how he relates the mechanical world of the
      tractor to the song of the whippoorwill, and extend your discussion to the larger
      philosophical theme of the image and its intimation of the complex interrelation-
      ship between the mechanical world created by humans and the world of nature.

Commentary

Charles Olson, *"Projective Verse,"* p. 896.

ALICIA SUSKIN OSTRIKER

The Change (p. 846)

Although contemporary American writer Ostriker is perhaps best known for her
essays on feminist studies, she is also a gifted poet. Her collection *The Imaginary Lover*
(1986) won the William Carlos Williams Award, and a later collection, *The Crack in
Everything* (1996), was a National Book Award finalist.

Questions for Discussion

1.   "The Change" has an energetic flow of language, but the mood of the poem is not
      joyous. What in the opening lines suggests that the poem will end in its disap-
      pointed acceptance of reality?

2.   What is Ostriker saying about the trees unable to "rip themselves up by the
      roots"? How does this compare to her daughter's behavior?

3.   Is the new behavior of her daughter presented as expected or typical? Does this
      make it less painful?

Topics for Writing

1.   "The Change" could be said to be "women's poetry." It is written by a woman
      about a moment in her life that would be felt by another woman. Discuss the poem
      from this point of view and comment on what the effect of the poem might be on
      a man reading it.

2.   MAKING CONNECTIONS   The automobile drive described in "The Change" is similar to the drive into the countryside that William Carlos Williams describes in his poem "Spring and All" (p. 1020) Compare the scene described in the two poems and contrast the use of this scene to present the themes that are the subject of each poem.

WILFRED OWEN

Dulce et Decorum Est (p. 836)

Owen was one of several poets who wrote of the tragedy of World War I. An entire generation of writers, European as well as English and American, began to create poetry out of the horrors of their experience. Among the English poets were Owen, who was killed shortly before the armistice; Edward Thomas, who was also killed; Robert Graves; and Siegfried Sassoon, who survived and wrote bitter memoirs. Among other poets were the Americans Joyce Kilmer and Alan Seeger, who were both killed. Many of the finest European poets who wrote of their time in the war — like the French writer Guillaume Apollinaire, who died of a head wound, and the Italian writer Giuseppe Ungaretti — were modernists who wrote in a contemporary idiom. The Americans and the English, on the other hand, wrote in traditional verse forms. Owen's war poetry was particularly shaped by his love for the verse mannerisms of the previous generation of poets, the group known as the Georgians. He was so talented that his later writing would probably have adopted a modernist technique, but he was never to have the opportunity to explore modernism.

Although Owen's poems sometimes seem constrained by the verse forms he used so faithfully, they are sustained by the clarity of his rage at what he and his men — he was an officer — were forced to endure. In the work there is also a sensitive love for the men with whom he served. Although he never could reveal his homosexual feelings, his writing, when it doesn't have actual fighting as its subject, often has an erotic undertone. This poem is one that is driven by his rage, and he uses the Latin phrase that every English schoolboy had to learn, *Dulce et decorum est pro patria mori,* or "It is a sweet and beautiful thing to die for one's country," as its mocking title and its angry conclusion.

Questions for Discussion

1.   What is the rhyme scheme of the poem? Is the meter consistent? Why is the last line shorter?
2.   Is the imagery of the first two lines, of old beggars and hags, created out of the sights and sounds of the trenches, or are they taken from another verse tradition?
3.   In lines 3 and 4, Owen has been forced to use an unnatural word order to create the rhymes. How would the lines read in normal word order?
4.   What does he mean by "blood-shod" in line 6?
5.   What is the figure of speech he uses for the German shells?
6.   The poem has many lines that respond to the sound of horror, and other lines use conventional poetic diction. What are some examples of the conventional imagery?

Topics for Writing

1.   Describe the horror of the situation in the poem and its effect on the speaker. Discuss the nature of antiwar poetry and consider whether it has had any effect on ending war.

2.   MAKING CONNECTIONS   Looking in other sources, find the war poems of Joyce Kilmer, Alan Seeger, Robert Graves, and Siegfried Sassoon, and compare them with Owen's poem, with attention to their poetic techniques as well as their sentiments toward war.

DOROTHY PARKER

Indian Summer (p. 718)
New Item (p. 777)
From *A Pig's-Eye View of Literature* (p. 777)

In the flush of enthusiasm that followed the brilliant careers of the women poets of the 1920s — writers like Edna St. Vincent Millay, Louise Bogan, and Elinor Wylie — there was also room for the irreverent voice of Parker, who used the same slightly old-fashioned verse forms and turned to the same eternal subjects of love and loneliness — but didn't take any of it seriously. In her introduction to Parker's *Collected Poems,* Colleen Breese writes,

> The era spanning the last decade of the nineteenth century and the first two decades of the twentieth was also a time of large-scale political movements and social changes among women. A new generation of women writers emerged . . . [who] did not feel bound to marry and have children as their life's work. Rejecting the traditional "women's sphere," they claimed for themselves the "male territory" of art. Many were fiercely determined not to be thought of merely as "women writers," and felt it necessary to distance themselves from other women. Gender was not part of the definition of who one was.
>
> Born into this tradition, Dorothy Parker, née Rothschild, said that her most fervent prayer had been "Please, God, don't let me write like a woman."

Parker, who was born in New Jersey in 1893, was drawn to the noisy world of New York in the 1920s and found a niche in the newly established magazine *The New Yorker.* She wrote poetry and stories, edited copy, and managed to find time to meet with other writers for lunch as one of the famed "Algonquin wits." She was beautiful, brilliant, professional, and helplessly insecure despite a successful career that took her finally to Hollywood and Academy Award nominations for screenwriting in the 1930s. There were problems with alcohol and men, there were suicide attempts, and the end of her life in 1967 was difficult and painful, but she dealt with everything with the same mordant humor and a refusal to take herself seriously. Her first collection of verse, *Enough Rope* (1926), was one of the most successful poetry volumes of the decade. Although her work has been continuously in print, Parker continued to doubt the importance of what she had achieved until the end of her life.

It is impossible to write about Parker without quoting at least one of her acerbic responses to something she found completely idiotic. For many years she wrote an unsigned column in *The New Yorker* under the heading "The Constant Reader," and one week she found herself reviewing A. A. Milne's new book about Winnie the Pooh. For her review, Parker reverted to baby talk, and her tart comment was "Tonstant Weader Fwowed Up."

Students will immediately understand that the humor in Parker lies not only in her refusal to take herself seriously. She is writing in the hallowed tradition of the English lyric, as were the women poets from whom she tried to distance herself, but she can't take this tradition very seriously, either. It is this tension between the care and delicacy of her verse and the mocking cynicism of her attitudes that keeps her work alive today.

INDIAN SUMMER

Questions for Discussion

1. This verse form is employed by many writers. Who are some of the writers in the anthology who use it?
2. The opening lines of the poem are in a traditional language, and we are not prepared for the modern slang of the final line. Is this the effect Parker was trying to achieve?
3. Parker was a master at rhyme, but she has teased the reader with the rhythmic shift in the word "theories" to create the rhyme in the first verse. Was this a conscious effect on her part?
4. Parker manages to achieve her effect with a poem that uses only two two-syllable words. Every other word in the poem has a single syllable. How does this help set the tone of the poem?

Topic for Writing

1. **MAKING CONNECTIONS**   The model for Parker's irreverent verses could have been A. E. Housman, since her word choice and line construction is very similar to his and her attitude toward love sometimes sounds like a conscious parody of Housman's. Compare this poem of Parker's with "Loveliest of trees, the cherry now" (p. 711) by Housman, and discuss the similarities and differences.

NEWS ITEM
FROM *A PIG'S-EYE VIEW OF LITERATURE: THE LIVES AND TIMES OF JOHN KEATS, PERCY BYSSHE SHELLEY, AND GEORGE GORDON, LORD BYRON; OSCAR WILDE; HARRIET BEECHER STOW; ALFRED, LORD TENNYSON*

Questions for Discussion

1. "News Item" instantly became a much-quoted classic. What is the distinctive quality of the poem that has made it so memorable? Is it the cleverness of the line or the surprise of the opinion expressed that gives the poem its humor?
2. What is she telling us about the men she mentions in the poem? Does she approve of their attitude, or is she angry?
3. In her literary epigrams from *A Pig's-Eye View of Literature*, it is clear that Parker is widely read in English and American literature. How do we know this from the poems?
4. Although there is sometimes a hint of malice in some of her dismissals, she also makes fun of herself. Is this the intention of the final line in her poem about Harriet Beecher Stowe?
5. Why does Parker call these poems "A Pig's-Eye View of Literature"? Is she attempting to lighten the sting of her wit by intimating that this is the point of view that a pig might have?

6. Are these poets that someone today might choose as a subject for epigrams? Why or why not?

Topics for Writing

1. Choose one of the literary epigrams and explain how Parker succeeds in bringing its subject to life.
2. Discuss why it would be necessary to have a comfortable familiarity of the work of these writers in order to describe them in an epigram.
3. Suggest a number of contemporary authors who might be the subject of epigrams, and clarify what it is about each of them that would be the motive behind the new poem.

LINDA PASTAN

To a Daughter Leaving Home (p. 820)

Although the poem is discussed extensively in Chapter 13, it might be useful to know that Pastan was born in New York City in 1932. She graduated from Radcliffe College, then earned master's degrees at Simmons College and Brandeis University. She began writing poetry in college, where her work won student awards, but following her marriage in 1953 and the birth of her three children, she gave up writing for many years. At her husband's encouragement she began writing again. Her first collection, *A Perfect Circle of Sun*, was published in 1971. Among her other books are *Setting the Table* (1971), *A Fraction of Darkness* (1985), and *An Early Afterlife* (1995). Many of her poems deal with her family's life, and they are written in an unadorned style that has the immediacy of a grocery list.

NITA PENFOLD

My Poems (p. 705)

Nita Penfold is a contemporary American writer whose work appeared in the landmark anthology of women's poetry *Claiming the Spirit Within* (Beacon Press, 1996).

Questions for Discussion

1. Penfold says of her poems that they are not "polite ladies." What is she telling the reader about them? Does the image of her poems as having "red-rough hands" and "ready grins" suggest that they have any specific feminine characteristics at all?
2. What is the term for a figure of speech in which something inanimate is given human characteristics by the writer?
3. What is Penfold telling her reader when she writes that her poems won't let her sleep "until they loose my soul"?
4. She says of her poems that they won't "keep my secrets." Is this something that the reader expects poems to do? Could the poem itself be considered the telling of a secret?

5. Is there a psychological intention in her use of the word "bindings," or does she mean some kind of literal cloth binding?

Topics for Writing

1. MAKING CONNECTIONS   Compare this poem with Alice Walker's "I Said to Poetry" (p. 707), and discuss how the figures of the poem, and of poetry itself, that they present are similar or different.
2. Although Penfold thinks of her poems as feminine, the adjectives she uses to describe them could almost be portraying rough, noisy boys. Discuss the apparent contradiction, and decide whether you agree or disagree with her portrayal.

FRANCESCO PETRARCA

Love's Inconsistency (p. 773)

The fourteenth-century Italian man of letters Francesco Petrarca (Petrarch) famously composed sonnets about his unrequited love for the mysterious Laura. The paradoxical quality of such unrequited love is captured in these lines. This sonnet has the typical Petrarchan octave of two quatrains rhyming *abbaabba*. But the sestet rhymes *cddcee*, with a less-than-typical concluding couplet that provides a summarizing similar to the couplets that end Shakespearean sonnets.

Questions for Discussion

1. Is love the only emotion that triggers such paradoxical extremes of feelings?
2. What parts of the poem do you find puzzling? The ideas, the sixteenth-century diction, or both?

Topic for Writing

1. Have the class break into three groups to write paraphrases. Have the first group paraphrase lines 1–4, the second 5–8, the third 9–12. Put the paraphrases up on the board, then have the class as a whole try to come up with a worthy paraphrase of lines 13–14, to make it fit well with the rest of the paraphrased poem.

SYLVIA PLATH

Morning Song (p. 998)
Daddy (p. 998)
Elm (p. 1001)

Students will find considerable help in approaching Plath's poetry in the text's biographical note and commentaries. Students should be encouraged to look at Plath's poetry from every possible angle and to be open-minded when interpreting meaning. Plath was a poet who took risks, and students will more fully understand and respond to her work if they take risks in their own reading of it.

MORNING SONG

"Morning Song" is the first poem in the *Ariel* collection, and although it describes a familiar domestic scene — a young mother at home with her first child — it does so in a series of startlingly original images. The poem displays many of the characteristics of confessional poetry, a form that Robert Lowell initiated in his 1959 collection *Life Studies* and that Anne Sexton was to take to further limits in the years after Plath's suicide.

Questions for Discussion

1. What is the meaning of the first line of "Morning Song": "Love set you going like a fat gold watch"?
2. What is the term for the figure of speech in the phrase "your bald cry" in line 2?
3. What does Plath mean in line 10, "your moth breath"?
4. What is the term for the figure of speech she uses in line 16, "swallows its dull stars"?

Topic for Writing

1. Analyze the details in "Morning Song" and discuss what the poem tells us about the speaker's daily life.

DADDY

Before students read the *Ariel* poems, they might find it helpful to read the commentary in Chapter 17 by Robert Lowell (p. 1060), who both influenced and was influenced by Plath. The *Ariel* poems have been analyzed and discussed many times, but this should not inhibit students.

"Daddy" inspired many later women poets to address their fathers in verse, but Plath's is still the most raw and brutal poem of them all. The pain and anger are so sharp that it is hard to believe that Plath's father died when she was eight years old and in many ways she never really remembered him. "Daddy" is her creation of her father, not her memory of him.

Questions for Discussion

1. What does Plath mean by the first lines, "You do not do, you do not do / Any more"?
2. What is the symbolism of her description of the father as a "black shoe" and the daughter as a "white foot"?
3. The abrupt "Achoo" at the end of the first stanza is meant as sardonic humor. What are some other instances in the poem when she is being grimly humorous? Why does she use humor in the poem? Is this black humor?
4. To what is Plath referring with "Chuffing me off like a Jew" in line 32?
5. Consider the various implied meanings in lines 58–59, "At twenty I tried to die / And get back, back, back to you." Do the emotions of these lines contradict Plath's other statements about the father in the poem?
6. Whom could she be describing in line 72, "The vampire who said he was you"?

Topic for Writing

1. Plath imagines the daughter as a Jew in "Daddy." Analyze the associations she develops through this Jewish identity.

ELM

The poems of Plath's written during her periods of disturbance are often difficult to interpret. If students understand that in this poem the protagonist speaking is the elm tree itself they will have much less difficulty discussing its fierce imagery.

Questions for Discussion

1. What is the "I" that is speaking in the poem? What is the "great tap root"?
2. Would this be considered an example of *personification*?
3. Why does the elm say that it does not fear reaching the "bottom"?
4. What is the sound of the sea the elm refers to? Have other poets also used this same metaphor?
5. What might Plath mean with her statement that "Love is a shadow"? Why does she suddenly suggest that the shadow has hooves?
6. Why does the tree say that it can "bring you the sound of poisons"? What could be the meaning of the image?
7. An elm makes a shrieking sound if it is tossed in a heavy wind, is this the poet's justification for outcries of her own?
8. How could the tree be "Scorched to the root"? Is it the sunset color of the tree Plath is describing or is it perhaps summer heat?
9. How could the tree be a bystander in a high wind?

Topics for Writing

1. Although this is a disturbing poem it is also a brilliant example of the poetic insights Plath brought to her writing in this period. Discuss figures of speech like love that has "gone off, like a horse" and show how she develops the image in the lines that follow. In the paper discuss other striking images like "the atrocity of sunsets" and "My red filaments burn and stand, a hand of wires."
2. A number of images in the poem present difficulties in interpretation. Offer some possible readings of lines like "Till your head is a stone, your pillow a little turf, / Echoing, echoing," "shall I bring you the sound of poisons?" or, writing about the fruit of the rain, "tin-white, like arsenic." Support your arguments by a close reading of the entire poem.
3. Compare the imagery of this poem with the other poems of Plath's in the anthology, relating them to each other and to what the student knows of Plath's own personal tragedy.

Commentary

Robert Lowell, "*Foreword to Plath's* Ariel," p. 1060.

EZRA POUND

In a Station of the Metro (p. 791)
A Pact (p. 810)

Pound's role in the development of modernist poetry was crucial and decisive. His early advocacy of the imagist movement led to a renewal of poetic language, and he was instrumental in bringing about the publication of the work of Robert Frost, T. S. Eliot, and William Carlos Williams. His editorial work on Eliot's *The Wasteland* helped make it one of the most influential poems of the period between the two world wars, and his own long work, *The Cantos,* influenced an entire generation of British and American poets.

Pound's artistic achievement, however, has been overshadowed by his political activities during World War II. He had been a resident of Italy for many years at the outbreak of the war and was an active supporter of Mussolini and his Fascist Party. During the war, Pound collaborated with the Italian government on a series of propaganda broadcasts supporting the Fascist war aims and approving of the extermination of Europe's Jews. He was captured by American soldiers and imprisoned at the war's end, but efforts to bring him to trial as a traitor led instead to his being declared mentally incompetent and unable to stand trial, and for more than a dozen years he was held in a psychiatric hospital. There followed a shrill, persistent debate among American writers, some supporting Pound's right to express himself as an artist and others who insisted he had to be tried for his crimes. Finally he was released and returned to Italy, where he isolated himself from most of his early associates. The debate has not ended with his death, and the new awareness of Holocaust crimes has only emphasized his culpability over half a century later.

Questions for Discussion

1. "In a Station" is usually considered the poem that most decisively influenced the growth of imagism. What are the characteristics of the poem that make it imagist?
2. Although the poem is very short, it still manages to create a mood and set a scene. How does the poem achieve this?
3. What aspect of its poetic syntax was to have an effect on younger poets? Do we still see this effect today?
4. What similarities does this poem have to the examples of haiku poetry in Chapter 11 (p. 788)?
5. In "A Pact," Pound writes that Whitman "broke the new wood, / Now is the time for carving." What does Pound mean by the "new wood"? What poetic means does Pound seem to have taken from Whitman's "new" way of writing?
6. What does Pound suggest with his comment "I have detested you long enough"?
7. Pound often was ambivalent about his American background. What is he declaring in the line "We have one sap and one root"?
8. Is there anything in the technique of the poem that shows the poetic influence of Whitman?
9. What is the connotation of the word "commerce" in the last line?

Topics for Writing

1. MAKING CONNECTIONS   Contrast the short imagist poem "In a Station" with a more characteristic poem of the period by William Butler Yeats and discuss the differences not only in technique but in the aims of the poet as well.
2. MAKING CONNECTIONS   Discuss the role of Walt Whitman in forming a distinct American consciousness as Pound perceived Whitman's place in the development of the new poetry.
3. Discuss the importance of older mentors in the development of a younger poet like Pound.

Commentaries

Ezra Pound, *"On the Principles of Imagism,"* p. 1065.
Ezra Pound, *"What I Feel about Walt Whitman,"* p. 1068.

Dudley Randall

Ballad of Birmingham (p. 755)

Randall was born in Washington, D.C., in 1914. He graduated from Wayne State University and the University of Michigan. As librarian and poet-in-residence at the University of Detroit, he became associated with active younger black writers. His activities included the founding of an important small publishing enterprise, Broadside Press, and editing the 1971 anthology *The Black Poets.* Although he has not published a large body of work, a collection of his poetry, *Litany of Friends: New and Selected Poems,* appeared in 1981.

Randall's "Ballad of Birmingham" was published in the midst of the civil rights struggles of the 1960s, and it was inspired by the tragic bombing of an African American church in Birmingham in 1963. White racists destroyed the church with dynamite, killing four small girls.

Questions for Discussion

1. What is the metric form of the poem? What elements of the poem's formal structure identify it as a ballad?
2. In line 7, when Randall describes "clubs and hoses, guns and jail," is he exaggerating the situation on the Birmingham streets?
3. Why has Randall described the death of only one of the girls?
4. What is the irony Randall intends to convey to the reader in lines 20 and 21?
5. Randall doesn't use the final verse of his poem to moralize or to accuse anyone of the girl's death. Why has he chosen not to end his poem this way?

Topics for Writing

1. It is unusual for a contemporary writer to use an older poetic form for a subject as violent and emotionally charged as a church bombing. Discuss the reasons that Randall may have turned to the form of the traditional ballad for the poem.
2. **MAKING CONNECTIONS** Compare this ballad with other ballads in the text and discuss the elements in style and language that the poems have in common; suggest some differences in Randall's modern poem.

Lou Reed

Chelsea Girls (p. 719)

Reed began his career as one of the lead singers with the New York rock band The Velvet Underground. With his solo album *Rock and Roll Animal,* Reed achieved recognition as one of the most important solo artists of the early 1970s. The Chelsea Hotel is still a large, shabby building on New York's Twenty-third Street, two blocks west of Fifth Avenue. It has long been a haven for artists and musicians who often have taken what became lifetime leases on their apartments. The poet Dylan Thomas stayed at the hotel when he visited New York, and it was also popular with many rock groups, since it was comfortably rundown, cheap, and permissive. The musicians attracted a casual group of women fans — "groupies" — who drifted from room to room and band to band, sometimes living for weeks along the hotel's bare tile corridors waiting for the next band to check in. Among many of its temporary and permanent residents, there was widespread drug use, sexual promiscuity, and, as a result, a high rate of gonorrhea and other sexual diseases. It is the groupies that Reed describes in the song's lyrics.

Questions for Discussion

1. Although most modern poets no longer use rhyme in their writing, rhyme is still closely tied to song lyrics. What are some of the reasons for this? What is the rhyme scheme for this song? In lines 5, 6, and 7, there is a repeated rhyme on a single word. What is the effect of the repetition on the rhythm of the song?
2. Describe the girls Reed has included in the song. Has he presented them as the desirable young women they see themselves as?
3. The lyric uses many terms from the drug scene and the street world. What are some of the terms, and how do they apply to the lyric?
4. What is Reed suggesting in the lines "She wants another scene / She wants to be a human being"?

Topics for Writing

1. Although this lyric was written to be sung, it is also very effective on the page as a poem. Discuss this relationship between a lyric and its melody, and suggest the reasons for the enduring quality of the melding of words and music.
2. **RESPONDING CREATIVELY**   The drug scene of the 1960s has left a broad imprint on our consciousness of that era, and we now have much more familiarity with the scenes that are described. Take one of the women described in Reed's verse and write a short, imagined sketch about what her life was like before she drifted into the hotel and what might have happened to her after she left the scene.

KENNETH REXROTH

The Heart of Herakles (p. 851)

When Kenneth Rexroth moved to San Francisco from Chicago in the 1930s he was known as a political activist, and in California he became involved in the arduous campaign seeking recognition for the controversial Maritime Worker's Union. In the 1950s and 1960s he was one of the first supporters of the Beat writers and was prominent in the poetry and jazz performances popular in San Francisco night clubs. In his later years his poetry was centered in the natural world of the California mountains.

"Herakles" is another spelling for Hercules, a legendary figure of enormous strength in Greek and Roman mythology. Rexroth has been reminded of the name by the sight of a constellation of stars, the Cluster of Hercules.

Questions for Discussion

1. What is Rexroth doing as he lies out in the night? Why are the mountains a good site for looking into the stars?
2. Is it possible for him to trace the movement of stars in his telescope or is it his consciousness of their movement that he traces?
3. Can he see the stars when his body is sleeping? Is it possible that as he writes only his "eyes and brain are awake"?
4. Is Rexroth describing a trance-like moment in the poem in the line "I can no longer / Tell where I begin and leave off"?

5. How does he personify the physical presence around him, the breeze, the grass, the earth, "the swarming stars"?

Topics for Writing

1. Rexroth was actively involved in the effort to protect the natural environment in California. Discuss his poem in terms of this movement, drawing on outside sources and quoting from the poem itself.
2. In the poem there is a reverence for the natural world which Rexroth identifies with. Discuss this feeling in connection with today's movement to protect the environment, citing statements by other figures like activist Al Gore that support Rexroth's stance, using quotations from the poem as an opening for the discussion.

ADRIENNE RICH

Aunt Jennifer's Tigers (p. 1002)
Diving into the Wreck (p. 1003)

For almost four decades Adrienne Rich has been one of the most conspicuous figures of the American literary landscape, both as a poet and as an active spokesperson for women's issues. She has played many roles and mirrored all of them in complex, emotionally charged poems. She graduated from Radcliffe in 1951, and she found herself almost immediately successful as a poet, winning the Yale Younger Poets Award in 1953. At about the same time she married and quickly had three children, all sons. The burden of motherhood and marriage to a Harvard faculty member weighed heavily on Rich, and despite a continuing series of grants, awards, and fellowships for her writing, she felt that her life was still waiting to begin. In the 1960s, she and her husband moved from Cambridge to New York, and she became deeply engaged in the anti–Vietnam War movement. She also began teaching in a program for disadvantaged children. Her poetry became more specifically political, and the form of her work, which had begun to be less formal in the late 1950s, moved closer to the new "confessional" style of writers like Robert Lowell and Anne Sexton.

By the end of the 1960s, Rich felt she had entered a new period in her life, and she ended her marriage. Tragically, a few months later her husband committed suicide. She was now the most attentively followed of the new group of feminist poets, and her book *Diving into the Wreck* was awarded the National Book Award for 1973. Three years later, she published *Twenty-one Love Poems*, a sequence of poems that celebrated a lesbian relationship that marked a new direction in her life. For several years she taught and edited the feminist lesbian journal *Sinister Wisdom*. Although illness has forced her to be less public in recent years, she continues to be a major force in today's literary world.

AUNT JENNIFER'S TIGERS

Although this is an early poem, already it confronts the somber truth of human mortality. Although her aunt will die, the tigers she has embroidered will continue their prance into the future, "proud and unafraid." There is also the suggestion of the feminist responses that came to characterize Rich's later poetry in line 3's inference, "They do not fear the men beneath the tree," and in lines 7 and 8, "The massive weight of Uncle's wedding band / Sits heavily upon Aunt Jennifer's hand." There is a further inference — perhaps unconscious on the poet's part — of this weight of her aunt's marriage in line 10, "Still ringed with ordeals she was mastered by." The use of "ring" in this line could refer

to the wedding ring of the previous stanza. Students will also note that the poem is written in closed rhyme form, but within the seeming restrictions of meter and rhyme the
poem has the immediacy and directness of the most successful lyric poetry written in
contemporary open forms. It is a poem that satisfies the reader with both the clarity and
poignancy of its theme and the skill of its writing.

Questions for Discussion

1. What is the meter and the rhyme scheme of the poem? Why does Rich vary the
    overall meter with metric feet of different stress patterns? Does this variety add to
    the effect of the poem? The poem also uses perfect end rhymes. Is there an exam-
    ple of enjambment?
2. What is the figure of speech that Rich employs with the image of the first line,
    "tigers prance across a screen"?
3. The reader senses the emotional division between the world of Aunt Jennifer's
    embroidery and the woman's own world, which is emphasized by the word "terri-
    fied" in line 9. How has Rich prepared us for this strong statement? Has she given
    us intimations of the "ordeals" that finally defeated her aunt?
4. Rich suggests that her aunt's embroidering was difficult work. Is the weight of the
    wedding band the reason that her needle was "hard to pull"?
5. Is there a contradiction between the first line's description that Aunt Jennifer's
    fingers "prance" as she works and the harsher emotional reality Rich suggests in
    the second stanza? Is this tension between the two situations resolved in the poem?
6. What is the inference in line 6's mention of the "ivory needle"?

Topics for Writing

1. The poem is often read as a statement of the enduring triumph of women's work
    and values. Discuss the poem with this theme in mind.
2. In the phrase "ivory needle," Rich suggests that Aunt Jennifer lives in comfort-
    able economic circumstances, which do not, however, ameliorate the emotional
    difficulties of her life. Discuss the choices women of her aunt's generation often
    were forced to make for economic security.

DIVING INTO THE WRECK

"Diving into the Wreck" is a powerful, sharp-edged poem that has been the subject of considerable critical discussion. Although what the poem describes, in physical
terms, is clear, there is less certainty about what Rich intends to be the poem's metaphor.
This reading by New York critic Jean Gould appears in *Modern American Women Poets*
and describes the action of the poem:

> . . . in "Diving into the Wreck" we watch the poet go about her deep-sea
> project. After reading a book of myths, loading a camera, and checking her
> knife blade, she dons the necessary gear: an absurd pair of flippers and a
> heavy, ill-fitting mask — and, all alone, she descends the ladder, rung by
> rung, that leads down into the depths, where the wreck that man has made
> of civilization lies waiting to be explored: what she came for — the wreck,
> not a story or a myth, but the genuine article. The metaphor is maintained
> throughout. After further description, now she has found the spot; she is
> there, both a mermaid with dark hair flowing and a merman in armor.
> Silently they circle about the wreck and dive into the hold. As both maid
> and man, in her duo-personality she examines the cargo hidden in barrels,
> half forced apart and left to rot. Finally, either by cowardice or courage —

perhaps by both — she finds her way back carrying her knife and camera with, most important, an old book of myths which doesn't contain their names. The significance of the conclusion is self-evident. (231)

The final imagery of the combined woman / man figure, neither of whom finds anything about him- or herself in the "book of myths" they have recovered from the wreck, makes it impossible to read the poem simply as a feminist description of the silencing of women. Also, although we assume that we are reading a reexamination of human history, there is nothing specific in the poem to make this clear. We have to follow her on her dive and learn from her what we can. Students will find that the poem is a complex, multifaceted experience, and repeated readings will help them navigate their way into its depths.

Questions for Discussion

1. What do we assume Rich means by "the book of myths" in line 1?
2. Why does she use the word "myths"?
3. How can we read "ladder" in line 13? The speaker has just told us that she is alone, but she says that many others have used the ladder. Is there a contradiction in the two statements?
4. What does she mean with the statement that "there is no one / to tell me when the ocean / will begin"?
5. What can we read into her description of the power of her mask in line 38?
6. In lines 46 and 47 she speaks of "many who have always / lived here." Does this contradict her description of what she is diving toward as "a wreck"?
7. What is she suggesting in the passage of line 83, "we are the half-destroyed instruments"?
8. What would we identify as "this scene" in line 90?

Topics for Writing

1. Explain the poem's extended metaphor and discuss its importance to the feminist debates of the 1970s.
2. Discuss the imagery of the poem and show how the details Rich has chosen reach a cumulative effect in the poem's final sections.

EDWIN ARLINGTON ROBINSON

Miniver Cheevy (p. 728)
Richard Cory (p. 729)

With Robert Frost, Robinson was long considered the quintessential New England voice in American poetry. He differed from Frost, however, in his concentration on the people of a specific New England community that he named Tillbury Town. His poetry has much of Frost's technical skill and edge, but his view of New England small-town life was considerably more pessimistic than Frost's portrait of life on the outlying farms. Robinson was born in Maine in 1869 and died in Boston in 1935, and the Maine town of Gardiner, where he grew up, was the model for Tillbury Town.

When he was a struggling writer, Robinson tried to support himself in New York City with a job as a time checker in the subways. It was not until his second book, *Captain Craig* (1902), was noticed and praised by President Theodore Roosevelt that his circumstances improved. Roosevelt made it possible for him to get a job in the New York Custom House, where he worked until 1910. Robinson was praised by other poets, and several of his poems have become part of the American poetic canon, but he always felt himself as isolated and out of step with newer trends. He was awarded the Pulitzer Prize three times, and his book *Tristram,* which won the prize in 1927, became that rarity in the world of poetry — a genuine best-seller — even though it was a difficult long single poem.

Although his later books are generally not considered to be his best work, there has long been a critical consensus on the poems that continue to be read. The anthologist and critic Louis Untermeyer, whose taste and industry through nearly fifty years of work was a major force in shaping American attitudes toward poetry, clarified the contemporary view of Robinson's work in the 1950 edition of his *Modern American Poetry:*

> In all [Robinson's early books] there is manifest a searching for the light beyond illusion. But Robinson's transcendentalism is no mere emotional escape; his temper subjects the slightest phrase to critical analysis, his intuitions are supported — or scrutinized — by a vigorous intellectuality. Purely as a psychological portrait painter, Robinson has given American literature an entire gallery of memorable figures: Richard Cory, who "glittered when he walked," gnawing his dark heart while he fluttered pulses with his apparent good fortune; Miniver Cheevy, frustrated dreamer, sighing "for what was not" . . . Luke Havergal, Cliff Klingenhagen, Reuben Bright, Annandale, the tippling Mr. Flood — they persist in the mind more vividly than most living people. Such sympathetic illuminations reveal Robinson's sensitive power, especially in his projection of the apparent failures of life. Indeed, much of Robinson's work seems a protest, a criticism by implication, of that type of standardized success which so much of the world worships. Frustration and defeat are like an organ-point heard below the varying music of his verse; failure is almost glorified in his pages. (117)

In the troubled period of the 1960s and 1970s, the figure of Richard Cory, who despite his seeming success "Went home and put a bullet through his head," seemed true enough that folksingers Paul Simon and Art Garfunkel set the poem to music. Robinson's disappointment with the world he found around him has echoes in the harsh irony of stories and novels by many younger writers, and the savage despair of his portrait of "Miniver Cheevy" is matched by the dark humor of many current American films.

Questions for Discussion

1. MAKING CONNECTIONS What is the verse form of "Richard Cory"? How is it similar to or different from the verse form of A. E. Housman (p. 771)?
2. The descriptions of Cory in lines 3 and 4 could have been found in other verse of the period, but the image of the next line, "he was always quietly arrayed," is distinctly in Robinson's own voice. Explicate that line.
3. Is there anything in the poem that prepares us for the suicide in the last line?
4. Is the suicide presented as justification for the despair of the other people of the town?
5. The unhappiness of "Miniver Cheevy" is presented with the laconic justification "he had reasons." What does Robinson mean?
6. The form of "Miniver Cheevy" differs from the form of "Richard Cory." What are the differences and their effect?

7. What are the two kinds of rhyme that alternate throughout the poem?
8. What is the meaning of lines 15 and 16, "He mourned Romance, now on the town, / And Art, a vagrant"? Why are "Romance" and "Art" capitalized?
9. Much of the poem is heavily sarcastic. What are some of the examples of sarcasm?

Topics for Writing

1. Discuss the view of life that Robinson presents in "Richard Cory" and "Miniver Cheevy" and relate this view to that of modern times.
2. Robinson has painted a ludicrous portrait of "Miniver Cheevy," but it is a portrait we all recognize. Discuss the poem's dark humor and its relevance as a portrait of someone living today.

THEODORE ROETHKE

My Papa's Waltz (p. 718)

The childhood memory in "My Papa's Waltz" is told directly: The narrator's father came home drunk one night and waltzed around the kitchen with him — in front of his disapproving mother — and then put him to bed. To turn this small anecdote into a poem, Roethke has written it as a modest lyric ballad, in four-line stanzas of iambic trimeter, rhyming *abab*. He demonstrates his skill by using feminine rhymes in lines 2 and 4 of the first and third stanzas, and masculine rhymes in these lines in the alternating stanzas.

The poem's emotional effect is achieved with the first line, "The whiskey on your breath," and, as the young boy is put to bed, the last line, "Still clinging to your shirt" — still hugging his father. Despite the confusion, awkwardness, and discomfort he feels, the boy still loves his father. To reassure readers of the poem's intentions, Roethke has the boy call his father "papa," and in line 5 he uses the verb "romped," with its connotations of pleasant play.

Questions for Discussion

1. In "My Papa's Waltz" Roethke creates a word in the phrase "Could not unfrown itself." What does he mean by this? In an alteration in the poem's simple diction he uses the word "countenance" instead of "face" to describe his mother watching them. Why?
2. Does the poem's language imply that this is a happy or an unhappy memory?
3. What can we infer about the age of the boy from the language Roethke uses?
4. What does the poet tell us about his father and mother in the poem? What does he suggest in the description of "a palm caked hard by dirt"?
5. In describing the waltz he uses the word "romped." Does Roethke intend to lighten the mood of the poem with this light-hearted descriptive word, or is he using it ironically?
6. Can we draw any conclusion about the boy's attitude from the final lines?

Topic for Writing

1. MAKING CONNECTIONS There are several portraits of a child's relationship to a parent in the anthology. Compare the emotions depicted in this poem to a poem such as Sylvia Plath's "Daddy" (p. 998) or Seamus Heaney's "Digging" (p. 970).

CHRISTINA ROSSETTI

Song (p. 717)

Although none of Rossetti's other writing caused as much critical debate as her long poem *Goblin Market,* her shorter lyrics had a wide readership during her lifetime. Her brief, careful poems have gone through periods of relative neglect, but the purity and subtle skills of her lyrics have assured her a larger role as today's readers reevaluate nineteenth-century writing. Her themes and poetic idiom were not at all uncommon, but in lines such as "Haply I may remember / And haply may forget," she displays a unique poetic voice.

Questions for Discussion

1. In "Song," is Rossetti expressing an indifference to love in the lines "And if thou wilt, remember, / And if thou wilt, forget"? What is her meaning in this seeming disinterest?
2. The "nightingale" in line 11 could be an allusion to Keats's "Ode to a Nightingale." Do you think this was Rossetti's intention?
3. What is she describing in lines 13–14, "And dreaming through the twilight / That does not rise nor set"?

Topics for Writing

1. The popular appeal of short lyric poems such as Rossetti's has long contributed to the role poetry plays in our culture. Discuss the place of the short, personal lyric in literature.
2. MAKING CONNECTIONS   Rossetti's poems share many of the themes of Emily Dickinson's. Select one poem by Dickinson that addresses similar ideas or expresses similar sentiments, and analyze how each poet uses language, style, and structure to develop this theme.

MURIEL RUKEYSER

The Sixth Night: Waking (p. 699)
Myth (p. 844)
Chapultepec Park / I (p. 1006)
Madboy's Song (p. 1006)
Salamander (p. 1007)
Waiting for Icarus (p. 1007)

Muriel Rukeyser always considered herself to be a social activist, though she did not join groups or close herself to a wide range of opinions and sympathies. Her writing is always an expression of a broad humanism, tempered with passion and understanding, and in her poetry she is as conscious of her own weaknesses as she is of the problems of others.

The Sixth Night: Waking

On first reading this short poem students may not realize that the sixth night to which Rukeyser is referring is (according to the book of Genesis of the Bible) the sixth night that God has labored with the creation of the earth. Adam and Eve are asleep under a tree, and with the word from God "Let meanings move," suddenly there is the beginning of poetry. Rukeyser is suggesting that poetry is among the first expressions of human life and as such it should be valued.

Questions for Discussion

1. What does Rukeyser mean by "That first green night of their dreaming"?
2. Why is "Tree" capitalized?
3. Does the phrase "Let meanings move" echo other phrases from Genesis?
4. What is the technical term we use to describe this kind of echoing?

Topics for Writing

1. Rukeyser emphasises the role that poetry plays in identifying and naming things we experience around us. Discuss this concept of the role of poetry.
2. Poetry is one of humankind's oldest forms of creative expression. Write on why poetry has its beginnings so early in our human shared experience.

Myth

This poem was written almost a decade after the challenging feminist statement of *The Feminine Mystique,* by Betty Friedan, which became the principal text of the so-called second wave of feminism. In this poem, however, she is not expressing anger but using humor and irony in addressing the question of women's identity, which had for centuries been allowed to disappear into the ambiguities of common assumptions.

Questions for Discussion

1. What is the form of this poem?
2. Why do you think that the writer chose to use the prose poem form for her poem?
3. What is the writer alluding to in her opening phrase, "Long afterward . . ."?
4. What is Oedipus demanding to know with his question "Why didn't I recognize my mother?"
5. Has the writer composed the riddle which the Sphinx asked Oedipus or is it from early myths and legends? What was the Sphinx trying to achieve by asking the question?
6. What word would you choose to describe the tone of the poem — comic, sardonic, sly?

Topics for Writing

1. Discuss the theme of this poem, the question of specific women's identities, within the context of the second wave of feminism. Clarify the differences between that generation of feminist activism with the first wave of feminism — with its focus on the right to vote — and the current direction of feminism, the so-called third wave — with its effort to open the discussions to lower-class and underprivileged women as well as lesbian, bisexual, and transgendered women.
2. The poem is presented as an allegory. Discuss the roles that the Sphinx and Oedipus play in their exchange and present this in terms of our expectations of the character of these two protagonists.

3. Discuss the implications in the plaint by Oedipus, "Everybody knows that," when he is referring to the inclusion of women in the generic word "Man."
4. Compare with another language the practice in English of using generic nouns as collective terms for men and women together.

CHAPULTEPEC PARK / I

Chapultepec Park is a popular park in Mexico City, which Rukeyser visited in the early 1940s. She uses this description of sunrise in the park as a way to introduce questions of social stratification since the people in the park are clearly poor and probably homeless. At the same time, she leaves the reader with a glimpse of a moment of personal affirmation through her own response to the beauty of this moment.

Questions for Discussion

1. Rukeyser is describing a particular moment in the park. What is the moment and how does she use her skills as a poet to bring the moment to her readers?
2. What kind of activities is the writer describing in the park? Would they also be activities in a city park in the United States? What are the differences?
3. What figure of speech is she using with the phrase "morning / Leaning over the . . . park"? How does she develop the implications of this phrase? What other figures of speech has she employed in the poem?
4. Some of what the poem describes is realistic detail, some is clearly symbolic. What is Rukeyser suggesting with her final line, "A young horse runs into the sunlight"? Does this suggest a real or a symbolic moment?
5. What is she telling the reader in her walk to the "Philosopher's Footpath"? Is this a real place in the park? Is she presenting it as a symbol for the moment in the park?

Topics for Writing

1. Although some critical thinking about poetry places it outside the frame of the time and place, this poem also reflects the specific place and the moment when it was written. Discuss the poem's setting in this particular social context.
2. Much of Rukeyser's writing is considered activist and this poem also suggests decisive attitudes about society. Discuss the images in the poem that indicate to a contemporary reader that this poem reflects Rukeyser's sympathies with people outside the usual social frame using specific references to moments she describes.
3. Discuss the poem's artistic technique — the methods used to bring Rukeyser's description of the morning in the park to Rukeyser's readers — using the terminology of poetic form and imagery as specific illustrations.

MADBOY'S SONG

The emphasis in a discussion of this poem should be on Rukeyser's employment of the word "Song" in the title. The form of the poem is drawn from the older tradition of literary songs that employ the alternation of stanza and chorus within a narrative presentation. Another interesting aspect of the poem is its employment of the tone of an earlier period, and its theme is a classic lover's complaint at his rejection by his love. Its diction and imagery suggest the style of the songs Shakespeare incorporated in his dramas. Rukeyser here is clearly turning to the style and mode of another time to write a poem that has modern implications.

Questions for Discussion

1. What is the form of the poem? Would this kind of poem have been written in an earlier period? Are there examples of poems like it in the anthology?
2. Discuss the rhyme scheme and whether the irregularities of the rhythm affect our perception of it as a rhymed poem? Do the occasional examples of near rhyme — "Whispers/sister", "car/water" obscure the use of perfect rhyme throughout the rest of the poem?
3. What does the line "One I loved, she put me away" indicate about the poem's subject? Is the boy's madness real or metaphoric?
4. In line 23 the poet includes a mention of a car, which is anachronistic in the poem's setting. Discuss Rukeyser's possible reasons for introducing this here.
5. What are the specific elements of a song that Rukeyser has used for the poem? Is the rhythm sufficiently regular to set it to a melody?
6. Is the boy's malady a familiar lament in the medieval court literature of the lover's rejection? What is the implication of the line "Once is enough to drown"?

Topics for Writing

1. **MAKING CONNECTIONS**   Compare this poem to the sonnet by Francesco Petrarca, "Love's Inconsistency" (p. 773), which also is a complaint by a rejected lover. Each of them is an excellent example of hyperbole, and this should be discussed in the writing.
2. Discuss Rukeyser's use of an older form to write a modern version of a classic lament and consider the question of why poets often return to poetic idioms that have been relegated to the past.
3. **MAKING CONNECTIONS**   Compare this poem to the occasional "lyrics" in Shakespeare's plays, discussing their themes and the forms and techniques employed by both writers.
4. **MAKING CONNECTIONS**   Using other sources discuss this poem in terms of the conceits employed by poets of the post-Elizabethan era, notably John Donne.

SALAMANDER

Although this is a small poem, writing that is sometimes termed a "finger exercise," it is an excellent example of the literary skill and sensitivity to words that a writer like Rukeyser represents.

Questions for Discussion

1. What are some of the visual images the poem suggests and how has the poet heightened their effect through the use of imagery, as in the phrase "a little taper of the flame for tail"?
2. Is this poem similar in style to the imagist poems in the anthology? Does it have some similarities to the haiku in the anthology?
3. What figures of speech has the poet employed in the poem? What is she telling the reader in her repetition of the word "red"?
4. Although this is a short poem, probably written quickly, it is obviously written by someone with considerable experience and confidence. What elements of the poem demonstrate this quiet mastery?
5. How does the poet compare the situation of the salamander to the bird? What is the implication of the place of the salamander in the natural environment?

Topics for Writing

1. MAKING CONNECTIONS   Compare this poem to the haiku and the ima-
    gist poems in the anthology and show how they are similar and how they are dif-
    ferent, citing specific examples from the poems.
2. Discuss the use of language and figures of speech, including metaphor, simile,
    and alliteration, for example, "Flickering red in the wet week of rain."

WAITING FOR ICARUS

  This is a poem in which the reader unconsciously supplies the story around which
the poem is structured, a form of narrative often called association. The legend of Icarus
is one of the staples of beginning education, both as an intriguing narrative and as a cautionary tale, and someone turning to Rukeyser's poem associates it with the familiar
story as they read. The readers also know something which they cannot share with the
young woman in the story. They know that the story has a tragic ending. Although the
woman is not aware of it, she is waiting in vain. Icarus has already flown too close to the
sun and fallen to his death.

  Someone who is familiar with this anthology may also associate this poem with
another poem based on the same legend, W. H. Auden's "Musée des Beaux Arts"
(p. 908).

Questions for Discussion

1. What do we call a tale like the story of Icarus and his father?
2. What is unique about a narrative like this that does not intend to point a moral les-
    son?
3. What is the emotional effect the writer has achieved by telling the story in the first
    person? Does the reader empathize with the woman's complaint?
4. Although the poet is recounting an ancient legend, she has brought the story into
    our own time. How has she achieved this?
5. We are presented with a "generation gap" between the mother's dire predictions
    of possible disaster and daughter's wish to make the same trial as her lover. What
    does this suggest to the reader in terms of the emotional effect of the poem?
6. How do we associate the woman's complaint in the poem with our knowledge of
    the legend's tragic ending?

Topics for Writing

1. MAKING CONNECTIONS   Compare this poem with the version of the
    Icarus legend by W. H. Auden, "Musée des Beaux Arts" (p. 908), in the anthol-
    ogy. Each version utilizes the familiar story to make a different statement about
    human beings, their indifference or their impatience. Contrast the different
    themes that the two poets found in the same narrative.
2. In the poem the young woman's complaints and Icarus's assurances of his safety
    are presented in classical male / female stereotypes. Discuss these stereotypes in
    lines like "He said the wax was the best wax" and "I would have liked to try those
    wings myself," and in the warnings from the woman's mother.
3. It is obvious from much of her writing that Rukeyser considered herself a femi-
    nist. Discuss the feminist ideas and attitudes that this poem represents, and set
    them into the larger context of the second wave of feminism, using specific exam-
    ples from the poem.

MARISA DE LOS SANTOS

Because I Love You, (p. 798)

Marisa de los Santos was born in Baltimore and grew up in northern Virginia. She received her M.F.A. from Sarah Lawrence College and her Ph.D. from the University of Houston. She teaches at the University of Delaware, and now lives in Philadelphia. This poem is from her collection *From the Bones Out,* published by the University of South Carolina Press in 2001.

Questions for Discussion

1. Why is the comma that ends the words of the title an important key to understanding the poem?
2. Is the moment she describes a common experience? Is this kind of fleeting impression something that poets often turn to as a subject?
3. What is the image de los Santos is describing when she writes of the cars "linked with short chains of light"? What is the term for this figure of speech?
4. What does she tell us about her other "loves," when she writes of boys reading on the beach or of crossing guards in white gloves? Are these true moments of love?
5. With the word "easily" in the next-to-last line of the poem, she tells us that there are different ways of loving. What does the word tell us about her love for the person named as "you" in the title?
6. Is this a simple poem?

Topics for Writing

1. Although the poem extends only to a moment when the poet glimpses someone else who also stops to look at the beautiful sky above the traffic, it captures in its few lines a larger truth about the nature of love. Discuss this concept and illustrate it with images from the poem.
2. The poem presents the contrast between the crowded highway and the scenes of the clouds and the moon above her. Write about the contradictions in these two realities, and show how the poet has drawn them together in her writing.

ANNE SEXTON

The Starry Night (p. 1008)
For My Lover, Returning to His Wife (p. 1009)

In his 1980 book *Alone with America,* critic Richard Howard emphasizes that Sexton's work is based almost entirely on her own experience. If you are a writer like Sexton, he says, "You must begin somewhere, though, generally with your life, above all with your life when it seems to you to welter in a particular exemplary status." Students will find that the first two poems contain no generalizations, no larger political or religious issues: Sexton's life is her subject.

THE STARRY NIGHT

"The Starry Night" describes a Van Gogh painting that moves Sexton so strongly that she feels she wants to die in just the way the night is depicted in the painting. She wants to disappear into the emotional vortex of the painter's vision. The painting itself was inspired by a Walt Whitman poem, so with Sexton's poem the response of writer to painter to writer has come full circle. The first two stanzas end with the same balladlike refrain, "Oh starry starry night! This is how / I want to die," and there is a rhyme between the third and seventh lines. The last stanza, however, seems to lose itself in the poet's emotional turmoil, and the poem ends with the despairing image "no flag, / no belly, / no cry."

Questions for Discussion

1. In "The Starry Night," why does Sexton say that the drowned woman slips *up* into the sky?
2. What might "The old unseen serpent" mean in line 10?
3. How would you paraphrase the poem's last lines, "no flag, / no belly, / no cry"?

Topic for Writing

1. MAKING CONNECTIONS   The anthology contains other examples of poets responding to paintings — for instance, W. H. Auden's "Musée des Beaux Arts" (p. 908) and Rita Dove's "Sonnet in Primary Colors" (p. 776). Analyze the ways in which the paintings are used in each of these poems, and discuss why poets sometimes write about paintings.

FOR MY LOVER, RETURNING TO HIS WIFE

Whatever may be the strengths or weaknesses of Sexton's poetry, she continually used her life in ways that no mainstream woman poet had ever done before. This confessional poem is quite literally what its title says it is. She is simply saying goodbye to someone she has loved who is returning to his marriage. In her laconic description of her feelings, she even manages to say wanly positive things about her rival.

Questions for Discussion

1. Although much of the poem is written in four-line stanzas of similar line lengths, the tone of the poem is loosely conversational. Do you miss formal elements in the poem, or does it achieve its effect through other means? What are some of the other means?
2. Is Sexton's grudgingly accepting image of her lover's wife — that she was "melted carefully down" for him — something we expect from her? What does she mean by "one hundred favorite aggies"? Does the word "aggies" have the effect Sexton intended of alluding to childhood, since it is no longer a common word?
3. Although she uses the word "dull" in her description of her lover's wife in line 7, is Sexton in fact being critical of her? Is there a more negative tone to the description of her in the next line, "as real as a cast-iron pot"?
4. The poet lists several specific examples of the wife's importance to her lover's marriage. What are they? Are they things considered typical of married life in modern-day New England?
5. How does Sexton respond to the reality of the lover's wife having borne him three children? Since Sexton had children of her own, is there a suggestion of empathy in this description?
6. Although she uses the word "bitch" in her description of the wife, there is almost an admiring tone in her summation of the woman's temperament. Was this intended?

7. Is Sexton's dismissal of her own claims on the man — that she is merely "a water-color" — genuine? How might she have portrayed herself in a more conventional poem?

Topics for Writing

1. MAKING CONNECTIONS   Discuss the elements of the poem that are unexpected or unconventional, even in our own permissive age. Compare it to an earlier woman's expression of love, for example, Elizabeth Barrett Browning in "How Do I Love Thee?" (p. 775).
2. MAKING CONNECTIONS   Discuss the confessional poetry of Sexton and Sylvia Plath, and compare it to the work of other confessional poets, such as Robert Lowell and Sharon Olds. Discuss the elements that make their poetry different from that of their predecessors.

WILLIAM SHAKESPEARE

That time of year thou mayst in me behold (p. 772)
Shall I compare thee to a summer's day? (p. 1011)
When to the sessions of sweet silent thought (p. 1011)
Let me not to the marriage of true minds (p. 1012)
My mistress' eyes are nothing like the sun (p. 1012)

Students will find biographical information and critical discussions of Shakespeare in "Conversations on *Hamlet* as Text and Performance" (p. 1621). They should also read Erica Jong's commentary, "Devouring Time: Shakespeare's Sonnets" in Chapter 17 (p. 1055).

In her essay, Jong describes the sonnets as "the 152 best poems in our language," but it took more than two hundred years for Shakespeare's verse to become so highly regarded. The sonnets were originally published in 1609; there was another edition in 1640; they appeared again in a collection of Shakespeare's writing in 1766, published in response to a new interest in the comedies. In 1789, when the publisher issued a new edition of the collected writings, he omitted the sonnets, saying, "the strongest Act of Parliament that could be framed would fail to compel readers into their service." It was not until the nineteenth century that the sonnets came to be regarded as an irreplaceable part of our literary heritage.

Most commentators on the sonnets agree that they were written in the 1590s, at the time when Shakespeare was writing his lighter plays. They have little of the darkness of his late tragedies, although, as Jong points out, they share the Elizabethan obsessions with time and mortality. Many efforts have been made to trace a story in the sonnets, and there have been almost as many efforts to prove that someone other than Shakespeare wrote them. Some of the difficulty with these interpretations, however, is that we generally read the sonnets in modernized versions, in which spelling, punctuation, and sometimes even words themselves have been altered. In original form, it is more obvious that many stylistic differences exist between the poems, indicating that they were written over a period of years. There is no suggestion that they were written or intended to be read as a story.

Shakespeare was a writer capable of assuming many guises and adopting many styles. The style of the sonnets is largely derived from Henry Howard, Earl of Surrey, who developed the form of the sonnet that Shakespeare used; from Sir Philip Sidney, whose sonnet sequence *Astrophel and Stella* was published in 1582; and from Edmund Spenser, one of the most important poets of the generation just preceding Shakespeare's and whose sonnet sequence *Amoretti* was published in 1595. The power of Shakespeare's sonnets lies in his refusal to comply with the thematic conventions his predecessors had developed. He expands the sonnet's emotional limits beyond the realm of courtly love and into contemplations of mortality and the nature of time. His technical brilliance takes the sonnet into dimensions of rhetorical inquiry that no poet before him had attempted.

THAT TIME OF YEAR THOU MAYST IN ME BEHOLD

Questions for Discussion

1. Scan the sonnet and discuss its metrical form and rhyme scheme. (This same form will fit the other sonnets as well.)
2. Discuss the sonnet's extended metaphor.
3. The sonnet contains several metaphors for death. What are they?
4. What is the meaning of "Bare ruined choirs" in line 4?
5. What is Shakespeare saying about night in line 7?
6. What is he saying about love in line 13? Paraphrase this line.

Topic for Writing

1. MAKING CONNECTIONS   Discuss the meaning of "carpe diem" in terms of this sonnet. Compare it to another carpe diem poem — for instance, Robert Herrick's "To the Virgins, to Make Much of Time" (p. 717).

SHALL I COMPARE THEE TO A SUMMER'S DAY?

Questions for Discussion

1. Nature is present in many guises throughout the sonnet. Discuss which references to nature are simply images and which are also metaphors.
2. What is the term for the figure of speech represented by *Death* in line 11?
3. What claim is Shakespeare making for poetry in the last two lines? Is this claim unique to this sonnet? Why would he use images that were part of the common poetic vocabulary of his time?

Topic for Writing

1. In the second line of the sonnet, Shakespeare praises his mistress for being "temperate." Discuss why the Elizabethans valued this as a virtue in women.

WHEN TO THE SESSIONS OF SWEET SILENT THOUGHT

Questions for Discussion

1. What mood is Shakespeare describing in the first line of the sonnet?
2. The first line is a classic example of alliteration. Discuss the alliteration of this and other lines in the sonnet.

3.   What does Shakespeare mean by "old woes new wail" in line 4?
4.   Describe what happens to the speaker's mood in lines 6–12.
5.   Paraphrase lines 10–12.

Topic for Writing

1.   Analyze and discuss how the speaker's unhappiness is manifested while he is in this mood.

LET ME NOT TO THE MARRIAGE OF TRUE MINDS

Questions for Discussion

1.   In the sonnet's concept of "the marriage of true minds," is Shakespeare denying physical love? What does he mean by the phrase?
2.   What qualities of love does Shakespeare describe in the sonnet?
3.   Discuss the conceit of line 4.
4.   What does Shakespeare mean by "his bending sickle's compass come" in line 10?

Topic for Writing

1.   **RESPONDING CREATIVELY**   Read Erica Jong's paraphrase in the commentary (p. 1055) and write a similar paraphrase for this sonnet.

MY MISTRESS' EYES ARE NOTHING LIKE THE SUN

Questions for Discussion

1.   Could this sonnet be described as an antilove poem? What saves it from this?
2.   Is this list of the mistress's attributes a conscious rebuttal of the clichés of the courtly sonnet? What was Shakespeare intending by writing in this manner?
3.   Is the sonnet meant to be humorous?
4.   Discuss the meaning of the last line.

Topic for Writing

1.   **RESPONDING CREATIVELY**   Write a modern antilove poem, using contemporary images in the way that Shakespeare used images in his sonnet.

Commentary

Erica Jong, *"Devouring Time: Shakespeare's Sonnets,"* p. 1055.

PERCY BYSSHE SHELLEY

Ode to the West Wind (p. 764)
Ozymandias (p. 774)

Students may not want to read the entire excerpt from Shelley's "A Defence of Poetry" in the commentary section (Chapter 17, p. 1069), but many of the essay's passages suggest a theory and a response to poetry that can help readers gain a fuller understanding of Shelley's writing. The first paragraph begins with "A poem is the very image of life expressed in its eternal truth" and ends with "Poetry is a mirror which makes beautiful that which is distorted." "Poetry is ever accompanied with pleasure," Shelley writes. "All spirits on which it falls, open themselves to receive the wisdom which is mingled with its delight. . . . Poetry is indeed something divine. It is at once the centre and circumference of knowledge; it is that which comprehends all science, and to which all science must be referred. It is at the same time the root and blossom of all other systems of thought; it is that from which all spring, and that which adorns all; and that which, if blighted, denies the fruit and the seed, and withholds from the barren world the nourishment and the succession of the scions of the tree of life." Few poets or critics have expressed a more exalted view of poetry and its powers.

ODE TO THE WEST WIND

The form of the poem, terza rima, is discussed in the text. In a note to the poem, Shelley said that it was largely composed in a forest outside of Florence on a windy, tempestuous day on which a thunderstorm eventually erupted.

"Ode to the West Wind" is long and complex, but students should not have any difficulty following Shelley's thought if they read the poem carefully, section by section. The generally accepted structural interpretation is that the first three sections conceive of the autumn wind as a dark presence bringing death to the earth. Throughout the poem the forceful wind is personified: The first section ends with "Destroyer and Preserver"; in the second section the wind is described as "Thou Dirge / Of the dying year" (lines 23–24); and the closing lines of the third section describe the wind's voice reaching even to the plants in the depths of the ocean, which on hearing the wind's voice "suddenly grow grey with fear, / And tremble and despoil themselves." Also, each of the sections ends with an invocation to the wind, "O hear!" which has the sound of a supplicant before an almighty power.

The last two sections suggest a life that is contained within the wind, beginning with Shelley's realization that the wind has the power to save him from difficulties and disappointments. He opens the fourth section, beginning at line 43, with the wish "If I were a dead leaf thou mightest bear," and the lines are carried forward with the dream that the wind could lift him and carry him in his "sore need." The images rush to a climax with Shelley's pained outcry "I fall upon the thorns of life! I bleed!" The entire section is an invocation to the wind, but the tone of Shelley's pleading has changed. He now identifies with the wind; he is no longer a supplicant. In the last line he has become "One too like thee: tameless, and swift, and proud."

In the final section, beginning at line 57, the wind becomes a life-giving force, capable of scattering Shelley's thoughts to the world just as it scattered the leaves in the first stanza. The wind, by scattering his words, will be a trumpet of prophecy to the slumbering earth. On a first reading, the last image of "O Wind, / If Winter comes, can Spring be far behind?" may seem simply to describe the change of seasons from the dying of autumn to the rebirth of spring. But as Shelley has made clear in the preceding lines, he now sees the wind as the deliverer of his words to the earth's people. "Spring" is not only the natural season; it is also a spring of Shelley's words.

Students will also better understand the poem if they are aware that it is essentially written in two modes. Through his continuous reading and his passionate commitment to poetry, Shelley was exceptionally learned, and at the time he was writing, the new concept of romantic poetry was still being formed. Although the mood of the first three sections is wild and driven, their structure and style are essentially of the late Augustan mode. Augustan poetry used elevated diction and personification, was preoccupied with large general truths, made extensive literary and classical reference, and avoided openly expressed subjective emotion. All of this describes the first three sections of "Ode to the West Wind." Beginning with the fourth section, however, the poem suddenly shifts into the personal and the subjective. It is now in the romantic mode. One of the poem's achievements is its successful fusion of the two styles.

Questions for Discussion

1. What is Shelley describing with "Pestilence-stricken multitudes" in line 5?
2. What is he telling the reader about the wind in the first three stanzas?
3. In the image of line 11, "Driving sweet buds like flocks to feed in air," he is using two interconnected figures of speech. What are they?
4. In the second section, what is Shelley suggesting when he writes that the leaves are spread on the stream of the wind?
5. What does he mean with his image, in lines 24–25, that the night will be "the dome of a vast sepulchre"?
6. In line 29 he says that the wind has wakened the Mediterranean "from his summer dreams." What is he telling us?
7. Who is the dreamer he describes in lines 33–34? What does he mean by "the wave's intenser day"?
8. What is Shelley describing with the image "Cleave themselves into chasms" in line 38?
9. What is he telling us about his childhood in lines 48–51?
10. What is he telling us about his life now in line 55?
11. What is he asking the wind to do when he asks it to make him its lyre?

Topics for Writing

1. Discuss the elements of the Augustan or neoclassical style in the poem's first three sections.
2. The final section, beginning with the line "Make me thy lyre," presents the poet as the instrument of the wind. Explicate Shelley's meaning in this section.
3. Leaves appear as symbol and metaphor throughout the poem. Analyze what this leaf imagery suggests about Shelley's poetic methods.

OZYMANDIAS

Questions for Discussion

1. "Ozymandias" is written in an irregular rhyme scheme that does not entirely fit either the Italian or the English models of the sonnet. What characteristics of the sonnet do we find in the poem?
2. In line 5, what is Shelley depicting with the phrase "sneer of cold command"?
3. Discuss some of the possible interpretations of line 8, "The hand that mocked them, and the heart that fed."

Topic for Writing

1. The poem is usually interpreted as a parable of the futility of human vanity and pride. Discuss the reasons for this interpretation.

Commentary

Percy Bysshe Shelley, "*From 'A Defence of Poetry,'*" p. 1069.

JOAN JOBE SMITH

Feminist Arm Candy for the Mafia and Sinatra (p. 831)
The Carol Burnett Show (p. 887)
Dancing in the Frying Pan (p. 888)

Joan Jobe Smith, who lives in Long Beach, California with her poet husband, Fred Voss, is one of a group of poets who in the 1960s and 1970s took much of their inspiration as young writers from the anarchic poetry of contradictory spirits like Charles Bukowski and the emerging Beat poets. They write in an immediate, everyday language, rather than the heightened poetic diction advocated by many academic poets. They consider their writing outside of the usual poetic channels, communicate with each other by Internet, and often publish each other's books. Smith's work covers a breadth of contemporary topics, but it is the poems she has been writing for some years about the period she worked as a go-go dancer that have had the widest circulation. For many readers, Smith's descriptions of the men for whom she danced have been a helpful counterpoint to typical depictions of masculine interest in women's bodies — in television, film, and much popular writing — that neglect the women's individuality or role consciousness. Smith was very conscious of what she experienced in her efforts to please the customers in the clubs, and she is one of the few women in these jobs who has chosen to tell of her experiences.

FEMINIST ARM CANDY FOR THE MAFIA AND SINATRA

Questions for Discussion

1. What is the form of Smith's poem? Could it be described as a prose poem? Why or why not?
2. How has the writer turned this anecdote about a friend's dismal experience into an expression of a larger idea with the distinctive presentation that we consider a poem? What are the points of emphasis and concentration that give this poem its shape?
3. Much of the language and syntax of the poem reflects the writer's own experience as a dancer. Do terms like "arm candy" continue to strike readers as "cool," or has the term been dated, like many other slang terms? What is the meaning of "arm candy"?
4. A term like "arm candy" uses a number of figures of speech. What are some of them?
5. Is Smith justified in questioning her friend's chances of success with her social agenda in her next job as a go-go dancer?
6. Is the writer being ironic in her suggestion that the workers in the sex industry might be eligible for the same benefits and work regulations as other workers?

Topics for Writing

1. Discuss the experience of Sindy as an expression of a woman's fate in a masculine world beyond her control.
2. MAKING CONNECTIONS Compare the social consciousness of this poem with poetry by other modern women poets who are represented in this anthology, among them Sylvia Plath, Ann Sexton, and Sharon Olds, all of whom write about their difficulties with masculine interpretations of women's roles.

3. MAKING CONNECTIONS   Contrast the poetic form and use of language in this poem with poetry by more academically oriented writers like Elizabeth Bishop, using examples to contrast their use of meter and rhyme, as well as figures of speech.

THE CAROL BURNETT SHOW

Questions for Discussion

1. Is the old TV variety show *The Carol Burnett Show* still familiar to television audiences through reruns or does a reader today have to guess at the association? What would be a comparable television presentation today? What would students suggest as a substitute?
2. Would the mother of a young woman today react with the same negative feelings to her daughter working in a sex club?
3. In her description of the work she and the other dancers do in the club, there is an element of the figure of speech known as *hyperbole*. How are readers made aware of this in the description? Are other figures of speech employed in the poem?
4. How does the poem achieve its feeling of rush and hurry? Is this something we usually expect from poetry?
5. This poem was written as the writer looked back at her experience with some detachment. Could she have written the poem at the same time it was happening? Would she have written a different poem?
6. What is there that is particular about her job that gives the reader a stronger feeling of the abuse she experienced? Would a reader react in the same way to a poem about women being badly treated in a job that was not related to the sex industry?

Topics for Writing

1. In an early chapter of this anthology, there is a discussion about the difference between the subject and the theme of the poem (p. 703). In this poem we have an example of this difference, since the *subject* of the poem is the writer's experience as a go-go dancer, but the *theme* of the poem is her relationship to her mother. Using examples, discuss these two elements of the poem, subject and theme, and show how the poet has used each of them as an emotional structure in the poem.
2. As someone who worked in the go-go clubs, Smith describes her experiences without making a moral judgment. Discuss this attitude and suggest explanations for it, at the same time contrast it with the negative attitude toward work in these clubs and the moral implications of the work by other people who have never patronized or worked in them.

DANCING IN THE FRYING PAN

Questions for Discussion

1. In the title of her poem the writer is making an *allusion* to a well-known phrase, what is the phrase? Why did she use it in this conext?
2. How does the writer make use of the poetic effect *onomatopoeia* in the poem? How does it add to the effect of the poem?
3. The poetry Smith has written about her experiences is written in a vernacular idiom, using elements of hyperbole and irony to heighten the essential impossibility of her situation. Does this use of everyday speech give the writing a quality of *authenticity*? Would the poem have been as effective if she had used a more consciously literary idiom?

4.   Is there a sense of *irony* for the reader in the difference between the reasonableness of the conversation with her agent and the ridiculous situations she is describing?

5.   In her hints of various reasons why she was fired by various club operators, there is a sense of a competition between the dancers for the audience's attention. What are ways she describes where she was unable to compete? Does this expose conventional views of work in the sex clubs as being essentially destructive to the worker's sense of individuality? How do we resolve the seeming contradictions between these two perceptions?

6.   The situation Smith describes, as she attempts to talk to her agent from the edge of a highway, is very humorous. Is humor an element that is often present in contemporary poetry? Why is there more emphasis on the more serious themes in poetry?

7.   In this poem the writer has chosen to emphasize the ridiculousness of the situation. Could she have written about the same situation in a tone of anger? Suggest some reasons why she has chosen to look back at the moment and laugh at what she experienced?

Topics for Writing

1.   In the poem, the woman writes that the irony of her situation is that she didn't know her experience as a go-go dancer ". . . was not going to be the worst job I would ever have." Suggest other jobs she might have had that could have been worse.

2.   A standard visual element in many television programs with themes of crime and detection is a night club scene in which go-go dancers are depicted on a background stage, often performing what is known as a "pole dance." Discuss and contrast the descriptions of the go-go girls' actual experience as presented in the poem and the depersonalized images presented in these television programs.

3.   In our society we become accustomed to masculine stereotypes and the depictions of their responses to go-go dancers and other entertainers in sex clubs. Discuss the emotions Smith describes in her poetry and contrast the feelings of the dancers themselves with these masculine images, quoting from her poetry.

STEVIE SMITH

Not Waving but Drowning (p. 714)

Smith, as both a poet and novelist, seems so much a part of London that it's a surprise to realize that she wasn't born there. She was born in 1903 in Hull, in the northeast of England, as Florence Margaret Smith, but moved to London when she was three and died there in 1971. She worked all her life as the private secretary to the managing directors of a large British magazine publisher, and she titled her first novel, published in 1936, *Novel on Yellow Paper,* as she'd written much of it in the office on the lined yellow sheets of her stenography pad. Her first collection of poems, *A Good Time Was Had by All,* was published the next year. Smith was very popular as a reader of her wry, witty writing on BBC Radio, and her books had a wide audience. "Not Waving but Drowning" is based on a newspaper story Smith had read about a group of friends who, while picnicking on the beach, waved cheerily back to one of their group who had swum too far out and was desperately signaling for help.

Questions for Discussion

1.   Is the drowned man accusing his companions of letting him drown?

2.   In line 7, are the man's companions attempting to justify themselves?
3.   In line 9, what is the drowned man saying about his life?

Topics for Writing

1.   Smith has taken a simple news story and transformed it into an allegory of the victim's life. Discuss how she has done this.
2.   Smith wrote this poem using both traditional and modern means, and the poem achieves the spontaneity of open-form verse within the stanza structure and a rhyme scheme of closed verse. Discuss how she accomplished this, analyzing the poem's meter and rhythm, including the notable half-rhyme of "moaning"/ "drowning."

GARY SNYDER

Straight-Creek — Great Burn (p. 852)
What Have I Learned (p. 878)

Gary Snyder's name usually is associated with the writers of the Beat Generation because of his portrayal in Jack Kerouac's popular novel *Big Sur* as the hiker and mountaineer Japhy Ryder. Snyder defines himself, however, as a West Coast regional poet with a firm belief in Buddhist doctrine. He is a passionate defender of the environment and in his writing has worked not only to make his readers aware of the uniqueness of the natural world, but also of its vulnerability as humanity takes for itself more and more of the planet's limited surface.

STRAIGHT-CREEK — GREAT BURN

Questions for Discussion

1.   Does the syntax of the poem follow the linguistic forms of standard English? What is different about Snyder's ways of organizing his images?
2.   How does Snyder intend us to interpret the poem's first word, "Lightly"? Are there a number of possible interpretations?
3.   Much of the poem is composed of brief images but Snyder also includes scientific explanations for some of what he is seeing. What is the meaning of the term "geosyncline" that he uses? Does it help the reader have a clearer understanding of what Snyder is describing?
4.   Snyder also uses poetic imagery to describe the moments, like the shift of the clouds he watches over his head, "Shining Heaven / change his feather garments / overhead." Does this image give the reader a stronger impression than the scientific term he used a few lines before? Why or why not?
5.   In the short verse beginning with the words "Shining Heaven," how has he made use of personification?
6.   This poem does not move in a linear pattern, instead the images are arranged in a pattern of association. Why has Snyder written it in this manner? Does it reflect the way he is seeing the mountains around him?
7.   In his last four lines, Snyder finishes his description of the birds' flight. What is he telling the reader about the relationship between the space of the world around him and the space of the poem itself? Is this an ending the reader could have expected?

Topics for Writing

1. Snyder's poem can be thought of as a mosaic of images, moving from one visual object to another. Discuss how he has given form to the poem with this seemingly random gathering of poetic material and suggest a philosophic statement that Snyder perhaps intended with this method of composition.
2. RESPONDING CREATIVELY   The poem is rich with imagery of nature. Separate the images he has created and from them construct the mountainside in its entirety, using Snyder's language where possible.
3. RESPONDING CREATIVELY   Using the poem's imagery, write a description of birds seen outside the window or in local trees and analyze the process by which the glimpse of the birds becomes a line of a poem.

GARY SOTO

Mexicans Begin Jogging (p. 1013)
Teaching English from an Old Composition Book (p. 1013)
Waiting at the Curb: Lynwood, California, 1967 (p. 1015)

Students will immediately recognize that "Mexicans Begin Jogging" is an ironic comment on the situation of immigrants — legal and illegal — along the border between the United States and Mexico. In the poem Soto pretends that none of the problems needs to be taken seriously. The title itself is a sardonic joke on Anglo Americans' obsession with health and fitness. The running Soto describes is a rush by Mexicans to flee from the border patrol, but the effort is presented as mere exercise. Soto uses strong images to reinforce the dilemma: He works "under the press / Of an oven yellow with flame"; as he runs through the streets he becomes the "wag to a short tail of Mexicans." The harsh reality — that the people with whom he is running for protection work in the fields in the summer as laborers — is emphasized by line 16, they "paled at the turn of an autumn sky."

In "Teaching English from an Old Composition Book," Soto again presents a picture of the difficulties of the immigrant experience, although in this poem the situation is less threatening. Here the speaker is trying to teach a language class with materials that are shabby and outdated. The humor is in the use of the term "Tally-ho," which is an old-fashioned phrase used almost exclusively in England. The poem is alive with details of the class and the speaker's role as a teacher, and there is a gentle, warm sympathy for the students and their situation, just as there was for the immigrants beginning their run in the first poem. Again, instead of anger at their situation, Soto brings wry compassion. The comic Cantinflas, in line 14, was a popular clown in Mexican films who portrayed a lively, bungling busybody.

Questions for Discussion

1. Why does Soto tell the story of "Mexicans Begin Jogging" as a joke?
2. Do any lines in the poem suggest that this might not be a joke?
3. What is Soto saying about the sociologist's description of Mexicans in line 18?
4. In "Teaching English from an Old Composition Book," what is Soto telling us when he describes the classroom's piece of chalk as "no larger than a chip of fingernail"?
5. What is Soto describing with "Knuckle-wrapped" in line 5?

6.   What is the speaker telling us about his students in the phrase "now smarter by one word" in the third stanza?
7.   In "Waiting at the Curb: Lynwood, California, 1967," what is Soto suggesting when he describes the woman inside the house calling to her husband that *Laugh-In* was coming on the television?
8.   Although the poem still expresses the difficulties of one culture adjusting to another, the tone is more one of resignation and acceptance than of anger or disappointment. Could students suggest some reasons for this?
9.   A woman inside the neighbor's house also calls to her husband that the popular television show is starting. What does Soto want us to understand from this?
10.   Although Soto has set his confrontation between father and daughter within the Mexican American community, could the situation he describes occur as well in other American cultural groups? Could this be considered a universal situation?
11.   Why doesn't the father raise more serious objections to his daughter's appearance?
12.   Why does the daughter, despite her father's final acceptance of her break from his own social norms, still say to herself that she will have to leave her family?

Topics for Writing

1.   Discuss whether it was necessary for Soto to use irony in "Mexicans Begin Jogging."
2.   After reading "Teaching English from an Old Composition Book," discuss the connotations of the final phrase of the second stanza, "a pantomime of sumptuous living."
3.   In "Waiting at the Curb: Lynwood, California, 1967," Soto is presenting an example of the process of acculturation that occurs within any multicultural society. Discuss the specific examples he has used to suggest this process, and discuss the poem's relevance for the particular situation of Mexican Americans in the United States today.
4.   In a short paper, set the father's objections to his daughter's appearance and her tastes in friends and music into historical perspective, comparing it with the social attitudes prevalent in American society at this time.
5.   **MAKING CONNECTIONS**   Compare Soto's work with work by other Hispanic poets in the anthology, such Martín Espada (p. 953). Discuss their sense of militancy and the reasons behind it, drawing some conclusions about possible resolutions of these problems.

MARCIA SOUTHWICK

A Star Is Born in the Eagle Nebula (p. 787)

Marcia Southwick's poem is an attempt to come to terms with grief, and in it she subtly creates a complex, loving portrait of the relationship that has ended with her husband's death. The poem was selected for *The Best American Poetry* anthology for the year 1999.

Questions for Discussion

1.   Is the subject of the poem the difficulty of cleaning oil from seabirds' feathers? Why does Southwick open with this news item?

2.   Does she seem to have someone whom she is addressing as she runs through her catalog of items and events? Is it her husband? Could the things she is presenting be used to create a portrait of him?

3.   In the closing lines she describes a picture in the newspaper of girls with soap bubbles, and she says of the moment the camera has captured, "Nothing earth-shattering." Does this tell us about the picture, and is it simply a comment intended for her husband, or does it hint at the anguish she is experiencing?

4.   Can we say the same thing about the later abrupt sentence, "That's the plot"?

5.   When she follows it with the incongruous "A life. Any life," is this again a veiled comment about her situation?

6.   Why has she chosen the mention of the birth of a star as the title for her poem?

7.   Why has she ended the poem by relating the story of a bittersweet drawing from a comic strip?

Topics for Writing

1.   The chaotic assortment of news items in Southwick's poem could be read as a time capsule that sets the poem into a moment of contemporary history. Discuss this aspect of the poem, and describe those objects that help define its moment.

2.   Elaborate on the suggestion Southwick makes at the end of the poem, that life ends in misunderstanding and loneliness, by drawing inferences from other things she has named in the poem.

BRUCE SPRINGSTEEN

The River (p. 721)

Born in New Jersey in 1949, Bruce Springsteen has enjoyed an extraordinarily successful career as a rock singer and songwriter since the 1970s, when the critic Jon Landau famously declared him the future of rock 'n' roll. Initially compared to Bob Dylan, Springsteen moved away from his early penchant for writing prolix and some-times enigmatic songs peopled with fantastic characters to develop his own persona of blue-collar hero, working-class rocker, and protest singer. His 1980 double album *The River* is his first work in which that persona emerges strongly. With its simple ballad style and stark lyrics about the decay of a working-class marriage and dreams, the title song foreshadows Springsteen's next album *Nebraska*. An acoustic album whose songs are bleakly peopled with losers and criminals, *Nebraska*'s overall style pays homage to Woody Guthrie's folk and protest music, a style Springsteen continues to revisit and explore to this day.

Questions for Discussion

1.   If the river is a symbol, what do you think it stands for? What other symbols or metaphors strike you as being important?

2.   "The River" was written more than thirty years ago. Does it seem relevant today? If so, what contributes to the relevance — the situation described, the language used, or something else?

3.   MAKING CONNECTIONS   Compare the lyrics and rhyme scheme of "The River" to other traditional folk ballads in the book or to other folk ballads you may know. What similarities and differences do you note? What do you make of them?

Topics for Writing

1. RESPONDING CREATIVELY   Rewrite "The River" as one of today's most popular musical artists would write or perform it. Alternatively, relate the events of the song as they might be reported in a newspaper after the last night the narrator and his wife go down to the river, or as a feature story on people struggling in a bad economy.

2. Listen to one of Springsteen's acoustic folk albums — for example, *Nebraska* or *The Ghost of Tom Joad* — and discuss his depiction of working-class people. Alternatively, write a comparison/contrast of working-class people depicted on those albums.

WALLACE STEVENS

Thirteen Ways of Looking at a Blackbird (p. 793)

Stevens was born in 1879, studied law at Harvard University and New York Law School, and, after an unsuccessful attempt to set up his own practice, became a legal counsel for the Hartford Accident and Indemnity Company in 1916. He remained with the company for the rest of his life, becoming a vice president in 1934. He was already writing poetry as a student, and he continued to write throughout his long business career. Stevens's bibliography might give the impression that his literary career began with the publication of his first book, *Harmonium*, in 1923, but this book and much of his other work until the late 1930s was published by coterie presses in small editions that failed to sell even their few hundred copies.

A useful approach to this enigmatic poem might be to gather thirteen critical ways of looking at "Thirteen Ways of Looking at a Blackbird." Here are three responses to the poem that may shed some light on its opacities.

> Like other American poets influenced by the *chinoiserie* of Imagism, Stevens turned for a time from Western models to Eastern ones, and wrote his set of serial "views" after the manner of Chinese and Japanese painters, calling his set "Thirteen Ways of Looking at a Blackbird." In writing this poem, Stevens discovered his affinity for the aspectual poem — a series of variations on a theme. . . . Each of the "parts" of [the poem] is equally valid. Visual experience, measuring the world by eye, thus becomes the equable model (since we do not privilege one glance over another) for modern perception and cognition alike. Implication, innuendo, eccentricity of perspective, and summary aphorism become the condensed vehicles for Stevens's multiple "ways of looking."
>
> — HELEN VENDLER, *Voices and Visions* (1987), 134

> As the color black becomes [in the poem "Domination of Black"] the color or trope of *ethos* or Fate, so in "Thirteen Ways" it also serves as the emblem of Ananke, of Fate conceived as Necessity, where again Emerson is the likeliest origin for Stevens. Section VIII seems to me the revelation of the poem's disjunctiveness:

> I know noble accents
> And lucid, inescapable rhythms:
> But I know, too,
> That the blackbird is involved
> In what I know

What the poet knows is poetry, *materia poetica* and poetry being the same thing for Stevens. But there is no *materia poetica* without the domination of the blackbird, for the blackbird is Stevens's first thinker of the First Idea. And so he mixes in everywhere, including the union of a man and a woman. He is our knowledge, to use Stevens's very American idiom, not just that it is snowing, but that it is going to snow.

— HAROLD BLOOM, *Wallace Stevens* (1977), 105

"Thirteen Ways of Looking at a Blackbird" . . . begins and ends in the snow; and the permanence of the blackbird in this otherwise destructive element makes it the chief instance of a persona who has indeed a mind of winter. This poem — perhaps the most systemic exercise in epistemology that Stevens ever indulged in . . . deserves careful explication. The poem begins in a cold, sublime setting. The speaker, or looker, is moved or disturbed by the eye of the blackbird. The rhythms are arranged to make "eye" a prolonged utterance to correspond with a prolonged and fascinated attention to it. The speaker is made self-conscious by the little blackbird's eye; he is not so much looking at the blackbird as being looked at by it.

— WILLIAM BURNEY, *Wallace Stevens* (1968), 32

Perhaps just as helpful is an unsigned comment by a *Time* magazine reviewer in 1953: "Few living poets can be as vivid and as vague, both at once."

Although his work began to be available in larger editions after World War II, Stevens has pretty much remained a poet's poet: Outside of the academic world he is largely read and studied by other poets, and it is these other poets who have made "Thirteen Ways" so important. Reprinted in popular anthologies since the 1940s, it has strongly influenced young poets both in Europe and America, and it continues to fascinate new writers. Perhaps the poem is more accessible to poets because they don't have to try to understand it: They can simply let its juxtapositions, inferences, inflections, and innuendoes work on their imaginations.

Stevens's *Collected Poems* appeared in 1955, the year of his death, and it won both the Pulitzer Prize and the National Book Award.

Question for Discussion

1.   MAKING CONNECTIONS   Read the text's linked sequence of three haikus by Bashō (p. 789). What similarities and differences are there between the style of Stevens's poem and that of the haiku sequence?

Topic for Writing

1.   RESPONDING CREATIVELY   Choose any subject and, in the style of Stevens, write a poem expressing your own thirteen ways of looking at it.

MARK STRAND

Shooting Whales (p. 854)

In today's attention to the fragility of our planet, there is also a disquieting aware-ness that it is increasingly difficult to resolve the conflict between the needs of the ever-expanding human population and the needs of the planet's other species for their own food and space on the earth. Mark Strand presents one of those moments of conflict with a clear comprehension not only of the event he describes, but also of the unease he expe-riences at the spectacle of the killing of the whales.

Questions for Discussion

1. What is plankton and why has it caused the turmoil in the bay?
2. What has caused the problems for the humans living along the shore?
3. Why does Strand use the word "play" to describe the movements of the whales? Is this a term which the whales themselves might agree with?
4. Why would the children be taken in the boats to witness the shooting? Is this still a custom in these coastal communities?
5. In the fourth verse, describing the whales from a child's point of view, does Strand express sympathy for the animals? Would a child understand enough of the situa-tion to feel sympathetic toward them? Is it a child's image to say that "the doors of their faces were closed"?
6. What is Strand describing in his image "the path that they made / shone after them"? Why has he turned to a poetic metaphor at this moment in the poem?
7. The whales seem to have left the Bay after the first round of gunfire. Why does Strand speak of their "eyes of mourning"?
8. Could the moonlight have been blown from his father's shoulders, as Strand describes? Could this image have been inspired by the poet's conscious use of imagery or by the child's artless imagination?
9. As he sleeps, why would the boy dream of the whales luring him downward? How could he imagine that the whales knew where he was?

Topics for Writing

1. In a short paper, describe the situation in St. Margaret's Bay and offer other ideas that might have made it possible to clear the bay without killing the whales.
2. There is an inference in the poem that the whales were intelligent enough to real-ize they were being hunted and to dive out of reach of the guns and swim out of the bay. In a short paper discuss this aspect of the conflict for the planet — the con-sciousness of the other creatures that they are being hunted and that somehow they must find ways to survive.
3. Although much of the poem's language is written in an unadorned, literal idiom, Strand allows himself more poetic freedom in the verse beginning "The whales surfaced close by." Describe the figures of speech that occur in the verse and dis-cuss why Strand might have chosen to write about the whales themselves with more colorful imagery.
4. Discuss the thesis that the boy's dream might be a moment of conscience that he shares unconsciously with many individuals who have witnessed the destruction of other species. Relate the idea to your own experience or the experience of friends.

WISŁAWA SZYMBORSKA

True Love (p. 800)

Szymborska, who was born in Poland in 1923, has always considered herself only one member of a talented group of Polish poets who matured in the years after World War II. The poets she feels are her peers are Czeslaw Milosz, Zbigniew Herbert, and Tadeusz Rozewicz. Both Milosz and Szymborska won the Nobel Prize, and her immediate response when she was notified was that the prize should have been given to all of them as a group. Her acceptance speech in 1996 was typical of her modesty and her continuing sense of wonder at the world around her:

> The world — whatever we might think when we're terrified by its vastness and our own impotence or when we're embittered by its indifference to individual suffering, of people, animals, and perhaps even plants (for why are we so sure that plants feel no pain?); whatever we might think of its expanses pierced by the rays of stars surrounded by planets we've just begun to discover, planets already dead, still dead, we just don't know; whatever we might think of this measureless theater to which we've got reserved tickets, but tickets whose life span is laughably short, bounded as it is by two arbitrary dates; whatever else we might think of this world — it is astonishing. (trans. Stanislaw Baránczak and Clare Cavanagh, in *Poems New and Collected* [1998] xv)

Her *Poems New and Collected,* published in an expanded edition in the United States after she won the Nobel, surprised everyone by having a modest sales success, but her writing is reaching a growing audience of American readers.

Questions for Discussion

1. The tone of "True Love" is a kind of bemused irony. Is the speaker serious when she asks in the first line, "Is it normal?"
2. What is she referring to in the lines "And their little celebrations, rituals, / the elaborate mutual routines"?
3. What is the poet telling us about human relationships when she writes, "It couldn't populate the planet in a million years"?
4. Is the ending of the poem a surprise? What has prepared us for it?

Topics for Writing

1. Discuss the use of irony in the poem and explain the different meanings in the last line, "Their faith will make it easier for them to live and die."
2. MAKING CONNECTIONS   Often the tone of a poem by Szymborska and a poem by Marianne Moore (p. 991) is similar. Compare their writing, pointing out what is different about each of them and what is compatible.

Alfred, Lord Tennyson

Ulysses (p. 745)

The qualities that impressed Tennyson's Victorian readers are strongly in evidence in this popular poem. It displays the sonority of expression, the ease of versification, and the poet's willingness to attempt themes with strong emotional values. In "Tennyson's Voyage of the Mind," an essay on "Ulysses," the contemporary American poet Richard Wilbur wrote,

> . . . in this complex and celebrated soliloquy there are . . . many voices — diverse tones, moods, assertions, and echoes that the reader is challenged to hear rightly and to attune to if he can. To be sure, a poem so handsomely written can easily be plundered for simple messages. Robert Kennedy, campaigning for the presidency, was given to quoting, " 'Tis not too late to seek a newer world"; that phrase and others are dear to commencement speakers, while "Old age hath yet his honor and his toil" had proven useful with more mature audiences. Tennyson himself tells us that "Ulysses may securely be taken as a heartbreaking poem written at a time of grief and despondency." It was begun a few days after the death of his dearest friend, Arthur Hallam. . . . It was "written under a sense of loss," Tennyson said, "and gave my feeling about the need of going forward, and braving the struggle of life." (Robert Pack and Jay Parini, eds., *Touchstones: American Poets on a Favorite Poem* [1996])

The figure of Ulysses is from Homer's epic poems of the Trojan War, the *Iliad* and the *Odyssey,* and this is one of several poems in the anthology that also take their themes from Homer. Students should turn to John Keats's "On First Looking into Chapman's Homer" (p. 803) and Margaret Atwood's "Siren Song" (p. 799), which humorously recounts an incident on Ulysses' homeward journey from Troy.

Questions for Discussion

1. In line 4, Ulysses describes the country's laws as "unequal." Is it unusual for a ruler to say this about his own country's laws? Could this be one of the reasons for his discontent?
2. What is he saying about himself in line 11, "I am become a name"?
3. Why would anyone who has traveled widely use the phrase that Ulysses does in line 18, "I am part of all that I have met"?
4. Ulysses seems to be dismissing everyday life as meaningless in his image in line 24, "As though to breathe were life." Is this a reasonable interpretation?
5. In line 33, Tennyson begins the second long section of the poem with the words "This is my son." Is it ever made clear in the poem to whom he is speaking? Could the poem also be interpreted as a soliloquy?
6. In line 42, what does Tennyson mean by "household gods"?
7. What is he describing in line 58, "Push off, and sitting well in order smite / The sounding furrows"?

Topic for Writing

1. Although he has been the subject of countless poems, plays, stories, films, and songs, Ulysses, as far as anyone will ever know, is only a character from Homer's imagination. Discuss how a character from a writer's imagination can become the subject of a broader analysis of human nature.

Dylan Thomas

Do Not Go Gentle into That Good Night (p. 784)

Thomas's poetry was written for what could be described as a musical instrument — his own voice. He was one of the great readers of poetry, and recordings of his readings probably sold even more copies than his books. If students have the opportunity to listen to such a recording, they will immediately understand the methods of his poetry. If no recordings are available, certainly the poems should be read aloud in class.

The meter of Thomas's poetry is always flexible, and at the same time it is obvious to the listener. It is always Thomas's ear that makes the final decision. In "Do Not Go Gentle into That Good Night," the basic meter is iambic pentameter, but the final line of the first stanza, repeated in three other stanzas, is heard as hexameter.

"Do Not Go Gentle into That Good Night" is, on the surface, an exhortation to live fully and bravely up to the moment of death. Each of the kinds of men he names — wise men, good men, wild men, and grave men — should rage with regret that they didn't make more of their lives. The poem could also be read, however, as Thomas's attempt to justify his uncontrolled wildness to his dying father, or his dismay and fear that his father is so near death. The power of the poem comes from these emotional undercurrents.

Questions for Discussion

1. In "Do Not Go Gentle into That Good Night," what does Thomas mean in line 5, "Because their words had forked no lightning"?
2. What is the contradiction he suggests in lines 10–11?
3. In line 17, is he asking his father to curse him, or bless him, or both?
4. What does he tell the reader about death in the term "that good night"?

Topic for Writing

1. In his descriptions of different types of men in "Do Not Go Gentle into That Good Night," Thomas contrasts the ambitions and dreams of each kind of man with the disappointment of these men's actual achievement. Explicate the disappointments Thomas finds here.

Fred Voss

I Once Needed a Chance Too (p. 832)

Although today's perception of poets is that they are associated with universities and much of their time goes to their reading tours and to writing, there has also been a tradition of poetry written by men and women who work at day jobs. Poet Philip Levine worked in the steel mills in his apprentice years and for a period Walt Whitman worked as a carpenter helping his father build houses in Brooklyn. Fred Voss has worked as a machinist for many years, though he takes occasional breaks for reading tours and gives as much time as possible to his poetry. He lives in Long Beach, California, with his wife, the poet Joan Jobe Smith, whose writing draws on her own experiences working as a go-go dancer. Voss's poem reflects the tensions in Los Angeles and its neighboring communities like Long Beach as they struggle to deal with gang violence and the tensions of a struggling immigrant society.

Questions for Discussion

1. What is nineteen-year-old Hector's social background? Does the word "barrio" make this background more specific?

2. Which of the two men is most unlikely as a machine-shop worker — the young barrio drop-out or the older middle-class, university-educated shop veteran? What has brought them together?

3. The poem is as stripped of ornamental effects as the machine shop where the men are standing, but it is a poem that strongly affects the reader. How does Voss achieve this?

4. Could Hector also read the poem? What does this tell us about the things that were positive in his background?

5. Do the two men also communicate on a non-verbal level? How do we know this? Is this something that happens often at a workplace?

6. Although the tone of the poem is conversational, Voss uses the words "violence," "madness," and "desperate." How do these words alert us to the seriousness of the moment?

7. Does the situation in the poem justify for the reader the immediate sense by the poet that the two men will for a time become "father and son"?

Topics for Writing

1. **RESPONDING CREATIVELY** Write a poem like this one based on a workplace experience of your own, using language that is comfortable, and recount your own contact with other workers as they began a new job.

2. **MAKING CONNECTIONS** Using outside sources, compare poetry with this kind of working-class orientation by writers like Philip Levine, Joan Jobe Smith (p. 831), and Walt Whitman (p. 1017) with this poem, discussing the contrasts between the writers as well as the similarities.

ALICE WALKER

I Said to Poetry (p. 707)

Walker was born and raised on a tenant farm outside a small town in Georgia. She has written that from her mother she received "the three magic gifts I needed to escape the poverty of my home town . . . a sewing machine, a typewriter, and a suitcase, all on less than twenty dollars a week."

Walker was a scholarship student at Spelman College in Atlanta, then continued at Sarah Lawrence College in New York, where her writing attracted the attention of poet Muriel Rukeyser. Rukeyser passed Walker's poetry on to her own literary agent, and her first book, *Once,* was published in 1965, shortly after her graduation. She has written a wide range of books of fiction, poetry, and essays. She won an American Book Award for her novel *The Color Purple,* which was made into a successful film. She lives in San Francisco.

In "I Said to Poetry," Walker is using the form of an imaginary dialogue between herself and Poetry to describe the emotions that prod her to write, pretending that she would give it up, if only Poetry would leave her alone.

Questions for Discussion

1. What is the language of "I Said to Poetry"? Why is it effective for this poem?
2. What is the term for her giving human characteristics to Poetry?
3. What are her reasons for wanting to be free of Poetry, at least for a time?
4. Is she serious in her protests when Poetry questions her?
5. What is the experience she describes, in Poetry's words, in the lines beginning with line 27, "Poetry said: 'But think about the time . . .'"?
6. Why does Poetry challenge her statement that she's going to "learn how to pray again"?

Topic for Writing

1. This poem is a carefully constructed presentation of the emotional forces that drive Walker to write. Discuss what she is saying about the emotions she feels, and decide whether other poets feel the same drive.

ED WEBSTER

From *San Joaquin Valley Poems: 1969* (p. 837)

Ed Webster was born in California in 1958, and in 1969 his family was living close to the Naval Air Station in the San Joaquin Valley where his father was a pilot. These poems were his attempt to describe his memory of the days that followed after his father had been assigned to the aircraft carrier *Oriskany* and sent into combat in Vietnam. The sequence of poems appeared first in *Western Humanities Review,* and it was selected for *The Best American Poetry 1995.*

Questions for Discussion

1. Why did the poet's father write about coyotes in his letter to his sons?
2. The poet uses the military term "mail call" for receiving a letter. What is he suggesting by using the term?
3. What does he mean by the phrase "anything telltale"?
4. How could the small boys pretend to accelerate so quickly? Is this also one way to deal with their sense of their father's danger?
5. Although both stanzas of the poem are written in open form, the poem Webster quotes that he wrote in grade school uses traditional rhyme. Is it usual for children to learn to write rhymed verse? Why would it be considered an expected skill?
6. What is he telling us about his father's situation as he sees "the tracer rounds drifting up / over Haiphong Harbor"?
7. At the time Webster remembers in the poems, he was only ten years old. At that age, would summer be distraction enough for him to forget his father's danger?

Topics for Writing

1. Webster's poems suggest that war has no reality for children and that other things can distract them from it. Discuss this idea and illustrate it with examples from the two stanzas.
2. MAKING CONNECTIONS   So few poets have chosen to write about the period in their lives when fathers or brothers or uncles were facing combat in their military service. Comment on this, and contrast it with the emotions expressed in

the poems of Howard Nemerov and Randall Jarrell, which attempt to deal with their own realities of fear and death.

PHILIP WHALEN

I Give Up (p. 879)

Philip Whalen was born in Portland, Oregon in 1923. He attended Reed College, where he was closely associated with two other young writers, Gary Snyder and Lew Welch. Following his graduation he moved to San Francisco where he became part of the emerging Beat Movement. In 1955, with Snyder, Whalen took part in the legendary Six Gallery reading, which introduced the new Beat consciousness to a larger audience. He became interested in Asian studies, and in 1966–67 he lived in Kyoto, Japan, studying Buddhism. He became a monk in 1973. After acting as head monk in a Santa Fe, New Mexico monastery, he returned to San Francisco to lead the Hartford Street Zen Center. He died in 2002 at the age of seventy-eight.

Questions for Discussion

1. Whalen's poem is always on the edge of hyperbole. What does this term mean and how does it apply to what Whalen has written?
2. Whalen has many dreams in the poem, what are some of them? Does the poem end with a happy dream?
3. He is sleeping beside someone as he is tormented by his dreams. Why can the other person not help him?
4. Is he being serious with his assertion that homicidal maniacs are prowling the suburbs? Is the poem itself entirely serious?
5. What did Whalen mean by "the happy phantom of my greatness"?
6. What is he inferring with the phrase "used-up words to read"? How does writing a word use it up?

Topics for Writing

1. In line 6 of the poem, Whalen talks of being pursued by "endless logical argument." Discuss the opposite of this kind of argument — spontaneous, random thought — and discuss why Whalen responds to this way of thinking. Use examples from the poem.
2. Whalen writes that the "happy phantom of [his] greatness / wakes and grasps [his] pen," suggesting that the writing he does is automatic, without thought. Discuss why some writers have shared this feeling and relate it to your own experience writing this paper.
3. MAKING CONNECTIONS Whalen is considered one of the early representatives of the Beat literary movement. Compare this poem to other examples of Beat poetry in the anthology and discuss why you do or do not feel that Whalen's writing relates to theirs, using examples from the poems to develop your argument.

PHILLIS WHEATLEY

On Being Brought from Africa to America (p. 839)

Wheatley's poems were published when she was about twenty, and because some time had passed since their writing, we have to conclude that she was only a teenager when she wrote them. Although in her own time the wonder was that a woman from Africa could write any kind of poetry at all, the wonder for readers today is that she was such an extremely precocious, talented young poet. Wheatley's poems are written in the high Augustan style, and in this example she reveals her mastery of the style's elevated vocabulary and complex structuring. If she had lived longer, her poetry would certainly have become more individual, but the writing she did have time to complete demonstrates a high level of accomplishment.

In her poignant short poem, "On Being Brought from Africa to America," Wheatley speaks in the personal voice of someone who has been a slave, and she goes as far as she dares to admonish those who are prejudiced against her, reminding them that as fellow Christians, "Negros" may also be welcomed into heaven.

Questions for Discussion

1. In the first two lines of "On Being Brought" the speaker describes herself as fortunate to have been brought from Africa. Why does she say this?
2. What is meant by "diabolic die" in line 6?

Connection

Robert Hayden, "*A Letter from Phillis Wheatley,*" p. 968.

Commentary

Robert Hayden, "*On Negro Poetry,*" p. 1050.

WALT WHITMAN

A Farm Picture (p. 710)
From *Song of Myself,* 1, 6, 50–52 (p. 1017)
A Noiseless Patient Spider (p. 1019)

Ezra Pound's commentary on Whitman in Chapter 17 (p. 1124) is particularly interesting because it reflects the opinion of most intellectuals of the modernist period.

A FARM PICTURE

In "A Farm Picture" Whitman presents the farm in terms of its prosperity and its tranquility, describing the door of the barn as "ample" and the barn itself as "peaceful." The dominant sound of the opening line is the assonance of the vowel sounds — *a, o,* and a closely similar *ou.* The vowel sounds of the line are then gently contrasted with the phrase "sun-lit pasture field," which emphasizes its *p* and *l* sounds, then the muted vowels return in the concluding line, which is a soft weave of *a*'s and *o*'s.

Questions for Discussion

1. "A Farm Picture" is just what Whitman says it is, a picture of a farm. Is it a realistic picture, or is there an element of idealization?
2. The poem was written in 1865, the last year of the Civil War. Could Whitman have intended to depict a dream of the coming peace?
3. It is unusual to use the adjective "ample" to describe a door. What is the poet suggesting with this image?
4. Is the use of assonance in the poem suggestive of the picture that Whitman is presenting?

Topics for Writing

1. **RESPONDING CREATIVELY**   Taking the three lines of "A Farm Picture," use the images of the poem to write a prose sketch of a contemporary farm that has some of the same details and images of Whitman's poem.
2. The meter of "A Farm Picture" is much more regular than was customary in Whitman's poetry. Discuss why he chose to write the poem in this more regular style.
3. **MAKING CONNECTIONS**   Read this poem as a response to John Keats's poem "To Autumn" (p. 734), and compare their use of imagery to describe their very different country scenes.

FROM *SONG OF MYSELF*, 1,6,50–52

"Song of Myself" opened the first edition of *Leaves of Grass,* although it was, like the other poems of the book, untitled. In all of the subsequent reworkings of the book, Whitman continued to place it at or near the beginning. The poem is a freely expansive introduction to the new forms of verse he had discovered, and it played a crucial role in the development of his contemporaries' new consciousness. It was obvious to his more perceptive readers, however, that he had presented more than a new way of writing a poetic line. What was even more crucial was that he had moved the person of the writer to the center of the poem. The subject of the poem? It was himself, and to emphasize the universality of this conception — that anyone contained the elements of the persona "myself" — the first edition did not include Whitman's name as author. He is listed only as holder of the copyright on the reverse of the title page. Lyric poets had turned to their own emotions and attitudes again and again throughout history, but always there was a presumed subject —Shelley's west wind, Keats's Greek vase. Now, the subject would be the creative artist him- or herself, and our own world of expression was permanently shaped by this new concept.

Students may be confused as to the exact meaning of the title of the book, *Leaves of Grass.* Although Whitman alludes to grass often in the poems, he doesn't speak of grass having leaves. The explanation seems to be that he was punning on a common printer's term. He had worked as an apprentice in a print shop as a teenager and he knew that a common term for throw-away proof sheet was "grass." What he was intimating in the title, as he first conceived it, was that the book was composed of "leaves" — an elegant term for pages — of scrap paper.

Questions for Discussion

1. **MAKING CONNECTIONS**   How does the composition of the poem differ from other nineteenth-century poetry in the anthology? Is there any precedent for this new style in earlier poems?

2. What does Whitman mean by the statement "form'd from this soil, this air"?

3. In Section 6 he makes several guesses as to the nature of grass. What are some of his guesses? What is his suggestion in describing it as a "hieroglyphic"? What does the "hieroglyphic" spell for him?

4. Is there a mystery in the question "Whose?" that Whitman asks about the name of the owner of his imagined grass?

5. In contemporary colloquial language, what is the poet describing in the terms "Kanuck, Tuckahoe, Congressman, Cuff"?

6. What are the hints he hears about the dead young men and women? Are his feelings about death consistent with nineteenth-century religious beliefs?

7. In Section 50, what is the "word unsaid"?

8. In Section 51, what does Whitman say about the past and the present? What does he mean when he says, "Look in my face while I snuff the sidle of evening"?

9. The phrase "my barbaric yawp" in Section 52 was applied at first to Whitman's writing in amused derision, but the term soon came to have a more positive meaning. What is he telling us with the term, and why does he say that it is "untranslatable"?

10. How does the hawk's accusations of Whitman's "gab" and "loitering" relate to the way Whitman has described himself in the opening lines of "Song of Myself"?

Topics for Writing

1. Although Whitman does not use any of the conventional poetic means to create his new lines, there is no question that what he is writing is poetry and not prose. Discuss what it is in the writing that makes this immediately obvious.

2. MAKING CONNECTIONS   Compare the poetic means Whitman uses in his poetry with the work of other poets of his period: for example, Lord Tennyson, Robert Browning, or Emily Dickinson. Present reasons that Whitman's style became so influential as the modern era approached.

3. MAKING CONNECTIONS   The concept of the self in Whitman's poetry is different from the persona of the writer in the work of the romantic poets. Compare the individuality expressed in "Leaves of Grass" with the persona of a poem by Percy Bysshe Shelley or John Keats.

4. Write a paraphrase of Section 6 with its descriptions of grass and its manifestations.

5. Discuss Whitman's statement that he will always be waiting somewhere for his reader to catch up with him, and that the reader may look for him "under [his] boot-soles."

A NOISELESS PATIENT SPIDER

There is a long tradition of verse that draws analogies between lower forms of life and human spiritual or moral issues. This brief poem offers interesting opportunities to compare the spider described in the first stanza with the speaker in the second. What both spider and speaker share is a condition of isolation. It's the work of the poetry — Whitman's imagery, line length, and diction — that make something profound and enduring out of the comparison.

Questions for Discussion

1. Discuss the similarities the speaker suggests between himself and the spider.

2. Discuss the various ways and words Whitman uses to convey a sense of isolation

and the efforts to overcome it. For example, why does he repeat the word "fila-
ment" three times in the third line?

3.   Comment on the varying line lengths — for example the short initial lines of each
stanza versus the lengthening lines of the rest of the stanzas — and on internal
rhymes and rhythms that carry the poem along and enhance meaning.

Topic for Writing

1.   Paraphrase the poem. What gets lost in the paraphrase?

Commentary

Ezra Pound, *"What I Feel about Walt Whitman,"* p. 1068.

A NOTE ON WHITMAN'S SEXUALITY

In the classroom the instructor may be questioned about Whitman's sexuality.
Was he homosexual? As we use the word today, no. Did he have some kind of same-sex
experience as a young man? Perhaps, but the mid–nineteenth century was a different
time from ours. Marriage to middle- or upper-class women was almost impossible unless
there was some sort of economic security, and relationships with these young women
were severely circumscribed by guardians, religious scruples, and the lack of adequate
methods of contraception. The cities thronged with prostitutes, and gonorrhea and
syphilis were widespread and virtually incurable. The list of nineteenth-century authors
who ended their lives insane from the effects of syphilis is discouragingly long. Whitman
does write specifically about masturbation, but he feels, like most reformers of his time,
that it is an evil practice that destroys the body, the mind, and the soul. In one poem,
"Spontaneous Me," as David S. Reynolds points out in *Walt Whitman's America: A
Cultural Biography* (1995), Whitman writes of nocturnal emission with some consciousness that the young man might experience "strange, half-welcome pangs, visions,
sweats," but the man at the same time feels "red, ashamed, angry."

Perhaps because of the prohibitions surrounding sexual expression there were
compensations in intense friendships between men and between women. The words that
Whitman uses can, in themselves, confuse his readers. "Lover" meant someone for
whom there were strong feelings of friendship. "Orgy" was simply a word for party.
Because of the crowding and inadequate housing, it was very common for a man to share
a bed with another man — or sometimes two or three other men — just as it was common for women to sleep together. If these men were sincere friends, there may have been
an embrace and some kisses. If anything more happened between young men, it was
often mutual masturbation. In our society a same-sex experience is interpreted to mean
that the parties are gay or lesbian. In Whitman's time it was simply considered an expression of one's irrepressible sexual urges.

But what do we know of any same-sex relationships that Whitman might have
had? The truth is, nothing. As Reynolds points out, "His sister Mary had five children:
although next to nothing is known about her, we know for certain five more things about
her sex life than about Walt's" (197). Did Whitman feel a strong emotional attachment
to a man, and did he have strong homoerotic desires? This seems certain from the poetry.
His friends when he was younger, however, were heterosexual, and a letter from a
woman at the time seems clearly to indicate that they had made love the night before. In
Washington in the mid-1860s he developed an intense emotional relationship with a
working man named Peter Doyle, who was young enough to be Whitman's son. In a
diary entry in 1870 he castigates himself for his intense feelings for Doyle, saying specif-

ically that Doyle feels differently. They were physically close, but it seems from his diary note that Doyle would not permit anything beyond the conventional expressions of friendly affection common at the time. The longest poetic expression of one man's love for another in nineteenth-century literature is Tennyson's elegy for his friend Arthur Hallam, *In Memoriam,* but contemporary readers did not assume that the relationship was sexual.

This still leaves the questions as to why Whitman is so widely considered to have been homosexual, and why his poetry has such a central place in the gay literary consciousness. In his own time, and for years thereafter, the difficulty most middle-class readers had with Whitman was what they considered his hopeless wallowings in sexual relationships with women. When an English writer, Arthur Symonds, questioned Whitman closely about what Symonds and other European writers felt were homosexual suggestions in the "Calamus" section in the third edition of *Leaves of Grass,* Whitman was stunned. He blustered and exaggerated in his denial, but there is no mistaking his dismay. What gay and lesbian communities have found in Whitman is a portrayal of love that is so open and so free that there is room for any expression of love. For this, and for the ambiguity of the love he expresses in some of his major poems, he will continue to be a voice that the homosexual community feels speaks for them.

Suggested Reading

Reynolds, David S. *Walt Whitman's America: A Cultural Biography.* New York: Vintage Books, 1995.

WILLIAM CARLOS WILLIAMS

The Red Wheelbarrow (p. 792)
Spring and All (p. 1020)
This Is Just to Say (p. 1021)
The Problem (p. 1021)

Williams's poetry emphasizes the personal, the local, and the domestic. Of the major modernist poets (H.D., Eliot, Pound, and Stevens), he is the least "literary." His poems contain no hidden motifs, symbolic inferences, or complex allusions. As he said of his own aims, "no ideas, but in things," and he described a poem as "a small machine made out of words."

THE RED WHEELBARROW

"The Red Wheelbarrow" was included in Williams's self-published collection, *Spring and All,* and was reprinted in a pamphlet of experimental poetry that was published in Europe the next year. In *Modern American Poetry, 1865–1950* (1990), Fred Moramarco presents a plausible reading of this much-discussed poem:

> His famous poem, "The Red Wheelbarrow," much anthologized and over-explained, is nonetheless an excellent example of his poetry. . . . It shows his sharpness of visual perception — the way he looks at the world with a painter's eye. The simple and direct message of the poem is the importance of observing carefully, of opening our eyes to the physical world around us.

. . . Apart from the first two lines, this little machine made of words is a nearly pure imagist poem that calls the reader's attention to a simple but precisely composed scene. The first two lines create a tension and tease us with an unsupported assertion — "so much depends / upon" — and the reader expects some important religious, scientific, or philosophical statement to follow. Instead there follows a simple painterly description of a bucolic scene. I say "painterly" because Williams constructs this poem almost as if it were a painting, isolating color, shape, object, texture, and relationship. Notice how the poem's scene unfolds, word by word — *red, wheel, barrow,* and so on — until the whole picture comes into view like a developing photograph. Once the picture comes into focus, the reader cannot help but refer back to the beginning of the poem and ask why it is that so much depends on these things. So much depends, Williams seems to be saying, on paying attention to the colors, shapes, textures, and relationships between the objects that are right in front of you, and what happened to be in front of him when he conceived this poem was a red wheelbarrow and some chickens. He took what was "close to the nose" and put it in a poem that invites the reader to do the same.

Question for Discussion

1.   What does Williams achieve with the phrase "glazed with rain"?

Topics for Writing

1.   Discuss the elements that make this an imagist poem.
2.   Analyze the ways in which the colors Williams uses in the poem relate to painting.

Spring and All

This poem first appeared in a book Williams paid to have published in the south of France, *Spring and All.* It consists of short prose paragraphs, poems, works-in-progress, opinions, and reflections. There is no order or structure to the book, and its mood reflects Williams's disappointment at what he felt was his failure as a writer. At this point he had no publisher, except for coterie literary magazines, and he paid for what books he did publish. He was also furious at the success of T. S. Eliot's *The Waste Land,* which had appeared the previous year. It is possible that Williams had the opening lines of Eliot's poem, "April is the cruelest month / Breeding lilacs out of the dead land," somewhere in his mind when he wrote "Spring and All." Certainly the theme of Williams's poem is suggested by these lines from *The Waste Land:* "What are the roots that clutch, what branches grow / Out of this stony rubbish?"

This poem is one of Williams's best, perhaps his finest single lyric. Its theme is one of poetry's oldest — the renewal of life that comes with spring — but Williams more than delineates what is there before his eyes. In the first thirteen lines he makes readers conscious of this moment of early spring as it lives in their memory. The adjectives of lines 14–15 — *lifeless, sluggish, dazed* — come as a natural extension of the bleakness the poet sees in the raw day. There is some ambiguity in the word "They," which begins (at line 16) what could be called the poem's second half. It is not until line 20 that the poet begins to name what he means by the word: "They" are the plants that come alive out of the devastation of winter. In the poem's unforgettable last lines, Williams describes these plants as "rooted," taking a new grip on the earth as they waken.

In the last images, or in the earlier description of the new growth entering the world "naked, / cold, uncertain," it is impossible to forget that Williams was a pediatrician who delivered thousands of babies into the world.

Questions for Discussion

1. Is there any symbolic meaning for "contagious hospital," or is that simply the road the speaker was driving that day?
2. Why does Williams use the noun "waste" in line 5?
3. In the first section the colors of the earth are "brown" and "muddy." What colors does Williams contrast these with later in the poem?
4. In line 19, what does he mean by saying that the wind is "familiar"?
5. In line 23, to what does the word "it" refer?

THIS IS JUST TO SAY

Williams is supposed to have left this note for his wife, Flossie, on the kitchen table. It is one of his most popular poems, probably because it evokes an image of emotional closeness and warm domesticity. Few modern poets have described anything in their lives as so comfortable and so ordinary, and at the same time — as he tells the reader that the plums were "so sweet / and so cold" — so filled with wonder.

Topic for Writing

1. This poem could just as well be written in prose form, as a note. Discuss whether it would still be a poem in that form.

THE PROBLEM

Questions for Discussion

1. What is the form of the poem? How is it different from other modern free verse? Although the subject of Williams's poem is a church building, has he used a *personification* in his descriptions of the church?
2. Does the form of the poem aid the reader in following the poem's message, or is it a hindrance? Why might Williams have chosen it for this poem?
3. By isolating single words in some of his lines, Williams has given them considerable emphasis. Does this also give the words an extra weight in the context of the poem?
4. What does Williams tell us we can learn from the church? Does he clarify this point? Is it enough for Williams that he simply presents the issue?
5. Why does he compare this old, modest church with the Parthenon, one of the most famous buildings in the world's history? Does the comparison seem valid?
6. Williams asks what it is that has made the building "indestructible." Does he answer his own question, or are we expected to infer the answer from his response to the building?
7. What strong forces might be involved in the preservation of the church?
8. How does Williams view the church? What are some of the descriptive words he uses to let us see his feelings about the church?
9. Why does he tell us that even if the church should "be tumbled down" nothing could replace it? Does this have a larger symbolic meaning that we can infer from the poem?

Topics for Writing

1. One of the aspects of the three-tiered line that Williams employs in this poem is that it causes the eye to think in terms of word units. In a short paper discuss how this affects our reading of the poem and also how it affects our understanding of the poem.
2. Williams describes the little church as simple in design, but "comparatively / indestructible," and then claims that the church may be falling into ruin and that nothing could replace it. How does Williams use this paradox to create a metaphor? Using examples from his descriptions of the building, show how the building can be regarded as a symbol of a larger idea.
3. It is has often been said that Williams is one of the most *American* poets of his generation. Discuss the poem from the point of view of the American ideals that the church represents and answer Williams's own questions about how the example of the church might be used to help guide the conduct of our lives and how the modest structure is "comparatively / indestructible"?

Commentary

Ezra Pound, *"On the Principles of Imagism,"* p. 1065.

WILLIAM WORDSWORTH

I Wandered Lonely as a Cloud (p. 743)
Ode: Intimations of Immortality (p. 1023)
The world is too much with us (p. 1029)

Students should read Wordsworth's Introduction to the second edition of his *Lyrical Ballads* in Chapter 17 (p. 1075). This essay not only provides insights into Wordsworth's writing but it also includes the poet's lengthy justification of the use of natural speech and idioms in poetry. If students substitute "ordinary, everyday life" for "low and rustic life" and "ordinary people" for "these men," they will realize that Wordsworth was anticipating much of today's poetry. We accept our ordinary language for the very reasons Wordsworth suggested — because we believe this language to be "a more permanent, and a far more philosophical language, than that which is frequently substituted for it by poets," by which he means a poetic language created by an educated elite.

I WANDERED LONELY AS A CLOUD

This is one of Wordsworth's best-known short lyrics, written after the ballad "We Are Seven." His subject is no longer "incidents and situations from common life." Instead, he is writing of his own emotional response to the beauty of nature. Students will remember the later section in his Introduction to *Lyrical Ballads*, when he declares that "all good poetry is the spontaneous overflow of powerful feelings." The next paragraph of the Introduction includes the statement that poetry "takes its origin from emotion recollected in tranquility," which is a precise characterization of "I Wandered Lonely as a Cloud."

In "I Wandered Lonely as a Cloud," written in 1804, he looks back and remembers the dazzling beauty of a bank of wild daffodils in bloom that he saw along a lake shore. He says that now when he is resting or thinking he will suddenly remember the beautiful sight and will feel the same pleasure. It is this that he meant by "emotion recollected in tranquility."

Questions for Discussion

1. In "I Wandered Lonely as a Cloud," what figure of speech is Wordsworth using in line 12, "Tossing their heads in sprightly dance"? What is the comparison?
2. In line 22 he describes the "bliss of solitude." What does this tell us about Wordsworth?

Topics for Writing

1. Discuss the ways in which two comments from Wordsworth's Introduction — "All good poetry is the spontaneous overflow of powerful feelings" and poetry "takes its origin from emotion recollected in tranquility" — are illustrated by this poem.
2. In "I Wandered Lonely as a Cloud," Wordsworth uses the word *dance, dancing,* or *dances* in each of the poem's four stanzas. Describe what he means by each use of the word.

ODE: INTIMATIONS OF IMMORTALITY

The instructor might find this interpretation by David Daiches helpful in beginning a classroom discussion of this long and difficult poem:

> In the "Immortality Ode" Wordsworth gave the most complete account of the balance sheet of maturity as he saw it: in a poem whose very fabric is remembered perception giving way to reflection, he charts the course of the developing sensibility. . . . The naive freshness of the child's awareness gives way to the more sober vision of the man; mediated by love, the child's perceptions in a strange world take on a meaning which, as he grows up, finally emerges as the recognition of profound human significance in nature. . . . [I]t is a record of the profit and loss of growing up. The poet is only born when the child's bliss gives way to the man's more sober but profound sensibility, which works through "relationship and love" rather than mere animal sensations. The poem is thus one of Wordsworth's most central and illuminating works. (From *A Critical History of English Literature,* Vol. 4 [1971], 881)

The epigraph to "Ode" is from Wordsworth's "My Heart Leaps Up," which students may have already read and discussed. If students read the text's introductory note to "Ode" carefully, they will note that its first four stanzas were written together, and that Wordsworth had difficulty completing the poem. These first four stanzas express a joy and spontaneity that Wordsworth seldom achieved in his other writing: the form of the stanzas themselves conveys this spontaneity. The stanzas are irregular in length: The first two are each nine lines long, then, as though he couldn't contain his running thoughts, Wordsworth makes the third eighteen lines long, and the fourth grows to twenty-two. Although there is a basic iambic rhythm to the lines, they are irregular in length and follow no regular rhyme scheme.

The poem's central theme appears in the fifth stanza, beginning with the line "Our birth is but a sleep and a forgetting," and a classroom discussion could help clarify Wordsworth's thesis. The first four lines contain the theme that he develops through the rest of the poem. He says in these lines that our earthly life is only an interruption in the divine life that all beings experience before birth. As he writes in lines 64–65, "trailing clouds of glory do we come / From God, who is our home." Then, in Daiches's phrase, life becomes a "record of the profit and loss of growing up." The child loses the memory of his or her divinity, slowly, inexorably, as he or she grows older.

Questions for Discussion

1. Could the first five lines be described as pantheistic?
2. What is Wordsworth saying in line 16, "sunshine is a glorious birth"?
3. Why, in line 22, does the speaker think of himself as "alone"?
4. How could line 26, "No more shall grief of mine the season wrong," be paraphrased?
5. In lines 39–40, what is he saying about his own response to the day?
6. What "tale" is he learning from the trees and the grass, and how does this relate to his central theme?
7. In line 72, what is suggested in the description of the young person as "Nature's Priest"?
8. In lines 82–84 the poet describes the role of a child's nurse as a keeper, and the child as an inmate. Is he saying the nurse is playing a negative role in the child's life?
9. What are some of the things the child is foreseeing in his "dream of human life"?
10. In lines 106–107, is Wordsworth suggesting that the child spends his life imitating what he sees of life around him? As Wordsworth has expressed the theme of the poem, would this be a step away from the child's divine memory?
11. Who is the "Thou" of line 108?
12. In line 155 Wordsworth speaks of "truths that wake, / To perish never." Are these truths the faith that was to be challenged a generation later by scientific discoveries?
13. What does Wordsworth mean by "splendour in the grass" and "glory in the flower"?
14. In line 199, "Another race hath been," is he saying that a life has been lived? And in "other palms are won," does he mean that there have been rewards for this life?
15. What does the poet mean when he writes in the last line that thoughts can be too deep for tears?

Topics for Writing

1. Discuss the metaphor of the heaven that precedes childhood as an "immortal sea," which Wordsworth describes in lines 161–167.
2. **MAKING CONNECTIONS** Compare lines 167–168, "And see the Children sport upon the shore, / And hear the mighty waters rolling evermore," with the image of the waters drawing down the shore and signaling the poet's loss of faith in Matthew Arnold's "Dover Beach" (p. 907).
3. Interpret the poem's last two lines in terms of something you have strongly experienced.
4. Analyze whether the poem could have been written in the same way, or written at all, after the questioning of religious faith that occurred in England only a generation later.

THE WORLD IS TOO MUCH WITH US

Although Wordsworth writes in the introduction to the *Lyrical Ballads* that he intended to write in a speech that was close to the language of the common person, this sonnet is clearly an example of his neo-Augustan style. The classical references would not have been out of place in a poem by John Dryden, who was writing a century before. It is also, paradoxically, an exuberant poem, though he is saying in it that everything in the speaker's life has been consumed by "Getting and spending." He says in the opening phrase, "The world is too much with us," that the grind of daily life is wearing us down with responsibilities and allegiances: "We have given our hearts away." It is not surprising that the poem was a classic among Victorian readers, who worried that in the rush of nineteenth-century life they were losing their simpler enthusiasms. It is the final, unexpected image of the pagan gods rising from the sea that makes the poem so memorable.

Questions for Discussion

1. What is the form of Wordsworth's sonnet?
2. Is "Getting and spending" a useful summary of our everyday business activities?
3. What is meant by "a sordid boon"?
4. What are the things the speaker lists that fail to excite him? What do they represent?
5. In the phrase "I'd rather be / A Pagan suckled in a creed outworn," is he suggesting that Christianity is one of the causes of his malaise?

Topic for Writing

1. The poem can be read as a plea to return to the older folk traditions that were closer to nature. Discuss the poem from this point of view.

Commentary

William Wordsworth, "*From the Introduction to* Lyrical Ballads," p. 1075.

JAMES WRIGHT

Evening (p. 1030)
A Blessing (p. 1031)
Milkweed (p. 1032)
Lying in a Hammock at William Duffy's Farm in Pine Island, Minnesota (p. 1032)

EVENING

In his essay "1945 to the Present" in the *Columbia Literary History of the United States* (1988), James E. B. Breslin placed Wright with a group of writers whom he called "deep image" poets, using a term that at that moment was the subject of some critical debate. He wrote,

> In an essay on Wright, Bly . . . complained that in the 1950s poetry was understood in America as "a climb over a wall into an enclosure," into, say, a peaceful public park. The beats responded by deciding to batter down the walls; the deep image poets responded by searching the grounds for caves, hidden spaces in which some ancient primitive life might persist. The cave recurs in the poetry of Bly and Wright as an image of the unconscious, a

source of mysterious spiritual and instinctual energies, the sacred ground of the imagination. For deep image poets, as Bly says of Garcia Lorca, "writing a poem" involves "a climb from (the poet's) own world into a wilder world." What results is a poetry, in two of Bly's key terms, of "leaping" and "images." (1094)

This concept of the poem as an exploration into the unconscious clarifies some of the most startling of the discontinuities in Wright's poetry, and also identifies the source of much of the magic that gives the poems their unique aura. The explanation could also apply almost directly to the poem "Evening," in which Wright goes out into the family garden to call his small son for supper and for a moment imagines that his son has been transformed into a magic figure — perhaps Puck, the eternal forest child trickster of popular English mythology.

Questions for Discussion

1. The poem is written in a complicated rhyme scheme that is repeated in each stanza. What is the pattern of the rhymes? Some of the rhymes are perfect, others are near or slant rhymes. List the rhyming words and identify the type of rhyme.
2. It is possible to scan the poem in a fairly regular meter of three stresses to the line, but there is such a free use of enjambment that the poem, heard aloud, seems much freer rhythmically. How might Wright himself have heard the meter?
3. Is there any suggestion that the vision Wright experiences in the garden is anything more than a flight of his imagination? Is there some implied meaning in the phrase "The wide lawn darkened so"?
4. What changes does he imagine in his son's appearance? What is he suggesting in his fantasy that he will hear his son sing in notes?
5. What is the poet telling us about the boy in lines 46–48, "Like one who understands / Fairy and ghost — but less / Our human loneliness"?
6. As the vision ends, he writes, "Laugh, and the charm was ended." Is it simply reality that has ended Wright's dream, or the sound of laughter? Is it his son's laughter or his own?

Topics for Writing

1. Discuss the nature of a magic vision and illustrate the discussion with examples from the poem.
2. **RESPONDING CREATIVELY** Paraphrase the vision of the poem, but present it from the mother's point of view. Wright suggests that she has been conscious of some change in the earth, so this should be the center of the new narrative.
3. **RESPONDING CREATIVELY** For a useful exercise in understanding rhyme, write a stanza in the same rhyme scheme and meter as the verses of the poem, clarifying the nature of the rhymes — perfect or slant — and the structure of the meter.

A BLESSING
MILKWEED
LYING IN A HAMMOCK AT WILLIAM DUFFY'S FARM IN PINE ISLAND, MINNESOTA

In his critical study *The Electric Life: Essays on Modern Poetry* (1989), Sven Birkerts devotes an entire thirteen-page chapter to a "sounding" of Wright's poem "Lying in a Hammock." It is a tribute to the subtleties and the stylistic implications of this seemingly simple poem that Birkerts finds so much in it to discuss, and it is also a recognition of the uniqueness of Wright's accomplishment that Birkerts concludes that the poem finally expresses more than his chapter can satisfactorily elucidate. Birkerts's chapter, however, holds many insights that will be helpful to students who want to explore the depths of Wright's poetry. In an introductory paragraph, Birkerts discusses those aspects of any poem that he feels must be examined before we will understand it:

> A successful poem — or a great poem, or a "realized" poem — is an inexhaustible repository of sonic and semantic events/interactions. When we read such a poem we cannot err on the side of attentiveness; no discrimination is too fine. This is not to say that the poet has *consciously* located subtle resonance: if all the effects were conscious we could pull them out just as he put them in, and after a while we would have come to the end of it. But the language web extends past the shifting boundary of the field of the conscious, and the poem-making process depends as much upon associative marriages sanctified by a feeling of "rightness" as it does upon rational choice. And there is no limiting the effects produced by the unconscious interactions. They cannot be invalidated through any appeal to the poet's intention. (140)

The unconscious associations we sense in Wright's poetry cause us to return again and again to the poems to find what draws us to them. For anyone reading Wright, the last line of "Lying in a Hammock" is perhaps the most obvious example of the surprises and challenges we encounter as we try to understand his work. The line is "I have wasted my life," and a hurried reading of the poem would seem to suggest that nothing in the earlier lines has prepared us for this bleak conclusion. For Birkerts, however, "The conclusion cannot be taken as something separate from the body of the poem. It has not been tacked on — it is integral" (150). In his elucidation of the elements of the poem that prepare us for the abruptness of the final line, Birkerts makes a distinction between those descriptive passages in the poem — like the opening image of the butterfly, which he describes as "neutral observation" —and words or terms with an emotional weight. The first of these descriptive words, as he points out, is "empty," in line 4, then comes the phrase "last year's horses" in line 9, and finally the penultimate line, "A chicken hawk floats over, looking for home." Students can look for these "chink(s) into the subjective," as Birkerts calls them, in the other poems by Wright in the anthology.

Birkerts also makes a very useful comparison between Wright's poetic techniques and the classic Chinese poetry that has been a source for him:

> For the Chinese poets . . . every passing moment represented a unique configuration of higher forces, forces that passed through both subject and object (to use the Western concepts). A subject could, by heeding the momentary alignment of external details . . . catch a glimpse of his own spiritual location. Thus, the Chinese poet very often announced in his title the place and occasion of the poem. He would then limn with a few precise strokes the particulars of his setting, and conclude with a line or two giving the pitch of his feeling. Continuity between self and surroundings was implicit: Description further characterized the feeling, while the feeling extended out into the landscape. "Lying in a Hammock" is, quite possibly, Wright's attempt to Americanize, or Midwesternize, elements of this tradition. (141)

These critical tools should aid students in their discussions and their writing about Wright's poetry.

Questions for Discussion

1. What is the reason for the specific description of precisely where Wright was lying when he conceived "Lying in a Hammock"?

2. If a student considers the tradition of Chinese poetry that Wright follows, what is the significance of his use of the definite article *the* in the opening lines, to describe "*the* bronze butterfly" and "*the* black trunk"?

3. What is Wright suggesting about the passage of time in the image of the horse dung illuminated by the sun in line 10?

4. Why did Wright title his poem about the two ponies "A Blessing"?

5. In lines 11 and 12 there is a seeming contradiction in Wright's description of the ponies, "They love each other. / There is no loneliness like theirs." How can we explain this contradiction?

6. What is the term for the figure of speech "the young tufts of spring" in line 14?

7. What is the speaker telling us about his emotions in the image of the last three lines?

8. In line 2 of "Milkweed," "I must have looked a long time," why is the speaker unsure how long he has stood looking down the rows in the corn field?

9. Does "It is all changed" in line 6 change our perception of the time he has stood in the field?

10. Is there some way of specifically identifying the "wild, gentle thing" described in line 8?

11. In line 9, what is he telling us about the thing he wept for, "Loving me in secret"?

12. Is the speaker himself unable to identify what he has lost, or is he withholding this information from the reader?

13. What image is the last line describing? Why does Wright use a direct article, "*the* other world"?

Topics for Writing

1. Discuss the implications of the last line of "Lying in a Hammock," "I have wasted my life." Justify your answer with examples from the poem.

2. **MAKING CONNECTIONS** Compare Wright's use of concrete details to suggest an emotional situation in his other poems in the anthology.

3. **MAKING CONNECTIONS** Compare the use of nature to describe emotional states in Wright's poems and in a poem like William Carlos Williams's "Spring and All" (p. 1020).

SIR THOMAS WYATT

They Flee from Me (p. 716)

Although the poem's final stanza ends ambiguously, "They Flee from Me" is one of the most frequently anthologized early English love lyrics. Much of the lyric poetry of Wyatt's century — and for some centuries to follow — used a highly formalized, allusive poetic diction for lyric poems about love, but the moment in which the woman the speaker loves slips off her gown and takes him in her arms is described in language as immediate, as expressive, and as direct as any love poem written today.

Questions for Discussion

1. Analyze the rhyme scheme of the first stanza. Is it used consistently for the other stanzas?

2. Although the meter of various lines is irregular, the shifts of stress in some of these lines are justified by Wyatt's use of a caesura. Discuss the lines in which these are used, among them lines 4, 16, and 18.

3. Nothing in the poem identifies what the poet sees with the image in the first stanza, the wild creatures that "stalked in [his] chamber." Some commentators have suggested that the image Wyatt has in his mind is of wild deer. What details elsewhere in the poem are suggestive of deer?

4. What is Wyatt saying in line 6, "To take bread at my hand"? Is this a metaphor for a physical action or for an emotional exchange?

5. Consider lines 19 and 20 in terms of the end of the relationship. The speaker is given leave to go; is it willing on his part? Does the word "newfangleness" imply that the woman is going on to new lovers?

Topic for Writing

1. The poem's last two lines can be read as ironically sarcastic or as resignedly accepting of the inevitable end of a brief relationship. Discuss the possible meanings of "served" and "deserved" and decide if the poem ends in anger or resignation.

ELINOR WYLIE

Village Mystery (p. 749)

Elinor Wylie was one of the group of women poets whose writing played a dominant role in the American literary scene of the 1920s. Their poetry is usually dismissed today because they chose to write in traditional verse forms rather than experiment with the new modernism, but they brought a technical brilliance and a personal commitment to these styles, and there is a wiry persistence to the best of their work. Wylie wrote both fiction and poetry, but as critic Louis Untermeyer wrote of her,

> It was as a poet that Elinor Wylie was most at home in the world, and it is as a poet that she will be remembered. Whether she spins a web of words to an elusive whimsicality, or satirizes herself, or plunges from the fragmentary to the profound, every line bears her authentic stamp. The intellectual versatility is eventually reinforced by spiritual strength, insuring permanence to work which 'preserves a shape utterly its own.' (*Modern American Poetry*, 1950 ed., p. 297)

Wylie was born in Somerville, New Jersey, in 1885, and her talents were quickly recognized by her family. They moved to Washington, D.C., when she was a teenager, and she studied art at the Corcoran Institute, still undecided as to whether she would become an artist or a poet. After an impulsive early marriage, she fled to England with another man when she was twenty-four, and her first collection of verse, *Incidental Numbers,* was published there in 1912. She returned to the United States in 1916, settling in Boston and Maine, and in 1921 the first collection of her mature work appeared, *Nets to Catch the Wind.* It was an immediate success, and it was quickly followed by a second collection, *Black Armour,* in 1923, and her first novel, *Jennifer Lorne.* In the summer of 1928, when she was again spending some time in England, she became seriously ill, and she returned to the United States in the autumn, suffering from partial paralysis. She died in December, at the age of forty-three.

Questions for Discussion

1. What are the rhyme scheme and the meter of the poem? Why would readers today classify it as a traditional poem?
2. What is Wylie telling the reader with the poem's title? Who is the protagonist of the poem? Is it the poet herself, or has she created a persona to narrate the incident?
3. Are there other elements of the poem that would suggest an affinity with traditional poetic forms? Is the tone of the poem contemporary with its period?
4. Is the form that Wylie describes a true "ghost," or is she describing a metaphoric figure? Does she give an explanation for its appearance?
5. Does the poem accept the presence of the ghost figure?

Topics for Writing

1. MAKING CONNECTIONS   Compare this poem with other lyrics written in this same form, such as "Loveliest of trees, the cherry now" by A. E. Housman (p. 711), and discuss the technical elements of their poetic forms, relating them to the period in which they were written.
2. MAKING CONNECTIONS   The poem expresses an unquestioning acceptance of the figure of a dead girl begging in her shroud. Discuss this conscious acceptance of the spiritual in the poem, and trace the appearance of other "ghost" figures in early poetry.

WILLIAM BUTLER YEATS

The Lake Isle of Innisfree (p. 1033)
Easter 1916 (p. 1033)
The Second Coming (p. 1035)

Yeats sometimes referred to himself as "the last romantic," by which he meant the last of the poets of the romantic school, and students will find much in his poetry to remind them of that earlier group of writers. By the time Yeats began to write, however, a century had passed since the romantics' technical innovations were new, and their idiom had been sifted and resifted until the force of discovery, the excitement with the new idiom and language, had sunk under the weight of repetition. If students have read Keats, Wordsworth, Shelley, and Blake, they will find that Yeats, as a young poet, often used imagery and language reminiscent of the romantics, but with little of their imaginative power. It was a conscious choice that some critics have called "self-conscious romanticism." In "Symbol as Revelation," an essay written in 1890, Yeats explained the poetic method he shared with several other younger London poets, among them his friends Arthur Symonds, Lionel Johnson, and Ernest Dowson:

> We would cast out of serious poetry those energetic rhythms, as of a man running, which are the invention of the will with its eyes always on something to be done or undone; and we would seek out those wavering, meditative, organic rhythms, which are the embodiment of the imagination, that

neither desires or hates, because it has done with time, and only wishes to gaze upon some reality, some beauty. . . . The form of sincere poetry, unlike the form of popular poetry, may indeed be sometimes obscure, or ungrammatical . . . but it must have the perfections that escape analysis, the subtleties that have a new meaning every day.

Their new poetry was to look back at the old, but, as he also wrote in the essay, the gift of poetry that Yeats's generation inherited was not intended "to mirror our own excited faces, or the boughs waving outside the window." Although Yeats's style became sharper and more clearly defined in later years, he kept to his dictum to write poetry that would not show his excited face or describe the tree limbs outside his window.

Between the 1890s and World War I, while Yeats and his group were developing their aesthetic, the younger modernist poets were sweeping away the last of the romantic tradition with their experiments in free verse, imagism, poetic diction, and theme. Yeats responded by rewriting a number of his earlier poems to eliminate some of the "wavering rhythms" he had previously advocated. For a short period he employed Ezra Pound as a secretary, but he fired Pound when he discovered that the younger poet was rewriting some of the poems Yeats was giving him to submit to publications in an attempt to make them more modern.

When he was in his late forties, Yeats began to write in a much stronger and more direct style. His life had seen so many disappointments that the tone of regret lingered, but he could be specific about political questions other than Irish independence, and he was able to address larger social issues. One of the considerations for the awarding of the Nobel Prize for literature is the writer's commitment to a more just society, and Yeats's writing — as a poet, playwright, and activist fighting for Irish freedom — certainly qualified him for the prize, which he won in 1924.

At the end of Yeats's life, his poetry was dominated by his belief in spiritualism, and he developed a system of symbols based on the messages he believed he was receiving from spirits.

THE LAKE ISLE OF INNISFREE

Yeats's father, the painter Jack Yeats, had read parts of Henry David Thoreau's *Walden* to him when he was a boy, and Yeats had always had a dream of living, like Thoreau, in a cabin beside a lake. The immediate inspiration for this poem was something Yeats glimpsed when he was walking in London. In his *Memoirs* he wrote, "I was going along the Strand, and passing a shop window where there was a little ball kept dancing by a jet of water, I remembered waters about Sligo and was moved to a sudden emotion that shaped itself into 'Lake Isle of Innisfree.'"

"The Lake Isle of Innisfree" became Yeats's most popular poem, which made him uncomfortable, as he had reservations about the sententiousness of the opening lines.

Questions for Discussion

1. The theme of the poem — a longing to return to a simple country life — is familiar, and Yeats has no new insight to add to the long inventory of poems with this theme. The poem's meter, however, is complicated. Students should scan the poem and discuss its unusual line lengths.
2. The use of a comma to mark the caesura in seven of the poem's nine long lines divides the lines into two units of three stresses each, and the two lines that lack the comma, lines 6 and 10, divide metrically into the same three-stress units. Discuss Yeats's possible reasons for writing the poem in the long lines he has chosen,

instead of in shorter lines that would emphasize the poem's implied meter. What effect would a shorter line length have on Yeats's rhyme scheme?

3. Discuss the use of alliteration in lines 4 and 10. Would the choice of the word "lapping" be classed as onomatopoeia?

4. Is Yeats describing a real cabin in line 2?

5. All of the nature images in the poem are clichés. Why did Yeats choose to fill the poem with these familiar phrases?

6. The phrase "Nine bean rows" in line 3 is a conscious allusion to Thoreau's *Walden*. Are there any other images that allude to Thoreau's Walden experience?

7. Describe what Yeats is saying with the last line, "deep heart's core."

Topic for Writing

1. The poem is a reverie about an imagined life in nature. Discuss the contrasts between Yeats's imaginary country life and the realities of country life.

EASTER 1916

Questions for Discussion

1. Although Yeats wrote the poem under the strain of his emotions following the tragedy of the Easter Day Uprising in Dublin, he still composed the poem with a regular rhyme scheme. What is the rhyme scheme he chose? In his turmoil, however, he was irregular and inconsistent in the rhyming. What are some of the examples of half-rhyme or near rhyme?

2. What is the event Yeats is describing? Why is he so disturbed by what has happened?

3. Who are the figures referred to as "them" in the first line? What is his attitude toward them at that point?

4. What does he mean by the lines "Being certain that they and I / But lived where motley is worn"?

5. The last two lines of the first stanza indicate that something momentous has occurred, "All changed, changed utterly." What is he referring to?

6. What is the meaning of the line "A terrible beauty is born"? Why has he used the adjective "terrible."

7. The phrase "a terrible beauty" is often used without reference to the poem. Why has the term taken on its own vitality?

8. Yeats refers to one of the men as "A drunken, vainglorious lout," but he also includes him in the poem. Why has he forgiven this person for his behavior before the events? Is this a common attitude when faced with a contradiction between an individual's character and their achievement? How is it justified?

9. What does Yeats tell him himself about this change in our perception of the imperfect individual who also has become a hero? Is the phrase "Transformed utterly" justified?

10. What is Yeats referring to in the line "Wherever green is worn"?

Topics for Writing

1. Set the historical background of the poem and discuss Yeats's personal response to the tragedy. He has been circumspect, however, in naming the men who were captured and executed, and their occupation of the Post Office in Dublin is not named openly. Discuss the difficulty Yeats faced as an Irishman writing a poem that to the English occupying forces could be considered revolutionary and dangerous.

2.   It is sometimes said that art should not involve itself with politics, but clearly Yeats's poem takes a different stand. Discuss this idea in terms of the poem and suggest whether or not the idea that art and politics should be kept separate is valid today.

3.   In the third stanza of the poem Yeats writes of the life that was going on at the same time as the events of the Easter uprising. Write a prose paraphrase of the poem outlining the story he has told and discuss each of the threads he has woven into his narrative, though he felt himself unable to write openly about what has happened.

4.   He excuses any actions of the men who were executed by terming their commitment to the struggle against English domination an "excess of love." Can his lines "And what if excess of love / Bewildered them till they died?" be interpreted to mean that for a revolutionary cause the end justifies the means? Discuss this statement in terms of the world today and its many unresolved revolutionary conflicts.

The Second Coming

Some poems can be read without placing them in a historical context, but this poem needs to be considered in terms of 1919, the year it was written. In 1919 a violent civil war was raging in Russia between the armies of the new communist government and the reactionary armies of the Right, who were aided by international brigades from more than forty nations. Communist insurgents in Berlin staged a near coup that was put down with brutal repression. In Ireland the first fighting had begun between the small bands struggling for independence from Britain and British soldiers and their loyalist allies. It could have been any or all of these events, along with the prolonged horror of World War I, against which Yeats was reacting in "The Second Coming," one of his most overtly political poems. He is so engaged in this poem that its form is rough, with ambiguities that are difficult to interpret.

In his own notes to this poem, Yeats identified "Spiritus Mundi" as "a general storehouse of images which have ceased to be the property of any personality or spirit." *Gyre* can be defined as a shortened version of the word *gyration*, which would clarify the image of the opening lines as a hunting falcon on a widening gyration beyond the voice of the falconer. An interpretation of this would be humankind losing touch with God. Yeats, however, felt the poem had a mystical symbolism based on a gyre, which Richard J. Finneran explains as "one-half of a symbol which consists of two intertwined cones, the base of each being the apex of the other. The movement of the gyres in opposite directions suggests the inherent conflict in existence" (in *The Collected Poems of William Butler Yeats* [1989], 493).

The poem alludes to the Christian doctrine that the second coming of Christ will occur on the Day of Judgment, when the world ends. To Yeats, it seemed that the world was already ending in a flood of violence, as he indicates in the famous line "Things fall apart; the centre cannot hold." It is difficult to know precisely what Yeats meant by the "rough beast" that was going to be born in Bethlehem, as Christ had been, but it could be interpreted as a metaphor for anarchy itself rather than any specific cause.

Questions for Discussion

1.   What is the form of the poem? Why did Yeats choose this form for a poem with this subject?
2.   Discuss the different interpretations of the first line.
3.   Is "Mere anarchy" in line 4 an example of understatement, or is "mere" meant as an adjective that would diminish the importance of "anarchy"?

4. What is Yeats saying in lines 7–8 about the situation facing the societies of the world?
5. Could line 14 be interpreted as an allusion to the statue of the Sphinx?
6. What does Yeats mean by his image of the beast in lines 14–17?
7. Explain the image of line 20.

Topics for Writing

1. Yeats writes in the poem that the anarchy rising around the speaker is a prophecy of a second coming. Discuss the images used to describe this anarchy.
2. Explain the meaning of lines 7–8, "The best lack all conviction, while the worst / Are full of passionate intensity," and discuss their relevance to current social problems.

From a Zuni Invocation (p. 850)

As the extermination of Native American peoples ground toward its inevitable conclusion at the end of the nineteenth century, there was a corresponding effort to preserve fragments of the disappearing cultures as nostalgic souvenirs of the centuries of life before the arrival of the Europeans. In what remained of the Native American lands, ethnographers — many of them amateur folklorists, others professionally trained and working for government agencies — began to collect native histories and chants. As an expression of this romanticism for the past, many native songs appeared in popular magazines and journals, but these were usually rewritten as the kind of rhymed verse in conventional stanzas that the readers regarded as poetry. None of the native peoples had developed their own written language, so the mainstream authors felt free to use the material in any way that suited their audience.

The field collectors working among the native tribes, however, generally retained their source material in the form they heard it. Many of the collectors were women and perhaps the best known was Frances Densmore, who came to the Lakota people with a primitive hand-wound cylinder phonograph that recorded as well as played back what the wax cylinder had preserved. The example of a Zuni invocation reprinted in *Literature and Its Writers*, 5e, was collected in the Southwest by Matilda Coxe Stevenson, and it was published in an ethnographic journal rather than in a popular magazine or newspaper. In these transcriptions of the chants as the collectors heard them, there is still the sound of the singers' voices, and the urgency of their prayer to the spirits of their world. It is as poignant now as it was more than a century ago. For a desert people, there was no greater need than water. Their invocation cries out for any sign of rain, and they dream of torrents of water that will move stones and uproot trees.

Most such invocations were chanted rather than recited and were often performed communally, accompanied by a hand drum. The Zuni lived in large earthenware structures called pueblos, and the references to ascending a ladder refer to a place set aside for the spiritual needs of the pueblo. The chant was to be performed as members of the community sat together, with the hope that when they descended again to the desert floor, they would hear the sound of thunder.

Questions for Discussion

1. Where do the Zuni people live and what is their surrounding environment?
2. What is the spirit presence they hope to reach with their invocation?
3. What does the chant suggest when it speaks of a body of water that "dried for our

passing"? What are we told by the repetition of the word "poor" many times?

4.   Why does the invocation ask for the earth to be shrouded in fog?

5.   What does the phrase "that we may inhale the sacred breath of life" tell us of their beliefs?

6.   What does the chant tell us when it invokes both a "great father" and a "great mother"?

Topics for Writing

1.   MAKING CONNECTIONS   The Zuni invocation, a prayer for rain offered up by people living in a desert, has an emotional urgency that distinguishes it from the more general pleas for the earth written by people living in cities with access to running water and supermarkets. Compare this invocation with another poem in this section and discuss these differences.

2.   For native peoples everywhere, their relationship to the earth is direct and binding. Discuss this idea, relating it to the specific needs and dreams of the Zuni people expressed in their chant.

3.   The invocation speaks of seeds and flowers and asks that their children "live and be happy." Discuss the larger metaphor that the seeds and flowers present, and relate it to the life of the Zuni as it is presented in the chant.

4.   RESPONDING CREATIVELY   Imagine a native group living in a different natural environment — for example, the Northwest tribes who live on the shrouded Alaskan coast, or the peoples of New England whose villages were in dark forest land — and compose a chant which would tell of their dreams and wishes for the natural world around them.

PART THREE

DRAMA

SOPHOCLES

Oedipus the King (p. 1155)

Sophocles' audiences would have been familiar with the general outline of the Oedipus legend. Such knowledge is necessary for students to recognize the series of dramatic ironies and foreshadowings contained in the play. Because of a prophecy that their son will kill his father and marry his mother, Laius, king of Thebes, and his wife, Jocasta, pin their newly born son's feet together and send him to be abandoned in the mountains. Pitying the infant, the shepherd entrusted with this task gives him to a fellow shepherd who passes him on to Polybos, king of Corinth, and his wife, Merope. The couple, being childless, raise Oedipus as their own. In adulthood Oedipus hears the same prophecy given to Laius, that he will kill his father and marry his mother and, believing Polybos and Merope to be his parents, leaves Corinth to avoid his fate. On his travels he is forced off the road by a chariot and treated uncivilly by its occupant. In his anger he kills both servants and passenger, who is (unbeknownst to him) his father, Laius. Oedipus continues on to Thebes, liberating it from the evil Sphinx by answering her riddle. He is rewarded with marriage to the widowed Jocasta and becomes king. They have four children together and prosper for some years until fortune takes a turn. Sophocles begins his play at this point in Oedipus's life. Thebes is suffering from a plague, and Oedipus is determined to save the city by uncovering the cause.

Sophocles opens the play with Oedipus at the height of his power. The central action is Oedipus's determination to save his city. As the play progresses he gradually discovers his damnation, ironically, by his own relentless insistence to uncover the truth. In a single day he falls from sovereignty and fame to a self-blinded degradation. The chorus draws from this the moral that one should never take good fortune for granted, but to see this as Sophocles' isolated theme would be an oversimplification. The students' first impression of Oedipus should be mostly positive as they observe his paternal care for his people. But they should also perceive his proud feeling of superiority, which will contribute to his downfall. The Greeks called this pride "hubris." It was such, perhaps, that led to Oedipus's violent response against the chariot that pushed him from the road. Though Laius was insulting, Oedipus's response was out of proportion, and he should be made to recognize his guilt. The Priest reminds us that although the people admire Oedipus greatly, he is still a man and not a god. Lest we forget, Sophocles points out the important role and power of the gods in the Parodos. Between each scene the chorus offers a commentary on events, directing both the mood and the audience's response.

Sophocles wishes us to consider the moral issues behind human action and to recognize the powers that operate on human affairs. On the surface Oedipus seems to be in conflict with the plague, then Tiresias, then Creon; but the central conflict of the play is between Oedipus and the gods. This leads us to the play's twin areas of interest:

Oedipus's character and Oedipus's fate. Sophocles cleverly and intricately weaves these two aspects of the narrative. Oedipus is neither wholly virtuous nor wholly blameless but is presented as a complex man who offers the audience an intellectual and moral challenge. He is partly a victim of fate and the "savagery of God," but his spirited character leads him to make errors that contribute to his downfall.

Students may find Tiresias a problematic figure, as we are shown slight motivation for what he chooses to divulge and when (Why not denounce Oedipus when he first came to Thebes? Why not tell him the truth clearly now?). It may help to remember that, as a mouthpiece for the gods, he may act as inexplicably as they. Oedipus's rage at Tiresias is partly justified by his noble determination to learn the truth that Tiresias, at first, refuses to tell.

Oedipus's suspicion of Creon is less easy to justify. At times Oedipus's fury is both precipitous and unreasonable, and his eventual suffering is partly justified as a punishment for such behavior. He holds on for some time to his belief that Tiresias's words are a plot against him, for this is easier to believe than accepting what is really indicated: that Oedipus has failed to escape the prophecy of the gods. Creon's defense underlines his character and offers a clear contrast to Oedipus. Where Oedipus's vanity insists on his being number one, Creon is satisfied with being number three in the chain of command. Creon is not a man to take risks; he waits and does nothing decisive that has not been corroborated by the gods. Supporting the community values of reason, order, and compromise that the chorus voices, he lives the safe life that men like Oedipus proudly eschew, and therein lies Oedipus's magnificence and his downfall.

The "shadow memory" that Jocasta's words spark from Oedipus marks the change from total blindness to truth to the beginnings of "sight." Despite Jocasta's insistence that all prophecy is false, both she and Oedipus are forced to recognize the folly of such a defense. Sophocles shows that disbelief is as difficult as belief when we learn Polybos is dead without being killed by his "son," and yet Oedipus still fears a marriage to Merope. Ironically, it is the giving of the prophecy itself that has ensured its completion; had Oedipus not been told he was in danger of killing his father, he may never have left Corinth. Just as the Sphinx destroyed herself when Oedipus answered her riddle, so, too, must Oedipus destroy himself when he finally solves his own. The two prongs of the gold pins with which he blinds himself recall the two prongs that Laius had used against him; thus Sophocles relates this expiation directly to Oedipus's sin of patricide.

One of Sophocles' major contributions to drama was his introduction of a third actor. This changes the whole dynamic of the play, allowing for far more dramatic interaction between the various characters. Thus, for example, we can have the Scene 2 confrontation between Oedipus and Creon interrupted and resolved by Jocasta, and the ironic reunion of the messenger and shepherd before the man they had worked to save as an infant and now provide with the information that will destroy him. *Oedipus* can be viewed as an ideal tragedy. Indeed, of all the plays he had seen or read, Aristotle chose *Oedipus* as the basis for many of his conclusions concerning the nature of tragedy. Oedipus is neither a criminal who loses our sympathy nor a saint whose treatment might lead us to outrage. He is a noble protagonist who encounters misfortune and brings misfortune on others, as Aristotle suggests, not through "vice" or "depravity" but by "error and frailty."

Caught in a tragic dilemma, Oedipus can either shirk his duty as king or try to rid the city of plague, but, for him, either course would be ruinous. This successful ruler is gradually devastated and, through his failure, finally exhibits his extraordinary human spirit by accepting responsibility and performing the required penance to save Thebes. Watching his downfall induces our pity and fear; his misfortunes are out of proportion to his faults, and yet these faults make him human enough to remind us of our own vulnerability. With Oedipus's spirited response, however, Sophocles ensures that we are not left in despair; Oedipus has courageously confronted powerful forces (both internal and external) with a dignity that reveals the depth and breadth of the human spirit in the face of defeat. Whereas comedy tends to show people at their worst, tragedy allows them to be at their best and so offers us hope.

SUSAN C. W. ABBOTSON

Questions for Discussion

1. Aside from determining the central action of the play, what important information do we learn from the beginning concerning the character of Oedipus, the people of Thebes, and the nature of the gods?
2. Trace the instances of dramatic irony that occur throughout the play. What do you feel their function might be?
3. What can be determined about Oedipus's character from his treatment of Tiresias and Creon? How does this relate to the events at the three-way crossroads?
4. Why does Oedipus so quickly decide that Creon has been plotting against him?
5. To what extent is Creon's defense against Oedipus's charges borne out by his words and actions in the play?
6. What functions does the chorus serve?
7. What are the chorus's views and beliefs and how do they differ from those of Jocasta? Can we accept the moral the chorus asserts at the close?
8. To what extent are the things that happen to Oedipus his own fault or the fault of others? Is he ever able to choose a course of action?
9. How true is the messenger's declaration that what has occurred was "evil not done unconsciously, but willed"?
10. What would have happened if Oedipus had died according to his birth parents' plan?
11. Why does Oedipus blind himself instead of committing suicide, as Jocasta does?
12. Although the situations and characters of *Oedipus the King* were devised long ago, in what ways are they still relevant in today's society?

Topics for Writing

1. On whom should we blame the misfortunes that occur in *Oedipus the King*: Laius and Jocasta? Oedipus? the shepherd who saved Oedipus as a child? Tiresias? the gods? fate? Sophocles? Write an essay that considers these possibilities and reaches some kind of conclusion.
2. Trace the images of light and dark, sight and blindness, knowledge and ignorance throughout *Oedipus the King*. Show how these relate to one another and what Sophocles intends for his audience to conclude by their use.
3. RESPONDING CREATIVELY Imagine that you are a psychiatrist who has conducted a series of interviews with Oedipus. Write what you consider to be a professional assessment of his character and condition, giving recommendations for future treatment.
4. RESPONDING CREATIVELY Write the story line for a modern-day equivalent of this play. Try to follow the dynamics of *Oedipus the King* as closely as possible.
5. MAKING CONNECTIONS To what extent is an understanding of the nature of tragedy important in any interpretation of *Oedipus the King*? In what ways does William Shakespeare's *Hamlet* (p. 1204) also fulfill this criteria of tragedy? Does Shakespeare tend to support or contradict Sophocles' assumptions?

6.   **MAKING CONNECTIONS**   Discuss the parallels between *Oedipus the King* and Henrik Ibsen's *A Doll House* (p. 1309).

Commentaries

Aristotle, *"On the Elements and General Principles of Tragedy,"* p. 1568.
Francis Fergusson, *"Oedipus, Myth and Play,"* p. 1574.
Sigmund Freud, *"The Oedipus Complex,"* p. 1581.

Suggested Readings

Bloom, Harold, ed. *Sophocles'* Oedipus Rex. New York: Chelsea, 1988.

Bushnell, Rebecca. *Prophesying Tragedy: Sign and Voice in Sophocles' Theban Plays.* Ithaca: Cornell UP, 1988.

Edmonds, Lowell. *Oedipus: The Ancient Legend and Its Later Analogues.* Baltimore: Johns Hopkins UP, 1985.

Gardiner, Cynthia P. *The Sophoclean Chorus: A Study of Character and Function.* Iowa City: U of Iowa P, 1987.

Hogan, James C. *A Commentary on the Plays of Sophocles.* Carbondale: Southern Illinois UP, 1991.

Keogh, J. G. "O City, City: Oedipus in the Waste Land." *Antigonish Review* 69–70 (1987): 89–112.

Knox, Bernard M. *Oedipus at Thebes: Sophocles' Tragic Hero and His Time.* New York: Norton, 1971.

O'Brien, Michael John, ed. *Twentieth Century Interpretations of* Oedipus Rex: *A Collection of Critical Essays.* Englewood Cliffs, NJ: Prentice, 1968.

Rudnytsky, Peter. *Freud and Oedipus.* New York: Columbia UP, 1987.

Seale, David. *Vision and Stagecraft in Sophocles.* Chicago: U of Chicago P, 1982.

Segal, Charles. Oedipus Tyrannus: *Tragic Heroism and the Limits of Knowledge.* New York: Twayne, 1993.

Senior, W. A. "Teaching Oedipus: The Hero and Multiplicity." *Teaching English in the Two-Year College* (December 1992): 274–79.

Sophocles. *The Theban Plays.* New York: Knopf, 1994.

Verhoeff, Han, and Harly Sonne. "Does Oedipus Have His Complex?" *Style* 18 (1984): 261–83.

WILLIAM SHAKESPEARE

Hamlet, Prince of Denmark (p. 1204)

On the surface, *Hamlet* is a "revenge tragedy" in the tradition of Thomas Kyd's *Spanish Tragedy.* The conventional pattern of such revenge tragedies depicts a ghost who calls for vengeance and an avenger who pretends to be insane at least part of the time and who eventually dies having completed his revenge. Shakespeare enriches this formula by making his avenger, Hamlet, an unusually complex figure and by exploring many themes beyond the act of revenge — themes ranging from suicide to the meaning of life. Students may approach this play from numerous angles and should consider a variety of the issues Shakespeare raises: How far do appearances deceive? Can truth ever fully be known? What is the nature of evil? To what extent should we accept human frailty and changeability? What makes an effective ruler? How does the notion of honor affect how we live? To what extent do guilt or innocence matter in a potentially predetermined universe? In what ways are our lives ruled by Providence or by our own natures?

The character of Hamlet and the difficulties he has in pursuing the revenge the ghost has demanded constitute the core of the play. Students should consider not only the evident changes and developments in Hamlet's character during the play but also the character of Hamlet before we first meet him. This can be pieced together from comments made by other characters and by clues dropped by Hamlet himself. Such a Hamlet was considered the "rose of the fair state" and equally adept as a courtier, soldier, and scholar. The Hamlet we initially meet has undergone a profound change and is evidently suffering from dark suspicions and depression. His father's death and mother's hasty remarriage have severely shaken his view of the world. By focusing on his only unguarded speech (when he talks in soliloquy), we can trace his development through despair, self-disgust, and, finally, self-knowledge. His first soliloquy is disjointed, full of whirling accusations and dismay. As time progresses his speeches become more ordered and orderly as he matures and comes to terms with the world in which he must live (and die). Hamlet's drive to know recalls that of Oedipus, and it is, ultimately, as destructive as Oedipus's — of both self and others. As with Oedipus, it is useful to consider what might be Hamlet's "tragic flaw," but beware of oversimplifying his character. Samuel Coleridge suggests that Hamlet suffers from an "overplus of the meditative faculty," an interpretation that could lead to a discussion regarding how an individual's will to act can be smothered by thinking too much about the action; Hamlet's difficulties, however, go deeper than this.

Old Hamlet's ghost provokes the first in a series of problems for Hamlet: Is this an authentic spirit or a devil sent to tempt him? Despite a "prophetic" feeling that the ghost speaks the truth, Hamlet has initial doubts about its authenticity, which is one reason he insists on getting further proof of its accusations. The ghost has been "prompted to [his] revenge by heaven and hell" — that is, by a sense of divine justice but also by anger. As it is impossible to disconnect the two, the act of revenge is both a moral and immoral choice.

Hamlet cannot ignore the moral problem of revenge that makes it difficult to redress a crime without becoming a criminal oneself. He is not afraid to die, but he is afraid of damnation — maybe even of the act of killing. But once he has firm proof that Claudius poisoned his father, he has no choice but to kill his uncle to restore his family honor. Honor and duty are powerful motivations in the play and strip many characters of their freedom of choice. Laertes must avenge his father and sister; to ensure this, he is drawn into using a deceit he would normally reject. Ophelia rejects Hamlet and spies on him out of duty to her father. Even Gertrude's obtuseness can be explained by her sense of duty to husband and monarch.

Students should be encouraged to make comparisons between the various kings and young men they see and hear about. Shakespeare intends for the characters of Old Hamlet, Old Fortinbras, Fortinbras, Laertes, and Horatio to act as foils to Hamlet. Young Hamlet is as unlike his father as Fortinbras is his. Whereas Fortinbras and Old Hamlet are men of passion, warriors who do not hesitate to throw themselves into conflict and justify it with notions of honor, Hamlet is caught between passion and judgment, which he thoughtfully recognizes are frequently at odds. He admires Horatio for his judgment, seeing him as a man who lives by reason and who refuses to allow passions to sway him. Yet can one live a full life in that way? Horatio is ever on the periphery of action: He survives to tell the tale, but he is not a player. The death of Hamlet's father paralyzes Prince Hamlet, while both Fortinbras and Laertes actively counter the deaths of their fathers: Fortinbras, through "noble" battle, ends with the crown of Denmark; Laertes, through dishonest schemes, ends with death.

The fight between Hamlet and Laertes over Ophelia's grave announces that Hamlet has changed since his voyage to England — he is readier for action. When Hamlet declares, "There's a divinity that shapes our ends / Rough-hew them how we will" (5.2.10–11), he has reached an important understanding. Although he has been unable to make sense of it, he can now accept that he must let fate guide him. All he can do is to attempt to live with honor, despite fate's demands. Hamlet fails in this as long as he fails to avenge his father. Shakespeare seems to suggest that people must simply accept whatever fate throws at them and try always to do their best. Hamlet's new maturity convinces us that he will now be able to meet such a challenge. Hamlet finally kills Claudius, not with a plan but on the spur of the moment, after witnessing the poisoning of his mother and Laertes' confession pointing out the king's additional treacheries. Claudius dies quickly with all his sins upon his head, unable to expiate himself, and Old Hamlet is avenged in full.

The very fact that a ghost walks the battlements is, as Horatio recognizes in the opening scene, an indication that something is wrong in Denmark. Throughout the play we find striking images of corruption, decay, and death. The evil, initiated by Claudius in killing his brother, reaches out to touch everyone, and Hamlet, as avenger, becomes the direct and indirect cause of further deaths and even the object of revenge himself. In order to purge Denmark of evil, Hamlet becomes a part of that evil and so must die along with anyone else who is contaminated. The difference between his death and that of Claudius is that his is a noble sacrifice, whereas Claudius's is merely an ignoble end. That Hamlet insists Horatio remain alive to tell his tale and to ensure that he is remembered honorably is an indication of this important distinction.

Claudius should not be viewed as a straightforward villain. Students should note that on the surface what he says often appears reasonable. It is only when we view his words in light of his guilt and suspicions that we recognize his more selfish and even sinister purposes. Claudius enjoys the pomp and show of kingship but is neither a fool nor a tyrant, despite Hamlet's criticisms. He consults his council and rules practically, negotiating rather than fighting. There is no doubt he committed a serious crime to gain this position, and his conscience troubles him, but in refusing to give up what he has gained he cannot repent. He recognizes Hamlet's popularity and cannot treat him too harshly if he is to maintain control (a control revealed to be tenuous, as the people take Laertes' side against him). He must eliminate Hamlet, however, once he realizes that Hamlet knows his guilty secret. Claudius's initial plan of sending Hamlet to England to be executed is thwarted by the pirate attack on the ship. Hamlet returns to Denmark unscathed, so Claudius expediently manipulates Laertes to assist in Hamlet's killing, displaying an enviable capacity for instant action. Like Macbeth, Claudius discovers that one crime can only lead to another and, in Shakespeare's ordered world, can only end in the perpetrator's death.

There has been much discussion regarding whether Hamlet plays at being mad or actually becomes mad, which fuels the debate over "appearance" but neglects the simple expedience of the decision to put on an "antic disposition." Hamlet's realization of danger is real, and his "madness" does help protect him (as it did the original Hamlet in the tale on which Shakespeare based his play). Polonius is long-winded (in his first speech it takes him thirty-two words to say "yes") but it is a mistake to dismiss him as a fool. Polonius is the king's chief minister and minion, adept at intrigue and spying, even on his own son. Polonius makes most sense when his character is read as a purely political figure. Thus, ethics and morality feature in his nature only insofar as they are politically expedient. At one point, Hamlet likens him to Jephthah, who sacrificed his own daughter (2.2.359), and we see Polonius quite willing to use his daughter to get information about a man who is threatening his king.

Ophelia should gain our sympathy as a victim. She is treated cruelly by Hamlet, who uses her to get at Gertrude and Claudius, and further used by her father as a spy against her former lover. Her entire life has been guided by men, but when their support disappears — after Polonius has been killed by Hamlet and Laertes remains in France — she collapses. The world of Hamlet is male dominated, and the women are given little opportunity for independence, which raises the question of whether they can be held responsible for their behavior. The men of the play seem to think not: The ghost, like Hamlet, is more concerned about Gertrude's incest than losing the crown, but both blame Claudius for Gertrude's actions. After all, their reasoning goes, she is only a weak woman from whom little more could be expected.

An uncut performance of *Hamlet* would run six hours, and although any performance nowadays will have been cut, students should be aware that there are no irrelevancies here. Every line contributes to our understanding of not just Shakespeare's time but our own time as well, for the human issues *Hamlet* explores have not changed as much as we would sometimes like to believe.

Susan C. W. Abbotson

Questions for Discussion

1. In what ways does the ghost influence Hamlet's decisions? Can Hamlet trust it? Should he?
2. What are the women's lives like at Elsinore? Are Ophelia and Gertrude responsible for what happens to them?
3. In what way can Laertes and Fortinbras be said to be foils to Hamlet's character?
4. Hamlet enjoys mocking Polonius, but is Polonius really a fool? Does he deserve to die? Do you believe that any of the characters who are killed deserve to die? If so, why?
5. Why does Hamlet so often delay killing Claudius? Why not kill him when he is praying?
6. Although it is a tragedy, there are many comic moments in *Hamlet*. What types of humor does Shakespeare seem to use, and when and why do such moments occur?
7. What is the difference between blank verse and prose, and why does Shakespeare switch between the two? In speaking to Horatio, Rosencrantz and Guildenstern, the audience, Claudius, Gertrude, and the Players, does Hamlet use verse or prose? What does his choice tell us about these relationships? Do any other characters alternate between verse and prose like this?
8. What are the functions of the theatrical troupe and its performance? How is "acting" a relevant issue to the play as a whole?
9. To what degree can Claudius be seen as simply evil? Does he not have any redeeming personal qualities? Is Claudius a bad king? Would Hamlet have made a better one if he had been elected?
10. Why does Shakespeare have Hamlet's return to Denmark take place in a graveyard? Has Hamlet changed while he has been away?
11. Under what circumstances could Hamlet be called both a hero and a villain? Who is ultimately responsible for the "unfortunate" events that occur in the play — events such as Hamlet's losing the crown, Polonius's murder, Ophelia's suicide, Laertes' trickery, Hamlet's death?
12. Do you consider *Hamlet* to be ultimately optimistic or pessimistic?

Topics for Writing

1.   How necessary is Fortinbras? Many productions of *Hamlet* have chosen to elimi-
     nate the character. Discuss how such an omission affects the dynamics of the play
     and explain how you feel this character ought to be presented.
2.   By analyzing the language, logic, and presentation of Hamlet's main soliloquies,
     outline the developments they exhibit of his growing control and understanding.
     In what ways can we say that the Hamlet at the close of the play is different from
     the Hamlet at the start?
3.   Compare and contrast two different productions of *Hamlet*. You may select from
     the number of film, television, or audio recordings available or, if possible, go see
     a live performance. Giving reasons, include an assessment of which version you
     think Shakespeare would have preferred.
4.   RESPONDING CREATIVELY   After reading Tom Stoppard's "Encore" for
     Hamlet (p. 1631) write a version of *Hamlet* that will take ten minutes to perform
     from beginning to end and yet encapsulate the longer play. Consider the key
     developments in each of the five acts and include any lines that you feel are inte-
     gral to the play's meaning. Other speeches can be paraphrased in whatever idiom
     you choose. You may leave out certain characters, but do not add any.
5.   MAKING CONNECTIONS   Compare the character of Claudius in *Hamlet*
     to that of Oedipus in Sophocles' *Oedipus the King* (p. 1155). Which seems more
     suited to being an effective ruler, and why?

Conversation on Hamlet as Text and Performance, p. 1621

Geoffrey Bullough, *"Sources of Shakespeare's 'Hamlet,'"* p. 1623.
Stephen Greenblatt, *"On the Ghost in 'Hamlet,'"* p. 1630.
H. D. F. Kitto, *"'Hamlet' and the 'Oedipus,'"* p. 1625.
John Keats, *"From a Letter to George and Thomas Keats, 21 December 1817,"* p. 1627.
Virginia Woolf, *"What If Shakespeare Had Had a Sister?"* p. 1628.
Tom Stoppard, *"Dogg's 'Hamlet': The Encore,"* p. 1631.
Photographs of 'Hamlet' in Performance, p. 1635.
Sir John Gielgud, *"On Playing 'Hamlet,'"* p. 1633.
John Lahr, *"Review of 'Hamlet,'"* p. 1637.

Suggested Readings

Alvis, John, and Thomas West, eds. *Shakespeare as Political Thinker*. Durham, NC:
     Carolina Academic P, 1981.
Bevington, David M., ed. *Twentieth Century Interpretations of* Hamlet: *A Collection of
     Critical Essays*. Englewood Cliffs, NJ: Prentice, 1968.
Bradley, A. C. *Shakespearean Tragedy*. New York: Penguin, 1991.
Cantor, Paul. *Shakespeare:* Hamlet. Cambridge: Cambridge UP, 1989.
Dean, Leonard F., ed. *Shakespeare: Modern Essays in Criticism*. New York: Oxford UP,
     1967.
Dion, Gregg. "Fortinbras, Our Contemporary." *Theatre Studies* 38 (1993): 17–27.
Dusinberre, Juliet. *Shakespeare and the Nature of Women*. London: Macmillan, 1975.
Frye, Northrop. *On Shakespeare*. New Haven: Yale UP, 1986.
Hopkins, Lisa. "'That's Wormwood': Hamlet Plays His Mother." *Hamlet Studies* 16
     (1994): 83–85.
Jones, Ernest. *Hamlet and Oedipus*. New York: Norton, 1949.
Kermode, Frank, ed. *Four Centuries of Shakespearean Criticism*. New York: Avon, 1974.
Kernan, Alvin B. *The Playwright as Magician*. New Haven, CT: Yale UP, 1979.
King, Walter N. *Hamlet's Search for Meaning*. Athens: U of Georgia P, 1982.

Lupton, Julia Reinhard. *After Oedipus: Shakespeare in Psychoanalysis.* Ithaca, NY: Cornell UP, 1993.

Maher, Mary Z. *Modern Hamlets and Their Soliloquies.* Iowa City: U of Iowa P, 1992.

Prosser, Eleanor. *Hamlet and Revenge.* 2d ed. Stanford, CA: Stanford UP, 1972.

Schoenbaum, Samuel. *William Shakespeare: A Documentary Life.* New York: Oxford UP, 1975.

States, Bert O. Hamlet *and the Concept of Character.* Baltimore: Johns Hopkins UP, 1992.

Wofford, Susanne L., ed. *Hamlet.* Case Studies in Contemporary Criticism Series. Boston: Bedford/St. Martin's, 1994.

Wood, Robert E. *Some Necessary Questions of the Play: A Stage-Centered Analysis of Shakespeare's* Hamlet. Lewisburg, PA: Bucknell UP, 1994.

Henrik Ibsen

A Doll House (p. 1309)

Seen by many as the unofficial "father of modern drama," Ibsen had a career that went through many phases. *A Doll House* is a pioneer work that attempts to portray controversial social issues in a realistic manner without recourse to melodrama or sentimentality. John Gassner describes Ibsen as "too radical" for the nineteenth century but "too conservative" for the twentieth. It is true that by today's standards Nora's rebellion may not seem so major, but in 1879 it was considered downright immoral to suggest that a woman could be capable of abandoning her husband and children. By showing Torvald's romanticized marriage to be an empty dream, Ibsen was exploding the conventional, sentimental Victorian ideals of the "little woman" and the "angel in the house." As Gassner suggests, Nora's leaving to pursue "self-fulfillment" challenges the traditional "sanctity of marriage" in its innate plea for "female emancipation." Students, however, should be warned against solely considering the issue of women's rights within the play, for Ibsen is not so narrowly focused. *A Doll House* asks us to consider issues of hypocrisy, pseudo-respectability, human nature, and the "life-lie" that go beyond gender. For Ibsen, the "life-lie" is an individual's greatest offense against himself and others. It occurs when we do not allow ourselves to live according to our true natures but hide behind idealizations and deceits: Both Nora and Torvald are guilty of this.

George Bernard Shaw's *The Quintessence of Ibsenism* (1891) did much to bring Ibsen to critical attention. Defining idealism as that which masks realities that are too unpleasant to face, and realism as that which unmasks the truth for the general audience, Shaw saw himself and Ibsen as "realists," for both liked to engage in the stripping away of masks. Shaw also introduced the idea of the "discussion play" as opposed to the "well-made play." A well-made play creates suspense through meticulous plotting that gradually releases information toward a final denouement; both Shaw and Ibsen felt this to be artificial. A discussion play can be equally well-crafted, but it leads to an unresolved discussion that supersedes the demands of plot and allows the audience to judge events for themselves. The heated controversies surrounding *A Doll House* indicate that this is an effective, early example of a discussion play. That Ibsen intended to disturb his audience and make them think is without question; that he does so without resorting to diatribe, and with such a well-crafted and entertaining piece, is a measure of his genius.

The realism of Ibsen's work goes beyond mere set detail, although that is an important aspect of how he wished his plays to be produced. Ibsen tries to create psychologically real people in commonplace social situations. One should not ignore his use of symbolism, but it does not negate the sense of reality he generates. The furnishings of the Helmers' "doll house" are an early indication of the owner's consumer mentality, where appearances count most. From its piano, etchings, and "well-bound" books to its stove and comfortable chairs, it is on the surface an ideal setting. But is it a real home or just the doll house of the title? The two doors to the room symbolize Nora's eventual options: One leads to Torvald's inner sanctum and the other to the outside world. Ibsen's symbols do not intrude so much as help point to what lies beneath the surface. Nora's desire for macaroons ensures we understand she is yet a child who needs to grow up; she is, after all, a willing "doll." The stripped and disheveled Christmas tree indicates the extent to which Nora has been shattered, though she continues to uphold a veneer of gaiety in front of others. The fact that Torvald will not even allow Nora to read the mail, locking it in a box to which only he holds a key, shows how far he has kept her apart from the outside world in order that she may remain under his total control.

Initially, Nora does deserve the incessant diminutives Torvald heaps on her, although one may resent the intellectual disdain such objectifications imply. She virtually twitters as she throws things around, leaving them for servants to pick up, and coyly flirts with her husband and childishly plays with her children: She is a "little lark," "a little squirrel," "a little featherbrain." Her frivolous world is in stark contrast to Torvald's cautious, ordered world of business. He naturally prefers the sanctuary of his study or of work, merely using his wife as an occasional diversion or entertainment. But his world will be shown to be as remote and cold as Norway itself, a strict world of men and law in which women are allowed no footage. As Nora develops, we see her being related, in contrast, to the warmer, more passionate climes of Italy. It is to Italy that she takes Torvald after showing some spirit in defying the male world and procuring the necessary funds. It is an Italian dance, the tarantella, that Ibsen uses to indicate her feminine growth and development into a woman. When Nora threatens to burst out as a woman in the tarantella, Torvald feels compelled to control her and quiet her down, although, to his consternation, his attempts are less than effective. He will not be able to comprehend or prevent her growth.

Although Nora is initially naive, she is not stupid, and Ibsen has prepared us from the start for her hidden depths. Students should note the difference between the way she talks to her husband and the way she talks to Dr. Rank or Mrs. Linde. Although she banters with all three, it is on different levels, and with different awarenesses. She is capable of both manipulating her husband, playing up to his expectations of her as a "featherhead," and fooling him: He thought her to be making Christmas decorations when she was really engaged in copying to make some extra cash. She eats macaroons in defiance of his commands and openly denies having done so. She has a spirit that has not yet been crushed, albeit the only independence she can achieve is through deceit and lying. Although Nora plays the childish role Torvald demands of her, we know that inwardly she resents it. We see this in the pride she displays over her "adult" actions of getting money and independently working to repay it. The fact that the law actually prohibited a woman from borrowing money without a male relative's consent is important. Norway is a patriarchal society, and it will not be easy for Nora to combat it alone. She takes an incredibly brave action in leaving at the play's end.

Nora wins our sympathy through her generous spirit and because of her domineering husband. Her generous nature is indicated from the start as she overtips the porter and earnestly tries to assist her old friend, Mrs. Linde. Her spending is noticeably on others and not on herself. Even the crime she has committed was done to restore her husband's health. He had thoughtlessly refused to raise the money they needed for the trip the doctor recommended, preferring instead to risk leaving his wife and newborn child without a husband and father. Nora's marriage has no pretense of equality — Torvald simply cannot envisage such a relationship. He selfishly runs their lives according to his own whims and does not feel it necessary to consider his wife's feelings. Nora is aware that their marriage is based on appearances and realizes she may need something to keep Torvald's interest once her looks have faded. What Ibsen is telling us is that a true marriage needs a deeper bond than Torvald and Nora have managed to create. Nora has invested a great deal in her marriage, far more than Torvald could ever recognize, but she has invested unwisely and will be forced to realize this sad fact.

We may ask why Nora decides to admit the forgery to Krogstad; he is only guessing and has no firm proof. Is it an act of defiance betraying her inner strength, or simple naiveté? Her natural impulse is for truth rather than deception; thus she instinctively answers Torvald's questions about Krogstad honestly and ensures Torvald's unfortunate decision to fire Krogstad. In her dealings with Krogstad, Nora finds herself swiftly out of her depth; she is too innocent and inexperienced in the ways of the world. She is unable to offer the appropriate defense, appealing instead to idealistic notions of honor and sensibility. She has some awareness of the power relations of the male world, but not enough to judge accurately how to deal with Krogstad. Torvald is similarly incompetent in his dealings, as he is too concerned with his ego to judge clearly. While we can sympathize with Nora's failings, it is harder for us to sympathize with Torvald, who misjudges through pompous pride rather than ignorance.

We see the irony as Torvald snobbishly condemns Krogstad, unaware that his condemnation is going straight to the heart of his wife. Torvald's own respectability is not so pure; we know that he turned a blind eye to his father-in-law's criminal practices and even helped to clear him. He can afford to live the life he does only because of sacrifices his wife has made — sacrifices he could never even acknowledge. He dismisses Krogstad not because of the man's reputation but for personal reasons; thus he invalidates any idea of merit being integral to a man's success. When Nora calls him "narrow-minded," she is blurting out a truth. Torvald is a hypocrite, and his emotionless calculations make him scarcely human.

Although a minor character, Dr. Rank performs a number of functions, one of which is as a foil to Torvald. In contrast to Torvald, he treats Nora with respect and an undemanding love. As a cynic, his commentary on the world is a realistic vision of its amorality. The morally corrupt do tend to fare better than the scrupulously honest, as the world itself is not concerned with honesty, just the appearance of it. Rank's father contracted syphilis from extramarital liaisons, and his son has congenital syphilis from which he will soon die. Thus he becomes an emblem of the way the older generation's depravity can continue to affect future generations. Similarly, Nora is right when she realizes that she must change before she can be a fit mother. She does not wish her children to suffer the same blindness and restrictions that have dominated her generation.

The scene in which Rank declares his love touches on many issues in the play. Confessing his love to Nora lifts a huge burden from Rank's shoulders, and after this he is noticeably buoyant, despite his impending death. This underlines the necessity for truth-telling, as secrets are a heavy burden. In addition, we gain further evidence that Nora is not so unaware of reality. Nora knew of Rank's love all along and is annoyed at his confession. While this love remained unspoken, she could pretend that it did not exist; after all, this is a world in which appearances take precedence over truths. Rank is a man with whom Nora has talked and behaved more openly, having been able to set aside her doll persona. By treating her as a real human being, he has been able to give her the companionship Torvald could not. Nora's fine sensibility is underlined by her refusal to take Rank's money once he has altered their relationship by declaring his passion.

Although we may initially be surprised at her refusal, her impulse is the right one, reinforced by the realization that Krogstad will not allow her to buy back the bond.

Mrs. Linde, meanwhile, can be seen as a foil to Nora. While Nora married into an idealized dream of love, Mrs. Linde first married because she felt responsible for her family. She gave up her true love for the financial security of a richer man who subsequently lost his money and died, leaving her to go out into the world and work to support her mother and younger brothers. Though harsh, this has perhaps been the making of Mrs. Linde; she has gained self-respect from her achievements. She is now a woman who can bind herself to a man she respects without losing that independence. Her misfortune has allowed her to tap her own hidden resources, and she may be the lead Nora must learn to follow.

Krogstad, the man Mrs. Linde once loved, is far more human than Torvald. He did not rest on scrupulous sensibilities when his family's well-being was at stake, a decision Ibsen does not actually condemn. Although Krogstad initially appears to be the villain of the piece, Ibsen turns the tables. Krogstad is scarred by life and knows the way of the world — that it is essentially corrupt and run by appearances. Respectability is a must for certain advancements in society, but it need be only a surface affair and is something that can be acquired rather than won with honor. Both Krogstad and Mrs. Linde have suffered in life, and both have learned from these blows to become attuned to the real ways of the world and be supremely practical people. In an interesting gender reversal, Mrs. Linde proposes to him as she persuades him that they need each other equally — and we cannot fault the honesty of this. Indeed, they exhibit the qualities on which a true marriage should be based: mutual honesty and respect rather than concealment and falsehood. Thus the woman who married for money and the man with the dubious reputation defeat our expectations as they turn out to be the examples of how to behave. Krogstad even takes pity on Nora and returns the bond so that he might be worthy of his new wife. Indeed, it is Nora and Torvald who have done everything wrong.

Torvald's image of Nora is a romantic fantasy. Indeed, it restricts Nora from being human as it denies her her own personality. She finally learns to reject Torvald's doll-like image of her as she realizes that this rejection is the only way she can reclaim her humanity. Torvald helps her in this decision by his reaction to her dealings with Krogstad: He completely condemns her, does not consider her altruistic motives, and only considers how he will be affected. Nora realizes that she has been the victim, also, of a romantic dream, having expected her husband to stand by her and even to nobly take the blame. She now realizes that such "a wonderful thing" is only fantasy. She needs to enter the real world so that she can discover how it operates and discover an identity for herself. Torvald tries to rekindle his dream world when he is assured there is no longer any threat from Krogstad, but Nora refuses to allow this retreat. She insists they face each other honestly. She recognizes her own fault in having allowed first her father and then Torvald to use her as a plaything, but she concludes that theirs is the greater fault for expecting her to fulfill such a role and for not allowing her to be any more than that. Torvald offers to teach her now but it is too late: She has lost respect for him. We must also seriously doubt that he has the ability to teach her, as he still has lessons to learn himself. He does offer to change, and she rightly judges that this can happen only if she leaves.

SUSAN C. W. ABBOTSON

Questions for Discussion

1. What can be assessed from a careful consideration of how the Helmers' home and home life are depicted?

2. In what ways does Nora change in each of the three acts? In what aspects does she remain constant? How is the Nora at the close of the play a better or worse person than she is at the start?

3. How does Torvald treat his wife? What lies at the heart of this treatment?

4. What kind of deceits does Ibsen suggest can be condoned and what deceits does he condemn? Is motivation an issue?

5. What is the function and significance of the following: the macaroons, the Christmas tree, the children's presents, the tarantella, the letter box, the idea of dolls and doll houses?

6. What is the role and function of Dr. Rank? How does his relationship with Nora contrast with her marital relationship?

7. What are the roles and functions of Krogstad and Mrs. Linde?

8. For which of the characters in the play can we feel any sympathy, and why?

9. How would having Nora stay instead of leave change the way we perceive the message of the play?

10. What aspects of this play seem to be particularly realistic and what aspects do not?

11. Could this be called a comedy or a tragedy? Does the play exhibit elements of either of those genres?

12. What do you think might happen next to these characters?

Topics for Writing

1. Contrast the relationship of Krogstad and Mrs. Linde with that of Torvald and Nora Helmer. Trace what we know of the changes each relationship goes or has gone through and assess which one Ibsen seems to prefer.

2. Using *A Doll House* as evidence, what does Ibsen seem to suggest about the nature of women and how they should be treated within the home and society in general?

3. **RESPONDING CREATIVELY** Imagine one year has passed and Nora returns home to visit her husband and children. Write a short story or play scene that illustrates this meeting. Consider how both Torvald and Nora may or may not have changed in the intervening year.

4. **MAKING CONNECTIONS** Compare *A Doll House* with Arthur Miller's *Death of a Salesman* (p. 1423) and assess how far each can be considered realistic and tragic. Bear in mind the playwrights' views on the nature of both realism and tragedy.

Commentaries

Henrik Ibsen, *"Notes for 'A Doll House,'"* p. 1591.
George Bernard Shaw, *"On 'A Doll House,'"* p. 1613.
Joan Templeton, *"Is 'A Doll House' a Feminist Text?"* p. 1615.
Liv Ullmann, *"On Performing Nora in Ibsen's 'A Doll House,'"* p. 1617.

Suggested Readings

Ahmad, Shaiuddin, and Angela Gawel. "The Politics of Money: Incomplete Feminism in *A Doll's House*." *Dalhousie Review* 70 (1990): 170–90.

Davies, H. Neville. "Not Just a Bang and a Whimper: The Inconclusiveness of Ibsen's A Doll's House." *Critical Quarterly* 24.3 (1982): 33–43.

Fjelde, Rolf, ed. *Ibsen: A Collection of Critical Essays.* Englewood Cliffs, NJ: Prentice, 1965.

Johnston, Brian. "Three Stages of *A Doll House*." *Comparative Drama* 25.4 (1991–92): 311–28.

Lebowitz, Naomi. *Ibsen and the Great World.* Baton Rouge: Louisiana State UP, 1990.

Lyons, Charles R., ed. *Critical Essays on Henrik Ibsen.* Boston: G. K. Hall, 1987.

McFarlane, James. *Ibsen and Meaning: Studies, Essays, and Prefaces 1953–87.* Norwich, CT: Norvik, 1989.

Quigley, Austin E. "*A Doll's House* Revisited." Modern Drama 27 (1984): 584–603.

Shafer, Yvonne, ed. *Approaches to Teaching Ibsen's* A Doll's House. New York: MLA, 1985.

———. *Henrik Ibsen: Life, Work, and Criticism.* Fredericton, NB: York, 1985.

Templeton, Joan. "*The Doll House* Backlash: Criticism, Feminism, and Ibsen." *PMLA* 104 (January 1989): 28–40.

Young, Robin. *Time's Disinherited Children: Childhood, Regression, and Sacrifice in the Plays of Henrik Ibsen.* Norwich, CT: Norvik, 1989.

SUSAN GLASPELL

Trifles (p. 1362)

This play is not about murder so much as marriage. Glaspell leaves us in no doubt that Minnie Wright killed her husband, but John Wright's death only provides the occasion of the play. Its focus is on the differing male and female reactions as they search for a motive. Glaspell contrasts male and female perspectives throughout the play and engages our sympathy firmly on the side of the women. While the men vainly seek signs of violent rage, the women, with growing empathy, are able to recognize the signs of quiet desperation under which many women of their time were forced to live. We are asked to witness Mrs. Wright's life rather than Mr. Wright's death, and we are shown that the true "crime" has been the way she was being subjugated and "destroyed" by her marriage. We never see Minnie Wright; we learn about her only through others' comments. This dramatic method serves the dual function of allowing her to avoid particularity and so serve as a symbol of all women trapped in loveless marriages, as well as ensuring that our attention is focused on the reactions of others.

The play's opening firmly sets the scene. The gloomy kitchen is where Minnie Wright struggled to stay sane, and the domineering men immediately take charge while the women remain on the periphery. We learn that John Wright said little and demanded the same from his wife. We can also recognize that he is not so different from these other men, who clearly see women as a subservient group whose concerns hold little importance. Thus in their search for hard evidence to convict Mrs. Wright, they will repeatedly overlook the existing evidence that the women uncover, dismissing it as mere "trifles." Mrs. Hale's early defense of Mrs. Wright against the belittling comments of Mr. Henderson foreshadows her growing sympathy and complicity with the "murderess."

According to the play, once a woman marries she loses her former identity, along with her maiden name, and becomes subsumed by her husband: Note how even the sheriff calls his wife "Mrs. Peters." The lives of Mrs. Peters and Mrs. Hale may not be quite as dreary as the life Mrs. Wright evidently led, but, as women, they are aware of the limitations that a patriarchal society has placed on their gender. Their husbands are a little more communicative, and both women have children to distract them, but their days are no less yoked to the home and the demands of their husbands. Standing in the kitchen, the center of every farm wife's existence, Mrs. Hale and Mrs. Peters soon piece together the clues to events that continue to elude the men. Before marriage, Minnie Foster had been singing and full of life; placed within the confines of her marriage, however — symbolized by the house she lives in "down in a hollow" where you "don't see the road" and the concentric bars of the log-cabin pattern of her quilt and the canary cage — she has had all the life strangled out of her. Her husband destroyed Minnie Foster, just as he destroys her canary. Her revenge, knotting a rope around his neck while he slept, eventually appears just. Mrs. Hale leads Mrs. Peters to a full understanding of the situation as she removes the clues they discover, unpicking the erratic stitching in the quilt and putting the dead bird in her pocket.

Having known Minnie from the past and being a neighbor who had neglected to visit for over a year, Mrs. Hale accepts her own guilt in not having helped Minnie. Guided by Mrs. Hale, both women now take on responsibility by removing evidence and lying to Mr. Henderson, the county attorney, about how the canary died. Mrs. Hale's final retort, "We call it — knot it, Mr. Henderson," becomes layered with significance. The words themselves sound defiant against Henderson's facetious tone, and she mocks him with the evidence that she and Mrs. Peters have found and that even now he continues to miss — the knot around Mr. Wright's neck being clearly related to such a quilting knot. The emphatic "*We* call it" further suggests the "knot" or bond that has been tied between these women and Minnie against the men. Glaspell wishes us to recognize the potential strength bestowed on women who forge such bonds — a strength that comes with unity. It is a strength that will allow them not only to withstand male subjugation but also, we hope, begin to forge an independent female identity.

As Barbara Ozieblo points out in *The Provincetown Players*, "Although Glaspell condones the breaking of those codes of behavior which strangle women, she does not alienate the men who make them up." *Trifles* is not antimale so much as an attempt to awaken audiences to the dilemmas of womanhood. Feminism was still in its infancy when the play was written, and even its supporters were at times ambivalent as to where it might lead. The rebellion of Glaspell's women is consequently minimal; Minnie is safely locked away in prison. Mrs. Hale and Mrs. Peters may protect her, but they do not speak openly to the men in her defense.

Susan C. W. Abbotson

Questions for Discussion

1. How do you explain the play's title?
2. How does the setting of the play contribute to our understanding of Minnie Wright's position?
3. How does the entrance of the characters distinguish between the men and the women?
4. How can Hale's description of Minnie Wright as she sits in her rocking chair be interpreted from a female point of view rather than the male one that Hale provides?
5. Is there any doubt that Minnie Wright killed her husband? In what ways might her trial be affected if Minnie Wright was facing a court at the close of the twentieth century rather than at its start?
6. How should we interpret the behavior of Mr. Henderson, the county attorney? Why is Mrs. Hale so annoyed by him?
7. In what ways can Mrs. Peters be said to be a foil to Mrs. Hale?
8. What are the main differences between Minnie Foster and Minnie Wright?
9. Is Mr. Wright so very different from the other men we witness in this play?
10. Why do the men miss all the real evidence, and why do the women cover it up?
11. Why do we never see either of the Wrights directly?
12. In what ways is Minnie Foster related to the canary?

Topics for Writing

1. Is Mr. Wright really so wrong? We are told John Wright was not a bad man, "he didn't drink, and kept his word . . . and paid his debts." Minnie Wright's murder of her husband would be condoned by feminist critics, like Catherine Belsey, as a "defiance of patriarchy." Was it a "crime" for Minnie to strangle her husband or simple justice?

2. In what ways does the ironic title of the play shape its meaning? Explain the full significance of the title as well as the symbolism of the house, quilt, bird cage, and bird.

3. **RESPONDING CREATIVELY**   The play ends with the suggestion that Minnie Wright may just manage to "get away with murder." Write a play script or short story depicting the trial that will take place and include as many of the characters from the play as possible. Consider how the time period in which this play takes place will be an influential factor regarding what occurs during this trial.

4. **RESPONDING CREATIVELY**   Write the diary of Minnie Foster/Wright from just before she met John Wright up until she is taken to jail.

5. **MAKING CONNECTIONS**   How does *Trifles* compare to the short story "A Jury of Her Peers" (p. 185), and in what ways has Glaspell changed the emphasis of her account? (See the student paper in Part Four, "Comparison and Contrast," analyzing Glaspell's story and play.)

6. **MAKING CONNECTIONS**   Compare the differences that are portrayed between the lives of men and women in *Trifles* and Henrik Ibsen's *A Doll House* (p. 1309).

Connections

Susan Glaspell, "*A Jury of Her Peers,*" p. 185.
Lynn Nottage, *POOF!* p. 1561.

Commentary

Leonard Mustazza, "*Generic Translation and Thematic Shift in Glaspell's 'Trifles' and 'A Jury of Her Peers,'*" p. 1598.

Suggested Readings

Alkalay-Gut, Karen. " 'Jury of Her Peers': The Importance of *Trifles.*" *Studies in Short Fiction* 21 (1984): 1–9.

Bach, Gerhard. "Susan Glaspell: Provincetown Playwright." *Great Lakes Review* 4 (1978): 31–43.

Ben-Zvi, Linda, ed. *Susan Glaspell: Essays on Her Theater and Fiction.* Ann Arbor: U of Michigan P, 1995.

Dymkowski, Christine. "On the Edge: The Plays of Susan Glaspell." *Modern Drama* 31 (1988): 91–105.

Makowsky, Veronica. *Susan Glaspell's Century of American Women: A Critical Interpretation of Her Work.* New York: Oxford UP, 1993.

Mustazza, Leonard. "Generic Translation and Thematic Shift in Susan Glaspell's *Trifles* and 'A Jury of Her Peers.'" *Studies in Short Fiction* 26 (1989): 489–96.

Noe, Marcia. *Susan Glaspell: Voice from the Heartland.* Macomb: Western Illinois UP, 1983.

Smith, Beverly A. "Women's Work — *Trifles?* The Skill and Insights of Playwright Susan Glaspell." *International Journal of Women's Studies* 5 (1982): 172–84.

Waterman, Arthur E. *Susan Glaspell.* New York: Twayne, 1966.
Zehfuss, Ruth E. "The Law and the Ladies in *Trifles." Teaching English in the Two-Year College* (February 1992): 42–44.

TENNESSEE WILLIAMS

The Glass Menagerie (p. 1374)

Students should not view *The Glass Menagerie* as realistic drama but as a memory play, as all we are shown is related through the lens of Tom Wingfield's guilty memory after he has abandoned his mother and disabled sister by going off to sea in search of adventure. Williams's staging captures this nostalgic mood with dim lighting, recurring musical themes, and screen images. Williams warns us that memory tends to distort, omitting or exaggerating details, and is an emotional rather than logical response to events. What we witness is a replay of Tom's earlier life as he recalls the formative moments of his past. The play is autobiographical in that Williams's early life followed a similar pattern: living in poverty with an absent father, dominated by a strong mother, wasting his talents working in a shoe factory and feeling guilt over neglecting his shy sister, Rose (who had been given a lobotomy in the absence of his protection). Just as Eugene O'Neill tries to explain and exorcise his family-related guilt in *Long Day's Journey into Night,* so does Williams in *The Glass Menagerie,* and both come to the same conclusion. Fear and guilt are inescapable, crippling, and reducing, but they are not things from which one can escape by physically running away. They are psychological and will travel with you.

Williams does not allow Tom to shoulder sole blame but insists we recognize how much others contribute to his torment. Amanda, Laura, and Tom are individually imprisoned, each isolated from the others in fantasy worlds of their own creation. Amanda is trapped in memories of the South and her childhood, possibly more imagination than fact, but both have now vanished in reality. She dresses in her old clothes in an effort to recapture her illusions and will sacrifice her daughter's potential happiness by co-opting Jim as if he were one of her own suitors. She cannot let go of the past because she cannot face the fact that her husband left her, and so she dwells on her memory of a happy and opulent life on a southern plantation before that occurred. An unforgiving woman whose son must always be the first to apologize after a row, Amanda can never forgive her husband for leaving. She lives in a fake world of sentimental illusion because reality would destroy her. She will not come to terms with her present urban dwelling and the poverty in which the family now lives. On the rare moments Amanda is forced to face reality, she is drained of vitality until she can retreat again into her nostalgia.

Laura, crippled and shy, hides, behind her difference from her mother, in a world created for her by her records and glass animals. Her records are old and in their antiquity create a euphoric past where she can be happy. Through her glass creatures she can create a safe and innocent world where she is in charge, in contrast to the scary, confusing world she glimpses outside her room. She effectively retires from life, and her awakening with Jim is only transitory. Neither the outside world nor her mother can accept her extreme sensitivity, but she does not reject the world so much as it rejects her. The only place she has left to live is in her fantasy world. Her home life has been gradually whittled away as first her father leaves and then Tom. Outside of her fantasy world she is utterly dependent, so much so that she must even ask her mother what it is she should be wishing for on the moon.

Tom feels trapped in a routine job that is crushing his sensitive spirit and desire to be a writer, but he cannot quit because he feels responsible for his family. Amanda constantly takes pains to remind him of this responsibility to keep him there. At work he is as isolated as Laura is at home, and home, to Tom, is a nailed-up coffin in which he has no life. He tells Laura about a stage magician he went to see who was able to get out of a nailed-up coffin and wishes that he too had this ability to escape. Tom cannot leave the home as cleanly as his father did, and his only escape is into dreams of adventure stimulated by the movies. Tom is aware that the movies are not real, but he tells himself that they might be as he can see no other form of escape. What he really wants is to live someone else's life as he has no idea what to do with his own.

When Tom finally does leave, it is only a physical escape, for he cannot psychologically leave his family behind. After the initial sense of freedom, disillusionment sets in and turns to guilt as his imagination transforms innocent and unconnected items into cruel reminders of his poor sister. Then Tom becomes totally trapped, a prisoner of his own remorse. Tom's only release is that of death, suggested in the play's closing image of the candles being extinguished. This is an ambiguous allusion to both the brief candle of life that Shakespeare has extinguished in *Macbeth* and to the home fire to which Tom can never return: The death could be Tom's or Laura's.

Tom's feelings of guilt for Laura are greater than Amanda's because he sees Laura's difficulties, whereas Amanda ignores them in order to avoid such guilt. Amanda is, in fact, in danger of seeming a monster. She relies on Tom as the family provider and so refuses to allow him any freedom, even though she knows he is unhappy. She dominates him as one would a small child by treating him like a small child, for allowing him the mind of an adult might lead to rebellion. As an adult, Tom does try to rebel, but Amanda quells such moments by reminding him of his particular responsibility to Laura. She forces her illusions on them and manipulates them to create her own ideal environment. Through dramatic posturing she ensures their guilt and uses that to force them both into doing what she wants.

Laura is as easily broken as her glass; her mother's attempts to relive her own youth through Laura completely desiccate Laura's last shreds of self-confidence. Amanda continually expects too much of Laura, especially because she refuses to acknowledge any of her daughter's problems. Yet Williams insists that there is "much to admire in Amanda," and we should include love and pity in our judgment of her. She is admirable in her endurance, for her life has not been easy. She was abandoned by her husband and left to rear two children on her own, one of whom needs special treatment. At the end of the play "her silliness is gone and she has dignity and tragic beauty" as she comforts her daughter. Amanda's use of "we" and "us" rather than "you" when talking of Laura denotes the strong bond she has forged with her daughter's future — she intends to hold onto Laura for life, but we need not see anything sinister in that, as Laura at least has someone to look after her. Amanda has been a failure all her life and tries to make up for this by organizing everyone around her and forcing them to be successes. What goes wrong with this plan is her limited imagination; she cannot accept the roads her children would choose and tries to manipulate them onto roads of her choosing — roads that are entirely unsuitable. Laura's job as a secretary and Tom's in the shoe factory are both utterly antagonistic to their natures.

This is not just a family tale, however, and Williams wishes us to consider what he believes are the root causes behind success and failure in people's lives. Occasional references to the outside world suggest that the Wingfields are not the only people to be leading illusory lives, for people ignore Spain's troubles and the impending world war by living lives of apparent gaiety. Even Jim as a representative of this outer world exudes a lost sense of promise and is not entirely honest. He enjoys Tom's company largely because he allows him to live on his past glories, having known him since his high school glory days. Jim's rise to fame has been restricted and quelled in the real world, but, like Amanda, he refuses to give in. He has the self-confidence that Tom lacks, so maybe he will make it. Meanwhile, he boosts that confidence by playing along with Amanda and drawing Laura out for a brief moment before getting cold feet and escaping down that fire escape in a way Tom can only dream about.

SUSAN C. W. ABBOTSON

Questions for Discussion

1. Considering Williams's production notes, how does he intend the screens, music, and lighting in the play to operate? Do you think they are effective?
2. How does the play's setting — with its alleyway, fire escape, and glowing photograph — contribute to its meaning?
3. How important is the use of memory in this play, and how does it affect the events we witness and the way the story is told?
4. How does Amanda control and manipulate her children, and to what ends?
5. Why does Tom spend so much time at the movies? Why does he find his job so difficult? How is he like his father?
6. According to what we are shown and told in the play, what are the differences between northern and southern values and ways of life?
7. Why is Laura unable to complete her secretarial course? What do we learn about Laura from where she chooses to go when she pretends to go to typing school? Why is the spotlight on her when Amanda and Tom are arguing?
8. Why is Amanda so concerned to get Laura a husband? Is there any irony in this?
9. What motivates Jim's behavior, and does he help Laura or set her back? How is he different from the Wingfields? Is he any more likely to succeed?
10. How does the symbol of the unicorn (whole and broken) work? Why does Laura give it to Jim? What other objects and events in the play appear to be symbolic?
11. How far has Tom achieved his dreams of escape and adventure by the end of the play?
12. How do the glimpses we get of events in the outside world relate to the play? In what ways can this play be said to be about failure and its consequences?

Topics for Writing

1. Analyze the images of imprisonment and escape in *The Glass Menagerie* and discuss how they relate to the central characters.
2. How far can the women in this play be considered "sympathetic" characters?
3. **RESPONDING CREATIVELY**   How would this play be different if it was related from one of the other characters' memories? Select your character and provide a commentary to frame one of the play's scenes in the same way Williams uses Tom throughout the play. You should consider how this scene might have affected your character and how this character might choose to color his or her memory.
4. **RESPONDING CREATIVELY**   Decide what you feel is the central message of *The Glass Menagerie* and write a poem describing this theme, linking together as many of the play's symbolic items and events as you can.
5. Memory is central to *The Glass Menagerie*. Describe how it influences the play and what Williams believes to be the power and importance of memory.

Commentaries

Benjamin Nelson, *"Problems in 'The Glass Menagerie,'"* p. 1605.
Tennessee Williams, *"Production Notes to 'The Glass Menagerie,'"* p. 1618.

Suggested Readings

Arnott, Catherine, ed. *Tennessee Williams on File.* New York: Methuen, 1985.
Griffin, Alice. *Understanding Tennessee Williams.* Columbia: U of South Carolina P, 1995.
Hirsch, Foster. *A Portrait of the Artist: The Plays of Tennessee Williams.* Port Washington, NY: Kennikat, 1979.
Jones, John H. "The Missing Link: The Father in *The Glass Menagerie.*" Notes on *Mississippi Writers* 20 (1988): 29–38.
Leverich, Lyle. *Tom: The Unknown Tennessee Williams.* New York: Crown, 1995.
Levy, Eric. "'Through the Soundproof Glass': The Prison of Self-Consciousness in *The Glass Menagerie.*" Modern Drama 36 (1993): 529–37.
Mann, Bruce. "Tennessee Williams and the Rose-Garden Husband." *American Drama* 1 (Fall 1991): 16–26.
Parker, R. B., ed. The Glass Menagerie: *A Collection of Critical Essays.* Englewood Cliffs, NJ: Prentice, 1983.
Spoto, Donald. *The Kindness of Strangers: The Life of Tennessee Williams.* Boston: Little, 1985.
Stanton, Stephen S. *Tennessee Williams: A Collection of Critical Essays.* Englewood Cliffs, NJ: Prentice, 1977.
Thompson, Judith J. *Tennessee Williams' Plays: Memory, Myth, and Symbol.* New York: Lang, 1987.
Usui, Masami. "'A World of Her Own' in Tennessee Williams' *The Glass Menagerie.*" Studies in Culture and the Humanities 1 (1992): 21–37.
Williams, Tennessee. *Memoirs.* Garden City, NY: Doubleday, 1975.

ARTHUR MILLER

Death of a Salesman (p. 1423)

Death of a Salesman covers the last twenty-four hours of Willy Loman's life. A victim of both a heartless capitalist society and his own misguided dreams, Willy's eventual suicide is presented in tragic dimensions. We learn of past events leading up to this moment by seeing Willy's memories acted out on the stage. The transitions between current action and memory are fluid, and occasionally the two occur simultaneously; some students will find this confusing. Writing in a style that has become known as "subjective realism," Miller carefully blends a realistic picture of a salesman's home and life in the post-Depression years of the early 1940s with the subjective thoughts that are going through the protagonist's head. He achieves the same blend of realism and expressionism that Eugene O'Neill had attempted in *Bound East for Cardiff,* and he develops it into a full-length play. Willy doesn't have flashbacks so much as immediate experiences in which time has clearly been dislocated. "The past," Miller suggests in his autobiography, "is a formality, merely a dimmer present, for everything we are is at every moment alive in us." The concepts of past and present are presented to the audience through careful staging and the suggestive use of scrims and lighting.

Miller's strong sense of moral and social commitment runs throughout the play. Heavily influenced by Ibsen, Miller follows a similar style of dramaturgy and displays the same zeal regarding social issues. The aims of *Death of a Salesman* are twofold. Miller wanted to write a social drama confronting the problems of an ordinary man in a conscienceless, capitalistic social system, and also to write a modern tragedy adapting Aristotelian theory to allow for a common man as tragic protagonist. Students should read the commentaries in which Miller explains why he feels Willy Loman is a tragic figure. We should not allow Willy's domestic situation to blind us to his tragic stature. Miller ties his definition of heroism to a notion of personal dignity. Willy is heroic because he strives to be free and to make his mark in society despite the odds against him. Although he is destroyed in the process, he is motivated by love, and his destruction allows for learning to take place. Through Willy's sacrifice, Biff is able to accept his father's love while recognizing the emptiness of the dream Willy espoused. Willy Loman had accepted at face value overpublicized ideas of material success, and therein lies his tragedy. His downfall and final defeat illustrate not only the failure of a man but also the failure of a way of life.

From the start of the play students should recognize that Linda is very worried and Willy is very tired. For all of Willy's talk, this is a couple at the end of their tether. Willy is like a wounded animal near the end of its life, trying to die with dignity. His whole life has been a sell-out, his sons have turned out badly, and his relationship with Biff has soured. Willy recalls his idealized past both to escape and attempt to discover what went wrong. He searches for the answer to a question he has asked all his life: How does one become successful? Willy has convinced himself that the answer is to be well-liked, and he passes this belief on to his two sons. Miller makes it clear, however, that being well-liked has little to do with success. In this world people get ahead through hard work (Charley and Bernard), inheritance (Howard), or sheer luck (Ben). Neither Howard nor Ben waste any time trying to be liked, and both are depicted as selfish, brusque, and rude.

Related by his recording device to cold technology, Howard foreshadows the hard-hearted businessmen who will decimate their work forces as cheaper automation takes over. Howard has not worked for his success; he merely inherited it from his father. He has no time for his father's old salesman and does not even listen to what Willy tries to tell him. Howard represents an uncaring and exploitative business world — a world in which being well-liked holds no relevance. He has used Willy up and now dismisses him without a qualm. His only evidence of humanity is his uneasiness at having to witness Willy's reaction to this dismissal.

When the real world forces its attention on Willy in this way, he swiftly retreats to his dream world, where he can seek Ben's advice. Ben, a self-made man, tells his tale of finding a fortune in the African jungle as if it were some kind of solution, but it is merely a boast. Ben is a selfish man, and he survives the jungle by plundering it. Willy and Ben's father had left a wife and two young sons to seek success in Alaska, and he was never heard from again. Ben similarly ignores family responsibility as he follows in their father's footsteps. Ben's hardness has helped him to survive, and he has chanced on a fortune by luck. Willy could never do what Ben has done, and so Ben's advice is useless to him. Willy blames Linda for holding him back from going with his brother, but would he have taken that risk if he had been free? No; he is too fearful. He is right to be scared; the chances of such success are small. Willy cannot be as selfish as his brother. He is not the perfect father, but he does love his family and accepts the responsibilities their existence demands.

Charley, on the other hand, is successful, content, and a nice guy. Charley is satisfied with moderate success without feeling compelled to be the best, and he doesn't take any short-cuts but relies on steady, hard work. He recognizes that one's humanity has nothing to do with one's level of success. Charley passes on his values to his offspring just as Willy does. As children, Biff and Happy idolized their father and looked down on Bernard for his more cautious lifestyle and belief in work. Students should recognize, however, that Bernard represents an ideal in the play. He works for his success and it is well-earned, but it is not the be-all of his existence. This is the lesson Willy refuses to learn. Willy's sons look to him for guidance, but he feeds them unrealistic dreams. His wife supports and loves him, but he has an affair. Willy fails as a salesman and as a husband and father because he has no strong values.

As a youth, Biff was led to believe that because he was well-liked, he could get away with anything. He begins to steal — a football from school, lumber for the house, a crate of balls from Bill Oliver. Willy is desperate that Biff should succeed in life, and so, instead of punishing him, he condones the thefts and makes excuses. Willy neglects to instill in his son moral values. Biff is successful in high school as a football player, but he never goes to college. Initially he had planned to retake the math course he needed to get into college, but when he catches his father with a mistress, Biff's self-confidence dissipates and he loses respect for his father. As a result, his belief in the fantasies his father has fed him cannot be maintained. Out in the real world, away from the destructive influence of his father, Biff begins to recognize his own true nature. He takes some time to learn, spending a stretch in jail, but he eventually replaces his father's dream with one of his own. Whether or not Biff can achieve his dream of working with the land is not as important as the fact that it is more suited to his nature. Biff has gained self-knowledge, and in recognizing his own mediocrity and insignificance, he may be able to build himself a happier life. It would have been better for Willy to work at something he was happy doing, like carpentry, instead of trying to be the number-one salesman.

Happy does not reach the same level of awareness as his brother. Since his childhood he has admired both his father and his older brother. His brother left home, but Willy remained as a role model, and Happy has become a pale imitation of his father. He is a dreamer, although his dreams are more selfish than his father's, and more limited. He has no depth, living a shallow life that he pretends is a lot more glamorous than it really is. He isn't really happy, but he pushes his inner discontent aside. Bereft of even the few decencies Willy retains, such as a conscience and a sense of responsibility, Happy cuts an entirely disreputable figure. Despite his supposed love and respect for his father, Happy has no compunction about leaving Willy behind in a bar when he is clearly distressed. Happy has no dignity or honor; he takes bribes from manufacturers and he sleeps with the fiancées and wives of men higher in the firm than he, possibly to get even with them for being more successful than he will ever be. What is worse, his faith in his father's dream remains undiminished at the close.

Linda's central importance is as a voice of protest and outrage against what is happening to her husband. She insists that "attention must be paid" to Willy and his suffering. As Linda recognizes, Willy is a human being, and it *is* a terrible thing that happens to him. Dreams, illusions, and self-deceptions feed the action of this play; Linda, in contrast, seems very much planted in reality with her concerns over house payments, mending work, insurance premiums, and her husband's care. She knows exactly what her sons are, and she makes no bones about telling them, especially when they hurt her husband.

Despite Linda's clear sight, however, she allows her family's dreams to flourish; she even encourages them. Why she does this is partly due to the ambivalent nature of such dreams. When Biff is led to dream that he and Happy can start a business on a loan from Bill Oliver, we see the family revitalized and Willy gain the strength to ask for a better job. For a time the dream is clearly less destructive than reality. But to feed the dream, Biff has to reinvent not only his own abilities but also his relationship with Mr. Oliver. Such dreams can never be fulfilled, as they are based on lies. Although the dream may grant strength while it is maintained, as soon as reality intrudes, the dream is shattered and lays the dreamer open to harsh disillusionment. But the question remains: Is it possible to live in dreams?

Linda tries to protect Willy from the truth, and his own blinders assist in his deception; it is difficult to judge their decisions. Charley tells us, "A salesman is got to dream," and seems to suggest that Willy had no other option. When Biff insists that the truth be told, Willy cannot listen and misses the point, fixating instead on the single element of Biff's love for him, which he then uses as justification for suicide. Miller ensures that even the consequences of this act remain as ambiguous as the dream that provoked it. We are given no assurance that Biff will accept the money, and there is great uncertainty that the insurance company will pay out.

Students will need to read the lengthy setting and character descriptions, as they offer valuable clues for interpretation. Willy is presented as living in a claustrophobic, urban setting indicative of the harsh life he has chosen. His home is surrounded by apartment houses that emanate a threatening orange glow. When memory takes over, this glow gives way to a more dreamlike background with shadowy leaves and music, evoking a happier, pastoral era. At the close of the play, however, we see the looming "hard towers" of the apartment building dominating the setting once more. Without Willy's memories, the dream of a happier, Edenic life cannot exist in this city.

Many of Willy's activities can be seen as highly symbolic. He plants seeds just as he plants false hopes: Both will die and never come to fruition, largely because the house has become too hemmed in by the city. The front porch constructed of stolen lumber is indicative of how their lives have been built of something false. Willy does not fit into the modern world of machinery, and the values he espouses, where deals are made with a smile and a handshake, are clearly those of a bygone age. To illustrate this point, Miller frequently depicts Willy's uneasy relationship with such machinery as his car, his refrigerator, and Howard's recording machine.

The names of characters can also provide insights. "Willy" is a childish version of the more adult "William," indicating an intrinsic immaturity in his nature. The Loman men all need to grow up and find true direction in their lives, especially Willy, with his unrealistic dream of wanting everyone to like him. The surname Loman has been read as indicating Willy to be a low man, common and insignificant. Miller, however, declares that this was unintentional, for he picked the name from a movie he had once seen: *The Testament of Dr. Mabuse.* For Miller, the name "Lohmann" evokes the voice of a "terror-stricken man calling into the void for help that will never come." Meanwhile, "Biff" seems to indicate an abrasive nature and someone who will have to fight to get what he wants, whereas "Happy" invokes a happy-go-lucky personality — even though we learn his is a deluded happiness.

Miller describes salesmen as "actors whose product is first of all themselves, forever imagining triumphs in a world that either ignores them or denies their presence altogether. But just often enough to keep the game going one of them makes it and swings to the moon on a thread of dreams unwinding out of himself." The "Death of a Salesman" is initially that of Dave Singleman. Willy idealizes Singleman's death but views it bluntly: The man passed away on a train still trying to make that big deal, and despite the many who attended his funeral, he died alone. A salesman must always be on the move, and such a life inevitably wears one down. Singleman was a salesman of the past who could still manage to get by on being liked; Willy attempts to emulate Singleman's life in a less sentimental age. Working against greater odds, Willy runs out of steam, and it is his death with which the play ends. His funeral is not nearly so well attended, indicating a society in which people are accorded less importance, which seems finally to invalidate Willy's insistence on personality being the key to success.

SUSAN C. W. ABBOTSON

Questions for Discussion

1. What kind of relationships do Willy and Charley have with their sons? What values do they teach to their offspring? Whom do you think is the better father, and why?
2. Why is David Singleman so important to Willy? What is the life of a salesman? What does Willy sell?
3. What were Willy's father and brother really like? Does Ben have the answer that Willy is looking for? How did Ben get rich?
4. Why is Bernard so much more successful than Biff and Happy? What are the differences between Bernard and Howard?
5. What sort of woman is Linda Loman? How far can she be held responsible for what happens to her husband?
6. What are the turning points in Biff and Willy's relationship?
7. Does Willy Loman ever fully face the truth about his own life and the lives of his two sons? Do either of his sons?
8. Describe the significance of the following: the surrounding apartment houses, the flute music, Willy's seeds, the porch, Willy's reactions to machines, the jungle Ben goes into, and the names of the Loman men.
9. How is Willy's suicide foreshadowed in the play? Will the insurance company pay out?
10. What is Miller saying about the nature of the American Dream and capitalism? Is Willy's death inevitable? Does the play support or reject Willy's beliefs?
11. Though Willy is ordinary in many ways, what qualities does he possess that make him special and worthy of our sympathy?
12. Is Willy a tragic hero? What does he do that determines your answer to this question?

Topics for Writing

1. Arthur Miller insists that he does not condemn the capitalistic system as a whole but only those elements of it that appear false or hypocritical. How does *Death of a Salesman* support or refute this assertion?
2. Harold Clurman has suggested that "the father in Miller's work is a recurrent figure regarded with awe, devotion, love, even when he is proved lamentably fallible and when submission to him becomes painfully questionable. The father is a godhead because he is the giver and supporter of life; he is expected to serve as an example of proper conduct, of 'good.' . . . He gives identity and coherence to our being, creates value." Bearing this quote in mind, describe Willy's relationship with his two sons and decide whether he is a good father.
3. RESPONDING CREATIVELY   The ending of *Death of a Salesman* is intentionally ambiguous. What do you think may happen to the Lomans after Willy's suicide? What lessons have they learned or failed to learn? Write a short story that explores these questions and attempts to answer them.
4. MAKING CONNECTIONS   Miller is very concerned about how tragedy should be presented. After reading his commentary "On *Death of a Salesman* as

an American Tragedy," illustrate the essential difference between Greek and modern tragedy using *Death of a Salesman* and Sophocles' *Oedipus the King* (p. 1155).

5.   **MAKING CONNECTIONS**   In *Death of a Salesman* and *A Raisin in the Sun* (p. 1493), Arthur Miller and Lorraine Hansberry both show an interest in the needs and difficulties of families. By comparing and contrasting the Lomans and the Youngers, outline what those needs and difficulties appear to be. Is there such a thing as a perfect family? Does either playwright suggest how this ideal might be accomplished?

Commentaries

Arthur Miller, *"From the* Paris Review *Interview,"* p. 1595.
Arthur Miller, *"On 'Death of a Salesman' as an American Tragedy,"* p. 1592.
Helge Normann Nilsen, *"Marxism and the Early Plays of Arthur Miller,"* p. 1608.

Suggested Readings

Aarnes, William. "Tragic Form and the Possibility of Meaning in *Death of a Salesman.*" *Furman Studies* 29 (1983): 57–80.
Anderson, M. C. "*Death of a Salesman:* A Consideration of Willy Loman's Role in Twentieth Century Tragedy." *Crux* 20 (May 1986): 25–29.
Bigsby, C. W. E. *Modern American Drama, 1945–1990.* Cambridge: Cambridge UP, 1992.
——, ed. *Arthur Miller and Company.* London: Methuen, 1990.
Bloom, Harold. *Willy Loman.* New York: Chelsea, 1990.
——, ed. *Arthur Miller's* Death of a Salesman. New York: Chelsea, 1988.
Burgard, Peter J. "Two Parts Ibsen, One Part American Dream: On Derivation and Originality in Arthur Miller's *Death of a Salesman.*" *Orbis Litterarum* 43 (1988): 336–53.
Carson, Neil. *Arthur Miller.* London: Macmillan, 1982.
Centola, Steven R., ed. *The Achievement of Arthur Miller: New Essays.* Dallas: Contemporary Research, 1995.
Corrigan, Robert W., ed. *Arthur Miller: A Collection of Critical Essays.* Englewood Cliffs, NJ: Prentice, 1969.
Martin, Robert A., ed. *Arthur Miller: New Perspectives.* Englewood Cliffs, NJ: Prentice, 1982.
Martine, James J., ed. *Critical Essays on Arthur Miller.* Boston: G. K. Hall, 1979.
Miller, Arthur. *The Theatre Essays of Arthur Miller.* Edited by Robert A. Martin. New York: Viking, 1978.
——. *Timebends: A Life.* New York: Grove, 1987.
Murphy, Brenda. *Miller:* Death of a Salesman. New York: Cambridge UP, 1995.
Roudané, Matthew C., ed. *Conversations with Arthur Miller.* Jackson: UP of Mississippi, 1987.
Weales, Gerald, ed. Death of a Salesman: *Text and Criticism.* New York: Viking, 1967.

LORRAINE HANSBERRY

A Raisin in the Sun (p. 1493)

Much of *A Raisin in the Sun*'s plot was drawn directly from Hansberry's own experience. Attempts were made to dissuade her family from settling in what was perceived as a white area, and while growing up, Hansberry saw the increasing tension between wanting to assimilate and maintaining pride in one's own culture. But the fact is, *A Raisin in the Sun* explores a variety of topics, from family dynamics and the generation gap to black identity and women's rights. Robert Nemiroff rightly describes the play as presaging a "revolution in black and women's consciousness." He insists that the play has not grown less relevant with the passing of time, as the issues with which it deals remain prevalent in American society. Hansberry's cast does not just depict relationships defined by race and gender but includes characters of different classes, ages, and nationalities, so that we can consider universal issues surrounding class, generations, and national development beside the more obvious issues of race and gender. It is the play's ability to maintain *and* to go beyond its author's racial identity that makes it so effective.

The aspirations, relationships, and desires of the Younger family are universal, and they make the Youngers recognizably human to an audience who would have been unused to seeing African Americans realistically depicted onstage. The play also raises key issues regarding relationships between spouses, generations, and human beings in general. A number of critics have seen color as almost irrelevant to the plot and declare Hansberry to be a universalist rather than a racial activist; in fact, she is both. If Hansberry had been overtly radical it is likely that the play would never have been produced. By submerging her racial commentary, Hansberry was able to get the play performed and to prove that African Americans had a place on Broadway and should no longer be dismissed. She writes about a specific black family — we can universalize them only because they are so realistic. And yet it would be wrong to downplay the Youngers' race, which is central to their existence. The Youngers are not just working class but African American working class, and the stakes in their struggle to make good are intensified by this fact.

Some critics have accused Hansberry of embracing white middle-class ideas and advocating assimilation. This assessment is unfair to Hansberry and her play. *A Raisin in the Sun* is as wary of assimilation as it is of finding all the answers in Africa — both are depicted as extremes. An effective value system for African American families becomes difficult to find as they try to balance African tradition and American experience. African Americans face what Bernard Bell calls "a biracial and bicultural identity." This suggests a "double-consciousness" that must allow mutually exclusive identities to be held in balance. Neither Africanness nor Americanness should be neglected, as each has something essential to offer. This consciousness creates some of the apparent contradictions within the play, such as the conflict between Mama's matriarchal rule (African) and Walter's patriarchal expectations (American). Hansberry does not wish us to take sides but to consider the potential within each tradition. Hansberry's opening description tells us that she wants the set to reflect "indestructible contradictions." It is, possibly, the ability to live with such contradictions that makes the Younger family so durable.

Although the Youngers' furniture seems ordinary and worn, in their home it evokes a sense of hope and pride. The audience should realize that even this modest apartment has been a hard-won achievement. Life for the Youngers is a constant struggle to keep ahead and to keep up appearances as they scramble to become part of the middle class. Hansberry wishes us to consider the dangers of becoming so involved with appearances that we neglect what lies beneath — qualities of love, dignity, and unselfish sacrifice. These are concepts that Walter and Beneatha, especially, need to understand. All the characters in the play are so centered on their own dreams that their vision is restricted, and they fail to recognize one another's dreams. As the play progresses we see the Youngers learn to recognize and accept one another's dreams and so strengthen the family.

The differences between Joseph Asagai and George Murchison are important, as is Beneatha's choice between them. While Asagai is the complete African, George is the assimilated American. George is not a character to emulate, as he refuses to recognize either the equality of women, wanting Beneatha as his "little woman," or the importance of his African heritage, dismissing it as irrelevant. He knows facts about Africa but has lost touch with its spirit and strength. Because of his wealth, he is satisfied with the status quo and so selfishly refuses to change. Such selfishness is antagonistic to African American development as a whole. George may have wealth, but he has no real identity of his own, and he lacks the vibrancy we see in Asagai's secure ethnic identity.

Asagai is showing the rich tradition of Africa not just to Beneatha but also to the audience. In the 1950s, when this play was first produced, his sophistication would have been at odds with many people's limited perception of Africans as savages. Yet we should recognize that Asagai is unable to recognize what might be seen as "American aspects" of Beneatha's character, for his experience is entirely African. Asagai cannot accept Beneatha's drive for independence, although he admires her spirit. In his own way he wishes to dominate her as much as George does. Beneatha needs to find her own identity, which will lie somewhere between the Americanness of George and the Africanness of Asagai.

Asagai does point Beneatha toward a central truth of the play — that every individual must make his or her own life. If you do not use your own resources, then what you receive will never truly belong to you. Life is a struggle that must be embraced, as any gain necessarily includes risk. The future is never guaranteed, but to maintain your dignity, you must strive to pursue what you feel is right. Asagai wants to take Beneatha to Africa, but his impulse is selfish. Beneatha's home is in America, and America needs her spirited input. We never learn if she accepts his invitation to go to Africa, but we should hope she refuses. Beneatha will not find her identity solely in Africa, because she is also American.

Students may ask the extent to which Beneatha's interest in African culture is just a fad — as her excursions into photography, acting, horse-riding, and the guitar seem to have been. Yet we can view each of these hobbies not as a waste but as a part of the necessary process of finding and expressing herself. Beneatha is right to suggest that African Americans need a better understanding of Africa as an important part of their heritage, but she must not ignore the fact that they live in America. Beneatha and Walter's exhibition of their African roots shows an important pride, but they also need to have pride in their American-born family and to recognize what their strength has achieved in six generations.

Beneatha has lessons to learn beyond her academic education, including a need for tact and a respect for her elders and their beliefs. Her ambitions rely heavily on financial support from her family, and their sacrifice should be acknowledged. Walter limits her by her gender, feeling she should be satisfied with being a nurse or a wife rather than a doctor. Her spirit allows her to rise above his opinion. Beneatha wants to be independent, and this aspect of her dream places her beyond even the understanding of Mama and Ruth. Mama and Ruth are not against female independence, but they do not see how it can be practically possible at this time, a question Hansberry leaves open to debate. Mama and Ruth do teach Beneatha an important lesson about love — a truth that, in her immaturity, she has not realized: Love is not necessarily peaceful or easy; like life itself, it is a constant struggle if it has any meaning.

At the start, Ruth seems prematurely aged and tired, ready to give in and accept the meager life she has. She has momentarily lost her passion to strive further up the social ladder. Ruth dislikes risks and wants a safe life, but safety allows for little progress. Although the rest of her family still has the energy and desire to want more, she has been worn down by hard work. She has borne a large burden, nurturing and providing for her family with little reward.

Ruth's resignation is in direct contrast to Walter's intensity: A fire burns within him, even if it is still immature and its flames are only nervous and fitful. His erratic quality sets him apart, differentiating him from the ordinariness and predictability that are beginning to crush Ruth's spirit. Ruth and Walter are at odds; she has given up and become indifferent to the outside world, whereas Walter refuses to give up his desire to be a part of wider society, as indicated by his interest in the newspaper. Ruth's dormant strength returns, however, as she refuses to give up the house that Mama buys. We learn that this has been her dream as much as Mama's, and she is able to reinforce Mama's slipping spirit. Evidently, some advances need more than individual strength, which underlines the importance of family connections. The Youngers live in a ghetto neighborhood, and Mama and Ruth's desire to move is valid: The kids chase rats in the street, and the apartment is not only cramped but infested with cockroaches. A better home will allow them more room to grow. The urgency of this move is emphasized by the discovery that Ruth will be having another child.

Mama's key attributes are her strength and her clear sense of direction. It was her and her husband's combined strength that brought the family this far. Hansberry is fully aware that black progress in America will not happen overnight but will be a lengthy process, just as it is for any social group forced to begin with next to nothing. Equality will take generations of struggle — each generation contributing a little bit to the progress. Mama's plant, which she so doggedly preserves, underlines both her desire to grow and refusal to give in. It also represents her dream — to have a house with a garden. The "Scarlett O'Hara" hat that Travis gives Mama is an indication of her development: In owning property, she has become akin to the mistress of the plantation rather than one of the slaves who worked there. Having provided a house, Mama needs to give her family space to grow. She initially declares, "We working folk not business folk," and so dismisses Walter's business dreams without fair consideration. She wants the family to progress, but she may selfishly want to be the instrument of change. Mama must allow her children control of their own lives. Still, although Mama is the head of the family at the start, it may not be so much a role she demands as one she must take, one Walter has yet to grow into. Beneatha calls Mama a tyrant, but after putting a deposit on the house, Mama soon gives her son control of the family fortune, which he consequently wastes. This underlines the important lesson that control or respect cannot be given; it must be earned.

Whether Walter is the central character of the play is debatable. Although his growth toward manhood is important, so, too, is Beneatha's search for selfhood. In a way, privileging Walter's development over Beneatha's is an acceptance of the very male supremacy Hansberry questions. The check that Walter hopes for is not his but his mother's: an insurance policy paid out on his father's death. Taking this money will not assert his manhood, for this is something he needs to achieve by his own resources. It is, perhaps, hard for him to live under his mother's roof, but he must earn his own way out. At the start of the play Walter is more talk than action, and Ruth is wise not to get sucked into his dreams; she has heard them too often, seen too little done to achieve them, and has little time for dreams. Walter's early assertions of control seem ridiculous as he still thinks like a boy, without regard for his responsibilities. He defies his wife by giving Travis money, but then he has to borrow money from his wife for his car fare. Walter's view of Africa is a romanticized one as he performs his tribal dance, but it allows us to see the inner potential in Walter, which has become buried by so much empty talk.

There is a strong critique of money throughout the play. Walter is obsessed with money and getting on, and he is slow to realize what manhood really requires. Although Walter seems at first to be empowered by money, we come to realize that his true empowerment comes from his denial of money and insistence on dignity. Like Arthur Miller,

Hansberry suggests that capitalism gets in the way of the real system of love under which people should live their lives. Walter erroneously believes that life is money, but Mama knows that freedom is more important, having been closer to a generation that had none. It is what one does with that freedom that will determine one's life. Walter needs to respect the past and his parents' achievements, but it is now his turn to achieve, and Mama must allow him the freedom to develop self-respect. It is Mama's self-respect that provides the roots of her strength. Mama allows Walter real control not when she gives him money but when she allows him the freedom to choose what to do about the house. If Walter were to accept Karl Lindner's money, it would be a major regression for the whole family. He would be playing the black stereotype from which they are striving to escape and ruin any chance of self-respect for the future.

Lindner interrupts Walter's naive optimism and provides a reality check. His character is subtle: Awkward and soft-spoken, he seems to offer little threat by himself. We should recognize, however, the larger community and power behind such a figure. Viewing his discomfort, we realize that what he is asking is wrong. Even he seems to real-ize this, but he cannot surmount his own prejudices. He uses platitudes to mask what he is doing, but no one is ultimately fooled. His commentary on empathy is ironically some-thing of which he is incapable. How, we should ask, are the Youngers, with their hard-working background, any different from those folk in Clybourne Park? How can Lindner be anything other than a complete racist? Walter's instinct to eject this man from his home is right, and this action will be more empowering than the money he got from Mama. Walter begins his second confrontation with Lindner fairly sheepishly, but he draws strength as he continues — partly from within himself and his own pride and partly from his family and a recognition of the dignity he owes them for their sacrifices. It is at this moment that we see the man in Walter: Now that he can give orders to others and expect them to follow, he has finally earned their respect.

There are dark aspects of the play that should not be overlooked. One such aspect (which may be seen as realism, although it has engendered some criticism) is Hansberry's depiction of a lack of black solidarity, with the inclusion of such unhelpful characters as Willy Harris and Mrs. Johnson. While Willy runs off with Walter's money, Mrs. Johnson's appearance as a gossipy, unhelpful neighbor further underlines the inability of these characters to assist one another. Mrs. Johnson seems motivated by jealousy, not wanting the Youngers to rise above her. In this way she is as guilty as George of wanting to keep the status quo. Beneatha is right to compare Mrs. Johnson to the Ku Klux Klan: Both are destructive to black development in America.

Hansberry also ensures that we realize how potentially dangerous it will be for the Youngers to move to Clybourne Park. It would be a mistake to see this play as having a happy ending. Hansberry purposefully leaves us uncertain as to what will happen next. Even Mama's emotion at the end, being inarticulate, remains ambivalent: Is it from pride in her son's growth, or could it indicate an element of fear toward the dangerous unknown into which her family is going? What indignities might the Youngers be forced to suffer in Clybourne Park, where they are clearly not welcome? What will Beneatha decide to do with her life, and will her gender restrict her choices? What these stage characters have achieved so far is only a fragment of what our society will need to ensure true equality for both African Americans and women.

SUSAN C. W. ABBOTSON

Questions for Discussion

1. To what degree does the Langston Hughes poem at the start help to explain the play's action and characters? Are all the options it suggests considered in the play? Whose dreams are being deferred?

2. What are the "indestructible contradictions" that Hansberry suggests should be evident in the set design, and why are they so important? In what ways could this whole play be said to rest in contradictions?

3. In what ways are the characters of Ruth, Beneatha, and Mama (Lena) different? Which would you say is the strongest? What is the play saying about women's consciousness and rights in the 1950s?

4. What are the similarities and differences between George Murchison and Joseph Asagai? To what extent is their nationality accountable for their differences? Whom do you feel would make the better partner for Beneatha?

5. The character of Mrs. Johnson did not appear in early productions of the play. What does her character add? In what ways can she be compared to Willy Harris?

6. How is Karl Lindner presented? How are we supposed to react to his character?

7. At what point does Walter Lee become the true "Head of the House"?

8. What kind of man was Walter Senior? How far does his insurance money create or solve problems? What is Hansberry's attitude toward wealth?

9. What kind of relationship exists between Walter and Ruth? How does each relate to their son, Travis? What is the importance of children in this play?

10. Explain how the following symbols operate in the play: Mama's plant, Mama's gardening hat, Walter's liquor store, Ruth's unborn child, the house in Clybourne Park, Walter's two dances.

11. What will life be like for the Youngers in Clybourne Park? To what extent is the ending of this play "happy"?

12. To what extent are Hansberry's views in the play on race and gender still applicable in today's society?

Topics for Writing

1. All the characters in *A Raisin in the Sun* are caught up in dreams of a better future. What is each character's dream and how does he/she plan/hope to achieve it? In what ways do some of these dreams conflict? Whose dreams do you believe to be the most important, and why?

2. What are the racial issues in *A Raisin in the Sun* and how are they portrayed? Give reasons for your decision on whether race is the play's central issue.

3. **RESPONDING CREATIVELY**   Write a letter from one of the Youngers to a close friend in which you describe their interpretation of the play's final scene. What happens to the family when they move to Clybourne Park? Try to be true to the characters as they are depicted in *A Raisin in the Sun*.

4. **MAKING CONNECTIONS**   *A Raisin in the Sun* and Arthur Miller's *Death of a Salesman* (p. 1423) both portray families who are struggling to survive and progress in a society that seems antagonistic to their dreams. In describing the forces operating on each family, decide to what extent these forces are internal or external and how this might affect our judgment of the families.

Commentaries

Lorraine Hansberry, "*An Author's Reflections: Willy Loman, Walter Younger, and He Who Must Live*," p. 1584.
Lorraine Hansberry, "*My Shakespearean Experience*," p. 1589.

Suggested Readings

Barthelemy, Anthony. "Mother, Sister, Wife: A Dramatic Perspective." *Southern Review* 21 (1985).

Brown, Lloyd W. "Lorraine Hansberry as Ironist: A Reappraisal of *A Raisin in the Sun*." *Journal of Black Studies* 4 (1974).

Carter, Steven R. *Hansberry's Drama: Commitment and Complexity.* Urbana: U of Illinois P, 1991.

Cheney, Anne. *Lorraine Hansberry.* Boston: Twayne, 1984.

Cooper, David O. "Hansberry's *A Raisin in the Sun*." *Explicator* 52 (1993): 59–61.

McKelly, James C. "Hymns of Sedition: Portraits of the Artist in Contemporary African-American Drama." *Arizona Quarterly* 48 (1992): 87–107.

Nemiroff, Robert, ed. *To Be Young, Gifted, and Black: Lorraine Hansberry in Her Own Words.* Englewood Cliffs, NJ: Prentice, 1969.

Seaton, Sandra. "*A Raisin in the Sun*: A Study in Afro-American Culture." *Midwestern Miscellany* 20 (1992): 40–49.

Washington, J. Charles. "*A Raisin in the Sun* Revisited." *Black American Literature Forum* 22 (1988): 109–24.

Wilkerson, Margaret B. "*A Raisin in the Sun*: Anniversary of an American Classic." *Theatre Journal* 38 (1986).

Lynn Nottage

POOF! (p. 1561)

Students should take careful note of the time of the play — the present — and the statement Nottage includes after stating that the play takes place in a kitchen:

> Nearly half the women on death row in the United States were convicted of killing abusive husbands. Spontaneous combustion is not recognized as a capital crime.

This one act play takes only about ten minutes to perform, and it could be read in its entirety in the classroom. Its most spectacular event occurs in the darkness just before the stage lights rise, as we hear Loureen and her abusive husband Samuel shouting at each other. It is the only time Samuel's voice is heard, because he makes his first stage appearance as "a huge pile of smoking ashes" in the middle of the kitchen. By damning him to hell, Loureen has caused his death by spontaneous combustion, a device Victorian novelists loved but largely unused in contemporary theater — except by Lynn Nottage, who employs it to excellent effect in her short play about marital abuse. She has rewritten Susan Glaspell's *Trifles* in modern terms for modern audiences, and her suggestion of explosive stage action in the pile of smoking ashes is probably much more in tune with a contemporary audience's expectations than dead canaries in cages and unfinished hand-sewn quilts.

Loureen is a sympathetic woman — at first appalled and repentant about what she caused to happen to her husband — at the end of the play she sweeps his ashes under the rug and calmly sits down to enjoy her roast chicken dinner in solitude. Loureen has expiated her sense of guilt through her conversation with her upstairs friend Florence. Their dialogue is the play. Nottage has no need for the men in *Trifles*. As a playwright she doesn't have to justify defending a woman whose life had been ruined by a tyrannical, physically abusive husband. Times have changed since Glaspell's historical moment, and the past quarter-century of women's groups and feminist advances have prepared today's audiences to accept the idea of the murderous unfairness of spousal abuse.

POOF! is a humorous title, and its casual outrageousness prepares the audience to overhear the conversation between Loureen and Florence almost as if we were in collusion with them. After we witness Loureen's initial fright and repentance, we trust her. She's no out-of-control homicidal maniac. She cared for her husband initially, but he was destroying her life.

Florence is also trustworthy. At first she can't believe that Samuel is the pile of ashes on the kitchen floor and that her good friend has done this to her husband, telling her "We're talking murder, Loureen, not oven settings." But she's also level-headed ("You've been watching too much television"), against drugs ("You smoking crack?"), and unswervingly loyal in her friendship. When she finally accepts Loureen's story, she is at first angry that her friend didn't keep the pact they'd made to leave their husbands together when things got too bad. She begs Loureen to come upstairs and say the same words that will cause her husband Edgar to spontaneously combust, but when Loureen refuses, Florence is as resigned as a good friend would have to be.

She also senses the moment when Loureen is strong enough to be left on her own, and they both smile and share a hug before Florence returns to her family upstairs in the apartment building. The play doesn't leave us with a sense that it is antimale; instead, it is about strong friendships between women. Marriage isn't the only worthwhile goal in women's lives. They are also independent creatures and entirely sympathetic human beings.

Questions for Discussion

1. Nottage is a black playwright, but she hasn't restricted *POOF!* to black actors, though she does use non-standard English dialect occasionally in her play. What does this suggest about the situation she dramatizes in her play?
2. What instances of humor do you find in *POOF!*? How do they help to universalize the play?
3. Which audiences do you think might take offense of Nottage's depiction of the positive consequences of female bonding and sisterhood?

Topics for Writing

1. **MAKING CONNECTIONS**   Compare and contrast *POOF!* with Glaspell's *Trifles* (p. 1362).
2. Google the phenomenon known as spontaneous combustion and write an essay describing some of its notable previous appearances in works of fiction and drama.

Connections

Susan Glaspell, "*A Jury of Her Peers*," p. 185.
Susan Glaspell, *Trifles*, p. 1362.

Commentary

Lynn Nottage, "*On Writing POOF!*," p. 1612.

APPENDIX OF
AUDIOVISUAL RESOURCES

FICTION

SHERMAN ALEXIE

Smoke Signals. 89 min., color, 1998. VHS, DVD. Based on Alexie's "The Lone Ranger and Tonto Fistfight in Heaven," and starring Adam Beach and Eve Adams. Directed by Chris Eyre. Distributed by Buena Vista Home Entertainment.

MARGARET ATWOOD

Atwood & Family. 30 min., color, 1985. VHS 3/4" U-matic cassette. An interview with Atwood filmed on her island retreat. Director Michael Rubbo attempts to discover what shapes and drives Atwood's writing. Distributed by the National Film Board of Canada.

Margaret Atwood [recording]. 2 cassettes, 1983. An interview with Atwood. Distributed by American Audio Prose Library.

Margaret Atwood. 52 min., color, 1989. From the Writers Talk: Ideas of Our Time series. An interview with Atwood in which she discusses feminism, mythology, autobiography, and other topics. Distributed by the Roland Collection.

JAMES BALDWIN

Interview with James Baldwin and Kay Bonetti [recording]. 1 cassette (56 min.), 1984. Baldwin discusses the role of the artist in Western culture. Distributed by American Audio Prose Library.

James Baldwin. 55 min., color, 1997. Part of the Great Writers of the Twentieth Century series. Covers Baldwin's life, from his youth in Harlem to his later years as an expatriate in Paris. Distributed by Films for the Humanities and Sciences.

James Baldwin: The Poet That You Produced [recording]. 1 cassette or CD (60 min.). Explores the passion and vision that fueled both the author's life and career. Features excerpts from Baldwin's speeches and readings from selected works. Distributed by Pacifica Radio Archive.

James Baldwin: The Price of the Ticket. 87 min., 1990. Documentary profile highlighting Baldwin's work and life — as both author and civil rights activist. Distributed by California Newsreel.

TONI CADE BAMBARA

Interview with Toni Cade Bambara and Kay Bonetti [recording]. 1 cassette (90 min.). The author discusses her writing style and political concerns. Part of the Women's Studies series. Distributed by American Audio Prose Library.

RUSSELL BANKS

Russell Banks [recording]. 1 cassette or CD (73 min.). Banks discusses his craft, focusing on the social and aesthetic visions that influence his work. Distributed by American Audio Prose Library.

RAYMOND CARVER

Raymond Carver. 50 min., color, 1997. VHS. Part of the Great Writers of the Twentieth Century series. Carver, his wife, and friends discuss Carver's fiction and his upbringing. Distributed by Films for the Humanities and Sciences.

Readings and Interview [recording]. 2 cassettes (120 min.). Distributed by American Audio Prose Library.

To Write and Keep Kind: A Portrait of Raymond Carver. 60 min., color and b/w, 1997. VHS. From the Voices of the West series, originally aired on PBS. A look at the life and work of Raymond Carver. Distributed by PBS Video.

ANTON CHEKHOV

Anton Chekhov. 30 min., b/w, 1999. VHS. A look at Chekhov's life and work. Distributed by Kultur International Films.

Anton Chekhov: A Writer's Life. 37 min., b/w, 1974. Beta, VHS, 3/4" U-matic cassette. A biographical portrait of the writer. Distributed by Films for the Humanities and Sciences.

The Lady with the Dog. 86 min., b/w, 1960. VHS. In Russian, with English subtitles. Starring Iya Savvina, Alexei Batalov, Alla Chostakova. Directed by Yosef Heifitz. Distributed by Facets Multimedia, Inc.

KATE CHOPIN

Kate Chopin: Five Stories of an Hour. 26 min., color, 1991. Five dramatic renditions of Chopin's "Story of an Hour." Distributed by Films for the Humanities and Sciences.

Kate Chopin's The Story of an Hour. 24 min., color, 1982. A dramatization of the short story, with an examination of Chopin's life. Distributed by Ishtar Films.

The Story of an Hour and Other Stories [recording]. 2 cassettes (2 1/2 hours), 1992. Read by Jean DeBarbieris. Distributed by Books in Motion.

See also "Women in Literature, The Short Story: A Collection" on manual page 366.

RALPH ELLISON

Ralph Ellison: The Self-Taught Writer. 30 min., color and b/w, 1995. VHS. Part of the Black Achievers Video series. An examination of Ellison's early years of poverty to his rise as a prominent writer. Distributed by History on Video.

LOUISE ERDRICH

Interview [recording]. 1 cassette (50 min.). Erdrich and her husband, Michael Dorris, discuss the centrality of a Native American identity to the author's work. Distributed by American Audio Prose Library.

Louise Erdrich and Michael Dorris. 27 min., color, 1988. VHS, 3/4" U-matic cassette. From the Writers Talk: Ideas of Our Time series. Erdrich and Dorris discuss their overlapping writing approaches, techniques, and themes. Distributed by the Roland Collection.

WILLIAM FAULKNER

The Famous Author Series: William Faulkner. 30 min., color, 1998. VHS. A look at the author's life and career. Distributed by Filmic Archives.

William Faulkner. 45 min., color. VHS. Faulkner's own words, archival photographs and footage, and fictionalized reconstructions are used to recreate the South of William Faulkner's era. Distributed by Films for the Humanities and Sciences.

William Faulkner: A Life on Paper. 120 min., color, 1980. VHS, 3/4" U-matic cassette. A documentary biography. With Lauren Bacall, Howard Hawks, Anita Loos, George Plimpton, Tennessee Williams, and Jill Faulkner Summers (the author's daughter). Distributed by Home Vision Cinema.

William Faulkner Reads [recording]. 1 cassette, 1998. Contains Faulkner's first readings of his work. Includes the author's Nobel acceptance speech and excerpts from *As I Lay Dying, A Fable,* and *The Old Man.* Distributed by HarperAudio.

William Faulkner's Mississippi. 49 min., b/w, 1966. VHS. Deals with Faulkner's life and works. Distributed by Benchmark Media.

GABRIEL GARCÍA MÁRQUEZ

Gabriel García Márquez. 44 min., color, 1998. VHS. García Márquez discusses his life and work. Distributed by Films for the Humanities and Sciences.

Gabriel García Márquez: A Witch Writing. 52 min., color. VHS. An in-depth interview with the author, presented in the form of a conversation with an old friend he has not seen for a long time. Distributed by Films for the Humanities and Sciences.

Márquez: Tales Beyond Solitude. 57 min., color. VHS. Profiles the Colombian author. Features footage from his life and clips from films on which he has worked. Distributed by Public Media, Inc.

A Very Old Man with Enormous Wings. 90 min., 1988. VHS. With Daisy Granados, Asdrubal Melendez, Luis Alberto Ramirez, Fernando Birri. In Spanish with English subtitles. Distributed by Wellspring Media, Inc. and Facets Multimedia, Inc.

CHARLOTTE PERKINS GILMAN

Charlotte Perkins Gilman: "The Yellow Wallpaper." 76 min., color. VHS. A dramatization of Gilman's story. Directed by John Clive and featuring Stephen Dillon and Julia Watson. Distributed by Films for the Humanities and Sciences.

The Short Story No. 1: The Yellow Wallpaper. 15 min., 1978. VHS. With Sigurd Wurschmidt, Tom Dahlgren, Susan Lynch. Distributed by the University of Nebraska-Lincoln, GPN.

See also **"Scribbling Women"** on manual page 366.

SUSAN GLASPELL

A Jury of Her Peers. 30 min., color, 1981. VHS, 3/4" U-matic cassette, special order formats. A dramatization of Glaspell's short story. Distributed by Home Vision Cinema.

NADINE GORDIMER

Nadine Gordimer. 95 min., color. VHS, 3/4" U-matic cassette. Gordimer discusses her craft. Distributed by the Roland Collection.

Nadine Gordimer: On Being a Liberal White South African. 30 min., color, 1994. VHS. From the Bill Moyers' World of Ideas series.

Gordimer discusses her experiences growing up as a white South African and shares her views on apartheid in South Africa. Distributed by Films for the Humanities and Sciences.

NATHANIEL HAWTHORNE

Nathaniel Hawthorne. 25 min., color, 1998. VHS. Three leading Hawthorne scholars analyze and interpret several Hawthorne works. Distributed by Films for the Humanities and Sciences.

Nathaniel Hawthorne: New England's Puritan Son. 16 min., 1993. VHS. Both a tour of places portrayed in Hawthorne's tales and novels and a discussion of the author's philosophy, life, and work. Distributed by Clearvue/ EAV Inc.

Nathaniel Hawthorne: "Young Goodman Brown." 43 min., color. VHS. An adaptation of Hawthorne's story shot on location in historic Salem. Commentary on the author's life and the Salem witch trials provides historical context. Distributed by Films for the Humanities and Sciences.

Young Goodman Brown. 30 min., color, 1972. Based on the story by Nathaniel Hawthorne. Distributed by Pyramid Media.

ERNEST HEMINGWAY

Ernest Hemingway. 30 min., color and b/w, 1993. VHS. Part of the Famous Authors series. Distributed by Kultur International Films.

Ernest Hemingway: A Life [recording]. Part 1, 11 cassettes, Part 2, 10 cassettes (1 hr., 30 mins. per cassette). Read by Christopher Hunt. Draws from Hemingway's diaries, letters, and unpublished writings as well as personal testimony from the people who played a part in the author's life. Distributed by Blackstone Audio.

Ernest Hemingway: Rough Diamond. 30 min., color, 1978. VHS. Recreates a day in the life of Hemingway through a simulated interview with a young reporter. "Hemingway" recalls details of his life and works. Distributed by Phoenix Films & Video.

Ernest Hemingway: Wrestling with Life. 100 min., color, 1999. An intimate portrait of the man behind the literary legend. Includes the reminiscences of friends and family closest to the author and Hemingway's own words, taken from his letters, novels, and unpublished work. Narrated by Mariel Hemingway. Distributed by A&E Home Video.

Hemingway. 300 min., 3 cassettes. VHS, DVD. A biographical portrait of the author, filmed on location in the places where he lived and worked: Paris, Venice, Pamplona, the Alps, the Caribbean, and the United States. Distributed by Lance Entertainment, Inc.

Hemingway. 18 min. VHS. Analyzes Hemingway's life and works with a special focus on his famous literary style. Distributed by Filmic Archives.

Hemingway — Grace under Pressure. 55 min., color. VHS, 3/4" U-matic cassette. A biography of the author using photographs, newsreels, and film clips. Examines the relationship between the author's life and works. Distributed by Films for the Humanities and Sciences.

Hemingway: Up in Michigan, the Early Years. 28 min., color, 1986. VHS. A literary biography of the writer. Distributed by Clearvue/ EAV Inc.

Introduction to Ernest Hemingway's Fiction. 45 min. VHS. Part of the Eminent Scholars series. Examines the way in which Hemingway's clipped, laconic writing style transformed English language and literature. Distributed by Facets Multimedia, Inc.

ZORA NEALE HURSTON

Zora Is My Name! 90 min., color, 1990. VHS. Originally aired on PBS's American Playhouse series. Presents the story of Hurston's life in the rural South of the 1930s and 40s, with Ruby Dee and Louis Gossett Jr. Distributed by PBS Home Video, Karol Video, Facets Multimedia, Inc.

SHIRLEY JACKSON

A Discussion of "The Lottery." 10 min., 1973. VHS. Based on Jackson's short story. Hosted by Dr. James Burbin, professor of English, USC. Distributed by Filmic Archives.

The Lottery. 18 min., color, 1980. VHS, Beta, 3/4" U-matic cassette. Part of the Encyclopaedia Britannica Educational Humanities Program Short Story Showcase series. Based on Jackson's short story. Distributed by the Encyclopaedia Britannica Educational Corporation.

JAMES JOYCE

James Joyce. 80 min., color. VHS. An authoritative documentary of the author's life and work. Distributed by Films for the Humanities and Sciences.

James Joyce. 50 min., color. VHS. Part of the Great Writers of the Twentieth Century series, produced by BBC Staff. Critics and those who knew Joyce recall his life and examine passages in his works in relation to actual events in the author's life. Distributed by Films for the Humanities and Sciences.

James Joyce's Women. 91 min., color, 1985. Beta, VHS. Actors portray Joyce's wife plus Molly Bloom and two other of his female characters. Adapted from her one-woman stage show and produced by Fionnula Flanagan. With Flanagan, Timothy E. O'Grady, Chris O'Neill. Distributed by Universal Studios Home Video.

FRANZ KAFKA

Kafka: Nabokov on Kafka. 30 min. VHS. Based on a novel by Kafka and featuring Christopher Plummer and Vladimir Nabokov. Distributed by Facets Multimedia, Inc.

The Metamorphosis. 58 min., color, 1994. VHS. Part of the Living Literature: Classics & You series. Based on Kafka's story. Distributed by RMI Media Productions, Inc.

The Metamorphosis of Mr. Samsa. 10 min., 1979. VHS, 3/4" U-matic cassette. Based on Kafka's famous short story. Produced by the National Film Board of Canada. Distributed by Home Vision Cinema.

The Trials of Franz Kafka. 15 min., b/w, 1993. VHS. Kafka's life and times, told in his own words. Narrated by Kurt Vonnegut. Distributed by Films for the Humanities and Sciences.

JAMAICA KINCAID

Interview with Jamaica Kincaid and Kay Bonetti [recording]. 1 cassette (60 min.), 1991. Distributed by American Audio Prose Library.

Jamaica Kincaid Reads [recording]. 1 cassette (60 min.), 1991. Kincaid reads excerpts from Annie John, Lucy, and At the Bottom of the River. Distributed by American Audio Prose Library.

JHUMPA LAHIRI

Interpreter of Maladies [recording]. 4 cassettes. Read by Matilda Novak. Distributed by Audio Editions.

D. H. LAWRENCE

D. H. Lawrence. 30 min., color, 1998. VHS. Traces the life and literary career of Lawrence. Distributed by Filmic Archives.

D. H. Lawrence: The Rocking-Horse Winner. 90 min., b/w, 1949. VHS. Starring John Mills, Valerie Hobson. Directed by Anthony Pelessier. Distributed by Films for the Humanities & Sciences.

D. H. Lawrence as Son and Lover. 52 min., color, 1988. VHS, 3/4" U-matic cassette. A biography culled from the writer's essays, letters, and autobiographical pieces. Distributed by Films for the Humanities and Sciences.

GUY DE MAUPASSANT

Boule de Suif and Other Stories [recording]. 3 hours. Read by Clive Francis and Tony Britton. Distributed by Listening Books (the National Listening Library, UK).

"The Necklace" by Guy de Maupassant. 20 min., color, 1980. Beta, VHS, 3/4" U-matic cassette, 16-mm film. Part of the Encyclopaedia Britannica Corporation's Short Story Classics series. A contemporary setting of the classic story. Distributed by Encyclopaedia Britannica Educational Corporation.

HERMAN MELVILLE

Bartleby: A Discussion. 28 min., color, 1969. VHS. A commentary by author Charles Van Doren. Distributed by Encyclopaedia Britannica Educational Corporation.

Bartleby, the Scrivener. 60 min., color. VHS, 3/4" U-matic cassette. Distributed by Maryland Public Television.

Herman Melville. 22 min., color, 1978. Beta, VHS, 3/4" U-matic cassette, 16-mm film. Ancillary materials available. Part of the Authors Series of biographies. Distributed by United Learning.

Herman Melville. 30 min., color, 1998. VHS. Part of the Famous Authors series. Distributed by Filmic Archives.

Herman Melville: Bartleby, the Scrivener. 59 min., color, 1987. VHS, 3/4" U-matic cassette. Distributed by Films for the Humanities and Sciences.

Herman Melville: Consider the Sea. 30 min., color, 1995. VHS. Deals with the author and his relationship with the sea. Major works discussed include *Moby Dick, Billy Budd,* and "Bartleby, the Scrivener." Distributed by Monterey Media, Inc.

Herman Melville: Damned Paradise. 90 min., color, 1986. VHS, 3/4" U-matic cassette. Documents Melville's personal and intellectual history. Distributed by Pyramid Media.

Herman Melville: "November in My Soul." 27 min., color, 1977. Beta, VHS, 16-mm film. A portrait of the author's life and writing. Narrated by John Cullum. Distributed by Phoenix Films and Video.

Melville. 22 min., color, 1992. VHS. Explores Melville's career and important works. Distributed by Filmic Archives.

See also "Great American Short Stories I, II, III" on manual page 366.

JOYCE CAROL OATES

Joyce Carol Oates [recording]. 1 cassette (29 min.), 1989. The author talks about her writing habits. Distributed by New Letters on the Air.

Joyce Carol Oates. 28 min., color. VHS. Oates discusses her craft and the major themes of her novels, short stories, and poems. Distributed by Films for the Humanities and Sciences.

Joyce Carol Oates: American Appetites. 30 min., color. VHS. Part of the Moveable Feast series. Distributed by Facets Multimedia, Inc.

Smooth Talk. 92 min., color, 1985. VHS. A film adaptation of "Where Are You Going, Where Have You Been?" starring Laura Dern and Treat Williams. Directed by Joyce Chopra. Distributed by Vestron Video.

See also "A Moveable Feast" on manual page 366.

TIM O'BRIEN

Best American Short Stories of the Century, Volume 2 [recording].

2000. Among others, O'Brien reads his short story, "The Things They Carried." Distributed by Houghton Mifflin.

TILLIE OLSEN

Tillie Olsen: "I Stand Here Ironing." 17 min., color. VHS. The author discusses her short story. Also featuring Peter Carroll.

EDGAR ALLAN POE

A Discussion of Edgar Allan Poe's "The Fall of the House of Usher." 12 min., color, 1975. VHS. Host Ray Bradbury discusses Poe's influence on contemporary science fiction.

Edgar Allan Poe. 1996. VHS. Part of the Famous Authors series. Distributed by Kultur International Films.

Edgar Allan Poe [recording]. 4 cassettes (6 hrs.), 2000. Twenty of Poe's poems and tales, including "The Cask of Amontillado." Read by Basil Rathbone and Anthony Quayle. Distributed by HarperAudio.

Edgar Allan Poe: Architect of Dreams. 30 min., color, 1991. VHS. A portrait of Poe's life and work. Distributed by Filmic Archives.

Edgar Allan Poe: A Light and Enlightening Look. 52 min., color, 1995. VHS. Part of the Writing Wonders series (Vol. 4). Featuring Elliot Engel and directed by Carlton A. Gilfillan Jr. Distributed by Media Consultants, Inc.

Edgar Allan Poe: The Principal Works. 4 cassettes (24 min./each). VHS, 3/4" U-matic cassette. Focuses on Poe's individual works and their relation to the author. Individual titles include "The Raven and

Other Poems," "The Tell-Tale Heart," "The Black Cat," "The Cask of Amontillado." Distributed by Films for the Humanities and Sciences.

Edgar Allan Poe: Terror of the Soul and the Cask of Amontillado. 60 min., color, 1995. VHS. A biography revealing Poe's creative genius and personal experiences through dramatic recreations of important scenes from his work and life. Includes dramatizations of Poe classics such as "The Tell-Tale Heart" performed by Treat Williams, John Heard, and Rene Auberjonois. Distributed by PBS Video.

The Fall of the House of Usher. 30 min., 1976. VHS, Beta, 3/4" U-matic cassette. Part of Encyclopaedia Britannica Educational's Short Story Showcase series. Based on Poe's story. Distributed by Encylopaedia Britannica Educational Corporation.

That Strange Mr. Poe. 18 min. VHS. Distributed by Thomas S. Klise Company.

The Time, Life, and Works of Edgar Allan Poe. 32 min., color, 1994. Explores Poe's life and work. Features excerpts from his works, including James Earl Jones reading "The Raven." Distributed by Clearvue/EAV, Inc.

LESLIE MARMON SILKO

Leslie M. Silko. 50 min., color. VHS. Part of the Native American Novelists series. The author discusses her background and writing. Distributed by Films for the Humanities and Sciences.

See also **"Native American Novelists"** on manual page 366.

JOHN STEINBECK

The Chrysanthemums. 22 min., color, 1990. VHS. Based on Steinbeck's short story. Distributed by Pyramid Media.

Introduction to John Steinbeck's Fiction. 45 min. VHS. Part of the Eminent Scholars series. Offers detailed discussion of Steinbeck's life, career, and views. Features Jackson Benson. Distributed by Facets Multimedia, Inc.

John Steinbeck. 30 min., color, 1998. VHS. Part of the Famous Authors series. An exploration of the life and work of Steinbeck. Distributed by Filmic Archives.

John Steinbeck and the American Experience. 45 min., color. VHS. A portrait of the author and the America he depicted. Distributed by Films for the Humanities and Sciences.

Modern American Literature: John Steinbeck. 45 min. VHS, Beta (with ancillaries). A portrait of Steinbeck's life and works. Features formal and informal scenes of the author's friends and family. Distributed by Omnigraphics, Inc.

AMY TAN

The Joy Luck Club. 136 min., color, 1993. VHS, DVD. Based on Tan's best-selling novel. Distri-buted by Buena Vista Home Entertainment and Hollywood Pictures Home Video.

JOHN UPDIKE

Contemporary American Literature: Understanding John Updike's Fiction. 41 min., color, 1990. A discussion of Updike's works. Distributed by Omnigraphics, Inc.

John Updike: "A&P." 30 min., color. VHS. A dramatization of Updike's short story, with John Updike and Donald M. Murray. Distributed by Films for the Humanities and Sciences.

John Updike: A Childhood in the U.S.A. 44 min., color, 2001. VHS. Updike discusses the impact of his childhood on his writing. Distributed by Films for the Humanities and Sciences.

John Updike: In His Own Words. 56 min., color, 1997. VHS. Updike offers his insights on the writing process. Distributed by Films for the Humanities and Sciences.

ALICE WALKER

Alice Walker. 33 min., color. VHS. The author discusses the civil rights movement in relation to her life and the themes in her writing. Distributed by Films for the Humanities and Sciences.

Alice Walker. 30 min., color, 1988. VHS. Walker discusses a variety of topics, including family violence and the position of black women in America. Distributed by Public Media, Inc.

Alice Walker: A Portrait in the First Person. 28 min., color. The author recalls important events from her childhood and explores the themes in her novels and poetry. Distributed by Films for the Humanities and Sciences.

Alice Walker Interview [recording]. 1 cassette (46 min.), 1981. Walker talks about art, politics, and feminist writing. Distributed by American Audio Prose Library.

In Black and White: Alice Walker. 31 min., color, 1992. VHS, 3/4" U-matic cassette. Walker discusses her life, career, and views. Directed by Matteo Billinelli.

Distributed by California Newsreel.

Visions of the Spirit: A Portait of Alice Walker. 58 min., color, 1989. Directed by Elena Featherstone and featuring Walker. Distributed by Women Make Movies, Inc.

See also "In Black and White: Conversations with African American Writers" on manual page 366.

EUDORA WELTY

Eudora Welty: "A Worn Path." 30 min., color, 1999. VHS. A dramatization of Welty's short story and an interview with the author. Distributed by Films for the Humanities and Sciences.

Eudora Welty Reads [recording]. 1 cassette (1 hr., 47 min.), 1998. Welty reads "Why I Live at the P.O.," "A Worn Path," "A Memory," and others. Distributed by HarperAudio.

WILLIAM CARLOS WILLIAMS

William Carlos Williams. 60 min. VHS. Part of the Voices and Visions series. Featuring Allen Ginsberg, Marjorie Perloff, and Hugh Kenner, the film explores Williams's life and work. Distributed by Facets Multimedia, Inc.

GENERAL RESOURCES

The American Imagination: The Lives and Works of Twelve American Writers. 116 min. Part of the Creating the American Dream series. Authors discussed include: Edgar Allan Poe, Henry David Thoreau, Walt Whitman, Mark Twain, Emily Dickinson, Willa Cather. Distributed by Thomas S. Klise Company.

The American Short Story Series. 19 tapes, color. VHS. Includes film adaptations of classic American short stories, originally aired on PBS. Includes stories by Mark Twain, William Faulkner, F. Scott Fitzgerald, Stephen Crane, James Thurber, Ring Lardner, Henry James, Ernest Hemingway, and more.

Author to Author: Contemporary Short-Story Writers. 40 min. A panel discussion of the contemporary short story, featuring George Garrett, Richard Bausch, Madison Smartt Bell, Alan Cheuse. Distributed by Facets Multimedia, Inc.

Great American Short Stories I, II, III [recording]. 7 cassettes per volume (90 min. per cassette), 1982, 1983. Includes "Bartleby, the Scrivener," "The Minister's Black Veil," "The Bride Comes to Yellow Sky," "The Birth-mark," and many others. Distributed by Books on Tape.

In Black and White: Conversations with African American Writers. 6 videocassettes, color, 1992. VHS. Interviews with African American writers: Alice Walker, August Wilson, Charles Johnson, Gloria Naylor, John Edgar Wideman, and Toni Morrison. Distributed by California Newsreel.

A Moveable Feast. 8 cassettes, 30 min./program, color, 1991. VHS. Hosted by Tom Vitale. Profiles of eight writers: Allen Ginsberg, Joyce Carol Oates, Li-Young Lee, Sonia Sanchez, T. Coraghessan Boyle, T. R. Pearson, Trey Ellis, W. S. Merwin. Distributed by Filmic Archives.

Native American Novelists. 4 videocassettes, 50 min. each, color. VHS. The Native American experience is portrayed in conversations with four Native American authors: N. Scott Momaday, James Welch, Leslie Marmon Silko, and Gerald Vizenor. Distributed by Films for the Humanities and Sciences.

Scribbling Women [recording]. 5 cassettes (500 min.), 1997. Featuring stories by Charlotte Perkins Gilman, Willa Cather, Susan Glaspell, Ann Petry, and others. Distributed by the Public Media Foundation.

Tell about the South: Voices in Black and White. 3 cassettes (220 min.), color and b/w, 1996. A showcase of esteemed southern writers, including Jean Toomer, Eudora Welty, William Faulkner, Erskine Caldwell, Zora Neale Hurston, Thomas Wolfe, Richard Wright, Carson McCullers, William Styron, Margaret Mitchell and more. Rita Dove narrates, and contemporary authors Pat Conroy, Alice Walker, and Willie Morris reflect on the southern experience. Distributed by Agee Films.

Women in Literature, The Short Story: A Collection [recording]. 8 cassettes, 60 min. each. 1982. Includes "The Story of an Hour" and other works by Kate Chopin, Edith Wharton, Willa Cather, Mary E. Wilkins Freeman, Sarah Orne Jewett, George Sand, Frances Gilchrist Wood, and Selma Laerloff. Distributed by Books on Tape.

POETRY

MATTHEW ARNOLD

See "Literature: The Synthesis of Poetry" and "Victorian Poetry" on manual pages 384 and 386.

W. H. AUDEN

The Poetry of W. H. Auden, Part I [recording]. 1 cassette (50 min.), 1953. Part of the YM-YWHA Poetry Center Series. Distributed by Audio-Forum.

The Poetry of W. H. Auden, Part II [recording]. 1 cassette (59 min.), 1966. Part of the YM-YWHA Poetry Center Series. Distributed by Audio-Forum.

The Voice of the Poet: W. H. Auden [recording]. 1999. Auden reads from his works. Distributed by Random House Audiobooks.

W. H. Auden. 30 min., b/w. VHS. Part of the Writers of Today series. Auden is interviewed by Walter Kerr. Distributed by First Run/Icarus Films.

W. H. Auden and Writers of the 1930s [recording]. 1 cassette (59 min.), 1953. Read by Stephen Spender. Distributed by Audio-Forum.

W. H. Auden Remembered [recording]. 1 cassette (56 min.). Read by Heywood H. Broun and Stephen Spender. From the Broun Radio Series. Distributed by Jeffrey Norton Publishers.

See also "The Caedmon Poetry Collection: A Century of Poets Reading Their Work" on manual page 383.

AMIRI BARAKA

Amiri Baraka. 27 min., color. VHS. Part of the Sounds of Poetry series. Bill Moyers and Baraka discuss the black experience in America, and Baraka reads his poetry. Distributed by Films for the Humanities and Sciences.

Amiri Baraka II [recording]. 1997. Baraka reads his poetry with a distinctive jazz flair and talks about his life and the influences on his work. Distributed by New Letters on the Air.

Amiri Baraka: A Conversation with Maya Angelou. 26 min., color. VHS. Produced by staff at the BBC. Baraka and Angelou discuss literature as a catalyst for political change. Distributed by Films for the Humanities and Sciences.

In Motion: Amiri Baraka. 1989. VHS. An exploration of Baraka as a writer and activist. Featuring Allen Ginsberg, A. B. Spellman, Joel Oppenheimer, Ted Wilson, Askia M. Toure and directed by St. Clair Bourne. Includes excerpts from Baraka's play *The Dutchman.* Distributed by Facets Multimedia, Inc.

See also "Sounds of Poetry Series" on manual page 386.

ELIZABETH BISHOP

Elizabeth Bishop. 60 min., color, 1988. VHS. Part of the Voices and Visions series. An exploration of the geographic spirit of Bishop's life and works. Distributed by Filmic Archives.

Elizabeth Bishop [recording]. 1 cassette (60 min.). 2000. Distributed by Random House Audiobooks.

Elizabeth Bishop and James Ingram Merrill reading their poems in the

Coolidge Auditorium, April 15, 1974 [recording]. 1974. Distributed by the Library of Congress.

See also "Voices and Visions" on manual page 386.

WILLIAM BLAKE

Blake Ball. 16 min., color, 1988. VHS. Uses the game of baseball as a metaphor to explore Blake's world. Distributed by Pyramid Media.

William Blake. 30 min., color, 1998. VHS. Part of the Famous Authors series. A biographical portrait of Blake's life and works. Distributed by Filmic Archives.

William Blake. 24 min., color, 1999. VHS. Part of the Pioneers of the Spirit series. A biographical look at Blake. Distributed by Vision Video.

William Blake. 52 min., color. VHS. An exploration of Blake's London that also addresses Blake's artistic achievements and continuing appeal. Hosted by Peter Ackroyd. Distributed by Films for the Humanities and Sciences.

William Blake: The Marriage of Heaven and Hell. 30 min., color, 1984. VHS. Dramatizes the life of Blake and his wife Catherine. With Anne Baxter and George Rose. Distributed by Explorations.

William Blake: Selected Poems [recording]. 2 cassettes (180 min.), 1992. Includes "The Tyger" and "A Poison Tree." Read by Frederick Davidson. Distributed by Blackstone Audio Books.

William Blake: Songs of Innocence and Experience. 20 min., color. Examines the social context, style, and language of "The Chimney Sweeper" poems.

Distributed by Films for the Humanities and Sciences.

See also "Introduction to English Poetry" and "Romantic Pioneers," on manual pages 384 and 386.

ANNE BRADSTREET

See "Great American Poetry" on manual page 384.

GWENDOLYN BROOKS

Gwendolyn Brooks. 30 min., b/w, 1966. 3/4" U-matic cassette, special order formats. Brooks talks about her life and poetry. No known distributor.

Gwendolyn Brooks I & II [recording]. 1 cassette (60 min.), 1984, 1988. Distributed by New Letters on the Air.

See also "Anthology of Negro Poets in the U.S.A. — 200 Years" and "Poets in Person," on manual pages 383 and 385.

ELIZABETH BARRETT BROWNING

Elizabeth Barrett Browning. 26 min., color. VHS. A profile of Browning in the form of an interview between the author's most recent biographer and an actress speaking lines drawn from the poet's journals and poems. Distributed by Films for the Humanities and Sciences.

Robert and Elizabeth Browning. 30 min., color, 1998. VHS. Explores the Brownings' famous literary romance. In an apartment on Wimpole Street actors perform poems by both of the poets. Distributed by Filmic Archives.

See also "Victorian Poetry" on manual page 386.

ROBERT BROWNING

Robert Browning: His Life and Poetry. 21 min., color, 1972. VHS, 3/4" U-matic cassette, special order formats. A dramatization of Browning's life and several of his poems, including "My Last Duchess." Distributed by International Film Bureau, Inc.

Robert Browning: Selected Poems [recording]. 4 cassettes (360 min.). Read by Frederick Davidson. Distributed by Blackstone Audio Books.

Robert and Elizabeth Browning. 30 min., color, 1998. VHS. Explores the Brownings' famous literary romance. In an apartment on Wimpole Street actors perform poems by both of the poets. Distributed by Filmic Archives.

See also "Victorian Poetry" on manual page 386.

GEORGE GORDON, LORD BYRON

Byron: Mad, Bad and Dangerous to Know. 26 min., color. VHS. The poet seems to stand just out of camera range as the program focuses on publisher John Murray and his offices filled with Byron memorabilia. Distributed by Films for the Humanities and Sciences.

Lord Byron: Selected Poems [recording]. 2 cassettes (180 min.). Read by Frederick Davidson. Distributed by Blackstone Audio Books.

See also "English Romantic Poetry" on manual page 383.

LEWIS CARROLL

Lewis Carroll: Curiouser and Curiouser. 50 min., color. A portrait of Carroll's life and works.

Distributed by Films for the Humanities and Sciences.

See also "Victorian Poetry" on manual page 386.

LUCILLE CLIFTON

Lucille Clifton. 60 min., color, 1996. VHS. Part of the Lannan Literary Videos series. Distributed by the Lannan Foundation.

Lucille Clifton and Mark Doty. 27 min., color. VHS. Part of the Sounds of Poetry series, featuring Bill Moyers. Clifton, Doty, and Moyers discuss topics related to poetry and racial issues, and Clifton and Doty read several of their poems. Distributed by Films for the Humanities and Sciences.

SAMUEL TAYLOR COLERIDGE

Coleridge. 19 min. VHS. Distributed by Thomas S. Klise Company.

Kubla Khan by Samuel Taylor Coleridge. 27 min., color, 1993. VHS. Part of the Guide to Understanding Literature series. Host Alan Gedalof leads discussion of Coleridge's romantic poem, examining the poet's claim that he based the work on a drug-induced dream he had. Distributed by Films for the Humanities and Sciences.

Samuel Taylor Coleridge: The Fountain and the Cave. 32 min., color, 1998. VHS. A biography of the poet, filmed on location. Distributed by Filmic Archives.

Wordsworth and Coleridge: The Lake Poets. 30 min., color, 1997. VHS. Part of the Master Poets Collection II. Distributed by Monterey Media, Inc.

See also "English Romantic Poetry" and "Romantic Pioneers" on manual pages 383 and 386.

COUNTEE CULLEN

See "Anthology of Negro Poets in the U.S.A. — 200 Years" on manual page 383.

E. E. CUMMINGS

e. e. cummings: A Poetry Collection [recording]. 3 cassettes (3 1/2 hrs.), 2001. cummings reads from his works. Distributed by Harper-Audio.

e. e. cummings: An American Original. 30 min., color, 1997. Part of the Master Poets Collection III. Set in a re-creation of Greenwich Village, the film provides a portrait of the poet's life and works. Distributed by Monterey Media, Inc.

e. e. cummings: The Making of a Poet. 24 min., color, 1978. VHS, 3/4" U-matic cassette. A profile of cummings told in his own words. Distributed by Films for the Humanities and Sciences.

e. e. cummings: Twentieth-Century Poetry in English: Recordings of Poets Reading Their Own Poetry, No. 5 [recording]. 1 cassette. Distributed by the Library of Congress.

See also "Caedmon Poetry Collection: A Century of Poets Reading Their Work" on manual page 383.

EMILY DICKINSON

Emily Dickinson. 22 min. VHS, Beta, 3/4" U-matic cassette. A film about the poet and her poems. Part of the Authors series. Distributed by United Learning.

Emily Dickinson: A Certain Slant of Light. 30 min., color, 1977. VHS. Explores Dickinson's life and environment. Narrated by Julie Harris and directed by Jean

McClure Mudge. Distributed by Monterey Media, Inc.

Emily Dickinson: Poems and Letters [recording]. 2 cassettes (2.25 hrs.), 1959. Read by Alexandra O'Karma. Distributed by Recorded Books.

Emily Dickinson: Selected Poems [recording]. 4 cassettes (360 min.), 1993. Read by Mary Woods. Distributed by Blackstone Audio Books.

Magic Prison: A Dialogue Set to Music. 35 min., color, 1969. VHS, 3/4" U-matic cassette. Dramatizes the letters between Dickinson and T. W. Higginson. With an introduction by Archibald MacLeish and music by Ezra Laderman. Distributed by Britannica Films.

Poems and Letters of Emily Dickinson [recording]. 1 cassette (39 min.). Read by Julie Harris. Distributed by HarperAudio.

The World of Emily Dickinson. 30 min., color, 1997. VHS. A dramatic presentation of Dickinson's "letters to the world." Featuring Claire Bloom, Jill Tanner, Cynthia Herman, and George Backman. Distributed by Monterey Media, Inc.

See also "Introduction to English Poetry," "Voices and Visions," and "With a Feminine Touch" on manual pages 384 and 386.

H.D.

The H.D. Trilogy Film. 115 min. VHS. A look at Hilda Doolittle's life and work through the life of Joanna McClure during the years 1990 through 1992. Distributed by Facets Multimedia, Inc.

JOHN DONNE

John Donne. 40 min., color, 1998. Part of the Great Poets series. An introduction to Donne's poetry in simple, shortened form with discussion and analysis of the poet's love songs and sonnets. Distributed by Filmic Archives.

John Donne: Love Poems [recording]. 1 cassette (90 min.), 1990. Distributed by Recorded Books.

John Donne: Selected Poems [recording]. 2 cassettes (180 min.), 1992. Read by Frederick Davidson. Distributed by Blackstone Audio Books.

The Love Poems of John Donne [recording]. 1 cassette (37 min.). Read by Richard Burton. Distributed by HarperAudio.

See also "Metaphysical and Devotional Poetry" on manual page 384.

RITA DOVE

Favorite Poets: Rita Dove [recording]. 1 sound tape reel (60 min.), 1999. Distributed by the Library of Congress.

Poet Laureate Rita Dove. 60 min., color, 1994. VHS. Dove talks to Bill Moyers about her life and work. Distributed by Films for the Humanities and Sciences.

Rita Dove I and II [recording]. 2 cassettes (29 min. each), 1985, 1993. Dove reads a selection of poems. Distributed by New Letters on the Air.

See also "Poets in Person" on manual page 385.

T. S. ELIOT

Modern American Literature: T. S. Eliot. 45 min. VHS, Beta (with ancillaries). A survey of Eliot's life and works with formal and informal scenes of his friends and family.

Modern American Literature: T. S. Eliot's "The Waste Land." 45 min. VHS. Covers Eliot's major poem with illustrations, original book jackets, and informal scenes of the author.

The Mysterious Mr. Eliot. 62 min., color, 1973. VHS, 3/4" U-matic cassette. A biographical film about the poet. Distributed by CRM Learning.

Thomas Stearns Eliot. 58 min. VHS. Part of the Modern World series. A discussion of Eliot's literary contributions and innovations with readings of the author's poems by Edward Fox, Eileen Atkins, and Michael Gough. Distributed by Facets Multimedia, Inc.

T. S. Eliot. 60 min. VHS. Part of the Voices and Visions series. Eliot reads his poems and others speak about him. Features Stephen Spender, Quentin Bell, and Frank Kermode. Distributed by Facets Multimedia, Inc.

T. S. Eliot: The Waste Land. 59 min., color 1987. VHS. Part of the Ten Great Writers of the Modern World series. Examines Eliot's poem and analyzes its continual appeal as an emblem of the twentieth century. Featuring Peter Ackroyd, Craig Raine, Stephen Spender, with readings by Michael Gough, Edward Fox, and Eileen Atkins. Distributed by Films for the Humanities and Sciences.

T. S. Eliot: Twentieth-Century Poetry in English: Recordings of Poets Reading Their Own Poetry, No. 3 [recording]. Distributed by the Library of Congress.

T. S. Eliot Reads [recording]. 3 cassettes (3 hrs.), 2000. Distributed by HarperAudio.

T. S. Eliot Reads "The Love Song of J. Alfred Prufrock" and Other Poems [recording]. 1 cassette (50 min.), 2000. Distributed by HarperAudio.

Understanding Eliot's The Wasteland. 45 min. VHS. Part of the Eminent Scholars series. Explores Ezra Pound's collaborative role in the making of the poem, as well as key motifs and passages. With A. Walton Liz. Distributed by Facets Multimedia, Inc.

See also "The Caedmon Poetry Collection: A Century of Poets Reading Their Work" and "Voices and Visions" on manual pages 383 and 386.

LAWRENCE FERLINGHETTI

The Coney Island of Lawrence Ferlinghetti. 60 min., 1999. VHS. Part of the Beat Box Set series. Ferlinghetti discusses his life and works. Also features interviews with Allen Ginsberg, Gregory Corso, Anne Waldman, Andrei Vosnesensky, and Amiri Imamu Baraka. Distributed by WinStar Home Video (Fox Lorber Films).

A Coney Island of the Mind [recording]. 1 CD (53 min.), 1999. The author reads his poetry with music composed and performed by Dana Colley. Distributed by Rykodisc.

Lawrence Ferlinghetti [recording]. 1 cassette (29 min.), 1987. Rebekah Presson interviews Ferlinghetti. Distributed by New Letters on the Air.

See also "Howls, Raps, and Roars: Recordings from the San Francisco Poetry Renaissance" on manual page 384.

CAROLYN FORCHÉ

Carolyn Forché. 65 min., color, 1990. VHS. Part of the Lannan Literary Videos series. Recorded in Los Angeles on February 12, 1990. Forché reads from her works. Distributed by the Lannan Foundation.

Carolyn Forché. 94 min., color, 1994. Part of the Lannan Literary Videos series. Recorded on May 24, 1994, in Los Angeles. Forché is interviewed by Michael Silverblatt. The poet discusses her concerns with the brutal events of the twentieth century and reads "The Angel of History" in its entirety. Distributed by the Lannan Foundation.

Carolyn Forché [recording]. 1 cassette (29 min.), 1989. Distributed by New Letters on the Air.

ROBERT FROST

The Afterglow: A Tribute to Robert Frost. 35 min., color, 1989. VHS, 3/4" U-matic cassette, special order formats. Starring and directed by Burgess Meredith. Distributed by Pyramid Media.

Frost and Whitman. 30 min., b/w, 1963. VHS, 1/2" open reel (EIAJ), 3/4" U-matic cassette. Will Geer performs excerpts from the two poets' works. Distributed by Camera Three Productions, Inc. and Creative Arts Television Archive.

An Interview with Robert Frost. 30 min., b/w, 1952. VHS, 3/4" U-matic cassette. Bela Kornitzer interviews Frost, who reads from his poetry. Distributed by Social Studies School Service.

Robert Frost. 10 min., color, 1972. VHS. A biographical sketch of the poet. Distributed by AIMS Multimedia.

Robert Frost. 60 min., color. VHS. Part of the Voices and Visions series. Features interviews with Frost, dramatizations of his work, and commentaries by poets Seamus Heaney, Alfred Edwards, and Richard Wilbur. Distributed by Facets Multimedia, Inc.

Robert Frost: A First Acquaintance. 16 min., color, 1974. VHS. An examination of Frost's life through his poems. Distributed by Films for the Humanities and Sciences.

Robert Frost: New England Autumn. 30 min., color, 1997. VHS. Part of the Master Poets Collection set. Distributed by Filmic Archives.

Robert Frost: Twentieth Century Poetry in English: Recordings of Poets Reading Their Own Poetry, No. 6 [recording]. Distributed by the Library of Congress.

Robert Frost in Recital [recording]. 1 cassette (52 min.) Distributed by HarperAudio.

Robert Frost Poetry Collection [recording]. 2 cassettes (1 hr., 40 min.), 2000. From the Poet Anniversary Series. Distributed by Harper-Audio.

Robert Frost Reads His Poems [recording]. 1 cassette (55 min.), 1965. Distributed by Audio-Forum.

Robert Frost's "The Death of the Hired Man." 22 min., 1979. VHS, Beta, 3/4" U-matic cassette. Part of Encyclopaedia Britannica Educational's Poetry series. Edited by Clifton Fadiman and produced by Jeanne Collachia. Distributed by Encyclopaedia Britannica Corporation.

Stopping by the Woods of Mr. Frost. 22 min. VHS. Distributed by Thomas S. Klise Company.

The Voice of the Poet: Robert Frost. 2003. Frost reads from his works. Distributed by Random House Audiobooks.

See also "The Caedmon Poetry Collection: A Century of Poets Reading Their Work," "Literature: The Synthesis of Poetry," "Poetry by Americans," and "Voices and Visions" on manual pages 383, 384, 385, and 386.

ALLEN GINSBERG

Allen Ginsberg. 50 min., color. VHS, Beta, 3/4" U-matic cassette. Part of the Writers on Writing series. A biographical portrait of the poet's life and work. Distributed by the Roland Collection.

Allen Ginsberg [recording]. 1 cassette (29 min.), 1988. The author talks about the Beat movement and his battle against censorship. Distributed by New Letters on the Air.

Allen Ginsberg: When the Muse Calls, Answer! 30 min., color. VHS. Part of the Moveable Feast series. Hosted by Tom Vitale. Distributed by Filmic Archives.

Allen Ginsberg and Friends. 60 min., color. VHS. Part of the Poetry Heaven series. Ginsberg analyzes the poetry of William Blake and reads from his own works. Also features poets Mark Doty, Robert Hass, Marie Howe, Yusef Komunyakaa, Li-Young Lee, and Louis Jenkins. Distributed by Films for the Humanities and Sciences.

Allen Ginsberg Meets Nanao Sakaki. 1988. VHS. Ginsberg and Sakaki meet in an East Village poetry performance space, the Gas Station, to discuss and perform their works. Distributed by Facets Multimedia, Inc.

Beat Legends: Allen Ginsberg. 92 min. VHS. Ginsberg reads from his works, sometimes accompanied by a mini-pump organ. Also offers historical background information related to the poems being read. Distributed by Facets Multimedia, Inc.

The Life and Times of Allen Ginsberg. 82 min., color and b/w, 1993. VHS. Chronicles the life of the poet with commentary from Abbie Hoffman, Ken Kesey, Jack Kerouac, Joan Baez, and others. Distributed by First Run/Icarus Films.

See also "Fried Shoes, Cooked Diamonds," "Howls, Raps, and Roars: Recordings from the San Francisco Poetry Renaissance," "A Moveable Feast," "Poets in Person," and "The Voice of the Poet Series," on manual pages 384 and 386.

LOUISE GLÜCK

Favorite Poets: Louise Glück [recording]. 1 sound tape reel (60 min.), 1999. Distributed by Library of Congress.

Louise Glück. 60 min., color, 1989. VHS. Part of the Lannan Literary Videos series. Glück reads and is interviewed by Lewis Mac-Adams. Distributed by the Lannan Foundation.

Louise Glück [recording]. 1 cassette (60 min.), 1992. Glück reads from her work. Distributed by the Academy of American Poets.

THOMAS GRAY

Elegy to Thomas Gray. 20 min. Beta, VHS, 3/4" U-matic cassette. A cinematic interpretation of "An Elegy Written in a Country Churchyard." No known distributor.

THOMAS HARDY

Hardy's Wessex. 60 min., color. VHS. Hardy experts explore the poet's life and discuss his works. Features footage shot on location in Hardy's birthplace, Dorset, excerpts from his novels and poems, and insights into the people and places that defined the poet's world. Distributed by Films for the Humanities and Sciences.

Poetic Voices of Thomas Hardy. 20 min., color. VHS. Examines the poet's shorter poems with a focus on the different voices and personae Hardy employs. Distributed by Films for the Humanities and Sciences.

Thomas Hardy. 30 min., color, 1998. VHS. Part of the Famous Authors series. A biographical portrait of Hardy's life and work. Distributed by Filmic Archives.

Thomas Hardy and Dorset. 15 min., color. VHS, 3/4" U-matic cassette. Sets the novels and poems in Hardy's birthplace, Dorset. Distributed by Films for the Humanities and Sciences.

See also "Introduction to English Poetry," "Romantics and Realists," and "Victorian Poetry" on manual pages 384 and 386.

ROBERT HAYDEN

Robert Hayden [recording]. 1 cassette (90 min.), 1976. The poet reads his work. Distributed by the Academy of American Poets.

SEAMUS HEANEY

Seamus Heaney: Looking Back. 52 min., color. VHS, DVD. Heaney reads and discusses his poems. Distributed by Films for the Humanities and Sciences.

GEORGE HERBERT

See "Introduction to English Poetry" and "Metaphysical and Devotional Poetry" on manual page 384.

ROBERT HERRICK

See "Introduction to English Poetry" on manual page 384.

A. E. HOUSMAN

See "Romantics and Realists" and "Victorian Poetry" on manual page 386.

LANGSTON HUGHES

Langston Hughes. 24 min., color. VHS. A biographical sketch of the poet. Distributed by Carousel Film and Video.

Langston Hughes: Dream Keeper and Other Poems [recording]. 1 cassette/CD, 1958. Distributed by Smithsonian Folkways Recordings.

Langston Hughes: The Poet in Our Hearts. 30 min., color and b/w, 1994. VHS, Beta, 3/4" U-matic cassette. Part of the Poetry Film series. Piri Thomas reads selected Hughes poems. Readings are illustrated by clips from current and historical films and photographs. Distributed by Chip Taylor Communications.

Looking for Langston. 65 min., 1989. VHS. A biographical look at Hughes's life and work. Director Isaac Julien's biography of the poet is interwoven with the poetry of Essex Hamphill and Bruce Nugent and archival footage and period music from the Harlem Renaissance. Distributed by Facets Multimedia, Inc.

The Voice of Langston Hughes: Selected Poetry and Prose [recording]. 1 cassette or CD (38 min.). Selections from the years 1925–32. The author reads poetry from *The Dream Keeper and Other Poems* and *Simple Speaks His Mind*, and he narrates his text from *The Story of Jazz, Rhythms of the World*, and *The Glory of Negro History.* Distributed by Smithsonian Folkways Recordings.

Voice of the Poet: Langston Hughes [recording]. 2002. The poet reads his works. Distributed by Random House Audiobooks.

See also "Anthology of Negro Poets in the U.S.A. — 200 Years," "Harlem Renaissance: The Black Poets," and "Voices and Vision," on manual pages 383, 384, and 386.

RANDALL JARRELL

The Bat Poet [recording]. 1 cassette (67 min.), 1963. Part of the YM-YWHA Poetry Center Series. Distributed by Audio-Forum.

The Poetry of Randall Jarrell [recording]. 1 cassette (67 min.), 1963. Part of the YM-YWHA Poetry Center Series. Distributed by Audio-Forum.

The Voice of the Poet: Randall Jarrell [recording]. 2001. Jarrell reads his works. Distributed by Random House Audiobooks.

BEN JONSON

See "Introduction to English Poetry" on manual page 384.

JOHN KEATS

John Keats. 30 min., color, 1998. VHS. Part of the Famous Authors series. A biographical portrait of the poet's life and works. Distributed by Filmic Archives.

John Keats — His Life and Death. 55 min., color, 1973. Beta, VHS, 3/4" U-matic cassette. Extended version of "John Keats — Poet" (see next). Explores the poet's affair with Fanny Brawne and the events surrounding his death. Written by Archibald MacLeish. Distributed by Encyclopaedia Britannica Educational Corporation.

John Keats — Poet. 31 min., color, 1973. Beta, VHS, 3/4" U-matic cassette. A biography of the poet, with excerpts from his letters and poems. Written by Archibald MacLeish. Distributed by Encyclopaedia Britannica Educational Corporation.

John Keats: Selected Poems [recording]. 2 cassettes (180 min.), 1993. Read by Frederick Davidson. Distributed by Blackstone Audio Books.

Poetry of Keats [recording]. 1 cassette (90 min.), 1996. Read by Sir Ralph Richardson. Distributed by HarperAudio.

GALWAY KINNELL

Galway Kinnell. 60 min., color, 1989. Part of the Lannan Literary Videos series. Distributed by the Lannan Foundation.

Galway Kinnell I & II [recording]. 1 cassette (60 min.), 1982, 1991. Distributed by New Letters on the Air.

The Poetry of Galway Kinnell [recording]. 1 cassette (33 min.), 1965. Part of the YM-YWHA Poetry Center Series. Distributed by Jeffrey Norton Publishers.

See also "Anthology of Contemporary American Poetry" and "The Power of the Word Series" on manual pages 383 and 386.

YUSEF KOMUNYAKAA

Yusef Komunyakaa [recording]. 1 cassette (29 min.), 1995. Rebeka Presson interviews Komunyakaa. Distributed by New Letters on the Air.

DENISE LEVERTOV

Denise Levertov. 60 min., color, 1994. VHS. Part of the Lannan Literary Videos series. Levertov reads and discusses her poetry. Distributed by the Lannan Foundation.

Denise Levertov [recording]. 1 cassette (29 min.), 1983. The author reads her poems and discusses political activism and the responsibility of a writer. Distributed by New Letters on the Air.

The Poetry of Denise Levertov [recording]. 1 cassette (37 min.), 1965. Part of the YM-YWHA Poetry Center Series. Distributed by Audio-Forum.

AUDRE LORDE

Audre Lorde: Black Unicorn [recording]. 1 cassette (29 min.), 1979. Distributed by New Letters on the Air.

ROBERT LOWELL

The Poetry of Robert Lowell [recording]. 1 cassette (28 min.), 1968. Part of the YM-YWHA Poetry Center Series. Distributed by Audio-Forum.

Robert Lowell. 60 min., color, 1988. VHS. Lowell reads and discusses his work in connection with his political passions. Distributed by Filmic Archives.

Robert Lowell: Reading Himself. 37 min., color. VHS. Ian Hamilton examines Lowell's interrelated life and works. Distributed by

Films for the Humanities and Sciences.

Robert Lowell: Twentieth-Century Poetry in English: Recordings of Poets Reading Their Own Poetry, Nos. 11 and 32–33 [recording]. Distributed by the Library of Congress.

Voice of the Poet: Robert Lowell [recording]. 2000. Lowell reads from his works. Distributed by Random House Audiobooks.

See also "Voices and Visions" on manual page 386.

ARCHIBALD MACLEISH

Archibald MacLeish. 30 min., b/w. VHS. Walter Kerr interviews MacLeish. Disributed by First Run/Icarus Films.

Archibald MacLeish: Twentieth-Century Poetry in English: Recordings of Poets Reading Their Own Poetry: Nine Pulitzer Prize Poets, No. 29 [recording]. Distributed by the Library of Congress.

See also "The Caedmon Poetry Collection: A Century of Poets Reading Their Work" on manual page 383.

ANDREW MARVELL

Andrew Marvell: Ralph Richardson Reads Andrew Marvell [recording]. 1 cassette. Distributed by Audio-Forum.

See also "Introduction to English Poetry" and "Metaphysical and Devotional Poetry" on manual page 384.

MARIANNE MOORE

Marianne Moore. 60 min., b/w. VHS. From the PBS Voices and Visions series. The life and career of Marianne Moore. With commentary by Grace Shulman. Distributed by Unapix Entertainment, Inc.

Marianne Moore: Twentieth-Century Poetry in English: Poets Reading Their Own Poetry [recording]. 1949. Distributed by the Library of Congress.

See also "Voices and Visions," on manual page 386.

SHARON OLDS

Sharon Olds. 60 min., color, 1991. VHS. Part of the Lannan Literary Videos series. Distributed by the Lannan Foundation.

Sharon Olds [recording]. 1 cassette (29 min.), 1993. Distributed by New Letters on the Air.

Sharon Olds: Coming Back to Life [recording]. 1 cassette (60 min.). Distributed by Jeffrey Norton Publishers.

See also "Poets in Person" and "The Power of the Word Series" on manual pages 385 and 386.

WILFRED OWEN

The Pity of War. 58 min., color. VHS, 3/4" U-matic cassette. Excerpts of Owen's letters, poems, and diaries that depict the horrors of World War I. Distributed by Films for the Humanities and Sciences.

DOROTHY PARKER

Voice of the Poet: American Wits: Ogden Nash, Dorothy Parker, Phyllis McGinley [recording]. 2003. The three poets read from their works. Distributed by Random House Audiobooks.

Sylvia Plath

Bell Jar [recording]. 2 cassettes (3 hrs.). Performed by Frances McDormand. Distributed by HarperAudio.

The Bell Jar. 113 min., color, 1979. VHS. Based on Plath's semiautobiographical novel. Distributed by Vestron Video.

Sylvia Plath. 60 min. VHS. Part of the Voices and Visions series. A portrait of the poet's life and work, including archival footage and an in-depth interview with Plath. Distributed by Facets Multimedia, Inc.

Sylvia Plath. 4 programs (30 min. each), color, 1974. VHS, 1/2" open reel (EIAJ), 3/4" U-matic cassette. A biographical examination of the poet and her work. Distributed by Camera Three Productions, Inc. and Creative Arts Television Archive.

Sylvia Plath: The Growth of a Poet. 30 min., color, 1997. VHS. Part of the Master Poets Collection III. Follows Plath's development as a poet and includes readings and excerpts from Plath's works. Distributed by Monterey Media, Inc.

Sylvia Plath: Letters Home. 90 min., color, 1985. VHS. Staged version of Plath's letters to her mother. Distributed by Films for the Humanities and Sciences.

Sylvia Plath, Part I: The Struggle. 30 min., color, 1974. Beta, VHS, 1/2" open reel (EIAJ), 3/4" U-matic cassette. A dramatization of Plath's poetry by the Royal Shakespeare Company. Distributed by Camera Three Productions, Inc. and Creative Arts Television Archive.

Sylvia Plath, Part II: Getting There. 30 min., color, 1974. Beta, VHS, 1/2" open reel (EIAJ), 3/4" U-matic cassette. Plath's poems are set to music by Elizabeth Swados and performed by Michele Collison. Distributed by Camera Three Productions, Inc. and Creative Arts Television Archive.

The Voice of the Poet: Sylvia Plath [recording]. 1999. Plath reads from her works. Distributed by Random House Audiobooks.

See also "Voices and Visions," and "With a Feminine Touch" on manual page 386.

Ezra Pound

Ezra Pound. 60 min. VHS. Part of the Voices and Visions series. An in-depth look at the poet's work. With Hugh Kenner and Alfred Kazin. Distributed by Facets Multimedia, Inc.

Ezra Pound: Poet's Poet. 28 min., b/w, 1970. Beta, VHS, 3/4" U-matic cassette. A profile of Pound and his influence on later poets. Distributed by Films for the Humanities and Sciences.

Ezra Pound Reads [recording]. 2 cassettes, 2001. Distributed by HarperAudio.

See also "The Caedmon Poetry Collection: A Century of Poets Reading Their Work" and "Voices and Visions," on manual pages 383 and 386.

Dudley Randall

Dudley Randall Reading His Poems [recording]. 1 sound tape reel (60 min.), 1975. Distributed by the Library of Congress.

ADRIENNE RICH

Adrienne Rich. 60 min. Recorded in Los Angeles on May 14, 1992. Rich speaks with Michael Silverblatt and reads from her works. Distributed by Facets Multimedia, Inc.

Adrienne Rich [recording]. 1 cassette (29 min.). 1995. Rebekah Presson interviews the poet, who reads from her work. Distributed by New Letters on the Air.

The Poetry of Adrienne Rich [recording]. 1 cassette (30 min.), 1980. Recorded at the YM-YWHA Poetry Center in New York. Distributed by Audio-Forum.

Voice of the Poet: Adrienne Rich [recording]. 2002. Rich reads from her works. Distributed by Random House Audiobooks.

See also "Poets in Person" on manual page 385.

THEODORE ROETHKE

The Poetry of Theodore Roethke [recording]. 1 cassette (36 min.). Part of the YM-YWHA Poetry Center Series. Distributed by Audio-Forum.

Theodore Roethke: Twentieth-Century Poetry in English: Recordings of Poets Reading Their Own Poetry, No. 10 [recording]. Distributed by the Library of Congress.

Words for the Wind: Poems Read by Theodore Roethke [recording]. 1 cassette/CD, 1962. Distributed by Smithsonian Folkways Recordings.

See also "Anthology of Contemporary American Poetry" on manual page 383.

CHRISTINA ROSSETTI

See "Victorian Poetry" on manual page 386.

ANNE SEXTON

Anne Sexton Reads [recording]. 1999. Sexton reads from her works. Recorded shortly before her death. Distributed by Harper-Audio.

The Poetry of Anne Sexton [recording]. 1 cassette (35 min.), 1964. Part of the YM-YWHA Poetry Center Series. Distributed by Audio-Forum.

Voice of the Poet: Anne Sexton [recording]. 2000. Sexton reads from her works. Distributed by Random House Audiobooks.

WILLIAM SHAKESPEARE

Poetry and Hidden Poetry. 53 min., color, 1984. VHS, 3/4" U-matic cassette. A micro-examination of Shakespeare's poetry and its hidden meanings. Produced by the Royal Shakespeare Company. Distributed by Films for the Humanities and Sciences.

Presenting William Shakespeare. 35 min., color, 1992. VHS. A look at Shakespeare's life, world, and literary works. Distributed by Filmic Archives.

Selected Sonnets by Shakespeare. 40 min., color, 1984. VHS, 3/4" U-matic cassette. Features readings by Ben Kingsley and Jane Lapotaire. Distributed by Films for the Humanities and Sciences.

Shakespeare: The Man and His Times. 47 min., color, 1991. VHS. Includes ancillaries. Features footage of significant places in the poet/playwright's life, archival illustrations, and commentary from historians. Distributed by Clearvue/EAV, Inc.

Shakespeare in London. 3 cassettes (240 min.). VHS. A historic re-creation designed to give students a behind the scenes look at Shakespeare and his era. Distributed by PBS Video.

Shakespeare's Sonnets. 150 min., color. VHS, 3/4" U-matic cassette. Includes readings of fifteen sonnets that reveal details of Shakespeare's personal life. With Ben Kingsley, Roger Rees, Claire Bloom, Jane Lapotaire, A. L. Rowse, Leslie A. Fiedler, Stephen Spender, and Arnold Wesker. Distributed by Film for the Humanities and Sciences.

Shakespeare's Stratford. 29 min., 1983. VHS. History and criticism. Distributed by Encyclopaedia Britannica Educational Corporation.

The Sonnets — William Shakespeare. 30 min., color, 1993. VHS. Part of the Video Interaction Shakespearean series. Distributed by RMI Media Productions, Inc.

William Shakespeare. 30 min., color, 1998. VHS. A biographical portrait of Shakespeare's life and works. Distributed by Filmic Archives.

William Shakespeare: A Poet for All Time. 30 min., color, 1997. VHS. A presentation of several of Shakespeare's best-known works on location in Stratford. Distributed by Monterey Media, Inc.

See also "Introduction to English Poetry" and "Medieval to Elizabethan Poetry" on manual page 384.

PERCY BYSSHE SHELLEY

Percy Bysshe Shelley. 30 min., color, 1998. VHS. Part of the Famous Authors series. A biographical portrait of Shelley's life and

works. Distributed by Filmic Archives.

See also "English Romantic Poetry" and "Introduction to English Poetry" on manual page 383 and 384.

STEVIE SMITH

Stevie. 102 min., color, 1978. VHS. Based on the play by Hugh Whitemore and the works of Stevie Smith. Starring Glenda Jackson, Mona Whasbourne, and Trevor Howard. Distributed by UAV Entertainment.

GARY SNYDER

Gary Snyder. 2 cassettes (60 min. each), color, 1989. VHS. Part of the Lannan Literary Videos series. Distributed by the Lannan Foundation.

GARY SOTO

Gary Soto. 60 min. VHS. Recorded on May 2, 1995. Soto reads from his *New and Selected Poems* and speaks with novelist Alejandro Morales. Distributed by Facets Multimedia, Inc.

Gary Soto I & II [recording]. 1 cassette (60 min.), 1982, 1992. The author reads his work and talks about the recent rise of Chicano literature. Distributed by New Letters on the Air.

See also "Poets in Person" on manual page 385.

WALLACE STEVENS

Voices of the Poet: Wallace Stevens [recording]. 2002. Stevens reads from his works. Distributed by Random House Audiobooks.

Wallace Stevens. 60 min., color, 1988. VHS. Part of the Voices and Visions series. A portrait of the poet's life and works, illustrated by archival footage. Distributed by Filmic Archives.

Wallace Stevens Reads [recording]. 1 cassette (47 min.), 1998. Stevens reads from his works. Distributed by HarperAudio.

See also "Voices and Visions" on manual page 386.

ALFRED, LORD TENNYSON

See "Victorian Poetry" on manual page 386.

DYLAN THOMAS

Dylan Thomas. 25 min., color, 1982. VHS, 3/4" U-matic cassette. A portrait of the poet. Distributed by Home Vision Cinema.

Dylan Thomas: A Portrait. 26 min., color, 1989. VHS, 3/4" U-matic cassette. A biographical film. Distributed by Films for the Humanities and Sciences.

Dylan Thomas: A Return Journey. 53 min., color, 1990. VHS. A dramatic portrayal of the poet on his lecture tour in the 1950s. Featuring additional biographical information delivered by actor/director Anthony Hopkins. With Bob Kingdom. Distributed by Direct Cinema, Ltd.

A Dylan Thomas Memoir. 28 min., color, 1972. VHS, 3/4" U-matic cassette, 16-mm film. A character study of the poet. Distributed by Pyramid Media.

Dylan Thomas Reading His Poetry [recording]. 2 cassettes (2 hrs.). Distributed by HarperAudio.

Dylan Thomas (Unabridged): The Caedmon Collection [recording]. 2002. Distributed by Harper-Audio.

More Dylan Thomas Reads [recording]. (90 min.), 1993. Distributed by HarperAudio.

The Wales of Dylan Thomas. 15 min., color, 1989. VHS, 3/4" U-matic cassette. Images of Wales in Thomas's poetry, prose, and drama. Distributed by Films for the Humanities and Sciences.

See also "The Caedmon Collection of English Poetry" on manual page 383.

WALT WHITMAN

Frost and Whitman. 30 min., b/w, 1963. VHS, 1/2 open reel (EIAJ), 3/4" U-matic cassette. Will Geer performs excerpts from the two poets' works. Distributed by Camera Three Productions, Inc. and Creative Arts Television Archive.

The Living Tradition: Ginsberg on Whitman. VHS. Allen Ginsberg discusses the life and poetry of Walt Whitman. Distributed by Clearvue/EAV, Inc.

Selections from Walt Whitman's Leaves of Grass [recording]. 1 cassette, 1957. Distributed by Smithsonian Folkways Recordings.

Walt Whitman. 10 min., 1977. VHS. Part of the Poetry by Americans series. Readings and a discussion of Whitman's life. Hosted by Efrem Zimbalist Jr. Distributed by AIMS Media, Inc.

Walt Whitman. 12 min., color. 3/4" U-matic cassette. Examines Whitman's poetic language. Distributed by Films for the Humanities and Sciences.

Walt Whitman: Endlessly Rocking. 21 min., color, 1986. VHS. Shows a teacher's unsuccessful attempts to interest her students in Whitman. Distributed by Clearvue/EAV, Inc.

Walt Whitman: Poet for a New Age. 29 min., color, 1971. Beta, VHS, 3/4" U-matic cassette. A study of the poet. Distributed by Encyclopaedia Britannica Educational Corporation.

Walt Whitman's Civil War. 15 min., color, 1988. VHS, 3/4" U-matic cassette. Discusses Whitman's perspective on the war. Distributed by Churchill Media.

See also "Poetry by Americans" and "Voices and Visions" on manual pages 385 and 386.

WILLIAM CARLOS WILLIAMS

William Carlos Williams. 60 min. VHS. Part of the Voices and Visions series. Featuring Allen Ginsberg, Marjorie Perloff, and Hugh Kenner, the film explores Williams's life and work. Distributed by Facets Multimedia, Inc.

William Carlos Williams: Twentieth-Century Poetry in English: Poets Reading Their Own Poetry [recording]. 1949. Distributed by the Library of Congress.

William Carlos Williams Reads [recording]. 1 cassette (43 min.), 1993. Distributed by Harper-Audio.

See also "The Caedmon Poetry Collection: A Century of Poets Reading Their Work" and "Voices and Visions" on manual pages 383 and 386.

WILLIAM WORDSWORTH

William Wordsworth. 28 min., color, 1989. VHS, 3/4" U-matic cassette. An examination of the poet's work set against the Lake District, subject for many of the poems. Distributed by Films for the Humanities and Sciences and International Historic Films, Inc.

William Wordsworth: William and Dorothy. 52 min., 1985. VHS, 3/4" U-matic cassette. Explores Wordsworth's poetry and his troubled relationship with his sister. Directed by Ken Russell. Distributed by Films for the Humanities and Sciences.

William Wordsworth and the English Lakes. 15 min., color, 1989. VHS, 3/4" U-matic cassette. Looks at Wordsworth's use of language. Distributed by Films for the Humanities and Sciences.

Wordsworth: Selected Poems [recording]. 2 cassettes (180 min.). Read by Frederick Davidson. Distributed by Blackstone Audio Books.

Wordsworth and Coleridge: The Lake Poets. 30 min., color, 1997. Part of the Master Poets Collection II. Distributed by Monterey Media, Inc.

See also "English Romantic Poetry," and "Introduction to English Poetry," and "Romantic Pioneers," on manual pages 383, 384, and 386.

JAMES WRIGHT

See "Poet's Night" on manual page 385.

SIR THOMAS WYATT

See "Medieval to Elizabethan Poetry" on manual page 384.

WILLIAM BUTLER YEATS

The Love Poems of William Butler Yeats. 30 min., b/w, 1967. Beta, VHS, 1/2" open reel (EIAJ), 3/4" U-matic cassette. Selections from the poet's works. Distributed by Camera Three Productions, Inc. and Creative Arts Television Archive.

Poems by W. B. Yeats: Spoken According to His Own Direction and Poems for Several Voices [recording]. 1 cassette/CD, 1973. Also features poems by Thomas Hardy, Robert Graves, and Gerard Manley Hopkins. Read by V. C. Clinton-Baddeley, Jill Balcon, and M. Westbury. Distributed by Smithsonian/ Folkways Recordings.

W. B. Yeats [recording]. 1 cassette (49 min.), 1953. Read by Stephen Spender. Distributed by Audio-Forum.

Yeats Country. 18 min., 1965. VHS, 3/4" U-matic cassette. Yeats's poetry with scenes of the places in Ireland that inspired him. Some biographical information included. Distributed by International Film Bureau, Inc.

See also "The Caedmon Collection of English Poetry" on page 380 and "Introduction to English Poetry," on manual page 383.

GENERAL RESOURCES

Anthology of Contemporary American Poetry [recording]. 1 cassette/ CD, 1961. Includes poems by John Ciardi, Richard Eberhardt, Theodore Roethke, Howard Nemerov, Galway Kinnell, Donald Justice, May Swenson, Richard Wilbur, Karl Shapiro, and others. Distributed by Smithsonian Folkways Recordings.

Anthology of Negro Poets in the U.S.A. — 200 Years [recording]. 1 cassette/CD, 1955. Includes the poetry of Langston Hughes, Sterling A. Brown, Claude McKay, Countee Cullen, Margaret Walter, and Gwendolyn Brooks. Distributed by Smithsonian Folkways Recordings.

The Beats: An Existential Comedy. 60 min., b/w, 1980. VHS. Examines the Beat poetry scene in late 1950s America. With Allen Ginsberg, Lawrence Ferlinghetti, Jack Hirshman, Stuart Perkott, Hisakawa Aya, Frank Rio, and Shirley Clarke. Directed by Philomene Long. Distributed by The Cinema Guild.

Birthwrite: Growing Up Hispanic. 57 min., color, 1989. VHS. Focuses on the achievements of Hispanic American writers. Includes the work of Alberto Ríos, Edward Rivera, Rolando Hinojosa, Alejandro Morales, Lorna Dee Cervantes, Tato Laviera, and Judith Ortiz Cofer. Distributed by The Cinema Guild.

The Caedmon Collection of English Poetry [recording]. 1998. Includes poetry by William Shakespeare, John Donne, John Milton, William Blake, Robert Burns, William Wordsworth, Samuel Taylor Coleridge, John Keats, Alfred Lord Tennyson, Robert Browning, Elizabeth Barrett Browning, Gerard Manley Hopkins, Thomas Hardy, D. H. Lawrence, Rudyard Kipling, Wilfred Owen, William Butler Yeats, T. S. Eliot, W. H. Auden, Dylan Thomas, and Ted Hughes. Distributed by HarperAudio.

The Caedmon Poetry Collection: A Century of Poets Reading Their Work [recording]. 2 cassettes (3 1/2 hrs.), 2000. Includes T. S. Eliot, W. B. Yeats, W. H. Auden, Edith Sitwell, Dylan Thomas, Robert Graves, Archibald MacLeish, e. e. cummings, Robert Frost, William Carlos Williams, Wallace Stevens, Ezra Pound, and others. Distributed by HarperAudio.

English Romantic Poetry [recording]. 2 cassettes (2 hrs.), 1996. Featuring works by Blake, Byron, Coleridge, Keats, Shelley, and Wordsworth. Distributed by HarperAudio.

Fried Shoes, Cooked Diamonds. 55 min., color, 1978. VHS. Documents a summer at the Jack Kerouac School of Poetics at the Nairopa Institute in Boulder, Colorado. Features such poets from the Beat generation as Allen Ginsberg, Gregory Corso, William S. Burroughs, Peter Orlovsky, and Timothy Leary. Distributed by WinStar Home Video (Mystic Fire Video).

Great American Poetry [recording]. 2 cassettes. Read by Vincent Price, Julie Harris, and Eddie Albert. Includes poetry by Taylor, Bradstreet, Bryant, Longfellow, Emerson, Whittier, Holmes, Whitman, Melville, Dickinson, Miller, Lanier, and Crane. Distributed by Audio Editions.

Haiku. 19 min., color, 1976. VHS. An overview of this poetic form. Distributed by AIMS Multimedia.

Harlem Renaissance: The Black Poets. 20 min., color. VHS. Discusses this era, including an examination of Georgia Douglas Johnson, Fenton Johnson, W. E. B. DuBois, and Langston Hughes. Distributed by Carousel Film & Video.

Howls, Raps, and Roars: Recordings from the San Francisco Poetry Renaissance [recording]. 4 CDs, 1993. Features the work of Allen Ginsberg, Kenneth Rexroth, Lawrence Ferlinghetti, Gregory Corso, and others. Distributed by Fantasy Records.

Introduction to English Poetry. 28 min., color, 1989. VHS, 3/4" U-matic cassette. Part of the Survey of English Poetry series. Introduces students to English verse, with readings from Chaucer, Shakespeare, Herbert, Milton, Swift, Blake, Wordsworth, Shelley, Emily Brontë, Dickinson, Hardy, Yeats, and Ted Hughes. Distributed by Films for the Humanities and Sciences.

Literature: The Synthesis of Poetry. 30 min. VHS. Hosted by Maya Angelou, who reads some of her own work as well as the poetry of Frost, Sandburg, and Arnold. Distributed by RMI Media Productions, Inc.

The Master Poets Collection. 12 cassettes (240 min.), color, 1998. VHS. Includes works by Brontë, Browning, Scott, Tennyson, Kipling, Wordsworth, Coleridge, Dickinson, Shakespeare, and Frost. Distributed by Film Ideas, Inc.

Medieval to Elizabethan Poetry. 28 min., color, 1989. VHS. Examines trends of the period, focusing on John Skelton, Thomas Wyatt, Tichborne, Nashe, Walter Raleigh, Marlowe, Drayton, and Shakespeare. Distributed by Films for the Humanities and Sciences.

Metaphysical and Devotional Poetry. 28 min., color, 1989. VHS. Part of the Survey of English Poetry series. Looks at the works of John Donne, George Herbert, and Andrew Marvell. Hosted by Sir John Gielgud. Distributed by Films for the Humanities and Sciences.

A Moveable Feast. 8 cassettes, 30 min./program, color, 1991. VHS. Hosted by Tom Vitale. Profiles of eight writers: Allen Ginsberg, Joyce Carol Oates, Li-Young Lee, Sonia Sanchez, T. Coraghessan Boyle, T. R.

Pearson, Trey Ellis, W. S. Merwin. Distributed by Filmic Archives.

Poet and Poem from the Library of Congress [recording]. 4 cassettes or CDs (240 min.). Grace Cavalieri's public radio series featuring poets visiting the library. Includes interviews with Robert Pinsky, Rita Dove, Louise Glück, and W. S. Merwin. Distributed by Pacifica Radio Archive.

Poetic Forms [recording]. 5 cassettes (300 min.), 1988. Includes the list poem, the ode, the prose poem, the sonnet, the haiku, the blues poem, the villanelle, the ballad, the acrostic, and free verse. Distributed by Teachers & Writers Collaborative.

Poetry: A Beginner's Guide. 26 min. VHS. Interviews contemporary poets and examines the tools they use. Distributed by Coronet, The Multimedia Company.

Poetry by Americans. 4 programs (10 min. each), color, 1972. VHS. Robert Frost, Edgar Allan Poe, James Weldon Johnson, and Walt Whitman. Narrated by Leonard Nimoy, Lorne Greene, Raymond St. Jacques, and Efrem Zimbalist Jr. Distributed by Filmic Archives.

The Poetry Corner. 4 cassettes (180 min.), color. VHS. From the Anyone for Tennyson series. Includes Chaucer, Ogden Nash, Carl Sandburg, D. H. Lawrence, Edna St. Vincent Millay, Emily Dickinson, e. e. cummings, Pope Masters, Sylvia Plath, and more. Distributed by Filmic Archives.

The Poetry Hall of Fame. 4 cassettes (240 min.), color, 1993. VHS. A collection of biographical information about and poems by the literary greats. Distributed by Filmic Archives.

Poets in Person: A Series on American Poets & Their Art [recording]. 14 programs (30 min. each), 1991. Thirteen poets in conversation, reading their poems, discussing their lives, work, and the changing styles in contemporary American poetry: A. R. Ammons, Allen Ginsberg, Karl Shapiro, Maxine Kumin, W. S. Merwin, Gwendolyn Brooks, James Merrill, Adrienne Rich, John Ashbery, Sharon Olds, Charles Wright, Rita Dove, and Gary Soto. Distributed by Modern Poetry Association.

Poet's Night [recording]. 2 cassettes. John Ashbery and other modern poets read works by themselves and others. Includes poetry by Ted Hughes, Robert Lowell, Randall Jarrell, Philip Larkin, James Wright, and more. Distributed by Audio Editions.

Poets Talking. 15 cassettes (29 min. each), 1975. 3/4" U-matic cassette. Fifteen American poets read and discuss their works. Includes Donald Hall, Galway Kinnell, Gregory Orr, Carolyn Kizer, Robert Bly, Louis Simpson, Marvin Bell, Jerome Rothenberg, Wendell Berry, Larry Fagin, W. S. Merwin, Robert Hayden, Howard Norman, Lawrence Raab, and Joyce Peseroff. No known distributor.

Portraits in American Poetry. 5 cassettes (94 min.). VHS. Biographical portraits of major American poets, including Walt Whitman, Emily Dickinson, Robert Frost, Carl Sandburg, and Sylvia Plath. Distributed by Thomas S. Klise Company.

Portraits in English Poetry. 4 cassettes (92 min.). Biographical portraits of major English poets. Distributed by Thomas S. Klise Company.

The Power of the Word Series. 6 programs (60 min. each), color, 1989. Beta, VHS, 3/4" U-matic cassette. Bill Moyers talks with modern poets: Quincy Troupe, James Autry, Joy Harjo, Mary Tallmountain, Gerald Stern, Li-Young Lee, Stanley Kunitz, Sharon Olds, William Stafford, W. S. Merwin, Galway Kinnell, Robert Bly, and Octavio Paz. Distributed by Films for the Humanities and Sciences.

Restoration and Augustan Poetry. 28 min., color, 1989. VHS, 3/4" U-matic cassette. Discusses the age of satire in England, including the Earl of Rochester, John Dryden, Jonathan Swift, and Alexander Pope. Distributed by Films for the Humanities and Sciences.

Romantic Pioneers. 28 min., color, 1989. VHS, 3/4" U-matic cassette. Part of the Survey of English Poetry series. Readings of poems by Christopher Smart, William Blake, William Wordsworth, and Samuel Taylor Coleridge. Distributed by Films for the Humanities and Sciences.

Romantics and Realists. 28 min., color, 1989. VHS, 3/4" U-matic cassette. Part of the Survey of English Poetry series. Discusses Thomas Hardy, Gerard Manley Hopkins, A. E. Housman, and Rudyard Kipling. Distributed by Films for the Humanities and Sciences.

Sounds of Poetry Series. 9 cassettes (243 min.), color. VHS. A nine-part series in which poets talk with Bill Moyers about the language of poetry. Includes Amiri Baraka, Robert Pinsky, Marge Piercy, Coleman Barks, Lorna Dee Cervantes and Shirley Geoklin Lim, Stanley Kunitz, Jane Hirshfield, Lucille Clifton, Mark Doty, and Deborah Garrison.

Distributed by Films for the Humanities and Sciences.

Treasury of American Jewish Poets Reading Their Poems [recording]. 7 cassettes, 1995. Includes the work of Dorothy Parker, Philip Levine, Anthony Hecht, Denise Levertov, Allen Ginsberg, and John Hollander. No known distributor.

Victorian Poetry. 28 min., color. VHS. Part of the Survey of English Poetry series. An examination of works by Alfred Tennyson, Emily Brontë, Christina Rossetti, Elizabeth Barrett Browning, Matthew Arnold, and Algernon Swinburne. Distributed by Films for the Humanities and Sciences.

The Voice of the Poet Series [recording]. Distributed by Random House Audiobooks.

Voices and Visions. 13 programs (60 min. each), color, 1995. VHS. Originally aired on PBS, the series explores the lives of some of America's best poets. Hosted by Joseph Brodsky, Mary McCarthy, James Baldwin, and Adrienne Rich. Programs include: Elizabeth Bishop, Hart Crane, Emily Dickinson, T. S. Eliot, Robert Frost, Langston Hughes, Robert Lowell, Marianne Moore, Sylvia Plath, Ezra Pound, Wallace Stevens, Walt Whitman, William Carlos Williams. Distributed by Unapix Entertainment, Inc.

With a Feminine Touch. 45 min,, color, 1989. VHS. From the PBS TV series. Readings from Emily Dickinson, Anne Brontë, Charlotte Brontë, Emily Brontë, Sylvia Plath, and Edna St. Vincent Millay. Read by Valerie Harper and Claire Bloom. Distributed by Monterey Media, Inc.

DRAMA

SUSAN GLASPELL

Literature on Film Series, Volume Nine. 23 min. VHS, 3/4" U-matic cassette. A dramatization based on Glaspell's play *Trifles.* Distributed by Phoenix/Coronet/BFA Films and Video.

Trifles. 21 min., 1979. VHS, Beta. Adapted from the play by Susan Glaspell. Distributed by Phoenix/Coronet/BFA Films and Video.

See also **"Scribbling Women"** on manual page 366.

LORRAINE HANSBERRY

A Raisin in the Sun. 128 min., b/w, 1961. VHS, DVD. With Sidney Poitier, Claudia McNeil, and Ruby Dee. Directed by Daniel Petrie. Distributed by Columbia Tristar Home Video.

A Raisin in the Sun. 171 min., color, 1989. VHS. With Danny Glover, Esther Rolle, and Starletta DuPois. Directed by Bill Duke. An "American Playhouse" made-for-television production. Distributed by Monterey Home Video.

A Raisin in the Sun [recording]. 2 cassettes (2 hrs., 21 min.). Dramatization performed by Ossie Davis and Ruby Dee. Distributed by HarperAudio.

Lorraine Hansberry: The Black Experience in the Creation of Drama. 35 min., color, 1975. VHS. With Sidney Poitier, Ruby Dee, and Al Freeman Jr. Narrated by Claudia McNeil. A profile of the playwright's life and work. Distributed by Films for the Humanities and Sciences.

Lorraine Hansberry Collection [recording]. 4 cassettes (6 hrs.), 2001. A collection of Hansberry's plays, speeches, and interviews. Distributed by HarperAudio.

To Be Young, Gifted, and Black. 90 min., color, 1981. VHS, 3/4" U-matic cassette, 16-mm film. With Ruby Dee, Al Freeman Jr., Claudia McNeil, Barbara Barrie, Lauren Jones, Roy Scheider, and Blythe Danner. A play about Hansberry's life. Distributed by Monterey Home Video.

HENRIK IBSEN

A Doll's House. 89 min., b/w, 1959. VHS. With Julie Harris, Christopher Plummer, Jason Robards, Hume Cronyn, Eileen Heckart, and Richard Thomas. An original television production. Distributed by MGM Home Entertainment and Facets Multimedia, Inc.

A Doll's House. 98 min., color, 1973. With Jane Fonda, Edward Fox, and Trevor Howard. Screenplay by Christopher Hampton. No known distributor.

A Doll's House. 39 min., color, 1977. With Claire Bloom, Anthony Hopkins, and Ralph Richardson. Distributed by AIMS Multimedia.

A Doll's House, Part I: The Destruction of Illusion. 34 min., color, 1968. Beta, VHS, 3/4" U-matic cassette, 16-mm film. Norris Houghton discusses the subsurface tensions in the play. Distributed by Encyclopaedia Britannica Educational Corporation.

A Doll's House, Part II: Ibsen's Themes. 29 min., color, 1968. Beta, VHS, 3/4" U-matic cassette, 16-mm film. Norris Houghton examines the case of characters and the themes in the play. Distributed by Encyclopaedia Britannica Educational Corporation.

Henrik Ibsen: Sphinx — Who Are You? 52 min., color, 1999. VHS. Seeks to understand Ibsen, known as "The Sphinx," by tracing his travels, examining excerpts from his writings, and studying his instructions for performance of his dramas. Distributed by Films for the Humanities and Sciences.

Ibsen's Life and Times: Youth and Self-Imposed Exile. 28 min., color. VHS. The conflict between individual and society is illustrated in scenes from *Ghosts*, featuring Beatrice Straight as Mrs. Alving. Includes a biographical segment on the playwright. Distributed by Insight Media.

Ibsen's Themes. 29 min., 1968. VHS. Examines the depiction of women and themes of denied love in selected scenes from *A Doll's House*. Distributed by Insight Media.

ARTHUR MILLER

Arthur Miller: A Conversation with Mike Wallace. 45 min., color, 1997. VHS. Miller candidly discusses his life and works with Mike Wallace. Contains previously unreleased photos and footage. Distributed by Films for the Humanities and Sciences.

Arthur Miller: An Interview. 76 min., color. VHS. Produced by BBC Staff. Miller speaks about his life and career. Distributed by Films for the Humanities and Sciences.

The Arthur Miller Audio Collection [recording]. 4 CDs (4 hrs.), 2002. Full cast recordings of *Death of a Salesman* and *The Crucible*. Featuring Lee J. Cobb, Dustin Hoffman, Mildred Dunnock, and Jerome Dempsey. Distributed by HarperAudio.

Death of a Salesman. 135 min., color, 1986. VHS. With Dustin Hoffman, John Malkovich, Charles Durning, and Stephen Lang. Directed by Volker Schlondorff. A made-for-TV adaptation of the play. Distributed by Facets Multimedia Inc. and Warner Home Video, Inc. and Orion Home Video.

Death of a Salesman [recording]. 2 cassettes (2 hrs., 16 min.), 1998. Performed by Lee J. Cobb and Mildred Dunnock. Distributed by Caedmon/HarperAudio.

Private Conversations on the Set of Death of a Salesman. 82 min., color, 1987. Beta, VHS. Part of the On Stage series. With Arthur Miller, Dustin Hoffman, Volker Schlondorff, and John Malkovich. This PBS documentary presents heated discussion between actor, director, and playwright. Various interpretations of the play emerge and viewers gain insight into how each part contributed to the final production. Distributed by Warner Home Video, Inc.

WILLIAM SHAKESPEARE

Hamlet. 153 min., b/w, 1948. VHS, DVD. With Laurence Olivier, Basil Sydney, Felix Aylmer, Jean Simmons, Stanley Holloway, Peter Cushing, and Christopher Lee. Voice of John Gielgud. Directed by Olivier. Photographed in Denmark. Cut scenes include all of Rosencrantz and

Guildenstern. Emphasizes Oedipal implications in the play. Distributed by Paramount Home Video, Baker and Taylor Video, and Home Vision Cinema.

Hamlet. 114 min., color, 1969. VHS. With Nicol Williamson and Anthony Hopkins. Directed by Tony Richardson. Distributed by Columbia Tristar Home Video.

Hamlet. 222 min., color, 1979. 3/4" U-matic cassette, VHS. Directed by Derek Jacobi. Distributed by Ambrose Video Publishing, Inc.

Hamlet. 135 min., color, 1990. VHS. With Mel Gibson, Glenn Close, Alan Bates, Paul Scofield, Iam Holm, and Helena Bonham-Carter. Directed by Franco Zeffirelli. Distributed by Warner Home Video, Inc., Baker and Taylor Video, and Facets Multimedia, Inc.

Hamlet. 242 min., color, 1997. VHS. With Kenneth Branagh, Kate Winslet, Julie Christie, and Charlton Heston. Directed by Kenneth Branagh. Distributed by Filmic Archives.

Hamlet. 111 min., color, 2000. VHS, DVD. With Ethan Hawke, Kyle MacLachlan, Sam Shepard, Diane Venora, Bill Murray, Julia Stiles, Liev Schreiber, Karl Geary, Paula Malcomson, Steve Zahn, and directed by Michael Almereyda. Almereyda keeps Shakespeare's language, but updates the play's setting to present-day corporate America. Distributed by Buena Vista Home Entertainment.

Hamlet, One: The Age of Elizabeth. 30 min. Beta, VHS, 3/4" U-matic cassette, 16-mm film. An introduction to Elizabethan theater. Distributed by Encyclopaedia Britannica Educational Corporation.

Hamlet, Two: What Happens in Hamlet? 30 min. Beta, VHS, 3/4" U-matic cassette, 16-mm film. Analyzes the play as a ghost story, a detective story, and a revenge story. Uses scenes from Acts I, III, and V to introduce the principal characters and present the structure of each substory. Distributed by Encyclopaedia Britannica Educational Corporation.

Hamlet, Three: The Poisoned Kingdom. 30 min. Beta, VHS, 3/4" U-matic cassette, 16-mm film. Observes that poisoning in the play is both literal and figurative and affects all the characters. Distributed by Encyclopaedia Britannica Educational Corporation.

Hamlet, Four: The Readiness Is All. 30 min. Beta, VHS, 3/4" U-matic cassette, 16-mm film. Hamlet is presented as a coming-of-age story. Distributed by Encyclopaedia Britannica Educational Corporation.

Rosencrantz and Guildenstern Are Dead. 118 min., color, 1990. With Gary Oldman, Tim Roth, Richard Dreyfuss, Iain Glen, Joanna Roth, Donald Sumpter, Sven Medvesck, Joanna Miles, Ian Richardson, John Burgess, and directed by Tom Stoppard. Based on Stoppard's 1967 play. Distributed by Buena Vista Home Entertainment and Facets Multimedia, Inc.

Shakespeare and His Stage: Approaches to Hamlet. 45 min., color, 1979. VHS. Includes footage of the four greatest Hamlets of this century: John Barrymore, Laurence Olivier, John Gielgud, and Nicol Williamson. Shows a young actor learning the role. Narrated by Gielgud. Distributed by Films for the Humanities and Sciences.

The Tragedie of Hamlet: Prince of Denmark. 24 min. VHS. Actors depict Shakespeare and his contemporary, Richard Burbage, rehearsing the play. "Shakespeare" gives a line-by-line analysis of scenes from the play along with insight into plot and character. Part of the Shakespeare in Rehearsal Series. Distributed by Coronet, The Multimedia Company.

William Shakespeare, Hamlet [recording]. 3 cassettes (3 1/2" hours), 1995. A Shakespeare Society Production. Distributed by HarperAudio.

SOPHOCLES

The Age of Sophocles, 1. 30 min., 1959. VHS, 3/4" U-matic cassette. Discusses Greek civilization, the classic Greek theater, and the theme of man's fundamental nature. Distributed by Britannica Films.

Antigone. 120 min., 1987. VHS, 3/4" U-matic cassette. With Juliet Stevenson, John Shrapnel, and John Gielgud. Staged version. Distributed by Films for the Humanities and Sciences.

Antigone: Rites for the Dead. 85 min., color, 1991. VHS, DVD. With Amy Greenfield, Bertram Ross, and Janet Eilber. Directed by Amy Greenfield. A retelling of Sophocles' tragedy through action, dance, and rock music. Distributed by Mystic Fire Video.

The Character of Oedipus, 2. 30 min., 1959. VHS, 3/4" U-matic cassette. Debates whether Oedipus's trouble is a result of character flaws or of fate. Distributed by Britannica Films.

Oedipus at Colonus. 120 min., color. VHS. With Anthony Quayle, Juliet Stevenson, and Kenneth Haigh. Staged version. Distributed by Films for the Humanities and Sciences.

Oedipus the King. 120 min., color. VHS. With John Gielgud, Michael Pennington, and Claire Bloom. Distributed by Films for the Humanities and Sciences.

Oedipus Rex. 20 min., 1957. VHS, 3/4" U-matic cassette. Sophocles' play, presented in a signed version for the deaf. No known distributor.

Oedipus Rex. 87 min., 1957. VHS. With Douglas Campbell, Douglas Rain, Eric House, and Eleanor Stuart. Based on William Yeats's translation. Directed by Tyrone Guthrie. Contained and highly structured rendering by the Stratford (Ontario) Festival Players. Distributed by Home Vision Cinema.

Oedipus Rex: Man and God, III. 30 min., 1959. VHS, 3/4" U-matic cassette. Deals with the idea that Oedipus, although a worldly ruler, cannot overcome the gods and his destiny. Distributed by Britannica Films.

The Recovery of Oedipus, IV. 30 min., 1959. VHS, 3/4" U-matic cassette. Deals with man's existence in between God and beast. Distributed by Britannica Films.

Sophocles, Oedipus the King. 45 min., color, 1975. VHS. With James Mason, Claire Bloom, and Ian Richardson. A production by the Athens Classical Theatre Company, with an English soundtrack. Distributed by Films for the Humanities and Sciences.

TENNESSEE WILLIAMS

The Glass Menagerie. 134 min., color, 1987. Beta, VHS. With Joanne Woodward, Karen Allen, John Malkovich, and James Naughton. Directed by Paul Newman. Distributed by Universal Studios Home Video.

The Glass Menagerie [recording]. 3 CDs (3 hrs.), 2000. Dramatization performed by Montgomery Clift, Jessica Tandy, and Julie Harris. Distributed by Harper-Audio.

In the Country of Tennessee Williams. 30 min., color, 1977. Beta, VHS, 1/2" reel, 3/4" U-matic cassette, 2" Quad. A one-act play about how Williams developed as a writer. Distributed by Camera Three Productions, Inc. and Creative Arts Television Archive.

GENERAL RESOURCES

Black Theatre: The Making of a Movement. 114 min., color, 1978. 3/4" U-matic cassette. A look at black theater born from the civil rights movement of the 1950s, 1960s, and 1970s. Recollections from Ossie Davis, James Earl Jones, Amiri Baraka, and Ntozake Shange. Distributed by California Newsreel.

A Day at the Globe. 30 min., 1977. VHS. Starts with a brief overview of early drama and of seventeenth-century England, then discusses the Globe Theater, using still images. Explains how actors, artisans, and other company members prepared for performances and presents dramatic readings, period costumes, music, and sound effects to help students envision how Shakespearean drama actually looked. Distributed by Insight Media.

The Elizabethan Age. 33 min., 1990. VHS. Includes teacher's guide. A discussion of the resurgence of enthusiasm for the arts and letters that swept seventeenth-century England. Uses original sources. Distributed by Clearvue/EAV, Inc.

The Theatre in Ancient Greece. 26 min., 1989. VHS, 3/4" U-matic cassette. Program explores ancient theater design, the origins of tragedy, the audience, the comparative roles of the writer/director and actors, and the use of landscape in many plays. Examines the theaters of Heroditus, Atticus, Epidauros, Corinth, and numerous others. Distributed by Films for the Humanities and Sciences.